# Murder at Ford's Theatre

## Chronicle of an Assassination

BRENDAN H. EGAN, JR.

**To order additional copies of this book, contact:**
Xlibris Corporation
1-888-795-4274
www.Xlibris.com
Orders@Xlibris.com
35265

# Contents

# PART 3

# PART I

# CHAPTER I

## *King Lincoln*

During his time as president, more people hated Lincoln than loved him. Even in the North, he was not very well liked. Members of his own cabinet did not hold him in high regard. Secretary of War Edwin Stanton referred to him as a baboon, a hick, and a giraffe. Attorney General Edward Bates called him unexceptional. He was not thought of as a political heavyweight. His political adversaries and members of his own party felt they could mock him without suffering any political repercussion. They were wrong.

Today, Lincoln is best known and loved as the president who guided the Union through the most horrendous ordeal of its young life. It was America's biggest war; a little more than six million Americans died (as compared to a quarter of a million in World War II – a war about the same length of time with a much larger population). Hardly a family, North or South, had not lost a loved one. Lincoln was adamant about the survival of the Union, and the human carnage continued as long as the war was fought. By fighting, the war between North and South devastated a generation, causing millions of deaths, lifelong disabilities, and grief to innumerable households. It was a sad generation that went on after 1865.

It was fear that caused Southerners to hate Lincoln from the time he was the Republican nominee. To the Southerner, Lincoln was not a person, but a symbol of the Republican party, a party they believed intended to infringe upon their property rights, change their social values, and destroy their way of life.

Southern newspapers before and after the election damned Lincoln and the Republican Party.[1] The *Richmond Enquirer* summed up Southern feeling when it editorialized, "The significant fact which menaces the South is not that Abe Lincoln is elected President but that the Northern people, by a sectional vote, have elected a president for the avowed purpose of aggression on Southern rights. The purpose of aggression has been declared. This is a declaration of war, committed by State officers, acting under the dictation of a popular vote."[2] The *Southern Recorder* wrote, "We do not fear Mr. Lincoln but we do fear the fanaticism he represents, the sectionalism that will triumph in his election, and the passions which his success will engender."[3] The *New Orleans Daily Crescent* called Lincoln "a thorough radical Abolitionist, without exception or qualification."[4]

Although Southerners feared the Republican Party for what they thought it stood for, some Southerners disliked Lincoln as a person. Edmund Ruffin wrote in his diary, "That the abolition convention at Chicago had not nominated Seward as expected, or Bates, or Chase, or Cameron, or Wade, who had been spoken of as the most probable alternate choices, but Lincoln of Illinois, inferior in ability and reputation to all – & whom no one had mentioned before. I am sorry they did not nominate their ablest man, Seward, & so make their success more probable."[5]

Many Northern Democrats considered Lincoln's unilateral measures against those who opposed him to be brutal, dictatorial, and unconstitutional. Lincoln's unilateral suspension of the writ of habeas corpus led to more than thirteen thousand arbitrary arrests of citizens suspected of ill-defined disloyal acts.[6] Lincoln suspended the writ in some areas as early as April 27, 1861, and throughout the nation on September 24, 1862. Many political prisoners were held without trial, and others were tried before military commissions where the normal rules of being presumed innocent until proven guilty did not apply. No less than Chief Justice of the United States Roger B. Taney warned Lincoln that such practices violated the Constitution and that only Congress could suspend the writ of habeas corpus. Taney felt that Lincoln's suspension of the writ was an unconstitutional seizure of congressional powers and that nonmilitary individuals would be subject to military courts or imprisonment without due process of law especially when the civil courts were in place and functioning. Taney felt that the suspension of habeas corpus would collapse the government and change it to a military administration.[7] Lincoln, however, saw his measures as absolutely necessary to preserve the Union.

As a result of the suspension of the writ, Dennis A. Mahony, the editor of Iowa's *Dubuque Herald*, was jailed for ten weeks for his editorials criticizing the federal government. His newspaper wrote that he had "not yet been made acquainted with the charges against him or confronted by his accusers. And still we are told that we must sustain the administration. Well, if we must, we must. 'Long live Abraham Lincoln who gives us more liberty than we know what to do with.'"[8]

On the other hand, Lincoln did tolerate some caustic criticism from the press and politicians and often restrained his commanders from overzealous arrests. Democrats exaggerated Lincoln's suppression of civil liberties, in part because wartime prosperity robbed them of economic issues and in part because Lincoln handled the slavery issue so skillfully. The Constitution protected slavery, but Lincoln asserted that in wartime, the commander in chief could abolish slavery in rebellious states as a military necessity.

\*　　\*　　\*

An example of how Lincoln dealt with dissidents was his prosecution of Clement Laird Vallandigham. Vallandigham was a handsome, vain, and impetuous lawyer from Ohio, who in 1845 became the youngest member of the state legislature (1845-47). He had gained notoriety as a congressman (1858-'63), with Southern sympathies, and strongly criticized the federal government's policy toward the Confederacy. He vehemently attacked Lincoln's war policies, earning the reputation as a leader of the peace movement and as a copperhead. Vallandigham opposed the Industrial Revolution – the growing federal control over state's rights, the military draft, the emancipation of slaves – he favored a negotiated peace with the Confederacy and swore that as long as he was a member of Congress, he would not vote one dollar that would cause one drop of American blood to be shed. Not everyone in his constituency agreed with him, and he lost his election in 1862.[9]

General Burnside, who was transferred to the Department of the Ohio on March 26, 1863, after his debacle at the Battle of Fredericksburg, saw the state as infested with bitter opposition to the government and the war. Not considering the political consequences of his actions, on April 13, General Burnside imprudently issued his famous General Order No. 38, which stated in part "all persons found within our lines, who commit acts for the benefit of the enemies of our country, will be tried as spies and traitors, and, if convicted, will suffer death." Almost immediately throughout Ohio, the order was criticized as illegal; and many Ohioans feared that it would lead to governmental abuse.

Vallandigham, not to be deterred by military orders, made a speech, denouncing Lincoln as a despot, railed against the draft, and advocated negotiating peace with the Confederate government. "King Lincoln," Vallandigham said, "had promoted this war to free blacks and enslave whites." He urged his audiences in a number of speeches to oust Lincoln in the next election and "hurl the tyrant from his throne." Vallandigham also told audiences that "Jeff Davis was a gentleman, which was more that Lincoln was."

Needless to say, Vallandigham was watched carefully by Burnside's detectives, and at a speech in Mount Vernon, Ohio, a plainclothes federal officer sat among the crowd taking notes on the antigovernmental rhetoric.[10] Three nights later, on May 4, 1863, a company from the 115th Ohio arrested Vallandigham at his home in Dayton. This was Lincoln's most controversial and mismanaged political arrest. When townspeople heard of the arrest, a crowd organized to free him. However, he was quickly taken to the train that had brought the soldiers and quickly left with their prisoner before the crowd could reach the station.

On May 6, Vallandigham was tried by a military commission, despite his valid protest that the military had no authority to try him because as a civilian only a civil court could try him. This very argument was to be repeated during the conspiracy trial after Lincoln was assassinated. However, the military tried him anyway, found him guilty, and sentenced him to incarceration at Fort Warren in Boston Harbor for the duration of the war. On May 11, George E. Pugh, Vallandigham's lawyer, applied to Judge Levitt of the United States Circuit Court in Cincinnati for a writ of habeas corpus, but his motion was denied. The sentencing put Lincoln in political dilemma. If he kept Vallandigham in a military prison, he would be a constant source of irritation and become a political martyr. So on May 19, Lincoln modified Vallandigham's sentence to banishment. Lincoln took advantage of Burnside's General Order No. 38, which stated that deportation "beyond our lines into those of their friends" was one of the penalties. This sentence would engender far less sympathy for Vallandigham and prevent him from becoming a martyr.

Criticized about the trial and sentence, Lincoln replied on June 12, 1863, "Must I shoot a simple-minded soldier boy who deserts, while I must not touch a hair of a wily agitator who induces him to desert?"[11]

\* \* \*

Northerners sympathetic to the Confederacy were labeled Copperheads by the press. The name implied that these men were like snakes, capable of striking without warning to hamper the federal war effort. Copperheads had the strongest hold in the Midwest because many people there were of Southern background. In the 1850s, the Knights of the Golden Circle, a secret copperhead organization, flourished and supported the political aspirations of the South.

Most Copperheads were conservative "Peace Democrats" who opposed a strong federal government and were proslavery. Copperheads thought that Lincoln's policies were destroying constitutional government, and they saw themselves as loyal citizens defending the government. These men saw the war as inexorably changing the society of rural America, states rights, and white supremacy. Although some Copperheads won local elections, they had little overall influence in war politics. For years after the war, however, the Democrats were tainted with charges of "copperheadism." As a group, Copperheads did not speak out much, and there were few arrests since military officials did not hesitate to use the power of arrest against civilians suspected of disloyal sentiments. The majority of Copperheads were satisfied with attending secret meeting, taking solemn oaths, exchanging passwords and recognition codes, and enjoying in each other's fellowship a righteous sense of being persecuted by evil forces. Not many Copperheads shed any of their own blood. They held peace meetings, passed out antiwar literature, gave refuge to soldiers who deserted, arranged draft riots, gave military information to Confederate agents, smuggled medicine and supplies to the South, and the more militant destroyed government property.

In Indiana in late 1864, Lambdin P. Milligan, a Copperhead, and others, were tried for treason. A military commission convicted Milligan of subversive activities including spying, organizing resistance to the United States, and conspiring to release Confederate prisoners. He was sentenced to be hanged.[12] The leadership of the Sons of Liberty, as the Copperheads were also known, was further demoralized by Lincoln's reelection that year.

*     *     *

Some people just disliked Lincoln because they viewed him as unrefined with his untutored Western frontier mannerisms and his ungainly appearance. The proadministration New York diarist, George Templeton Strong, in late January 1862 commented on the president's lack of social polish, "He is a barbarian, Scythian, yahoo, or gorilla, in respect of outside polish but a most sensible, straightforward, honest old codger. The best President we have had since old Jackson's time, at least, as I believe . . . . His evident integrity and simplicity of purpose would compensate for worse grammar than his, and for even more intense provincialism and rusticity."[13]

Newspaperman Henry Villard believed that if fashionable New Yorkers did not know who Lincoln was, they would have been ashamed to be seen on the street with him.[14]

People who hated the war and the measures Lincoln took to win it were eager to believe that he was as vulgar as he was unrefined. Many thought Lincoln an uneducated boor, filthy in his habits, and obscene in all his ways, particularly in his Western humor.

Many Democrats who did not believe that Lincoln was a tyrant did consider him incompetent. Maria Lydia Daly, a New York diarist, in her diary entry of July 16, 1862, wrote,

> The Judge is going to Washington. He says that poor Stanton has to bear the blame of the foolish acts of President Lincoln, who, since the taking of Norfolk, thinks himself a general, and goes about with his compasses in his pocket. He is thinking about being reelected. Can our countrymen be so blind, so stupid, as to again place such a clod, though an honest one, in the Presidential chair?[15]

From her June 18, 1863, entry Mrs. Daly wrote:

> Another rebel raid into Pennsylvania by Lee has been more successful than the last. Our wretched Administration have allowed all the three-years' men to return without making any provision whatever to replace them. Truly God has a controversy with this people. He raises for us no deliverer. There is not one honest, clever man left: at least such are not permitted to have influence. One would not admit the men who rule us in Washington, with the exception of Chase and Seward, even into the drawing room.[16]

*     *     *

One of the issues for which Lincoln was disliked by many contemporaries was his stand on emancipation. Some, such as Samuel F. B. Morse, the inventor and painter, believed that emancipation was unconstitutional and unwise; Morse thought it tended "to divide the counsels of the North, and unite the South, and render the restoration of the national Union next to hopeless."[17]

Racism was behind many of the attacks on the emancipation policy. Many northern editors severely criticized Lincoln. Chauncey Burr, editor of the New York magazine the *Old Guard,* maintained that unless Lincoln and the other black abolitionist traitors were stopped, the United States would become a "mongrel concern of whites, negroes, mulattos, and sambos . . . instead of a Federal Union of white men, we shall become a nation of mongrels, the most degrading and contemptible the world ever saw . . . . It is certain that we are fighting not to free the negro but to degrade and destroy ourselves by amalgamation with the lowest of all the human races."[18] A month later, Burr wrote that no patriot could rejoice at news of Union military victories because those victories supported the despised abolitionist policy.[19]

Later in 1864, Burr compared the two presidential candidates: "McClellan is a Christian and a gentleman. Lincoln is a barbarian and a buffoon. McClellan is humane and tolerant in all his instincts and rules of action. Lincoln is infernal and implacable in every feeling and purpose. The difference between them may be defined to be precisely that between a human being and a fiend . . . for Lincoln is an infernal. His face is a faithful chart of his soul, and his face is that of a demon, cunning, obscene, treacherous, lying and devilish." He concluded his article by saying that "the government is in the hands of fiends – cast them into outer darkness.[20] This from a New York editor.

A democratic newspaper in Kansas wrote, "The simple question to be decided is whether the white man shall maintain his status of superiority by supporting the Democrats or be sunk to the level of the Negro by supporting the Republicans."[21]

Racial hate poured from the words of a Maryland journalist, William Wilkins Glen, who was outraged that a Negro preacher, H. H. Garnett, was allowed to preach in the House of Representatives. "Is he a John the Baptist – and who is to come after him. Shall we have a civilized gorilla next? Last week a negro was admitted to practice in the Supreme Court. How long before Lincoln will invite them to diplomatic dinners and lead the way to table with a greasy wench hanging on his arm."[22]

Another issue that engendered a great deal of hatred of Lincoln was the formation of black infantry units. No other federal policy produced such an emotional reaction in the South. The policy of organizing and arming blacks into military units caused a firestorm of hate and fear throughout the Southern states. Southern blacks and former slaves were taken as volunteers into the Union Army, and white Southerners feared that putting black infantry in the federal army might inspire a massive slave rebellion. On August 21, 1862, the Confederate War Department issued General Order No. 60 "that [Union] Major-General Hunter and Brigadier-General Phelps be no longer held and treated as public enemies of the Confederate States, but as outlaws; and that in the event of the capture of either of them, or that of any other commissioned officer employed in drilling, organizing, or instructing slaves, with a view to their armed service in this war, he shall not be regarded as a prisoner of war, but held in close confinement for execution as a felon at such time and place as the President shall order."[23]

*   *   *

Many Northerners kept diaries of their political thoughts. One woman in Lincoln's hometown of Springfield, Illinois, wrote in her diary entry of July 3, 1863,

> Tomorrow will be the glorious fourth. I trust my poor country will be in a better state in another year. National affairs present a gloomy aspect at present. Our money is fast losing its value. Our armies have again been defeated. Thousands and thousands of lives have been sacrificed yet nothing accomplished. The south is still unsubdued. What shall we do? Will the President have the face to call for another draft? Can he ask more men to lay down their lives for nothing? Surely he will not, yet this is feared and the terrible scourge may be just begun. God help us . . . Our only hope is in a Democratic President, or an uprising of the people to demand their rights as free men.[24]

Marcus Mills Pomeroy, editor of the *Wisconsin LaCrosse Democrat*, wrote: "May Almighty God forbid that we are to have two terms of the rottenest, most stinking, ruinworking small pox ever conceived by friends or mortals in the shape of two terms of Abe Lincoln's administration." If Lincoln should be elected, Pomeroy will go on "to misgovern for another four years, we trust some *bold hand will pierce his heart with dagger point for the public good.*" After Lincoln's death, Pomeroy proposed an epitaph: "Beneath this turf the Widow Maker lies, Little in every thing, except in size."[25]

Perhaps more was at stake in the presidential election of 1864 than in any other in American history. The election would determine whether or not the American experiment in popular government would succeed. It would also determine whether or not slavery would be abolished, for Lincoln's Emancipation Proclamation would be meaningless in an independent Confederate States of America.[26] An enormously unpopular president, Lincoln was despised and ridiculed from all political directions, including his own Republican party. His conscription of five hundred thousand more men to fill depleted Union armies only caused more Northern criticism. If Sherman had not taken Atlanta, Sheridan had not defeated Confederate General Early at Cedar Creek in the Shenandoah; and Admiral Farragut not been victorious at Mobile Bay, Lincoln might have lost the election. Even with the positive influence of these victories, Lincoln only received 55 percent of the vote.

The wartime stress and criticisms were taking their toll on Lincoln. In 1864, the thought of not seeking another term as president occurred to him. He told a friend, "This war is eating my life out. I have a strong impression that I shall not live to see the end." There was formidable opposition to Lincoln throughout his party. The

Republican conservatives thought him a radical, and the liberals thought him a failure. In Congress, liberal Republicans mocked Lincoln as a "simple Susan" who dragged his feet on every significant war measure. "This vacillation and indecisiveness of the President has been the real cause why our well-appointed armies have not succeeded in the destruction of the rebellion."[27] In reality, Lincoln was even more aggressive than his generals.

Clement C. Clay Jr. wrote to Richmond on November 1, 1864, from Montreal: "All that a large portion of the Northern people – especially in the northwest – want to resist the oppressions of the despotism at Washington, is a leader. They are ripe for resistance, and it may come soon after the Presidential election. At all events, it must come, if our armies are not overcome and destroyed or dispersed. No people of the Anglo-Saxon blood can long endure the usurpations and tyrannies of Lincoln."[28] From the Southern point of view, the time for Northern resistance to Lincoln had come; it was the Confederacy's best chance to avoid what was now recognized as an otherwise inevitable defeat.

# CHAPTER 2

## *Who Would Want to Kill Me?*

On December 26, 1860, Horace Greeley wrote a letter to Lincoln's law partner William Herndon, "I tell you I think today an even chance that Mr. Lincoln will not be inaugurated Washington on the 4th of March.[29]

Lincoln did make it to the presidential office, but threats to his safety were ongoing. After being in office just five weeks, the English actress Jean Davenport, wife of Colonel Frederick W. Lander, brought information to Lincoln about a plot. On the evening of April 18, 1861, Mrs. Davenport, accompanied by an older woman, called at the executive mansion and asked to see the president. She told John Hay, his secretary, "It is about a matter concerning his personal safety."

Lincoln had retired for the night, but young Hay was only too happy to talk to the attractive Mrs. Davenport. He had seen her on the stage, and he listened to her story if only to hear her cultured voice and English accent. Davenport told a tale of meeting a young gentleman friend from Virginia who was in the city to buy a new saddle, and he had told her that he and six others, including someone named Ficklin, would shortly do something that would "ring through the world." Davenport "concluded that the President was either to be assassinated or captured."

Hay smiled reassuringly. "I will tell Mr. Lincoln about your story."

After the two women left, Hay told Lincoln of the visit and of her extraordinary story and warning. Characteristically, Lincoln listened politely but did not take the warning seriously but just "quietly grinned."[30]

John Bigelow, the consul general in Paris, had heard rumors, even as far away as France, about plots to assassinate Lincoln. Bigelow wrote to Secretary of State Seward in June 1862 about these rumors. Seward wrote back to Bigelow,

> There is no doubt that from a period anterior to the breaking out of the insurrection, plots and conspiracies for purposes of assassination have been frequently formed and organized. And it is not unlikely that such an one

as has been reported to you is now in agitation among the insurgents. If it be so it need furnish no ground for anxiety. *Assassination is not an American practice or habit, and one so vicious and desperate cannot be engrafted into our political system.*

This conviction of mine has steadily gained strength since the Civil War began. Every day's experience confirms it. The President, during the heated season, occupies a country-house near the Soldiers' Home, two or three miles from the city. He goes to and comes from that place on horseback, night and morning, unguarded. I go there unattended at all hours, by daylight and by moonlight, by starlight and without any light.[31]

Ever since Lincoln's election in November 1860, people had sent threatening letters or planned violence against him. He received hate mail, some saying that he would never live to be inaugurated. Some of these threatening letters came to Lincoln in Springfield before he even left for his inauguration in Washington. One such letter came from Lynchburg, Virginia, dated January 18, 1861:

Dear Sir,

I have heard several persons in this place say that if you ever did take the President Chair that they would go to Washington City expressly to kill you. For your wife and Children sake don't take the Chair if you do you will be murdered by some cowardly scoundrel.

Other sample letters read:

May the hand of the devil strike you down before long – You are destroying the country. Damn you – every breath you take –

January 4, 1864, from New York: "The same who warned you of a conspiracy Nov. 18th 1862 is now compelled in inform you, that, Your days are numbered, you have been weighed in the balance and found wanting. You shall be a dead man in six months from date Dec. 1863. Thus saith the good Spirit."

November 1864: "When you remember the fearful, solemn vow that was taken by us, you will feel there is no drawback-Abe must die, and now."[32]

Well-meant warnings in 1860 did not affect Lincoln's actions: "As I have every reason to Expect that you will be our next President – I want to warn you of one thing – that you be Exceeding Careful What you Eat or Drink as you May be Poisoned by your Enemys as was President Harrison and President Taylor."[33] (Undoubtedly a reference to the suspicion of the time that those two presidents had met such a death.)

A laborer in West Virginia reported overhearing a conversation: "That the plan was all made that if old Abe was Re alected [*sic*] we are agoin [*sic*] to kill him and I am the man that it agoin [*sic*] to do it with your help."[34]

Another letter sent by a poorly educated concerned citizen warned, "Mr. Lincoln Sir i rite to you to tell you to be on your gard du not eeat every Thing you have orded to be brought be Carful not to be Posined by those rufings Mr. Lincoln Sir i hope that the Lord Will Spair Your Life to mak the the Country in A beter [*sic*] Condison."[35]

On October 17, 1860, a man from Chester, Pennsylvania, wrote, "I now endeavor to do all I can to put you on your gard. When you cross Masons & Dix. line keep you eye's OPEN and look out for your enimeys or they will poison you or do something to take your life. Same as they tried to serve Old Buc. Look, Sharp"[36]

From Columbus, Indiana: "Dr. Sir – Allow me to suggest to you that you are and will be until the end of your Presidential term in personal danger from Border Ruffians at all times – I have heard some of them say that you should be killed – You owe it to your friends but more particularly to your Country to use great caution at all times and under all circumstances-We must not-we cannot lose you-The anxiety of your friends here and our Country's good is my excuse for troubling you."[37]

As the war progressed, threats to Lincoln's life increased. They came in speeches by Peace Democrats, in daily letters to the president, and in Copperhead editorials. William O. Stoddard, another of Lincoln's secretaries, called these letters "abuse, scurrility, threats" and "utter insanities." He referred to them as "the brutalities, enmities, and infamies of the President's letter-bag."

Henry Villard, a friend of Lincoln's and a frequent guest in the White House, wrote that "letters threatening his life are daily received."[38]

Lincoln said of the letters, "Soon after I was nominated in Chicago, I began to receive letters threatening my life. The first one or two made me a little uncomfortable, but I came at length to look for a regular installment of the kind of correspondence in every week's mail . . . . There is nothing like getting used to things!"

"I know I'm in danger, but I am not going to worry about it," Lincoln repeatedly stated over the Civil War years. "As to crazy folks, I must take my chances," Lincoln once told Hay.[39] Lincoln did keep the letters with assassination threats that got through his staff and filed them in a large envelope marked "Assassination."[40]

A samplings of the envelope's contents reveals the naivete, anger, and coarseness of the writers:

> Never expect to occupy the White House (when you get into it it will be a
> Black House) for that is only intended for Southern Gentlemen and not for
> Black Republicans and mulatto scamps. (Charleston, South Carolina)

Your death would greatly benefit the whole country. (Robert Kemmeck, Carrollton, Georgia)

Dear Sir: Caesar had his Brutus, Charles the First his Cromwell. And the President may profit by their example. From one of a sworn band of 10, who have resolved to shoot you in the inaugural procession on the 4th March 1861. (Vindex, Washington, DC)

Sir: You will be shot on the 4th of March by a Louisiana Creole. We are decided and our aim is sure. (A Young Creole)

God damn your god damned old Hellfired god damned soul to hell you god damned old Abolition son of a bitch. (Pete Muggins, Fillmore, Louisiana)[41]

Edward D. Neill, another of Lincoln's secretaries, retained in his files a letter from an acquaintance in St. Paul who wrote to report a frightening rumor that "he has heard that the President if re-elected, would be assassinated by the 'knights' [of the Golden Circle]." The writer's advice was "to put the Prest. on his guard." In a letter from Gloversville, New York, dated February 1865, "God knows I have hated you, but God knows I cannot be a murderer. Beware of the ides of March. Do not, like Julius Caesar, go to the Senate unarmed. If I did not love my life, I would sign my name."[42]

\*　　\*　　\*

Two of Lincoln secretaries wrote that

From the very beginning of his Presidency Mr. Lincoln had been constantly subject to the threats of his enemies and the warnings of his friends. The threats came in every form; his mail was infested with brutal and vulgar menace, mostly anonymous, the proper expression of vile and cowardly minds. The warnings were not less numerous; the vaporing of village bullies, the extravagances of excited secessionist politicians, even the drooling of practical jokers, were faithfully reported to him by zealous or nervous friends. Staff gave no notice to most of these letters. In cases where there seemed a ground for inquiry it was made, as carefully as possible, by the President's private secretary and by the War Department, but always without substantial result. Warnings that appeared to be most definite, when they came to be examined proved too vague and confused for further attention . . . . He had himself so sane a mind, and a heart so kindly even to his enemies, that it was hard for him to believe in a political hatred so deadly as to lead to murder. He would sometimes laughingly say, "Our friends on the other side would make nothing by exchanging me for Hamlin."[43]

Lizzie Keckley, Mary Lincoln's black seamstress and companion, remembered that "frequent letters were received warning Mr. Lincoln of assassination, but he never gave a second thought to the mysterious warnings. The letters, however, sorely troubled his wife. She seemed to read impending danger in every rustling leaf, in every whisper of the wind."

Mary Lincoln was continually fearful for her husband's safety. His fatalism in the matter only added to her nervous suspicions that assassins were only waiting to murder him.

Mary Lincoln would ask, "Where are you going now, father?" as she observed him putting on his overshoes and shawl.

"I am going over to the War Department, mother, to try and learn some news [about the war]."

"But, father, you should not go out alone. You know you are surrounded with danger."

"All imagination. What does any one want to harm me for? Don't worry about me, mother, as if I were a little child, for no one is going to molest me." And with a confident, unsuspecting air, he would go out alone.

For weeks when trouble was anticipated, friends of the president would sleep in the White House to guard him from danger.[44]

Leonard Swett warned him so often against the dangers of exposing himself to potential assassins that it became a sore subject between them. Lincoln once said to his friend, Swett, "I cannot be shut up in an iron cage and guarded. If I have business at the War Office, I must take my hat and go there; and if to kill me is within the purposes of this rebellion, no precaution can prevent it. You may guard me at a single point, but I will necessarily be exposed at others. People come to see me every day and I receive them, and I do not know but that some of them are secessionists or engaged in plots to kill me. The truth is if any man has made up his mind that he will give his life for mine, he can take mine."[45]

On another occasion Lincoln said, "I will be careful. But I cannot discharge my duties if I withdraw myself entirely from danger of an assault. I see hundreds of strangers every day, and if anybody has the disposition to kill me he will find opportunity. To be absolutely safe I should lock myself up in a box."[46]

Indeed, if Lincoln had acted as if he were in constant fear for his life, he could not easily have held public receptions. He could not have escaped the pressures of the White House by afternoon drives or visits to the soldiers' home or attendance at the theater.

\* \* \*

There were Confederate proposals to kill Lincoln.

In June 1861, Camille La Valliere De Kalb sent two letters to the confederate secretary of war L. P. Walker, proposing to blow up the federal capitol "at a time when Abe, his minions, and the Northern Congress are all assembled together."

The two men met, and De Kalb requested that he be commissioned as a colonel of topographical engineers and paid a million dollars to carry out the plan. Walker delayed any decision because he wanted to investigate De Kalb. De Kalb wrote again to Walker, giving his background and explaining his plan more fully. But Walker still was doubtful and conferred with Judah Benjamin, the Confederate treasurer. Together they decided that the plan should not be given any more consideration.[47]

Jefferson Davis received and rejected many letters from people proposing the assassination of Union officials. In a letter dated September 12, 1861, Henry Clay Durham offered "to dispose of the leading characters of the north." He admitted, however, that his method would be "quite an underhanded manner of warfare." On the back of the letter was the word "file." Later on August 17, 1863, Durham, now sergeant of Company I, Sixty-third Georgia Infantry, again wrote, "I propose, with your permission, to assist in the organizing a number of select men, say not less than three to five hundred, to go into the United States and assassinate the most prominent leaders of our enemies; for instance, Seward, Lincoln, Greeley, Prentice." On August 24, this letter was also filed without action.[48]

Private Robert Stanton, Company D, Fifth Texas Infantry, wrote a letter to Confederate Secretary of War James Seddon asking for approval to "remove at once and forever those persons who fill high places in the North." However, Seddon replied that "the laws of war and morality, as well as Christian principles and sound policy forbid the use of such means."[49]

Jefferson Davis received many letters during his presidency from individuals offering their services for various covert operations. One example is from a man only identified as N. L. Oldham, dated February 5, 1865, offering to burn enemy vessels to "annoy and harass the enemy." This letter, like all the others, Jefferson filed away and not acted on.

*   *   *

After the Lincoln assassination, stories real or imagined, were reported to the War Department. One such report came from Captain Levi Wells, who reported on a conversation he had with a Mrs. Martha Hunter of Martinsburg, Virginia. Hunter reported that something would happen on the fourth of March that would very much help the rebel cause. When Captain Wells asked her to explain, she became "embarrassed and would not explain."[50] Rumors of assassination plots were everywhere.

*   *   *

On January 26, 1861, the House of Representatives took note of the many rumors and formed a select committee to investigate secret societies and any assassination plots. The committee began hearings on January 29 and called twenty-four witnesses. Some of the witnesses were General Winfield Scott; Colonel Charles P. Stone, inspector general of the District of Columbia militia; Jacob Thompson, secretary of the interior;

Enoch Lowe, former governor of Maryland; Thomas H. Hicks, the incumbent governor of Maryland; James G. Beret, the mayor of Washington; Dr. Cornelius Boyle, head of the Washington branch of the National Volunteers; and two Baltimore members of the National Volunteers, Cipriano Ferrandini and Otis K. Hillard. (Ferrandini, in fact, engineered a plot to shoot Lincoln in Baltimore.)

Testimony dealt with Lincoln's safety and was taken until February 13, which was also the day the electoral votes were counted. The committee issued its report on February 14, stating that there were no secret organizations having the goal of attacking the Capitol or any part of the federal government.[51] The committee was wrong. There were groups that were violently opposed to the inauguration of Lincoln and to the Republican government in Washington. Editorials, speeches, and other documentation indicated there were Northern Democrats, Copperheads, and Southern sympathizers who wanted to destroy the government of Abraham Lincoln.

*   *   *

On February 11, Lincoln left his home state to go to Washington. He said farewell to the citizens of Springfield, Illinois, "I now leave, not knowing when, or whether, I may return, with a task before me greater than that which rested upon [President] Washington."[52]

To demonstrate his confidence in the citizens of the border states and to cultivate their confidence in him, Lincoln favored taking a southerly route to Washington. However, his advisors were against this route; and for political reasons, they decided that the inauguration journey was to pass through the major cities of the North. The final leg of the trip would be a stop in Harrisburg, Pennsylvania, on February 22 and then on to Baltimore arriving about eleven o'clock in the morning. Then go on to Washington the same day. In these larger cities, Lincoln would meet a larger number of influential politicians whose support he had to have.

Major David Hunter, later a Union general, was a member of the presidential party on that train trip from Springfield to Washington. Months earlier, he learned of a plot to assassinate Lincoln, and on October 20, 1860, Hunter wrote a letter warning Lincoln that "your success and safety being identified with the great Republican cause, the cause of peace, union and conservatism; must be my apology for addressing you. On a recent visit to the east, I met a lady of high character, who had been spending part of the summer among her friends and relatives in Virginia. She informed me that a number of young men in Virginia had bound themselves, by oaths most solemn, to cause your assassination, should you be elected. Now Sir, you may laugh at this story, and really it does appear too absurd to repeat, but I beg you to recollect, that on 'the institution' these good people are most certainly demented; and being crazy, they should be taken care of, to prevent their doing harm to themselves or others. Judicious, prompt and energetic action on the part of your Secretary of War, will do doubt secure your own safety, and the peace of the country."[53]

Hunter was not the only military officer who was concerned about Lincoln's safety. Another officer from the adjutant general's office, in Kalamazoo, Michigan, wrote, "Serious apprehensions exist in the minds of many of your friends, with regard to your personal safety, either at your inauguration or immediately following it. Entertaining similar views, I do accordingly tender to your Excellency a Regiment of well equipped-well, organized, and well officered citizens soldiers at present attached to the Military force of Michigan."[54]

There were some who perceived a threat to Lincoln's life and were willing to do something about it. One such person was George P. Bissell of Hartford, Connecticut, who, on December 30, 1860, wrote Lincoln offering protection: "Having seen threats that you shall not be inaugurated on the 4th of March next & having this morning seen letters from Republicans at Washington which give a very dark picture I write to offer you my services. If you say the word, I will be there with from twenty to one thousand men, or one hundred, (any reasonable number) organized & armed."[55]

Senator Seward, soon to be the secretary of state, wrote to Lincoln on December 28, 1860, "There is a feverish excitement here which awakens all kind of apprehensions of possible disturbance and disorders connected with your assumption of the government . . . . Habit has accustomed the public to anticipate the arrival of the President elect in this city about the middle of February, and evil minded persons would expect to organize their demonstrations for that time. I beg leave to suggest [that you] drop in the City a week or ten days earlier."[56]

Joseph Medill, who ran the *Chicago Tribune* from 1855 to 1899, also warned Lincoln that secessionists were planning to disrupt the inauguration in Washington:

> The evidences of my ears and eyes are forcing me to believe that the secessionists are seriously contemplating resistance to your inauguration in this Capitol. There is certainly a secret organization in this city numbering several hundred members having that purpose in view – sworn armed men, and bunches or lodges affiliated with them in design, extend south to Richmond, Raleigh & Charleston . . . . The Union & loyal sentiment of her citizens [Baltimore] is gradually giving way, and the vicious rabble are getting control. If things go on there for the next 60 days as they have for the last 30, the city will be under the complete control of Disunion Vigilance Committees and a reign of terror will domineer over that city . . . . There are other plans discovered such as to prevent the counting of the electoral votes in February, but this part of the scheme depends upon their ability to prevent your inauguration in the Capitol, and that depends, they admit (say), on the position that Maryland and Baltimore will take between now & then . . . and if Maryland gives way your friends will have to fight their way with the sword from the Pa. line to the Capitol . . . . I am not writing to you as an alarmist, but still I would not be true to my duty to you, to fail to warn you of what the enemy seems to be doing.[57]

Baltimore was indeed a dangerous place for Lincoln to go. E. B. Washburne, who later met Lincoln's train when it secretly arrived in Washington from Baltimore, wrote a worried letter on January 10 to Lincoln, "To my observation things look more threatening to-day than ever. I believe Va. and Maryland are both rotten to the core. We have had one of our friends from N. Y. in Baltimore, sounding matters there, and he gives most unfavorable reports. Great danger is to be apprehended from that quarter. The very worst secessionists and traitors at heart, are pretended Union men, and we have found out that one of these very men, has been in consultation with Corwin as to how to protect this city!!!"[58]

At the outbreak of the war, there was no military guard at the White House. Colonel Charles Halpine,[59] a member of General Halleck's staff, wrote, "I have many times entered the mansion, and walked up to the rooms of the two private secretaries, as late as nine or ten o'clock at night, without seeing or being challenged by a single soul. There were, indeed, two attendants, one for the outer door, and the other for the door of the official chambers; but these . . . were, not infrequently, somewhat remiss in their duties."[60]

One evening in late 1862, Lincoln came to General Halleck's private quarters to protest – half jocularly, half in earnest – against a small detachment of cavalry (Company K, 150th Pennsylvania) that had been detailed to guard him. Lincoln was annoyed that the men had been assigned to guard his carriage when he went to and returned from the soldiers' home.[61] Lincoln complained that he and Mary "couldn't hear themselves talk" because of clatter of the soldier's sabers and spurs; and Lincoln noted the guards were new recruits and very awkward, and he was more afraid of being shot by them accidentally than by someone making an attempt on his life.[62]

In October 1863, Governor Tod of Ohio visited the White House and was shocked at the lack of protection for Lincoln. He immediately applied to and received from the War Department permission to organize one hundred mounted bodyguards. The company, named the Union Light Guard, was composed of selected Ohioans all mounted on "fine black horses." Their responsibilities were to "guard the front entrance to the White House grounds, and to act as an escort to the President whenever he went out in his carriage, or when he rode on horse-back, as he often did during the summer."[63]

In addition to these mounted guards, an infantry company guarded the south side and east and west ends of the White House.

*    *    *

During the Civil War years, there were no telegraph facilities in the White House, so Lincoln had to walk to the military telegraph office, which was in the War Department Building, to get the latest battlefront news. Lincoln spent more time there than at any other place outside the White House. Lincoln generally made this trip in the morning, afternoon, and late at night. There he kept in touch with the events of the war; and during great battles, he spent many a sleepless night there. For most of the war, Lincoln had no protection at all during his nightly walks to the telegraph office. Lincoln would go over to the telegraph office alone; however, under orders for Secretary Stanton, he was not allowed to return unescorted.

The president disliked these security arrangements and sometimes evaded the guards on his nightly walks or asked the soldiers to stay behind. Stanton was constantly cautioning Lincoln to be more aware of the dangers around him. But Lincoln was a difficult man to control and continued to walk alone from the White House to the War Department during the night.

Stanton was infuriated by Lincoln's lack of caution and was bewildered by his refusal to accept security arrangements. Did he not care about his own life?

Sergeant Henry W. Knight, a guard assigned to the War Department, recalled that one dismal rainy night Lincoln said to his escort, "Don't come out in this storm with me, boys. I have an umbrella and can get home safely without you."

"But Mr. President," a soldier objected, "we have positive orders from Mr. Stanton not to allow you to return alone, and we dare not disobey his orders."

"No, I suppose not," agreed Lincoln. "If Stanton should learn that you had let me return alone, he would have you court-martialed and shot inside of twenty-four hours."[64]

Early in the summer of 1864, some of the soldiers of the Ohio company who were guarding Lincoln were restless and eager to see action with Grant. There came a time that summer when Lincoln was at the soldiers' home, one of the soldiers approached Lincoln about a change of service. Lincoln as was his custom answered the soldier with a story, "Well, my boy, that reminds me of an old farmer friend of mine in Illinois, who used to say he never could understand why the Lord put the curl in a pig's tail. It did not seem to him to be either useful or ornamental, but he guessed the Lord knew what he was doing when he put it there. I do not myself," he said, "see the necessity of having soldiers traipsing around after me wherever I go, but Stanton, who knows a great deal more about such things than I do, seems to think it necessary, and he may be right. And if it is necessary to have soldiers here, it might as well be you as someone else. If you were sent to the front, someone would have to come from the front to take your place.

"It is a soldier's duty to obey orders without question, and in doing that, you can serve your country as faithfully here as at the front, and I reckon it is not quite as dangerous here as it is there." The other soldiers, upon hearing of their comrade's unsuccessful effort to get a transfer, had a laugh, but none of the other member of that company ever again asked for a transfer from Lincoln.[65]

\*   \*   \*

Ward Hill Lamon, Lincoln's friend and legal associate from Danville, Illinois, was now Lincoln's self-proclaimed bodyguard and was constantly at his side. Lamon went to the chief of the Washington Metropolitan Police and convinced him to detail four special duty officers to the executive mansion. They wore civilian clothes and carried concealed weapons. Part of their duty was to accompany the president on his walks to the War Department, escort him to the theater, and outside of Lincoln's bedroom door.[66]

Lincoln continued to allow anyone who called at the White House to be sent upstairs to his study. He wanted to continue living his life as if he were still a private lawyer in Illinois. Lamon had a different point of view; he sent a memo to Lincoln saying, "I fear that there are eavesdroppers and traitors lurking about, [the White House] I would suggest that no one be allowed upstairs except such as you permit after they're sending up their cards." Lincoln ignored this warning.[67]

Meanwhile, threatening letters continued to be received at the White House. Those letters that Lincoln did receive he kept in a bulging folder in a special pigeonhole in his battered upright desk at the White House. Most of the threats that arrived in Lincoln's mailbag were destroyed; Stoddard, another of Lincoln's secretaries, apparently did destroy all the letters that came across his desk.[68]

The White House secretaries did not pass on all the letters because they thought that most of the anonymous threats and warnings came from deranged cranks and that assassins would not write to broadcast their intentions. A stoical Lincoln simply shrugged and declared "that if anybody was bad enough to kill him there was nothing on earth to prevent it."[69] He could only die once, he stoically told Secretary of the Navy Gideon Welles; and he was determined "not to suffer from continual apprehension."[70]

Stoddard recounted an incident in the White House involving some of Lincoln's hate mail – a "dignified, elderly man" waiting for an audience with Lincoln saw Stoddard, whose responsibility it was to open the incoming mail, disposing of some of the letters quickly. The visitor spoke up, saying, "Is that the way you treat the President's mail? . . . What would the people of the United States think, if they knew that their communications to their Chief Magistrate were dealt with in this shameful manner?"

Stoddard offered the visitor "a handful of the selected letters . . . . He took the awful handful and began to read, and his red face grew redder. Then it was white with speechless wrath. Perhaps he had never before perused anything quite so devilish in all his life."

"You are quite right, sir," he gasped, as he sank into his chair again. "Young man, you are right! He ought not to see a line of that stuff! Burn it, sir! Burn it! What devils there are!"[71]

If the threatening letters had been investigated rather than ignored and destroyed, security around Lincoln may have been more visible and organized. Lincoln's secretaries, however, were accustomed to the threats and ignored them, especially when so many threats were made; and the threatened violence never materialized. And as Stoddard wrote, "The assassination idea had taken possession of so many minds that not many days would pass without the coming of some kind of epistolary threat or warning."[72]

# CHAPTER 3

## *The Next Man Will Be Just as Bad for Them*

Lincoln's security was primitive, and because of the federal government's inexperience, much of it was haphazard. Security was supplied by the War Department; Stanton; the governor of Ohio; the Washington Metropolitan Police Department; and a private body guard, Ward Lamon. Too many agencies were employed, and responsibility was divided. Lincoln often went to public places unattended because he did not want to isolate himself from the public. Over and over, Lincoln demonstrated through words and deeds his fatalism and indifference to his own security.

George Healy, a leading American portrait painter of the nineteenth century, created the portrait of Lincoln that is now considered to be the best likeness of him. To pass the time while he was being painted, Lincoln would frequently launch "into anecdotes and reminiscences . . . . Now and then Lincoln would reveal some of his inter thoughts. He confided that the protection insisted upon by his guards irked him. Sometimes, he said, he managed to elude them, but felt so repentant when he realized their anxiety that he promised them each time 'to be more careful.'"[73]

Lincoln once told Francis Carpenter, "I do not see what the Rebels would gain by killing or getting possession of me. I am but a single individual, and it would not help their cause or make the least difference in the progress of the war. Everything would go right on just the same." And replying to the cautions of those around him, Lincoln responded, "If they kill me, the next man will be just as bad for them."[74]

In a conversation with Charles Halpine, Lincoln said, "Now, as to political assassination, do you think the Richmond people would like to have [Vice President] Hannibal Hamlin here any better than myself: In that one alternative, I have an insurance on my life worth half the prairie – land of Illinois. And besides if there were such a plot, and they wanted to get at me, no vigilance could keep them out. We are so mixed up in our affairs, that – no matter what the system established – a conspiracy to assassinate, if such there were, could easily obtain a pass to see me for any one or more of its instruments. To betray fear of this, by placing guards, and so forth, would only be to put the idea into their heads, and perhaps lead to the very result it was intended to prevent. As to the crazy folks, Major, (Halpine) why I must only take my chances-the worst crazy people I at present fear being some of my own too zealous adherents."[75]

Threats to Lincoln's life also came from the North. A Northern Copperhead editorial in 1864 *Beaver Dam Argus* (Wisconsin) read, "History shows several instances where people have only been saved by the assassination of their leaders, and history may repeat itself in this country. The time may come when it will be absolutely necessary that the people do away with such rulers the quickest way possible." An August 20, 1864, editorial of the *Wisconsin LaCrosse Democrat* stated, "And if he [Lincoln] is elected . . . for another four years, we trust some bold hand will pierce his heart with dagger point for the public good."[76]

In November 1864, Lt. Waldeman Alston, Company G, Eleventh Kentucky Cavalry, offered his services for covert action in the North. In June 1864, under the command of General John H. Morgan, he had been captured while on a raid in Kentucky. He escaped, made his way into Canada, and attempted to return to the Confederacy; but en route he became infected with yellow fever. While recovering from this disease in Sulpur Springs, Virginia, he wrote to Jefferson Davis, "I now offer you my services, and if you will favor me in my designs, I will proceed, as soon as my health will permit, to rid my country of some of her deadliest enemies, by striking at the very heart's blood of those who seek to enchain her in slavery. I consider nothing dishonorable having such a tendency."[77] No one in the Confederate government took his scheme seriously and never replied.

Another plot was offered by Major Joseph Walker Taylor, a cousin of Jefferson Davis's first wife. He had been wounded at the battle of Fort Donelson in February 1862. While convalescing in Louisville, he conceived a plan to go into Washington and capture Lincoln. He traveled to Washington by train and stayed with his uncle, Union General Joseph Taylor. Walker Taylor was one of four brothers who fought in the war, two on the side of the North and two on the side of the South. Later he attended a White House reception where he was introduced to Lincoln as Mr. Taylor of Kentucky. President Lincoln asked about his wounds, and Taylor replied that he received them at Fort Donelson. Lincoln commented on Taylor's bravery. Taylor watched the President's routine and, in the early summer, laid his plan before President Davis. The kidnapping would take place while Lincoln was traveling to his summer quarters at the soldiers' home. Davis, however, rejected the abduction scheme on the ground that Lincoln, a "western man" and former wrestler, would certainly resist capture, with a high probability that Lincoln would be killed. "I could not stand the imputation of having consented to let Mr. Lincoln be assassinated. Our cause could not stand it . . . . No, sir, I will not give my authority to abduct Lincoln."[78]

Davis said much later that Taylor was "the only man who ever talked to me on the subject of his [Lincoln's] capture or at least the only one who I believed intended to do what he proposed." Jefferson Davis spoke to his wife, Varina, about Taylor's idea, saying that "Taylor was a brave man and of course did not see that Mr. Lincoln could not be captured alive." After Davis explained to Taylor that "the plan was impracticable for that reason if for no other," Taylor agreed to drop it because he "would not lend himself to a plan of assassination any more than I would."[79]

The Confederate secretary of war believed that "the laws of war and morality, as well as Christian principles and sound policy forbid the use of such means." After the Kilpatrick-Dahlgren Raid in February and March of 1864, Confederates captured documents showing that the Union planned to burn Richmond and kill Jefferson Davis. The documents may have been forged; but, forged or not, people in the South held Lincoln responsible for the proposed assassination of Davis.[80]

*    *    *

During the winter of 1863-'64, Confederate Colonel Bradley Tyler Johnson proposed a plan to General Hampton to take 250 Maryland cavalrymen across the Potomac River above Georgetown and make a lightning raid on the soldiers' home to capture Lincoln. General Hampton, after several discussions, gave his approval. The Confederate spies in Washington had kept Richmond authorities current on the disposition and strength of the federal units in and around Washington.

At that time, it was well-known that President Lincoln frequently spent summer nights at the soldiers' home, taking advantage of the cooler nights. In fact during his presidency, Lincoln spent up to a quarter of his nights at the soldiers' home. The plan called for a selected group of five cavalryman to capture Lincoln, cross the Eastern Branch of the Potomac River into Southern Maryland, and then cross the Potomac River back into Virginia. The main body of soldiers would cut the telegraph wires, block the roads between Washington and Baltimore, and then move back through Western Maryland to Virginia. If that means of retreat were cut off, Johnson was to go up into Pennsylvania and then west to West Virginia.[81] All these movements were to distract the pursuing federal armies from the direction the captured president would be taken.

The plan fell through when the Union's General Sheridan advanced upon the Confederate capital. Colonel Johnson and his battalion, preparing for the abduction mission, received orders to join General Early at once to act as rear guard. General Early did reassure Johnson that as soon as Union General Hunter could be driven from Lynchburg, Johnson could return to his plan of capturing Lincoln.

But fate took another turn.

Johnson was promoted to brigadier general after General Williams E. Jones was killed in battle on June 5, 1864, and was assigned to command his brigade. The plot to capture Lincoln was abandoned because General Sheridan's Army of the Shenandoah destroyed Early's army and with it any plans to capture Lincoln.

The plan had obvious defects since the raid was to have been carried out without firm knowledge that Lincoln would actually be at the soldiers' home on the night of the raid. The plan may have been abandoned when it was fully explored or when Johnson became brigadier general, and other duties took up his time. At any rate, the operation could never have been carried out because Secretary of War Seddon and Jefferson Davis denied approval. The political and military consequences of abducting Lincoln would have been enormous and would have affected the course of Confederate history.[82]

Taylor, Bradley, and later John Wilkes Booth, all proposed to capture Lincoln as a military strategy to change to direction of the war. Kidnapping a private citizen was a civil matter; however, capturing the commander in chief of the armed forces in time of war was quite another. Capturing (the Southern point of view) or kidnapping (the Northern point of view) the commander in chief in time of war was definitely under the jurisdiction of military law. All the kidnapping plots were designed to affect military operations and hopefully the outcome of the war.

One thing that the Taylor, Bradley, and Booth schemes had in common was the escape route. They all involved going through Southern Maryland and crossing the Potomac into Virginia. This route was favored because throughout the entire war, the Confederate Signal Bureau had a number of underground routes through Southern Maryland that involved crossing the Potomac into Virginia.

*　　*　　*

Private citizens warned Lincoln of assassination plots, but Lincoln encouraged his staff to ignore them. One letter cautioned Lincoln that there were "hordes of Secesh-sympathizers" around Washington who would not hesitate to shoot him on his rides to the soldiers' home. "If, you value your life! do, I entreat of you, discontinue your visits, out of the City."[83]

Although there were Copperhead editorials, threatening letters, and real and imagined plots of abduction and assassination, there may have been one attempt on Lincoln's life at the soldiers' home. The home, about three miles from the White House, had been established by General Winfield Scott for Mexican War veterans. Lincoln found it a quiet place where he and his family could escape the city heat.[84] Private John W. Nichols, Company K, 105th Pennsylvania Volunteers, who later was to become head of the Omaha Fire Department, was one of Lincoln's bodyguards from the summer of 1862 until 1865. His company had been assigned to guard the White House and the soldiers' home. Nichols reported that Lincoln "persistently refused an escort, imagining himself perfectly secure."

Nichols at the home described the possible assassination attempt.

I was doing sentinel duty at the large gate through which entrance was had to the grounds of the Home. The grounds are situated about a quarter of a mile off the Bladensburg road, and are reached by devious driveways. About 11 o'clock I heard a rifle shot in the direction of the city, and shortly afterwards I heard approaching hoof-beats. In two or three minutes a horse came dashing up, and I recognized the belated President. The horse was very spirited, and belonged to Mr. Lamon, marshal of the District of Columbia. The horse was Mr. Lincoln's favorite, and when he [the horse] was in the White House stables he [Lincoln] always chose him. As horse and rider approached the gate, I noticed that the President was bareheaded. After assisting him in checking his steed, the President said to me: "He came pretty near getting away with me, didn't he? He got the bit in his teeth before I could draw the rein."

I then asked him where his hat was, and he replied that somebody had fired a gun off down at the foot of the hill, and that his horse had become scared and jerked his hat off.

I led the animal to the Executive Cottage, and the President dismounted and entered. Thinking the affair rather strange, a corporal and myself started in the direction of the place from where the sound of the rifle report had proceeded, to investigate the occurrence. When we reached the spot where the driveway intersects with the main road we found the President's hat – a plain silk hat – and upon examining it we discovered a bullet hole through the crown. The shot had been fired upwards, and it was evident that the person who fired the shot had secreted himself close to the roadside. We listened and searched the locality thoroughly, but to no avail. The next day I gave Mr. Lincoln his hat and called his attention to the bullet hole. He rather unconcernedly remarked that it was put there by some foolish gunner, and was not intended for him. He said, however, that he wanted the matter kept quiet, and admonished us to say nothing about it. We all felt confident that it was an attempt to kill him, and a well-nigh successful one, too. The affair was kept quiet, in accordance with his request. After that, the President never rode alone.[85]

The increased threat to Lincoln's safety was now so apparent that Lincoln was forced to accept a military escort to and from the soldiers' home. Barracks for a company of the Seventh Independent Company of Ohio Volunteer Cavalry were quickly built near the White House, and henceforth, both of the president's residences were patrolled by cavalry. Lincoln, however, often foiled this security by slipping away in his carriage, so protection was by no means complete.[86] Lincoln also walked in the late afternoon through Washington with no guards or escorts but his friends Frank Carpenter and Noah Brooks.

\*   \*   \*

Lamon carried two revolvers and a knife in the defense of Lincoln. During the fall of 1864, Lamon did not sleep at home a single night. He left home about ten o'clock at night to go to the White House where he remained during the night without Lincoln's knowledge.[87]

In November, Washington's chief of police William B. Webb assigned a small force of four policemen as bodyguards for Lincoln. The four men were Elphonso Dunn, Thomas Pendel, Alexander Smith, and the soon-to-be-infamous John Parker. Not long after the police guard's arrival, Thomas Pendel took the position of doorkeeper; and on January 4, 1865, William H. Crook was added to this police detail. These men were all armed with revolvers and worked on a rotating schedule. Two men were on duty from eight in the morning to four in the afternoon. They guarded the approach to the president in his office or elsewhere in the building and accompanied him on walks. At four o'clock, another man went on duty and remained until midnight, or later if Mr. Lincoln had gone outside the White House and had not returned by that time. At twelve, the second night guard went on duty until he was relieved at eight in the morning. The night guards were expected to protect the president on his way to and from the War Department and to patrol the corridor outside his bedroom while he slept.[88]

This extremely small contingent, spread thinly over the course of Lincoln's day, amounted to an acknowledgement of potential danger but was inadequate. The men were ill trained. Lincoln consented, but "he wished as little show as possible of this precaution." Lincoln wanted the guards to wear civilian clothes, and no mention was made of their appointment in the newspapers. They "walked with him, not behind him. The President was simple in his manners; he was in the habit of talking freely with any one who wished to speak to him. So it happened that a passer-by had no way of knowing that the man in plain clothes who walked by Mr. Lincoln's side was any other than the casual friend, office-seeker, petitioner, adviser, who helped to fill up every minute of the President's waking time."[89]

It was difficult to distinguish real conspiracies from empty boasting and from mere rumors growing out of barroom confidentialities. Warnings and threats of danger were common; however, some of them were investigated. "Warnings that appeared to be most definite," wrote the president's secretaries, "when they came to be examined proved too vague and confused for further attention."[90]

\*   \*   \*

Southern civilians also had plans to bring about the death of Lincoln. Confederate George Washington Gayle, a forty-three-year-old Alabama lawyer with extreme views on slavery and the rebellion, placed an advertisement in the *Selma Dispatch* on December 1, 1864,

> One Million Dollars Wanted to have Peace by the 1st of March.-If the citizens of the Southern Confederacy will furnish me with the cash, or good securities for the sum of one million dollars, I will cause the lives of Abraham Lincoln, Wm. H. Seward, and Andrew Johnson to be taken by the 1st of March next. This will give us peace, and satisfy the world that cruel tyrants can not live in a 'land of liberty.' If this is not accomplished, nothing will be claimed beyond the sum of fifty thousand dollars in advance, which is supposed to be necessary to reach and slaughter the three villains. I will give, myself, one thousand dollars toward this patriotic purpose. Every one wishing to contribute will address Box X, Cahawba, Alabama.[91]

Not a good idea since Lincoln was assassinated four months later, and Gayle was arrested in Alabama on May 25, 1865. He maintained that the advertisement for the assassination of government leaders was nothing more than a joke and came as a result of a banquet speech. That speech, he claimed, was later printed in the *Selma Dispatch*. He claimed that not one dollar of pledged money was ever paid to this assassination fund. Gayle was indicted on conspiracy to assassinate the president, and he was tried and convicted in the South.

Finally on April 27, 1867, Gayle received a full pardon after many endorsements and petitions on his behalf. President Johnson and Secretary Stanton believed him to be a harmless and eccentric Southerner.[92]

* * *

There may have been a bombing plot against the life of President Lincoln. William H. Snyder, a Confederate enlisted man from General Gabriel J. Rains's Torpedo Bureau had information about a possible bombing plot. He told the story to Colonel Edward H. Ripley, Ninth Vermont Infantry, who led one of the first federal units into Richmond on April 4, 1865.[93] Ripley thought him a "more than usually intelligent and a fine-appearing man," and during their conversation, Snyder told Ripley that he felt that the war "was hopeless . . . [and] his conscience told him every life taken now was in a way a wanton murder."[94]

Ripley recalled the meeting,

> He knew that a party had just been dispatched from Rains' torpedo bureau on a secret mission, which vaguely he understood was aimed at the head of the Yankee government, and he wished to put Mr. Lincoln on his guard and have impressed upon him that just at this moment he believed him to be in great danger of violence and he should take greater care of himself. He could give no names or facts, as the work of his department was secret, and no

man knew what his comrade was sent to do, but of this he was convinced,
that the President of the United States was in great danger.[95]

Ripley had his adjutant, Captain Rufus P. Staniels, take Snyder's statement under
oath. Ripley then sent a message asking Lincoln, who was still in Virginia near City
Point, for a meeting. Lincoln replied that they could meet at nine the next morning,
April 5 aboard the flagship *Malvern*, where Lincoln was staying. At the meeting, Snyder
waited outside of Lincoln's cabin while Ripley discussed Snyder's statement and the
dangers to Lincoln by the Torpedo Bureau. Ripley urged the president to listen to
Snyder to hear the story firsthand. Predictably, Lincoln replied, "No, it is impossible
for me to adopt and follow your suggestions. I deeply appreciate the feeling which has
led you to urge them on me, but I must go on in the course marked out for me, and I
cannot bring myself to believe that any human lives who would do me harm."[96]

Lamon believed that "there never was a moment from the day he crossed the
Maryland line, up to the time of the assassination, that he was not in danger of death
by violence, and that his life was spared until the night of the 14th of April, 1865, only
through the ceaseless and watchful care of the guards thrown around him."[97]

"Four year of threats and boasting, of alarms that were unfounded, and of plots
that came to nothing thus passes away; but precisely at the time when the triumph
of the nation over the long insurrection seemed assured, and a feeling of peace and
security was diffused over the country, one of the conspiracies, not seemingly more
important than the many abortive ones, ripened in the sudden heat of hatred and
despair."[98]

Noah Brooks recounts that one night in 1864 as he and Lincoln were walking
back to the White House from the War Department, he thought he saw a figure of a
man dodging behind a nearby tree. "As we passed in safety, I came to the conclusion
that the dodging figure was a creature of the imagination." This incident began a
conversation in which Lincoln said to Noah Brooks, "I long ago made up my mind
that if anybody wants to kill me, he will do it. If I wore a shirt of mail, and kept myself
surrounded by a body-guard, it would be all the same. There are a thousand ways of
getting at a man if it is desired that he should be killed."[99]

Hate for Lincoln had been growing since his first inaugural. This atmosphere of
hate, coupled with four years of civil war, and Lincoln's own indifference to his safety,
set the stage for America's first presidential assassination.

# CHAPTER 4

## *For It Did Look So Cowardly*

Baltimore was a city of Southern sentiment trapped behind Union lines. Central and eastern Maryland was largely of confederate sympathy, and Lincoln later used brute military force keeping it in the Union.

In late summer of 1860, William Byrne, a Baltimore businessman, created the National Volunteers to work for the election of John C. Breckinridge.[100] But when Breckinridge lost, Byrne had no trouble persuading his group to prevent Lincoln's inauguration. Lincoln, blissfully unaware that there were such men as Byrne who would do him harm, was scheduled to pass through Baltimore on February 23 on his trip from Illinois to Washington. Using the Northern Central Railroad, he was to come from Harrisburg, Pennsylvania, and arrive at Baltimore's Calvert Street Station at about noon. From the station, Lincoln would take a carriage through the streets of Baltimore to the home of a railroad executive for lunch. In the early 1860s, many of the nation's railroad tracks were of different gauges. And this was the case in Baltimore; in order to get to Washington, a traveler had to switch trains.

Byrne and his group planned to kill Lincoln as his carriage passed from one train station to another. The plan was that Lincoln was to be shot by multiple assassins, who would then escape into the crowd. But on the evening of the twenty-first, Lincoln learned of the plot to assassinate him, and at the urging of General Scott and Secretary of State-designate Seward, agreed to pass through the city unannounced during the early morning hours of February 23.

In January 1861, Samuel M. Felton, president of the Philadelphia, Wilmington, and Baltimore Railroad, received information from social worker Dorthea Dix of reported rumors in the Baltimore slums that secessionists in Maryland planned to isolate Washington. They planned to burn the bridges north of Baltimore as well as Maryland's Havre de Grace train ferry on the Susquehanna River. Alarmed, Felton sent this information to General Winfield Scott in Washington. Felton continued to receive reports of plots against his railroad; and finally, fearful of damage to railroad property, retained the Chicago detective Allan Pinkerton.[101]

By February 3, Pinkerton was in Baltimore with detectives Harry Davies, Kate Warne, and Timothy Webster, who was later hanged in Richmond as a Union spy. Pinkerton sent Warne and Davies to the Barnum Hotel. It was, he found, a well-known gathering place for Southern sympathizers. The two, posing as Southerners with strong secessionist views, found it easy to infiltrate secessionist organizations.

Pinkerton, meanwhile, secured office space at 44 South Street and set up his cover as a stockbroker under the name John H. Hutcheson of Charleston, South Carolina. Within days, he had unearthed evidence of a plot to kill Lincoln. Baltimore police chief Marshal George P. Kane was an active Southern supporter, so Pinkerton concluded that the police could not be trusted in the event of an emergency. He was right, Kane later became a Confederate officer.

Pinkerton's other agent, Timothy Webster, joined a sessionist cavalry unit, near Havre de Grace, Maryland, and uncovered a plan to destroy bridges and other railroad property. Meanwhile Kate Warne was using her feminine charm to infiltrate Baltimore's social elite.

Pinkerton's investigators discovered that a barber at the Barnum Hotel, Cipriano Fernandina, was behind the assassination plot. He was a member of Byrnes National Volunteers and had recently been called before the congressional select committee, which was looking into possible assassination plots in early February. One of Pinkerton's detectives was invited to attend a meeting where Fernandina outlined a plan to assassinate Lincoln at the Calvert Street Station.

Alarmed by the threats of assassination, Pinkerton sent a warning letter to Norman B. Judd, general counsel of the Chicago and Rock Island Railroad. Judd, a leader in the Illinois Republican Party, was on the train with the Lincoln party en route to Washington. Pinkerton's agent, William H. Scott, caught up with the Lincoln entourage at Cincinnati and handed Pinkerton's letter to Judd at breakfast on February 13. Judd decided not to warn Lincoln or others in the party until he got more details from Pinkerton. As Lincoln's train roared eastward, Pinkerton and his detectives continued to probe the pro-Confederate activities in Baltimore.

One aspect of Pinkerton's investigation was his office neighbor at 44 South Street, a broker named James H. Luckett. Luckett arranged a meeting between Mr. Hutcheson (Pinkerton) and the barber, Cipriano Ferrandini, at John Barr's saloon on South Street. Also present at this meeting was William H. H. Turner, clerk of the Baltimore Circuit Court. Luckett introduced them to Pinkerton as Captain Ferrandini and Captain Turner, and Ferrandini told Pinkerton about how the group planned to kill Lincoln when he came through Baltimore.

As soon as Pinkerton could get out of the meeting, he sent another warning letter to Judd, which reached him at Buffalo. Pinkerton recommended that Lincoln change his travel plans and come through Baltimore secretly and at night. Pinkerton was not sure whether Judd understood the gravity of the situation or even whether he believed Pinkerton at all. So Pinkerton directed Kate Warne to take a train to New York on February 18. She carried another letter addressed to Judd and a letter of introduction to Edward S. Sanford, American Telegraph Company president, in case the cooperation of the telegraph company would be needed. It took Warne a little over a day to get to New York, and it was not until seven thirty the next evening that she was able to meet with Judd.

In her room at the Astor House, Warne showed Judd Pinkerton's letter, which urged Lincoln to change his travel plans. Judd finally became alarmed enough to take action. He told Warne that he was going to call in the New York City Police, but Warne persuaded him to wait. No one, she said, was able to handle the situation but Pinkerton. Pinkerton would, she said, be in Philadelphia on February 21.

Judd agreed, and Warne returned to Baltimore on the next train to report to Pinkerton about the meeting. Up to this point, Norman Judd was the only one on the Lincoln train who knew of the plot.

As planned, on February 21 about 7:00 PM, Pinkerton and Felton met with Judd in room 21 of Philadelphia's St. Louis Hotel. Felton first explained what Pinkerton was doing for the railroad in Baltimore. Then Pinkerton told about the plot against the president. Judd listened carefully and then agreed with the men that it would be risky for Lincoln to pass through Baltimore during the day as scheduled.

"I want you, Mr. Pinkerton, to talk to the President personally," Judd said.[102]

The two went to the Continental Hotel, and after some difficulty in making arrangements, the meeting got underway at 10:15 p.m. in Judd's room with only Lincoln, Judd, and Pinkerton present.

"You must leave for Washington tonight," Pinkerton said flatly after he told his story. Lincoln, however, refused, "I am scheduled to raise a flag over Philadelphia's Independence Hall in the morning and I have to appear in Harrisburg in the afternoon. I cannot break these engagements." Lincoln surveyed the disappointed faces of the two men. Then said, "I will, however, leave with Pinkerton in the evening."[103]

Lincoln's conference with Pinkerton and Judd ended at 11:00 p.m.; and upon his return to the hotel, Lincoln met Frederick Seward, son of Senator Seward. Young Seward delivered a letter dated Washington February 21 from his father: "My son goes express to you – He will show you a report made by our detective to General Scott – and by him communicated to me this morning. I deem it so important as to dispatch my son to meet you whenever he may find you – I concur with Genl Scott in thinking it best for you to reconsider your arrangements. No one here but Genl Scott, myself & the bearer is aware of this communication."[104]

Frederick Seward's trip to Philadelphia was the result of a parallel investigation by detectives sent to Baltimore by John A. Kennedy, superintendent of the New York City Police, on February 1, 1861. These New York detectives also quickly penetrated the secessionist apparatus. David S. Bookstaver, a New York detective, posing as a music agent, soon confirmed the conspiracies. The detectives' instructions were to report secretly to Colonel Charles P. Stone, inspector general to General Winfield Scott, and, from him, to Senator Seward. Young Seward left for Philadelphia carrying General Scott's report and a letter from Seward to Lincoln. Independently, Kennedy's detectives picked up much the same information as Pinkerton's men and came to the same conclusion.[105] The confirming reports made Lincoln decide to pass quickly through Baltimore and to arrive in Washington unannounced.[106] Young Seward, much relieved, sent a message to his father saying that "his advice had been taken."[107]

Later that night in Judd's room, Pinkerton, Sanford, Colonel Scott, Felton, Lamon, and railroad and telegraph officials anxiously worked through the night in to develop a plan to get Lincoln into Washington safely.[108] The key element in Pinkerton's plan was secrecy: A train, with a private car, was to be ready at Harrisburg with the telegraph line to Baltimore disconnected and other lines closely watched. At dusk, Lincoln would slip away from the hotel and leave by the train. When the train got to Baltimore, a carriage would take him across town to a sleeping car hooked to the regular Baltimore and Ohio train. Pinkerton and Warne would provide security from Philadelphia to Washington, arriving in Washington at 6:00 a.m.[109]

The train with Mrs. Lincoln and children, in which Lincoln would have ridden would go on to Baltimore as scheduled with Judd and the military escort on board for protection.

Lincoln's train left Harrisburg for Philadelphia at 10:55 p.m., where Pinkerton and Warne met them. There was a small layover, so Pinkerton had a private carriage waiting and drove Lincoln around the city until it was time to board the train. When it was time, the Lincoln entourage boarded the last car. Half of the car had been curtained off with the pretext that it was for Kate Warne's sick brother. The four of them occupied this part of the sleeper for the journey to Baltimore.

The train arrived in Baltimore at three thirty in the morning. The sleeping cars were uncoupled and pulled over the connecting line to the Camden Street Station. There in the early morning hours, Lincoln made his connections aboard a Baltimore and Ohio train for Washington. Everything went as planned, and just after six on the morning of February 23, Lincoln arrived in Washington. He was met by Congressman Elihu Washburne, who had been sent by Seward, and taken by carriage to the Willard Hotel.[110]

Lincoln, who was roundly criticized in the press for avoiding Baltimore always regretted the way he had entered Washington. "It was," he said "a grave mistake in listening to the solicitations of a professional spy and of friends too easily alarmed." Lincoln frequently upbraided Judd "for having aided him to degrade himself at the very moment in all his life when his behavior should have exhibited the utmost dignity and composure."

Later Lincoln told Lamon, "You know I have always told you I thought you an idiot that ought to be put in a straitjacket for your apprehensions of my personal danger from assassination. You also know that the way we skulked into this city, in the first place, has been a source of shame and regret to me, for it did look so cowardly!"[111]

# PART 2

# CHAPTER 5

## *He Had a Winning Personality*

The Booths were an Anglo-American family of stage tragedians. The father and three of his sons made significant contributions to the American theater. The family patriarch, Junius Brutus Booth, made his debut in London in 1813.[112] With his portrayal of Richard III in 1817, he became one of England's most famous tragedians. He left England to pursue an acting career in America. Abandoning his Beligian wife, Adelaide, and five-year-old son, Richard, he left with his mistress. She was Mary Ann Holmes, a London flower girl. The couple arrived in Norfolk, Virginia, on June 30, 1821.[113]

Holmes presented herself as Mrs. Booth to all her new acquaintances and began to bear children with great regularity. Junius Brutus Booth Jr., the first of ten children, was born in Charleston, South Carolina, in 1821.[114] Although Junius became an actor, he was even more successful as a theater manager.

Rosalie Ann, born in 1823, was throughout her life an introvert, who did not relate well to others. The family politely referred to her as an invalid. Rosalie stayed at home with her mother until 1885 when her mother died.[115]

Edwin Thomas Booth, born in 1833, followed in his father's footsteps and became a tragedian of international reputation.[116] At the age of sixteen, he debuted with his father. In 1854, he toured Australia with actress Laura Keene, and in 1861, he performed in London. Edwin also managed the New York's Winter Garden Theater from 1863 to 1867; acted a record one hundred consecutive performances in the role of Hamlet, an unheard of feat in those days; and built New York's Booth's Theater after the Winter Garden burned down.

John Wilkes Booth, born in Bel Air, Maryland, on May 10, 1838, was the ninth child. Like his father and two of his brothers, he also became a noted Shakespearean actor. He excelled at portraying the sound and fury that excited audiences.

In 1842, Junius' son by Adelaide, Richard, came from London to visit his father. Later, Richard reported to his mother about his father's common-law wife, Mary Ann, and his half brothers and sisters. Adelaide had not seen her husband since 1821 but must have heard in theater circles that her husband had a family in America. In fact, it is most likely that she sent her son Richard to America to confirm the rumors. After receiving this news from her son, Adelaide Booth left Liverpool and arrived in New York on October 31, 1846. After arriving in America, Adelaide wrote an angry letter to her sister, Terese, in England, "Nobody here has any notion that I am the wife of the famous tragedian." She also wrote that her lawyer would "fall on his [Junius] back like a bomb."

Adelaide wanted her part of the fortune Junius had amassed, and she planned to win a considerable amount of money when she filed for divorce, charging adultery.[17] The divorce was not challenged, and on April 18, 1851, the divorce was granted. Still, Adelaide had trouble letting go. When she died in Baltimore on March 9, 1858, her tombstone read, "Wife of Junius Brutus Booth Tragedian." On John Wilkes Booth's thirteenth birthday, May 10, 1851, Junius Sr. married Mary Ann Holmes. The Booth househould was a loving one; however, the prevailing traits of Booth family members seems to have been those of alcoholism and bouts of depression.

John Wilkes Booth was baptized and first attended day schools near his Baltimore home. In 1849 when he was eleven years old, he attended a Quaker boarding school twelve miles from his home. Three years later, he boarded at an Episcopal school for one year in Catonsville, Maryland. During that year, John became fast friends with Samuel B. Arnold, son of a wealthy Baltimore baker. Arnold later was the first to be recruited by John Wilkes in September 1864. At the age of fifteen, Booth's education ended.

Junius Brutus Booth Sr., who stayed active in the theater until his death on November 30, 1852. He was buried in a Baltimore cemetery; however, on June 13, 1869, Edwin Booth purchased lots at the Green Mount Cemetery in Baltimore, and bodies of family members from other cemeteries, including that of his father, Junius Sr., were reinterred there. Green Mount Cemetery eventually held all the Booth children except Edwin and Junius Brutus Jr.

Mary Ann Booth continued to farm the Bel Air estate after her husband died. But the responsibility of running the farm fell to John Wilkes.[118] But John knew little about farming, and the farm failed. His mother then had to lease out the land, slaves, and animals. The Booth family continued, however, to live on the property. Mary Ann and the young Booths got a firsthand view of how others treated slaves and horses when their tenant took over the farm. The Booths were horrified to see their slaves and horses worked to exhaustion.

One day, Mary Ann and two of her daughters, Rosalie and Asia, argued with the tenant over the treatment of the Booths' slaves and horses. The tenant farmer told Booth's mother to mind her own business. When John was told of the argument, he went to talk to the tenant farmer to get more reasonable treatment for the slaves and animals. Booth also asked for an apology for the manner his tenant had used in speaking to Booth's mother and sisters.

"Will you go up to my house this moment with me and apologize to my mother and sisters for the abusive names you have called them?" Booth asked.

"First find your ladies!" the tenant growled. Then to justify his actions, he said, "Do you think I am going to lose my share of these crops just to save a lot of lazy dumb beasts and thick-skulled niggers from being tired? Apologize! I won't!"

"Then I'll whip you like the scoundrel that you are!" cried Booth, and he struck the man over the head with a stick. "I knocked him down, which made him bleed like a butcher," he wrote an old school friend. "He then warranted me and in a couple of weeks I have to stand trial. For assault and battery."[119] A local magistrate came out to the Booth farm and, after some discussion, ordered the Booth family to keep the peace.

John, unlike his older brothers, Junius Jr. and Edwin, wasn't trained in acting by his father and never appeared on the stage with him. Edwin, who some felt surpassed even his father in distinction, recognized John's talent and innovation and felt that he could have made "a brilliant mark in the theatrical world."[120]

Booth's acting career began at the age of seventeen on August 14, 1855. John, having acted in his first play, immediately went to tell his favorite sister, Asia, about it. He had acted as Richmond in *Richard III* at the St. Charles Theatre in Baltimore. The play was a benefit performance for John Sleeper Clarke, a boyhood friend of Edwin's. Clarke later became a successful comedian and married Asia.[121] The theater was under the management of Laura Keene, who later starred in the play *Our American Cousin*, during the course of which John Wilkes Booth assassinated President Lincoln. She and Edwin Booth knew one another at the time and were on very unfriendly terms, having fought over a business matter during a previous engagement.

Booth's mother was, as expected, not happy about John's becoming an actor. Although she had married an actor, and two of her other sons were actors, she had hoped that her favorite son would take up a more stable and socially acceptable career. But John had been bitten by the acting bug.[122]

John Clarke helped Booth get hired by at the William Wheatley Arch Street Theatre. The season ran from August 15, 1857, to June 19, 1858. The theater season began in late summer and ended the following June because in summer the theater became too hot, and there was no way to cool the building. Booth worked the next two seasons at the Old Marshall Theatre in Richmond; in those two years, Booth learned about the theater and the art of acting.[123]

Booth was excited about fulfilling his dream of becoming an actor; however, he was also becoming obsessed with Southern issues. He had grown up in an area of Southern sentiment, and now he took every opportunity to loudly proclaim his beliefs in Southern rights. Increasingly he wanted to gain Southern approval and acclaim. George Wren, an actor who had known and acted with Booth in Richmond, characterized Booth as a man "strongly Southern."[124]

\*　　\*　　\*

In 1859, two events occurred that changed Booth's Southern sympathy to fanaticism – John Brown's raid on Harpers Ferry and his subsequent hanging.

Brown was captured, tried, and, as expected, found guilty and sentenced to hang. The execution was to take place in Charlestown, Virginia, on December 2. No one knew whether his supporters would try to rescue him, and so militias were ordered to Charlestown to maintain order.

In Richmond on November 24, Booth was on break from rehearsals. For a long time, he had been nursing his anger against abolitionists. Booth believed the role of slaves was subjugation. He, like many whites of the time, saw slaves as subhuman and certainly did not want them freed. He accepted the theory of white Southern males that if freed, the black man would lust after white woman and "mongrelize" the white race. With these ideas heavy on his mind, Booth, idling his time between rehearsals, caught sight of the Richmond Grays and the Richmond Blues as they were marching down the street. They had been assigned duty at Charlestown by Governor Wise of Virginia to guard John Brown and the men captured with him. Booth impulsively asked if he could join the Grays, and Captain Louis J. Bossieux allowed him to join as a private and issued him a uniform. Booth was thrilled. When asked how the play would proceed without him, he replied, "I don't know and don't care."[125]

A correspondent of the *Richmond Enquirer* who came to report on the militiamen in Charleston wrote, "Amongst them I notice Mr. J. Wilkes Booth, a son of Junius Brutus Booth, who, though not a member, as soon as he heard the tap of the drum, threw down the sock and buskin, and shouldered his musket and marched with the Grays to the reported scene of deadly conflict."[126]

On December 2, 1859, the day of John Brown's execution, Booth was less than fifty feet from the gallows. Brown had written a note and had given it to his executioners: "I John Brown am now quite certain that the crimes of this guilty land will never be purged away but with Blood. I had as I now think vainly flattered myself that without much bloodshed it might be done." Strange words coming from someone who personally initiated and participated in much bloodshed. Unfortunately for thousands of young men, this prophecy would later become true. Two days after Brown's execution, the militia returned to Richmond, and Booth went back to the theater.[127]

Booth's career took off, but so did his tendency toward injury. On October 1, 1860, Booth began a tour with Matthew Canning's company as Romeo. On October 12, Booth was scheduled to play Hamlet but did not appear because Canning had accidentally shot him while attempting to let the hammer down on a pistol. Booth had received a "flesh wound in the thigh;"[128] however, the next day, Booth played Charles DeMoor in *The Robbers*. The exertion may have been too much for him though; it was five days before he returned to the stage reciting the funeral oration of Marc Anthony. The acting company then traveled to Montgomery, Alabama, without Booth. He joined them five days later. He performed in Montgomery until December 1 and then left for Philadelphia to see his sister.

Asia, now married to John Clarke, was delighted to see her brother but was concerned about his health. She wrote a letter saying, "John is home. He is looking well, but his wound is not entirely healed yet: he still carries the ball in him."[129]

By January 21, 1861, Booth was feeling well again and performed in Rochester and then on to Albany's Green Street Gayety Theatre where opening night went well. However, the next day, while playing Pescara in *The Apostate*, Booth fell on a dagger, the point cutting him in the right armpit. This accident kept him off the stage for a week. When he returned to the play, his right arm had to be tied to his side. Despite his wound, the reviews were good: "His acting was so fearfully real in some of the scenes as to cause a thrilling sensation to pervade the audience."[130]

On Booth's first morning in Albany, he expressed his strong Southern sentiment in public at the Stanwix Hotel. He had created such a loud disturbance that the manager of the theater at which Booth was performing was approached, and it was suggested that Booth had better tone down his rhetoric. The treasurer of the theater, Mr. Cuyler, promptly told Booth that if he continue to express his Southern sentiments "in public, not only would he kill his engagement, but endanger his person."[131] Booth agreed, but privately, he seethed with contempt for Northern audiences. Booth performed in Maine and then went back to Albany where he was injured again, but this time not on stage.

After his last performance on April 27, Booth was ending an affair he was having with the actress Henrietta Irving.[132] They were both staying at the Stanwix Hotel. Irving, however, felt that there had been an understanding that he would marry her and was angry when he told her the relationship was over. She pleaded with him to continue the relationship, but when he refused, she drew a knife and rushed at him. But Booth threw up his arm and only received a minor cut. Irving returned to her own room and in a show of anger cut herself. However, after seeing her own red blood oozing from her pale skin, she stopped, having inflicted only a superficial wound.[133]

\* \* \*

During this time, near the beginning of the war, a twist of fate connected Robert Lincoln and Edwin Booth. Robert Lincoln was standing on the platform of the Pennsylvania Railroad Station in Jersey City. He was in line watching passengers in front of him purchase their sleeping car reservations from the conductor at the door of the train. Robert Lincoln later described the incident,

> The platform was about the height of the car floor, and there was of course a narrow space between the platform and the car body. There was some crowding, and I happened to be pressed by it against the car body while waiting my turn. In this situation the train began to move, and by the motion I was twisted off my feet, and had dropped somewhat, with feet downward, into the open space, and was personally helpless, when my coat collar was vigorously seized, and I was quickly pulled up and out to a secure footing

on the platform. Upon turning to thank my rescuer, I saw it was Edwin Booth, whose face was of course well known to me, and I expressed my gratitude to him, and, in doing so, called him by name.

Robert Lincoln was understandably grateful to Edwin Booth for saving his life and told many people of the incident during his lifetime.[134]

\*    \*    \*

Booth spent considerable time on the road. For the 1861-1862 season, he appeared in Buffalo, (October 28 to November 9), Detroit (November 11 to 18), Cincinnati (November 25 to December 7), Louisville (December 9 to January 4), St. Louis (January 6 to January 18), Chicago (January 20 to February 1), Baltimore (February 17 to March 8), New York (March 17 to April 5), a return to St. Louis (April 21 to May 3), Boston (May 12 to May 23), Chicago again (June 2 to June 21), and closed the season in Louisville (June 25 to July 1).

In the 1862-1863 season, Booth appeared in Lexington for two nights (October 23 and 24), then Louisville (October 27 to November 8), Cincinnati (November 10 to November 22), Chicago (December 1 to December 20), St. Louis (December 22 to January 3), Boston (January 19 to February 13), Philadelphia (March 2 to March 14), Washington (at Grover's Theatre, April 11 to April 18) and the Washington Theatre (April 27 to May 9), St. Louis again (June 15 to June 26), and closing in Cleveland (June 30 to July 3). The fighting days at Gettysburg and Vicksburg.

In 1863, Booth was still traveling full time for theater engagements. He performed in Boston (September 28, 1863, to October 10), Providence (October 17), Hartford (October 20, 21, and 22), Brooklyn (October 24 and 26), New Haven (October 27 and 28) and then went on to Ford's Theatre in Washington (November 2 to November 14). From Washington, Booth went to Cleveland (November 26 to December 5).

As early as 1862, Booth was reviewed with high praise. The *New York World* raved that Booth was "a star of real magnitude."[135] The *St. Louis Daily Missouri Democrat* called him "the greatest tragedian in the country."[136] The next year, the *National Intelligencer* said, "He stands without a rival. Mr. Booth's acting in the fifth act of *Richard* is truly great . . . in his battle scenes he is far ahead of any actor living."[137]

Despite his acclaim, Booth had still not mastered self-control. Just nine months after vociferously speaking out in Albany, he did the same thing in St. Louis with more serious results. At the Ben Debar Theater where he had an engagement beginning December 22, 1862, he loudly and publicly proclaimed that he wished the "whole damned government would go to hell." Booth was held by Lieutenant Colonel Henry L. McConnell, the provost marshal for the Department of Missouri, and was only released upon taking the oath of allegiance to the Union and paying a fine for his disloyal expressions.[138]

During the war years, entertainment of any type drew large crowds. Despite his political indiscretions, Booth was the darling of the era. When he opened as Richard III at Washington's Grover's Theatre on April 11, 1863, he was billed as:

THE PRIDE OF THE AMERICAN PEOPLE
THE YOUNGEST TRAGEDIAN IN THE WORLD
who is entitled to be denominated
A STAR OF THE FIRST MAGNITUDE
Son of the great
JUNIUS BRUTUS BOOTH
and brother and artistic rival of
Edwin Booth
Who is engaged to commence this evening
and who will remain
ONLY SEVEN NIGHTS[139]

Afterward, the *National Republican* dubbed Booth's debut "a complete triumph. He has already taken the hearts of the people by storm."[140] A day later, the paper added that his playing created a sensation. "His youth, originality, and superior genius have not only made him popular but established him in the hearts of Washington people as a great favorite."[141]

Booth was also admired by many fellow actors. In April 1863, a young English actor Charles Wyndham (later knighted), said of Booth, "A marvelous man, he was one of the few to whom that ill used term of genius might be applied with perfect truth . . . . John Wilkes Booth has a greater natural gift than his brother Edwin." Wyndham believed that Booth had a "divine flash, amazing materials, extraordinary presence and magnetism . . . seldom has the stage seen a more impressive or a more handsome or a more impassioned actor." He described Booth as having "sweeping black hair, a figure of perfect youthful proportions and the most wonderful black eyes in the world." In addition, he was "witty, magnetic, a great raconteur, and he could hold a group spellbound by the hour . . . . He was the idol of women."[142]

John Adam Ellsler, who managed the Cleveland Academy of Music where Booth had performed, wrote, "Had he lived, would have stood head and shoulders above all the artists of his time."[143]

John T. Ford, agreeing with Ellsler and wrote of Booth, "Doubtless he would have been the greatest actor of his time if he had lived . . . . People waited in crowds after the performance to catch a glimpse of him as he left the theater."[144]

\*     \*     \*

Booth was a student of the theater with successful suggestions about revolving platforms, cutaway sets showing more than one room in the same house, and new lighting and sound ideas. He rewrote *The Marble Heart* so it became one his most reliable vehicles, and he put songs into plays that previously had no music. He had directorial instincts and offered ideas to his directors and fellow actors.[145] John Wilkes Booth was not satisfied with light fluffy roles; he actively sought Shakespearean roles in which he could show his acting talents. He approached Shakespearean parts with a drive and intensity that set him apart from other actors of his day. Booth was intense on stage and always strived for realism. Once in a rehearsal of a sword fight between Richard and Richmond in *Richard the Third*, Booth shouted at his opponent, "Come on hard! Come on hot! Hot, old fellow! Harder – faster!" As fate would have it in this rehearsal, Booth was hit with the sword across the forehead. Actor McCollom, his opponent, seeing Booth's face running with blood, shouted, "Oh, good God! Good God!"

Booth calmly replied, "That's all right, old man! Never mind me – only come on hard, for God's sake and save the fight!"[146]

Actress Clara Morris remembered Booth as "so young, so bright, so gay, so kind" with a magnetically charming and winning personality. "In his case there was nothing derogatory to dignity or to manhood in being called beautiful, for he was that bud of splendid promise, blasted to the core before its full triumphant blooming – known to the world as a madman and an assassin, but to the profession as 'that unhappy boy.'"[147]

Many years after Booth's notorious act, many of his contemporaries could at last bring themselves to write about him and his personality.

Morris later wrote, "It was impossible to see him and not admire him; it was equally impossible to know him and not love him . . . . My! What a dashing, elegant, handsome fellow he was, with his perfectly formed figure, graceful in every movement, his pale dark face and his big flashing dark eyes, which had all the lights and changes which are supposed to be possible only to the deeper blue eyes. He was gentleman in speech, manner and thought as he was in bearing. He was a great favorite with the men and the women adored him."[148]

Morris gave another instance of Booth's personality, "He was rushing from the theatre one day, and as he plunged ahead he upset in the street one of the dirtiest and most ragged little gutter snipes I have ever seen. The child was so dirty as to be repulsive. He was not hurt, but he stumbled and fell. Mr. Booth stooped, picked the little fellow up and set him on his feet, carefully dusted his ragged clothes, took his handkerchief and wiped the urchin's nose, which sadly needed it, placed a quarter in his hand, and then heartily kissed this little fellow twice and squarely on the mouth. A father could not have been more tender or more gentle with his own child. The child probably thought more of his quarter than he did of his kisses, but let me tell you there were many handsome, well-bred, and wealthy ladies in the land, married as well as unmarried, who would have done many foolish things for one of those kisses."[149]

Another actress described Booth as "the most perfect Romeo, the finest I ever saw, was the brother, Wilkes Booth. He was very handsome, most lovable and lovely. He was eccentric in some ways, and he had the family failings, but he also had a simple, direct, and charming nature. The love and sympathy between him and his mother were very close, very strong."[150]

John was never lonely for feminine companionship. Catherine Winslow wrote that "the stage door was always blocked with silly women waiting to catch a glimpse, as he passed, of his superb face and figure."[151] Journalist George Alfred Townsend wrote that women of all ages and social classes pursued Booth more than he to them.[152] Many women were attracted to Booth, and many opportunities arose for him to be with members of the opposite sex. Hotel maids made his bed with extra care, and laundry girls vied with each other to deliver his clothes. Waitresses at restaurants made "swift and gentle offerings of hot steaks, hot biscuits, hot coffee, crowding about him like doves about a grain basket, leaving other travelers to wait upon themselves or go without refreshment."[153]

He received thousands of love letters. "He was the idol of women," wrote the actor and later British baronet Charles Wyndham. "His conquest embraced the sex, and with no effort. They would rave of him, his voice, his hair, his eyes."[154]

Actress Jennie Gourlay described Booth as "a gentleman, a high-minded, cultured man . . . . A very handsome man, perhaps the handsomest I ever saw." A contemporary point of view by Gourlay was that "Lincoln's kindness of heart and goodness are well understood now but in those bitter days of strife and blood many of his countryman, north and south, thought him a tyrant. They claimed he was careless of the blood that was shed."[155]

John Deery, an owner of a billiard saloon and a national champion of the game, wrote, "Few men have known John Wilkes Booth better than I have known him, and, despite his terrible crime and deplorable ending, no man have I ever known who possessed a more winning personality . . . . John Wilkes Booth always kept his own counsel. He never used to gossip about his professional work, nor boast of his stage career as is the general custom of actors."[156]

But Booth had a more volatile side. On one occasion near the beginning of the war, Booth was riding in a train with John Sleeper Clarke. Booth did not like Clarke, had opposed his marrying Asia, and had often urged Asia to get a divorce. During the train ride, Clarke spoke disparaging of Confederate President Jefferson Davis. At this, Booth "sprang up and hurled himself upon Clarke, . . . catching him by the throat." After some pushing and shoving, he shouted at Clarke, "Never, if you value your life, never speak in that way to me again of a man and a cause I hold sacred!" Later Clarke passed "the matter off as a harmless temporary aberration."[157] Edwin Booth could not understand his brother John's attitude about the southern cause, and they constantly argued about the Civil War. Edwin supported Lincoln – the war effort and had voted for Lincoln – while John was adamantly pro-Confederacy.

\*      \*      \*

Booth held racist views but did not subscribe to blacks being treated cruelly. His sentiment became clear during the New York City draft riots in July 1863. Just after the battles of Vicksburg and Gettysburg, New York erupted into the worst riots in its history. The protest against Union conscription had turned into an ugly three-day killing spree from July 13 to 16. The federal government called for volunteers into the federal army; but when the number of volunteer's dwindled in 1862, the federal government ordered state governors to draft men into state militias. On March 3, 1863, the Union Enrollment Act decreed that all able-bodied men from the age of twenty to forty-five were subject to the draft. Because men who could pay $300 or supply a substitute could avoid conscription, only the rich could afford to escape the draft, making the Civil War look like a rich man's war but a poor man's fight.

Of all the disturbances in the North, the New York City riots were the bloodiest. Angry mobs, largely of Irish descent who felt the war was about freeing the blacks who would then take their jobs, battled police and militiamen. At least a thousand people were killed, most of them black men, women, and children. Military units fresh from the battle of Gettysburg restored order, and the draft resumed in August.

When the riots began, John Wilkes Booth was in New York City visiting his brother, Edwin. While there, John took Adam Badeau's (a personal friend of Edwin and later Union general) servant and hid him in the basement for days. Booth was enraged by the cruelties of the riot, but he did regard blacks as a subrace and did not want them to be freed.[158]

\*　　\*　　\*

On Monday, November 9, 1863, Booth performed in *The Marble Heart* with President and Mrs. Lincoln in the audience seated in the fateful box where seventeen months later Booth would assassinate him.

On this cold November night, the Lincolns took with them the two daughters of the U.S. minister of Russia, Cassius M. Clay. Eight cavalrymen escorted the carriage. It was not a pleasant ride. As the carriage bounced along the uneven road, the body of the car chanced to swing low to the ground, and an iron hoop lying on the road was caught under it. The sharp end of the hoop came slicing up through the carriage seat, right between Mary Lincoln and her husband. Mary began to scream, thinking that the carriage was being attacked. The driver, hearing Mary's calls for help, pulled the carriage to a halt and, seeing no assassins about, looked under the carriage.

"It's only a piece of metal caught underneath!" he called out; and pulling the hoop free, he threw it to the side. Then he bounded back up on the front of the carriage and, after a nod from the cavalry captain, whipped up the horses. The party proceeded again toward the theater.

Mary Clay, one of the minister's daughters, sat quietly through the whole incident, but as they proceeded again, she spoke, "Mr. Lincoln, in Russia, no czar would travel a St. Petersburg Street without cavalry escort and police along the route. Do you think the few cavalrymen we have riding with us tonight are enough?"

"I don't like having an escort at all," he replied. "But I tell you, I believe when my time comes, there is nothing that can prevent my going, but the people will have it." (Meaning Lincoln's security escort)

Booth played two roles in the play that evening, Phidias and Raphael. One was that of a villain – it was a plumb of a role, and one that Booth played to the hilt. Booth, who had come to regard Lincoln as his nemesis, saw him and came so near that he could not resist venting his anger through his role. As his part required that he threaten another character in the play, Booth made his way very near the presidential box and screamed the threats, putting his finger very close to Lincoln's face. Booth found three occasions to shout threats while pointing at Lincoln.

At last, Mary Clay could not resist saying, "Mr. Lincoln, he looks as if he meant that for you!"

Lincoln, who never brought himself to think ill of anyone, smiled and patted her hand. "Well, he does look pretty sharp at me, doesn't he?"[159]

*   *   *

Booth accepted an engagement at the Union Theatre in Leavenworth, Kansas, beginning on December 22, 1863 and ending December 31. After finishing his engagement, he rode a steamer to St. Joseph, Missouri, on his way to his next engagement in St. Louis. There he was stranded by a fierce snowstorm. In order to raise money to continue his trip to St. Louis, Booth gave a night to dramatic readings.[160]

But the trains out of St. Joseph were not running. So the next day, Booth paid one hundred dollars to hire a sleigh with four horses. Booth was determined to get to St. Louis, and when he learned that the railroad was operating from Breckinridge, he set out with his sleigh. When he finally arrived in St. Louis, he gave only five performances.[161]

Next Booth performed in Louisville and then at Nashville for two weeks at the Wood's Theatre beginning on February 1, 1864. In Nashville, Booth became acquainted with William A. Browning, Governor Andrew Johnson's secretary. (On April 14, 1865, the day of the assassination, Booth attempted to see Johnson or Browning, leaving his calling card at the hotel desk.) From Nashville, Booth traveled to Cincinnati but arrived with a severe cold on February 15, 1864. Because of his illness, on February 17, Booth's role was taken by an understudy. The Cincinnati engagement ended on February 26. On February 22, Booth wrote to Richard Montgomery Field saying, "I have been very sick here, but am all right again. Thank God".[162]

Booth had a relapse and had to start his New Orleans engagement one week late. Apparently his poor health was affecting his acting, since the next day a reviewer wrote,

"Mr. J. Wilkes Booth is as yet an actor of more promise than of actual performance, and time, care and study, may yet develop in this really promising young actor those evidences of stage talent that made his father so famous, and that have already made his brother Edwin so great a favorite."[163]

On March 20, Booth was still not up to par. A New Orleans paper wrote, "Schiller's tragedy *The Robbers* is no favorite of ours, and what we saw of the performance of it at the St. Charles last night did not recommend it. Mr. Booth's Charles de Moor we have seen far excelled by actors who were not stars."[164]

Booth continued to have problems with illness. The next day, the *New Orleans Times* stated that Booth's raspy voice was affecting the quality of his performance. His voice was hoarse when he portrayed Othello and two days later when he played Macbeth. His voice continued to deteriorate through a performance of the *Merchant of Venice*. His performances of March 26, 27, and 28 were canceled because of illness.

On Sunday, March 27, the *New Orleans Times* contained the following:

> Notice – The management of the St. Charles Theatre regret to inform the public that in consequence of the severe and continued cold under which Mr. Booth has been laboring for several days, and at the suggestion of his medical adviser, he is compelled to take a short respite from his engagement. Due notice will be given of his next appearance.

On Tuesday night, however, Booth returned to the stage although his voice had not recovered. The following Sunday, April 3, his New Orleans engagement ended.[165] Since his sleigh ride from St. Joseph to Breckinridge in January, Booth had been constantly ill.

Booth then took a twenty-two day respite before beginning his last extended engagement on April 25 and closing on May 27. It was the longest engagement of his acting career.

During this Boston engagement, Booth met and began to court a beautiful sixteen-year-old Boston girl named Isabel Sumner. Of this romance, only six letters survive, and all were written by Booth to Isabel.

The letters show that Booth was captivated by the beautiful teenager. How the two met is not recorded; however, it is likely that they met at the theater. They exchanged photographs, and Isabel kept an autographed photo of Booth throughout her life. Booth gave her a pearl ring with the inscription "J. W. B. to I. S." on the inside of the band. On one occasion, she sent him flowers while he was in New York City. She must have felt strongly about Booth because least once, she traveled to New York by herself to meet him, something proper young ladies never did.

Booth wrote in his first letter to Isabel, "How, shall I write you; as lover, friend, or brother. I think so much of you, that (at your bidding) I would even try to school my heart to beat as the latter."[166] And a week later, he wrote, "Indeed, I thought you had forgotten me, and I had no idea how much I cared for you till the last week or so."[167]

There was a period when no letters were exchanged, and Booth feared that Isabel did not want to be involved with him. He wrote on July 24, "God forever bless you Isabel, I will trouble you no more, if you say the word, but can never, never cease to think of you as something pure and sacred, A bright and happy dream, from which I have been awoke to Sadness."[168]

From this point, Booth performed only three more times.[169]

Junius Brutus Booth Jr. arrived back on the East Coast from California in June 1864. Junius has been in California since 1852 working as an actor and theater manager. He was surprised to discover that his brother, John, was so sympathetic to the Southern cause. In the end, Edwin and Asia's husband, John Sleeper Clarke, would not discuss politics with John because they considered him a monomaniac on the Southern cause.

In August, the Booth family gathered at Edwin's home[170] in New York, as they occasionally did, and John, true to form, caused a particularly passionate argument.[171] John, to Edwin's chagrin, criticized Lincoln's appearance, his coarse manners, salty jokes, and his folksy character as a disgrace to the office of the presidency. Booth maintained loudly that Lincoln was destroying slavery by "robbery, rapine, slaughter and bought armies" (referring to foreigners in the Union Army). John proclaimed that if Lincoln were reelected, he would overthrow the Constitution and become king of America. "You'll see – you'll see, that reelection means succession," he once told Asia.[172] Edwin became so angry at his brother's intense remarks about Lincoln and the Union that he forbade any more discussion about the war in his home in order to maintain peace during family gatherings.

*     *     *

In 1863, Booth had an engagement in Cleveland at the John Ellsler's Academy of Music from November 26 to December 5. While in Cleveland, Booth struck up a personal friendship with John Ellsler, and from this friendship, they became business partners in the Dramatic Oil Company. Early in 1864, John Ellsler, Thomas Mears, and Booth acquired rights to three and one-half acres along the Allegheny River near Franklin, Pennsylvania. Booth hired a friend, Joseph H. Simonds, as his business agent to manage the enterprise.[173]

Booth, along with Simonds, was in Franklin on June 10 and June 29, 1864, and stayed at the McHenry House in Meadville, Pennsylvania. Simonds testified, "I accompanied him to the oil regions in June, 1864, for the purpose of taking charge of his business there."[174] Booth and Ellsler spent most of July living near the well site.

Years later, Ellsler wrote that "as the time for the fall [theater] season approached, we settled up our business and parted at Meadville, Pa., wishing each other Godspeed. It was our last handshake. I never saw him again."[175]

# CHAPTER 6

## *Mary Eugenia Surratt*

Mary Surratt grew up on her parent's tobacco farm in what is now Clinton, Maryland. Her parents, Elizabeth Anne and Archibald Jenkins, were married on June 4, 1821. They quickly had three children in four years; and then unexpectedly and unfortunately for the growing family, Archibald died in the fall of 1825. Mary Elizabeth was the second of the three children. John Zadoc, her older brother, was born on February 2, 1822; Mary in 1823; and James Archibald in 1825. After her husband's death, Mrs. Jenkins continued working the farm and managed their eleven slaves. She found that she was good at running the farm and even bought more land.[76]

Mrs. Jenkins was determined that her daughter would have a proper education, so she entered Mary into the Academy for Young Ladies, run by St. Mary's Catholic Church in Alexandria.[77] Mary was a rather plain-looking girl with dark hair and with the unfocused stare of someone with poor vision. Throughout her life, her vision continued to decline; until by age forty, she moved about in a softly focused world in which images were never fully seen, and small things, like threading a needle by gaslight, became impossible. Mary's poor vision would later play a part in her conviction in the Lincoln's conspiracy trial.

Mary was not Catholic, but during her four-year stay at the Academy for Young Ladies, she converted to the Catholicism. Typical of new converts, Mary quickly became the evangelist of the family.

On August 20, 1838, Mary Jenkins was named the godmother at the baptism of her nephew, Henry Randolph Webster, at St. Mary's Catholic Church. Mary entered her name on the baptismal certificate as Maria Eugenia Jenkins. She probably chose "Eugenia" in honor of Sister Eugenia Maginnis, a teacher at the Academy for Young Ladies. Mary, strong willed and with youthful enthusiasm, converted her mother and her brother, John Zadoc, and his wife.

In 1839 when Mary was sixteen, she met John Harrison Surratt. John Surratt, raised by Richard and Sarah Neale, was twenty-seven years old at the time he decided he wanted Mary as a wife. On August 6, 1840, he bought a marriage license, and only weeks later, the couple were married. Mary had married John Surratt on the condition that he convert to Catholicism. Mary got pregnant immediately, and on June 2, 1841, she gave birth to Isaac Douglas Surratt on June 2, 1841. Elizabeth Susanna "Anna" Surratt was born on January 1, 1843, and John Jr. on April 13, 1844.[78]

John Surratt Sr. managed the farm of his foster father, Richard Neale, known as Pasture and Gleaning after Neale's death in September 1843. John Surratt was already on a downhill course financially; he did not manage the farm or his finances well and was in debt from 1843 until the day he died. These debt when carried through to 1865 would contribute to Mary Surratt's execution. Mrs. Neale, on May 27, 1845, conveyed her title to the tract of land known as Pasture and Gleaning to John Surratt Sr. Sarah Neale was baptized in the Catholic faith on June 27, 1845, undoubtedly through Mary's efforts, and died shortly after on August 6, 1845.

For the next few years, Mary and Christina Edelen began a fund-raising drive for the construction of a Catholic church in Oxon Hill, Maryland. Their work resulted in St. Ignatius Catholic Church being built on donated land in 1850.[79]

On the whole though, Mary's life went from bad to worse. Mary was miserable; her husband was beginning his slow decent into alcoholism; and then, the year after the joy of St. Ignatius's being completed, the Surratt's home caught fire. The structure was totally destroyed. Luckily, no one was hurt, but now the family needed a place to stay. They ended up moving in with Mary's cousin, Thomas Jenkins; his wife Charity; and their six children. The situation was less than comfortable, and John Surratt cast about for what he could do next. He did not want to invest money to rebuild his house since he had not made a very good living managing the farm. He decided not to rebuild the burned-out home but to build a new dwelling, one that included a tavern and public room. Surratt Sr. had decided to become a tavern keeper. Until the tavern was built, the Surratt family remained with the Jenkins.

In January 1852, Surratt Sr. purchased 287 acres of farmland from Charles B. Calvert. Surratt didn't have enough money and owed a balance of $279.21. The tavern, built on this property at a crossroads, was completed in October. It had nine rooms – five on the first floor and four on the second – the kitchen was an attached room on the right side of the house.

Mary could not bring herself to move the children into the new tavern. Instead, she packed up her things and returned to Pasture and Gleaning. Since the house had burned down, Mary moved into the only structure available – the vacant servant quarters. Mary and the children stayed on the old farm for six months and while John blustered and swore, trying to get them to move in with him. At last, he was able to sell the old property, and Mary had to move. She had no place to go but to the newly built tavern. With all the stress in her life, Mary began to experience headaches.

The tavern was in Prince George's County, Maryland, about twelve miles from Washington and directly on the road from Washington to Bryantown. Because the tavern was at a crossroads, it soon became a way station for local farmers and travelers in Southern Maryland. Behind the house was a fruit orchard and farmland where the family grew grain, vegetables, fruits, and other crops for themselves and for market. Across the street was a blacksmith and wheel maker's shop.

On September 23, 1852, a license was issued to John Surratt to manage a tavern. The tavern's central location led to its being designated the polling place for the Ninth Election District, and in October 1854, the local post office for the new town of "Surrattsville" operated out of the front room of the tavern.

In time though, John Sr. became his own best customer. He was drunk most of the time, so Mary had to take on the job of managing the tavern.[180] Mary once wrote to a Catholic priest about her husband saying that "he is drunk almost every day and I fear there is but little hope of his ever doing any better."[181]

Mary, anxious to get her daughter an education and away from the tavern, asked for financial help from Father Finotti, and with his help, Anna was enrolled at St. Mary's Female Institute in Bryantown, Maryland, from 1854 until 1861.[182]

Surrattsville was a small town, and the local entertainment was gossip. Because Mary was miserable and married to an alcoholic, rumors soon began that Mary and her confessor, Father Joseph Maria Finotti, were romantically involved. Religion was all she had left to fall back on, so it was highly unlikely that anything improper passed between the two young people. However, rumors were voiced so blatantly that church officials sent Father Finotti to Boston to put an end to the gossip.[183]

Now cut off from friendships inside and outside the home, Mary devoted herself to her children. In 1855, she made arrangements for tuition grants for her two sons, Isaac and John, to go to St. Thomas Manor. The boys, aged fourteen and eleven, only studied there for two years because St. Thomas Manor closed due to financial problems. By January 1858, Mary, through another Catholic priest, Father Wiget, found employment for Isaac in Baltimore, away from the tavern.

On September 2, 1859, John Jr. enrolled at St. Charles College in Howard County, Maryland. John, who was studying to be a priest, was an outstanding student and a member of the Society of Angels, an organization of honor students. John stayed at the school until the death of his father in August 1862.[184] At this school, John Surratt first meets and befriends Louis Weichmann, who will play an important part in Mary Surratt's eventual execution.

In the meantime, Anna was excelling at school; she was a member of the prestigious Enfant de Marie Society, wrote very well, and had many friends.[185]

By 1859, John Surratt Sr. continue to fall more and more into debt. To pay off some bills, he sold seventy-five acres of land to John Nothey, a neighbor, and twenty-five acres to Francis Lawson Goddard.

Isaac returned from Baltimore on March 4, 1861, inauguration day, and told his frightened mother that he was going to Texas. On May 7, he joined the Thirty-Third Texas Cavalry; he survived the war but did not return until after his mother was executed.

The Surratt family, like most of their neighbors, were Southern in sympathy, so when mail service ended between the North and South, the Surratts made the tavern into a relay station for Confederate couriers. John Surratt Sr. was "an impetuous Southerner, full of intense prejudice and hate toward the Yankees . . . out-spoken in his convictions, and proud of every Southern victory."[186]

Major William Norris of Baltimore County and chief of the Confederate Signal Service had couriers transport letters, dispatches, Northern newspapers, and medical supplies, using the tavern as a way station. The couriers, heading South, collected and dropped off letters and dispatches on their way to Richmond and did the same on their return trip. Places like the Surrattsville tavern were important in the courier system.

On Tuesday, August 21, 1862, John Surratt Sr. died, and this led his son John Surratt Jr., now eighteen years old, to leave his studies. On September 1, he replaced his father as postmaster of the Surrattsville post office.

John Sr. had left his family in financial difficulties. Their farm was mortgaged, and the family had to pay off his debts. It was during this time the John Jr. joined the Confederate courier service. His pro-Confederate sentiment was known by those in that area of Maryland and, as the local postmaster, was the obvious choice for operating that section of the courier route.

John Jr. often went to Washington to sell fruits and vegetables from his farm at the public market in Washington. On one of these trips in the spring of 1863, John ran into Louis Weichmann, his former schoolmate from St. Charles College. After leaving St. Charles College, Weichmann had taken a teaching position at St. Matthew's Institute for Boys in Washington.[187] John Surratt and Weichmann resumed their friendship, and John invited Lou to return with him to Surrattsville.

On April 3, 1863, John and Lou Weichmann made a trip together to St. Charles College. They saw Weichmann's old friend, Father Mahoney, and during this visit, Weichmann introduced John Surratt to Henri Beaumont de Sainte-Marie, who now taught in a Catholic school nearby. Sainte-Marie told them that he wanted to work in Washington, and later, Weichmann helped him get an assistant teaching position at St. Matthew's school. One month later, de Sainte-Marie embarrassed Weichmann by leaving without any notice.[188] Sainte-Marie will later betray John Surratt to the American consulate, while Surratt was in hiding after the assassination, as a Papal Zouaves.

Young Surratt lost his position as the local postmaster because of an altercation there on election day 1863. And so a pro-Union man Andrew V. Robey became the new postmaster in the tavern. Now John Surratt had to carry the mail in and out of the South without the use of the Surratt Tavern as a drop-off point. John's courier duties became more dangerous, and he began making more frequent trips between Washington and Richmond.

The tavern did, however, remain a stop in the Confederate courier route; they just didn't talk to the new postmaster. The tavern was designated by the Signal Corps of the Confederate army as an official station on one of the secret lines of communication established between Richmond and Washington. Thomas Conrad and other rebel spies, agents, scouts, and blockade-runners stopped often at the Surratt Tavern on trips between Washington and the signal station on the Potomac.[189]

Meanwhile, Louis Weichmann's fortunes improved. In early January 1864, Weichmann found better paying employment in the office of the Commissary General of Prisons. There he earned eighty dollars a month – forty-two dollars a month more than when he had taught at St. Matthew's Institute.[190] Surratt frequently visited Weichmann at his boardinghouse where he was introduced to another boarder, General Albion Paris Howe of the United States Artillery. General Howe will eventually become a member of the military commission that will try and condemn John's mother.

As time went on, the responsibility for the farm and tavern became too much for Mary. The daily grind was exhausting, and Mary may have been afraid of the influence that living in a public house was having on her daughter, Anna, who was growing into a pretty teenager. So Mary decided to lease out the tavern and move to Washington. Previously, Mary's late husband had, on December 6, 1853, bought a townhouse on H Street in Washington for four thousand dollars.[191]

Mary planned to convert the three-story unit into a boardinghouse and take in boarders to make ends meet. Mary was getting older, her eyesight was deteriorating, and both of her sons were in the war effort for the Confederacy. In September, Louis Weichmann visited the Surratt house and tavern for a second time, and during this visit, John told Weichmann his mother's planned to lease the tavern to John Lloyd and begin operating a private boardinghouse in Washington. John invited him to board there, and Weichmann cheerfully accepted. He agreed to pay thirty-five dollars a month for food and lodging and moved in on November 1.[192]

In December, John M. Lloyd began leasing the tavern for five hundred dollars. Lloyd, married to Mary Elizabeth Mohoney, a daughter of a tailor in Washington, was a Southern sympathizer. He was a former bricklayer, a member of the Washington Day Police Force, then a farmer, but always a Southern sympathizer. John Surratt stayed at the tavern between the time Lloyd signed the agreement and the time he actually began management of the tavern.[193]

It was on the first day of October 1864 that Mary and her daughter, Anna, moved to the boardinghouse at 541 H Street, NW.[194]

The H Street townhouse was sandwiched between a narrow alley and the home of Hugh B. Sweeny, a local banker. Out front between the walk and the street was a maple sapling, and in the backyard was the family well. The building had three stories, and in 1865, there was a long wooden stairway along the entire front of the building from street level to the main entrance on the second floor. From this entrance, a long hall extended the length of the building along the right inside wall. Close to the back of the house, stairs rose up all three stories. The street-level entrance, an "English basement," had a public sitting room, a dining room, and a kitchen in the rear.

The second floor family sitting room, with a fireplace, was at the front of the house where Mary Surratt entertained guests. Behind this sitting room was a more private parlor, which gave the only access to two identical bedrooms approximately ten feet by ten feet. One could only get to the bedrooms by going through the parlor. Mary occupied one of these bedrooms and nineteen-year-old Honora Fitzpatrick the other. She had come to the boardinghouse on October 6; her father was a collector for several Washington banks.[195]

On the third floor, John Surratt and Louis Weichmann shared the back bedroom and were boarders; John Holohan and his family occupied the front bedroom and foyer. In the attic were two bedrooms with dormers facing the street. These rooms occupied by Anna and her cousin, Olivia Jenkins.[196]

The boardinghouse was in the center of the city and within walking distance of all the hotels, theaters, and government buildings. Mary was excited that she could walk to St. Patrick's Catholic Church at F Street between Ninth and Tenth streets where Father Jacob Ambrose Walters presided.

But because of John Surratt Sr.'s legacy of debt, Mary was never able to be debt free. On January 1, 1852, Surratt Sr. had purchased 287 acres from Charles Calvert, and Mary still owed the Calverts on the property in 1865. In 1852, Charles Calvert received two notes from Surratt Sr., each for $398.50. Over the years, these notes had accumulated so much interest that on January 19, 1865, Mary at last was obliged to mortgage the H Street house to pay $1,000 on the debt. However, in April, Mary was still deep in debt, and George Calvert demanded that Mary honor the $764.53 still outstanding on the Surratt house and tavern.[197] Mary's subsequent trips to Surrattsville to straighten out this problem would lead to her arrest and execution.

In November and December, Mary was advertising for lodgers in the *Washington Star*.[198] And John Jr. in January 1865 deeded over all of his shares of the family property to his mother, after conspiring with Booth to kidnap Lincoln.[199]

# CHAPTER 7

## *Kidnap the President*

At the end of his Boston engagement, Booth visited his brother Edwin in New York. Even though John's political views greatly differed from those of his brother, Edwin was kind and hospitable toward John, hoping that by being generous, he might soften his brother's strongly held Southern rhetoric. From Edwin's home, John made several trips to the oil regions of Venango County, Pennsylvania, where he had invested money.

By the summer of 1864, Booth felt that the North was slowly strangling the South with its superior manpower.[200] Booth found in his hatred for the Union cause, and specifically Lincoln himself, a path to greatness. The South was low on manpower, and the North had a seemingly limitless supply. If Southern prisoners of war could be freed, Booth felt that the South could still win the war. He would kidnap his nemesis, Lincoln, and ransom him for soldiers to save the day for the Confederacy.

Booth did little more than criticize Lincoln until August 1864. But then Atlanta fell, and Lincoln's reelection seemed likely. Booth resolved that he had to do something at last for his devoted Confederacy. The war was quickly ending, and soon it would be too late. Soon his one great opportunity to save the Confederacy and gain fame would be gone.

Booth focused all his anger, hate, and personal frustration on Lincoln. As the head of the Northern government, it was easy for Booth to see him as the source of all his dissatisfaction and anger. He felt that Lincoln was a "false president," who clearly was "yearning for kingly succession." The collapse of his oil investments coupled with this pro-Confederate sentiments contributed to his hatred of Lincoln.

Booth had always been vocal about his pro-Southern sentiments and were well-known in Boston, New York, Washington, and other cities. He was not shy about sharing his political views with anyone who would listen. He was too vocal about his sentiments to be of any covert use to the Confederacy. With a frenzy of righteous indignation, Booth set about creating a scheme to kidnap Lincoln. Booth was sure that if he spirited Lincoln to the Richmond, the president could be ransomed for thousands of Southern prisoners of war.

Booth, who was becoming more and more emotionally isolated, saw himself as planning and executing this plan. Booth was an intelligent man with well-known, strong, pro-Confederate sentiments – "an ardent lover of the South and her policy, an upholder of Southern principles." Although he spent the war as an itinerant actor, mostly in Northern cities, he yearned for wartime glory. He promised his mother that he would not enlist; and as a well-paid actor, this promise was not hard to keep. He embellished on his wartime exploits to his sister, Asia. Booth told her that he had smuggled quinine into the Confederacy.[201] He may have tried using his money for the purchase of quinine, but there is no evidence that he ever took possession of the medicine and physically carried it through Union lines to Confederate authorities. In the same conversation with his sister, Booth says that Grant "has given me freedom of range without knowing what a good turn he have done the South. *Not that the South cares a bad cent about me, mind-a mere peregrinating play-actor,*" This remark a clear indication that Booth, at one time, tried to approach the South and had been rebuffed. Booth's closing in his "To Whom It May Concern" letter of November 1864 stated that he was a Confederate *presently acting on his own*. There is no indication that the Confederate Secret Service wanted a relationship with Booth.

\*　　\*　　\*

The first documented evidence of Booth's conspiring against Lincoln is in Baltimore at the Barnum's hotel between August 8 and 3, probably closer to the eighth. "Booth set up a meeting with two old school friends, Michael O'Laughlen and Samuel Arnold.[202]

Early in John Wilkes Booth's youth, he wrote a series of letters to William O'Laughlen (1838-1915). Booth had attended a Baltimore grammar school with William and his younger brother, Michael O'Laughlen (1840-1867).

O'Laughlen, who lived with his widowed mother at 57 North Exeter Street, had been in Company D, First Maryland Infantry, and been discharged because of a disability. He also admitted after his arrest on April 17, 1865, that he had been a member of the Knights of the Golden Circle, but he told his interrogators that he had not been active during the past four years.[203]

Samuel Arnold had worked in the South as a civilian but returned to Maryland in February 1864. "I came," he said, "ostensibly to see my mother who was very ill. To restore her to health I promised to remain . . ."[204] Arnold was at his father's house in Baltimore when he received a surprise message to come see Booth at the Barnum Hotel. "I had not seen Booth since 1851, when we parted with one another at school."

Arnold arrived before O'Laughlen, and Booth greeted him, offering him a drink and cigars. They first talked of "escapades of school boy days" and then of "the present war." When O'Laughlen arrived, Booth introduced him as "a former acquaintance from boyhood."

Now that all three were together, Booth began to speak of what he had in mind. To solve the Confederate manpower shortage, Booth proposed that Lincoln be captured while he was traveling to or from the soldiers' home on the outskirts of Washington. Booth argued that the plan was easy to carry out and that it was "purely humane and patriotic in its principles," devoid of selfish personal ambition, and legitimate as an act of war.[205]

Booth talked more about the viability of the plot, but there was some debate. However, after a little more wine, the two men agreed to join Booth in his plot. The meeting over, Booth told the two that he was going to New York to take care of his personal finances.

Booth's plan was in principle the same as that proposed earlier by Bradley Johnson to Wade Hampton and Jubal Early. Booth's plan also resembled that approved by Secretary of War Seddon, who sent a group seven months later under the command of Captain Thomas N. Conrad to Washington in mid-September 1864 to explore such possibilities.

From Baltimore, Booth took the train to New York, but while he was there, he had an attack of erysipelas. The bacterial infection, susceptibility to which often runs in families, causes sudden fever, shivering, and then a sharply defined and painful inflammation of the skin and underlying tissue. Booth suffered the attendant headaches and then apathy and restlessness. In the midst of all this misery, he suffered another attack of bronchitis.[206] He ended up recuperating for about two weeks.

Booth, knowing that if his kidnap plan should take place, he would become a wanted man, began to put his affairs in order. Feeling well enough to travel, Booth went to Franklin, Pennsylvania, to sell his speculative oil leases. Joseph H. Simonds, Booth's business agent, closed out all of Booth's oil leases by September 27. Booth was a better actor than a businessman because he "never realized a dollar from any interest possessed in the oil region. His speculations were a total loss." His losses amounted to $6,000, and Booth paid all the expenses on the transfer and the conveyances of the properties.[207]

Also he had a one-third interest in property along the Allegheny River, of this he bequeathed a third to Joseph and two-thirds to his brother Junius Booth Jr. To his sister, Rosalie, he bequeathed some stock.

\*   \*   \*

Having settled most of his affairs in New York, Booth gathered up his trunk of stage costumes and took a train for Canada. On the way, Booth stopped in Newburgh, New York, arriving late Saturday night, October 16. The next morning, Booth bought clothes at a local clothing store. Booth got back on to a Canadian-bound train and settled back into his seat. And as the scenery slipped by, he became immersed in his own dark thoughts. About noon, he crossed the Hudson River on his way to Canada, arriving in Montreal on October 18, and promptly registered at St. Lawrence Hall, the unofficial Confederate headquarters.

Booth did not go to Montreal for ten days just to ship his wardrobe trunk to Richmond via Nassau and by coincidence just happen to stay at St. Lawrence Hall. The trip was made just weeks after he closed out his oil investments with a loss of $6,000 and soon after his meeting with Arnold and O'Laughlen in Baltimore with a scheme to kidnap Lincoln. Booth went to the St. Lawrence Hall in Montreal to make contact with Confederate authorities. Booth was confident that the Confederate government would welcome his plan and protect him once the plan was carried out.

Because of Booth's well-known pro-Confederate passion and his prestige as a nationally known actor, he may have tried to speak to Clement C. Clay or Jacob Thompson during his Montreal stay. However, Thompson and Clay were in Quebec City on October 14, unsuccessfully seeking a conference with Governor General Lord Monck. The two Confederate representatives planned to leave Quebec City on October 15 and would have to travel through Montreal to their respective destinations in Canada. Clay to St. Catherines and Thompson to Toronto.[208]

Clay arrived in St. Catherine's by October 19, (one day after Booth arrived in Montreal) and so Booth did not see him. Thompson arrived at the Queens Hotel in Toronto on October 21. There is no documentation that Booth met him, only that he passed through Montreal during the early part of Booth's stay in that city.

Booth was desperate to talk to any Confederate official, so he was fair game for a rogue by the name of Patrick C. Martin. Martin was a Baltimore liquor dealer and a blockade-runner. A Federal War Department letter dated July 24, 1862, protested government dealing with his firm and described him as "an uncompromising rebel of the 19th of April notoriety."[209] Martin, who had been in Montreal since the summer 1862, spent his time buying and shipping supplies to the Confederacy via Montreal and Halifax. There are numerous references to Martin in Confederate records and in the Official Records of the Union and Confederate Navies.[210] Martin had contacts with the Confederate Secret Service and may have been loosely connected to it.[211]

After all his self-promotion with the Confederate Secret Service, Booth finally did receive from Martin (not a Confederate official) a letter of introduction to Dr. William Queen, an elderly physician in Southern Maryland on the edge of the Zekiah Swamp some six miles out of Bryantown in Charles County. Booth expected Dr. Queen in turn to help him find local support, contacts, and possible escape routes. Booth's cover story was that he was interested in buying land in that area.

Booth arranged to have his wardrobe trunks shipped to the island of Nassau and from there to Richmond through the federal blockade. Booth wanted his wardrobe in Richmond after his flight from Washington with the president of the United States as hostage. He sent the wardrobe via the *Marie Victoria*, a seventy-three-foot schooner. It departed Montreal on or about November 18, 1864, bound for Halifax, but two weeks later ran aground in a storm near Bic, Quebec. All aboard were lost in the St. Lawrence River, including one Patrick C. Martin.[212]

Booth also saw George Sanders in Montreal. Sanders was a member of the Virginia convention that passed the ordinance of secession, and he was also a member of the Confederate Congress.[213]

George Sanders had sought to arrange a peace conference in early July 1864 at the Clifton House on the Canadian side of Niagara Falls. The purpose of the conference was to embarrass the Republican party and to affect the November elections. Lincoln ignored the conference, and the planned conference never took place.

General John A. Dix, commander of the New York district, sent Colonel Ambrose Stevens, his intelligence officer, in civilian clothes to the Clifton House. There he discovered that Confederate agents, Copperheads, and peace Democrats were among the conference delegations. He reported to General Dix that one of the Confederate peace commissioners was proposing a scheme to assassinate Lincoln just before the November elections. When Lincoln was told, he wanted the proposed plot kept secret since he felt that the publicity would do more harm than good.[214]

Sanders was not respected by the official Confederate representatives in Canada. Clement Clay, second only to Jacob Thompson in the Confederate Canadian mission, wrote that "George N. Sanders is at Niagara Falls, representing himself as sent by our government to encourage peace. He actually talked to my informant of calling a peace meeting of citizens of the US and CS to devise joint action for that end. I hope he will not do so silly a thing, but wish he were in Europe, Asia or Africa." In another letter, Clay concluded, "I suppose George has gone to Montreal to indulge his great and glorious pretensions of luck, liberty and independence."[215]

With Sander's reputation among the Confederates in Canada of being something of a loose cannon, it is not surprising the Booth would see such a man. Sanders, a native of Kentucky, was widely known as "a man of wild and impractical thoughts."[216] When Booth was staying at the St. Lawrence Hall, George Sanders was registered at the Ottawa Hotel. There where three witnesses at the conspiracy trial who testified that they had seen Booth with Sanders in Montreal at this time.[217]

George Sanders had a history of advocating political assassinations. He was appointed by President Pierce as consul to London in June 1853. Sanders left for London in November before the Senate's confirmation to it. The Senate at first rejected his nomination but later confirmed it. In London, Sanders associated with European radicals, including Giusepe Mazzini (a political theorist and republican revolutionary who fought for Italian unification and was called the prophet of Italian nationalism), and Giuseppe Garibaldi (one of Italy's most famous military heroes, fighting in South America and Italy and a protege of Mazzini). Sanders agreed with Mazzini's "theory of the dagger" that tyrannicide was justified and once wrote a letter advocating the killing of Louis Napoleon "by any means, and by any way it could be done".[218]

Sanders was also involved in a plot to assassinate Louis Napoleon, a plot that culminated in what is now called the Fronde affair.[219]

On September 22, 1855, Sanders spoke at a meeting in New York, which was held to celebrate the rise of the French Republic of 1792. The *New York Herald* reported this meeting on the front page the next day and quoted Sanders as saying "he was of the Ledru-Rollin school, he was for death to tyrants, and he was for the guillotine."

George Sanders's son, Major Reid Sanders, died at Fort Waren, Boston, as a prisoner of war.[220] One month later, Sanders met Booth. Because of his son's death while in the custody of the Union and because he advocated political assassination, States' rights and Confederate independence, Sanders could very possibly have become a supporter of Booth's kidnap scheme.[221]

A contemporary, Francis Lieber, wrote that Sanders was a man with "few if any principles, with little regard for right and wrong, a rabid republican in Europe's Liberty, Equality, Fraternity but strictly for slavery in the Southern States." In 1864, Sanders claimed that he had been authorized by President Davis in 1862 to carry on negotiations to end the war, but a letter from Jefferson Davis later denied this.[222]

Sanders had reckless views about what constituted legitimate covert actions upon the North. His ideas threatened Canadian neutrality. He and Clement Clay had organized the St. Albans raid with Jacob Thompson advising against it.[223]

It is not surprising that the Confederate government had very little to do with him and that the Canadian representatives thought he was a rogue. It was only natural that Booth would gravitate to him while in Montreal.

On October 27, Booth was at the Ontario Bank in Montreal; he deposited $455 and purchased a bill of exchange. He asked the teller, "I am going to run the blockade, and in case I should be captured, can my captures make use of the exchange?"

The teller told him "they could not unless he endorsed the bill, which was made payable to his order." Booth bought a bill for $300 and paid in American gold. Ultimately he never spent it; the bill of exchange were found on Booth's body at the time of his death.[224]

The next morning, October 28, Booth left for New York. When he got there the next day, he signed the papers releasing him from his oil interests.

\*     \*     \*

On October 19, 1864, under the command of Lt. Bennett H. Young, twenty-two Confederate soldiers in Quebec crossed the border and rode fifteen miles to raid three banks in St. Albans, Vermont. The raiders stole approximately $200,000 and unsuccessfully tried to burn the town down, but townspeople turned out in force and defended their small town. In the ensuing gun battle, one citizen was killed and several others wounded. The raiders made off with the money, but an angry posse, quickly put together by the federal provost marshal from Burlington, pursued them across the Canadian border. The posse caught up to the fleeing Confederates and took several of them captive, including Lieutenant Young. However, the provost marshal's celebration at the capture was short lived; since he was on Canadian soil, local authorities forced him to turn the raiders over to them. By October 23, fourteen of the raiders were in Canadian custody. They were sent to Montreal where authorities would decide whether they should be extradited as criminals.[225]

Canadian proceedings began on November 2 but soon recessed. Lieutenant Young claimed that the action he and his band of raiders undertook was an act of war, not robbery and murder. Young wanted an extension so that he could get documentation that his raid had been approved in Richmond. By mid-December, the presiding judge ruled that he had no jurisdiction in the case and ordered the prisoners released; however, the $200,000 was to be returned to St. Albans.

The release of the raiders was an outrage to many in the United States, and under political pressure, the Canadian government acceded and again issued a warrant for the arrest of the raiders. Many of the raiders had prudently made themselves scarce, and only five could be found to be arrested, including Lieutenant Young. But on January 11, proceedings were recessed again. The raiders wanted thirty days to get documentation from Richmond confirming that they had acted as soldiers in the Confederate army.

The St. Albans raid and its aftermath later played a role in why Sarah Slater and John Surratt were in Canada. If it were not for the St. Albans raid, John Surratt would not have been in Elmira, New York, on the night of the assassination, a fact that surely saved his life.

\*    \*    \*

Beginning on October 29, Booth stayed in New York about a week; during that time, he met Samuel Chester, a fellow actor he knew. Booth began a slow cultivation of Chester and told him about sending his wardrobe trunk to Richmond. Booth again saw Chester in New York on November 25 when they acted together in *Julius Caesar.*

During December, Booth saw Chester periodically with Booth telling him of a "big speculation" he was involved in but always being evasive when asked what the speculation was. At one time, Chester claimed that Booth told him that he was speculating in farms in Southern Maryland and urged him to join him.[226]

Late in December or in early January, Booth again traveled to New York, continuing his recruitment of Chester. Booth at last decided that the time was ripe. The two were on a walk together talking about old times and ended up having dinner and drinks at a local pub. They carried the drinking to another saloon and then took a walk up Broadway. Booth used this opportunity to mention again what he had hinted at for the last two months. Further along in the walk, Booth finally told Chester that the speculation was a conspiracy to capture the heads of the Union government, including the president. Chester had not expected this. He was shocked and frightened, thinking the conspiracy was an impossibility. Booth continued to recruit Chester up to mid-February, but Chester continued to refuse; and he was growing more and more uneasy at Booth's insistence. Chester was fearful that should Booth actually carry out his scheme, he might be implicated, especially since he knew of the plan beforehand. Chester saw the dark outline of the scaffold looming against the night sky.

*　　*　　*

Southern Maryland bounded by the Potomac River and the Atlantic Ocean was a pro-Confederate area filled with people who hated the Northern cause and accepted and abetted Confederate couriers in their journeys to and from the South. No battles were fought in this area, and Union and Confederate forces largely ignored it because it was of no strategic value. The pro-Confederate population did provide manpower and support not only to the Confederate courier system but also to smugglers and to men wanting to join the Southern armies. Through these Marylanders' efforts, dispatches ran easily to and from Canada, and Northern newspapers could be read by Richmond authorities within twenty-four hours of publication.

The federal government did patrol the area with troops and gunboats; however, because of the many creeks and inlets that bordered the Potomac, it was not difficult for Confederate couriers to avoid detection.

On Friday, November 11, Booth traveled to Bryantown to visit Dr. Queen. Booth carried with him the letter of introduction from Patrick Martin. Dr. Queen, a member of the Confederate underground in Charles County, was cordial, and Booth spent that night with the Queen family. The next day, Booth visited the doctor's son-in-law, John C. Thompson.[227] Booth lied when he told them that he had made a lot of money in Pennsylvania oil and was now interested in purchasing land in Southern Maryland.

It is also during this trip that Booth became acquainted with Samuel Mudd.[228] On Sunday, November 13, Booth accompanied Queen and Thompson to St. Mary's for church services. It was here that Thompson introduced Booth to Dr. Mudd. Dr. Mudd usually attended Sunday services at his own church, St. Peter's, near his home, but apparently had come to St. Mary's just to meet Booth at the invitation of Dr. Queen.

Booth returned to Dr. Queen's home and traveled to Washington the next day Monday, November 14. Two days later, he made a deposit of $1,500 at Jay Cooke's Washington bank.[229] Later that day, Booth traveled to Baltimore to join his brother Junius on a trip to New York City. They were going to rehearse with Edwin for *Julius Caesar*. The three bothers had agreed to appear together for a one-night performance on November 25 with the proceeds going to erect a statue of Shakespeare in New York's Central Park.

Two thousand people were in attendance that night at the Winter Garden with tickets selling for as high as five dollars, which was about what an enlisted man earned in the Union Army per month. Mary Ann Booth with other members of the Booth family saw the play from a private box. Junius Jr. played Cassius, Edwin played Brutus, and John portrayed Mark Anthony. The play was reviewed in the *New York Herald*, which said, "Brutus was individualized with great force and distinctness, Cassius was brought out equally well, and if there was less of real personality given to Marc Anthony, the fault was rather in the part than in the actor . . . [John] played with a phosphorescent passion and fire, which recalled to old theatergoers the characteristics of the elder Booth."

That same night, a group of Confederates from Canada attempted to burn New York City by setting fires in several hotels. The play was interrupted at the beginning of the second act by a fire at the nearby Lafarge Hotel. Edwin Booth, hoping to prevent panic, appealed to the audience to remain quietly seated until the end of the play.

Lieutenant Colonel Robert M. Martin of the Tenth Kentucky Cavalry commanded the arsonous Confederate unit. Martin was capture in October 1865 but was pardoned by President Johnson in 1866. Two other men under his command were not so lucky – they were captured, tried, and executed. They were John Yates Beall who was hanged at Fort Columbus on February 24, 1865, and Robert Cobb Kennedy who was hanged at Fort Lafayette on March 25, 1865.[230]

New York City residents were furious over the attempt to burn their city. The fires had not, in the end, been very successful. There had been smoke in some hotels and less than a thousand dollars in damage in others. But the arson caused concern in other Northern cities that the Confederacy might be intending to attack civilian property.[231]

Confederate Secretary of State Benjamin was embarrassed and angry about the arson mission. It had been hideously bungled and turned into a political nightmare with unfavorable stories in the newspapers. The selection of targets – hotels, which were not military installations – did the South no good even if every hotel had burned to the ground. The most the raid accomplished was to anger Northerners against the Southern cause without destroying the crucial military installations, trains, or arsenals that would have made the mission worthwhile.

Although Jefferson Davis and Judah Benjamin felt that their Confederate representative in Canada, Jacob Thompson, was wasting their money in foolish, poorly thought-out schemes, they kept him in office so he could complete another poorly thought-out plan. He was trying to convince many Northerns to trade their paper money for gold and to accumulate the precious metal as protection against the collapse of the North; Benjamin asked him to concentrate on that operation and to cease all other operations. The scheme was to use $100,000 to buy gold, hoping to cause financial panic and a run on the New York gold market. The paltry sum used was, of course, inconsequential to the gold market as a whole, and the plan failed pitifully.

The Confederates in Montreal made more bizarre attempts to damage the Union's ability to wage war. In late December 1864, they attempted to derail a Union train carrying high-ranking Confederate prisoners. The idea was to free the prisoners and take them to Canada. No one seemed to consider the possibility that the captive Confederates might be killed in a successful derailment. It was snowing heavily when they reached the site of the planned derailing. Only then did they discover that no one had brought a crowbar to pull up the tracks. The would-be derailers laid a small iron rail on the track with the idea that the train would jump the tracks. As the train rushed by, it merely brushed the rail aside and continued down the tracks.

These same bungling Confederates then came up with the idea of kidnapping Vice President Andrew Johnson and demanding as ransom the release of all Confederate prisoners. The vice president was visiting in Louisville, Kentucky. The plan was for one man to engage Johnson in conversation in his room about a possible government job. A second accomplice with a pistol would then rush through the door left unlocked by the first man. The vice president would be bound and gagged, his overcoat placed over his head and shoulders, and the men would carry him away, saying they were taking a sick friend to the hospital. The plotters hired a closed carriage for the job but had to postpone the abduction the first night because no driver showed up. On the second night, the pair stealthily crept down the hall to the vice president's door. They knocked. Everything was perfectly planned, except that the vice president had left for Cincinnati after lunch that day.[232]

\*   \*   \*

After the Winter Garden performance in New York City, Booth went to Philadelphia to visit Asia. There he left a packet, saying, "Lock this in your safe for me. I may come back for it, but if anything should happen to me, open the packet alone and send the letters as directed, and the money and papers give to their owners." Asia accepted the packet without question. It was not unusual for people who traveled a lot to speak of possible accidents, since travel was risky and dangerous, and a traveling actor was constantly exposed to the possibility of a fatal accident. Asia promised to lock up the packet.[233]

Next Booth set about buying the equipment he needed for the kidnapping. Between November 16 and December 12, 1864, he returned to New York City and obtained two carbines (seven-shot Spencers), revolvers, three knives, and two pairs of handcuffs. All these, Booth stowed in his trunk for the train trip back to Washington. On the way, however, he began to worry that the weight of his trunk would attract attention. So he stopped in Baltimore and asked Arnold to take some of the weapons and send them to him in Washington by express.[234]

On December 12, Booth checked back into the National Hotel in Washington.

\*   \*   \*

On Saturday, December 17, Booth returned to the Bryantown and stayed the night at the home of Dr. Queen. The following day, after church services at St. Mary's, Booth met with Dr. Mudd at the Bryantown Tavern and was introduced to Thomas Harbin (alias Thomas Wilson), a Confederate courier. After Booth excitedly explained his kidnap plan to the two men, Harbin thought Booth was "a crazy fellow" but agreed "that he would give his cooperation."[235]

The Confederacy only had four months left of its existence; Richmond was surrounded by Grant's army and was in complete chaos, including its communication system with the outside world.

From the Bryantown Tavern meeting, Booth returned with Dr. Mudd and spent the night at his home. The next morning, Booth told Mudd that he wanted to buy a horse. The horse would be used in the kidnapping plot. Mudd mentioned that his neighbor, George Gardiner, had several for sale, so Booth and Mudd went to the Gardiners. Booth told the story that he needed the horse to travel over the roads of Southern Maryland to look at land sites to buy, with Mudd standing silently by. Gardiner offered Booth a young mare, which Booth rejected. When Gardiner brought out an old dark-bay saddle horse with one eye. A price was agreed upon, and Booth bought the horse. He felt the need to explain his choice and said that he intended to use the horse for only one year. Booth paid eighty dollars in cash, and the horse was to be delivered to Bryantown the next morning, Tuesday, December 20.[236]

The next morning, Booth and the horse were back in Washington and, later that day, cashed a check for $100 at Cooke's Washington bank. However, he did not return to the National Hotel that day. Instead he visited his favorite prostitute, nineteen-year-old Ella Turner Starr (alias Ella Turner and Fannie Harrison). Booth, although he was courting a respectable girl, Lucy Hale, spent much of his spare time with Ella. She even accompanied him on one of his trips to Pennsylvania. He stayed with Ella at her sister's bordello,[237] reveling in her fresh beauty and sexuality. When Booth died, one of the five photos he had on him was one of Ella Starr.[238]

Booth finally checked into the National Hotel on December 22.

*　　*　　*

On December 23, Dr. Mudd rode to Washington with his cousin Jeremiah T. Mudd to do some Christmas shopping and to buy a new stove for his wife, Frances. Night had just fallen when they arrived. The two stabled their horses near the Navy Yard and then checked in at the Pennsylvania House. After dinner at a nearby restaurant, they went drinking at Brown's Hotel and then the National Hotel. Dr. Mudd left his cousin drinking at the hotel and went walking down Pennsylvania Avenue where he ran into Booth on the street.[239]

Booth was delighted to see his new Confederate contact. Booth had learned of a young confederate courier named John Surratt. Now Booth wanted to meet Surratt. During the conversation that followed, Booth asked Mudd to introduce him to John Surratt. Mudd had known John Surratt for sometime; he had been at the Mudd farm more than a dozen times as a Confederate courier on his way to and from Virginia. Surratt often ate at the Mudd home but always slept "out in the woods" since Mudd did not want his servants or field hands to be aware of Surratt's illicit activities.[240] Booth's network of confederates were falling into place.

Booth and Mudd walked along Seventh Street toward the Surratt boardinghouse and by chance met John Surratt and Louis Weichmann, who were out for some Christmas shopping. Mudd introduced Booth to Surratt, and Surratt introduced Weichmann to the group.

Booth invited the three men to his room at the National for drinks and cigars. The three quickly agreed and walked the short distance to the hotel. Booth was at his most charming. At one point in the evening, Booth asked Surratt to help him draw a route from Washington to the Potomac. He told Surratt that he had become lost on his latest visit to Southern Maryland and wanted to get the roads straight, especially the route from Washington to the Potomac. Booth sketched out a crude map on the back of an envelope and asked Surratt to check whether it was correct.

Weichmann, who sat slightly apart, heard and saw nothing of this interchange, except that Booth was "drawing lines on paper." Booth and Mudd excused themselves and went out into the hallway to talk. Then they called to John Surratt to join them, leaving Weichmann alone and miffed at being excluded.[241]

Later, Mudd asked the others if they wanted to return with him to *his* hotel. They all readily agreed and bundled up to walk to the Pennsylvania House where they settled into the downstairs sitting room.

At ten o'clock, the gathering broke up, and the next morning, Mudd and his cousin continued Christmas shopping. Mudd did purchase the stove for his wife and made arrangements to have it shipped home. After a little more shopping, Mudd and Jeremiah went back to the Navy Yard at about three o'clock for their horses and rode home.[242]

The next day, Christmas Eve, Booth left Washington for New York where the Booth family would be gathering.

*　　*　　*

On Christmas day, McVicker, a Midwestern theater manager, wrote to Booth from Chicago, asking, "What do you say to filling time weekly with me, May twenty-ninth? I have not yet filled your time in January and see no chance of doing so with an attraction equal to yourself. There are plenty of little fish but I don't want them if I can help it. So, if you can come then, come at the above date."[243] It meant that Booth was still popular and in demand as an actor in the major cities. His reputation among theater managers and his popularity with the paying public was as strong as ever. But Booth was too busy plotting the kidnapping of Lincoln to accept McVicker's offer.

# CHAPTER 8

## *He Was a Crazy Fellow*

During the last six months of the war, Farragut attacked and destroyed the Confederate warships defending Mobile, Alabama, and the city itself was captured the following April, closing the Confederacy's last major gulf port. Sherman took Atlanta in September and then Savannah in December. In early November, Southern forces suffered a pounding defeat at Chattanooga, and by February, Sherman's army was plowing through South Carolina and Columbia, the state capital, soon to go up in smoke. In the Shenandoah Valley, General Sheridan was cutting and burning a broad path through the Confederacy's breadbasket. He defeated Confederate General Jubal Early at Cedar Creek and continued the destruction of crops and livestock, severely cutting off Confederate supply lines to its armies.

It was all but over for the South, and all but Confederate diehards knew it. One of those diehards was John Wilkes Booth. He was spending all his time and energy on trying to get his kidnap scheme together. On returning from his Christmas visit with his family, Booth stopped at Baltimore to arrange with Samuel Arnold to buy a horse and buggy and to transport it to Washington. While in Baltimore, he collected the rent on the Hartford County farm, signing the receipt on December 30. On New Year's Eve 1864, Booth arrived back in the Washington by train. Around January 11, Arnold and O'Laughlen arrived in Washington with the horse and carriage. They stabled the horse at Naylor's stable and then registered at Rullman's Hotel. They were both caught up in the plan that Booth was preparing. About a week later, they left Rullman's and rented a room from Mary Van Tine at 420 D Street.[244]

With the exception for two performances, both in Washington, Booth no longer did any acting; he was consumed by his plan that would save the Confederacy and skyrocket him to greatness. He turned down acting jobs, saying that he was spending all his time keeping up with his Pennsylvania oil dealings. Young Arnold told his parents that he "was in the oil business with Booth" when asked what he was doing to earn a living.

On the evening of January 1, 1865, Booth paid his first visit to John Surratt at his mother's boardinghouse. The visit was friendly and cordial, and from then on, Booth became a frequent visitor at the Surratt home. Mary's daughter, twenty-two-year-old Anna, and the other ladies staying at the house were attracted by Booth's charisma and good looks. John Surratt wrote to his cousin Belle Seaman in New York that he and Anna were going to a "regular country hoe down" and that the Smithsonian Institution had had a fire. He then wrote, "I have just taken a peep in the parlour. Would you like to know what I saw there? Well, Ma was sitting on the sofa, nodding first to one chair, then to another, next the piano. Anna is sitting in a corner, dreaming, I expect, of J. W. Booth. Well, who is J. W. Booth? She can answer the question. Miss Patrick [Honora], playing with her favorite cat, a good sign of an old maid, the detested old creatures. Miss Dean fixing her hair, which is filled with rats and mice.

"But hark! The door bell rings and Mr. J. W. Booth is announced. And listen to the scamperings. Such brushing and fixing."[245]

The Ms. Dean who Surratt referred to in his letter was Mary Apollonia Dean from Alexandria, Virginia, a ten-year-old who came to board at the Surratt house, a little after Christmas 1864, while attending the Visitation School for Girls, a Catholic school.

Anna and Honora were so excited by their acquaintance with the handsome actor that they each bought a photograph of Booth at a local gallery. Thrilled with her purchase, Anna hung it in her bedroom.[246]

When her brother John saw the picture of Booth on Anna's wall, he had instant misgivings. When the kidnap scheme came to fruition, John Surratt knew that they all would be wanted men. Surratt wanted no ties between his sister and Booth, and of course, he could not tell her why. He could only demand that she tear up the picture and throw it in the fire. If she refused, he would take it from her.

Anna was outraged; rebelling against her brother's inexplicable demand, she hid the portrait behind a framed picture given to her by Louis Weichmann. After the assassination, when the boardinghouse was searched, Booth's picture was found where Anna had hidden it. She also took to writing his name repeatedly on pieces of paper.

Booth's visits reveal a great deal about Booth and John Surratt. They both knew they were about to engage in a scheme that would make them notorious wanted men if they succeed and dead men if they fail. Yet they, and other conspirators, often met at the boardinghouse. They were both, despite their experiences, rather naive, not realizing that they were putting Mary Surratt and the other boarders at risk. John Surratt was somewhat aware of this when he told his sister to get rid of Booth's photo. To Surratt's way of thinking, Booth's photo was a danger to the household, but he did not have the presence of mind to realize that frequent visits by all the conspirators was an even greater threat to his family.

On December 30, John Surratt got a job with the Adams Express Company. On January 13, he asked his employer for a day off so he could take his mother to the Surratt Tavern on business. Since he had only been on the job for two weeks, the company refused his request, and they refused Mary herself when she made the same request the next day. When John heard that the company refused his mother's request, he was furious. He quit the job, not even returning to pick up his back wages.[247]

Sometime in January 1865, John Surratt decided to help John Wilkes Booth abduct President Lincoln and set about getting contacts in the area along the planned escape route. On January 14, he met Thomas Harbin at Port Tobacco, Maryland, and arranged for him to help the fugitives when the time came. This small town on Port Tobacco Creek ran into the Potomac River. With its small streams and inlets, the creek was an ideal hiding place for blockade-runners and Confederate agents going to and from Richmond.

On another trip to Port Tobacco that same month, John Surratt was introduced to George Atzerodt. Atzerodt, originally from Prussia (now northern Germany), was born on June 12, 1835, and came to the United States in June 1844. He had spent most of his adult life in Charles County, and so he knew the area well. He was short, stout, and round shouldered with unkempt brown hair and a goatee. His rough appearance gave him the air of slow-wittedness. Atzerodt had been working with his older brother, John, who had a carriage painting shop in Port Tobacco. With the start of the Civil War, the business failed, and George began his blockade-running across the Potomac River, a profession that provided a lucrative income. He lived with a woman and fathered one child by her.

John Surratt had used many blockade-runners to ferry him across the Potomac River to and from Richmond; he recruited Atzerodt. John knew Atzerodt was a skilled blockade-runner and that he was familiar with the back roads of Maryland. In Atzerodt's confession of April 25, 1865, he says, "John H. Surratt came after me in the winter . . . it was after Christmas."[248]

At Port Tobacco, Surratt bought a boat for $250 from Richard Smoot and James Brawner. The understanding was that Judge Frederick Stone would hold $125 of the amount in trust until the boat was used and then pay off the balance.[249] Atzerodt hid the boat at Goose Creek and later moved it to Nanjemoy Creek where Charles and George Bateman, two blockade-runners, looked after it.

\*    \*    \*

Lewis Thornton Powell was born in Alabama in 1844.[250] His father, a farmer and part-time Baptist preacher, later moved the family to Live Oak Station in northern Florida. As soon as the war broke out in 1861, Powell and his two brothers enlisted. Powell joined the Second Florida Infantry on May 30, 1861. At this time, he was below the legal enlistment age of nineteen; however, he convinced his family to allow him to enlist. The war was not kind to the Powell family. Oliver was killed at the battle at Murfreesboro in 1863, and George lost his leg during the siege of Petersburg.

Although Powell was a giant of a man and appeared sturdy and tough, he quickly ended up in the hospital within two months of enlistment. In November 1862, he was in the hospital again. On June 23, 1862, he reenlisted for the duration of the war and received a $50 reenlistment bonus. He fought in a number of battles – several in the Peninsula Campaign, Second Battle of Bull Run, Antietam, Chancellorsville, and Fredericksburg.

Powell was still with the Second Florida Infantry when he was captured at Gettysburg after being wounded in the right wrist.[251] Because his injury was not very debilitating, he was soon acting as a nurse at the Twelfth Army Corps Field Hospital. In a Hemingwayesque scenario, he became involved with a nurse.

Her name was Margaret Branson. She was a strong secessionist and had volunteered her services to nurse the wounded. She once declared, "I have never taken the Oath of Allegiance . . . . I have always been a Rebel sympathizer."[252] During her stay in Gettysburg, she only nursed the Confederate wounded.

So it happened that thirty-one-year-old Margaret Branson nursed nineteen-year-old Powell. When Powell was transferred as a prisoner of war to the Pratt Street Baltimore West Hospital, Margaret Branson promptly left Gettysburg and returned to Baltimore.[253] Five days later, Powell and about nine other prisoners escaped. Chief steward of the hospital, Samuel S. Bond, reported, "It was the general belief that they were assisted in their escape by this Miss Branson."[254]

After his escape from the Baltimore hospital, Powell made his way south to Warrenton, Virginia, where he joined Mosby's Rangers.[255] The battalion was quartered in civilian houses, and Powell lived at the various homes of members of the Payne family. In late November 1864, Powell's unit was involved in a skirmish with Union troops and captured Captain Richard Blazer. The four rangers responsible for that capture, including Powell, were assigned to escort Captain Blazer to Libby Prison in Richmond.[256]

On Christmas 1864, Powell helped save two federal soldiers from an angry mob. Six captured Union soldiers were left in Powell's custody. Powell, however, did not stay with his charges but took his horse and went off on an errand. While he was gone, fellow Confederate soldiers were angry because the house that had been burned by the Federals killed four of the prisoners. When Powell returned and discovered what had happened, he took the remaining two prisoners to safety.

Powell left Mosby's Rangers sometime in early January 1865 and returned to Baltimore to be with Margaret Branson.[257]

On January 13, Powell appeared before Lieutenant Maguire, the provost marshal, at the Fairfax Court House, Virginia. Lieutenant Maguire, in turn, sent Powell to the local military headquarters in Alexandria where, as a confederate, he would have to take the oath of allegiance. Powell, not wanting to give his true name, told officials that his last name was Payne, the name of the family with which he had stayed. Powell gave two reasons for his using the name "Payne." The surname of Payne was familiar in Fauquier County, and Powell wanted to claim to be from a section of the country where he was familiar with the people and geography.[258]

Powell took the oath of allegiance on January 13 and was issued a pass and parole.[259] Powell then left for Baltimore and Margaret Branson.

As soon as Powell arrived in Baltimore, he called on Margaret. For ten days, Powell stayed at Baltimore's Miller Hotel, then he moved into the Branson boardinghouse at 16 North Eutaw Street where he was introduced to the other boarders as Mr. Payne. The Branson house was a safe house for Confederate couriers.[260]

During this time, Powell became acquainted with David Preston Parr, who owned the Mr. Parr's China Halls, which catered to an upper-class clientele.[261] Parr operated a Confederate safe house and aided the courier system that went through Baltimore. Parr introduced Powell to a Confederate courier named John Surratt, and through Surratt, Powell was introduced to John Wilkes Booth.

\* \* \*

Meanwhile, Louis Weichmann was still yearning to finish his studies for the priesthood. To do so, he needed a letter of permission from the Reverend John McGill, bishop of Richmond. The letter arrived January 17, 1865, on a flag-of-truce ship, giving Weichmann the permission he needed. He made plans to attend St. Mary's Seminary in Baltimore beginning September 1, 1865. The Lincoln assassination and the conspiracy trial prevented these studies.[262]

Surratt and Weichmann traveled to Baltimore on January 21 and both checked into the Maltby House, room 127. Weichmann had gone to Baltimore to see Father Paul Dubreuil at St. Mary's Seminary.[263] Surratt went to see David Preston Parr. Four days later, Surratt made another trip to Richmond.[264]

\* \* \*

Maryland, it must be remembered, was a slave state bordering the Union capital, Washington, on the north and east. Maryland, as well as Kentucky and Missouri, had to be held by the federal government at all costs. Control of Maryland was vital to the safety of Washington. Eastern Maryland, because of its geography, was the ideal underground route for smugglers and Confederate couriers. Throughout the war, they delivered dispatches from Canada and newspapers from Northern cities to Richmond. Federal cavalry patrolled the roads on the eastern shore, and gunboats patrolled the rivers to maintain order and catch couriers and blockade-runners. But federal patrols were easy for Confederate sympathizers to avoid because they sparsely populated the area and the many hiding places in the swamps and numerous creeks. Eventually martial law was declared in eastern Maryland, and the cavalry enforced military rule.

Booth planned his escape route after the assassination to be through Southern Maryland. Some crossing points on the Potomac would put Booth well into Virginia not very far from Richmond. Booth's projected route was the most logical because it very closely matched the underground system already in use for getting people, dispatches, newspapers, and mail across the Potomac and into the Confederacy.

\* \* \*

In January, David Edgar Herold was brought into the conspiracy. Herold was born in 1842 in Washington. His family was well-off financially, and David had studied pharmacy at Georgetown College and at the prestigious Rittenhouse Academy in 1859. But despite his family money and education, young Herald was immature and untrustworthy. He worked for several druggist during the next five years, but he had a reputation for being unreliable. Dr. Samuel A. McKim considered Herold "a very light, trivial, unreliable boy; so much so that I would never let him put up a prescription of mine if I could prevent it."[265]

Herold's father, who died in October 1864, wrote, "Under no circumstances shall the duty of settling my estate devolve upon my son David."[266] Herold's familiarity with Southern Maryland where he did his bird hunting made him an ideal guide in the kidnapping plot.

David Herold knew all the players long before Booth developed his kidnapping and assassination schemes. He had known Booth since the spring of 1863 when they met at one of the drug stores where Herold was working. He had known John Surratt about nine years. He had met George Atzerodt four years previously during one of his hunting trips to Southern Maryland. And Herold acknowledged meeting O'Laughlen in Baltimore through Atzerodt. Herold also knew Weichmann; they had first met at the Surratt Tavern in the spring of 1863.

Herold lived with a friend in Washington, DC, for eleven months in 1864. That fall took two to three months off from work to go partridge hunting. After this hunting season, he went to live with his mother, "looking for a situation."[267]

The plan to kidnap Lincoln now included John Wilkes Booth, John Surratt, Lewis Powell, David Herold, George Atzerodt, Michael O'Laughlen, and Samuel Arnold as the principals and Samuel Mudd and Thomas Harbin who agreed to help in a supportive role. Were there others? In inquiry for the trial, Major Thomas T. Eckert, an assistant of Secretary Stanton, visited the USS Montauk and the prison a number of times to question Powell, who responded, "All I can say about this is, that you have not got the one-half of them."[268] Booth frequently had exaggerated the number of people involved (as he did with the unsuccessful recruitment Samuel Chester), and Powell took at face value Booth's exaggerated claims and considered the people he met in Baltimore and others such as Chester and Thomas Harbin as members.

On January 20, 1865, John Wilkes Booth performed at the Grover Theatre in *Romeo and Juliet*. The *Washington National Intelligencer* said:

He is full of genius . . . . We have never seen a Romeo bearing any near comparison with the acting of Booth on Friday night. His death scene was the most remarkable and fearfully natural that we have seen for years upon the stage . . . . His elocution was faultless.[269]

*　　*　　*

On a trip to New York at the end of January, Booth stopped off in Philadelphia and reclaimed the sealed envelope he had left with Asia Booth Clark for safekeeping. It was a long rambling letter addressed "To Whom It May Concern." While in New York, he added his signature to the letter but in a different ink from that used in the body. On his way back to Washington, Booth stopped by the Clarks' again and left the envelope, signed with his name J. Wilkes Booth.

On February 9, 1865, Booth again is travelling to Philadelphia and New York. Before he left Washington, he wrote a letter to Orlando Tompkins, a theater owner in Boston, requesting him to reproduce a dozen of Booth's favorite photographs and to forward them to Edwin in New York City. Booth continued in the letter, "This is very important as there are several parties whom I would like to give one."[270] This is a strange request, perhaps Booth wanted to give them to family and friends, knowing he would not be returning to the North.

Booth saw his sister one more time when he stopped in Philadelphia on February 10 on his way to New York.

*　　*　　*

In early February, George Atzerodt returned to Washington after a trip to Southern Maryland. He stayed at the Surratt boardinghouse, and there he met and became close friends with Weichmann.[271] The ever-inquisitive Weichmann did not understand the relationship that John Surratt and Atzerodt had with Booth. When Weichmann asked Atzerodt what the three of them were doing, Atzerodt said Booth intended to rent the Washington Theatre and employ him as a ticket agent. At another time, Weichmann asked Surratt the same question and was informed that Booth was preparing him for a theatrical career in Richmond. During January, February, and March, Booth was a daily visitor at the Surratt boardinghouse.

Atzerodt stayed only a few days at the boardinghouse before he was kicked out. Mary had found several bottles of liquor in his room. When her son returned home, she told him that she didn't want "Port Tobacco" (as she called him after the town he came from in Maryland) to stay there any longer.[272] Anna said of Atzerodt that "they [Anna and her mother] did not care about having him brought to the house," that she didn't care about having "such sticks brought to the house; that they were not company for her."

* * *

The temperature was twenty-six degrees on February 7 when the Holohan family moved into the boardinghouse. Irish-born John Holohan and his wife, Eliza Jane Smith, were married on June 21, 1850. He was three years her senior, and by 1865, they had two children – Mary, age fourteen, and Charles, age twelve. Holohan made his living procuring substitutes for drafted men and had previously worked in the post office and as a stonecutter. The marriage was rocky and once Eliza had had her husband arrested for assault.[273]

With the Holohans, Mary's boardinghouse was finally filled to capacity. With the rooms full, Mary hired a woman to pick up the wash on Mondays and return it on Wednesdays.[274]

* * *

As a Confederate courier, John Surratt came in contact with other Confederate agents, some of whom stayed at the boardinghouse or the tavern. Two of these agents were Gus Howell and Sarah Slater. The comings and goings of these two in March 1865 played an important role in the fate of the Surratt family.

Gus Howell enlisted in the Confederate army in Fredericksburg, Virginia, on June 25, 1861, but was discharged for disability on July 16, 1862. Whatever his disability, it did not prevent him from becoming deeply involved in the Confederate underground in Maryland. Federal forces patrolling the Potomac River arrested him on October 24, 1862, and charged him with "transporting rebels from Maryland to join the rebel army." Howell was paroled and quickly arrested again on January 29,1863, in Upper Marlboro, Maryland. A month later, Howell was released again and was back in Maryland on the Potomac River working as a blockade-runner. Howell has been called "one of the most effective Confederate spies and blockade runners along the Potomac."[275]

In early February 1865, Howell was assigned as escort for Sarah Antoinette (Nettie) Gilbert Slater, a courier. Slater was an attractive, married twenty-two-year-old from North Carolina, who spoke French fluently. She was to take papers from Richmond to Montreal and left on January 31. Her mission was to deliver documents concerning the captured St. Albans raiders to a Montreal judge. The documents confirmed that the raiders were, at the time of the raid, Confederate soldiers.[276]

With an escort, Slater traveled the usual courier route along the Richmond, Fredericksburg, and Potomac Railroad to Milford Station and Bowling Green in Virginia. At Port Royal, Virginia, she crossed on the Rappahannock River ferry. This is where on February 2 she met Gus Howell near the mouth of Mattox Creek on the Potomac River. Howell relieved the original escort. They crossed the Potomac River into Maryland and made their way to Washington. From there, Howell escorted Slater to the European Hotel in New York City. After leaving Mrs. Slater in New York City, Howell returned to Washington, arriving February 19 to await Slater's return, and stayed at the Surratt boardinghouse. From New York City, Slater continued on alone to Montreal by train with her documents. In the early morning hours of February 15, 1865, Slater registered at St. Lawrence Hall in Montreal, as Mrs. N. Slater of New York.

Slater delivered her documents, and two days later, she was on her way back to Richmond with urgent dispatches. John Surratt was assigned to meet her in New York and take her to Washington and then to the Surratt boardinghouse from which Howell planned to escort her through Maryland to Virginia.

On the afternoon of February 22, Sarah Slater and John Surratt arrived in Washington. Slater left immediately for Richmond with Howell and Atzerodt. At Port Tobacco, Atzerodt rowed them across the Potomac to Mathias Point, Virginia.

Accompanied by Howell, Slater made a second trip to Canada in early March. It was on Slater's trip that on March 8, Confederate Secretary of State Benjamin wrote in his ledger, "Payment in gold to defray expense of dispatch messenger to Canada: $100."[277] However, Gus Howell did not complete the journey with Slater all the way from Richmond to Washington.

So it was that Sarah Slater arrived by herself at the Surratt boardinghouse a few days later with the ever-helpful Weichmann bringing her trunk into the house. Weichmann was infatuated with the comely courier and quizzed Mrs. Surratt for information about her. Mary Surratt threw caution to the wind and revealed to Weichmann that Slater "was a blockade runner or bearer of dispatches." But, Mary maintained, Mrs. Slater was perfectly safe. If she got into trouble, there was no danger because "she could immediately apply to the French consul" for help, "speaking French as she did."[278] This was not true; Slater would have had to be a citizen of France to obtain the protection of the French embassy. That night at Mary's behest, Weichmann gave up his bedroom for Slater, and he slept in the chilly attic. Slater left the following morning, leaving her "dainty slippers" in the bedroom where they were found and treasured by Weichmann.

From Washington, Slater left with John Surratt by train for New York. She then went on alone, arriving in Montreal on March 17 and left Montreal March 22, with replies from General Edwin Lee who was then head of the Confederate government's delegation in Canada. When she went to New York, a member of the underground sent a letter to John Surratt to come and get her.[279]

John Surratt escorted Slater back to Washington on the morning of March 25 with the dispatches for Richmond. Later that day, John involved his mother by taking her with Sarah Slater by carriage to the Surratt Tavern, now operated by Lloyd. There, Lloyd informed them that Gus Howell had been captured by federal cavalry the night before. Howell was to have escorted Slater to Richmond. Had the cavalry unit been delayed just one day, they would also have captured Sarah Slater and her dispatches as well as Mary and John Surratt.[280]

John Surratt now took it upon himself to escort Slater all the way to Richmond. While at the Surratt Tavern, he met David Barry, a local who lived only a mile and a half from the tavern. Barry wanted to see Lieutenant Charles Keyworth, a Confederate signal corpsman in Port Tobacco, who might have received news about Barry's two sons who were under the command of General Robert E. Lee. Barry asked John Surratt if he could go as far Port Tobacco with him, and Surratt agreed if Barry would return the horses and carriage to Washington. Barry readily agreed. Surratt told Barry "that he intended to see a lady he had in charge across the Potomac river, and if necessary, to Richmond." John Surratt introduced Slater as Mrs. Brown. Barry was curious about "Mrs. Brown," and tried to get a good look at her. Barry could only tell that she was under thirty and was a slim delicate woman with dark eyes and hair. Barry could not see her face well because she kept her veil down nearly all the time. This incautious sharing of his courier activities was probably owing to Barry's Southern sympathies. Nonetheless, Surratt did not fully appreciate how allowing his activities to be known by casual acquaintances, and involving his family in his travels could endanger his mission and their well-being. Surratt did escort Sarah Slater to Richmond, and Barry returned Booth's horses and carriage to Howard's livery in Washington on March 26.[281]

Meanwhile, Mary Surratt, who was still at the tavern, visited her former servant, Rachel, and then her brother, Zadoc Jenkins. Mary returned to Washington by stage with Zadoc's daughter, Olivia, who would be visiting with her over the Easter holidays.[282]

When Barry returned the horses the next day in Washington, he also visited Mary Surratt at her boardinghouse. He delivered a letter to her from John, telling her he had gone to Richmond.[283] Booth and Atzerodt were at the Surratt boardinghouse when Barry arrived, and they also learned of Howell's arrest and John's trip to Richmond.

Slater and John Surratt arrived in Richmond on March 29, finishing her second round trip to Montreal. With them, they had dispatches from Edwin Lee for Secretary of State Benjamin. Using the name "Harry Sherman," Surratt checked into the Spotswood House on the evening of March 29.[284]

On March 31, Confederate Secretary of State Benjamin reimbursed Surratt ten twenty-dollar gold pieces to pay expenses for their last round trip to Montreal.

Benjamin then gave Slater and Surratt another assignment. They would go to Montreal to deliver to General Edwin Lee dispatches containing specific instructions for the disposal of Confederate funds into English banks.[285] On April 1, John Surratt and Sarah Slater left Richmond. Two days later, Richmond fell to General Grant.

The two couriers arrived in Washington late on the afternoon of April 3. John Surratt visited his mother and while there exchanged the gold coins given to him by Benjamin for greenbacks with boarder John Holohan. John Surratt felt that he could continue his courier duties indefinitely. Then the bombshell fell. One of the servants in the house told him that a detective had been looking for him. Was it in connection with the kidnapping plot, his Confederate courier activities, or something unrelated? Quickly John left the house with Weichmann but did not return home for fear of being picked up by the police.

Slater and Surratt left Washington for New York early the next morning by train, stopping in New York. There he called at Edwin Booth's elegant home, asking for John Booth. He was told that he had gone to Boston where Edwin was playing an engagement. Surratt continued to Montreal; however, Sarah Antoinette "Nettie" Slater disappeared for a time from the historical record.

*   *   *

Detectives found a letter among Booth's possessions when they searched his room at the National Hotel after Lincoln was shot. The letter was dated "N.Y. 20th Feby/65" and delivered to "J. W. Booth, esq."

The letter began,

> I regretted not to have again seen you [Booth] on Saturday and yesterday could not find out Mr. Edwin Booth's house as his name is not in the Directory. As Lewis is anxious to have had a conversation with you relative to the order for shipping the horses, as well as the Ile [?] question. With regard to the former may I beg you to find out as soon as convenience will allow if the thing is possible, and if so, write me such a letter as I can show the Gentleman (who wishes to procure the order) and I will go at once to Washington and give the particulars. However, I may say the desire of the owner of the horses is to send them to Paris. He is a strong Union man in a good position here . . . . [signed] J. J. Redford[286]

Taken literally, the letter makes no sense. However, the letter was not about shipping horses. One interpretation may go as follows: Lewis Powell was anxious to have a conversation with Booth about the kidnap plan (shipping the horses). He wanted an update on whether the kidnapping was still planned (if the thing is possible). The words "I can show the Gentleman (who wishes to procure the order)" seem to refer to another member of the kidnap plot. "I will go at once to Washington and give the particulars" may be code for his going to Richmond to inform the Confederate government of the plan. "The desire of the owner of the horses is to send them to Paris" could refer to taking the kidnapped Lincoln to Richmond. "He is a strong Union man" seems to be code for a Confederate man since Booth had no Union men among the plotters.

The letter also clearly shows that as of February 20, the Confederate government was not aware of Booth's scheming since the writer was going to go to Richmond and give the government there "the particulars." This interpretation of the letter is based on the assumption that the writer is talking about the conspiracy to kidnap. Another interpretation could be made if one assumed that the writer was talking about quinine and the subject was smuggling.

*   *   *

In late February, Powell left the Bransons and went to the Surratt boardinghouse. Introducing himself as Mr. Wood, he asked whether Mr. Surratt was in. Weichmann, who answered the door, told him that John Surratt was not at home, so Powell then asked to see Mrs. Surratt.[287] Weichmann went to the parlor where Mary, who was sitting with her daughter and another lady, announced Mr. Wood. Powell told Mary Surratt that he knew her son, and after some social conversation, she invited him to stay for dinner and spend the night. Because the dining room was not yet cleaned up, Powell ate in Weichmann's room. Weichmann took the stranger his dinner on a tray and asked him where he was from. Powell, forgetting his persona, replied that he was from Baltimore and that he was "a clerk in the china store of Mr. Parr." Powell was referring to Preston Parr, the Confederate agent in Baltimore who had introduced John Surratt to Powell. Powell spent the night and then left early the following morning.[288]

Powell's masquerade as Mr. Wood, a Baptist minister, was unconvincing. Anna Surratt assessed his demeanor and, in her opinion, found him to be "a perfect fool" who she believed did not possess "his five senses."[289]

There was a time when John Surratt showed concern for the safety of his mother and sister. On the evening of Powell's last stay at the Surratt boardinghouse when the household had gathered together, Lewis Powell made a remark alluding to plans to abduct the president. John immediately took Powell aside and told him never to say anything like that again in the presence of his mother or his sister. John continued by saying that his mother and sister knew nothing about the affair, and furthermore, he didn't want them to know anything.[290]

*   *   *

Lucy Lambert Hale, daughter of Senator John P. Hale of New Hampshire, lived with her parents and sister at the National Hotel when the family was staying in Washington. The younger of two daughters, Lucy, was twenty-four in 1865, pretty, precocious, and slightly chubby. (John Ford once called her stout.) She had become infatuated with the handsome young actor, John Wilkes Booth. Photographs of five women were found in Booth's diary after he was killed, and Lucy's photo was one of them.

John P. Hale, a graduate of Bowdoin College, was quite gifted in debating and public speaking. In New Hampshire, John Hale had been a courtroom lawyer and was best known for defending those who refused to return fugitive slaves to their Southern master. He was elected to the House of Representatives and later to the Senate.

Hale held strong abolitionist views and was twice the presidential candidate of the Free Soil Party, which opposed the extension of slavery into the new territories. Senator Henry S. Foote of Mississippi said on the Senate floor that if Hale ever came to Mississippi, "he could not go ten miles into the interior before he will grace one of the tallest trees of the forest, with a rope around his neck, and with the approbation of every virtuous and patriotic citizen; and, if necessary, I should myself assist in the operation." With a quick wit, Hale mocked Foote's angry outburst. He thanked his Mississippi colleague for his "hospitable invitation" and suggested that Foote come to New Hampshire where people would be very interested in his views and debating with him to elicit the truth. After this incident, Senator Foote became known in the North as Hangman Foote.[291]

Hale was defeated in the November 1864 elections and asked Lincoln for a foreign ministership. Lincoln, who wished to "break his fall" from the loss of his Senate seat, had Secretary of State Seward appoint Hale as ambassador to Spain. He was first considered for an ambassadorship to France; however, that post was considered too sensitive to give to Hale, and Spain was the political compromise. Hale was to begin his new post in the spring of 1865.

Lucy liked attention, and she liked to flirt. Then she met the womanizing John Wilkes Booth, the "handsomest man in America." She fell in love with Booth, who was charming and, because he was an actor, not quite what her parents wanted for her. Naturally Lucy wanted to marry him. Booth, who knew that this match would never take place because of his abduction plans, agreed to marry Lucy as soon as she returned from Spain, where she was accompanying her father and mother. Lucy planned to come back to the United States in one year.

Lucy was also charming and charismatic. Oliver Wendell Holmes, a Harvard undergraduate and future U.S. Supreme Court justice, met her on a Maine vacation. In April 1858 when she was eighteen years old, he wrote to her at her Hartford boarding school saying that after parting from her, he was "so cross that no one could come within a mile of" him for three days because he missed her so. Less than a week later, he wrote, "Dear Miss Hale (need that formality be kept up any longer?)." Holmes wrote saying how happy he was to learn that no young men in Connecticut could go riding with her, for school rules forbade it. "This affords me huge satisfaction." In wartime Washington, Lucy lived at the National Hotel with her parents and her sister, Elizabeth, who was six years older. During the war, Holmes, a captain in the U.S. Army, occasionally had duties that brought him to Washington, and on these visits, he renewed his acquaintance with Lucy.[292]

In the winter of 1858-59, Lucy was studying at a boarding school in Boston where she met Robert Lincoln. Robert felt that he and Lucy were very close, for he wrote to her a very possessive note in April 1864. Lucy had accepted an invitation from a fellow student at Robert's school to attend class day. Robert wrote, "Mr. Anderson [Robert's friend] informs me that he has invited you to our Class-day. If you will promise to be good and not allow any freshman to be presented to you, I have not the slightest objection in the world to your accepting his invitation."[293] When she was in Washington; moreover, he sent her flowers.

Robert Lincoln was an impressive catch on his own terms and would go on to be one of the most successful presidential progenies in American history.

In 1869, John Hay, one of President Lincoln's secretaries,[294] wrote Lucy Hale from Madrid of his thoughts of her,

> I came back from the station wondering if there were anyone else in the world just like you; one of equal charm, equal power of gaining hearts, and equal disdain of the hearts you gain. The last glance of those mysterious blue-grey eyes fell upon a dozen or so of us and everybody but me thought the last glance was for him. I have known you too long. Since you were a school-girl – yes, even in those early days you were as puzzling in your apparent frankness and real reserve as you are today. You know how I love and admire you. I do not understand you, nor hope to, nor even wish to. You would lose to me something of your indefinable fascination if I knew exactly what you mean.[295]

Lucy Hale met Booth at the National Hotel. Like most other government officials, the Hales did not have a private home in Washington. Booth also lived at the National when he was in Washington, so it was inevitable that he would eventually meet Lucy. Many times, Booth gave dramatic readings in the hotel parlor. Booth and Hale were often together, and it was Lucy who began to see their relationship as serious. In the mid-1800s, there was a social stigma attached to actors and their way of life. Neither Lucy nor her parents liked the fact that Booth was an actor; even though he was a great tragedian actor, Senator Hale wished for someone more worthy of his daughter.

That John was an actor, Lucy told him, was the only thing she didn't like about him. Quick witted, he replied, "If only you weren't an abolitionist."[296]

Despite their differences, Booth actively courted Lucy. On February 13, Booth wrote her a valentine. He was in New York at his brother Edwin's house; his brother Junius was also there. In a letter dated "Tuesday, Feb. 1865," Junius wrote his sister, Asia, that "John sat up all Monday night [February 13] to put Miss Hale's valentine in the mail – and slept on the sofa – to be up early & kept me up last night till 3 1/2 AM – to wait while he wrote her a long letter & kept me awake by every now and then using me as a dictionary."[297]

"Will you marry me?" Booth asked Lucy. After agreeing to the proposal, Booth asked Lucy not to tell anyone of their engagement. Lucy agreed. Although the Hales did not know of this secret engagement, the Booth family did. Mary Ann Booth wrote a letter to her son,

> The secret you have told me is not exactly a secret, as Edwin was told by someone, you were paying great attention to a young lady in Washington – Now my dear boy, I cannot advise you how to act – you have so often been dead in love and this may prove like the others, not of any lasting impression – you are aware that the woman you make your wife you must love and respect beyond all others, for marriage is an act that

cannot be recalled without misery if so entered in . . . . You are old enough and have seen so much of the world, to know all this, only a young man in love does not stop to reflect and like a child with a new toy – only craves the possession of it – think and reflect – and if the lady in question is all you desire – I see no cause why you should not try to secure her – her father, I see he has his appointment, would he give his consent?[298]

After Booth's death, Lucy, still devoted, wrote broken-hearted letters to Edwin.[299]

# CHAPTER 9

## *Today We Kidnap the President*

Booth was growing impatient, waiting to carry out the kidnapping. He knew that the longer he waited, the more chance something could go wrong. Sure enough, on March 12, Powell was arrested and charged with being a spy. But the incident had nothing to do with Booth or his plans.

Powell had assaulted a black maid at Branson's boardinghouse. Powell's reason for the assault was "because she insulted me." Powell had told the woman to clean his room, and she had responded angrily that she was no slave and deserved respect. At this, Powell's prejudice and rural Southern upbringing boiled to the surface, and he beat the maid, whose name was Annie. Annie went straight to the police and told them not only of the assault but also of Powell's activities with the Confederate Secret Service. When Powell was arrested, it was not for assault and battery, but for being a spy.[300]

Despite this arrest, Powell (using the name of Lewis Payne) was paroled on March 14 and ordered to remain north of Philadelphia for the duration of the war.[301] Powell attempted to erase the words "to go north of Philadelphia and remain during the war."[302] Had Powell obeyed the terms of the parole, he would have escaped execution four months later. But, instead, as soon as he was released from custody, Powell went to the Branson house and from there to David Parr's china shop where he found the following telegram waiting for him:

D. Preston Parr
210 W. Baltimore Street
Baltimore, Md.
March 14, 1865, 11:40 a.m.

Immediately telegraph if my friend is disengaged and can see me this evening in Washington.

Harrison Surratt
541 H. Street, bet. 6 & 7 Sts.[303]

That afternoon, Parr spoke to Powell and, on Powell's behalf, sent a telegram to John Surratt saying, "He will be over in the six P.M. train."

Powell arrived at the Surratt house that evening for the second time.[304] Although he had a distinctive physique and face, he introduced himself to the same people he had seen before as Mr. Paine, a Baptist preacher. Although he was dressed in a gray suit and black tie, he fooled no one except Mary Surratt, who couldn't see very well.[305] Weichmann showed the young man to the parlor where Mary, Anna, and Honora Fitzpatrick were sitting. In the course of conversation, one of the young women recognized Powell and addressed him as Mr. Wood, but he ignored her. He told the women that he had been imprisoned as a rebel in Baltimore and "that he had taken the Oath of Allegiance, and was going to become a good and loyal citizen."[306] While Anna played the piano throughout the evening, Powell played "a social game of cards with the young ladies."[307] He stayed at the boardinghouse for three days.

John Surratt returned home late the following day and went to his bedroom, which he shared with Lou Weichmann. Later that evening, Powell knocked at their door. Weichmann, who was writing at the table, called to enter. Powell pretended that he didn't know Surratt. After greeting Weichmann, he then asked if the man seated on the bed was Mr. Surratt. Weichmann said that he was. Powell needed to talk to Surratt about the kidnap plot, but he did not want to talk in from of Weichmann, so Weichmann was asked to leave the room so that Powell could talk privately with Surratt.[308]

John Surratt affirmed to Powell that Booth was trying to pull a group together in Washington. Now he was recruiting Powell, the last member of Booth's group.

On March 13, Booth in Washington sent a telegram to O'Laughlen, No. 57 North Exeter Street, Baltimore. The telegram read, "Don't fear to neglect your business. You had better come at once." O'Laughlen came to Washington on March 15. That evening, Booth invited all his people to the expensive Gautier's restaurant on Pennsylvania Avenue.

This was a busy day for Booth. First he arranged for Surratt and Powell to occupy the presidential box at Ford's Theatre to see the play *Jane Shore* that evening. Booth had reserved the box (combined boxes 7 and 8) so that Surratt and Powell would become acquainted with the layout and the theater in which he planned to capture Lincoln. Booth invited two of Mrs. Surratt's boarders to accompany the men to the play – seventeen-year-old Honora Fitzpatrick and ten-year-old Mary Apollonia Dean. It was better that the two men be accompanied by the two females to avoid looking conspicuous. All attended the theater as Booth planned. Booth himself came into the box during the performance, spoke to Surratt and Powell for a moment, and then left.[309]

Undoubtedly Booth had come to see that all was going as planned and to remind Surratt and Powell of the meeting later that evening. After the play, Booth hosted his oyster dinner; Thomas Harbin, the only other known figure to agree to help Booth, was not at the meeting.[310]

At the dinner, Booth presented a new plan to the group. He planned to seize Lincoln from the presidential box at Ford's Theatre, handcuff him, lower him by rope to a darkened stage, and carry him out the back door of the theater. Lincoln had been a strong wrestler in his youth, and the whole idea of lowering him on a rope was ludicrous.

The plan was absurd, and Arnold was the first to object to the idea as suicidal. How could anyone hope to get the president down on to the stage in front of an audience containing hundreds of federal soldiers, take him out the back entrance passed the actors, out the back alley, and then expect to escape through Washington – a town occupied by troops, police, and cavalry patrols – to a guarded Potomac bridge with no one pursuing them? Arnold was disgusted at the "utter impracticability" of the scheme. He later wrote, "I wanted a shadow of a chance for my life and I intended having it."[311]

Challenged by Arnold, Booth threatened to shoot him and shouted, "Do you know you are liable to be shot, [remember] your oath!"

"Two can play at that game!" Arnold shouted back with temper running high.

The others at the gathering agreed that Booth's plan was ridiculous, so Booth finally withdrew his idea and returned to the original plot of capturing the president on the way to the soldiers' home. Paranoia crept into the group. Some felt that "the suspicion of the Government had been aroused [sic], from the fact that double stockades were being erected at the bridge crossing the Eastern Branch on the Prince George's side of the river." The conspirators wondered whether this meant that the government suspected that a kidnapping was planned. At last, they decided that their plans had not been discovered. The meeting finally broke up "about 5:00 o'clock in the morning."[312]

The plot to kidnap Lincoln, as conceived by Booth, had no chance of success. On its face, the proposed plan was foolishly ineffective and never would have received approval at any level in the Confederate government, including Montreal. The plot would have been the biggest and by far the most important covert operation in the short history of the Confederate States of America, an operation that the Confederate States of America would have depended upon for its very existence. Booth was a loose cannon, a dreamer unable to project the consequences or chances of success of his scheme. Booth's statements, "They do not give a bad cent about me," and calling himself "a Confederate at present doing his duty upon his own responsibility" indicate that Booth's unrealistic ideas had indeed been rejected by Confederate authorities, if in fact they were ever aware of them.

The next day, Booth was riding passed Rullman's Hotel and saw Arnold in company with O'Laughlen. Booth, after calling O'Laughlen and talking with him, spoke to Arnold. Booth apologized for what he had said at the meeting. He remarked that Arnold must have been drunk to object to his proposed plan. Arnold felt his anger flash. He had not, he told Booth, been drunk as Booth and the others may have been. Arnold affirmed his objection and said that at the end of the next week, he was ending his connection with Booth and his crazy plans.[313]

\* \* \*

The following day, March 17, Booth saw his chance to put his original plan into action. He was visiting some fellow actors, John Mathews, James W. Wallack, and E. L. Davenport. Davenport mentioned that his company was performing *Still Waters Run Deep* for wounded soldiers at the Campbell General Hospital that very afternoon. Campbell Hospital had a hall that was "capable of holding five hundred persons."[314] Davenport mentioned that the president had been invited to attend the matinee at the hospital that was on the same road that led to the soldiers' home but a little closer to Washington.

"Why don't you come, Booth?" Davenport asked. "You'll see a good performance."

Booth could hardly believe his good fortune. He was so excited that he could actually put his kidnap plan into operation that he did not check the information Davenport gave him. As it turned out, Lincoln had only been *invited* to the hospital performance, but he never went. Had Booth read the *National Intelligencer,* he would have found out that Lincoln could not attend the Campbell Hospital presentation because he was scheduled to present a captured battle flag to Governor Oliver Morton of Indiana at the National Hotel, Booth's hotel![315]

Booth responded quickly to what he thought was his golden opportunity to use his original kidnapping scheme. He would capture Lincoln, ride with him over the Navy Yard Bridge, and then race through the countryside of Southern Maryland to Virginia. Hidden boats would be waiting to take the kidnapped Lincoln across the Potomac River.

Booth quickly gathered his fellow conspirators and told them "to be in readiness at 2. o'clock" [in the afternoon]. At two, Booth and the conspirators got into a carriage and went to a rendezvous at a tavern near the hospital.[316]

When John Surratt and the others had left the boardinghouse to abduct the president, Mary was distraught. "On the way to dinner, I met Mrs. Surratt in the hall," Weichmann said. "She was weeping bitterly. Go down Mr. Weichmann, and make the best of the dinner that you can. John [Surratt] is gone away, John is gone away."[317] Mary was very upset because she suspected that her son was doing something more dangerous than courier duties. Living with her son through the war years, Mary knew of John's courier duties.

The would-be kidnappers began to arrive at a nearby tavern – Arnold and O'Laughlen, then Atzerodt and Powell, and finally Booth and Surratt. The plan was to stop Lincoln's carriage as he returned to Washington from the play. Lincoln and his driver would be overpowered and handcuffed. After subduing and binding Lincoln, the conspirators would then race through Southern Maryland to the Potomac River.

Herold would join them as they passed the Surratt Tavern.[318] Herold took a carriage with two double-barreled shotguns, two Spencer carbines, one pistol, ammunition, a dirk, a sword, a rope, and a monkey wrench and drove to the Surratt Tavern.[319]

Meanwhile the six conspirators drank together and went over their plans. Booth left them and rode his horse to Campbell General Hospital to find out when the performance would be over.[320] Arriving at the hospital, Booth found Actor-Manager E. L. Davenport during intermission.

"Hello, Ned," he said. "Who's in the house?"

Davenport mentioned some people.

"Did the old man come?" [meaning Lincoln]

Davenport said he had not, and John turned to go.

"You are in a great hurry," Davenport replied, watching Booth's nervous step.

Booth turned, his face damp. "Yes, I'm trying a new horse and he is rather restive," Booth lamely replied.[321] Having learned the awful truth, Booth turned abruptly and remounted. Had the plot been discovered? Even now, the federals might be closing in on the group back at the tavern!

Booth jumped on his horse and galloped back to the tavern where the other conspirators waited. He arrived very excited, telling the others that Lincoln had never shown up for the performance. Even now, Booth exclaimed with some fear; authorities might be on the way to arrest the conspirators. They must split up and go their own way.

"Our movements," Booth announced, "are being watched.[322] Frightened, the men needed no further urging. Each knew that if he were caught, he would be hanged.

After the aborted attempt, Surratt, Powell, and Booth returned to the Surratt boardinghouse, which would have been the absolute worst place to hide if the authorities had really been after them. Surratt arrived first and ran up to his bedroom, which he shared with Weichmann. Weichmann was surprised to see Surratt rush in with such a frightened look on his face. Weichmann recalled that Surratt was "very much excited and waved a Sharpe's revolver around and yelled that he would shoot anyone who came into the room." It was doubly surprising when Powell burst into the room soon followed by Booth.

Booth, a riding whip in one hand, nervously walked several times around the room, eyes flashing, jaw set. He was about to speak and then noticed Weichmann. He motioned to the other two, and the excited trio left and climbed the stairs to the attic. There they were alone and argued about whether they had been discovered and what they should do. After a half hour of getting nowhere, they left the boardinghouse separately.[323]

When Booth finally returned to his hotel, he discovered that Lincoln was there giving a speech. Booth stood in the audience, steaming at his mistake. From the balcony, Lincoln was speaking of a report that the desperate South was going to take black men into its army. With hatred in his eyes, Booth stared up at the balcony where Lincoln stood.

An acquaintance, Thomas Richardson, saw Booth and started up a conversation. "Have you come to hear the great Lincoln speak?" Then he asked, "Don't you think Mr. Lincoln looks pale and haggard?"

"Yes, he does," growled Booth with a furious look.[324]

Meanwhile, at the Surratt Tavern, Herold was unaware that the kidnapping plot had not taken place. He played cards with some locals in the small barroom and waited for the conspirators to arrive with the kidnapped Lincoln. After a while though, Herold began to suspect something had gone wrong. Anxiously he gathered up his things and rode to the small village of T. B. about five miles south of Surrattsville. When Booth and the captured Lincoln still had not arrived, Herold spent the night at the local hotel.[325]

The following morning, Saturday, March 18, Surratt and Atzerodt rode first to Surrattsville and then toward T. B. to get Herold. But early that morning, Herold decided to return to Surrattsville. He met the two on the road. They all returned to the Surratt Tavern where they got a drink at the bar. They asked John Lloyd to keep the wrench, rope, and rifles that Herold had strapped to his horse.

Lloyd gave an emphatic no, saying that he did not know of any good hiding place for the rifles in the tavern. Surratt, who had lived in the building for many years, showed Lloyd that the rifles could be concealed by hanging them from the rope tied in the attic so they dangled between the inner and outer walls of the dining room.[326] He told Lloyd that they would call for the rifles within a few days. The rifles, however, stayed hidden until late on the night of the assassination.

This incident ended Booth's fantasy of kidnapping Lincoln. Many of Booth's gang were disillusioned and most went their separate ways. Surratt left two days later to meet Sarah Slater in New York City. Powell was in New York City on March 20, and Booth left for New York on March 21. Arnold and O'Laughlen returned to Baltimore on March 20 looking for jobs there.[327] Arnold decided to have nothing more to do with Booth's wild schemes and got a job with J. W. Wharton at Old Point Comfort. He had applied for the position on March 24 and was accepted on the thirty-first.[328] Herold and Atzerodt, who had no incomes, stayed in Washington. Atzerodt by Sunday, March 19, was staying at the Pennsylvania House, half a block from Booth at the National Hotel.[329]

After this, Booth was the only conspirator to visit the Surratt boardinghouse, and at this time, he asked Atzerodt to sell some of the horses.

\*       \*       \*

The day after the abortive kidnapping attempt, Booth played Pescara in *The Apostate* at Ford's Theatre. Booth had committed himself to John McClullough to play in his benefit night.[330] This acting appearance was his last. Booth had given John

Surratt two passes to the play, and Surratt attended with Weichmann. After the play, Booth had drinks with Herold and Atzerodt at the tavern adjoining Ford's Theatre. Later the two men joined Weichmann, John Surratt, and John Holohan at Kloman's saloon, near Eighth and E streets.[331]

*  *  *

On the evening of March 21, Booth took the seven-thirty train to Baltimore on his way to New York. He went to Barnum's Hotel and wrote a note to Arnold, asking him to call upon him at the hotel.[332] He wrote that if Arnold rejoined the group for just a week and their plans were unsuccessful, then they would disband forever.

Booth did not hear from Arnold, and he continued on his trip to New York City where he stayed at the St. Nicholas Hotel. He was there to see Edwin Booth's one hundredth performance as Hamlet and to visit Lucy Hale.

On Friday, March 25, Booth, returning to Washington from his New York trip, stopped at the home of Arnold's parents in Baltimore, only to find that Arnold was at his brother's farm. When Arnold finally came home, his parents told him that Booth had called and gave Arnold the four-day-old note.[333]

The note filled Arnold with consternation. He did not think Booth would be successful in kidnapping Lincoln, and Arnold was beginning to see the liability of being associated with him. Then Arnold imprudently sent Booth a reply, telling him to wait until Richmond approved his plan. Booth kept this letter, leaving it in his trunk where it was later found by investigators and led to Arnold's life sentence.[334]

Booth did not give up on his kidnap project. He spoke to Powell and found that he was still willing to proceed. Booth at once set about getting accommodations for Powell back in Washington. He sent a cryptic telegram to Weichmann for John Surratt asking for the address of the Herndon House.[335] Powell was later to board there.

*  *  *

Mary Ann Booth continued to be troubled and anxious over her son John and his mysterious comings and goings. She was left to her own imagination as to what he was up to, and she wrote to him immediately after his departure from New York,

> My dear Boy:
>
> I have just got yours. I was very glad to hear from you. I hope you will write often. I did part with you sadly, and I still feel sad, very much so. June [Junius Jr., her eldest son] has just left me. He stayed as long as he could. I am now quite alone. Rose [Rosalie, her eldest daughter] has not returned yet. I feel miserable enough. I never yet doubted your love and devotion to me – in fact I always gave you praise for being the fondest of all my boys,

but since you leave me to grief I must doubt it. I am no Roman mother. I love my dear ones before country or anything else. Heaven guard you, is my constant prayer.

Your loving mother,
M. A. Booth[336]

\*　　\*　　\*

By March 27, Powell had returned to Washington from New York and checked into the Herndon House. A room had been reserved for him by John Surratt.[337] This time, Powell registered using the alias of Kincheloe; it was the name of an officer in one of Mosby's units.[338] Powell remained at this address until the assassination.

Booth, anxious to regroup his band of conspirators, telegraphed O'Laughlen in Baltimore and said, "Get word to Sam. Come on, with or without him, Wednesday morning. We sell that day sure. Don't fail."

O'Laughlen and Arnold were no longer interested in kidnapping Lincoln and did not go to Washington. Booth had read in the *Washington Star* of March 27 that President and Mrs. Lincoln had reserved boxes for several operas at Ford's Theatre. When Booth saw this, he foresaw opportunities to kidnap Lincoln. There was, in fact, no imminent opportunity to kidnap Lincoln. Booth had botched this second attempt before it even started. Lincoln was not even in Washington. He had left for City Point, Virginia, on the twenty-third aboard the *River Queen* to observe with Grant firsthand the last days of the Confederacy.

Booth's chances for glory and to save his beloved Confederacy was fleeing away. Booth now gave up his plan to kidnap Lincoln, and on April 1, he took an evening train to New York. He told Atzerodt he was going to Canada.

The Confederates were well aware of Lincoln's arrival at City Point. The Confederate courier system was extremely efficient, and Northern newspapers found their way quickly into Southern hands. The *Richmond Sentinel* of March 30, 1865, carried a story from the *New York Herald* of March 27, stating that Lincoln was "still with the armies on the James River."

\*　　\*　　\*

The Confederacy was in its last days, Richmond was expected to soon fall, and Lincoln wanted to be close to the front lines. On March 23, 1865, Lincoln, accompanied by his wife and Tad, with William Crook and Charles Penrose as bodyguards departed Washington to visit General Grant at his headquarters. Away from the pressure of Washington, this trip was as close as Lincoln got to a vacation as president.[339]

While in Virginia, Lincoln spent time with his wife on carriage rides through the countryside. She needed her husband's constant reassurance of his love and support – throughout the war she had endured constant and unjust accusations that she was a rebel spy whose sympathies were with the Confederacy. Mary Lincoln had lost a brother and a beloved half-brother, Alex, to the Confederate cause.

Mary Lincoln was high-strung, insecure, and self-centered. Washingtonian high society had greeted her as a country bumpkin when she and the president first came to Washington, and Mary never forgave them. She had spent most of her time in attempts to prove herself regal – she had renovated the White House and had given countless soirees at which she appeared in queenly splendor. But the circle of people who might actually call her "friend" was small. Indeed, her only constant companion was Mary Keckley, her black seamstress.

Mary Lincoln, always very jealous in regard to her husband, made an absolute fool of herself at City Point twice! On March 25, she made an excursion from City Point to the front of the army. On this occasion, General Grant had ordered all officers' wives to the rear because of heavy fighting. However, when the fighting subsided, Mary Lincoln and Julia Grant boarded a special military train, giving them their closest glimpse of war. Along the route, twisted and mangled soldiers in blue and gray gave the wives a gory glimpse of war. The railroad only went part of the way. To finish the journey, the men rode horseback and the wives rode in a converted ambulance.[340] During some polite conversation, Colonel Badeau mentioned that the wife of General Charles Griffin also had a special presidential permit to visit the front lines. At this news, Mary was suddenly furious.

"What do you mean by that, sir?" Mrs. Lincoln exclaimed. "Do you mean to say that she saw the President alone? Do you know that I never allow the President to see any woman alone?"[341]

Colonel Badeau and Julia Grant stared at Mary Lincoln in shocked silence. Despite their attempts to calm her, Mrs. Lincoln demanded that the carriage be halted.

"Let me out at once. I will ask the President if he saw that woman alone!"

Apprehensive about a public display of anger, Colonel Badeau and Mrs. Grant finally convinced Mary Lincoln to wait until the whole party reached their destination. When the ambulance arrived at the review site, General Meade rode up to pay his respects. But Mary immediately and bluntly cut off his pleasantries. "Who," she demanded, "gave Mrs. Griffin permission to be up front with the President?"

Shocked at her behavior, Meade replied that it was Secretary of War Stanton who had granted the permission.[342]

The scene Mary made was "distressing and mortifying" to Julia Grant.[343]

Mary's behavior did not improve. The next day, Mary Lincoln and Julia Grant were to go to a grand review of the Army of the James, then commanded by Major General Edward Ord. Lincoln rode out from City Point to the review grounds on horseback. The two ladies again traveled in an ambulance, escorted again by Colonel Badeau. Badeau, humiliated by Mary's behavior the day before, had asked Colonel Horace Porter to join the party, in hope that another officer's presence might curb future outbursts from Mrs. Lincoln. Lincoln was with Major General Edward Ord for a review of the troops.

The converted ambulance crawled along the muddy corduroy road. When Mary and Julia arrived, the review had already begun. Mary, however, saw General Edward Ord's wife in a chic feathered Robin Hood cap, riding by the side of the president. Mrs. Ord was strikingly beautiful and a competent horsewoman. When Mary Lincoln saw this, "her rage was beyond all bounds."

"What does that woman mean by riding by the side of the President? And ahead of me? Does she suppose that he wants her by the side of him?" she raved.

Mary's carriage was standing in a sea of mud, but she demanded to be let out, and hiking up her skirt, she tramped through the mire toward the mounted group, which included Mrs. Ord.

"There come Mrs. Lincoln and Mrs. Grant," said the unsuspecting Mrs. Ord to the people she was with. "I think I had better join them." She rode to the two women and was greeted by Mary with insults that horrified her. Mrs. Lincoln exhibited no discretion, calling Mrs. Ord "vile names in the presence of a crowd of officers." Colonel Badeau and Colonel Porter stood by helplessly, unable to deflect Mrs. Lincoln's rage, hoping "that nothing worse than words occurred."

Upon hearing Mary Lincoln's abusive language, Mrs. Ord burst into tears.

When President Lincoln at last came to collect Mary, he tried to calm her, but she would not allow her anger to be assuaged. She wanted deference – and she wasn't getting it.

Later at City Point, chairs had been set out, and a tired Julia Grant reached them first and sat down gratefully. However, Mary Lincoln, seeing herself as the grande dame of the occasion, again let her ire get the better of her. "How dare you be seated until I invite you . . . . I suppose you think you'll get to the White House yourself, don't you?"

Mrs. Grant, who could hardly comprehend such rudeness, calmly replied that she was happy with her present position and that it was far greater than she ever expected just a few years ago.

"Oh! You had better take it if you can get it. 'Tis very nice!" Mary Lincoln replied sharply.

For the next three days, Mary Lincoln remained "indisposed" aboard the *River Queen*. Suddenly it was announced that she would return to Washington.

Is it any wonder that in just over two weeks, Julia Grant strongly objected to going to Ford's Theatre with the Lincolns on Good Friday, April 14? Julia had developed an intense dislike for Mary Lincoln as had Mrs. Stanton, wife of the secretary of war.[344]

Mary got back to Washington on April 2, but by April 5, she had assembled an entourage of supporters to accompany her on a return trip. When she sailed back to City Point, Mary was accompanied by the Marquis de Chambrun and Senator Charles Sumner of Massachusetts, both personal friends of the Lincolns. Also with her were

Senator and Mrs. James Harlan of Iowa; their daughter Mary, whom Robert Lincoln married in 1868; and Elizabeth Keckley, Mary Lincoln's seamstress and confidante. The group arrived at City Point about noon the next day. Later that day, Mary Lincoln and her party, without her husband, visited Richmond.[345] However, the next day, Abraham Lincoln joined his wife and the new guests and traveled to Petersburg by railroad. They spent the day visiting the sick and wounded in camp hospitals, and Lincoln spoke to local citizens about his reconstruction ideas.

The Lincolns and their guests left City Point on April 8 on the steamer *River Queen*, and they arrived near sunset on Sunday, April 9, to the news that Lee had surrendered.[346]

# CHAPTER 10

## *The Plan Has Changed*

It was on Sunday, April 2, that General Lee notified President Davis that it was impossible for his army to hold Richmond. This news was the beginning of the end of the Confederacy. Davis received this news at St. Paul's Church and hurried back to his home. There he gathered his papers and fled the city by train. Davis, knowing that Richmond would soon fall, had his wife and children leave Richmond the previous week.

That first week of April, Booth was in Boston, and Atzerodt was in Washington, taking Booth's horses from stable to stable trying to sell them. Meanwhile, John Surratt and Sarah Slater arrived in Washington on the Leonardtown, Maryland, stage at about four o'clock on April 3. But John did not go to his mother's boardinghouse until about eight-thirty that evening. John told his mother that Sarah Slater had returned with him from Richmond and that Slater was staying at the Metropolitan Hotel and would leave for Montreal the next day.[347]

At dinner, Susan Mahoney, a black servant, who joined the Surratt household on April 1, told John that a detective had been to the house asking where John was.[348] This news startled him, and he knew that the boardinghouse was no longer a safe place for him. Later John told his mother that he and Weichmann were going out. But John Surratt did not return. He slept in a Washington hotel and left with Slater on an early train the next morning for New York City. John felt that since detectives had been around looking for him, it was safer for him not to return home.[349]

Mary was devastated when Weichmann returned that evening and told her that John would not be coming home – that he was leaving the next morning with Slater. John had asked Weichmann to say good-bye to his mother for him.[350] Mary began to be frightened for her son's safety.

On April 4, on the way to Montreal, Surratt tried to see Booth at his New York home. But Booth was not there. Servants told him that he had gone to Boston. While Slater disappears from the historical record, by April 6, Surratt had checked into the

St. Lawrence Hall as John Harrison in the same hotel where General Edwin G. Lee had taken up residence. (Harrison was Surratt's middle name.)[351]

On Wednesday, April 5, Mary received a note from her son, John. In this letter, mailed from Springfield, Massachusetts, he wrote that he would be staying for a day because he had overslept and missed his train connection. After she read the note, Mary "pitched it on a window sill" and was unable to locate it later.[352]

Later that day, Surratt met with Edwin Gray Lee. General Lee, acting as Judah Benjamin's military attaché, had just arrived in Montreal on April 3, replacing Jacob Thompson and Clement C. Clay. Surratt gave Lee dispatches, detailing how Confederate funds in Canada would be transferred to banks in England.[353]

In Boston, Booth visited a shooting gallery and practiced with a pistol. He also settled some real estate transactions and went to see his brother Edwin who was in Boston playing *Hamlet*.[354] During this visit, John, true to form, got into another political argument with Edwin about the Civil War, and John's last words to Edwin were, "Good-bye, Ned, you and I could never agree upon that question"

On April 7, John Wilkes Booth returned to New York City where he again saw Samuel Chester. The two went out drinking, an activity Booth had lately indulged in more frequently. Liquor again made Booth more indiscrete than usual. As the two sat drinking in the House of Lords pub, he exclaimed, "What an excellent chance I had to kill the President, if I had wished, on inauguration day! I was as near the President on that day as you are to me." Booth had been able to get that close because he had obtained a pass from Lucy Hale.

Chester was rattled and asked, "What good would that do?"

And Booth replied, "I could live in history." The next day, Booth returned to the National Hotel.[355]

\*    \*    \*

Lee's army had surrendered. His men had stacked their arms at Appomattox, and Lee had told his troops to go home, obey the law, and put in a crop. The bulk of the Confederate army now consisted of a small army under the command of General Joseph Johnston in North Carolina. And Johnson was at this time preparing to surrender to William T. Sherman.

That night, the air was filled with the booming of cannons. Federal troops just outside of Washington fired many rounds in celebration. The next morning, the cannonading continued with troops firing off nearly five hundred shots. People were firing off guns in a delirium of joy; at last, the war was over! Every flagstaff displayed the stars and stripes; and men, women, and children cheered – the great rebel General Robert E. Lee had surrendered! With the fall of Richmond the week before and now the news of General Lee's surrender, life in Washington was one continuous celebration.[356]

One observer wrote that "in Washington City we were already hoarse with shouting the day before. The bells and cannon clanged and boomed with hoarseness greater than usual. The news of the collapse of the rebellion rolled and surged over the country like a rushing mighty wind. The strain of anxiety which for four long years had rested upon the nation like a nightmare dream, had been lifted. Millions of firesides, upon hill-tops and in valleys, glowed with a brighter luster as news of victory floated in the air."[357]

The next evening, April 10, a crowd of about three thousand gathered below one of the White House balconies. Many calls were made for Lincoln to appear and make a speech. When he failed to appear, the crowd only cried out louder. When Tad appeared at a second-story window, a great cheer rose, certainly delighting the youngster. Finally President Lincoln came out on to the balcony to say a few words, and the crowd cheered him with "absolute madness."

Lincoln told the crowd he was going to make a formal speech the next evening. "I shall have nothing to say if you dribble it all out of me before." The crowd laughed and applauded. Lincoln continued, "I see you have a band of music with you. I propose closing up this interview by the band performing a particular tune which I will name. Before this is done, however, I wish to mention one or two little circumstances connected with it. I have always thought 'Dixie' one of the best tunes I have ever heard. Our adversaries over the way attempted to appropriate it, but I insisted yesterday that we fairly captured it. I presented the question to the Attorney General, and he gave it as his legal opinion that it is our lawful prize." At this wit, the crowd laughed and applauded again.[358]

That evening, all government buildings and the whole city were lit with candles, and rockets and fireworks were shot off into the sky. Every public building had been decorated, and the whole length of Pennsylvania Avenue had been decorated with flags and lights.[359] People were in a state of frenzy at the fall of Richmond. April 10 was proclaimed a legal holiday, a national day of thanksgiving.[360]

Across the Potomac River in Arlington, Virginia, was the former estate of Robert E. Lee. It consisted of many acres of land presided over by a white mansion with a pillared entry. When Lee refused the position of general of the Union Army and decided instead to support the Confederacy, he had had to abandon his home. Union officials wasted no time in seizing the estate – the official reason being for nonpayment of taxes. To ensure that Lee could never again live in the beautiful house, the Union converted the property into a cemetery for Union soldiers. The graves were placed across the plantation and as close to the front door as possible.

Now at the conclusion of the war, thousands of ex-slaves gathered to celebrate their emancipation on the brilliantly lit estate.

Upon hearing that the South had been defeated, Mary Surratt drew down the shades and closed the blinds, like one in mourning. "Her house was gloomy and cheerless," said Weichmann. "To use her own expression, it was 'indicative of her feeling!'"

\*　　\*　　\*

Booth spent the afternoon of April 10 visiting at the Surratt house. He was there to see if John Surratt had returned from escorting Sarah Slater to Canada. During his visit, Annie Ward, a teacher at the Visitation School, arrived. She had received a letter from John Surratt that day. Annie read the letter to Mary, Anna, and Booth. Mary could not read the letter herself because of her poor eyesight.[361]

Later Weichmann and Booth were discussing the war when Booth uttered, "No, it is not gone up yet!" He drew out a map from his pocket, spread it on to a table, and showed Weichmann the "different routes which Johnston would take to the mountains" to continue the war.

Fatefully that evening, Mary asked Weichmann if he would take her to Surrattsville the following day on business.[362] She wanted to go to Surrattsville to see John Nothey, a local farmer, who had owed her $479 for thirteen years for having purchased property from her late husband. The money would be used to pay a debt to Charles Calvert, who was pressuring her to pay an old debt.[363] He agreed; and so the next morning, April 11, Mary sent Weichmann to the National Hotel to ask Booth if she could borrow his horse and carriage. Weichmann learned when he arrived that Booth had sold them. However, he gave Weichmann ten dollars to hire another carriage for Mary Surratt. Booth was well off, generous, and friendly to the mother of John Surratt.

It was about nine o'clock when Weichmann and Mrs. Surratt started out in the rented carriage for the tavern, which was ten miles from the Washington Navy Yard Bridge. It would take several hours to get there.

On the way out of Washington, Weichmann and Mary drove through Uniontown (now a section of Washington called Anacostia). There they happened to pass John Lloyd going the other way in his buggy with his sister-in-law, Emma Offutt. The buggies halted, and Mary spoke briefly to Emma about Gus Howell's being in prison and how she wished he would take the oath of allegiance.[364]

After the chance encounter with Lloyd, Mary and Weichmann continued on to the Surratt house and tavern. She sent a message to John Nothey, asking him to meet her at the tavern at two o'clock.

While waiting for a reply, Mary visited with Bennett F. Gwynn and was invited to stay for the midday meal. Gwynn, a wealthy farmer with a 325-acre plantation, was a Southern sympathizer whose eldest son had been killed at age seventeen while serving in the Confederate army. Mary enjoyed the visit, and Captain Gwynn returned to the tavern with her. He wanted to help her by speaking to Nothey himself. When the three got back to the tavern, Nothey was waiting.[365] On Mary's behalf, Gwynn spoke privately with Nothey, but he was not successful in getting him to pay the debt that day.[366] So Mary returned to Washington empty-handed at about six in the evening.

\*　　\*　　\*

Booth, who had arrived back from New York on April 8, heard with consternation the news of the fall of Richmond. On the night of April 11, Booth walked through the jubilant city with Lewis Powell and David Herold, seeing the crowds and hearing the cheers. They walked toward the White House where Lincoln would speak. At Fourteenth Street and Pennsylvania Avenue, they ran into the songwriter Henry B. Phillips, who asked them to join him for a drink.

"Yes anything to drive away the blues," Booth said, never turning down the opportunity to drink.

"What is giving you the blues?" Phillips asked, astounded.

"This news is enough to give anyone the blues," Booth replied.[367]

When Powell and Herold Booth left Phillips, he finally arrived at the White House grounds to hear Lincoln's speech. A large crowd had been gathering there to hear Lincoln speak. When the president at last stood on a balcony, he received a tremendous and continued ovation.[368]

Lincoln had written out his whole address and read it by the light of a candle held by Noah Brooks.[369] Seven-year-old Tad sat at his father's feet, collecting the sheets of manuscript as his father finished with them and let them drop. Lincoln spoke of clemency for the South, thanksgiving that the long war was over, and his future policy toward the seceded states, particularly Louisiana. Lincoln told the crowd that he wanted to restore citizenship to the Southern people as soon as politically possible. Lincoln's plan was that if 10 percent of the qualified voters of a state took an oath of allegiance to the federal government, the state could return to the Union and send congressmen and senators to Washington. Lincoln wanted all the states to put the war behind them. As for the freed slaves and the possibility of giving them the vote, Lincoln said, "If universal amnesty is granted to the insurgents, I cannot see how I can avoid exacting in return universal suffrage, or at least suffrage on the basis of intelligence and those who have served our cause as soldiers in the field."

Ms. Harris, who was later be in the presidential box at the time of the assassination, was at the White House that night as a guest of Mrs. Lincoln.

In the darkness, Booth grabbed Herold's arm and hissed, "That means nigger citizenship! Now by Christ, I'll put him through. That is the last speech he will ever make!" Booth turned to Powell and asked him to shoot Lincoln as he stood on the balcony. But Powell refused to take the risk, and Booth's voice began attracting attention. Frightened, Powell and Herold persuaded him, after some difficulty, to leave.[370]

It was on this night that Booth changed his kidnap plan to one of assassination, and the statement, "This is the last speech his will ever make!" reflected his state of mind. Booth was ready and eager to do something "great and decisive" for the Southern cause. Booth's words and actions showed that he was psychologically prepared to assassinate Lincoln by April 11 and was only waiting for an opportunity. This opportunity came about noon on April 14 when he learned that Lincoln would attend Ford's Theatre that night.

Capturing Lincoln was no longer feasible. Richmond had fallen, and General Lee had surrendered to General Grant, so there was nowhere to bring a captured president. But Booth thought the South might regroup and fight on.

When he talked with a friend, Edward Person, on April 13, Booth said he had "the biggest thing on his hands that had ever turned up and that there was a great deal of money in it."[371]

John Wilkes Booth was twenty-six years old and considered to be the handsomest man in Washington. He was charming, intelligent, and well liked by others. He had an established career and was capable of making up to three hundred dollars a week – a great deal of money at the time. He was engaged to Lucy Hale, a young lady of the highest social standing in Washington's social circles, and had countless sexual liaisons. Many men in the North or South would have loved to be in his position. Booth had fallen into a depression, and each day starting about April 5, he was drinking a great deal of liquor. He went to a saloon owned by John Deery every day either in the afternoon or in the evening. He was no longer acting, the war was not going his way, and he stepped up his liquor intake; he sometimes drank a quart of Brandy in less than two hours.[372]

"We are all slaves now," Booth told Harry Ford after Lee had surrendered. "How could Lee have given up? When he had accepted the sword put in his hands, he had sworn he would never surrender it."

"Yes," Ford said, "but Lee was a brave general and a gentleman and must have known what he was doing."

"A very good General but I don't like the way he surrendered!" Booth barked back. Booth claimed that he himself was as good and as brave as Lee. At this, Ford smiled, "Well you have not got three stars yet to show it."[373]

Edwin A. Emerson was standing in front of Ford's Theatre on April 13 when Booth walked up. The two fell into conversation, and Booth took the cane Emerson was carrying, put it across his shoulders, and held each end in his hands.

"Ned," Booth began, "did you hear what that old scoundrel did the other day?" What are you talking about?"

"Why, that old scoundrel Lincoln," Booth said. "He went into Jeff Davis's house in Richmond, sat down and threw his long legs over the arm of a chair and squirted tobacco juice all over the place. Somebody ought to kill him!" A few moments later, Booth pulled down on the ends of the cane as it rested across his shoulders. It snapped into four pieces. He looked at them blankly and then handed them to Emerson, who no doubt was unhappy about his broken cane.[374]

Later that day, Booth walked along Pennsylvania Avenue when he chanced to meet a schoolgirl from New York who he knew. She was on an extended visit to Washington with her mother. They had heard Booth recite in the parlor of the National, and Booth had spoken to them of the need for clear speech. The young girl, whose name was Ms. Porterfield (and later Mrs. William A. Brown) told him excitedly she was headed for a shop to buy candies. Booth, perhaps already inebriated, misunderstood.

"What do you want with more candles?" he demanded. "The windows are full of them now, and when they are lighted I wish they would burn every house to the ground. I would rejoice at the sight . . . . I guess I'm a little desperate this morning, and, do you know, I feel like mounting my horse and tearing up and down the streets, waving a rebel flag in each hand till I have driven the poor animal to death."

She felt that "something was wrong with the man; he was so deeply wrought up . . . . His excited and vehement speech startled me." She had never seen him in such a state; Booth had been so amiable and pleasant in the past. She started to say something when he quickly interrupted her.

"Don't you study Latin at school?"

She said yes.

"Then tell me this: Is tyrannis spelled with two n's or two r's?"[375]

\* \* \*

Booth was not alone in thinking that the release of captured Confederate soldiers could keep the Southern war effort afloat. Although Richmond had fallen, Edwin Lee refused to believe that the war was over. To the North, the war seemed as good as over after Appomattox on April 9; but many Southerners, like President Davis and General Edwin Lee, expected the struggle to continue. Of the surrender at Appomattox, General Edwin Lee wrote, "I cannot and will not believe that because General Lee was compelled to surrender 22,000 men, we therefore have no more armies and can wage war no more."[376] The Confederacy still had armies in the field although the largest of the remaining Confederate armies, General Johnson's, was about to surrender in North Carolina.

The North held thousands of Confederate prisoners of war who, if freed, could continue the fight, and Edwin Lee thought that an increase in available soldiers could yet save the Confederacy. General Edwin Lee considered the New York prisoner-of-war camp at Elmira a possible source of manpower for the South.

With this in mind, he spoke to Surratt about this possibility, and Surratt agreed to secretly survey the Federal prison at Elmira for a possible escape attempt.[377] This was Surratt's first true spy mission, prior to this, he had been just a courier, albeit a very clever one. John Surratt left Montreal for Elmira on April 12 and arrived there the next day. Once there, he was to survey the physical layout of the camp, including the roads leading to the camp, the location of the guard stations, possible escape routes, and the amount of stored munitions.[378]

On April 13 and 14, Surratt bought clothes in Elmira, and the clerk noted down his purchases. On April 15, Surratt went to another clothier to buy some white shirts and, while there, learned of the Lincoln assassination. The sweat broke out on his face as he realized that his connection with Booth put him in great peril. Surratt immediately decided to get out of the country. He took a train north for Canandaigue, New York, and spent the night at the Webster House. The next day, no trains were operating because it was Easter Sunday, but on Monday morning, he crossed into Canada at the Rouses Point Bridge. He again registered at the St. Lawrence Hall as John Harrison, and he gave his report and drawings of the Elmira Prison to Edwin Lee.[379] Unbeknownst to him, detectives were already hot on his trail.

There was even a $25,000 reward for him. On April 17, the day Surratt registered at the St. Lawrence Hall, detectives James A. McDevitt and Holohan, along with Weichmann, left Washington for Montreal to search for him.

Frightened, Surratt moved his hiding place several times. He first hid at the home of John Porterfield, a former Nashville banker, and from there to a Montreal tailor, John J. Reeves, for two days. From there, he was taken by canoe to the south shore of the St. Lawrence River to St. Liboire (thirty-four miles east of Montreal) where he was sheltered in Father Charles Boucher's home.

On September 16, 1865, Edwin Lee and Beverly Tucker arranged passage for Surratt as Mr. McCarty on a ship bound from Quebec to England. Later Surratt went to Italy where he enlisted as John Watson in the Papal Zouaves. A fellow Zouave, Henry Sainte-Marie, who had known Surratt in Maryland before the war betrayed Surratt and sent word to the local U.S. consulate. The Department of State moved on the matter slowly and delicately because they didn't want to appear to be infringing on papal authority. At last the pope's guards arrested Surratt, but after, he had a spectacular escape, involving a leap off on a high cliff into water below. Surratt was later rearrested as his boat was docking in Alexandria, Egypt, on November 27, 1866.[380]

*     *     *

On the afternoon of April 13, Booth visited Grover's National Theatre. Booth had appeared there in April 1863 and January 1865. He came into the office and interrupted C. Dwight Hess and the prompter of the theater as they read a manuscript. Oblivious to his own presumptuous behavior, Booth sat in a chair and started talking about the illumination of the city that night.

"Is Grover's going to be illuminated tonight?" he asked.

"Yes, it is," said Hess, somewhat surprised and annoyed by the interruption. "And tomorrow night we are going to have an even bigger display for the anniversary of the fall of Fort Sumter."

Booth at last came out with his real question, "Will the President be invited?"

"Yes," Hess replied, not knowing the motivation behind this deadly question. "But the invitation will go to Mrs. Lincoln since she arranges all the President's theater going." Then Hess stopped abruptly and stared at Booth. It was so unlike Booth to just walk right in uninvited, much less force a conversation. The peculiarity of it struck Hess immediately. Hess put his script away and then turned to Booth.

"John, when are you going to Richmond again?" he asked since he knew John had Southern sympathies.

"I never shall go to Richmond again! I never shall go to Richmond again!" Booth exclaimed.[381]

During the evening of April 13, Booth, readying himself to assassinate Lincoln, asked John Deery, one of Booth's many friends and owner of a billiard parlor, a personal favor to purchase a box seat at Grover's Theatre for Friday night's performance of *Aladdin! Or His Wonderful Lamp.*

Booth suggested that Deery let one of his employees attend to the matter. Deery was surprised at his request as he knew Booth had the freedom of any theater in Washington and could obtain a box from Grover simply by asking for it. Deery mentioned this to Booth who replied that he did want to put himself into a situation of accepting free tickets, which he knew would be proffered to him if he personally sought to buy the tickets. Booth was explicit in saying that the messenger must not accept any other box than the one he had specified. The box Deery was instructed to buy adjoined the box Lincoln would be in if he accepted Grover's invitation instead of Ford's.[382]

Herold went home the night of April 13, his last night home.

\* \* \*

On April 5, Secretary of State Frederick Seward went out in a carriage with his family. It was a pleasant ride, except the door of the carriage kept opening. At last, the coachman halted the horses and climbed down off the carriage to fix the problem. As he stood on the pavement, the horses bolted, racing driverless through the street. Secretary Seward leaned forward, attempting to grab the loose reins, but he missed and fell forward into the street. A cavalry officer eventually halted the runaway carriage; and Fanny, Seward's daughter, leaped out and ran back to where her father lay unconscious and severely injured.

At first, she thought that her father was dead. He was alive, although his right arm was broken close to the shoulder, his jaw was fractured, and his face lacerated. As part of his treatment, Seward had his lower jaw and neck encased in a heavy leather-and-steel fitting. It was this casing that later saved his life when Powell attacked him. He was at his home on Lafayette Square recuperating when Booth sent Powell to observe the comings and goings of the house.

Booth told Powell to make himself familiar with Seward's home. So on the morning of April 13 and again the next morning, Powell visited the Seward home, flirting with a pretty chambermaid during these visits.[383]

\* \* \*

On Thursday morning, April 13, Honora Fitzpatrick went to confession with Mary at St. Patrick's Catholic Church, and ten-year-old Appollonia's parents arrived to take her to Virginia for the Easter holidays.[384] And so the youngster was spared the police roundup at the Surratt boardinghouse two days later.

# CHAPTER 11

## The Happiest Day of My Life

The Lincolns were the first presidential couple to make a habit of theater going and to invite artists to the White House not only to entertain, but to be honored guests. Mary Lincoln in particular loved the excitement of the stage and seemed fascinated by actors and singers. However, after the assassination, Mary Lincoln never went to a performance in a theater or concert hall again.[385]

Lincoln's only relief from the war and the multitude of people who demanded his time was the theater. Sometimes he went to a comedy to enjoy a "hearty laugh."[386] Mary Lincoln was a great theater buff, long before she met her husband. As a young girl, she had told a schoolmate that as far as a future husband went, "her choice should be willing and able to let her see as much of the theater as she wanted, and beyond that she did not expect to be too particular."[387]

At one time, Mary had her husband defend a theater company that had arrived in their town. Local preachers riled against the stage and were successful in getting passed a law calling for high fees for the acting company to get a permit to perform. Young Abraham Lincoln volunteered to help the company file an appeal at Mary's request. He spoke eloquently for the actors and won the court decision, getting the tax rescinded. In the acting company was Joseph Jefferson, who later introduced Edwin Booth to Mary Devlin and who he later married.

The president's youngest surviving son, Tad, often recommended plays to his father. Tad once convinced his father to attend a patriotic spectacle at Grover's Theatre – a performance Tad had seen several times. At the performance, Lincoln was surprised when, for the final chorus, Tad came on stage wearing a little uniform, waving a flag, and singing, "We are coming, Father Abraham, three hundred thousand more, shouting the battle cry of freedom!" Lincoln enjoyed his son's performance.[388]

Lincoln, self-taught and widely read, also enjoyed reciting lines from Shakespeare. He would recite these lines from memory to the artist F. B. Carpenter, who was commissioned to do a large painting of Lincoln signing the Emancipation

Proclamation. At one sitting, Lincoln rendered the opening soliloquy from *Richard III*, and of this incident, Carpenter later wrote, "I could not refrain from laying down my palette and brushes, and applauding heartily, upon his conclusion, saying at the same time, half in earnest, that I was not sure but that he had made a mistake in the choice of a profession."[389] He also enjoyed the performance of comedian Jeems Pipes, whose repertory included "comic imitations of a stammering man." Lincoln told him that he had known a man who invariably whistled when he stammered. Lincoln gave an imitation of the man's habit, and the comedian liked the concept. He rehearsed it until he had mastered it to Lincoln's satisfaction and then added it to subsequent performances.[390]

Lincoln went to the theater even when he was tired. He knew that if he remained at the White House, there would be no relief from incessant visitors. As it was, Lincoln had visitors up and including the time he got into his carriage to go to the theater.

Lincoln saw Edwin Booth in *The Merchant of Venice, The Fool's Revenge,* and *Ruy Blas.* When Lincoln saw John Wilkes Booth in the *Marble Heart* on November 9, 1863, presidential secretary John Hay thought John gave a "tame" performance.[391] The *Washington Evening Star* took a different point of view saying that "the romantic young actor by his earnestness, his vigorous grasp of genius, and his fervor of style, claims the most brilliant honors of his art.[392] Lincoln "rapturously" applauded Booth's acting, said the reporter George Alfred Townsend, and said he wanted to meet him.[393]

For most of his presidency, Lincoln went to the theater with his wife and guests, but without a guard, his only attendant was Charles Forbes, an unarmed carriage footman.[394]

Lincoln disliked the security arranged for him and constantly complained about all the protection that officials around him had ordered. He felt that it was important that the people know he was not in constant fear of death. "I determined when I first came here [to the White House] that I would not be dying all the while," Lincoln said.

He was not an easy person to guard even when precautions were taken.[395]

Early in the war, mounted guards were posted at the carriage entrances of the White House, and sentries were stationed at the foot gates. But Lincoln protested that armed guards made him seem imperial, and he discontinued the arrangement. Stanton later prevailed upon the president to have a cavalry detachment accompany him on trips between the White House and the soldiers' home and around Washington.[396]

But frequently, Lincoln would manage to leave the executive mansion for his summer residence at the soldiers' home without the cavalry escort. The escort, upon realizing that Lincoln had left, then would have to hurry to overtake him. When important military events were progressing, Lincoln would visit the War Department before going to bed. Generally he went alone in the dark of the night even at late hours. Lincoln, who was determined to live without fear, continued to operate as if no harm could befall him.

There was little or no security at the executive mansion or at Lincoln's summer residence on the grounds of the soldiers' home three miles to the north. Anyone with or without an introduction could see the president after business hours. When the doorman went off duty early in the evening, anyone could enter the White House, pass a cleaning woman, knock on a few doors, and find the president of the United States. Once a "modest shopkeeper whose home was not far from the Smithsonian Institution" decided to see Lincoln. He entered the White House and found him, casually dressed. Lincoln politely invited the visitor to sit down and talk.[397]

Congressman Cole Cornelius wrote in his memoirs that in the summer of 1864, "unlike the time when Congress is in session, there were very few callers on the President; (when Congress is adjourned) in fact he was frequently quite alone. He was always found in his room on the second floor at the southeast corner of the building. The weather being warm, his door was usually if not always open. Anyone could enter at pleasure and unannounced as I was accustomed to . . . . There was no guard posted about the premises and no attendant upon the President, that I could see, other than the ordinary servants and perhaps the usher, who was rarely at his post."[398]

\* \* \*

April 14 began as a day of rejoicing. The United States flag was again raised at Fort Sumter in South Carolina. Exactly four years before it had been lowered when federal forces under Major Robert Anderson had surrendered to General P. T. G. Beauregard. Ceremonies were held, and Henry Ward Beecher, a nationally known Presbyterian minister, spoke at Fort Sumter of the reunification of the country, and the end of the "war of brothers." Lincoln was invited to the celebration ceremonies at Fort Sumter but fatefully declined the invitation.

Although it was Good Friday, a day of religious sobriety, even the most devout felt joy and thanksgiving – the killing was ending, and soon husbands and sons would be coming home. Peace, so long desired, was at last close at hand.[399]

\* \* \*

On this Good Friday, Mary Surratt again went to early mass with Weichmann. They walked the few blocks to St. Patrick's. After the services, Weichmann went to work, and Mary returned to the boardinghouse. There she found a letter from George Calvert demanding payment of the debt that Mary owed him.[400] Mary immediately decided to take a trip to Surrattsville to speak to John Nothey about the debt that he owned to her so that she in turn could pay Calvert.

At around ten that morning, Secretary Stanton gave the remainder of the day off to government employees who wished to attend Good Friday religious services, and so Weichmann again went to church, this time to St. Matthew's. He got home about noon where he had lunch and retired to his room.

At about two o'clock, Mary Surratt knocked on his door. "I have a letter here from Mr. George Calvert and I find it necessary to go into the country to see about a debt due me by John Nothey. Would you have any objections to driving me down?" Weichmann quickly accepted and left to rent a horse and carriage for the trip. Mary got her things together and told Eliza Holohan that she would be back in time to attend evening Mass with her.

Meanwhile, Booth was making his arrangements for that evening. He stopped by the boardinghouse to see whether John Surratt had returned and instead found Mary on the verge of leaving for Surrattsville. The timing could not have been more perfect for him. He gave Mary some field glasses all wrapped up in brown paper. "Will you give this to John Lloyd?" he requested with a winning smile.[401]

Booth also asked Mary to deliver a message to John Lloyd. In this era of no telephones, it was common practice for people to deliver messages to others if it was on their way. Booth was handsome, charming, and had been a guest at the boardinghouse frequently; certainly Mary would have agreed to carry a message and package for him. After all, that was her destination.[402] Had Booth arrived just a little later, he would have missed Mary.

When Weichmann arrived with the rented carriage at approximately two thirty, Mary got into the carriage; and Booth, still there, mounted his horse.[403]

Mary and Weichmann arrived at the Surrattsville tavern around four o'clock. Mary's brother, Zadoc, was there, but Lloyd was not. Mary showed Zadoc the letter that she had received from Calvert. After discussing this with his mother, Zadoc agreed to help by paying interest on the judgments Mary had against her.[404] Since Nothey did not arrive, Mary decided to leave him a threatening note. She had Weichmann write it out since her eyesight was so bad. The note asked Nothey to pay his debt to her within ten days, or she would sue him.[405]

Now Mary had the package and the message, and no one to give them to. Lloyd was not at home. But even as Mary pondered this, Emma Offutt, Lloyd's sister-in-law, showed up in a buggy. Mary gave Emma the package and asked her to give it to Lloyd.[406]

Emma told Mary that Lloyd was attending a trial in Upper Marlboro, Maryland. In February, he had gotten into fight at the tavern; and a patron, Edward Perrie, had stabbed him. However, when Lloyd arrived in Marlboro on the fourteenth, he found that the case had been continued to the November term of the Prince George's Country Circuit Court.

Lloyd didn't return directly home from Marlboro, instead, he took the opportunity to drink and play cards.[407] Then he bought some fish and oysters to take home. When he did return to Surrattsville, Lloyd was accompanied by James Lusby, who remembered that "Mr. Lloyd and I returned from Marlboro to Surrattsville together. He was very drunk on that occasion."[408] Richard Sweeney, who rode on horseback part of the way back to Surrattsville with Lloyd, noted that Lloyd "was considerably under the influence of liquor, and he drank on the road."[409] Captain Bennett Gwynn, who saw Lloyd on the road about five miles from Surrattsville, confirmed this by saying Lloyd "had been drinking right smartly."[410] Emma Offutt in her testimony said that "Lloyd was very much in liquor, more so than I have ever seen him in my life."[411]

At about five-thirty, Captain Gwynn arrived at the Surratt Tavern from Upper Marlboro.[412] At that time, Mary told him about the letter that she had received from Calvert that morning. Then she gave Captain Gwynn the note Weichmann had written for her and asked Gwynn to deliver it to Nothey.[413]

Captain Gwynn politely agreed to deliver it, however, because his wife was ill he first would stop at his house to see how she was doing. Captain Gwynn was about to help Mary into her carriage when he notice that the undercarriage of the buggy was damaged. He called to Joseph Knott, the barkeeper, and asked him to get some rope, then explained to Weichmann how the carriage could temporarily be repaired with rope.[414]

Mary Surratt was leaving when Lusby arrived, slightly ahead of Lloyd. Lusby said, "I saw Mrs. Surratt just as she was about to start to go home. Her buggy was standing there at the gate, when we drove up, and she left in fifteen or twenty minutes after that."[415]

Captain Gwynn left, and then the very drunk Lloyd arrived. Had Mary left only a few minutes earlier, the later case for hanging her would have been weaker. Mary went over to greet Lloyd, and the two went into the kitchen with Weichmann following. Lloyd was unloading the oysters and fish that he had brought from Marlboro and invited Mary and Weichmann to stay for supper. The two declined the invitation, perhaps because Lloyd was so drunk. They said that they had to get back to Washington because of the weather, and indeed it was about the time Weichmann and Mary returned to the house damp from a light drizzling rain.[416]

Mary returned from the trip exhausted and hungry. With Olivia Jenkins, Honora, and Anna, Mary ate a late dinner in the dining room.[417]

The high point of the evening for Mary was that another letter had arrived from John. It had been mailed to Anna Ward and delivered that afternoon. Anna had read the letter and told Mary that it was from Montreal that John liked the city, had visited a famous French cathedral, and had purchased a pea jacket for ten dollars in silver. John wrote that board was $2.50 in gold! John wrote that he might go to Toronto and then signed the letter "John Harrison."[418]

Later, her daughter Anna, not feeling well, went to her room, and Mary and Eliza Holohan prepared to attend evening church services. They left the house on foot about nine fifteen for the Good Friday services. Services generally lasted until ten o'clock or later, which explains why Mary and Eliza started for church at such a late hour. The wind blew freezing rain against their faces, and the air was unseasonably cold. They had walked only a few houses when Eliza remarked that it was a "heavy disagreeable night," and the two decided to go back to the house. They talked for a few moments, and then Eliza went to her room, and Mrs. Surratt stayed in her parlor.[419]

By ten o'clock that evening, the house was quiet.

\*    \*    \*

At eleven o'clock on the morning of the fourteenth, Lincoln convened a cabinet meeting with secretaries Seward Jr., Stanton, McCullough, Welles, Speed, and Postmaster General Dennison. Frederick Seward, normally his father's assistant, held his father's position temporarily because of his father's accident on April 5. At the meeting, Lincoln made it clear that he wanted no prosecution of any rebel leaders and would not be sorry to have them escape out of the country.

"Frighten them out of the country, open the gates, let down the bars, scare them off, shoo!" he said, waving his hands. "Enough lives have been sacrificed, no one need expect me to take any part in hanging or killing these men, even the worst of them."

The cabinet agreed that the Union must be restored, including the role of U.S. federal courts, the postal system, customs and harbor controls, and the opening of Southern seaports to commerce. Seward reported that there was "little diversity of opinion, except as to details."

The mundane details of reconstruction were discussed, such as the Treasury Department taking possession of the custom houses and collecting the revenues, the War Department garrisoning or destroying the forts, the Navy Department occupying the harbors and taking possession of the navy yards and ships, the Interior Department sending out surveyors and land and Indian agents, the postmaster general reopening the post offices, and the attorney general reestablishing the federal courts. These proposals would set the power and machinery of the federal government in motion in the former Confederacy.[420]

Toward the end of the meeting, the president asked for any news from Sherman, and Grant replied he was "hourly expecting word."[421] Lincoln remarked that he expected the news to be favorable, "for he had last night the usual dream which he had preceding nearly every great and important event of the War."

It was a recurring dream that came to him before the firing at Fort Sumter and before the battles at Bull Run, Antietam, Gettysburg, Stone River, and Vicksburg. "I had this strange dream again last night, and we shall, judging from the past, have great news soon. I think it must be from Sherman." In Lincoln's dream, he had a vague sense of being "in a singular and indescribable vessel, but always the same, and that he was moving with great rapidity toward a dark and indefinite shore."

The cabinet listened as Lincoln described his dream and his interpretation. One cabinet member suggested that the dream foretold of a great victory, meaning that the war was on the verge of being won. Someone else said the dream was just a coincidence. Young Seward offered the opinion that at each of the previous times the president had had the dream, there had been possibilities of great change and that Lincoln had therefore had feelings of uncertainty that surfaced in his sleep.

"Perhaps," Lincoln replied to them politely. "Perhaps that is the explanation."[422]

The news would be good since Confederate General Joseph E. Johnston was at that moment preparing to surrender his army. Johnston had written to Sherman that to continue to fight would constitute murder, not battle.

At the end of the meeting, young Seward reminded the president that the new British minister, Sir Frederick Bruce, was waiting to be received for presentation of his credentials. Lincoln paused for a moment and then said, "Tomorrow at two o'clock."

"In the Blue Room, I suppose?" asked Seward.

"Yes, in the Blue Room. Don't forget to send up the speeches beforehand. I would like to look them over."[423] This appointment, of course, would never be kept.

After the cabinet meeting, Grant privately spoke to Lincoln. Grant had declined Mary Lincoln's invitation of the previous night to accompany the president and herself "to drive around with us to see the illumination." This invitation had not mentioned Mrs. Grant. Now on the morning of April 14, Mrs. Lincoln invited both the Grants to the theater.[424] Julia Grant, seething about Mary's tirade against Mrs. Griffin and Mrs. Ord and about herself being accused of disrespect and envy, visited Mrs. Stanton and discussed the carriage and theater invitations with her. Mrs. Stanton shared with her that she did not have social relations with Mrs. Lincoln. That and the City Point incidents decided the matter.

Reenforced by this encounter, Julia Grant was refusing to participate in an social occasion in which Mary Lincoln was involved. And so it was up to General Grant to respectfully decline the invitation. As an excuse, Julia quickly planned a trip to New Jersey to visit their children.

To ensure his cooperation, Julia sent her husband a note the morning of the cabinet meeting, reminding him that she wanted to leave for New Jersey. The note was delivered during the cabinet meeting. When Grant spoke to Lincoln about the plans to visit the children, he showed the note to Lincoln. It was a good excuse to get out of the theater invitation.

After the cabinet meeting, Lincoln told his wife that the Grants would not be joining them at the theater. Originally Mrs. Lincoln had invited Speaker of the House of Representatives Schuyler. But believing that the Grants would come, she had rescinded the offer, telling Colfax that "therefore I shall have to waive, all ceremony & request you to accompany us some other evening soon."[425] Unaware of how her behavior was perceived by others, Mary reinvited Colfax. Colfax, understandably, declined; he maintained that he was making arrangements for a western trip and leaving the next day, therefore, could not accept. Colfax had seen Lincoln in the early morning of the fourteenth and later that day, just before Lincoln left for the theater. Colfax remembered that Lincoln's face was alive with smiles as he talked about the war's end. Colfax thought that a great burden had been lifted from Lincoln, and it seemed to be "the happiest day of his life."[426]

Robert Lincoln had arrived that morning from Grant's staff in Virginia in time for breakfast with his parents. He had spent much of the war at Harvard. Only recently and over his mother's objections, he had enlisted in the army. His father, however, had made sure that he would be safe. He had young Lincoln assigned to General Grant's staff. Robert told firsthand of the surrender ceremonies at Appromattox he had attended although he had been outside the room where the two generals met. Robert also showed his father a recent photograph of General Lee, which he had obtained in Virginia. Lincoln looked at the picture of Lee and commented, "It is a good face; it is the face of a noble, noble, brave man. I am glad the war is over at last."[427]

Mary wanted Robert to come to the theater that night with them, but Robert declined. He was exhausted, not having slept in a bed for weeks, and wanted to retire early.

Because of the lateness of the invitation and because few people wanted to accompany Mary on social occasions, she had difficulty putting together a theater party. Mary invited the Stantons, but the secretary of war declined. Stanton did not want Lincoln to attend; he felt that "Mr. Lincoln ought not to go, it was too great an exposure."[428] In addition, Mrs. Stanton absolutely refused to go anywhere with Mary Lincoln!

Lincoln tried to help by inviting William A. Howard, the Detroit postmaster, but he was leaving Washington that evening.

Mr. and Mrs. William H. Wallace, governor of Idaho Territory, declined because he was very tired.

Richard Yates could not accept because he had other engagements with friends that evening.

George Ashmun of Massachusetts refused the invitation, saying he had a previous engagement.

The Marquis Adolph de Chambrun declined because he did not want to "attend a theatrical performance on Good Friday."

Governor Oglesby and General Haynie were the last to be invited, but they both had a prior obligation.[429]

\*     \*     \*

When the National Hotel maid came into Booth's room on the morning of April 14, she found his bed still made up. The evening of April 13, Booth did not return to his room but stayed with Ella Starr, his favorite prostitute, in the bordello where she lived with her sister at 62 Ohio Avenue. Through an alcoholic haze and pangs of guilt about not writing more frequently to his mother, he sat down at 2:00 AM on the fourteenth and wrote a letter. He composed a few lines reassuring his mother that he loved her and that nothing was going on – "indeed I have nothing to write about. Everything is dull."[430]

After leaving Ella, Booth returned to the National Hotel dining room for breakfast. Afterward he entered into the parlor and talked with Lucy for a few moments. Then had a shave at Charlie Wood's barbershop near the hotel and dropped by the Grover's Theatre to see whether Lincoln had gotten tickets there.[431]

Sometime that morning before 11:00 AM, Booth met Thomas R. Florence of the *Daily Constitutional Union* on the sidewalk and had a quick conversation. Booth spoke of going to Canada for some engagements and then of his losses in Pennsylvania oil investments.[432]

By eleven o'clock, Booth was back at the National Hotel where Henry E. Merrick, a clerk at the hotel, noticed Booth in the hotel office and thought "he looked unusually pale."[433]

At about 11:30 a.m. that morning, Booth went to Ford's Theatre where he had an arrangement with the management for his mail to be delivered when in Washington. Before entering the theater, Booth went behind the theater and was seen by Mary Jane Anderson, a black woman, who live in one of the alley houses. When Booth came around to the front of the theater, Harry Ford, the theater's treasurer, was standing at the door.

Ford called out, "There comes the handsomest man in Washington!"

Booth grinned, and the two men went inside, and Ford gave Booth his mail. Ford knew of Booth's aversion to jokes about the Confederacy and decided to tell a practical joke at Booth's expense. He remarked, "The President will be here tonight with General Grant. They've got General Lee a prisoner, and he's coming too. We're going to put him in the opposite box."

Booth, startled by this sudden information, maintained the presence of mind to reply wittily, "I hope they are not going to do like the Romans – parade their prisoner before the public to humiliate him."

Ford's Theatre was not informed about the Grant's cancellation where a box had been reserved for the foursome. Mary Lincoln, while yet unaware that the Grants had canceled, had sent a White House messenger to reserve a box in both their names. The messenger arrived at Ford's Theatre at about 11:00 a.m., and Clay Ford wrote notices for the afternoon papers (the *Washington Evening Star* and the *Republican*), announcing that the Lincolns and Grants would be attending that evening's performance.[434]

Good Friday was always a slow theater night, and in addition, the weather was unseasonably cold and windy with dark clouds and occasional rain. The president's and Grant's appearance was expected to bring in more theatergoers. William DeMotte and several colleagues were among the theatergoers that had heard that Lincoln and General Grant would attend Ford's Theatre that night, and they decided that they would "make use of the occasion to see these noted men."[435]

Booth sat down to read his mail, but he hardly saw the letters before his eyes. He was thinking of the performance that evening.

"Are you sure Lincoln and Grant will be at the evening performance?"

"Yes, they are surely coming," replied Ford.[436]

The play that night was the comedy *Our American Cousin* and was to be the last performance of and benefit for actress Laura Keene.[437]

Booth felt his heartbeat faster at the news of where Lincoln would be that night. He went outside the theater and sat down on a bench.

The actor Harry Hawk, who would be appearing in the play that night, came by and saw Booth contemplating what to do about the information he had just learned.

"How do you do, Mr. Booth?" asked Hawk.

"How are you, Hawk?" Booth replied to the actor's greeting, hardly noticing the man.

Booth stood, nodded politely, and went back inside the theater. He watched the rehearsal. Booth was familiar with the play; he studied the action, the scenes, and the change of backdrops. He had been sitting quietly in the darkened seats, watching, when at last he saw what he was looking for. Toward the end of the play was a scene with only one actor on the stage. Not only that, the actor had a long soliloquy that would afford Booth the time he needed. That would be the opportune moment to shoot Lincoln. Booth converted his kidnap plan to an assassination plan – he salvaged parts of the original for his murder plot. He would shoot Lincoln from behind; jump to the stage, a drop of about ten feet, an easy accomplishment for the athletic Booth, then run out the back door to his waiting horse. After giving this idea some thought, he went through the back door to look at the alley. He was seen by another black woman, Mary Ann Turner, whose front door fronts to the back of Ford's Theatre.[438]

Booth began to organize all the parts of a plan for assassination. He was in the mood for drastic measures. His frustration and alcohol consumption had given him a new direction. Now he had an opportunity to simultaneously kill the two individuals he believed responsible for the Confederacy's impending defeat. To further ensure the possible resurgence of the Southern armies and to inflict the greatest damage on the hated federal government, Booth made a decision to also kill Vice President Andrew Johnson and Secretary of State Seward.

By killing these three, Booth in his warped mind reasoned that he would save the South and redeem himself for four years of inactivity. He was sure the Confederacy could continue to fight if these four men died, leaving the Union leaderless.[439]

By noon, Booth was at the stable of James W. Pumphrey at 224 C Street across from the National Hotel. He had rented stalls there for his horses when he had put together his kidnapping plan. He had since sold the horses, but the lease on the stable was still good.

Pumphrey noted that Booth "came to my stable about 12 o'clock of the 14th of April last, and engaged a saddle-horse, which he said he wanted about 4 or half-past 4 that day. He had been in the habit of riding a sorrel horse, and he came to get it, but that horse was engaged, and he had in its place a small bay mare, about fourteen or fourteen and a half hands high."[440]

*   *   *

When Ford's Theatre learned that General Grant would be attending that evening, staff began enlarging and specially decorating the presidential box in Grant's honor. This single box, which was actually two boxes, numbers 7 and 8, was on the right side of the theater as one faces the stage and on the same level as the balcony. These two boxes were usually separated by a partition about seven feet high and three inches thick. They were accessible by a small corridor about four feet wide and ten feet long, running behind the first box and ending at the second. Each box could accommodate up to four people; however, when the partition was removed, the combined boxes could accommodate ten to twelve people.

That afternoon, the theater's builder James J. Gifford, Edmund Spangler, and young Joseph "Peanuts" Burroughs removed the partition between the boxes and converted them into a single box. Burroughs was a handyman whose nickname came from his selling peanuts to theater patrons.

For decorations, two flags were draped on either side of the exterior, two additional flags were draped over the velvet-covered balustrade, and a Treasury Guard's regimental flag (white spread eagle and stars on a blue background) was placed at the center post above the American flags. A framed engraving of George Washington was brought from the reception room and placed on the box's exterior center pillar. For the foursome, the box was supplied with a chair, a velvet sofa, three velvet armchairs, and a rocking chair.[441]

While Spangler was working on the partition, he made derogatory remarks about Lincoln.

"Damn the President and General Grant!" Spangler exclaimed recklessly.

"What are you damning the man for – a man that has never done any harm to you?" Burroughs replied.

"He ought to be cursed when he got so many men killed," responded Spangler.[442] He could not know then that these words would come back to haunt him.

\*     \*     \*

After leaving Pumphrey's stables, Booth walked toward the Willard Hotel on Pennsylvania Avenue and Fourteenth Street. But he stopped at the Kirkwood House, two blocks south of the Willard. Atzerodt had registered there, according to Booth's instructions. Atzerodt took room number 126 shortly before eight o'clock that morning.[443] Earlier Booth had told Atzerodt "to go to the Kirkwood and get a pass from Vice President Johnson." A pass would allow the conspirators to move into Southern Maryland without problems at the guard posts at the bridges.[444]

But Atzerodt had not gotten the pass, and now Booth was at the Kirkwood hoping to get a pass from either the vice president or his secretary, William A. Browning. Booth had met Johnson and Browning in Nashville. But when Booth inquired for them, the hotel clerk informed him that neither was in. Booth wrote on a card, "Don't wish to disturb you: are you at home? J. Wilkes Booth." The clerk placed the card in Browning's box. [445] From the Kirkwood House, Booth walked down Pennsylvania Avenue and entered the dining room of the Willard Hotel. The Grants were staying at the Willard, and Booth saw Julia Grant and her young son, Jesse, eating lunch. Booth took a seat across the room from them.

Mrs. Grant noticed Booth but did not recognize him. What she saw was "a man with a wild look" staring at her from across the room. Later, Mrs. Grant would write that she was positive that the man was Booth.[446]

Booth did not order lunch at the Willard. He was satisfied with staring angrily at Mrs. Grant. He then returned to the National where he had lunch with Lucy's mother, whose husband was now the minister-designate to Spain, and Mrs. Temple, a Washington socialite. The women said they wanted to go to Ford's Theatre that night to see *Our American Cousin*. Booth, knowing what he had planned for that evening and not wanting his fiancée's mother to see it, advised them not to go. He told him that actors would not give a good performance to a small audience, and since Good Friday meant a small audience, "the play would drag on that account." The two women, thanking him for his insight, decided that they would go to the theater the following night.[447]

*     *     *

After the cabinet meeting, General Grant planned to leave on the four o'clock train to Burlington, New Jersey. Mrs. Grant told him of the incident at lunch. "When I went in to my lunch today, a man with a wild look followed me into the dining room, took a seat nearly opposite to me at the table, stared at me continually, and seemed to be listening to my conversation."

"Oh, I suppose he did so merely from curiosity," her husband replied.[448] Grant himself was quite used to such attention. He had been admired and at times even mobbed by people since his victory over Lee. The day before, he had started to walk from his hotel room to the War Department. When he was recognized, a crowd began to form. Grant was the hero of the American people, and praise was heaped upon him. It was only after the police arrived that Grant had been able to continue on his way.

Later that afternoon, the wife of General Rucker arrived with her carriage to take the Grants to the railroad station. They had not ridden far, however, when a man rode passed them on a dark horse. The horseman rode a little ahead the carriage and turned around and looked back into the carriage. Julia Grant recognized him at once, exclaiming, "That is the same man who sat down at the lunch table near me. I don't like his looks!"[449] The horseman rode on.

At the station, the Grants boarded the private car of Mr. Garrett, president of the Baltimore and Ohio Railroad. When Booth saw Grant driving to the station, this was his first indication that Grant would not be a the theater that night. Grant eluded his planned assassination.

*     *     *

Lincoln told his wife he wanted to take a carriage ride later in the afternoon. Mary, always ready to make each occasion a social event, asked whether he wanted any guests to accompany them. But Lincoln said, "No, I prefer to ride by ourselves today."

At about two o'clock, President Lincoln and his wife had lunch in their upstairs quarters. Later Lincoln returned to his office to see visitors and to handle the endless work of the presidency. Lincoln met briefly with Vice President Johnson. He met also with former senator and now Minister-designate to Spain John P. Hale, who was in Washington to receive his instructions from the State Department.

Secretary of the Navy Welles had called Hale's appointment as minister to Spain, "a position for which he is eminently unfit." The ministership was a political appointment recommended by "a majority of the Union Senators." It was, however, being given as a political plum for Hale's past years as a senator.[450]

On the morning of the fourteenth, Hale went to the White House to bid farewell to the president, whom he had known since their days together in the Thirtieth Congress, when Lincoln served his one term in the House of Representatives. Their relationship had never been close, but always friendly. Hale had been an ardent abolitionist, and he spoke of Lincoln as a man of unexcelled "honesty and patriotism," whose single aim was "the welfare of the country."[451] At this meeting, Hale asked Lincoln for "an act of clemency and kindness" for a New Hampshire man, who had fraudulently represented items in the sale of war supplies. Lincoln went along with Hale's request for a pardon, which was typical of Lincoln's desire to heal the wounds of war.[452]

Lincoln, as was his custom, visited the telegraph office at the War Department on the afternoon of April 14 accompanied only by White House guard William H. Crook. This afternoon, he wanted to see if there had been any news of Johnston's surrender to Sherman. During this walk, Lincoln said, "Crook, do you know, I believe there are men who want to take my life. And I have no doubt they will do it."

"Why do you think so, Mr. President?" Crook asked.

"Other men have been assassinated" was the reply.

"I hope you are mistaken, Mr. President."

"I have perfect confidence in those who are around me, in every one of you men. I know no one could do it and escape alive. But if it is to be done, it is impossible to prevent it," Lincoln said fatalistically.[453] Lincoln had expressed this thought many times before. When on inauguration day, Stanton cautioned Lincoln about security; Lincoln told him, "Stanton, it is useless. If it is the will of Providence that I should die by the hand of an assassin, it must be so."[454]

While at the War Department, Lincoln told Stanton of his theater plans for that night, and Stanton again urged the president to give up the theater party. Lincoln asked Secretary Stanton whether Major Eckert, one of Stanton's able assistants and an officer noted for his physical strength, might accompany him to the theater that night.

"Well, Stanton," Lincoln said, "I have seen Eckert break five pokers, one after the other, over his arm, and I am thinking he would be the kind of man to go with me this evening. May I take him?" In the incident Lincoln described, Eckert had once demonstrated the poor quality of the cast-iron pokers at the War Department by breaking five of them across his left arm.

However, Stanton refused to let his assistant accompany Lincoln. Stanton wanted to discourage Lincoln from going to the theater at all and so claimed that he had some important work for Eckert that night and could not spare him. Later, Lincoln asked Eckert himself whether he could attend. But Eckert, knowing Stanton's views, declined. Both Stanton and Eckert were at home when informed of the assassination.[455]

Also Captain Beckwith, General Grant's telegrapher and cipher operator, (1862-1865) wrote, "Secretary Stanton upon learning of the arrangements for the theater party, promptly registered most strenuous objections to the plan . . . . He [Lincoln] made light of his Secretary's fears."[456]

Lincoln returned to the White House accompanied by Crook; before entering, Lincoln turned for a moment and said, "Good-bye, Crook," an unusual remark for him. He normally say, "See you later."[457]

*   *   *

Sometime after leaving Julia Grant at the Willard Hotel, Booth went back to the Kirkwood House to see if Johnson had returned. There, Booth talked with Atzerodt and was told that the vice president had not yet returned. After Booth left, Herold arrived and went to Atzerodt's room. They talked for a few moments and then left for Naylor's livery stable. Atzerodt rode a horse that he had hired from another stable, and Herold walked. At Naylor's, Atzerodt turned his horse over to the foreman, John Fletcher, and asked him to have it ready at ten o'clock that evening. Herold took this opportunity to rent a horse. Herold returned alone at four o'clock and asked for the horse he had hired. He agreed to have it back at the stable by nine o'clock that evening. Fletcher would never see that horse again. Herold's keeping the horse out after nine o'clock would be the cause of early suspicion and the unraveling of the conspirators' names.

Booth was busy arranging the assassination. It is now between 2:00 and 2:30 PM, and he had just seen Mary Surratt and gave her the small package and a message to deliver to Lloyd. He then went to the stable behind Ford's Theatre to arrange for sheltering the bay mare he had hired from Pumphrey. Near three o'clock, the two black women who lived in the alley houses – Mary Jane Anderson, for the second time that day, and Mary Ann Turner, her next door neighbor – saw Booth. He was talking with a woman. Rehearsal at Ford's that day was in the afternoon, and Booth may have been talking to a cast member of *Our American Cousin*. Mary Jane Anderson gave a little of her feelings about Booth when she later testified that "I stood at my gate and looked right wishful at him."[458] Adding herself to the multitude of Booth's female admires.

Booth then went into the theater where he saw Ed Spangler and Peanuts Burroughs working on the two upper boxes, arranging them for the accommodation of the presidential party. Seeing that work was being done on the presidential box, Booth was satisfied that Lincoln would indeed be there that evening.[459]

Inside the theater, Mames Maddox, Ford's Theatre property manager, caught sight of Booth and asked jovially if he'd like to get a drink at the Star Saloon next door.

"No thanks," Booth answered. "I've a touch of pleurisy, and I don't think I'll drink anything." But later, he said he'd walk over with Maddox, Burroughs, Spangler, and young Ferguson, a callboy who alerted actors when to go onstage.

In the saloon, Maddox had a glass of beer and Ferguson a sarsaparilla. With that, Booth said, "I think I'll reconsider and have a glass of ale." "He was", Ferguson writes, "everybody's friend up to the moment of his revelation of sinister motives."[460] Afterward, Booth paid the bill, and they all left, the theater employees going to dinner before the evening performance.

As Booth left the Star Saloon and headed for Pumphrey's stable, he met Joseph Hazelton, a twelve-year-old boy, who sold programs in front of Ford's Theatre. A small conversation ensued in which Booth asked, "Well, Joseph, have you made up your mind yet to become an actor?"

I don't know, Mr. Booth, Perhaps I wouldn't do for the stage."

"Try it, Joseph, when the time comes," Booth urged, "Try it. You have the face of an actor, the features of the young Byron. The world will think better of the actor some day and treat him more liberally." As Booth was walking away, Hazelton recalls that Booth turned back and said, "We have been good friends, Joseph, eh? Well, try to think well of me and this will buy you a stick of candy." And Booth then gave Hazelton a coin. Hazelton did become an actor and worked as such for some fifty years.[461]

At about four o'clock, Booth walked the five to six blocks to the National Hotel where he asked Henry Merrick, the day clerk, for some paper and an envelope. Merrick jesting with Booth asked "if he had made a thousand dollars" that day.

Booth replied, "No, but I have worked hard enough to have made ten times that amount."

Merrick let Booth use the office to do his writing. Booth tried to think through the alcohol that he had continued to drink that day. "Merrick, is this the year 1864 or 1865?"

"You are surely joking; you certainly know what year it is," Merrick replied.

Booth answered, "Sincerely, I am not." Merrick told him it was 1865, and Booth resumed writing. Only then did Merrick notice something troubled and agitated in the actor's appearance; Merrick found this "entirely at variance with his usual quiet deportment."[462] Booth was writing a letter to the *National Intelligencer* explaining his reasons for the assassinations. When he had finished and sealed the envelope, he said good-bye to Merrick and walked across the street to Pumphrey's stable to get the bay mare he had rented.[463]

Booth rode up Pennsylvania Avenue and turned right onto Tenth Street to the Ford's Theatre where he spoke first James Maddox and then to James P. Ferguson, owner of the restaurant next to Ford's. Ferguson was on the porch of his restaurant when Booth shouted to him, "See what a nice horse I have got!" Booth turned his horse around and then said, "Now, watch: he can run just like a cat!" And he headed back toward Pennsylvania Avenue.[464]

It was nearly four thirty when Booth stopped on Pennsylvania Avenue, across the street from Grover's Theatre, to greet Charles Warrick, a fellow actor who had recently been sick. During Warrick's illness, Booth had frequently visited him.

Moments later, Booth met and spoke to John Matthews.[465]

Matthews was appearing at Ford's Theatre that night. "John," Matthews asked, "have you seen the prisoners?"

They all paused for a moment to watch a long line of ragged stragglers from Lee's army being marched through the street under guard.

"Yes, I have." Booth, ever dramatic, put his hand to his forehead. "My God! I no longer have a country! This is the end of constitutional liberty in America." Booth's melodramatic performance must have been confusing; everyone knew he was living quite well in the enemy camp. Booth leaned over the horse's neck, took Mathews's hand, and privately asked, "I wish to ask you a favor; will you do it for me?"

"Of course," Matthews replied, not bothering to ask what the favor might be.

"I have a letter which I wish you to deliver to the publishers of the *National Intelligencer* tomorrow morning, unless I see you in the meantime. I may leave tonight, and it will not be much trouble for you to deliver the letter." Booth stressed that delivering the letter was very important and that he hesitated to trust it to the mails. Matthews Assured Booth that he would deliver the letter.

Just then, an open carriage rumbled passed them going up Pennsylvania Avenue. Matthews exclaimed, "Why, there goes General Grant. I thought he was coming to the theater tonight with the President this evening!" Booth turned in the saddle, and his face paled. Passing by was the carriage carrying the Grants to the railroad station.[466]

Booth thundered after the carriage. When he had passed it, he reversed his horse and looked directly into the faces of Ulysses and Julia Grant. The carriage went on its way to the Baltimore and Ohio station where the Grants would depart for New Jersey. It is only now, about 4:30-4:45 p.m. that Booth learns that Grant would not be at the theater with the Lincolns.

Booth was definitely startled by the departure of Grant. Now he worried that Lincoln also might have changed his plans.

After seeing the Grants leave, Booth hurried to the Kirkwood House to check on the whereabouts of the vice president. There he met John Devenay. Devenay testified that he saw Booth "on the steps of the Kirkwood House . . . on the night of the 14th of April, between 5 and 6 o'clock."

"When did you get back from Canada?" Devenay asked.

"I have been back for some time," Booth said peevishly. He searched for a way to escape Devenay. "Well, I will see you later." But before Booth could leave, Devenay asked, "Are you going to play here again?"

"No, I am not going to play again; I am in the oil business." Booth replied and pushed passed Devenay into the hotel.[467]

Booth managed to get away and into the hotel where he learned that Johnson was still not in. Disgusted, Booth returned to the stable behind Ford's Theatre to leave his horse. Then he entered the theater through the back door. There he asked Spangler for a halter for his horse. Spangler, however, was very busy preparing the theater for the evening performance and spent another stagehand to find a halter. When at last the man returned, Spangler did take time out to go to the stable with Booth to put the halter on the horse. Spangler also started to take off the saddle, but Booth said, "Never mind, I do not want it off."[468]

Booth, now feeling the need for alcoholic support, asked Maddox, Peanuts, and Spangler to join him at the bar next door for a drink. Booth paid for the round of drinks, and after one drink, Maddox, Burroughs, and Spangler returned to their work at the theater.

Alone again, Booth went to the National Hotel to have dinner with Mr. and Mrs. Hale, their daughter Lucy, Mrs. Temple of Washington, and an English lady who was visiting Washington. As they waited in a parlor, Mrs. Temple recalls that Booth "seemed to be in good spirits" and recalled "nothing whatever excited in Booth's manner." He knew that this meeting with his fiancée was going to be his last. Booth took Lucy aside; and for a few moments, they talked before being called to dinner. He took out his watch when they finished dinner and said, "I must go." He said good-bye to Lucy and the group and started to leave, but then he came back to the table. In a theatrical view of himself, he took Lucy's hand and quoted Hamlet, "Nymph, in thy orisons be all my sins remembered." He kissed her hand and left. Later that night as the group was parting, Mrs. Temple remembered saying to Lucy, "My dear, you look exquisitely lovely tonight, sweeter and prettier than I ever saw you."[469]

Sometime after seven o'clock, Booth left the National Hotel; and by seven thirty, he was having another drink, this time with William Withers, director of the orchestra at Ford's. Withers knew Booth well – he had played billiards with him the night before the assassination – and also knew President Lincoln and had taught Tad how to play the drums.[470] "During the conversation . . . about different members of the theatrical profession," Withers said, "I laughingly remarked that Booth would never be as great as his father. An inscrutable smile flitted across his face as he replied, 'When I leave the stage, I will be the most talked about man in America.'"[471]

# CHAPTER 12

## *Entire Absence of All Safeguards*

It was three o'clock in the afternoon when Lincoln and his wife left on their carriage ride. They took a route along the Potomac, and Lincoln was in high spirits. Mary Lincoln wrote of the carriage ride,

> Down the Potomac, he was almost boyish, in his mirth & reminded me, of his original nature, what I had always remembered of him, in our own home – free from care, surrounded by those he loved so well & by whom, he was so idolized. That Friday, I never saw him so supremely cheerful – his manner was even playful .... During the drive he was so gay, that I said to him, laughingly, "Dear Husband, you almost startle me by your great cheerfulness." He replied, "And well I may feel so, Mary, I consider this day, the war has come to a close" – and then added, "We must both, be more cheerful in the future – between the war & the loss of our darling Willie – we have both, been very miserable".[472]

Lincoln was hopeful that now that the war was over, he and Mary would have some peace and happiness. He thought that after his presidency, he would return to Illinois and open a law office in Springfield or Chicago and pass the rest of his life in solitude.[473] Lincoln's carriage returned along the damp streets of Washington to the White House. His afternoon ride with his wife had been quite pleasurable. He was in good spirits, and as they arrived at the White House, he saw Governor Richard J. Oglesby and General Isham Haynie walking toward the Treasury.

"Come back, boys, come back!" he called.

The men smiled their hellos and came toward him. Together they all went inside the White House. Soon they were listening as Lincoln regaled them with readings from the writings of political humorist Petroleum U. Nasby (David Ross Locke) – the initials of course spelled "pun" – on the most likely end of the war. Then Lincoln asked the two men if *they* would like to go to the theater with him, but Oglesby and Haynie declined, saying that they were off to a meeting of the Illinois senatorial and congressional delegations at Willard's.

As Lincoln was about to give further renditions of Nasby, they must have given a sigh of relief as a servant came in to inform Lincoln that dinner was served.

"The President is expected at the theater and has to eat," the servant informed the two guests. Oglesby and Haynie left very close to six o'clock, and the Lincolns had their last dinner together. The Lincolns usually ate at seven o'clock; however, on this evening they ate a little earlier.

Noah Brooks visited briefly, and although he was suffering from a bad cold, Lincoln invited *him* to the theater, but Brooks also declined, saying that he did not feel well and wanted to go to bed early.

The president signed a few papers, including the appointment of the territorial governor of Nebraska. The card of Senator William Stewart of Nevada was brought up with a note saying that Stewart wished to introduce an acquaintance to him. Lincoln, however, sent back, "I am engaged to go to the theater with Mrs. Lincoln. It is the kind of engagement I never break. Come with your friend tomorrow at ten, and I shall be glad to see you. A. Lincoln."[474]

The card of Representative George Ashmun of Massachusetts was brought up, and Lincoln sent back a card of his own, "Allow Mr. Ashmun & friend to come in at 9 A. M. tomorrow. A. Lincoln, April 14, 1865."[475]

Mary Lincoln had spent the day asking people to go to the theater with her, and she was growing desperate. But she at last found a couple who would say yes. They were Harry Rathbone and his fiancée (and stepsister), Sarah Harris. Mary also arranged for Tad to see the play *Aladdin! Or His Wonderful Lamp* at Grover's Theatre.

Senator Stewart and Searless also wanted to see the president that night and arrived at the White House as Lincoln was leaving to pick up his guests. Lincoln told both senators that he would see them in the morning.[476]

Lincoln had one more visitor as he got into his carriage. Former congressman Isaac Arnold of Illinois came walking up and asked to speak to him.

Lincoln was brisk. "Excuse me now, I am going to the theater. Come and see me in the morning."[477]

The Lincolns rode to pick up their guests with only the coachman; Francis Burke; and valet, Charles Forbes. Lincoln's bodyguard for that night, John F. Parker, was to meet the president at the theater and had already walked to Ford's Theatre seven blocks away. Thomas Pendel, the doorman at the White House, told Parker to meet the president there "and you see him safe inside."[478] As usual, Lincoln refused to have a military guard with him when he went to places of entertainment or to church. He wanted "to go as free and unencumbered as other people."[479]

The presidential couple went first to the home of Senator and Mrs. Ira Harris at Fifteenth and H Streets to pick up their young guests. Clara was the daughter of the senator, who was one of Lincoln's most ardent supporters. Senator Harris had been a

New York State Supreme Court justice and was elected to succeed William H. Seward when the latter became secretary of state. Mrs. Pauline Rathbone Harris was Senator Harris's second wife. The former Mrs. Rathbone of Albany had a son, Henry, who had been seventeen when his father died. The family was left a large fortune earned in the manufacture of stoves. The senator's marriage to the former Mrs. Rathbone made Clara Harris and Henry Rathbone stepsister and stepbrother. The two young people fell in love and became engaged in early 1865. Major Henry Rathbone was twenty-eight, and Clara was twenty-three and a friend of Mrs. Lincoln. Clara Harris had been at the White House during Lincoln's speech on Tuesday night.[480]

\*     \*     \*

Michael O'Laughlen with his friends Bernard Early, Edward Murphy, and James Henderson came to Washington on April 13 to celebrate the end of the war. They arrived at five o'clock and spent the remainder of the day having a good time. The four men were together on Friday April 14 until eight o'clock that evening.[481] They were all together except when Henderson went into a barbershop to get a shave. While he was in there, O'Laughlen and Early walked down to the National Hotel. There O'Laughlen went in, leaving Early standing in front of the hotel. O'Laughlen said he would be back in fifteen minutes and then went in and asked at the desk for Booth. But Booth was not in. So O'Laughlen returned to Early, and when the two men got back, Henderson was still in the barber's chair.[482]

O'Laughlen did not succeed in contacting Booth, and for Good Friday night, O'Laughlen had a solid alibi. He and his friends were at the bar at Rullman's Hotel. He was sitting at the bar when news of the assassination reached them.[483]

At the same time, Samuel Arnold was 120 miles away in Fortress Monroe, Virginia, where he was employed as a clerk for John W. Wharton.[484]

\*     \*     \*

Atzerodt spent the afternoon doing what many young men did for entertainment in those days – he drank. He did this drinking at several restaurants along Seventh Street and then returned to the Kirkwood House between five thirty and six o'clock. A clerk told him that a young man had called for him and would come by later. Atzerodt knew that the young man could only be Herold, so Atzerodt sat in the lobby and waited.

At last, Herold returned, and he told Atzerodt that Booth and Powell wanted to see him immediately at the Herndon House. Obediently the two young men went to the meeting. They must have wondered what Booth had to say to them. The war was all but over, so kidnapping the president could not be useful. They knew, however, that Booth was generous, and at the least there would be free drinks. At this meeting, when the men had all assembled in his room, Booth revealed his plan to kill

Lincoln instead of kidnapping him. Quickly Booth handed out assignments to each of the conspirators. Booth was to assassinate Lincoln, Atzerodt the vice president, and Powell (with Herold as guide) the secretary of state.

Powell accepted his role and was undisturbed by the quickness of the organization of this plot, the lack of planning and coordination, and the fact that he had no idea what streets to take to escape across the bridge into Virginia. However, Atzerodt immediately balked at the change in plans. "I only agreed to help kidnap the president," Atzerodt asserted. "I'm not going to kill anybody."

"It's too late!" Booth reminded Atzerodt. "You're in it! If caught they will hang us all!"

Herold's only responsibility was to act as guide for Powell. The murders were to be synchronized to happen shortly after ten o'clock. That is when Booth estimated the play would have only one actor on stage.

The men at last left Booth. He felt he had cowed them to his will. Booth needed more alcohol. He went to Taltavull's Star Saloon adjoining Ford's Theatre and fortified himself with another drink.[485]

From the saloon, Booth went back into Ford's Theatre. There he spoke to Henry Ford in the box office and confirmed that the Lincolns were still scheduled to see the performance that night.[486] Booth was elated that his plan was working. Now he only had to wait. He would kill a man soon – it was nerve-wracking. He spent the rest of the evening going back and forth from Ford's Theatre to the saloon next door. Booth's anxiety and alcohol consumption continued to increase. When at curtain time the Lincolns had not arrived, Booth agonized over whether the president had canceled at the last minute. Booth continued to drink at the bar. Robert Gourlay, brother of Jeannie Gourlay, who played Mary Meredith in the play that night, saw Booth drinking in the saloon during the intermission after act 1, which ended about nine o'clock.

During one of his trips between the theater and the saloon, Booth went to the stable in the alley behind the theater to get the bay mare. He led the mare up the alley to the back of Ford's Theatre. He opened the rear wooden door and called several times for Spangler, but instead the actor J. L. Debonay appeared.

"Tell Spangler to come to the door and hold my horse," Booth demanded.

Debonay could see Booth had been drinking, and certainly he wondered at Booth's offensive behavior. But he repeated the message to Spangler, who was working as sceneshifter on stage left. Spangler, seeing that he was not needed by the play for the moment, went outside and obediently held the reins for the man who had treated him to a number of drinks. Booth went in the back door of the theater. He wanted to walk behind the set to get to stage left and asked Debonay if he could cross the backstage. Debonay answered that it was in use as a dairy scene in act 2 – Booth would have to go under the stage and come up on the other side.

Meanwhile Spangler called to Debonay, "Tell Peanut John to come here and hold this horse, I have not time. Mr. Gifford is out in front of the theatre, and all the responsibility of the scene lies on me."

Peanut John was attending the stage door. He kept out those not authorized to be backstage. "Spangler," he shouted, "I cannot hold the horse. I have to stay by the door!"

Spangler replied, "Hold the horse, and if there is any difficulty lay the blame on me." Peanut John took the reins from Spangler and huddled down on a carpenter's bench near the back door.[487] It was cold, and a light rain made the back alley a very uncomfortable place.

Intermission began and people began strolling into the vestibule and bar. Booth went outside into the crowd, and to his horror, he saw the president's carriage at the curb. Lincoln might leave the theater at intermission! If that should happen, the assassination plot would fall apart. But when the crowd returned to their seats, the carriage stayed empty. Booth celebrated in the Star Saloon by calling loudly for brandy. Many who saw him thought he was getting drunk. Farther down the bar, the president's coachman, Francis Burke, and his valet messenger, Charles Forbes, were having a drink with guard John Parker. Parker was supposed to be in the theater, guarding Lincoln.

Booth at last slammed down his empty glass on to the bar and went out in front of the theater again. One of the things he had failed to bring with him was a pocket watch, so he did not know how close to ten o'clock it was. Not knowing unnerved him.

"What time is it?" Booth asked Buckingham, the night doorman at Ford's.

Buckingham had no watch. "Sorry, Mr. Booth, you'll have to go into the lobby and look at the clock." Booth frowned and went inside. Then he returned and asked for a chew of tobacco. Booth, however, was too nervous to stay talking. He went back to the saloon for a quick drink and then walked back to the theater.[488]

At one point, Booth was standing in front of the theater when Captain William Williams of the city mounted police came by. They knew each other, and Williams asked, "John, join me for a drink?"

"No!" he replied, "I promised to look at Laura Keene in a particular scene."

Williams went into the bar by himself.

A little after ten o'clock, Booth entered the bar again. He needed more alcohol to catapult him toward the fateful moment. Taltavull later said, "I saw him go out of the bar alone, as near as I can judge, from eight to ten minutes before I heard the cry that the President was assassinated."[489]

Meanwhile John Miles, a black employee of Ford's Theatre, was "up on the flies, about three and a half stories from the stage"; gazing out of a nearby window, he could see Peanut John "lying on a bench holding the horse."[490]

The third act had begun as Booth entered the lobby for the last time. Jeannie Gourlay (Mary Meredith in the play) later remembered that "he was so pale, that I thought he was ill."[491] Booth passed Buckingham for the last time that night, went up the stairs, and moved behind the audience along the crescent-shaped aisle.

\*　　\*　　\*

One of the security guards originally detailed to guard Lincoln was George W. McElfresh. His orders were, "When the President went to the theatre I should get there as soon as possible, take a seat at the box door, and let no one enter without first sending in his name or card, and I often stopped people that I knew to be particular friends of the family, until I had announced them."[492] But McElfresh, exhausted by the night shift, was transferred to another position about a month before the assassination. McElfresh later speculated, "If the officer that took my place had carried out the orders given me I don't think Booth could have gotten into the President's box."

As it was, John Parker was new to the job, having held the position for only eleven days. Curiously, it was because of Mrs. Lincoln that he was at Ford's that evening – Parker replaced Thomas Pendel, who had been promoted to doorkeeper. Mrs. Lincoln had fired the previous doorkeeper for delaying to take a notice to the newspapers about a reception. That night, Parker was wearing civilian clothes and carrying a .38 Colt revolver.[493]

Mrs. Lincoln's mood was festive and was prepared to enjoy herself that evening. She wore an elegant light gray silk spring dress, a dark bonnet, and a black velvet coat. The president was dowdy as usual in a black frock coat and silk top hat. In his pockets were spectacles in a silver case, an Irish linen handkerchief with "A. Lincoln" embroidered in red, an ivory pocketknife trimmed in silver, and a velvet eyeglass cleaner. His brown leather wallet, lined with purple silk, contained, among other things, eight newspaper clippings favorable to him and a Confederate States of America five-dollar bill with Jefferson Davis on its face.

At the theater, Lincoln greeted Joseph Hazelton, who distributed the programs. He had once been introduced to Lincoln at the White House. "Joseph, I am glad to form your acquaintance, and I trust I shall always deserve your regard," the president had said and, twice thereafter, had greeted him by name at theater visits.[494] The program Joseph handed to the four members of the presidential party was for *Our American Cousin* by Tom Taylor. It starred Laura Keene, a well-known actress and theater producer. She was demanding of her employees and known for her temper tantrums, paying her bills on time, and paying high wages. As manager of her own theaters in several cities, she put on extravagant productions, involving herself in all aspects of the theater including scenery design and production, lighting, costumes, and props.

*Our American Cousin*, popular in the 1860s, was a silly farce with bizarre characterizations, far-fetched assumptions, and puns and misunderstandings. The plot involved a New England Yankee who became heir to an English fortune, a mother seeking to marry off her daughter to the American, a silly British lord who distorted language and concepts and got nothing straight, a con artist who attempted to get the money, and a sweet heroine who captured the Yankee's heart.

It was just the sort of play that the president loved, affording an opportunity for a few laughs and relaxation.

The Lincoln's and their guests arrived at the theater late. At about 8:30 PM, the Lincolns, Miss Harris, and Major Rathbone climbed the staircase leading to the rear of the crescent-shaped balcony. To stage left was the door to their box overlooking the stage. A peculiar feature of the theater box was that it had two doors because the box's space was often divided by a movable partition into two spaces. Whenever Lincoln attended the theater, the partition was removed so that he could enjoy a double box.

As the presidential party sat down, Laura Keene as Mrs. Trenchard was on stage, trying to explain to the dim-witted Lord Dundreary the point of a joke. He kept saying he couldn't see it.

"Well, anyone can see that!" she ad-libbed, gesturing toward the presidential party and dropping a curtsy. The audience of some 1,700 broke into applause as the band, under William Withers Jr., played "Hail to the Chief."

Lincoln bowed to the audience for a few moments and then sat in the rocking chair. Mrs. Lincoln sat in a chair to his right.[495] Miss Harris sat in a chair beside her, and Major Rathbone sat on the small sofa at the far end of the box.

Parker had never seen a performance of *Our American Cousin* and, expecting the evening to be uneventful, was watching it from a seat in the balcony below his post at the door to the passage leading to the president's box. In addition, during the intermission, he and Forbes, the valet, approached Francis Burke, Lincoln's coachman, and asked him to take a drink with them. The three went next door for a drink. When the final act began, Parker was either in his baloney seat or still in the bar.

\* \* \*

There were many rumors of assassination plots in the Civil War years, and probably several real plots existed. The White House and the War Department could not take them all seriously. Lamon expressed the feelings of many at the time:

> It seems almost incredible that the apprehensions of danger to Mr. Lincoln should have been shared by so few, when one thinks of the simplicity of his domestic habits, the facilities at all times afforded for a near approach to his presence, and the entire absence of all safeguards for the protection of his person, save the watchfulness of one or two of his most immediate friends. "But the truth is, the crime of assassination was so abhorrent to the genius of Anglo-Saxon civilization, so foreign to the practice of our republican institutions, that little danger was apprehended.[496]

At the time of Lincoln's assassination, Lamon was in Richmond at Lincoln's insistence, helping the planning for the opening of the Virginia legislature. Lincoln had just returned from Richmond, and while there, he had started the process of reconstruction by allowing the Virginia legislature to convene. However, "there had arisen some complications," and Lincoln asked Lamon, being a Virginian, to go to Richmond and move this process along.

When Lee surrendered at Appomattox, there was popular jubilation. Grant had given General Lee terms that reflected the spirit of the second inaugural address. Lincoln walked the streets of Richmond unharmed, and Lincoln's plans for reconstruction were defined and proceeding smoothly, especially in Louisiana. The White House guard Crook later wrote, "It did not seem possible that . . . there could be danger. For my part, I had drawn a full breath of relief after we got out of Richmond, and had forgotten to be anxious since."[497]

Lincoln did go to the theater on the night of April 14, 1865, and so did John Wilkes Booth, his assassin.

# CHAPTER 13

## *Stop That Man*

The play went on.

It was not difficult for Booth to get into the presidential box. When at last it was time and with only one actor on stage, Booth, feeling invincible with alcohol, went to the outer door of the box.

Shortly before Booth's arrival, Simon P. Hanscom, editor of the *Washington National Republican*, had called at the president's box to deliver a document. The editor had been to the White House, and when told Lincoln was at the theater, he delivered a "dispatch" to the president there. In his newspaper, he reported that the only one present at the door was Charles Forbes, Lincoln's messenger and footman.[498]

Many events of that night are shadowed in confusion.

William O. Stoddard, one of Lincoln's secretaries, maintained that he saw Booth present his card to Forbes and said that Lincoln had sent for him, and so he was allowed to enter the presidential box.[499]

In another version by Captain Roeliff Brinkerhoff (later general), Booth spoke to no one; he just walked in. Brinkerhoff wrote:

> When one of my friends called my attention to the President's box, with the remark, "There's a reporter going to see Father Abraham," I looked and saw a man standing at the door of the President's box, with his hat on, and looking down upon the stage. Presently he took out a card case, or something of this kind, from his side pocket and took out a card. It is said that he showed it to the President's messenger outside, but I saw nothing of the kind, in fact I saw no other man there aside from those seated in the audience. He took off his hat, and put his hand upon the door knob, and went into the little hall or corridor, back of the box. Presently, I cannot say how soon, it may have been two, three, or five minutes, I heard a pistol

shot. I turned to the President's box and saw a man flash to the front with face as white as snow, and hair as black as a raven.[500]

Captain Oliver C. Gatch had also seen Booth near the passage to the presidential box. Gatch remembered,

It was during a lull in the action of a scene, that my brother and I, cramped from long sitting in one position, rose from our seats to stretch ourselves. While we were standing in the aisle close to the wall, my brother called my attention to a young man who seemed to be watching the play from a position against the wall near the entrance to the President's box. My brother remarked [about] this young man's striking appearance, and I agreed with him, thinking him the handsomest man I had ever seen. He had a haughty demeanor, but his face was so calm that one would never have thought of suspecting him of any dreadful purpose. I noticed, though, how his eyes flashed and how sharp was their contrast to his pallid countenance. Presently, I saw him edge toward the box without changing his attitude, and then enter the passage way and close the door behind him. Almost instantly the house was startled by the loud report of a pistol shot.[501]

James P. Ferguson, who operated a restaurant "adjoining Ford's Theater on the upper side", had attended the performance that night in order to see Grant and had "secured a seat directly opposite the President's box, in the front dress circle." Ferguson recalls,

Somewhere near 10 o'clock, during the second scene of the third act of *Our American Cousin*, I saw Booth pass along near the President's box, and then stop and lean against the wall. After standing there a moment, I saw him step down one step, put his hands on the door and his knee against it, and push the door open, the first door that goes into the box.[502]

On this point, Booth may have the last word. In his diary entry for April 14, he wrote, "I struck boldly and not as the papers say. I walked with a firm step through a thousand of his friends, was stopped, but pushed on." Booth supports that he was questioned by Charles Forbes before he was allowed to go into the passageway leading to the presidential box. It was well-known that it was Lincoln's habit to invite actors to his box for conversation, so it is understandable that Forbes let Booth pass. Even if Parker had been at his post, he also might well have let Booth see the president.

Once in the passageway to the presidential box, Booth closed the door behind him. He braced it shut with a piece of wood (part of a dismantled music stand), one end was jammed into a hole carved in the wall, the other was against the door so it could not be opened from the outside. At the end of a ten-foot passageway, the door to the presidential box was ajar.

Mary Lincoln was sitting affectionately close to her husband, holding hands. Mary leaned against him and whispered, "What will Miss Harris think of my hanging on to you so?"

Lincoln replied, "She won't think anything about it."[503]

These were his last words.

On stage, Harry Hawk as Trenchard was alone. His voice echoed across the wooden floor of the stage. "Don't know the manners of good society, eh? Wal, I guess I know enough to turn you inside out, you sockdologizing old man-trap."

It was one of the funniest lines in the play, and the audience laughed uproariously. Booth drew a small derringer from his coat pocket; jerked the door open; and with one stride, he was only a few feet from the seated president. Booth stretched his arm straight, aiming the pistol. Then, without hesitation, he pulled the trigger. The laugh partially drowned the sound of the detonation that sent a bullet into Lincoln's head.

The fatal shot entered behind Lincoln's left ear, traveled more than seven inches, shattered the orbital plates of both eye sockets, then halted in the right front hemisphere of his brain.[504]

Major Rathbone's back was to the door when Booth fired his derringer; but at the report of the pistol, he turned and saw the assassin. Rathbone jumped up and lunged for Booth, who pulled out a dagger and tried to stab him. Rathbone parried the blow by striking the knife upward with his arm; but in doing so, he received a long cut from his elbow to his shoulder. Ms. Harris and Mrs. Lincoln sat momentarily stunned as Booth rushed passed them, jumping over the railing and on to the stage. As he was about to jump, Rathbone grabbed at Booth's coat but held it only for a moment before losing his grip. As Booth went over the edge, Rathbone shouted, "Stop that man!"[505]

Booth crouched as he fell off balance, falling on to one knee and put out both hands to break the fall. He rose and exclaimed, "Sic semper tyrannis!" (The Virginia State motto meaning, "Thus always to tyrants!") Booth chose these words because they were the words that Shakespeare gave to Brutus when he struck down Caesar.[506]

He stood up quickly with the "easy agility of an athlete."[507] This statement is significant because it was made before anyone knew that Booth later had a broken ankle. There is reason to now believe that Booth broke his ankle in a fall from his horse somewhere between the bridge crossing into Maryland and the Surratt Tavern.

*     *     *

Standing alone on stage, Harry Hawk saw Booth jump the ten to twelve feet from the president's box, land on stage, and sink briefly to one knee before rising to wave a knife.[508]

After the audience heard the gunshot, what happened next is considerably less certain since many of the patrons that night give conflicting statements.[509]

Most witnesses claimed that Booth turned to the audience and shouted, "Sic semper tyrannis!" Other witnesses who later wrote of the assassination claimed that Booth added another phrase or said something entirely different. The statements of the theater patrons that evening on what they saw and heard varied widely. Booth's phrases most frequently quoted after "Sic semper tyrannis!" are "The South is avenged!" "Revenge for the South!" "I have done it!" and "Virginia is avenged!" There were other witnesses who stated that Booth said nothing. William Flood and Police Superintendent A. C. Richards remembered that Booth shouted "Sic semper tyrannis!" twice while crossing the stage.[510] Dr. Samuel R. Ward, a student at Georgetown University employed at the Treasury Department, had purchased four tickets after reading in the newspaper "that General and Mrs. Grant would accompany" Lincoln to the theater that night. Ward wrote many years later that he read statements by people claiming to have been present that Booth "did not shout 'Sic Semper Tyrannis' but I am sure that he did." However, Dr. Ward does claim that Booth shouted those infamous words while on the presidential balcony before he leaped to the stage.[511]

The sound of the gunshot confused the audience. Some thought it was a shot from outside the theater in postwar celebration, others thought it was an accidental discharge, and still others thought it was part of the play. The confusion over what caused the sound gave Booth the few extra seconds he needed to escape from the crowded theater.

"My God, that's John Booth!" Harry Hawk said. He watched as Booth dragged himself up on one knee and heard Booth shout, "The South shall be free!" Then Booth came toward Hawk waving the knife. Hawk did not know what Booth had done, but seeing the knife flash in his direction, Hawk turned and ran from the stage to his dressing room.[512]

At first, the audience took the shot and sudden appearance of Booth onstage as part of the play. The doorkeeper, John Buckingham, looked at the stage when he heard the shot, saw a man leap down, and recognized him when he stood up.[513] Harry Ford was in the treasurer's office when he heard the shot. He "opened a little window that looked into the theater, [and] saw Booth crouching on the stage with a knife in his hand. Even then," he remembers, "we could not tell what had happened, and no one seemed to know. We thought at first that some one had insulted Booth and he had pursued the man across the stage. A few minutes which seemed an hour, passed before the terrible truth was known."[514]

Edwin A. Emerson, waiting backstage to go on, heard the shot but was not alarmed – he thought it was the sound of a set being shifted. Emerson continued to read his script; however, he looked up in time to see Booth leap from the presidential box. Emerson recalled, "He caught his spur in a flag draped under the box and fell heavily, but this did not prevent him from rushing frantically down to the footlight, brandishing a large bowie knife in his hands, and crying 'Sic semper tyrannis!'"[515]

Backstage, John Mathews, who still had the letter Booth had given him for the *National Intelligencer*, heard what sounded like a shot and decided it was a bit of stage business to frighten the idiotic Lord Dundreary. New stunts at his expense had been added to the play in the past. "That is done for the purpose of frightening Dundreary," Mathews thought and waited for some reaction.[516]

Standing at stage right was young William J. Ferguson; he was to go on next with Laura Keene. Ferguson later wrote, "Almost without pause he recovered himself [from the jump] and arose, . . . Apparently unhurt, three feet to a stride, he rushed across the stage . . . towards where [we] were standing." Ferguson stepped back, and Booth went between him and Keene. "In all, possibly a minute had passed between the time of the pistol report and the moment when he rode out of sight."[517]

During this time, the orchestra leader, William Withers, argued with Ms. Keene about a new song, which had been scheduled to be performed between the first and second acts but which Ms. Keene had decided should be postponed. Withers said he knew Booth and Lincoln, and as he told investigators later, "I knew him [Booth] intimately, and we had played billiards the very night before. I also knew Mr. Lincoln pretty well, for I had taught little Taddy how to play the drum, and he used to drum for the guards."[518]

When Ferguson stepped back, Withers was left standing in Booth's path. Withers describes what happened next:

> I was returning to the orchestra, when I heard the report of a pistol. I stood with astonishment, thinking why they should fire off a pistol in *Our American Cousin.* As I turned round I heard some confusion, and saw a man running toward me with his head down. I did not know what was the matter, and stood completely paralyzed. As he ran, I could not get out of his way, so he hit me on the leg, and turned me round, and made two cuts at me, one in the neck and one on the side, and knocked me from the third entrance down to the second. The scene saved me. As I turned, I got a side view of him, and I saw it was John Wilkes Booth. He then made a rush for the back door, and out he went. I returned to the stage and heard that the president was killed.
>
> Where I stood on the stage was not more than a yard from the [rear] door. He made one plunge at the door, which I believe was shut, and instantly he was out.[519]

Dr. Charles Taft, one of the doctors to attend to Lincoln that night, recalls that after Booth fell to the stage, he sprang "quickly to his feet with the suppleness of an athlete."[520]

For a brief moment, the audience waited for the play to go on.

In the box, Mrs. Lincoln was momentarily stunned by the shot from Booth's pistol. She saw a man rush by her and leap over the balustrade on to the stage.[521]

Rathbone shouted, "Stop that man!"

Ms. Harris immediately echoed him, "Stop that man! Won't somebody stop that man!"

After being bumped by Booth, Laura Keene stepped from the wings on to the stage, and looking up at the presidential box, she called, "What is it? What is the matter?"

"The President is shot!" exclaimed Ms. Harris.

At these words, Mary Lincoln stood up and began to scream hysterically.[522]

It was clear now what had happened; and in an instant, the theater was in an uproar. Actress Helen Truman, who played the daughter Augusta, described the scene:

> Mrs. Lincoln's screams turned the house into an inferno of noise. There will never be anything like it on earth. The shouts groans, curses, smashing of seats, screams of women, shuffling of feet and cries of terror created a pandemonium that must have been more terrible to hear than that attending the assassination of Caesar. Through all the ages it will stand out in my memory as the hell of hells.[523]

E. A. Emerson, who played Lord Dundreary, described what came next, "In the pandemonium which followed, no one seemed to know just what to do."[524] People began jumping up on to the stage and began breaking the music stands and instruments of the orchestra. There was a crush as spectators from the rear pushed forward, knocking some people down. Laura Keene, seeing this surge toward the stage and fearing a riot, shouted to the audience, "Order, order!" And added, "For God's sake, have presence of mind and keep your peace, and all will be well." This appeal fell on deaf ears.[525]

Twenty-three-year-old Dr. Charles Leale heard the shouts that the president had been shot. Leale had been a doctor for six weeks, graduating in March 1865 from Bellevue Hospital Medical College in New York, and was presently stationed at the Army General Hospital at Armory Square. In civilian clothes that night, he went to aid the president. He made his way across the balcony to where men were trying to force open the door to the presidential box. Because of their pushing, it was hard for Major Rathbone to loosen the piece of wood jamming the door. When the outer door finally opened, people poured through, making it difficult for Leale to get inside. When Leale at last could enter, he saw Rathbone holding his wounded arm and asking for help. Leale put his hand under his chin, looked into his eyes, determined that he was in no immediate danger, and went to Lincoln. When Leale identified himself as an army surgeon, Mary Lincoln immediately asked, "Oh, Doctor! Is he dead?"

Leale looked at her startled and then began to examine Lincoln; his job made all the more difficult by Mary's screams. He turned to the men crowding the passageway and hollered out for someone to get water. Leale first looked for a knife wound, thinking Lincoln, like Rathbone, had been stabbed. It was difficult to examine the president because he was still in a seated position, so Leale had him gently lowered on to the floor, Leale holding the injured head. At Leale's direction, someone opened Lincoln's coat and shirt down to his belt. Leale searched the wounded president, but there was no knife wound. He ran his fingers through Lincoln's blood-matted hair and at last found the bullet wound. Leale removed a clot of blood immediately to relieve pressure inside the brain.

Meanwhile, from an orchestra seat, Dr. Charles Taft got up on to the stage, announced that he was a doctor, and asked to be lifted up so that he could climb into the presidential box.[526]

Laura Keene, always a strong-willed person and anxious to know what had happened, raced out of the theater to the alley on the building's south side, up the stairs of the adjoining building, and through a door on to the balcony level near the passageway to the box. From there, she elbowed her way into the president's box and knelt down by his head. Keene was a social acquaintance of the presidential couple, and Mary Lincoln had on several occasions invited Keene to the White House.

Once in the box, Keene appealed to Dr. Leale to allow her to hold Lincoln's head. Dr. Leale granted the request, and she sat on the floor of the box and held his head in her lap.[527]

Leale knew what a great responsibility he had taken on – he must do everything to keep the president alive. Certainly Leale's own heart raced when he saw that Lincoln had stopped breathing. At once, Leale straddled him, opened Lincoln's mouth, and extended two fingers to depress his tongue to allow him to breathe. Lincoln did begin to breathe, but shallowly. To help Lincoln breathe, Leale had two men raise and lower the arms to expand the thorax while Leale pressed the president's diaphragm to force air in and out. He also pushed his right hand beneath the sternum to stimulate the heart. A feeble heartbeat resulted. After a while, it was apparent that Lincoln could continue independent breathing.

Also during these hectic moments, someone brought brandy to the box; and Leale slowly poured a small amount of brandy into Lincoln's mouth. The president was able to swallow.

"How is he?" was the question constantly asked.

"His wound is mortal," Leale announced. "It is impossible for him to recover."

Later Dr. Taft praised Leale for his quick judgment; because of Leale's actions "Mr. Lincoln did not expire in the theater within ten minutes from fatal syncope [lowering of blood pressure]."[528]

Although more experienced doctors presented themselves, Leale, as the first to attend the patient, was by protocol the physician in charge. Leale directed that the president be removed from the crowded box. The president's carriage had been ordered to take him to the White House, but both Dr. Leale and Dr. Taft felt that Lincoln would not survive jouncing the seven blocks to the White House over Washington's rough streets.

The two doctors wanted to make the president more comfortable by taking him to some nearby bed. With the crush of people in the hallway, Leale was force to call out, "Guards, clear the passage! Guards, clear the passage!"[529] There were plenty of volunteers to carry the president. Lincoln was lifted by hands slipped under his body and carried down the winding front stairs to the street and then across the crowded street. Union soldiers cut a path through the chaotic mob of theater patrons who had spilled out into the street. Soldiers and theatergoers ran in confusion. There were close to 1,700 patrons at Ford's Theatre that night, and they were spilling out of the theater and running.

Across the street, Henry Safford, who occupied an apartment on the second floor of the building, stood in front of the house, holding a lighted candle. In response to shouts of "Where can we take him?" Safford responded, "Bring him in here!" and waved them over to the Petersen House. It had been twelve to fifteen minutes since Lincoln had been shot, and continually, Dr. Leale removed clots from Lincoln's wound even as the bearers carried Lincoln across the street. Each time Dr. Leale removed a clot, the president's breathing seemed to improve. All around them was a crowd of people.

Safford directed the people carrying Lincoln to the best room in the building – it was a 9 1/2 by 17 1/2 foot room that had been rented to William T. Clark of Company D, Thirteenth Massachusetts, five days earlier. Clark had been assigned to duty in the Quartermaster's Department. Clark was away at the time and did not return until Sunday.

Clark's modest room held only a bed, table, several chairs, and a bureau on which were photographs of Clark's two sisters and his mother. On the wall was a photographic reproduction of Rosa Bonheur's *The Horse Fair* and engravings of J. F. Herring's *The Village Blacksmith*, *The Stable*, and *The Barnyard*.

Clark had left the room neat and clean. The bed had clean sheets and a worsted Irish bedspread. As the bearers moved through the narrow corridor to the room, Mary Lincoln momentarily lost sight of her husband. She began to scream, "Where is my husband? Where is my husband?" Mary's screams had a telling effect on everyone as the bearers laid Lincoln on the little bed. He was so tall that he had to be laid diagonally across the bed.

\* \* \*

The scene that night was described by the Marquis Adolph de Chambrun: "Opposite the theater where the crime had just been committed, a cordon of troops had been drawn up in front of the small house to which the President had been carried. The soldiers were crying like children but were also dangerously exasperated." It was utterly impossible to get through the line or even to approach it. The tension was so great that at the smallest movement by a bystander, thought Chambrun, a soldier would have fired without hesitation.[530]

Emotions on the street were running high that night as the president lay dying in the Petersen House. The crowds that night irrationally assumed that the actors were responsible for the assassination. There were cries of "Hang the actors!" A storekeeper near Ford's Theatre who spoke out, saying the assassination was not their fault, was nearly hung by a mob. He had a rope around his neck when he was rescued by soldiers.

Senator William Steward was on the streets that night and wrote that "a bloody battle which would have shocked humanity was averted a thousand times that night by a miracle."[531] Dr. Taft wrote of the ugly mood of people on the street. "One man who ventured a shout for Jefferson Davis was set upon and nearly torn to pieces by the infuriated crowd."[532] It seemed that the whole of Washington was out in the streets. Rumors began to spread that Steward and Stanton were killed, that Grant was shot on his way to Philadelphia, and that Vice President Johnson was murdered at the Kirkwood House. Rumors were rife: Lee's surrender at Appomattox had been repudiated and was part of a military strategy to attack Washington, the entire Cabinet had been assassinated, the war would go on, and prisoners in the Old Capitol Prison had broken out and were going to burn the city.

Many people left the theaters, hotels, and restaurants where they had been celebrating and gathered in frightened crowds. Because they were desperate for information, rumors spread quickly. Cavalry riding through the streets to unknown destinations contributed to people's sense of impending danger. By daybreak, however, the fear and rumors were replaced by anger and the need for revenge.[533]

The crowd outside of Ford's Theatre and the Petersen House grew larger and angrier. Some of the military commanders on-site took command of the situation and ordered cavalry to control the crowds. Units of the Union Light Guard arrived to clear the streets, and guards were posted. Other troops under the command of General Christopher Augur, commander of the Department of Washington, were mustered out; and soon the entire city was under military control.[534]

\*     \*     \*

The presidential box, which now would be treated as a crime scene, was not sealed off. Anyone could come in and search the area. William Kent, a government employee, had entered the presidential box immediately after Dr. Leale that evening. Kent had earlier lent Leale his pocketknife so that Leale could cut Lincoln's coat and shirt. Later that evening, Kent could not find the key to his room; and thinking that it may have dropped out of his pocket when he pulled out his knife for Dr. Leale, Kent returned to the presidential box to look for it. Instead, he found Booth's derringer.

Kent turned the derringer over to Lawrence A. Gobright, Washington telegraphic correspondent of the Associated Press, who in turn gave it to the police.[535]

The senselessness of the assassination was apparent to many. Senator Orville Browning noted in his diary:

The Marshal W. H. Lamon has several times within the last two months told me that he believed the President would be assassinated, but I had no fear whatever that such an event would occur. I thought his life of very great importance to the rebels. He was disposed to be very lenient and merciful to them and to smooth the way for their return to their allegiance. I thought him the best friend they had among those in authority and that they were beginning to appreciate that fact, and that his life would be dear to them as to us. It seemed to me that the people in rebellion had many reasons for desiring the continuance of his life, none to wish his death, and I did not think any of the disaffected among us could be insane and fiendish enough to perpetrate the deed.[536]

George T. Strong, on the other hand, wrote in his diary for April 15, "I have been expecting this. I predicted an attempt would be made on Lincoln's life when he went to Richmond; but just now, I should have said the danger was past."[537]

The *New York Times* on April 17, 1865, reported that Secretary of State Seward had information on a conspiracy to assassinate the president and others, but that these rumors "were so common that the admonition was disregarded," with the editors adding in hindsight "though but for Mr. Seward's serious accident precautionary steps would have been taken."[538]

# CHAPTER 14

## *That Awful Night*

At about the same time that Booth pulled the trigger at Ford's Theatre, Powell and Herold arrived at Secretary of State Seward's house near Lafayette Park. Powell had come armed with a pistol and knife, and Herold was to wait outside while Powell murdered Seward. Then he would lead Powell out of Washington. Although Powell had been in Washington a number of times, he still did not know his way around the city. Sixty-three-year-old Seward was in bed recovering from his carriage accident. Powell's plan was to gain entrance to the house by posing as a messenger delivering medicine from Dr. Tuillio Verdi, Seward's physician.

Ten o'clock that night, Dr. Norris, one of Seward's doctors, examined the secretary of state and left. The gaslights were then turned low, and the household was settling down for the night. Upstairs, Fanny Seward was reading to her father from the *Legends of Charlemagne*, and Seward was beginning to fall asleep.[539]

Fifteen minutes later, Powell rang the doorbell; and William Bell, the nineteen-year-old black servant, answered the door.

"I bring medicine sent by Dr. Verdi," Powell said. But Bell declined to let Powell in, at which he protested, "The medicine must be delivered to Seward personally. I must deliver it."

Powell realized by Bell's demeanor that arguing was useless. All at once, Powell pushed passed Bell into the hall and raced up the stairs. When Powell reached the third floor, he was met by Frederick Seward Jr. who had come out of one of the rooms. Astonished at seeing the tall stranger, Seward Jr. blurted out, "What are you doing in the house?"

"I have to deliver medicine in person," Powell replied. But the words came out unconvincingly; and young Seward, angry and suspicious, told Powell that the secretary was asleep. "He cannot be disturbed. Just leave the medicine!" young Seward said tersely.

Fanny in her father's room heard the commotion and opened the door to the hallway. Powell peered behind her and saw Seward. Quickly he asked, "Is the secretary asleep?"

"Almost" was her reply. Immediately Frederick Seward pushed her back inside and closed his father's door.

He turned to Powell. "Well if you will not give me the message, go back and tell the doctor I refused to let you see Mr. Seward. I am his son, and the assistant secretary of state. Go back and tell the doctor that I refused to let you go into the sickroom because Mr. Seward was sleeping."[540]

"I must see him! I must see the Secretary of State personally!" Powell insisted in vain. At last Powell realized that he was not to be admitted.

Disingenuously, Powell said, "Very well, sir, I will go."

He started down the stairs and then suddenly turned, pulled out an 1858 Whitney navy revolver, and fired at young Seward. But the revolver misfired. Powell, a powerfully built man, rushed at young Seward, bludgeoning him with the gun butt. Powell fractured Seward's skull, but young man was still conscious and grabbed Powell. The two struggled on the landing. They crashed against the door to Seward's room; it flew open, and the two fell into the dimly lit room.

Downstairs, Sergeant Robinson of the Eighth Maine Volunteers, who had been assigned as Secretary Seward's nurse during his recuperation, heard Fanny's scream. He rushed up the stairs and into Seward's room. As he entered, Powell, knife in hand, slashed him on the forehead, sending him to the floor. Powell, with a gun in one hand and a knife in the other, threw Fanny out of the way. Powell jumped onto Seward's bed and began to slash Seward about his face and neck with the knife.

At first, Fanny thought that this must be a "fearful dream," then she began screaming.[541] Robinson got to his feet and, seeing Powell on the bed, jumped on to his back. But Powell was big and powerful and stabbed twice into Robinson's shoulder.

From his bedroom, Augustus, another of Seward's sons, heard Fanny's screams and ran to his father's room. Augustus, who had just awoke, saw the two men struggling on the bed. In the dim light, he thought the nurse was trying to murder his father. Augustus grabbed Sergeant Robinson, giving Powell a chance to get free. For his efforts, Augustus was stabbed in the head and left hand. In the ensuing melee, Powell shouted, "I'm mad, I'm mad!" apparently realizing for the first time exactly what he was doing.

Secretary Seward had rolled off the bed toward the wall and out of harm's way. The protective brace around his neck that supported his fractured jawbone saved him from the brunt of Powell's knife attack although he did receive one serious cut on the right cheek from his ear to near his mouth. Powell at last realized that the situation was quickly getting out of hand and that he might soon be trapped in this small room. He broke away and raced down the stairs.

At that moment, Emerick Hansell, a State Department messenger, arrived at the front door of the Seward residence. Powell in his panic stabbed the unsuspecting Hansell in the chest, just missing his lungs but leaving him severely wounded and bleeding. Powell ran out into the street, leaving his Whitney revolver and brown hat behind.[542]

Powell ran to his horse and looked around wildly for Herold. Herold, hearing Bell and the screams from the Seward house, panicked and fled without waiting for Powell. Bell, hearing the scuffle upstairs, had rushed into the street, shouting, "Murder! Murder!"

Powell with the mayhem behind him ran out of the house and mounted his horse; but in his haste, he dropped his silver-mounted bowie knife. The knife, decorated in a Florida alligator motif and the words, "The Hunter's Companion – Real Life Defender," was found the next morning opposite Secretary Seward's house.[543]

To avoid suspicion, Powell at first kept his horse at a walk. However, with Bell still sounding the alarm, Powell soon raced off into the night at a gallop, leaving the five wounded people behind.[544]

Herold's flight left Powell without a guide. To escape Washington, Powell would have to cross one of the two bridges across the Eastern Branch of the Potomac – the Navy Yard Bridge or the Bennings Bridge. The bridges were only a half mile apart; but without Herold, Powell was quickly lost – he had no idea of the layout of the city. The conspirators had agreed to meet about ten miles southeast of Washington and from there to escape to Virginia crossing the Potomac River.

Powell rode his horse so hard that night that the horse fell and became lame. Powell and the horse reached one of the many hospitals in Washington, Lincoln Hospital, just east of the capitol. At a little after one o'clock, Lieutenant John F. Toffey found the horse "by the dispensary of the hospital" and found "the horse was blind of one eye." He "noticed that he was a little lame" and that "the sweat was pouring off him and had made a regular puddle on the ground."[545] Powell had ridden the one-eyed horse Booth had purchased from George Gardiner, Dr. Mudd's neighbor.

After leaving the horse, Powell, confused and frightened, climbed a stout tree and spent the night there. When day broke, Powell "heard the rush of cavalry and peering forth, saw them distinctly as they passed by on their search for the murderers. This rush of cavalry continued all day long, so Powell remained in the tree." The next night, Powell tried to "escape to Baltimore and proceeded in the darkness of night in that direction." He may have thought that the Branson sisters would take care of him; whatever his motivation, Powell got lost again.[546]

*   *   *

Early that evening, Secretary of War Stanton visited Seward. Upon returning home, he dismissed his servants and was undressing for bed when a messenger arrived to tell him about the attack on Seward. Stanton's wife, who answered the front door, told her husband, "Mr. Seward is murdered!"

"Humbug! I left him only an hour ago" was Stanton's first reaction.

Still he hurried, went downstairs, and, after being convinced of the assault by the messenger, took a carriage to Seward's house. There he found the injured secretary of state and Secretary of the Navy Gideon Welles, who had just arrived. He told Stantion that the president had been shot and was still at the theater.[547]

Those who were sent to tell what happened to Seward met those who told of what had happened to Lincoln. The news brought panic to Washington in the hours after the assassination.

Welles and Stanton left immediately to go to the president's side. They ordered General Montgomery C. Meigs, quartermaster general, who had also arrived, to take charge of Seward's house.[548] He, like many others, thought that no harm could come to him. He did, however, think that others might be in danger and ordered guards at the homes of all the cabinet members and of Vice President Johnson. Then Stanton, Wells, and Justice Cartter left in a carriage with a cavalry escort that Meigs ordered for their safety.[549]

A little after eleven o'clock, they arrived at the theater and found that Lincoln had been moved across the street to the Petersen House. The little room where Lincoln lay unconscious was becoming more and more crowded with people who felt they ought to be present at the event. Guards outside the building had to struggle with an ever-growing crowd of people who also wanted to go in.

Stanton did a quick assessment and took immediate charge of the situation. He set up a command post in one of the rooms of the Petersen House.[550]

Stanton was convinced that he faced a rebel plot and that the war had resumed. Decisively, he put military posts in and around Washington on alert. With Lincoln unconscious and dying and Vice President Johnson unable to assume authority until Lincoln's death, the task of running the government defaulted to Stanton. Soon cavalry patrols were racing through the streets of Washington. On Stanton's orders, Justice Cartter began to write down statements from individuals who had been in Ford's Theatre.

*     *     *

Atzerodt took his mare to Naylor's livery stable about one o'clock that afternoon to be stabled and fed. From April 3 to 12, Atzerodt had stabled the brown one-eyed horse there that Powell would later use. John Fletcher, the foreman, asked Atzerodt what had become of the one-eyed horse, and Atzerodt replied "that he had sold him in Montgomery County."

A little before seven that evening, Atzerodt returned to the stable and had his horse saddled. "If I stay until morning, how much are you going to charge me again?"

"Only fifty cents more," Fletcher replied.

Atzerodt left without the horse and returned at about seven thirty in the evening and requested that Fletcher "not to take the saddle or bridle off that mare until ten o'clock, and to keep the stable open for him."

At ten o'clock when Atzerodt came back at the stable, Herold had not yet returned with the horse as he had promised. Atzerodt asked Fletcher "to have something to drink with him." Fletcher readily agreed. He wanted to ask about the horse Herold had not returned. The two went down to the nearby Union Hotel. Fletcher had a beer, and Atzerodt "took some whiskey"; and then they returned to the stable. As Atzerodt mounted the mare to leave, Fletcher said, "Your acquaintance is staying out very late with our horse."

"Oh!" Atzerodt answered, defending Herold. "He will be back after a while."[551]

Fletcher did not find him convincing and decided that the two were trying to steal his horse. When Atzerodt rode off, Fletcher followed him on the chance he would see Herold. Atzerodt went to the Kirkwood House, and Fletcher "watched until he came out, and mounted the mare again. He went along D Street, turning north at Tenth Street."[552]

Atzerodt had told Booth outright that he did not want to assassinate Johnson and made no attempt to do so. He had protested that he had never agreed to kill anyone. Atzerodt probably recognized that it was too late to save the Confederacy with political assassinations, or he realized the folly of what he had been asked to do. Lincoln was right when he said that anyone who set his mind to kill him could do so but that they would hang for it.

In any case, Atzerodt rode off; and Fletcher returned to Naylor's livery stable. Meanwhile, Fletcher did not give up trying to find his horse. He set out on foot:

> I came upon Pennsylvania Avenue close to Willard's; and then I saw Herold riding the roan horse belonging to Mr. Naylor that I had hired him. The horse seemed as if he wanted to go to the stable. I thought, if I could get close enough to him, that I would take the horse from him; but I expect he knew me by the light of the gas – the lamp at Willard's corner. He began to move the horse away a little. Said I, "You get off that horse now! You have had that horse out long enough." He put spurs into the horse, and went up Fourteenth Street.

Fletcher returned to the stable to get a horse. He began to search for Herald though the streets of Washington. Fletcher continues:

> On the south side of the Capitol. I there met a gentleman coming down; and I asked him if he saw any men going up there, riding on horseback. He said yes, and that they were riding very fast . . . . I followed on until I got to the Navy-Yard Bridge and the guard there halted me, and called for the sergeant of the guard. He came out, and I asked him if a roan horse had crossed that bridge, giving him a description of the horse, saddle, and bridle, and the man that was riding."

"Yes, he has gone across the bridge," responded Sergeant Cobb of the Third Massachusetts Heavy Artillery. During the war, all bridges heading south out of

Washington had been closed at sunset. Regulations were still in force but greatly relaxed. On April 13, Lincoln had ordered the end of restrictions on travel between Washington and the former Confederate states.

"Did he stay long here?" asked Fletcher.

"He said that he was waiting for an acquaintance of his that was coming on," Cobb responded, "but he did not wait, and another man came riding a bay horse or a bay mare, right after him."

"Did he tell you his name?"

"Yes, he said his name was Smith."

Then Fletcher asked if he could cross the bridge after them.

"Yes, you can cross, but you cannot return."

"If that is so, I will not go," decided Fletcher. Reluctantly he turned around and returned to the city.[553]

When Fletcher returned to the city, he looked at his watch and noted that it was ten minutes to twelve. He stopped at Murphy's stable to see the foreman, Dorsey, and asked whether Herold's "roan horse had been put up there."

"No," Dorsey replied, "but you had better keep in; for President Lincoln is shot, and Secretary Seward is almost dead."

Fletcher, shocked, returned to the stable and put up his horse. It was one thirty when he sat on a chair outside the office window. He heard from people passing on the sidewalk that men riding horseback had shot President Lincoln.

Suddenly Fletcher put it all together – Atzerodt had left the stable strangely late at night, and Herold had kept out a horse. Fletcher's suspicions were aroused. He stopped a passing cavalry sergeant and told him all that had happened. The sergeant, in turn, told Fletcher to go to the local police station. So Fletcher walked over to the station where he spoke to Detective Charles Stone, who listened carefully and then took him to see General Augur.

Fletcher told the general Herold's name, description, and age and that he had pursued Herold to the Navy Yard Bridge.

In Augur's office was the saddle and bridle from Powell's horse, which Fletcher recognized immediately. General Augur asked the description of the horse that had worn that saddle and bridle, and Fletcher told him of the one-eyed horse. Fletcher did not know Atzerodt's name, but he did have it in a card file back at the stable.

General Augur and Detective Stone immediately knew they were on to Lincoln's assassins and took Fletcher back to his stable to get Atzerodt's name off the card. The connection to the conspirators was being made – names were beginning to appear. Fletcher had given General Augur Atzerodt's and Herold's name.[554] Fletcher told General Augur that Herold and Atzerodt were acquainted.

By two o'clock, General Augur had four names: John Wilkes Booth, identified as the man who shot Lincoln; John Surratt was identified as a close friend of Booth and suspected of the attempted murder of Secretary of State Seward; David Herold; and George Atzerodt.

General Augur knew Herold had crossed the Navy Yard Bridge; and from Sergeant Cobb, he later learned that a man giving his name as Booth had also crossed the bridge close to eleven o'clock. The Navy Yard Bridge had been officially closed at nine o'clock, after which, it was up to the discretion of the guard on duty to permit passage.

General Augur ordered the Thirteenth New York Cavalry, commanded by Lieutenant David Dana, provost marshal at Fort Baker, to look for the men in Prince George's County.

Acting on Fletcher's information to Detective Charles Stone, Superintendent of Police Richards, sent his own search party into Prince George's County and brought Fletcher along.

Police were able to trace George Atzerodt from information on his stable card. They went to the Pennsylvania House where he said he was staying. John Greenawalt, the proprietor, told them that Atzerodt had stayed the one night and had left very early that morning without paying his bill.

*   *   *

John Lee, a military detective, was sent to the Kirkwood House that night by Washington Provost Marshal James R. O'Beirne to check out the security where Vice President Andrew Johnson was staying. While in the barroom Lee learned that a suspicious-looking man had taken a room the previous day. The hotel register showed that G. A. Atzerodt, Charles County, had room number 126 and had signed in before eight o'clock on the morning of April 14. Lee at once went to the room and tried the door, but it was locked.

"Get the key to this door!" Lee commanded.

When the clerk could not find a key, Lee eyed the door purposefully. Then he backed up and rushed at the door, shoulder first. There was a mighty thud and then a cracking of the thin veneer that held the latch, and the door flew open.

The room was empty. Lee found a black coat, a "revolver, loaded and capped, and three embroidered handkerchieves – one with the name "Mary R. E. Booth," another with the name "F. M. Nelson" (Herold's brother-in-law), and another with the letter *H* in the corner. There were three boxes of Colt's cartridges and some personal items. The most damning item of all was in the pocket of Atzerodt's coat. It was a bankbook; on the inside of the book was inscribed "Mr. J. Wilkes Booth in account with the Ontario Bank, Canada, 1864: October 27; by deposit, cr. $455." There was also a map of Virginia.[555]

Atzerodt, however, never actually slept at the Kirkwood. The night of the assassination, he stayed at the Pennsylvania House. These items connected Herold, Atzerodt, and Booth.

*   *   *

William A. Browning, President Johnson's private secretary, told investigators that between four and five o'clock in the afternoon of the assassination, he had found Booth's card in his box; the card for the vice president was mistakenly given to him.[556] Browning had known Booth when he was playing in Nashville and thought perhaps Booth remembered him and was in town to do a play.

"It is from Booth; is he playing here?" Browning remarked to the clerk when he picked up the card.[557]

*   *   *

Vice President Johnson was at the capitol most of the morning of the fourteenth. He saw Lincoln that afternoon, had dinner at the Kirkwood House at five o'clock, and did not leave the hotel that evening. Former governor Leonard Farwell of Wisconsin and inspector of inventions in the patent office asked the vice president to join him at the theater that night; however, Johnson had declined, and Farwell had gone to Ford's Theatre by himself.

In the theater, as soon as Farwell realized that Lincoln had been shot, he ran to the Kirkwood House. Breathless, he burst into the hotel lobby and shouted at the desk clerk to guard the stairs. Farwell ran up to suite 65 and began beating on the door, shouting, "Governor Johnson!" Farwell was forgetting for the moment that Johnson was no longer military governor of Tennessee. "Governor Johnson! If you are in this room, I must see you!"

"Farwell, is that you?" replied Johnson.

"Yes! Let me in!"

Johnson opened the door; and Farwell pushed by him, slammed the door shut, and fastened the lock. "Lincoln has been shot." Guards, on Stanton's orders, soon began to assemble around Johnson's room. With Secretary of State Seward already seriously wounded, no one knew just how widespread the assassination plots were.

Farwell went back to Ford's Theatre to get more firsthand information about Lincoln's condition. When he reported back to Johnson on Lincoln's grave condition, Johnson decided to go to Lincoln's side. He met opposition from his guards – such a trip would be too dangerous. Major James R. O'Beirne, the provost marshal of the District of Columbia, offered Johnson troop protection; but Johnson declined. Like Lincoln, he felt that no harm would come to him.

Johnson left the Kirkwood House accompanied only by Farwell and O'Beirne. The three went to the Petersen House, where Johnson paid his respects. However, he did not stay long, knowing that Mary Lincoln detested him.[558]

# CHAPTER 15

## *He Belongs to the Angels Now*

In the front parlor of the Peterson House, Mrs. Lincoln sat on a horsehair sofa with Ms. Harris. Mary Lincoln spent the evening shrieking and crying.

She stared at the blood spattered across Harris's dress. "Oh, my husband's blood, my dear husband's blood!" Mrs. Lincoln kept screaming. It was not, however, President Lincoln's blood; it was that of Major Rathbone from his knife wound. Lincoln had bled very little. When Major Rathbone had fainted, Ms. Harris had come to his aid, wrapping her handkerchief around his wound. Rathbone was later given medical attention and driven home.

"Oh, why didn't he kill me? Why didn't he kill me? Kill me! Kill me! Kill me too!" screamed Mrs. Lincoln. Periodically, to everyone's discomfort, she got up and went into the small room where her husband lay.

"Do live! Do speak to me!" Mary Lincoln pleaded with her unconscious husband. "Live but for one moment to speak to me once, to speak to our children." She turned to one of the men. "Send for Tad; he will speak to Tad; he loves him so!"[559]

Tad, who had been watching *Aladdin! Or His Wonderful Lamp*, starring the actress Effie Germon, at the Grover's Theatre, had been whisked away when the news of Lincoln being shot arrived. Then the assistant manager at Grover announced to the audience that Lincoln had been shot. No one knew how serious Lincoln's wound was. Tad was immediately brought back to the White House and was met by doorkeeper Thomas Pendel.

Tad cried, "Oh, Tom Pen! Tom Pen! They have killed Papa dead. They've killed Papa dead!"[560]

Pendel took the anguished child to his bedroom and sat with him until the boy fell asleep.

Back at Grover's Theatre, the assistant manager telegraphed Leonard Grover, the owner, who was in New York. He told Grover what had happened, at which Grover was shocked and appalled.

"Thank God, it wasn't ours" was Grover's reply.[561]

\* \* \*

In the meantime, Judge Cartter quickly received reports about who had shot the president. Harry Hawk told what he knew. Laura Keene, whose intellect was quite sharp, said that she did not know who had fired the shot but that she did know who had jumped from the box.

There was never any doubt about what had occurred. The murder was not committed in the dark of night; but in a well-lit theater in front of seventeen hundred theatergoers, many of them knew Booth.

As Judge Cartter began to take testimony of witnesses, he realized he needed someone proficient in shorthand. General Augur called out to the crowd for anyone who knew stenography; and James Tanner, hearing of the request, volunteered his services. Tanner rented a room in a house adjoining the Petersen House.

Tanner, who had lost both legs below the knee at the Second Battle of Bull Run, used artificial legs and a cane. After recuperating from his wounds, he then studied at Ames's Business College in Syracuse, New York, and later obtained a position with the Ordnance Bureau of the War Department in Washington. Tanner started at midnight taking down witnesses' statements, and he finished up at about 1:30 AM. In Tanner's opinion, only fifteen minutes had gone by before he had taken "testimony enough down to hang Wilkes Booth, the assassin, higher than ever Haman hung."[562] And in a Washington police log, there was an entry for eleven o'clock, naming Booth as the assassin.[563]

\* \* \*

The Grants arrived in Philadelphia about midnight. They were going to cross the Delaware River by ferry and continue their journey to Burlington but paused at the Bloodgood's Hotel near the ferry station to get something to eat. It was here that General Grant received a telegram telling him of the assassination of Lincoln. Immediately, Grant ordered a train to take him back to Washington. Because the details of getting the train would take hours, General Grant took his wife to Burlington, only an hour away, and returned to Philadelphia in time to board the train to Washington. Stanton telegraphed General Grant in Philadelphia and cautioned him to watch closely "all persons who come near you in the cars" and to have an engine "in front of the train to guard against anything being on the track."[564] He arrived there around ten o'clock the next morning.[565]

By midnight, Stanton had sent telegrams naming Booth as the assassin to all federal military forts and batteries in the Washington area and had armed guards to protect the vice president.[566]

Stanton sent messages on Lincoln's condition to General John A. Dix, the commanding general in New York City. According to protocol, important military or government news would be distributed to the press through General Dix's office. The first message to Dix sent at two fifteen in the morning did not mention Booth. The second, sent at three twenty that morning, did. Stanton notified other government officials and posted military guards to protect them from possible assassination. He thus insured the security of the city as he assessed the extent of the conspiracy against the government. He also investigated the attempt on Seward's life as well as interviewing eyewitnesses. Stanton waited four hours to notify the press the identity of the assassin. He was distracted and delayed by his other activities.

The *New York Tribune* beat Stanton's announcement and was the first on the street with the news of the assassination and later with naming Booth as the assassin.[567]

The federal government was unprepared for the massive manhunt it was to undertake. Although the investigation started quickly, it was uncoordinated. The investigating agencies through jealousy or inefficiency were reluctant to share information. When reward money was posted, it soon became every investigator or soldier for himself.

Before midnight on April 14, the naval station at St. Inigoes, Maryland, the telegraph station closest to Port Tobacco near the mouth of the Potomac, was warned that "an attempt has been made this p.m. to assassinate the President and the Secretary of State" and that the parties to the assassination "may escape or attempt to escape across the Potomac."[568]

*   *   *

Robert Lincoln, who had declined his mother's invitation to go to Ford's Theatre because he was exhausted, was in bed at the White House when his father was assassinated. When the news reached him, Robert immediately went to the Petersen House and stayed by his father until he died the next morning.

For the rest of his life, Robert Lincoln believed that had he gone to the play with his parents, he would have had a good chance of sounding the alarm before Booth could shoot. As the junior member of the theater party, Robert would have been sitting in the back of the box, and Booth would have had to pass him in order to approach the president with his small derringer.[569]

*   *   *

Almost immediately, Stanton, as well as the public, assumed that the assassination was the result of a grand Confederate conspiracy hatched in Richmond. After the brutal and costly war, it was natural for people in the North to believe that the Confederate government was involved in the act.

On the night of April 14, William Eaton, a War Department detective, searched Booth's room at the National Hotel and seized Booth's trunk. He turned it over to Lieutenant William H. Terry of the War Department.[570] Among the papers in the trunk was the March 27 letter from Arnold suggesting to Booth that they delay their plans and that Booth not "act rashly or in haste." Arnold had implicated himself by writing, "I would prefer your first query, go and see how it will be taken at Richmond, and ere long I shall be better prepared to again be with you."[571]

At 4:44 AM, Stanton wired Major General Dix, commander of the Union Army in Maryland, "It appears from a letter found in Booth's trunk that the murder was planned before the fourth of March, but fell through then because the accomplices backed out until 'Richmond could be heard from.'"[572]

A Confederate cipher was also found in Booth's room. It was the standard Vegenere alphabetical square used by the Confederacy to encipher and decipher communications. Although Booth possessed the cipher and knew how to use it, no communications from him have ever been found in the Confederate archives, nor are there any first person statements that Booth ever used the cipher.[573]

"Damn the rebels, this is their work," Secretary of the Navy Gideon Welles said to his wife after learning of Lincoln's assassination.[574] Edward Bates, former attorney general, wrote that Booth's cry of "Sic Semper Tyrannis" may have been "a clue to the unraveling of a great conspiracy, for this assassination is not the act of one man; but only one scene of a great drama."[575] Another cry, which typified the feeling of many, was expressed by David McDonald, "Damned – eternally damned – be the assassin! Doubly damned be the instigators to the crime. May the infernal gods sweep them all to hell in a hurricane of fire!"[576]

Secretary Stanton and the judge adjutant's office were only too willing to believe in a high-level Confederate conspiracy rather than that the men involved had acted on their own. Dripping revenge, General Boutwell wrote to General Butler: "If there be evidence connecting any of the rebel leaders with the plot to assassinate the President, indictments should be found that we may follow them to other countries. It is not unlikely that Davis, Breckinridge and Benjamin had a hand in the business."[577]

Stanton and others were concerned that news of the assassination might cause federal troops to carry out wanton reprisals against Confederates. To prevent any type of reprisals, news of the assassination was withheld from the armies in the South for a few days.

\*     \*     \*

During the vigil at the Petersen House, Mary Lincoln was becoming more hysterical. Repeatedly she kept crying, "Why didn't he kill me?" Her screams were putting everyone on edge. At last, Robert Lincoln sent a messenger to the home of Senator James Dixon of Connecticut to ask Mrs. Dixon, a close personal friend of Mary Lincoln, to come comfort his mother. She was in bed when the messenger arrived, but she dressed quickly and hurried to Mary Lincoln's side when she learned of the shooting and that Mrs. Lincoln needed her.[578] Mrs. Dixon stayed all that early morning with Mary, and at intervals, she helped Mary walk to her husband's bedside.

Throughout the night, doctors continued to examine Lincoln; however, there was nothing they could do for him. The bullet had driven an inch-wide piece of bone three inches into his brain. The doctors put mustard plasters and hot water bottles on the wound. The damage to his brain was irreparable, and the doctors could only make Lincoln as comfortable as possible as he lay dying. When symptoms indicated pressure under the wound, Dr. Leale cleared the opening of the clots so blood could flow and relieve pressure on the brain.[579]

During that night, Dr. Leale held Lincoln's hand so that if he recovered consciousness, he would know someone was with him and "that he was in touch with humanity and had a friend."[580]

The light rain that had been falling the previous evening increased in the early morning hours of April 15, and by dawn, the rain was drenching the crowd that jammed the streets from F Street to Pennsylvania Avenue. Tanner finished transcribing his notes, and Lincoln's breathing became more difficult.

Throughout the night, Mrs. Lincoln made repeated trips from the parlor to the bedside of her dying husband. To save her further emotional pain, "clean napkins were laid over the crimson stains on the pillow" when she came in. On her last visit to see her husband, Mary fainted. After being revived, she pleaded with Lincoln, "Love, live but for one moment to speak to me once, to speak to our children!"[581]

Sixteen physicians saw Lincoln that night and perhaps as many as sixty-five people went into and out of the room. These included several congressmen and cabinet officers.

One of the many people crowded into Lincoln's room when he died was Assistant Secretary of the Treasury Maunsell B. Field. He described Lincoln's last moments:

> About 7 o'clock a change occurred, and the breathing, which had been continuous, was interrupted at intervals. These intervals became more frequent and of longer duration, and the breathing more feeble. Several times the interval was so long that we thought him dead, and the surgeon applied his finger to the pulse, evidently to ascertain if such was the fact. But it was not till 22 minutes past 7 o'clock in the morning that the flame flickered out. There was no apparent suffering no convulsive action, no ratting of the throat, none of the ordinary premonitory symptoms of death. Death in this case was a mere cessation of breathing.[582]

Rev. Phineas D. Gurley, the clergyman of the New York Avenue Presbyterian Church, began to pray. At the end of his prayer, he said, "Thy will be done. Amen." "Amen," the others in the room echoed. At this point, Stanton said, "He belongs to the angels now."[583]

Stanton had often been considered cold and uncaring; however, on that night, he had tears rolling down his cheeks. Corporal Tanner later remembered, "I knew it was only by a powerful effort that he restrained himself and that he was near a break."[584]

One of the young surgeons present reverently placed silver half dollars upon Lincoln's eyes to keep them closed, and the white bedsheet was drawn up over Lincoln's face.[585] Mary Lincoln continued to sob and moan. She leaned on the arm of Robert, who escorted her to her carriage. As she was leaving the Petersen House, Mary looked across the street at Ford's Theatre and said, "Oh, that dreadful house! That dreadful house!"[586]

The gears of government began to slowly grind forward to organize the greatest manhunt in American history. In the Petersen House, Stanton set up a headquarters to hunt for the assassin. Stanton told Tanner "to take charge of the testimony" he had written down.[587] By telegraph, Stanton alerted military commanders of the assassination and ordered them to arrest and detain all suspicious individuals. After Lincoln died, the cabinet assembled, with the exception of Seward and McCulloch, in the back parlor of the Petersen House. There they signed a letter prepared by Attorney General Speed to Vice President Johnson, officially informing him of the president's death and that he was now president.[588]

The cabinet assembled in the Kirkwood House to witness Johnson's taking the oath of office as president of the United States. The ceremony was brief, and all witnesses were deeply moved by the circumstance that had brought them there. At noon, Johnson's first cabinet meeting was held at Secretary McCulloch's office in the Treasury Building. Johnson asked all the cabinet members to retain their positions. Because Seward was still unable to resume his position as secretary of state, Johnson appointed William Hunter (chief clerk of the State Department) as acting secretary of state until Seward recovered from his wounds. Johnson also began arrangements for Lincoln's funeral.[589]

Lincoln was being seen in a different light now. Because of his horrific death, Lincoln's image was making the transition in most people's minds from a hated buffoon to a beloved martyr. They wanted revenge.

# CHAPTER 16

## *This Appalling Crime*

When John Wilkes Booth was pulling the trigger, mother was in New York, Asia was in Philadelphia awaiting the birth of a child, Junius Jr. was playing in Cincinnati, and Edwin was in Boston.

The reaction in Washington to the news of the assassination that Saturday morning neared the point of group hysteria. Most of it out of fear that the South had somehow regrouped and was preparing to invade Washington. Mobs of men wandered the streets prepared to kill anyone known to have "secesh" feelings or who did not advocate the most violent punishment for the conspirators.

Booth was widely condemned. On Easter Sunday, from churches across the country, Booth was denounced as "an accursed devil . . . fiend . . . miserable, wretched assassin . . . demon in human form . . . debased assassin." In Massachusetts, a minister who did not deliver a sermon on the assassination was summarily dismissed by his congregation.

Booth was widely condemned in Europe, where kings and queens feared and hated assassins. "In the night the shadow of a great and ghastly crime had passed over the land," wrote the *Times of London* New York correspondent. Booth was thought of as the vilest assassin known to history and would own an "immortality of infamy."[590]

Expressions of sympathy began to arrive not only from every state but from all over the world: the Duke of Brunswick, the Corps Legislatif of France, Count Bismarck and the Prussian House of Deputies, His Highness Aali Pacha of Turkey, Queen Victoria, and the Empress Eugenie called the assassination a "horrid crime . . . cowardly, cruel atrocity . . . odious act, appalling tragedy."[591]

It was not only in the North that Booth was universally condemned but also in the South. "The heaviest blow which has ever fallen upon the people of the South has descended," said the *Richmond Whig*. "The assassination was an appalling, deplorable calamity, a terrible blow to the South."[592]

From Virginia, Governor Pierrepont wrote to Stanton:

Loyal Virginia sends her tribute of mourning for the fall of the Nation's President by the hands of a dastardly agent of treason, who dared to repeat the motto of our State at the moment of the perpetration of his accursed crime.[593]

On April 16, 1865, General Ewell and sixteen other Confederate generals who were prisoners of war at Fort Warren, Massachusetts, wrote the following letter:

Lieut.-Gen. U.S. Grant,
Commanding U.S. Army.

General:

You will appreciate, I am sure, the sentiment which prompts me to drop you these lines. Of all the misfortunes which could befall the Southern people, or any Southern man, by far the greatest, in my judgment, would be the prevalence of the idea that they could entertain any other than feelings of unqualified abhorrence and indignation for the assassination of the President of the United States and the attempt to assassinate the Secretary of State. No language can adequately express the shock produced upon myself, in common with all the other general officers confined here with me, by the occurrence of this appalling crime, and by the seeming tendency in the public mind to connect the South and Southern men with it. Need we say that we are not assassins, nor the allies of assassins, be they from the North or from the South, and that coming as we do from most of the States of the South we would be ashamed of our own people, were we not assured that they will reprobate this crime.

An endorsement by Major Appleton was attached to the letter and forwarded by General Hoffman to General Grant.

"The general officers confined at this post as prisoners of war have, from the moment of the reception of the news, expressed their regret for the loss of President Lincoln, and their utmost horror of the act and detestation of his murderers."[594]

In Memphis, "nearly the whole city was trapped in the habiliments of mourning and the sorrow owned to be universal." General Banks gave a speech in that city in which he said of Lincoln, "In the President you have lost a friend, a protector, who, while he vindicated the rights of the nation, was not willing that a hair on your heads should be harmed beyond what necessity demanded." [Applause][595]

John Nicolay, one of Lincoln's secretaries, returned from Cuba on April 17 and on April 18 wrote to his wife about the atmosphere of Washington after the assassination:

Our ship arrived safely at the Navy Yard at about 2 1/2 P.M. yesterday. I cannot describe to you the air of gloom which seems to hang over the city.

As I drove up here from the Navy Yard almost every house was draped and closed, and men stood idle and listless in groups on the street corners. The Executive Mansion was dark and still as almost the grave itself. The silence and gloom and sorrow depicted on every face are as heavy and ominous of terror as if some greater calamity still hung in the air, and was about to crush and overwhelm everyone.

This morning the house is deeply draped in mourning, and the corpse is laid in state in the East Room, where great crowds are taking their last look at the President's kind face, mild and benignant as becomes the father of a mourning nation, even in death. The funeral will take place tomorrow.[596]

In the midst of mourning, rumors spread of attempts against Stanton, Secretary of the Interior John P. Usher, Senator Charles Sumner, Chief Justice Salmon P. Chase, and Judge Advocate Joseph Holt. Military guards were placed at all their homes and offices.

\*   \*   \*

When Jefferson Davis arrived in Charlotte, North Carolina, news of the assassination had not yet been delivered. A crowd, including some soldiers who recognized Davis, quickly gathered and asked him to speak. Davis gave a speech acknowledging that the condition of the Confederacy was poor. However, Davis was truly the last Confederate. "The cause is not yet dead!" he shouted to the audience. "And only show by your determination and fortitude that you are willing to suffer yet longer, and we may still hope for success."

After the speech was given, Major John C. Courtney, a telegraph operator, handed Davis a telegram from his Secretary of War Breckinridge.

It read: "President Lincoln assassinated in the theatre in Washington . . . Seward's house was entered on the same night and he was repeatedly stabbed and is probably mortally wounded." After Davis read it, he had the telegram read to the crowd. Some cheered but most realized the gravity of the news. Davis gave a stern look of reproof to those in the crowd who had cheered. All accounts of that day agree that Davis voiced regret at Lincoln's assassination.

At first, Davis did not know whether to believe the news. During the war, rumors were numerous and generally unfounded. While still in Charlotte, North Carolina, Davis met Breckinridge on Saturday, April 22, and asked whether the news about Lincoln's assassination was true. Breckinridge said it was. Breckinridge also thought that the assassination "had cost the South her best friend in this dark hour."[597]

According to Stephen R. Mallory, the Confederate secretary of the navy, Davis said, "I am sorry. We have lost our noblest and best friend in the court of the enemy . . . I certainly have no special regard for Mr. Lincoln, but there are a great many men of whose end I would much rather hear than his. I fear it will be disastrous for our people, and I regret it deeply."[598]

Davis knew Lincoln to be a kinder, gentler man than his replacement, Andrew Johnson, from whom he expected less.[599] Davis later said, "Next to the day of the fall of the Confederacy, the darkest day the South has known was the day of the assassination of Abraham Lincoln."[600]

The next morning, Davis attended St. Peter's Episcopal Church and heard from the minister that the assassination was "folly and wickedness, a blot on American civilization, infamy."

Davis was captured on May 10 and brought to Macon, Georgia, on May 13. Major General James Wilson, the commanding general in the region, informed Davis of the conspiracy charges against him for the assassination; and he replied, "I have and there is one man who knows it to be a lie."

"By 'one man,' I presume you mean some particular, man?" asked the general.

"I do, I mean the man [Andrew Johnson] who signed the proclamation, for he knows that I would a thousand times rather have Abraham Lincoln to deal with, as President of the United States, than to have him."[601]

Davis's wife, Varina, wrote in her memoirs that upon hearing of the assassination from General Breckinridge, Davis said, "I am sorry to learn it. Mr. Lincoln was a much better man that his successor will be, and it will go harder with our people. It is bad news for us."[602]

In August 1907, Jefferson Davis's daughter, then Mrs. J. A. Hayes, wrote a letter to General William J. Palmer. In part, she wrote:

I was a small child at the time, and, like most Southern children, I looked upon Lincoln as the arch-enemy of my country; and, thoughtlessly, as the servants and guards around us were rejoicing, I ran to my father with what I supposed would be good news to him. He gravely and gently took me in his arms and explained to me that this terrible deed was done by a crazy man who, no doubt, thought he was the savior of the South, though really her worst enemy. My father added, "Always remember, my little daughter, no wrong can ever make a right. The South does not wish her rights to come through dastardly murder, but through fair fight." Then he sighed deeply and said: "This is the bitterest blow that could have been dealt to the Southern cause. Lincoln was a just man and would have been fair and generous in his treatment of the Southern people; his successor is a man we can expect nothing from."[603]

As a leader of a new nation trying desperately to gain recognition in Europe, it is unlikely that Davis would approve an assassination plot. European leaders would have condemned the action of a national leader kidnapping or killing another nation's head of state. In addition, Jefferson Davis was a fairly conservative and conventional leader; it would not have been within his sense of honor to kill another head of state. Southern assassination of Lincoln would have been very counterproductive by arousing public opinion in the North.

Jefferson Davis wrote in a letter dated May 11, 1878, from New Orleans saying that "the news (of the assassination) was to me very sad, for I felt that Mr. Johnson was a malignant man, and without the power, or generosity which I believed Mr. Lincoln possessed . . . . The fact was, that without any personal regard for Mr. Lincoln I considered him a kind hearted man, and very much to be preferred by us to his successor Mr. Johnson: but had it been otherwise nothing could have made me willing to adopt assassination as a means to be employed." Later in the letter, Davis wrote about attempts on his life and concluded that "neither I, or those associated with me, believed Mr. Lincoln to be particeps criminis."[604]

Robert E. Lee at first refused to hear the details of what had happened. When he finally did learn, he felt "the event one of the most deplorable that could have occurred. Not only had the scheme not been known in the South, but if it had been, it would have received the most severe condemnation."[605]

Lee gave an interview with the *New York Herald*; the paper reported regarding Lincoln's assassination: "The General considered this an event in itself one of the deplorable that could have occurred. As a crime it was unexampled and beyond execration. It was a crime that no good man could approve from any conceivable motive. Undoubtedly the effort would be made to fasten the responsibility of it upon the South; but, from his intimate acquaintance with the leading men of the South, he was confident there was not one of them who would sanction or approve of it."[606]

Later Lee wrote that the assassination was "a crime previously unknown to this country and one that must be deprecated by every American."[607]

General Edwin G. Lee, Confederate military attaché in Montreal, wrote in his diary for April, "News of Lincoln's death came this morning, exciting universal shock." Lee crossed out "shock" and substituted "horror and amazement."[608]

In Charleston, former governor William Aiken, the South's largest slaveholder before the war, said of the assassin, "Our expression of disgust for the dastardly wretch can scarcely be uttered. Can it be believed that in the nineteenth century a human being could be found to have in his bosom so diabolical an idea? The heart sickens."[609]

And from the *Baltimore Intelligencer*: "We are heavily overburdened by the affliction which has befallen us," where four years earlier a plot to assassinate President-elect Lincoln had been laid. "We are too much oppressed with the weight of grief to find words expressive of our horror and agitation. We are overwhelmed by the shock of a crime whose enormity baffles description." The editor poetically wrote that "he has exchanged the laurel wreath of time for the crown of immortality."[610]

There were some who praised Booth and felt that Lincoln got what he deserved.

John S. Wise wrote, "Perhaps I ought to chronicle that the announcement was received with sentiments of sorrow. If I did, I should be lying for sentiments sake. Among the higher officers and the intelligent and conservative men, the assassination caused a shudder of horror at the heinousness of the act and at the thought of its possible consequences; but among the thoughtless, the desperate, and the ignorant, it was hailed as a sort of retributive justice. In maturer years I have been ashamed of what I felt and said of that awful calamity."[611]

The *Galveston Daily News* wrote that "inspired by patriotic impulse and believing he was ridding the world of a monster, his name will be inscribed on the roll of true-hearted patriots along with Brutus and Charlotte Corday." The *Chattanooga (Tennessee) Daily Rebel* wrote: "Abe has gone to answer before the bar of God for the innocent blood which he has permitted to be shed, and his efforts to enslave a free people."[612]

\*　\*　\*

On April 17, General Sherman received a telegram telling him of the assassination as he was about to board a train to meet Confederate General Johnston under a flag of truce to discuss terms of surrender. As soon as Sherman was alone with Johnston, he showed him the telegram – the news had not yet reached Johnston's army in North Carolina. Johnston read the telegram; "Perspiration came out in large drops on his forehead, and he did not attempt to conceal his distress. He denounced the act as a disgrace to the age." Johnston immediately said that he hoped Sherman "did not charge it to the Confederate Government." Sherman told Johnston that he did not believe he or Lee "could possibly be privy to acts of assassination; but I would not say as much for Jeff. Davis, George Sanders, and men of that stripe."[613]

When the Sherman's troops were finally told of the assassination, there was a universal grief among them. "I never before or since have been with a large mass of men overwhelmed by one simple emotion," wrote General Putnam. "The feeling with all was the loss not only of the great Captain but of the personal friend, of him who was for the troops, as for the whole country, Father Abraham."[614]

\*　\*　\*

The English actor Charles Wyndham, at one time a close friend of John Wilkes Booth, was in England when news that Booth shot Lincoln arrived. At first, Wyndham refused to believe the reports; however, after some thought later, he said,

> Calling to mind the extraordinary man as I had known him I could conceive of his committing some such desperate, mad act in one of his frenzied moments. Wyndham reasoned, that Booth must have thought he was "committing a heroic deed, one that would cause his name to be handed down as that of a national deliverer . . . . I can imagine how he threw himself into his terrible work, I can see the theatric manner in which he performed it, 'Sic semper tyrannis!' he cried, and the madman had not overborne the actor

in his gesture as he pronounced his exultation over the frightful crime . . . .
There was but one John Wilkes, sad, mad, bad John Wilkes."[615]

\*      \*      \*

Actress Charlotte Cushman was a close friend of the Seward family and always
stayed at their home when performing in Washington. She was in Rome when she
learned that Lincoln and Secretary Seward had been attacked. It was Cushman
who two years earlier, on stage with Booth, had accidentally opened up the surgical
incision on Booth's neck when they embraced onstage. "In our country," she said,
"in these modern times it is too theatrical a thing to be done by an American!"
When she heard that Booth was the assassin, she wrote in a letter, "I cannot keep
from weeping. The horror makes my blood run so cold as to bring the tears to my
eyes and cheeks . . . . I am unable to think or to feel or to do anything else but sit
and clasp my hands in dread and fear. My heart feels as though it were cramped
up in a vise."[616]

\*      \*      \*

Across the country, the news of the assassination arrived with the morning
newspaper. Lincoln had been shot and could not recover, were the first reports. John
Ellsler, who the previous year had been involved with Booth in oil speculation in
Pennsylvania, wrote that after reading the newspaper at breakfast in Columbus, Ohio,
he was unable to move or speak, then he felt as if he were on fire.[617]

Actress Clara Morris and her roommate, Hattie, were draping their front window
with black cloth in memory of Lincoln when a passerby told them who had killed
the president. Hattie, who was holding tacks between her lips as she put up the cloth,
almost swallowed when she laughed at the absurdity. Clara laughed and told the man
that this was not a subject to joke about.

Later, Ellsler knocked at their door; "his eyes were dreadful, they were so glassy
and seemed so unseeing." Clara knew that he was devoted to his children and could
only imagine that one of them must have been hurt.

"What is it?" Clara asked. "Oh, what has happened to them?"

Ellsler sat down and very faintly asked, "You haven't heard anything?"

Hattie knew at once what he was talking about. And she also guessed now that
the news about Booth was true.

"A man, he lied though, said that Wilkes Booth, but he did lie, didn't he?" Hattie
replied.

"No, No! He did not lie, it's true!"

When the truth was at last confirmed, the two burst into tears. After recovering
from this emotional moment, Ellsler said, "So great, so good, a man destroyed, and
by the hand of that unhappy boy! My God! My God!"

Clara reminisced about the Booth who had joked with her about her Grecian costume in *The Marble Heart* and of the Booth who had kissed a dirty child in the street after accidentally knocking him over, and as Morris had written, "He knew of no witness to the act." She called him "poor, guilty, unhappy John Wilkes Booth!"[618]

\* \* \*

In Philadelphia, twelve-year-old John Drew of the Drew-Barrymore theatrical family told his mother that Lincoln had been assassinated.

"Are you sure?" she asked. When he assured her of the fact, she sat wordlessly for a moment. Then from her desk, she took out a letter Lincoln had sent her in 1862, thanking her for providing the presidential party with seats at the Arch Street Theatre. She gazed at it silently for a time and asked without raising her eyes, "Who did such a monstrously wicked thing?"

Young John Drew told his mother it had been John Wilkes Booth.

His mother cried out, "No!" She thought of Edwin Booth, who had often been a guest at the Drew home.

"No!" she cried out. "It is unthinkable! The brother of one so kind . . . Will our profession ever atone?"[619]

\* \* \*

Early on the morning of April 15, a friend of Booth's, Billy Baron, brought the news of Lincoln's assassination with Booth as the assassin to Ella Turner Starr at the bordello run by her sister. Ella who loved Booth obsessively, went to her bed, and put Booth's picture under her pillow. She covered her face with a cloth soaked in chloroform, but was soon discovered, and a doctor was summoned. She was revived, but told her doctors she did not thank them for saving her life.[620] She did not know that Booth was less devoted to her. He carried the pictures of five women on him throughout his escape odyssey – Starr was not one of them.

Among Booth's effects later was found a note from Ella to John Wilkes, which reads as follows:

My darling Baby

Please call this evening as soon as you receive this note I will not detain you five minutes for gods sake come

yours truly
E S

if you will not come
write a note the reason why
Washington Feb 7th [1]865[621]

This note led detectives to the bordello. In the sweep of arrests of all people who knew Booth, all the ladies of the house were arrested.

\*     \*     \*

John T. Ford was in Richmond, under a War Department pass, visiting an uncle (the oldest brother of his mother) whom he had not seen since the war began. The news was not publicly announced in Richmond until Monday morning in the *Richmond Whig*. However, Ford talked to a relative on Sunday afternoon who told him that President Lincoln was assassinated in Washington by Booth.

Ford laughed. "Edwin Booth is in Boston!" It never occurred to Ford that Edwin's brother John was in Washington. "I treated the matter with not the slightest credence. It was only on Monday morning, before the boat leaving the wharf, that I got a newspaper and learned the actual fact." The boat Ford took was returning him to Washington via Baltimore harbor.[622] As an acquaintance of Booth Ford, he was arrested at home in Baltimore and only released on June 1.[623]

# CHAPTER 17

## Find the Murderer

It was not until four o'clock on the morning Lincoln died that Stanton issued a statement officially naming Booth the assassin.

Stanton had ordered Major Thomas T. Eckert to return to the War Department telegraph office and send a telegram to General Grant, summoning him back to Washington immediately. The telegram reached Grant at Philadelphia as he was about to leave for Burlington, New Jersey. Stanton sent Grant another telegram at three o'clock, informing him of Lincoln's and Seward's condition and that "investigations strongly indicate J. Wilkes Booth as the assassin of the President." Stanton begins the telegrams with "The President still breathes, . . ." yet calls Booth an assassin by the third paragraph.[624]

During the night, General Augur sent telegrams to outlying commands. Two were to Brevet Brigadier General William W. Morris, temporarily commanding the Eighth Army Corps, Baltimore, naming Booth as Lincoln's assassin.[625]

Throughout the night of the fourteenth and into the next day, Stanton organized the investigation into the assassination and the hunt for Booth. At Stanton's disposal were the Washington police force, headed by Almarin C. Richards; the military police attached to the provost marshal's office, headed by James R. O'Beirne; cavalry in and around the city, commanded by Major General Christopher C. Augur; the War Department's own secret service agents; and the detectives and spies attached to the Bureau of Military Justice.

These agencies, however, felt no great need to cooperate among themselves. They were plunged into furious competition because of the hope of promotion and large rewards. For all their efforts, the government uncovered surprisingly little about Booth's escape route due in no small part to the lack of cooperation among the agencies.[626]

In the first hours following Booth's attack, with so much happening in Washington and with so many rumors circulating about what might happen next, it was impossible for Stanton and his aides to subject their problem to the calm and intelligent analysis that many modern-day assassination scholars say they should have given it. Stanton and others had no reason to conclude that Booth would continue to ride in a southerly direction. There was no way of knowing whether Booth would try to escape by going through Montgomery County, Maryland, and then attempt to seek help from John Mosby or turn north to Baltimore, Philadelphia, New York, and on to Canada. Or he might continue as first reported through Southern Maryland, crossing the Potomac into Virginia.

Stanton's delay of three hours in naming Booth the assassin is reasonable, considering that sending an angry citizenry after the wrong man would have been irresponsible. A delay of three hours was perhaps not excessive. Similarly, Stanton felt censorship of news about the assassination sent out of Washington was justified to prevent panic or mob rule throughout the country. Although the assassination of Lincoln was one of the most sensational stories in American history and came at a time when many people were already emotionally overwrought, there were remarkably few lurid reports of the assassination in the press.

Despite Booth's escape plans, his timing and itinerary were altered by an unforeseen event – his broken ankle.

*　　*　　*

Just after the assassination, Parker slipped away in the pandemonium that reigned in the theater; and he was not heard from again until six o'clock the next morning. Parker walked into the police station after drinking the night away with a woman named Lizzie Williams, a "woman of the street." The charges against her were immediately dropped. However, the question remains, why did Parker bring her in hours after the assassination? Parker may have arrested her so that he would not arrive at the police station empty-handed. Or he was angry at her for refusing services to him.

On May 1, 1865, charges were brought against Parker for neglect of duty.[627]

A trial was held before a Metropolitan Police board on May 3. No known record of the trial remains, and charges against him were dropped on June 2. The charges could have been dismissed because Lincoln, who disliked the attention given to his safety, dismissed Parker and told him to take a seat and enjoy the play. This order would have been in character for Lincoln. Parker, like others, probably had decided that since the war was over, he could relax his guard – why not see Laura Keene in her final performance?[628] Whatever the reason, Parker remained on active duty on the police force. He even continued on the White House security detachment until May 10, a week after his police board trial, when he returned to the police department. On May 24, records there show that he arrested a woman for soliciting and that she was convicted and fined ten dollars.

Parker's poor performance as a policeman did not end on April 14. Twice more, he was taken before the police board. On November 22, 1865, Parker was accused of conduct unbecoming a police officer. On July 27, 1868, a supervisor found him sleeping on duty. Parker claimed he was ill. Finally, Parker was discharged from the Metropolitan Police on August 13, 1868.

William H. Crook years later wrote, "I have often wondered why the negligence of the guard who accompanied the President to the theater on the night of the Powell has never been divulged .... Yet, had he done his duty, I believe President Lincoln would not have been murdered by Booth .... Had Parker been at his post at the back of the box-Booth still being determined to make the attempt that night – he would have been stabbed, probably killed. The noise of the struggle – Parker could surely have manage to make some outcry – would have given the alarm."[629]

William H. Crook continued saying that John F. Parker had "confessed to me the next day that he went to a seat at the front of the first gallery, so that he could see the play."[630] Crook maintained that Parker's responsibility was to remain in the little passageway outside of the presidential box and to guard the president.[631] However, another guard, Tom Pendel, later wrote that Parker's instructions were only to see Lincoln safely into the theater. This is in keeping with Lincoln not wanting guards with him at church or the theater.

*　*　*

After stabbing the orchestra leader, Booth ran out of the theater's rear entrance into the area known as Baptist Alley. There young Burroughs sat on a stone bench holding the reins of Booth's mare.

As Burroughs held Booth's horse and sat on a carpenter's bench, he heard the report of a pistol. "I was still out by the bench," Burroughs testified, "but had got off when Booth came out. He told me to give him his horse. He struck me with the butt of a knife, and knocked me down ... and rode off immediately."[632]

Booth lost no time in making his escape. He dashed out the alley on to F Street, then careened on to Ninth Street, cutting through the park at Judiciary Square, skirted the grounds of the capitol building, and raced down Pennsylvania Avenue to Eleventh Street to cross at the bridge near the naval station.

The ride had taken only a few minutes by the time he caught sight of the bridge. The he slowed down. When Booth arrived at the bridge and Sergeant Cobb approached "to see if he was a proper person to pass."

"Who are you, sir?" Sergeant Cobb asked.

"My name is Booth."

"And where are you coming from?"

"From the city," replied Booth, forcing himself to reply calmly; then Cobb asked where he was headed.

"I'm going home." Sergeant Cobb asked where his home was.

Booth replied that "it was in Charles [County]." Sergeant Cobb asked him what town.

"I don't live in any town.

"You must live in some town."

"No, I live close to Beantown, but not in the town."

"Why are you out so late?" Sergeant Cobb asked, knowing his orders were that no one was to pass after nine o'clock.

Booth replied that he had had somewhere to go, and he thought he would use the moon to ride home by.

Sergeant Cobb considered all of Booth's answers and his demeanor and decoded that "he was a proper person to pass."

Sergeant Cobb described what happened next,

> In perhaps five or seven, or, at the outside, ten minutes, another person came along [Herold]. He did not seem to be riding so rapidly as the first, or his horse did not show signs of it as much as the first. I asked who he was, and he said that his name was Smith [David Herold], and that he was going home; that he lived at the White Plains. I asked him how it was that he was out so late. He made use of a rather indelicate expression, and said that he had been in bad company .... After his explanation, I allowed him to pass .... Afterward, a third horseman [Fletcher] rode up, and made inquiry after a roan horse; after a man passing on a roan horse. He made no inquiry about the other horseman who had passed first.[633]

It was thought at the time the name Booth had given to Sergeant Cobb was a ruse to put pursuers on the wrong trail.

Polk Gardiner was on the Bryantown Road that night on his way to Washington. At about eleven o'clock on Good Hope Hill, just outside Washington, he met two horsemen, one about half a mile behind the other, and both riding very fast. The first (Booth) asked Polk if a horseman had passed ahead; he then asked about the road to Marlboro and whether it turned to the right. Polk told him to keep straight ahead.

As the second horseman (Herold) rode up, teamsters were passing at the time, and Gardiner saw the second horseman ask them whether a horseman had passed ahead.[634]

On his mad ride in the dark on an unfamiliar horse, Booth drove the animal to stumble and fall. The heavy beast fell, breaking Booth's left tibia bone. This unforeseen event changed Booth's plans.

Herold finally caught up with Booth at Soper's Hill about eight miles south of Washington and not far from the Surratt Tavern. The two men continued on together, but Booth was in great pain from his broken bone. At last, the two, riding more slowly because of Booth, arrived at the tavern.

In 1865, sixty-eight batteries, defensive fortifications, and forts surrounded Washington, and Booth passed two of them, Forts Baker and Wagner. Both forts had telegraph lines to the War Department, but no one had alerted these outposts.

Around midnight, messages were finally sent to all forts; but by then, Booth and Herald were arriving at the Surratt Tavern. Herold dismounted, went inside, and found Lloyd, the alcoholic barkeep, still up and drinking by himself. Booth, not wanting to dismount and remount because of the broken leg, stayed mounted, but he had difficulty staying seated.

"Lloyd for God's sake, make haste and get those things!" Herold yelled. Herold was referring to the carbines and ammunition that John Surratt had brought to the tavern March 18 and that were hidden inside the wall in the dining room. Herold only wanted one of the carbines since Booth was hurt and in no condition to use one.

Lloyd looked at Herold, who he knew, and then at Booth, who he did not know. Then, drunk as he was, Lloyd retrieved one of the carbines, the ammunition, and the field glasses, which he gave to Herold. Booth was sweating and groaning with pain, and Herold got a bottle of whisky from the tavern and gave it to Booth. Booth took the bottle gratefully and drank while still sitting on his horse.[635]

\* \* \*

The news of the assassination had quickly spread throughout Washington. Police arrived at the National Hotel to search Booth's room. "We all laughed at the absurdity of such a thing," remembered Walter Burton, the night clerk. "All night long," he continued, "I watched the door, confidently expecting to see Booth come walking in blithe and smiling, to give the lie to this foul story." Burton had been a friend of Booth's, often chatting with him at the hotel desk; frequently the two drank liquor and smoke cigars together. Burton, who had walked home with Booth from the capitol to the hotel on inauguration day, had not suspected that Booth was displeased with the election.[636] Burton eventually realized the seriousness of what the detectives were saying.

Mrs. Temple, the Washington socialite who had had lunch with Lucy Hale and her mother, described that evening as people at the National Hotel gradually become aware of what was happening,

I was aroused by an indefinable noise that served to wake, but was not loud enough to startle one. Doors were slamming all over the house, and a murmur of voices was heard. I thought at first that some one was sick, and that a doctor was being hurriedly sent for; but the noise still continuing, I imagined that there must be a fire in the vicinity. This idea caused me to jump up at once and open the window, and I heard the sound of many horses' feet striking the pavement in a full run, but no fire bells or alarms; but still the inexplicable sounds continued. The rebels have stormed the city was the next impression, and with that I hastily threw on my wrapper and hurried to my parlor. There was no one there, and I kept on until I got to the grand salon, and there I found a crowd of people, mostly like myself guests of the hotel.[637]

Lucy Hale had awoke because of the slamming doors and voices; she dressed and went to the salon. When she heard the dreadful news of the assassination and Booth's involvement in it, she screamed and fainted before any one could reach her.[638] Lucy was carried to her hotel room.

The scene at the National Hotel was typical of what was happening around Washington that night. Mrs. Temple continued, "That night of horror seems like a frightful dream to me now. None of us retired, but sat in the parlor in a kind of dumb terror . . . not until the gray dawn came stealing in did we retire sick at heart and with heavy, wet eyelids."[639]

*     *     *

Two hours after his last breath, Lincoln, covered by a white sheet and a flag, was returned to the White House in a hearse. The horse-drawn hearse was led by an officer on foot carrying an unsheathed saber and flanked by ten privates marching with arms reversed. William Doster who was standing at Pennsylvania Avenue and Fifteenth Street when the hearse went by, later wrote, "Never before or since have I heard a crowd as that was, composed mostly of negroes, men and women, utter so loud and piercing a wail, as these mourners uttered, when the body passed close to them. It seemed as if the whole world had lost a dear, personal friend whose loss was not to be repaired."[640]

When Lincoln's body arrived at the White House, Mrs. Lincoln went from room to room, refusing to enter, for in each one, something reminded her of her assassinated husband. "Oh, no, not there. Oh, I couldn't go in there." Finally Mrs. Dixon and Mary Jane Welles, wife of the secretary of the navy, prevailed on Mary to go to her bedroom. At about eleven o'clock that morning, Elizabeth Keckley, responding to Mrs. Wells request to visit Mary, arrived at the White House. (Three messengers had been sent out that night for Mrs. Keckley; but because they had had an incorrect address, none of them had found her.) When Keckley arrived, Mrs. Welles left, saying that she had to go to her own family.

Keckley found Mrs. Lincoln giving forth "the wails of a broken heart, the unearthly shrieks, the terrible convulsions, the wild, tempestuous outbursts of grief from the soul." Only Tad was able to calm her.

"Don't cry so, Mama! Don't cry, or you will make me cry, too! You will break my heart."[641] She refused all sympathy calls except those of Secretary Stanton and Senator Sumner.

On Easter morning in the White House, workmen began preparing the East Room for the president's funeral; but the sounds of a wooden platform being built for the coffin utterly unnerved Mary Lincoln as she lay upstairs. She requested that the construction be stopped; however, work continued but quietly.

There was a memorial service at the White House, which was decorated with a mass of flowers, and a cross of lilies at the head of Lincoln's casket and roses at the foot. When it was over, Lincoln's body was taken in a hearse to the capitol.

On April 19 at sunrise, cannons all over Washington began to fire at one-minute intervals, and all businesses were closed in the city. At noon, the city's church bells began to toll. The bells of Washington and Georgetown and Alexandria rang. The procession from the White House to the capitol was led by the Twenty-second U.S. Colored Infantry followed by other Union military units and civilian groups. Lincoln was laid in state in the capitol. His body lay in the Capitol rotunda were two endless lines of slow-moving mourners formed an ellipse as they passed around the coffin and joining again as they passed the coffin. The lines never stopped.[642]

\*     \*     \*

Police, military detectives, and whole regiments of troops scoured Southern Maryland and Northern Virginia to pick up the trail of Booth and his accomplices. General Augur sent cavalry to all outlying counties to block off roads and search houses.

Stanton recruited detectives from other jurisdictions. At one o'clock on the morning of April 15, Stanton telegraphed John H. Kennedy, chief of police of New York, "Send here immediately three or four of your best detectives." Stanton also called in Colonel H. S. Olcott and sent a telegram to New York, asking Colonel LaFayette C. Baker, chief of the United States Secret Service, "Come here immediately and see if you can find the murderer of the President."[643]

Baker arrived in the Capital with his cousin, Lieutenant Luther B. Baker, and immediately had handbills posted offering reward money. "The common council of Washington, have offered a reward of $20,000 for the arrest and conviction of these assassins, in addition to which I will pay $10,000."[644]

On April 20, 1865, Stanton issued a proclamation,

> $100,000 Reward
>
> The murderer of our late beloved President, Abraham Lincoln is still at large. $50,000 reward will be paid by this department for his apprehension in addition to any reward offered by municipal authorities or State executives.
>
> $25,00 reward will be paid for the apprehension of John H. Surratt, one of Booth's accomplices.
>
> $25,000 reward will be paid for the apprehension of David C. Herold another of Booth's accomplices.

Liberal rewards will be paid for any information that shall conduce to the arrest of either of the above named criminals or their accomplices.

All persons harboring or secreting the said persons or either of them or aiding or assisting their concealment or escape will be treated as accomplices in the murder of the President and the attempted assassination of the Secretary of State, and shall be held to trial before a military commission and the punishment of death.

Let the stain of innocent blood be removed from the land by the arrest and punishment of the murderers.

All good citizens are exhorted to aid public justice on this occasion. Every man should consider his own conscience charged with this solemn duty, and rest neither night nor day until it is accomplished.[645]

At Stanton's order, James B. Fry, the provost marshal general of the army, ordered all provost marshals in the North to question everyone leaving for Canada or Europe. For a time, Stanton was in control of the government and the army although Johnson had been sworn in that morning. With Congress not in session, the Civil War not yet completely over, and the general public enraged over the assassination, Stanton could temporarily justify almost any action he wanted to take.

\*     \*     \*

In the early morning hours of the fifteenth, soldiers and civilians walked the streets of Washington emotional and agitated about President Lincoln's being shot. The crowds were loud and boisterous; so all the residents, including Mary Surratt, knew about the assassination.[646]

Chief of Police Richards "soon thereafter obtained information that John H. Surratt was often in company with these men and then that Booth had often visited or called at Mrs. Surratt's house."[647]

As soon as Richards learned this, he pulled together a small group of detectives, and they visited the Surratt boardinghouse. Richards half expected to find Booth and Surratt hiding there. At the least, he expected to get information and leads about where the men could be found. Detectives McDevitt, Clarvoe, Bigley, and Kelly got on their horses and took a ride to H Street.

They arrived between 2:00 and 2:30 a.m. and banged on the door.

Weichmann answered and was surprised to see a handful of detectives sizing him up sternly, demanding to search the house, and asking for Mary Surratt.

"I will fetch her," Weichmann said, but the detectives followed right behind him. Weichmann walked through Mary's parlor and knocked on her bedroom room.

"Ask them to wait a few minutes and I will open the door," Mrs. Surratt called back.[648]

When Mary opened the door, one of the detectives introduced himself as John Clarvoe of the Metropolitan Police and asked where John Surratt was.

Mary replied, "John is not in the city, sir. He is in Canada – I just received a letter from him."

"Where's the letter," demanded the detectives. But she could not produce the letter because she had thrown it, she thought, on to a window sill; and now, when she looked, she could not find it.[649]

The detective asked her when she had last seen Booth, and she replied honestly that it had been about two o'clock Friday afternoon.

The detectives continued searching all three floors of the house. The sound of their shoes could be heard thudding around the two upper stories. Finally they left when they did not find the two men.

That Saturday morning, boarders John Holohan and Weichmann read in the newspaper, "The man, Surratt, who is believed did the bloody work at Secretary Seward's has for many years been branded a desperado of the worst kind."[650]

After reading the newspapers, Weichmann and Holohan realized that they were at risk of arrest; they lived in the same boardinghouse as the "desperado." It would be better, they decided, if they went to the police and gave information voluntarily. Weichmann knew that being a close friend of John Surratt as well as a boarder at the Surratt boardinghouse was not going to look good for him. The two men went to the Metropolitan Police Station where Weichmann was immediately arrested. Weichmann was cooperative from the beginning, and he and Holohan went with detectives Clarvoe and McDevitt in search of Booth and Herold. They first went to Herold's parents' house where Mrs. Herold gave them a photograph of her son. With the picture in hand, the detectives with Weichmann in tow rode into Maryland looking for the assassins. They found no one and returned to Washington about eight o'clock. That night, Weichmann slept on the floor of the police station.[651]

Saturday night was a bad night for everyone at the boardinghouse. Arrests seemed imminent. In the morning, Eliza Holohan hurriedly took her children and left the boardinghouse to stay with her mother. She returned Monday morning to get the family belongings.[652] Also that morning, about 10:00 a.m., a detective took John Holohan and Weichmann to the boardinghouse where Weichmann "went to his room and changed his clothes." Then they all left.[653]

\*   \*   \*

That Sunday, Susan Mahoney, a servant of Mrs. Surratt's, told her aunt, Mary Ann Griffin, that during the night, she was feigning sleep and overheard things at the boardinghouse. She was sure that the people staying there were all involved in the assassination. Filled with excitement, Mrs. Griffin told her employer, John H. Kimball, who told General Augur. Although Susan Mahoney's claims were unsubstantiated rumors by a naive servant, she and Mary Ann Griffin were rewarded with $250 each;

and Kimball received $500. It was rationalized that since the erroneous information led to the arrest of Lewis Powell, the rewards were justified.[654]

\*     \*     \*

Near eight thirty on the evening of April 17, Major H. W. Smith, under orders from Colonel Wells, was to take Captain Wermerskirch, detectives Devoe and Rosch, and a detachment of five soldiers to search the boardinghouse again; this time he was looking for evidence connecting anyone there to the assassination. At the same time, Smith was to "arrest Mrs. Surratt and all in the house." Eliza Holohan had indeed gotten out of the house just in time!

The detachment drew up in front of the H Street house. One of the detectives ran up the wooden stairs and banged on the door. Mary Surratt cautiously pulled open a window and peered out. She had extremely poor vision and could not see in the dark.

"Is that you, Mr. Kirby?" she asked, thinking it was her neighbor.

"No, but open the door at once, if this is Mrs. Surratt's house!"

Mary opened the door, and Major Smith rushed in.

"Are you Mrs. Surratt?" asked Smith.

"I am the widow of John H. Surratt," Mary replied.

Then the major added, "The mother of John H. Surratt Jr.?"

"I am."

Then the major announced, "I come to arrest you and all in the house and take you for examination to General Augur's headquarters." General Christopher Augur was commander of the Twenty-second Army Corps, which included all Union troops in the Washington area.

No one was permitted to leave the house, not even the servants. The two detectives, Devoe and Rosch, went downstairs to guard any servants there.

Major Smith turned to Mary and asked for her keys and told her the house would be under military guard. Mary dutifully handed him the keys and then took the men into the parlor and introduced the women who were assembled there. At this time, detectives Sampson and Morgan arrived to help those already there.[655]

The detectives arrested everyone and were preparing to leave when there was a sudden knock at the door. Who would be knocking on the door this late at night?

Major Smith ordered Wermerskirch and Morgan, "Both of you go out into the hall and stand behind the front door. Wermerskirch, when the doorbell rings, you unlock it and open it. I'll be standing in the parlor doorway to the hall."

The men positioned themselves, and the door was carefully opened. Major Smith stared at the muddy figure in the doorway. It was a tall man carrying a pickax. Smith stepped into the hall, his hand on his firearm.

It was Powell.

Tired, dirty, cold, and hungry after three nights in the outdoors, Powell had come to the only place he thought he might be able to hide. This nocturnal visit by Powell sealed Mary Surratt's fate. His timing was fatal. Powell had covered his head with a shirt sleeve and was holding a pickax he had stolen.

Powell stood in the doorway; then comprehension gradually crept across his face, as he realized he had walked into a house full of police.

"I guess I have mistaken the house," Powell said, turning to go.

"No, you have not," the major answered.

Detective Morgan stepped from behind the door and asked, "Whose house are you looking for?"

"Mrs. Surratt's," Powell said, unable to think quickly enough to feign having knocked on the wrong door.

"This is the house. Come in at once." The major loosened his pistol in its holster, and Powell did as he was told. Captain Wermerskirch shut and locked the door and dropped the key into his pocket.

Under Major Smith's questioning, Powell, trying to create an acceptable story, said that Mrs. Surratt had hired him off the street to dig a gutter the next day. He said he had come at this late hour so Mrs. Surratt could give him "directions about digging the gutter the next morning." His story was simply not believable.

Major Smith returned to the parlor. "Mrs. Surratt, please step here for a moment."

Obediently, Mary came in and peered at Powell. Because of her poor eyesight, she took him for a "tremendous hard fellow with a skullcap on and with a weapon in his hand." And she did not recognize him and thought the pickax was a weapon.[656]

Major Smith told Mary who the man claimed to be, and she listened with growing indignation. She raised her right hand and said, "Before God, sir, I do not know this man, and I have not seen him before, and I did not hire him to come and dig a gutter for me."[657]

Honora Fitzpatrick peeked through the parlor door at Powell. Although she had normal vision, she did not recognize him either. Only later at General Augur's office did Honora recognize him when the skullcap was taken off his head.[658]

When Powell was asked to identify himself, he produced the verification copy of the oath of allegiance he had taken as "Lewis Paine" in Baltimore on March 14.[659]

Major Smith told Powell, "Your story does not hang together," and was arrested.[660]

Mary and Anna Surratt, Honora Fitzpatrick, Olivia Jenkins, and Powell left the house under arrest.

Anna Surratt may have been correct in her earlier observation about Powell that he "did not possess his five sense." Approaching the house without wondering why police and military were stationed outside, why carriages (to transport those arrested) were outside the boardinghouse, and why the house was still brightly lit close to midnight, shows that Powell did not evaluate the situation with much perception.[661]

\*       \*       \*

When Mary Surratt's boardinghouse was searched, the photographs of Davis; Stephens; Beauregard; Stonewall Jackson; and Union generals McClellan, Grant, and Hooker were found. A photograph of Booth was found hidden behind a framed copy of Anna Surratt's picture, *Morning, Noon, and Night*. Weichmann had given this picture to Anna, and she had hidden Booth's photograph there after her brother John had told her to throw it out.

Mary Surratt told General Augur that she had not seen her son, John, "since the 3rd of April." She did admit that "Mr. Booth has been coming to our house about two months; sometimes he called twice a day; we found him very much a gentleman." Mary Surratt described the family's relationship with Booth, "I think my son invited him home the evening he was introduced to him. I did not hear him mention how he came to know him. My son is a country-bred young gentleman. I was not surprised that he should make the acquaintance of such a man as Mr. Booth because I consider him capable of forming acquaintances in the best society. I never thought a great deal of his forming Mr. Booth's acquaintance because he called very frequently when my son was not there; he called upon the rest of us sometimes."[662]

She said that everyone was surprised that Booth had killed the president. "We often remarked that Mr. Booth was very clear of politics; he never mentioned anything of the kind, and it was a subject that we never indulged in."

When Mary was asked her political sentiments, she said, "I don't pretend to express my feeling at all; I have often said that I thought that the South acted too hastily; that is about the amount of my feeling, and I say so again."[663] After the questioning, Mary was taken to the Old Capitol Prison.

On April 28, Mary was interviewed again, this time by Colonel Henry Steele Olcott. She told him that Booth frequented her house often, and Atzerodt had boarded there once as had Payne alias Wood. But she continued to deny all knowledge of assassination.

On the subject of "shooting irons" that Lloyd claimed Mary told him to have ready, the interview went as follows:

Q. What did you say about any shooting irons or carbines?
A. I said nothing.
Q. Any conversation of that kind? Did you not tell him (Lloyd) to have shooting irons ready, that there would be some people there that night?
A. To my knowledge, no conversation of that kind passed.
Q. Did you know any shooting irons were there?
A. No, Sir, I did not.[664]

Olcott reported that Mrs. Surratt "repeats substantially the story that she told on her first examination." The colonel concluded, "She denies in toto having had any conference with Lloyd about firearms, or any conversation with Booth, Herold, or others about the projected assassination or having known that her son was implicated in it, or of having done anything prejudicial to the public interest. Her manner throughout was cool and collected."[665]

Lewis Powell was identified by Augustus Seward, the oldest of Seward's sons, and by William H. Bell, the black servant who had answered the door at the Seward residence. So by four thirty in the morning, Powell was in chains aboard the gunboat *Saugas*.

On the night of April 18, John Lloyd was arrested in Surrattsville and taken to Bryantown where Provost Marshal Colonel H. H. Wells had set up his headquarters. At first, Lloyd refused to say anything against Mrs. Surratt because by speaking against her, he would incriminate himself in aiding Booth's escape. Only after intimidation and threats of torture did he give the desired testimony.

John T. Ford was also arrested on April 18 and detained at the Old Capitol Prison. Ford later wrote concerning Lloyd, "Several there said that after his arrest in the country, he had been threatened with torture, and intimated that he had to say what he did to secure relief." Lloyd shared with Ford that he had agreed to testify against Mrs. Surratt only after he had "suffered extreme duress at the hands of his captors."

This type of witness coercion occurred with other prisoners also. Ford wrote that "while in the Carroll Prison, I recall the handcuffing of a witness named Howell, a former blockade-runner, who bore the irons on his wrists for many days in my presence. When asked why he was ironed, he replied: 'I suppose because I won't say what I don't know. They wish to make me incriminate those that I know nothing against.'"[666]

Honora Fitzpatrick was released from prison on April 19; however, she was returned to prison three days later. The men who had rented horses to the assassin as well as customers of the bordello where Ella Turner lived and the actors and employees at Ford's Theatre were rounded up and incarcerated.

\* \* \*

The full power and might of the U.S. federal government was set to finding John Wilkes Booth and David Herold. The rewards were so great that many people reported seeing him in such places as Pottsville and in three other Pennsylvania towns, in Brooklyn, and in Chicago where the police arrested a McVickers Theatre actor who resembled him. Rumors spread that he was still in Washington in secret passages below Ford's Theatre and in the streets disguised as a black woman. A man on crutches was seen entering a Pennsylvania Avenue house between Eleventh and Twelfth Streets, and at once, police and soldiers came to search every residence on the block.

When two Confederate officers being escorted through Washington appeared, a shout came from the crowd, "Booth!" and the mob became belligerent. The two

Confederates were hurried into the office of the provost marshal. General Spinner and the minister-designate to Spain, John Hale, were on the scene and went out to the crowd offering assurances that neither of the men was Booth.[667] But the crowd did not disperse, and eventually the two prisoners were taken through a rear door to nearby Old Capitol Prison.

*　　*　　*

It was announced in the press that Lucy Hale was Booth's undeclared finance. In a paragraph buried deep in an article about the assassination investigation, the *New York Tribune* of April 22 stated, "The unhappy lady, the daughter of a New England senator, to whom Booth was affianced, is plunged in profoundest grief: but with womanly fidelity is slow to believe him guilty of this appalling crime, and asks, with touching pathos, for evidence of his innocence."[668]

Mrs. Temple, a close friend of the Hales, was, during the period between the assassination and Booth's death, a constant companion to Lucy. Mrs. Temple, said, "I did the best I could to calm her, and finally succeeded. She wrote a letter to Booth telling him she loved him and concluded by saying she would marry him even at the foot of the scaffold."[669] Her passion was misplaced since Booth had willingly sacrificed their relationship for his assassination scheme and spent his last night in Washington with Ella Turner, who was in love with him.

Also Booth told John Matthews, "Think of it, John, that at my time of life – just starting, as it were – I should be in Love!" Matthews continued by describing Booth's love for her as follows: "He loved her as few men love. He had a great mind and a generous heart, and both were centered upon this girl, whom he intended to make his wife. Her picture was taken from his person after he was killed." Booth's love for Lucy did not stop him from seeing many other woman, including Ella Starr, and Lucy's photo was only one of five that Booth had on him when he was killed.[670]

Senator Hale applied all his influence to keep his daughter's name out of the papers. He had his friends write letters to editors saying that there was no truth to the stories about his daughter, that she had hardly known the assassin, and that she had had no personal relationship with him.

*　　*　　*

By this time, Lincoln's body had been brought to a special black-draped train of eight cars. Six were for mourners, one was for the guard of honor, and one was for his coffin and that of his son Willie. The engine, covered in black, started out on the 1,662 mile journey to Springfield. The train proceeded at a steady twenty miles an hour, and all along the route, guns fired in salute and bells tolled. Beside the tracks, people crowded to see the train go by. Entire towns turned out at all hours of the day and night. Of the thirty million people of the North, seven million saw the train slowly pass, and one and a half million people filed by as Lincoln laid in state in a dozen cities.

* * *

Major General Winfield Scott Hancock published an appeal to black people to help find the assassins,

Headquarters Middle Military Division,
Washington, D. C., April 24, 1865.

To the Colored People of the District of Columbia and of Maryland, of Alexandria and the Border Counties of Virginia:

Your President has been murdered! He has fallen by the assassin, and without a moment's warning, simply and solely because he was your friend and the friend of our country. Had he been unfaithful to you and to the great cause of human freedom he might have lived. The pistol from which he met his death, though held by Booth, was fired by the hands of treason and slavery. Think of this, and remember how long and how anxiously this good man labored to break your chains and to make you happy. I now appeal to you, by every consideration which can move loyal and grateful hearts, to aid in discovering and arresting his murderer. Concealed by traitors, he is believed to be lurking somewhere within the limits of the District of Columbia, or the States of Maryland and Virginia. Go forth, then, and watch, and listen, and inquire, and search, and pray, by day and by night, until you have succeeded in dragging this monstrous and bloody criminal from his hiding place. You can do much; even the humblest and feeblest among you, by patience and unwearied vigilance, may render the most important assistance. Large rewards have been offered by the government, and by municipal authorities, and they will be paid for the apprehension of the murderer, or for any information which will aid in his arrest. But I feel that you need no such stimulus as this. You will hunt down this cowardly assassin of your best friend as you would the murder of your own father. Do this, and God, whose servant has been slain, and the country which has given you freedom, will bless you for this noble act of duty.

W. S. Hancock
Major General U.S. Volunteers,
Com'dg Middle Military Division[671]

* * *

The federal government was in chaos after the assassination, and the pursuit of the conspirators was haphazard.[672] The federal government was unprepared for an event of this magnitude. It took time for those involved to realize the entirety of the situation and get organized. The early stages of the investigation and pursuit of the assassins was haphazard but conducted with the full force and power of the U.S. government. Washington Police Chief Richards telegrammed the police departments of Baltimore, Philadelphia, New York, and Alexandria, saying, "J. Wilkes Booth the tragedian is the person who shot the President this evening at Ford's Theatre. He made off on horseback probably towards Baltimore."[673]

On April 17, the *New York Times* wrote, "There have been a dozen rumors of Booth's capture but so far as can be learned from the authorities, not only has he not been captured but they are not even too certain in which direction he made his escape." There were also reports that Booth was believed to be heading toward the Canadian border, and at the same time, there were rumors that he had never left Washington and demands were made that the military conduct a house-to-house search of every dwelling in the city.

Baltimore Provost Marshal James L. McPhail and two of his detectives immediately began to search for Booth in Baltimore. McPhail had known the O'Laughlen family for thirty years and knew that O'Laughlen was a friend of Booth's. By late Saturday afternoon, McPhail had the names of Samuel Arnold and Michael O'Laughlen. McPhail sent a telegram to Washington.

April 15, 1865

C.A. Dana
Asst. Secy of War

Sir: Samuel Arnold and Michael O'Laughlen, two of the intimate associates of J. Wilkes Booth, are said to be in Washington. Their arrest may prove advantageous. Both are well known in Washington and were formerly in the rebel army."

The War Department now knew who the "Sam" was in the letter found in Booth's trunk at the National Hotel.

McPhail telegraphed Assistant Secretary of War Charles A. Dana on April 16 that he had traced Samuel Arnold, another friend of Booth's, to Fortress Monroe. Fifteen minutes after receiving McPhail's telegram, Dana responded, "Arrest Samuel Arnold, suspected of being concerned in the murder of the President."[674]

Arnold was arrested on April 17 at Fortress Monroe, Virginia. He had been there since the first of April working as a clerk for a sutler, John Wharton. When Arnold was interrogated, he readily admitted his part in the plan to kidnap Lincoln. On April 18, in Marshal James McPhail's office in Baltimore, Arnold gave a written statement of his part in the plot.[675]

O'Laughlen knew that he was wanted and surrendered himself to Baltimore policeman William Wallace on April 17.[676] McPhail followed orders to bring O'Laughlen by train "in double irons" to Washington.[677]

*　　*　　*

All military telegraph lines were operational the night Lincoln was assassinated. One commercial line between Washington and Baltimore, the People's Line of Washington Telegraph Company, was deliberately suspended for about two hours by William C. Heiss, a station manager. Heiss thought that the assassination might be a signal for a general uprising in the South, so he shut down the telegraph line to prevent the news from reaching Southern sympathizers. He also claimed that he thought federal troops would begin reprisals against Southern sympathizers once they heard of the assassination. Heiss reasoned that shutting down the commercial and limiting telegraphic communication solely to the military would allow "that proper measures could be taken to obviate, head off, or control any such reprisals."[678]

There were many competing commercial telegraph companies in Washington at that time, so Heiss's shutting down of the telegraph line did not affect the outcome of the manhunt for the assassins.

Eckert later explained why he made no investigation, "It did not at the time seem to be sufficiently important, as the interruption only continued about two hours. I was so full of business of almost every character that I could not give it my personal attention . . . . I could not ascertain with certainty what the facts were without making a personal investigation, and I had not time to do that."[679]

# CHAPTER 18

## *A Fearful Calamity Is upon Us*

John Wilkes Booth was eminently successful in his profession, extremely likable, engaged to a senator's daughter, on the best of terms with his family (except for political discussions with Edwin), and a man with many friends. He was sociable and generous, and he was universally admired and liked by the members of his profession. However, he was also opinionated and a loudmouth on the subject of the Confederacy. He voiced political sentiments inappropriately, could flare up in an instant, saw himself as a player on the stage of life, and acted theatrically. He followed sexual urges but never felt any long-term commitment, and he was obsessed with gaining approval on a grand scale.

Junius Brutus Booth, their father, had a serious mental condition. John's brother, Edwin, has a deeply troubled personality. Rosalie was silent and withdrawn; she lived with her mother until she died and then lived as a recluse.

The youngest member of the family, Joseph, had suffered from childhood from what he self-diagnosed as "melancholy insanity." Junius Jr. wrote to his brother Edwin, (October 20, 1862, from San Francisco), "Jose seems an enigma. but I think I can guess him. I would not say so to Mother but I am afraid he is not sound in mind. His insane manner of enlisting & subsequent conduct in England & his departure for Aust. seem to point that way. Mind I do not say positive insanity but a crack that way. Which father in his highest had, & which I fear runs more or less thro' the male portion of our family, myself included."[680]

Junius Jr. was so concerned with his own possible insanity that he never did anything on impulse but thought everything through. This was never said about brother John.

In a letter dated March 22, 1862, John Wilkes Booth wrote to his business agent, Joseph H. Simonds, saying, "No news yet of Joe. Have hunted every place I can think of. I can't tell what to do, poor Mother will take it so hard."[681] In early 1862, Joseph left for England "to see my brother Edwin there, and with the intention of seeing my grandmother." Joseph did finally write his mother and told her he was in England. Shortly after this letter, on or about July 15, 1862, Joseph left Gravesend, England, for Australia. He returned to San Francisco in June 1864 and, through his brother Junius, secured a job as a letter carrier with Wells Fargo.

Joseph sailed from San Francisco on April 13, 1865, and did not hear of the assassination until the ship docked in Panama. He was told that a man named Booth had killed the president, but "I did not think anything of that. I knew there was a hundred Booths." Later, when more information became available, he realized that the assassin was his own brother, John.[682]

\* \* \*

Mary Ann Booth learned of the assassination and of her son's role in it from the newspapers. As she read the paper, she cried and thought of the family's honor, "O God, if this be true, let him shoot himself, let him not live to be hung! Spare him, spare us, spare the name that dreadful disgrace!"[683]

\* \* \*

Edwin Booth was on the stage in Boston playing Sir Edward Mortimer in *The Iron Chest*. Edwina, his daughter by Mary Delvin, was almost four years old; she was away visiting her cousins, the Clarkes, in Philadelphia. Marion, Junius Jr.'s daughter, was also visiting the Clarkes. Rosalie Booth and Mary Ann Booth were at Edwin's house in New York.

Edwin Booth was told of the news of the assassination by his valet James Brown.[684] They were visiting Orlando Tomkins on Franklin Square. Tomkins, a druggist by education, managed the Boston Theatre from 1862 to 1878 when his son Eugene Tompkins took over the management of the theater. It was through the theater that Orlando knew Booth. Booth apparently was appreciative of Orlando's work in helping in the purchase of some real estate on Commonwealth Avenue in Boston, for on April 6, 1865, Booth took Orlando to a local Boston jewelry store known as Jones, Ball & Poor and not only bought a gold ring for him but also inscribed a message "JWB to OT"[685]

The *Philadelphia Press* remarked that "for Edwin Booth, indeed, we feel the profoundest pity. That he was a sincere Union man, we personally know. That he possessed talent of a high order is equally certain. Yet, now by the dastardly crime of a brother that name, which the genius of his father had rendered so illustrious in the annals of the stage, and of which his own talent was conserving and advancing the reputation is stamped with so foul a blemish that he must henceforth be unable to appear *under that name before the public of the United States*." [Italics by newspaper] The article went on to speculate that perhaps one day Edwin might change his name because "no man bearing the name of the criminal shall within our lifetime be permitted to appear before an American audience.[686]

Henry C. Jarrett, the manager of the Boston Theater, sent a letter to Edwin on April 15,

> A fearful calamity is upon us. The President of the United States has fallen by the hand of an assassin, and I am shocked to say suspicion point to one nearly related to you as the perpetrator of this horrid deed. God grant that it may not prove so! Out of respect to the anguish which will fill the public mind as soon as the appalling fact shall be fully revealed, I have concluded to close the Boston Theatre until further notice. Please signify to me your cooperation in this matter. In great sorrow, and in haste, I remain, yours very truly, Henry C. Jarrett.[687]

Edwin replied,

> With deepest sorrow and great agitation, I thank you for relieving me of my engagement with yourself and the public. The news of the morning has made me wretched, indeed, not only because of a brother's crime, but because a most justly honored and patriotic ruler has fallen in an hour of national joy, by the had of an assassin. The memory of the thousands who have fallen in the field in our country's defense cannot be forgotten by me, even in this, the most distressing day of my life. While mourning, in common with all other loyal hearts, the death of the President, I am oppressed by a private woe not to be expressed in words. But whatever calamity may befall me and mine, my country, one and indivisible, has my warmest devotion.[688]

Edwin's attitude, as expressed in this letter, did much to soften public sentiment concerning him and other members of the Booth family.

Edwin and Orlando Tompkins took a train from Boston to New York to see Mary Ann Booth at Edwin's home. Friends and family had gathered to greet Edwin upon his arrival. William Bispham wrote that Edwin was "stricken to the ground. Nothing but the love that was poured out for him by his friends saved him from madness. For days his sanity hung in the balance."[689]

Edwin was very disturbed to receive hate mail threatening his life and to burn down his home.[690] When he learned that he was to be arrested like his brother Junius and brother-in-law John Clarke, friends interceded on his behalf, and Edwin was instead put under house arrest. U.S. Marshals came and searched Edwin's house. They also read his letters in an effort to find incriminating evidence. Finally Edwin wrote a sorrowful letter, which he paid the newspapers to print,

My Fellow Citizens:

It has pleased God to lay at the door of my afflicted family the lifeblood of our great, good and martyred president. Prostrated to the very earth by this dreadful event, I am yet but too sensible that other mourners fill the land. To them, to you, one and all, go forth our deep, unutterable sympathy; our abhorrence and detestation for this most foul and atrocious of crimes.

For my mother and sisters, for my remaining brothers and my own poor self there is nothing to be said except that we are thus placed without any agency of our own. For our present position we are not responsible. For the future, alas; I shall struggle on in my retirement bearing a heavy heart, an oppressed memory and a wounded name, dreadful burdens, to my too welcome grave."[691]

\* \* \*

John Sleeper Clarke was shaving when he heard a scream from his wife, Asia. He ran to her and found her in bed with a newspaper, describing John Wilkes Booth as the assassin. She, as well as her siblings, could hardly believe that John had killed Lincoln; their father had raised them to hold all life sacred. He had not even allowed animals to be killed on his farm. Asia was still crying when the doorbell rang and a U.S. Marshal came to arrest Clarke.

John Clarke later wrote:

On the Saturday Afternoon following the assassination of the President, Mrs. Booth, the Mother, came to my house from New York. The whole family was of course much depressed and excited. On the Sunday Afternoon we thought of the envelope, and Mrs. Booth, my wife, and I determined to open it. We found the letter which was published – and for his Mother a letter, 5-20 bonds to amount of $3000. Phila. City 6s to the amount of $1000 – and an assignment of some oil land in Penna. to his brother Junius, and nothing more. I kept these papers in my possession during Monday, thinking that probably the authorities would enquire at the residences of his family for his papers-no one called. On Tuesday I handed them over to the United States marshal suggesting to him that if consistent I should like him to cause to be published the letter for his mother as in that he exonerated his entire family from any sympathy with his secession propensities, I was surprised the next day to find the other letter published and not the one for his mother which I suggested should be made public. Upon the arrival at my house of Junius B. Booth on Wednesday 19th of April from Cincinnati, I casually remarked at such a time a Booth entering my house might cause a talk, whereupon Junius instantly desired that his arrival should not be made known.[692]

The government ordered Asia to go to Washington; however, her pregnancy made travel impossible. She had to get a medical certificate testifying to her condition. Because she was the sister of John Wilkes Booth, it was difficult for her to find a doctor who would come to her house to certify her condition. In the end, Asia stayed in her home guarded by police.

Edwin Booth wrote to Asia, telling her to "think no more of him as your brother; he is dead to us now, as he soon must be to all the world, but imagine the boy you loved to be in that better part of his spirit, in another world."[693]

The people of Philadelphia turned their backs on the Clarkes. Few friends came to see them, and some who did visit arrived in secrecy.

*   *   *

The day of the assassination, Junius Brutus Booth Jr. was working at the Pike's Opera House in Cincinnati. He was staying at the Burnet House. When he came down on the morning of April 15, the desk clerk, Emil Benlier, seeing he was about to leave the hotel, told not to go out into the street.

"Why?" Junius asked.

"Haven't you heard the news?"

Junius said no, and Benlier at first was hesitant and did not want to tell him. However, when Junius pressed him for an answer, Benlier told him that his brother John had killed Lincoln.

"He was," Benlier later said, "the most horrified man that I ever saw, and for the moment he was overcome by the shock."

Benlier suggested that Junius go back to his room. Luckily, Junius followed his advice, for a short time later, a mob of "fully five hundred in number" came into the hotel.

"They would have hanged him in a minute if they could have laid their hands on him," Benlier later noted. Smuggled out of the hotel, Junius Booth was later arrested.[694]

# CHAPTER 19

## I Broke My Leg

After picking up the weapons and liquor at the Surratt Tavern, Herold and Booth rode off to the home of Dr. Samuel Mudd. Mudd, like most people in Southern Maryland, had very strong pro-Confederacy sentiments and strongly advocated state's rights. He support the Southern cause during the war, an attitude very common of Southern Maryland. In Prince Georges County, where Surrattsville was located, one single voter cast a Lincoln ballot in the 1860 election.

The doctor's house was some sixteen miles from the tavern. Cold rain continued to fall as the two men approached the farm. It was a dark miserably cold morning, and all was quiet and dark in the house. It was nearly four o'clock when Herold slid down off his horse, strode up the porch steps, and banged on the door.

Samuel Alexander Mudd was born on December 20, 1833, at Oak Hill, the farm of his father Henry Lowe Mudd Sr. Mudd Sr., a successful tobacco farmer in Charles County, Maryland, owned several hundred acres of farmland and close to a hundred slaves to work the tobacco fields. Tobacco crops were second only to cotton in the South.

At age seven, young Samuel attended public school for two years. Then his father hired a private tutor to educate all his children at home.

At age fourteen, Mudd studied for two years at St. John's College in Frederick, Maryland. There Mudd met his future wife, Sarah Frances Dyer (1835-1911) who was attending a girl's academy nearby. Mudd attended Georgetown College in Washington from 1850 to 1853. He then studied medicine and surgery at Baltimore Medical College.[695] He graduated in 1856 and married Sarah Dyer on November 26, 1857.

The young couple bought 218 acres of nearby land and had a house built there. Between November 1858 and January 1864, the Mudds had four children. Mudd made a living as a tobacco farmer and part-time county doctor. He had as many as eleven slaves on his farm to work the tobacco fields.

Hearing the banging on the door, Mudd dragged himself out of bed and opened the door. Herald anxiously began telling about Booth's injury. Herold's story was that Booth's horse had fallen on him, breaking his leg. Mudd, who knew Booth, having met him three times previously, immediately brought the two inside.

Shortly after arriving, Herold asked Dr. Mudd if their horses could be put into the stable – Herold was afraid that the one he was riding might break away if not confined. Dr. Mudd said yes and had his servant put the horses in the stable.

A candle lit the room into which Mudd led Herold and Booth. Shadows dance across the wall as Mudd rummaged through a drawer for more candles. The doctor swept a table clear and helped Booth stretch out on it. Mudd pulled off Booth's above-the-knee riding boots, which were designed to be interchangeable for both feet. The one on his left foot was impossible to pull off because of the swelling around the broken bone. Mudd took some heavy shears and cut the leather down the side. The boot was tossed aside. This action would later cost him dearly when it was later recovered by a Union officer. Inside the boot Mudd threw aside was printed "H. Lux, Maker 465 Broadway. J. Wilkes."

Mudd discovered that Booth had a simple fracture of the fibula (the smaller bone of the lower leg) about two inches above the ankle. It was not a life-threatening injury, but the break could become a serious injury if Booth continued to ride. To recover, Booth needed continued medical care and rest. Mudd, having no splinting supplies on hand, used splints fashioned from an old box.

Booth was also suffering from back pain due to Booth's position on his horse because of his broken ankle and long hours of riding, but Mudd could do nothing more for him, except to order rest. So Booth was carried upstairs to the room he had slept in just a few months before.

Mudd, a competent physician, had examined Booth – a man he had seen and talked with only weeks before in a hotel room in Washington and who had actually slept in his house only months before. He could not have been fooled as to Booth's identity. Mudd knew Booth. There is the November 13, 1864, meeting at St. Mary's Church when Booth is first introduced to Mudd by John Thompson; the second meeting in Bryantown on December 18, 1864, when Mudd introduced Booth to Harbin; and finally the December 23, 1864, meeting in Washington when Mudd introduced John Surratt to Booth.[696]

Day dawned only hours later, and by seven o'clock the next morning, Herold with Dr. Mudd and his wife, Frances, sat down to breakfast. Herold did not mention the assassination of Lincoln, but instead he spoke casually of his hunting in the area. Herold appeared relaxed as he told how he had been "frolicking around for five or six months."

Mrs. Mudd, unable to listen to such lack of industry, replied that "all play and no work makes Jack a bad boy. Your father ought to make you go to work!"[697]

"My father is dead," Herold replied blandly.

Mrs. Mudd had prepared a hearty country breakfast for her guests. But Booth showed no signs of descending the stairs. At last, Mrs. Booth prepared a tray and had her servant bring it upstairs. But Booth could not eat. Back in Washington at 7:22 that morning, Abraham Lincoln died.

Sometime during Booth's stay, Dr. Mudd suggested that if Booth's leg did not improve, he should see Dr. Richard H. Stuart, a Confederate sympathizer who lived on the Virginia side of the Potomac.[698] Later when Dr. Mudd was questioned by a federal officer, he lied saying he did not know Booth; he said, "His friend urged me to attend to his leg as soon as possible, as they were very anxious to get to Washington, and then, it is my impression, he inquired if they could reach some point on the Potomac, where they could get a boat to Washington." This lie hurt Mudd when Dr. Stuart, questioned by federal authorities, swore that "Dr. Mudd had recommended them to me."[699]

After breakfast, Herold asked the shortest way to the Potomac River, and Mudd told him that it was in the direction of Zekiah Swamp. That morning, Booth shaved off his mustache. He was in pain all that day and did nothing more than lay in bed until he left in late afternoon.

After lunch, Herold, knowing the pursuers were not far away, announced that they must be on their way. Booth and Herold wanted to rent a carriage for Booth to ride in, and Mudd suggested that Herold come with him to nearby Bryantown to find a rental. Mudd needed to go to Bryantown anyway to mail some contraband mail he had previously received.[700]

Meanwhile, Mrs. Mudd brought lunch up to Booth, but he still did not feel good enough to eat. Mrs. Mudd did not give up. Later she came up again with "some cake, a couple oranges, and some wine."

"How are you feeling?" she asked.

"My back hurts me dreadfully," Booth moaned. "I must have hurt it when the horse fell and I broke my leg." He groaned pathetically, "Is there was any brandy in the house."

"No but we have was some good whiskey."

But Booth declined, and Mrs. Mudd went downstairs.[701]

During this time, Dr. Mudd and Herold rode first to Oak Hill, the farm of Henry Lowe Mudd Sr., Mudd's father. There Herold hoped to borrow a carriage for Booth. But the family would not rent him their carriage – the next day was Easter, and they would need it to go to church. Mudd and Herald then set out for Bryantown.

Throughout the day, nearly two thousand cavalry were combing Southern Maryland in search of the two fugitives. The manhunt was gaining momentum, and the army believed that Booth was making his escape there. And Bryantown was no safe place for the fugitives. A detachment of the Thirteenth New York Cavalry commanded by Lieutenant David Dana had arrived in Bryantown about noon on Saturday.

Around two o'clock, Herold and Dr. Mudd approached Bryantown where they caught sight of some cavalry. Suddenly Herold changed his mind about going into town. He and Booth would forget about the carriage and use the horses after all. Mudd must have looked at him oddly; the young man had just gone to a lot of time and energy and now, as they neared renting stables, decided not to get a carriage after all. Mudd, confused by Herold sudden reversal, continued alone into town with his mail.

Herold, frightened by the sight of soldiers around town, headed back alone, avoiding arrest in Bryantown. Somewhere around Oak Hill, he got confused and rode about the roads trying to make out which way to go. At last, he came upon a freed black man, Electus Thomas, who pointed the way back to the Mudd farm.[702]

When Mudd rode into Bryantown, it was more crowded than usual. People were talking, and Union cavalry were everywhere. It was here that Mudd first learned of the assassination. Mudd saw the headlines of the *Washington Intelligencer* for that day.

LINCOLN ASSASSINATED
ACTOR BOOTH HUNTED
ACCOMPLICE STABS SEWARD
NORTH STUNNED BY TRAGEDY

While in Bryantown, Mudd bought some supplies, including some calico. He had a conversation with the owner of the local general store about the assassination, who remarked that the assassination was very tragic. "Yes," Mudd replied, "I am sorry to hear it."[703]

Mudd was shocked at the news and suddenly realized the position in which he found himself. He knew Booth had seen him at least three times, and Booth was being treated at his farm for a broken leg. Mudd was a known Confederate sympathizer involved in the Confederate courier system, so going to the cavalry in town was out of the question. Mudd hurriedly left Bryantown and followed the main road to his home. However, on the way, he stopped at the house of Francis R. Farrell sometime between four and five o'clock.[704]

There he met John F. Hardy, who was visiting, at the gate. Mudd claimed to stop by to see Hardy to buy some rail timber. However, Hardy had no rails to sell; he had already sold them to Sylvester Mudd, his cousin. Quickly, Mudd told Hardy the news about the president and Seward. Hardy testifies, "I remember that Booth's name was mentioned in the same connection, and I asked him if it was the man who had been down there, and was represented as Booth. His reply was that he did not know whether it was that man or one of his brothers; he understood that he had some brothers. That ended the conversation except that he said it was one of the most terrible calamities that could have befallen the country at this time . . . . He said nothing to me in that conversation about two strangers having called at his house, and remaining there all day."[705]

Hardy, much excited at the news, called out Farrell, who was still in his house, and he joined in the conversation.

Mudd told Farrell that he "was very sorry that this thing had occurred, very sorry." Farrell was convinced. "From his appearance, I think he was entirely in earnest in expressing his sorrow for the crime."[706] Mudd rode away after staying only about fifteen minutes.

Meanwhile, Herold, having found his way back, explained to Mrs. Mudd why he had returned without a carriage. Then he bounded up the stairs to tell Booth of the cavalry in the area. Booth, with pain convulsing through the broken bone, understood that they must move on and hide. Booth made his way down the stairs and out the door to the horses. Mrs. Mudd thought as Booth painfully hobbled downstairs that "so much of his face as could be seen presented a picture of agony."

"It was not a good idea for Booth to leave in that condition," Mrs. Mudd said, unaware of the Lincoln's assassination.

"If he suffers much we won't go far, I will take him to my lady-love's not far from here," Herold replied.

After much careful lifting and pushing, Herold got Booth up on to the horse. Before they could leave; however, Mudd galloped up to the farmhouse. He was frightened and visibly upset by the presence of federal soldiers searching for Booth.

"How dare you endanger me and my family!" he yelled at Booth and told him that he wanted them off his property "forthwith!" In a matter of minutes, they were gone.[707]

Mrs. Mudd stood there staring at her husband, stunned. She had no idea why he had changed so suddenly from a genial host to a furious evictor. After the two fugitives had disappeared from sight, Mudd told his wife all he had learned that Booth had assassinated Lincoln and that the countryside was swarming with Union cavalry.

Mudd and his wife discussed the mater at length. Booth was weak and possibly would not get far in his escape. Would Booth give Mudd's name to the federals to retaliate for throwing him out? To avoid this possibility, Mudd decided that he would go the next morning and tell a version of the story that was less damaging. After a long discussion with his wife, Mudd decided that in the morning, he would report the incident "to the soldiers"[708]

*    *    *

Easter Sunday was cold with overcast clouds.

In churches across the country, clergymen sermonized about the assassinated president. Many people were filled with mixed feelings – for the devoted Christian Easter is a happy event, and yet it was juxtaposed with the murder of Lincoln. Should they rejoice over the resurrection, or mourn over their fallen president? Easter was draped in black that year.

Samuel and Frances Mudd ordinarily attended morning service at St. Mary's. But this Sunday, Mrs. Mudd stayed at home, and Dr. Mudd attended St. Peter's Church. The same one where in November he had been introduced to Booth. Mudd's father,

Henry Mudd, had donated the land on which the church was built; and Samuel Mudd knew members of St. Peter's congregation. The church was only a few miles from his farm, and Mudd arrived early before the ten o'clock service. He found himself talking to Benjamin Gardiner. According to Gardiner, Mudd told him that "there were two suspicious persons at my house yesterday morning. I paid no particular attention to what he said about suspicious persons, because since the war commenced we have always had in our neighborhood deserted soldiers constantly, and detectives and soldiers of the United States, and we could hardly tell who they were."[709]

Dr. George D. Mudd testified for the defense. He said that "I was at church on Sunday, the 16th; it was then known that the President had been assassinated, but no one to my knowledge, supposed that Booth had crossed the river; this at least was my impression . . . . I saw Dr. Samuel Mudd at church. On returning home he overtook me, and I rode with him as far as his house."[710] During this ride, Samuel Mudd told him that two men had visited him. "Dr. Samuel A. Mudd had informed me that two suspicious parties came to his house a little before daybreak on Saturday morning; and that one of them had, as he said, a broken leg, which Dr. Samuel Mudd bandaged . . . that these parties stated that they came from Bryantown, and were inquiring the way to the Rev. Dr. Wilmer's; that while there one of them called for a razor and shaved himself, thereby altering his appearance; that he improvised a crutch or crutches for the broken-legged man, and that they went in the direction of Parson Wilmer's . . . . That Dr. Samuel Mudd went from his house with the younger of the two men (Herold) to try and procure a carriage to take them away from his house; that he went down the road toward Bryantown and failed to get one, and that they left his house on horseback."[711]

George Mudd was eager to help. He told Mudd that he knew Lieutenant Dana and volunteered to tell him of the visit of the two strangers, but because it was Easter Sunday, they would wait until Monday.[712]

\* \* \*

Lieutenant David D. Dana (younger brother of Assistant Secretary of War Charles A. Dana) was commanding the cavalry headquartered at Bryantown. Dispatched from Washington, he had led his unit to search Prince Georges and Charles counties. Washington police under Major A. C. Richards, army detectives under General Christopher Augur, and the secret service agents of Lafayette C. Baker, all under Stanton's control, were also searching for Booth.

At this time, the detectives and agents did not know that the assassin had a broken leg, and so no one thought that the injured stranger was Booth. Had the federal government known that the assassin had a broken leg, this would have been a vital piece of information in their manhunt for Booth. Not a single eyewitness reported seeing Booth limp as he fled across the stage. And now Mudd knew who the assassin was and that he had a broken leg, but he continued to say that the two men who visited his farm were strangers to him. This lie would haunt him in future months and years.

Lieutenant Dana decided to follow up on this information, so the next day, he sent Lieutenant Alexander Lovett to interview Dr. Mudd[713] Lieutenant Lovett arrived at the farm with George Mudd and a small squad of cavalry on Tuesday, April 18. After talking to Dr. Mudd, Lovett felt that the doctor was not completely honest. Lovett noted that "Dr. Mudd . . . did not at first seem inclined to give us any satisfaction . . . . On asking him who the man with the broken leg was, he said he did not know; he was a stranger to him. The other, he said, was a young man, about seventeen or eighteen years of age. Mudd said that one of them called for a razor, which he furnished, together with soap and water, and the wounded man shaved off his mustache."[714]

Samuel Mudd was sinking deeper and deeper into suspicion with every lie he told.

On April 21, Lieutenant Lovett returned to the Mudd farm. Mudd grew more and more alarmed at the questions he was asked. Then he realized that the soldiers were going to search the house only then did he remember the boot that he had cut from Booth's leg. He told his wife to go upstairs and bring down the boot. Mudd quickly explained he had cut it off the man's leg in order to set it. Lovett turned down the top of the boot and saw the name "J. Wilkes" printed in it. Lovett called Mudd's attention to it, and Mudd claimed he had not taken notice of it before. "At the second interview, he still insisted that the men were strangers to him."

When Lovett continued to point out the many discrepancies in his story, Mudd subsequently said "it was Booth."[715]

Dr. Mudd also lied to Lovett about the direction the two fugitives had taken when they left. He said that Booth and Herold had ridden off in the direction of the Zekiah Swamp, when in fact, the two had left traveling south and made a wide sweep around Bryantown.

The ruse backfired when, a few days later, Provost Marshal O'Beirne followed Helold's and Booth's tracks; they led him directly south of Mudd's farm near Oak Hill, the home of Henry Lowe Mudd Sr., Samuel Mudd's father. Since Dr. Mudd had directed the troops in an easterly direction, O'Beirne concluded that the doctor was lying and had aided Booth in his escape. Also in taking a wide sweep of Bryantown, Booth and Herold avoided the Thirteenth New York Cavalry.[716]

It was not until April 21 when Mrs. Mudd brought out Booth's boot that the War Department fixed its attention on "lame man" sightings, and one of those led directly to Booth's capture.

No eyewitness reported seeing Booth limp as he fled across the stage. It was only when Mrs. Mudd turning over Booth's boot to Lieutenant Dana on April 21 that there was any indicated that Booth had broken his ankle. The broken leg was important, but how did it happen? Historian Michael Kauffman has researched some points to consider:

1) Eyewitnesses at Ford's Theatre gave no indication of the break, except to say that the assassin landed on the stage off balance after leaping from the presidential box. One example is W. J. Ferguson (the young actor standing next to Laura Keene just off stage about to go on when Booth shot Lincoln) writes that after Booth's jump from the presidential box "apparently unhurt, three feet to a stride, he rushed across the stage toward the point in the first entrance where Miss Keene and I were standing." And later (in the same article) said, "I think I have made it clear that there was no time for the slightest delay in Booth's progress from the time of his fall to his disappearance in the alley, the distance on the stage level, about seventy-five feet, having been covered at a running pace, in not more that half a minute."

2) During his escape, Booth told everyone that he had broken his leg when his horse stumbled and fell on him. This accident apparently occurred after Booth crossed the bridge out of Washington and before he met up with Herald. He even said this to John Lloyd who knew about the assassination.

3) David Herold spoke of the stumbling horse; Herold said that Booth told him "that his horse had fallen or he was thrown off and his ankle sprained." Not yet realizing that the ankle was broken.

4) When Booth mounted his horse in Baptist Alley (and had trouble with the skittish mare), his left leg bore all the weight and torsion of his body, getting on a skittish horse on the left side with a broken left ankle is near impossible, yet he indicated no pain at the time.

5) Sergeant Cobb at the Navy Yard Bridge, who saw Booth twenty minutes after the shooting, noted that the assassin's voice was smooth and that he appeared at ease. Everyone Booth met subsequently said that Booth's voice was cracked in pain.

6) Dr. Mudd said that Booth's pants were muddy when he arrived on the morning of April 15.

7) Thomas Davis, a farmhand at Dr. Mudd's, told detectives that Booth's mare had a badly swollen left front shoulder and a fresh cut on its leg. Davis fed and cared for the horse during Booth's visit.

Booth wrote in his diary after he had read a newspaper article condemning his actions as cowardly and stating that he was the villain of the century. Booth may have been writing to justify his actions and at the same time to live out some high drama – breaking an ankle while leaping from the presidential box is more dramatic than falling off a stumbling horse.[717]

Lt. Dana arrested Mudd that day at his home. Mudd had created problems for himself because he was caught in a number of lies. It would be more than four years before the doctor would see his children again. His wife, Francis, whom he called Frank, visited him in prison in Washington. About a week after his arrest, Dr. Mudd wrote a letter to his wife,

Carroll Prison
April 29, 1865

My dearest Frank:

I am very well. Hope you and the children are enjoying a like blessing. Try and get some one to plant our crop. It is very uncertain what time I shall be released from here. Hire hands at the prices they demand. Urge them on all you can and make them work.

I am truly in hopes my stay here will be short, when I can return again to your fond embrace and our little children.

Soldiers were later stationed at the Mudd farm. They showed their disdain for the man who had aided and abetted Booth by breaking open the meat house and eating the meat. They burned the fences, destroyed the wheat and tobacco crops, and pulled boards off the corn house so the corn fell out on to the ground. What crops they did not eat were trampled upon.

# CHAPTER 20

## Atzerodt

A little after ten o'clock on the night of April 14, Atzerodt entered the Kirkwood House. Booth had told him to kill Vice President Johnson, but Atzerodt did not want to be an assassin. After a few drinks in the hotel's bar, he abandoned the assignment. Atzerodt rode to the capitol and beyond it to the Pennsylvania House on C Street for another drink. He returned the horse to Keleher's stable at about eleven o'clock. By then, people were learning of the news of Lincoln's assassination. Suddenly, Atzerodt, through a alcohol haze, was beginning to panic; he could easily be connected to Booth. Fearful that he would be arrested, Atzerodt knew he must get away and hide. He knew that through his association with Booth, he would be arrested. Atzerodt took a horse-drawn streetcar headed toward the Navy Yard and there met two men he knew, Washington Briscoe and John Yates. Briscoe, who had known Atzerodt for seven or eight years, saw him as he got on to the car between eleven thirty and twelve o'clock. Atzerodt, distracted, did not at first recognize Briscoe. Briscoe, however, recognized him and moved toward him. Briscoe asked him if he had heard the news.

Atzerodt said he had heard, but his mind was elsewhere. He was at his wit's end. Where could he hide? He pleaded three time with Briscoe to let him sleep in his store that night, but Briscoe three times "told him he could not."[718] Atzerodt rode the Navy Yard car back downtown. He decided to get a room at the Pennsylvania House and sneak out early in the morning because he had no money to pay the bill. It was then past two o'clock in the morning.

From the streetcar, Atzerodt then walked up 4 1/2 Street. As he was walking toward the Pennsylvania House, he met a stranger who asked where he could find a hotel. Atzerodt told him to come along with him.[719]

The stranger's name was Samuel Thomas.

John Greenawalt, the manager, later described that evening,

"I had just come in the house myself, and had gone to my room. About five minutes afterward a servant came up with a five-dollar bill and said, 'There is a man come in with Atzerodt who wants lodging, and wants to pay for it. So I went down and gave the man his change.'"

"Atzerodt asked for his old room, and I told him it was occupied. I told him he would have to go with this gentleman. So I gave this Thomas his change, and told the servant to show him to his room, and Atzerodt was going to follow him, when I said, 'Atzerodt, you have not registered.' Said he, 'Do you want my name?' I replied, 'Certainly.' He hesitated some, but stepped back and registered, and went to his room . . . . He got up about 5 o'clock and left the house, so the servant told me. A lady who was stopping at the house had given orders for a carriage to take her to the 6:15 train. She left before I got up, and as the servant was going out of the door, this man Thomas went out and asked the way to the railway depot. He had no baggage."[720]

Atzerodt left shortly afterward and walked toward Sixth Street. As the servant came back from getting the carriage, he met Atzerodt and said to him, "What brings you out so early this morning?"

"Well," he said, "I have got business." He left without paying his bill."

"The servant told me they came in together; but that is the only reason I had for thinking they came together. I told Atzerodt that he would have to room with that man, and he had no objection . . . . I do not know why Atzerodt and the man Thomas got up at the same time in the morning. They did not occupy the same bed."[721]

By eight, Saturday morning, Atzerodt walked to 49 High Street in Georgetown to the firm of Matthews & Company where he wanted to sell his watch. But John Caldwell, the manager, declined. Atzerodt, who needed money to make his escape, then begged Caldwell to lend him $10.

"I have not the money to spare," Caldwell said dryly.

Atzerodt had only one thing of value, and that was his revolver.

"Lend me $10, and take this as security, and I will bring the money or send it to you next week," said Atzerodt. Caldwell thought the revolver was good security and loaned him the money.[722]

With this cash in hand, Atzerodt decided to make his way to the farm of his cousin, Hartman Richter, who lived near Germantown, Maryland. Atzerodt had lived on this farm as a boy.

On his way out of Washington, Atzerodt visited a widow, Lucinda Metz, at 182 West Street and stayed for breakfast. Then he took a stage that ran from Washington to Rockville, Maryland. Atzerodt was the only passenger that morning when the stage left the Georgetown stop at Cunningham's Tavern at High and O streets. Just past Tennlytown, near the Washington/Maryland line, the stage was halted at a military checkpoint.

Atzerodt looked out the stagecoach's window, saw the soldiers getting ready to check passengers, and immediately opened the door and hopped out. He walked up to the checkpoint and started small talk with the sergeant in charge. Before long, Atzerodt asked the sergeant to have some hard cider with him at the nearby sutler's store. (A sutler is one who sells his goods/wares to soldiers in a moving army.) After Atzerodt and the Union sergeant finished drinking, Atzerodt asked William Gaither, a local farmer, for a ride. Gaither, being a friendly sort, gave him a seat in his wagon – only later did Gaither learn who the young man was.[723]

When authorities learned that Atzerodt was involved in the assassination and that he had slipped by the checkpoint, the sergeant who had drunk cider with him was arrested and charged with dereliction of duty.

About dark that Saturday, Gaither let Atzerodt off at John Mullican's tavern and blacksmith shop three miles north of Rockville. Gaither then went off toward his farm, and Atzerodt had a few drinks at Mullican's. It was dark when he set out on foot for Germantown. About eleven o'clock that evening, Atzerodt arrived at the Old Clopper Mill on Great Seneca Creek. Atzerodt knew the miller, Robert Kinder, from previous visits, and he asked Kinder to let him stay for the night. Kinder, not knowing Atzerodt was wanted, agreed. For this friendly act, Kinder was later arrested on April 28 and only released from the Old Capitol Prison June 3.

Walking his last few miles to the Richter farm, Atzerodt dropped by the farm of Hezekiah Metz between ten and eleven o'clock on Sunday morning. There he ate, and Metz inquired about the latest news of the assassination, and the men discussed whether Grant had been shot or not. Metz had heard that Grant had been shot on the train. Atzerodt, unable to resist implying that he knew quite a bit about the whole affair, said, "If the man that was to follow him had followed him, it was likely to be so."

Atzerodt told people that his name was Andrew Attwood, and only the Richters and a few boyhood friends knew his real name.[724] After enjoying the Metz's hospitality, Atzerodt finally departed, reaching the Richter farm between two and three o'clock on Sunday afternoon. "He [Atzerodt] remained at my house from Sunday till Thursday morning, and occupied himself with walking about, working in the garden a little, and going among the neighbors . . . . When he was arrested he seemed very willing to go along," Richter later testified.[725]

Meanwhile, on April 19, Hezekiah Metz was talking with a neighbor, Nathan Page, a local informer for the Union military's underground network. During the conversation, Metz told Page of the Sunday conversation with Atzerodt. The more Metz and Page discussed the conversation, the more unusual it seemed. At about two o'clock, Page was at the home of James W. Purdun, just north of Germantown, and told him about Metz's suspicious guest. Soon Purdun set out for the federal garrison at Monocacy Junction to report the matter to Captain Solomon Townsend. On the road, Purdun met Private Frank O'Daniel, Company D, First Delaware Cavalry. O'Daniel had been to nearby Clarksburg to retrieve his overcoat and was on his way back to his unit. Purdun asked O'Daniel to carry the message about the Atzerodt (Attwood) conversation to Captain Townsend. By the time the message was delivered, Atzerodt was at the Richter farm.

Back in camp, O'Daniel passed Purdun's message on to Sergeant George Lindsley, who took it to Captain Townsend. Townsend was skeptical because Purdun had previously sent him worthless information. So Townsend recommended that Major E. R. Artman, the post commander, to ignore the information. Artman agreed, but by nine o'clock on the evening of April 19, Major Artman changed his mind and ordered Captain Townsend to send out a detail to arrest George Atzerodt alias Andrew Attwood.

Sergeant Gemmill, First Delaware Cavalry, with a detail of six men, arrested Atzerodt on April 20 at about 4:00 A.M., at the Richter farm in Germantown.[726]

Gemmill's detail brought Atzerodt and Richter back to his unit at Monocacy Junction where Major Artman quickly established that Attwood was really George Atzerodt, wanted in connection with the assassination. The soldiers had at first considered the assignment to find and arrest Atwood undesirable. However, in the end, the arrest made all members of the detail richer when the reward money was distributed.[727] Information leading to the arrest of Atzerodt had been passed from Metz to Page, to Purdun, to Private O'Daniel, to Sergeant Lindsley, to Captain Townsend, and to Major Artman.

At 11:30 PM, April 20, George Atzerodt and Hartman Richter were brought aboard the gunboat *Saugus*.

# CHAPTER 21

## *With Every Man's Hand against Me*

As Atzerodt was fleeing Washington, and Powell was hiding in trees, Booth and Herold left the Mudd farm heading south. Their original plan was to go to the home of William Burtles on the east side of the swamp. Burtles was active locally in pro-Confederate activities in Charles County, Maryland. Booth got Burtles name from Mudd and knew of his Southern sympathy. However, a few miles south of Bryantown, the two men got lost in the darkness. About nine o'clock, they stumbled upon the home of Oswald Swann, a black man who owned a fifty-acre tobacco farm. Swann was raised in Charles County and knew the area well. They asked Swann for directions to William Burtles's farm and learned that they were only about two miles away. They offered two dollars to Swann if he would lead them to the farm, and Swann agreed. Before they left, Swann gave the hungry men some whiskey and bread.

On the way to Burtles's farm, Booth and Herold had second thoughts and instead wanted to be taken to the home of Samuel Cox. Cox was one of the leaders of the Confederate underground in Southern Maryland.

Swann relates, "They asked me if I could take them to Capt. Cox, if so they would give me $5 more. I took them. One was a small man, and the other was lame and had a crutch."[728] As they rode along the twelve-mile journey to the Cox farm, Herold began to worry – Swann himself might turn them in. At last Herold rode up next to Swann and threatened: "Don't you say anything. If you tell anybody you will not live long!"

The three reached Rich Hill, the Samuel Cox farm, a little after midnight. Cox, a wealthy slave owner, was a Confederate sympathizer.[729] He came to the door with a candle and spoke to Herold while Booth waited at the gate on his horse. After a few moments, Cox walked over to Booth and out of hearing of Swann. Booth told who he was and showed the India ink mark J. W. B. on his hand to prove it. Cox, realizing he had the president's assassin before him, led the two men into the house. Cox was willing to help, but he was concerned that his black servants would see Booth and

Herold and tell someone. So Cox told the two fugitives to sleep outside. He gave them food and a blanket and arranged for his overseer, Franklin Robey, to guide them to a spot thick with pine about one mile west of his house.[730] Meanwhile, Swann was standing just out of earshot watching the whole transaction.

When Booth and Herold came out to leave, one of them said for Swann's benefit, "I thought Cox was a man of Southern feeling!" Herald hoped that Swann would think Cox was turning the men away without help. Swann helped Booth mount his horse, and then Swann rode back to his farm.

Booth and Herold slept in the nearby pine thicket that night. Cox told them that more help would be on the way. The person he sent would whistle a particular tune so the men would recognize him as a friend.

*   *   *

Thomas A. Jones was a Southern overseer of about forty-five of age, a nonsmoker and nondrinker, a widower with several children, with no formal education. Jones, who lived on a farm only a few miles from Cox's farm, gave this account, "When Annapolis was a greater place than Baltimore, and the Patuxent Valley the populous part of Maryland, the main roads and ferries to all-powerful Virginia were on the lower Potomac." For geographical reasons, this portion of Southern Maryland was used "as the nearest safe point for spies and go-betweens" to cross from Maryland and Confederate Virginia. Jones had been asked "to carry the Confederate mail from Canada and the United States to Richmond. Jones replied that the risk was too great" and declined. However, Jones's heart was in the Confederate cause and said he would help in other ways. Throughout the war, Jones was active in the Confederate courier system. His mission was to get spies, messengers, and couriers of contraband mail across the Potomac River on their trips to and from Richmond. In the fall of 1861, Jones was arrested and imprisoned for six months.

Jones eventually became the chief signal agent of the Confederacy in Southern Maryland. "One portion of Jones's business was to put the New York and Northern newspapers every day into Richmond. These newspapers would go to Bryantown post-office, or sometimes to Charlotte Hall post-office, and would generally reach the Potomac near dusk, and being conveyed all night by the Confederate mail-carriers, by way of Port Royal, would be in the hands of the rebel Cabinet next morning, twenty-four hours only after the people in New York were reading them, . . . Jones heard of the murder of Lincoln on Saturday afternoon, April 15th . . . . On Sunday morning, the 16th of April about nine o'clock, a young white man (Samuel Cox, Jr.) came from Samuel Cox's to Jones's farm . . . . He told Jones that Colonel Cox wished him to come immediately to his house, about three miles to the north . . . . Jones mounted his horse and went to Cox's."[731]

There Cox said, "Tom, I had visitors about four o'clock this morning."[732]

Jones asked who and why the visitors had come.

"Cox related that on the previous night the assassin of President Lincoln had come to his house in company with another person guided by a negro, and had asked for assistance to cross the Potomac River; and," said Cox to Jones, "you will have to get him across." Cox told Jones where the fugitives were concealed and explained how he should give a signal by whistling, otherwise, the two men might fire on him.[733]

Cox exclaimed, "Tom, we must get those men who were here this morning across the river . . . . Can't you put those men across?"

"Sam, I will see what I can do."[734]

Jones set out for the pine thicket where the fugitives were hiding. On his way, he came upon Booth's bay mare, still saddled and bridled and grazing in a small clearing. Jones tied the horse to a tree since a stray horse would certainly be noticed. Then he made his way into the pine forest and whistled the way Cox had described. At this, Herold came out into a clearing holding his carbine cocked. "Who are you, and what do you want?" Herold demanded.

"I come from Cox, he told me I would find you here. I am a friend. You have nothing to fear from me," Jones replied.

Herold led him to Booth, who was lying on the ground with his head supported on his hand, partially covered by a blanket. Pistols and a knife were lying beside him. Booth was very pale and suffering intensely from his broken leg. But Jones remembered, "I have seldom, if ever, seen a more strikingly handsome man."[735]

Booth was very anxious to read the newspapers. "He seemed very desirous to know what the world thought of his deed," Jones remembered.[736]

Jones told Booth, "You must remain right here, however long, and wait til I can see some way to get you out; and I do not believe I can get you away from here until this hue and cry is somewhat over. Meantime I will see that you are fed."[737]

Jones told Booth that he had seen a horse grazing nearby, and Booth said it belonged to him. Jones told him that they would have to get rid of the horses or the animals would certainly draw attention. "Besides, there was no way to feed the horses."[738]

When Jones returned to the farm and told Cox that the horses might give the two fugitives away, Cox sent Franklin Robey, his overseer to dispose of them. Roby located both horses and rode them out into the deep water of a marsh and then shot them.[739] They sank out of sight and were never found.

Booth and Herold spent six days and five nights in the pine forest. The weather continued, chilly, damp, and unpleasant. Booth's broken leg became infected, and he developed a fever. To make matters worse, the two could not light a fire for fear its flame or smoke might give their location away. Jones continued to visit them daily, generally about ten o'clock in the morning. Jones always kept his visits to Booth and Herold short, visiting put him in great personal danger and could be hanged as an accomplice if caught. In all the times that Jones visited, "Booth did not rise from the ground at any time" until he was finally put on Jones's horse the night he left to cross the Potomac.[740]

On Tuesday, April 18, after delivering bread, butter, ham, a flask of coffee, and newspapers to Booth, Jones went to Port Tobacco. It was the traditional day for the transaction of public business in the county. Jones mingled in the square and became "satisfied that nothing was positively known." Later that day in the barroom of the Brawner Hotel, Jones met Captain William Williams. Williams was the Washington mounted policeman who, moments before Abraham Lincoln was shot, had asked John Booth in front of Ford's Theatre to come for a drink. Now Williams invited Jones to drink with him. Williams said, "I will give one hundred thousand dollars to anyone who will give me the information that will lead to Booth's capture."[741]

"That is a large sum of money and ought to get him if money can do it," Jones replied.

Although Jones did not think there was any change in his expression, Williams's suspicions were aroused.[742]

Jones was finally arrested and questioned, but he revealed nothing. He had seen the handbills ordering all citizens to join in the hunt for the assassin "and that to furnish bread and water to him [Booth] meant death." Jones did worry about his complicity, but it did not occur to him to turn Booth in. Jones never regretted losing out on the reward money that might have been his although Jones did believed that the assassination of Lincoln was a severe blow to the South's hopes for reconstruction.[743]

In response to why he did not turn in Booth for the reward money, Jones later wrote, "But, thank God, there was something I still possessed, something I still could call my own, and its name was Honor."[744]

\* \* \*

Jones came every day to the pine forest with food and newspapers. Booth read about the unanimous condemnation of his deed and that he was denounced as a wretch, a cutthroat, and other loathsome names.

Booth was shocked at public reaction to what he had done; he had heard Northerners and Southerners denounce Abraham Lincoln as a tyrant, a despot, and a military dictator. They had complained of a rigged election and political arrests. Throughout the most devastating war in American history, men on both sides had blamed the war and loss of life on Lincoln. Booth felt moved to defend his killing of Lincoln. He had with him a little appointment book from 1864, and in it he wrote furiously explaining why he had shot Lincoln. It was typical of Booth to describe his situation theatrically. So he described April 15 as the Ides, in reference to the Ides of March, when Caesar was assassinated in Shakespeare's *Julius Caesar*.

"Friday the Ides. Until today nothing was ever thought of sacrificing to our country's wrongs. For six months we had worked to capture. But our cause being almost lost, something decisive and great must be done. I struck boldly and not as the papers say. I walked with a firm step through a thousand of his friends, was stopped, but pushed on. A colonel was by his side. I shouted 'Sic semper.' In jumping broke my leg. I passed all his pickets. Rode sixty miles that night, with the bone of my leg tearing at every jump."

"I can never repent it, though we hated to kill. Our country owed all her troubles to him, and God simply made me the instrument of His punishment. I care not what becomes of me. I have no desire to outlive my country. The night before the deed, I wrote a long article and left it for one of the editors of the National Intelligencer, in which I fully set forth our reasons for our proceedings. He or the Govmt."[745]

At this point, Booth stopped writing his exaggerated and incorrect account. There was no colonel at Lincoln's side. Booth did not break his leg in jumping, he passed only one guard post, and he did not ride sixty miles that night.

Booth did not know that his letter to the *National Intelligencer* was never delivered, that Matthews had destroyed the letter.[746]

*   *   *

The weather continued, cold, foggy, and misty, and Booth's leg became more inflamed and swollen from neglect and exposure.[747] The ground was continuously wet, and the dampness made life miserable for Booth and Herold. Once Booth and Herold crouched in fear at the sound of tramping horses and clanking sabers as a body of cavalry passed not two hundred yards away.

On one of his daily visits, Jones told them that on Thursday, April 20, they would cross the Potomac. Booth and Herold were excited about continuing their escape; however, on that day, Jones canceled the crossing because Union cavalry was still in the area. The cavalry was visiting every house in lower Maryland.

On April 21, Jones went to the town of Allen's Fresh, which was just a cluster of a few houses. There he overheard a cavalry officer, John R. Walton, say, "We have just got news that those fellows have been seen down in St. Mary's County."[748] Jones, elated, watched as the cavalry rode off in that direction. Because the area would now be free of Union cavalry, Jones immediately made plans to transport Booth and Herold across the Potomac that night. He rode out to the pine thicket and told them to be ready that evening.

A light mist fell throughout the day, and it was near evening when Jones went to the pine forest. This time, however, he did so with extra care: It was the first time he had visited the hiding place at night. Men traveling after dark in the days following the assassination always drew suspicion, and Jones was very cautious, also he did not want to be shot.

"Now, friends," Jones said to the two men, "this is your only chance. The night is pitch dark and my boat is close by. I will get you some supper at my house, and send you off if I can."[749]

Jones had planned well for this crossing. He had his former slave, Henry Woodland, go out on the Potomac each morning to fish for shad. Jones wanted the boat used so that it would be seen on a daily basis and not arouse suspicion among the federals.

Jones also had Woodland bring the boat to Dent's Meadow every evening after the fishing.

With considerable difficulty, Herald and Jones lifted Booth on to Jones's horse. Booth was in great pain and could not help groaning.[750] By the time the three were mounted and rode off to Jones's farm, it was dark. Part of the trip was over a public road, and this was especially hazardous for the fugitives: they had to pass two houses. In one, there lived a black family whose children were always looking to see who passed. The other house had dogs that usually barked at anyone's approach. But the children did not appear, and the dogs did not bark. So the men passed safely. About ten o'clock, they arrived at Jones's farm.[751]

When the three stopped at Jones's front door, Jones said, "Wait here while I go in and get you some supper, which you can eat here while I get something for myself."

Booth asked pathetically, "Oh, can't I go in and get some of your hot coffee?"

"My friend," Jones replied, "it wouldn't do. Indeed it would not be safe. There are servants in the house who would be sure to see you and then we would all be lost. Remember, this is your last chance to get away."

Jones went in and spoke to Henry Woodland. "Did you bring the boat to Dent's Meadow, and leave it there?" Woodland replied that he had.[752]

Jones asked how many shad Woodland had caught that day, and Woodland replied, "I caught about seventy, master."[753] Before leaving, Jones gave food to Booth and Herold.

When at last they left, Jones and Herold walked, and Booth rode. A few hundred yards from the river, they were halted by a strong fence, which they were unable to take down.

They could not have brought the horse past the fence; the path beyond was a steep incline down to the Potomac. It was difficult enough to get Booth down off his horse, but then Jones and Herold had to carry him down the steep and narrow path. The way was filled with jerking and sudden stops until at last they reached the water's edge. There they found the boat Woodland had left. "It was a flat bottomed boat about twelve feet long, of a dark lead color." It was about ten thirty that Friday night, exactly one week since Booth had shot Lincoln.[754]

Herold and Jones got Booth into the boat. Then Jones showed them how to cross the river using a compass that had been brought along by Booth. Jones said, "Keep the course I lay down for you, and it will bring you right into Machodoc Creek. Row up the creek to the first house, where you will find Mrs. Quesenberry, and I think she will take care of you if you use my name."[755] Quesenberry, a Confederate sympathizer, had aided many Confederate agents during the war.

As Jones pushed the boat into the river, Booth said, "Wait a minute, old fellow," and offered Jones money for the boat. Jones replied that he would take only the cost of the boat – eighteen dollars – which Booth paid.[756]

The two men thanked Jones for his help; then Herold started rowing across the two-mile wide Potomac. The journey was dangerous because the Union Navy's Potomac Flotilla patrolled the river and the Chesapeake Bay.

On April 23, Swann was talking to Joseph Padgett that the search for Booth and Herold around Bryantown was useless because they were no longer in the area. Padgett drew the rest of the story from him and then took Swann to see John Young, a detective on Colonel Henry Wells's staff in Bryantown.[757]

After Swann told his story to detectives, Samuel Cox was brought in for questioning. At eleven o'clock that night, Cox was interrogated by Colonel Wells. At first, Cox "denied all knowledge of the two men." Colonel Wells told Cox that "he could have until four o'clock the next morning to reflect . . . . At 4 A.M. the next morning he was brought up by the guard and said he desired to talk with the Colonel and the first expression he made use of was that it was no use concealing the fact that the two men were at his house, but that he did not know who they were."[758]

For his seven dollars, Swann went to the Old Capitol Prison on April 27 and was not released until May 17.

On April 26, Cox was sent to the Old Capitol Prison. On the twenty-eighth, Cox was interrogated again, this time by Colonel Henry Olcott. Olcott also ended the interrogation at the point where Cox said he turned away both men at the door. Cox was released on June 3.[759]

*   *   *

Out on the river, Booth and Herold quickly became confused by the many inlets and lost their bearings in the dark. During the attempted crossing, Booth and Herold came close to either the *USS Juniper* anchored off Persimmon Point or the *USS Heliotrope*, which was moving upstream. Booth wrote in his diary the next day, "Last night being chased by gunboats til I was forced to return wet, cold, and starving, with every man's hand against me." If the gunboat was the *USS Heliotrope*, it may have seemed to Booth that the gunboat was giving chase.

Booth and Herold put to shore on the morning of April 22 still on the Maryland side of the Potomac. They had gone nine miles west of Dent's Meadow instead of eight miles south to Machodoc Creek. A strong incoming tide had swept the boat up the river.[760] When they came ashore, Herold knew where they were – Nanjemoy Creek. Herold had hunted there and recognized that they were close to Colonel John J. Hughes's farm. While Booth hid on shore, Herold walked to the Hugheses' home. Hughes knew Herold and also knew that he and Booth were wanted for the assassination. However Hughes sympathized with the two fugitives and gave Herold some food, but he refused to let Herold into his house.

Disappointed, Herold took the food back to Booth, and then the two waited for sunset to try crossing the river again. At this time, Lincoln's funeral train was on its way west.

On the twenty-second, Booth wrote a long involved theatrical complaint in his diary,

> After being hunted like a dog through swamps, woods and last night being chased by gunboats till I was forced to return wet, cold and starving, with every man's hand against me, I am here in despair. And why? For doing what Brutus was honored for, what made Tell a hero. (After sending an arrow through an apple placed on his son's head by order of the Austrian governor Gessler, the Swiss patriot used a second arrow to kill the despot.) And yet I, for striking down a greater tyrant than they ever knew, am looked upon as a common cutthroat. My act was purer than either of theirs. One hoped to be great himself, the other had not only his country's but his own wrongs to avenge. I hoped for no gains. I knew no private wrong. I struck for my country and for that alone. A country groaned beneath this tyranny and prayed for this end, and yet now behold the cold hand they extend to me. God cannot pardon me if I have done wrong. Yet I cannot see any wrong except in serving a degenerate people. The little, the very little, I left behind to clear my name, the governmt [sic] will not allow to be printed. (Apparently Booth is referring to the letter he gave Matthews.) So ends all. For my country I have given up all that makes life sweet and holy, brought misery upon my family, and am sure there is no pardon in the heaven for me, since man condemns me so. I have only heard of what has been done (except what I did myself) and it fills me with horror. God, try and forgive me and bless my mother. To night I will once more try the river, with the intention to cross; though I have a greater desire and almost a mind to return to Washington, and in a measure clear my name which I feel I can do. I do not repent the blow I struck. I may before my God, but not to man.
>
> I think I have done well, though I am abandoned, with the curse of Cain upon me, when, if the world knew my heart, that one blow would have me great, although I did desire no greatness.
>
> To night I try once more to escape these bloodhounds. Who, who can read his fate? God's will be done.
>
> I have too great a soul to die like a criminal. Oh may he, may he spare me that and let me die bravely.
>
> I bless the entire world. Have never hated or wronged anyone. This last was not a wrong, unless God deems it so and its with him, to damn or bless me. And for this brave boy with me who often prays (yes before and since) with a true and sincere heart, was it crime in him, if so why can he pray the same I do not wish to shed a drop of blood, but "I must fight the course" Tis all thats left me.[761]

After sunset, Herold and Booth again set out to cross the Potomac. But for the second time, Booth and Herold did not reach their goal of Machodoc Creek. For whatever reason, a gunboat, daylight, or just lost again, they landed near the mouth of Gambo Creek, a stream about one mile north of Machodoc Creek and about one mile from the widow Elizabeth Quesenberry's farm.[762] Quesenberry's farm was not far from the Potomac River, and during the war, the farm had been a station for Confederate signal agents working in Southern Maryland.

At sunrise, Herold went looking for the Quesenberry house known as the Cottage while Booth stayed behind in the flat-bottom boat.

When Herold arrived, Mrs. Quesenberry was not at the farm, but her daughter Alice was. Herold asked her to send someone to get Mrs. Quesenberry. While waiting for Mrs. Quesenberry, Herold thought of what their next move might be. Now that he and Booth had crossed into Virginia, they had no more need of the boat. He offered the boat Alice. The boat was later found and put on a gunboat and carried to Washington.[763]

At last, Mrs. Quesenberry returned, and Herold inquired if she would rent or sell "him and his brother a conveyance to take them" into the country. Mrs. Quesenberry refused. To her surprise, Herold replied courteously and bid her farewell. Quesenberry, taken aback and regretting her uncharitable reply, "called to him and asked him if he had anything to eat." He replied no, and she promised to send some food down to where the boat was tied.

At the Quesenberry house was Thomas Harbin (stepbrother of Thomas Jones), a Confederate agent who had been in on the abduction scheme. He brought the food down to Booth in a satchel belonging to Mrs. Quesenberry.[764]

Harbin knew Booth. They had met at the December 1864 meeting at the Bryantown Tavern. When he saw it was Booth who was Herold's "brother," Harbin's only concern was to get rid of the two men as quickly as possible. Aiding the fugitives could put a hangman's rope around his neck. Harbin told Booth to go to the home of Dr. Richard Stuart some eight miles away and that they could pay William Bryant, a local farmer, to take them there.

Herold saw that the farmer, William Bryant, was going to be their only way of continuing their escape. Herold left at once to talk to Bryant, arriving about 5:45 PM. Herold offered the farmer ten dollars to take the two fugitives to Dr. Stuart's home. Bryant quickly agreed to the money offered, saddled two horses, and went to Booth who "was sitting down on the open ground." Bryant asked about the broken leg, and Herold quickly replied, "He got it broke in Richmond in a fight; a horse threw him and broke his leg, and he was paroled to go home."[765] Bryant then took the two fugitives to Dr. Stuart's farm.

Dr. Stuart was considered the richest man in King George County and was a relative of Robert E. Lee, two of whose daughters had stayed with him for part of the war. His wife had served as a bridesmaid at Lee's marriage to Mary Custis.

During the war, Dr. Stuart had been arrested twice for assisting Confederate spies and couriers.

It was after dark when Booth, Herold, and Bryant arrived at the home of Dr. Stuart. Herold knocked on the door, and when Dr. Stuart answered, Herold told him, "We are Marylanders in want of accommodations for the night." Herold again told the story that the injured man was his brother and had a broken leg. He was treated in Maryland by Dr. Mudd, who referred them to him for further medical aid. Stuart knew that a man with a broken leg had killed Lincoln and now at night before him was a man with a broken leg.

Stuart dryly said that he had company for the night and had no room for more guests. Herold continued to plead for a room for the night and something to eat. Herold pleaded with Dr. Stuart that if he knew of their circumstances, he would understand the urgency of their need for shelter.

"I don't want to know anything about you!" Stuart sharply replied. "It is impossible for you to stay here!"

You are a physician," Herold said. "It is your duty to attend to this man's broken leg."

"I am not a surgeon!" Stuart growled.

Herold asked if Stuart could arrange transportation for them to Fredericksburg, and Stuart again declined. However, Stuart did reluctantly decide to give the two some supper.

Dr. Stewart was firm in his refusals and had no desire to hear anything that they had to say. Herold asked if Stewart knew of anyone who could take them to Fredericksburg, and Stuart suggested a free black man named William Lucas who lived nearby and "sometimes hired out his wagons." Perhaps Lucas would take them in for the night and provide transportation in the morning.

At this point, Stuart suggested that Booth and Herold go into the house to get dinner.

As Booth and Herold disappeared into the house, Stuart caught Bryant by the sleeve and demanded, "Who are those two men?"

Bryant lied and said that they had come to him from the marsh and asked if he could get them to Dr. Stuart's place.

"It is very strange, I know nothing about the men, I cannot accommodate them, you will have to take them somewhere else." The doctor was not fooled, he guessed who his uninvited guests were and wanted them as far away as possible.

Stuart went to the kitchen where the two were eating and told them, "The old man's waiting for you, he is anxious to be off, it is cold, he is not well and wants to get home."

Booth and Herold knew by his tone that they were being thrown out. But they were not in a position to protest, so they left.[766]

Bryant took them to William Lucas's home, which was nothing more than a one-room cabin. Lucas was asleep when the barking of his dogs awakened him. Bryant identified himself, and Lucas opened his door and found himself looking at Booth and Herold. Herald, now desperate, demanded, "We want to stay here tonight!"

"You cannot do it," Lucas replied. "I am a colored man and have no right to take care of white people. I have only one room in the house and my wife is sick."

Herold, however, was not to be put off. "We are Confederate soldiers, we have been in service for three years, we have been knocking about all night, and don't intend to any longer; we are going to stay!" Booth slid from his horse and hobbled into the cabin.

Lucas saw that he had no means to stop them. Booth's carbine was dangling from the saddle. "Gentlemen, you have treated me very badly," he said.

Booth pulled out a knife. "Old man, how do you like that?" he asked.

"I do not like that at all. I was always afraid of a knife," Lucas replied.

"We were sent here, old man," Booth announced. "We understand you have good teams."

Lucas replied that they could not have the team, for he had hired hands coming in the morning to plant corn.

Booth lost his temper; he was in a bad mood from the pain of his broken and infected leg and from being turned away at every house. He was furious that a black man was now refusing him.

Booth treated the black man as he had treated slaves back home in Baltimore; he ignored and discounted them. "Well, Dave, we will not go on any further, but stay here and make this old man get us his horses in the morning."

Lucas, who believed their story that they were soldiers, remarked, "I thought you would be done impressing teams since the fall of Richmond,"

"Repeat that again!" Booth said angrily. Lucas did not.

With intimations of violence from two white men, there was nothing for Lucas to do but get his wife up. They spent the cold night on the cabin porch while Booth and Herold slept in their bed.

The next day, Lucas asked for and received twenty dollars for his wagon horses, and it was agreed that his son Charlie would drive them. His son, who lived nearby, arrived and was told he would drive the two to Port Conway. Herold gave Mrs. Lucas the money as they left.[767]

Now into its eleventh day, the Booth/Herold manhunt was continuing with all the force the federal government could bring. Investigators were arresting people who had helped Booth. John Lloyd and Dr. Samuel Mudd were already arrested; and soon Captain Samuel Cox, Thomas Jones, Rose Quesenberry, and Dr. Richard Stuart were arrested. Literally hundreds of other people were also arrested, including actors and other theater people, friends and relatives of Booth, men who resembled Booth, and others the military suspected might be involved.

It was now Monday, April 24, and Booth's goal was Port Conway, ten miles away, where he intended to cross the Rappahannock River into Port Royal. Charlie Lucas drove Herold and Booth toward the small settlement of Port Conway, which consisted of a few houses, a little church, and a ferry. The town's only claim to fame was that it was the birthplace of President James Madison.

Sometime during that morning, Charlie Lucas drove the wagon up to the little ferry. Living at the ferry were the newly married Mr. and Mrs. Williams Rollins. Rollins was at the river preparing to go fishing and was checking his nets. Herold jumped down out of the wagon and asked Rollins if he would take them in his fishing boat across the few hundred yards of water to Port Royal. Rollins replied that he had to see to his nets, but he promised to let the ferryman, James Thornton, on the other side of the river know there were passengers waiting. By noon, the tide would be high enough for the ferry to cross the river, so Booth and Herold waited.

Charles Lucas Jr. was about to leave and return the horses and wagon to his father when Booth ordered him to wait while he wrote a reproachful letter to Dr. Stuart, which he wanted delivered. Booth was still filled with anger because of Dr. Stuart's abrupt reception to him. Booth had expected help from the doctor because he was a Southern sympathizer. Booth had torn a page from his diary and wrote a melodramatic letter to Dr. Stuart.

> Dear Sir:
>
> Forgive me, but I have some pride. I hate to blame you for your want of hospitality; you know your own affairs. I was sick and tired, with a broken leg, in need of medical advice. I would not have turned a dog from my door in such a condition. However, you were kind enough to give me something to eat, for which I not only thank you, but, on account of the reluctant manner in which it was bestowed, I feel bound to pay for it. It is not the substance but the manner in which kindness is extended that makes one happy in the acceptance thereof. The sauce to meat is ceremony; meeting were bare without it. Be kind enough to accept the enclosed two dollars and a half (though hard to spare) for what we have received.
>
> Yours respectfully,
> Stranger.
> April 24, 1865

By offering to pay for the food, Booth had insulted Stuart as a Virginia gentleman. The quote "The sauce in meat is ceremony. Meeting were bare without it" was from *Macbeth,* and here, Booth was pointing out that although Stuart had finally consented to feed them, his manner of offering the food was just as important as the offer itself. Booth felt very strongly that Stuart had fallen short in Southern graciousness and wanted to berate the doctor for his rudeness.[768]

Booth's insulting note later supported Stuart's claim that he had not assisted Lincoln's assassin.

As Booth and Herold waited for the ferry, three ex-Confederate soldiers, heading home, arrived on horseback, William Jett, age eighteen from the Ninth Virginia Cavalry; Absalom Bainbridge, also eighteen; and Mortimer Ruggles, twenty-one. (Ruggles father was Confederate General Daniel Ruggles.)[769]

Herold got out of the wagon with its two very wretched-looking horses and approached the men. To his great relief, he found that the men were Confederate soldiers. Herold told them that his name was Boyd and that his brother, he motioned in the direction of Booth, who was watching fearfully from the wagon, had been wounded in the leg while escaping from prison. Herold continued his fabrication telling them that their Negro driver, Lucas, had refused to take them any farther. Herold said that he and his brother were anxious to get on their way and would the three men help them. Ruggles immediately volunteered for the men's help.

Meanwhile, Booth was watching from the wagon. Herold, he thought, had been talking to the three strangers too long. With great difficulty and pain, he managed to climb from the wagon. Grabbing his crutch, he hobbled toward the men. When he got fairly close to the group, he looked suspiciously at Herold and then said to the men, "I suppose you have been told who I am."

Ruggles, thinking Booth meant that Herold had said that they were Confederate soldiers escaped from prison, said, "Yes."

Instantly Booth drew his revolver. He sternly, and with the utmost coolness, admitted being John Wilkes Booth, the one who had assassinated Lincoln. He announced that he was worth $175,000 to the man who captured him as stated in recent newspapers.

The Confederate trio looked at him in amazement. They thought that the man who killed Lincoln had been already captured. The news of his capture might have been one of the many rumors circulating, or perhaps they confused the news of the capture with that of Powell and Atzerodt. When the confusion was finally resolved, the three men agreed to help, saying that they were not going to take "blood money."

At these words, Booth replaced his revolver. "Thank you, my friends." He told them about his broken ankle, and with that, Booth was helped on to Ruggles's horse. At last the ferry arrived, and the five men were taken across the river.[770] Lucas then drove his wagon back to his father's house.

Jett was familiar with the Virginia county and promised to find Booth a place to stay to rest his broken leg.

"God bless you!" said Booth, his face wincing with the pain of his broken and infected leg.[771] Booth's ankle smelled of infection, and the skin was black and inflamed. He was in bad shape, physically.

Booth, Herold, and the three Confederates arrived on the other side of the river at about one o'clock.

The deeper into Virginia Booth went, the more he began to believe he could escape. Upon crossing the Rappahannock, Booth exclaimed, "I'm safe in glorious old Virginia, thank God!" Booth now had about thirty-six hours to live.

# CHAPTER 22

## I Am among Friends Now

Jett rode ahead to look for a place for the two fugitives to stay. He had only gone about two blocks when he came to the home of Randolph Peyton. Peyton was not home; however, his two spinster sisters, Sarah Jane and Lizzie, were.

"Can you shelter a gentleman who had been wounded," Jett asked.

"I will," Sarah Jane replied, and Jett left to get Booth and Herold. Sarah Jane was a Southern lady with a sense of Southern hospitality; however, when she saw the dirty, disheveled, and unshaven duo in her front yard, she had second thoughts. She said that her brother was out of town, leaving only her and her sister in the house, and that it would not be proper to board two strangers when their brother was not in the house. Sarah Jane suggested they go see Richard Garrett as he was a kind old man and always good for a favor. His house was just four miles outside of town along the road to Bowling Green.

Once again, Booth was rejected in Virginia. Jett then went to the home of George Catlett; however, Catlett was not at home.

The three Confederate soldiers and Booth and Herold had three horses among them. Herold, Jett, Bainbridge, and Ruggles shared two horses while Booth rode alone because of his injury.

"Now, boys," said Jett to the two fugitives, "I propose to take our friend Booth up to Garrett's house. I think they'll give him shelter there and treat him kindly."

"Whatever you deem best to do with me, my friends," replied Booth, "I'll agree to be satisfied."

"Jett understands this country," said Ruggles, "and I think that it will be well to act as he directs."

"I'm in your hands," said Booth. "Do with me, as you think best."

After a few minutes further conversation, the five men on three horses left Port Royal for the Garrett farm. Booth was disappointed by the rejections he received and by the public's reaction to what he had done. As they rode, Herold spoke of

Lincoln's assassination, but Booth cut him off by saying it was nothing to brag about. Booth thought about going to Mexico, for he said he saw the South had no refuge for him. When Ruggles asked if Europe was not a possibility, Booth said that European monarchs did not like to harbor assassins since they set examples.[772]

At about three o'clock in the afternoon, the men arrived at the gate leading to the farmhouse. It was on Monday, April 24. The Garrett house was a two-story dwelling with a wide front porch and a brick chimney at either end. The farm had a large front yard and outbuildings; to one side, there was a tobacco barn with wide-open spaces slats; and slightly to the rear of the house were two smaller structures used as corncribs. Behind it was an apple orchard.

The house was some distance from the main road, and when the men reached the gate leading into the farm, Herold decided that he would go on with the Confederate trio as far as Bowling Green to buy a pair of shoes. Herold and Bainbridge stayed at the gate while Jett and Ruggles accompanied Booth down the path to the house.

Booth rode a short distance when he turned to look back at Herold and Bainbridge; he lifted his slouch hat from his head, waved it, and shouted back, "Good-by, old fellow . . . come and see me again. I shall always be pleased to see you both!"

"I'll be with you soon, John," returned Herold, "keep in good spirits."

"Have no fear about me, Herold," Booth replied. "I am among friends now."[773]

The elder Richard Garrett was on the porch as the three men approached. Jett saw him and called, "Mr. Garrett, I suppose you hardly remember me."

"No, sir, I believe not."

"My name is Jett, I am the son of your old friend Jett of Westmoreland County." Then Jett introduced Booth as John W. Boyd, a soldier wounded at the battle of Petersburg. "He is trying to get to his home in Maryland. Can you take care of him for a day or two until his wound will permit him to travel?"

Garrett, congenial and eager for news from passersby, agreed. Booth was helped off his horse and put on to the veranda. Garrett's wife, sister-in-law, and children turned out to see the visitors. There was John, seventeen; William K. fifteen; Richard, eleven; and Joanna.

Young Richard Garrett asked Booth whether his leg pained him.

"Yes, it has not properly been cared for and riding has jarred it so that it gives me great pain." Booth remained on the porch, talking to two of Garrett's sons, John, who had just returned from Appomattox; and his younger brother William. Later, Booth had supper with the family and then spent a quiet evening with them. At nine o'clock, Booth was taken to one of the upper rooms in which the Garrett boys slept. He lay for the first time in ten days on a comfortable bed and slept. It was his last full night of sleep. He had less than twenty-four hours to live.

The next morning, young Richard Garrett, who slept in the same room, saw that Booth had two large revolvers and a pearl-handled dagger.

The weather on Booth's last day alive was sunny and warm.

That morning, Mrs. Garrett spread some quilts under an apple tree in the front of the house for Booth to lie upon, and Booth talked and amused himself with the Garrett children. Booth (whom the children called Mr. Boyd) entertained them with his pocket compass. The children watched in amazement as Booth moved the compass needle with his knife.

A little before noon, Booth returned to the house and asked young Richard to get down a large map that hung on a wall. The boy did as requested and spread the map out on the floor. Booth knelt down and studied it. Booth, not caring that this was not his map to draw on, took a pencil and began marking a route to Norfolk and then to Charleston and Savannah. Richard asked where he was planning to go.

"To Mexico," Booth replied.

"Why?" responded the young boy. "I thought last night you were going to join Johnston's army in North Carolina." Which is what he had told the family the previous evening.[774]

Booth ignored the child's question and continued looking at the map.

\* \* \*

After Herold left Booth at the Garrett farm that Monday afternoon, he and Bainbridge stopped at a tavern called the Trap. It was an old tavern and brothel managed by widow Martha Carter and her four daughters. Later Jett and Ruggles caught up with them, and after a meal and "other entertainment" from the four daughters, the four men left for Bowling Green, six miles away.

Their first stop there was the Star Hotel. Jett was courting sixteen-year-old Izora Gouldmen, the owner's daughter. That night, Ruggles and Jet stayed at the hotel, and Herold and Bainbridge went on to visit Joseph Clarke, a friend of Bainbridge's who lived on a farm about three miles away. Herold was delighted to stay the night there in a clean warm bed.

The next day around noon, Herold and Bainbridge returned to the Star Hotel. It was early in the afternoon when the men decided to take Herald back to the Garrett farm. Jett stayed in Bowling Green, so the three men rode two horses. On the way back, they stopped again at the Trap to drink. Only eight miles away, the pursuit force under Doherty was at the Port Royal ferry. Within a few hours, the cavalry would be at the Trap.[775]

At about four o'clock, Bainbridge and Ruggles left David Herold at the Garrett farm and introduced him as Mr. Boyd's cousin, David Harris. Booth now had about twelve hours to live.

Herold brought back the news that only some straggling Confederate cavalry were to be found at Milford, a short distance away. Also by this time, General Joseph E. Johnston had surrendered to General Sherman.

Garrett's eldest son, John, had gone to have his boots repaired at a shoemaker's shop about a mile from the house. While he was there, he saw a newspaper that a friend had brought from Richmond describing the Lincoln assassination. The paper described the reward of $50,000 for the capture of John Wilkes Booth.

John Garrett returned home, and during lunch, young John told the family about the reward posted in the paper.

The elder Garrett indignantly stated that he didn't believe the president had been assassinated. "It is some idle report started by stragglers." The son, however, was insistent and repeated the story of Lincoln and the reward. Garrett's second son, Robert, said he would turn in the assassin for the reward money.

Booth turned to him and asked, "If he were to come this way, would you inform against him?" Robert replied he would, for he could sure use the money.

Booth showed no emotion at all and said that he had heard Lincoln's assassin had been captured between Baltimore and Philadelphia and had been taken to Washington.

Garrett's daughter, Joanna, expressed the view that the man who killed the president must have been well paid for it. At this, Booth immediately replied, "It is my opinion he wasn't paid a cent, but did it for notoriety's sake."

Booth had told the Garretts that he was a Marylander, so naturally they asked him whether he had ever seen the Booth who had shot Lincoln.

"I saw him once in Richmond," said Booth, "about the time of the John Brown raid."

"Is he an old or a young man?" asked another.

"Well," answered Booth, "he was rather a young fellow." The elder Garrett informed them he had never heard of any Booth except the great actor, Edwin Booth.

Booth smiled at that remark. Perhaps he remembered his previous remark in Washington, "When I leave the stage for good, I will be the most famous man in America."[776] No one in the Garrett family suspected that the assassin John Wilkes Booth was in their mist. John Wilkes Booth was still the great actor.

After the meal, he and the two older Garrett boys went into the yard where they practiced shooting their pistols at a post in front of the house. Booth joined them and, with his broken infected leg, still hit the target each time; and the boys were impressed by his marksmanship.

Meanwhile, Ruggles and Bainbridge rode on toward Port Royal. Just outside of town, however, they met a soldier from Ruggles unit. He told the two that if they had not gotten their paroles and did not want to be captured, they had better turn back. Ruggles was told that the town was full of Yankees searching for Booth and that the federal cavalry there knew that Booth had crossed the river the previous day. The two frightened men turned immediately and rode back to the Garrett farm.

As they approached the farmhouse, they saw Booth lying on the lawn in front of the house. As soon as he recognized them, he arose and hobbled toward them, "Well, boys, what's in the wind now?"

Ruggles and Bainbridge told him about the federal cavalry in Port Royal and that they knew he had crossed the river the day before. They suggested to Booth that he hide out in the woods.[777]

Booth turned around to look for Herold, but he was nowhere in sight as indeed was no one else. He then straightened himself up to his full height and replied, "I'll do as you say, boys, right off. Ride on! Good-by! It will never do for you to be found in my company." Then as if he had conceived a desperate resolve, he said theatrically, "Rest assured of one thing, good friend, Wilkes Booth will never be taken alive."[778] Ruggles and Bainbridge immediately rode off to the east in the direction of Essex County.

Booth hurried as best he could to the house and asked Richard Jr. to rush upstairs for his pistols. Herold appeared, and Booth told him of the danger. Booth and Herold then went out back of the house and into the woods.[779]

As the two hid in the woods, they heard the Union cavalry pound past the Garrett driveway as they made for Bowling Green. When they had gone by, Herold and Booth, feeling somewhat safer, returned to the farmhouse.

Herold asked Garrett if he thought federal cavalry was crossing at the ferry, but Garrett was doubtful. However, when Jim, a young black man, arrived from Port Royal, he confirmed that cavalry had been at Port Royal when he left.[780]

The Garretts' were astounded at the behavior of their guests. Booth and Herold had now lost their credibility with the Garretts. The fugitives' suspicious behavior frightened them.[781]

The Garretts demanded an explanation, and Herold said, "I will tell you the truth, over there in Maryland the other night we got on a spree and had a row with some soldiers and as we ran away we shot at them and I suppose must have hurt somebody." Booth added that he was afraid the Yankees were going to make him take an enforced oath of loyalty to the Union.

It was a weak story, and the Garretts did not believe it. The federals weren't going to send a couple of dozen cavalrymen after two fellows who had been on a spree or to force a cripple to take the loyalty oath. The Garretts had children in the house as well as Mrs. Garrett's sister, Lucinda Holloway, a schoolteacher. They did not want to get between the cavalry and these two armed men. And so the Garrett men told the two to leave – they were no longer welcome.

Herold, not completely understanding the family's anger and fear, asked to rent the family's horses and a wagon to get to the Fredericksburg railroad station. John Garrett coldly refused. He suggested that their neighbor, a black man named New Freeman who lived nearby, might help them. But when one of the children went to summon him, he was not home. Sunset had passed, and Booth pled that since they had no way to leave that they be allowed to stay the night in the house.

"No gentlemen, you can't stay in the house," Garrett growled.

"We could sleep under the front porch," Herold suggested.

"No!" Garrett replied. "The dogs on the place would bite you."

"Well," asked Herold, "what's in the barn, then?"

It was finally agreed that the two could sleep in the tobacco barn but had to leave first thing in the morning.

The tobacco barn was a convenient place to put the unwanted guest since furniture and beds hidden there from any invading forces could be used. The barn was built with slats with narrow spaces between them so that air could circulate and dry tobacco leaves. It was possible to stand close to the tobacco barn and see inside and similarly from the interior one could see out through the openings.

And so on the night of April 25, about eight or nine o'clock in the evening, Booth and Herold bedded down in the tobacco barn.[782]

Young John Garrett, his brother William, and their father, were still uneasy, especially since Booth and Herold had firearms. They discussed the possibility that the two strangers might steal their horses in the middle of the night. John and William decided that they would lock the barn's door and spend the night in one of the corncribs between the tobacco barn and the stable to keep watch.[783]

# CHAPTER 23

## *Useless, Useless, Useless*

In Washington, the manhunt was gearing up. About midafternoon on April 24, Canadian-born Lieutenant Edward Doherty of the Sixteenth New York Cavalry received orders to report to Colonel Lafayette C. Baker, chief of the National Detective Police. Doherty was to have an officer and twenty-six enlisted men with three days' rations ready for an assignment.[784] This was not Lieutenant Doherty's first time tracking Booth – he had been on other forays into Northern Virginia. Doherty hurried to the barracks, had "boots and saddles" sounded, and in less than half an hour reported to Colonel Baker. The lieutenant was not enthusiastic about his men. They were deadbeats from other companies of the regiment. To Doherty, they were men who made excuses to stay in camp instead of fighting, or they were either sick or pretending to be sick. Colonel Baker was responding to a report that two men had been seen crossing the Potomac. A report had been received by Major James O'Beirne from Captain S. H. Bequeath at Port Tobacco, who telegraphed to Washington that two men had been seen crossing the Potomac River. They weren't Booth and Herold though. They were Tom Harbin and Joseph Baden, presumably on their way to the Quesenberry farm where Harbin was on April 23. The report caused forces to focus on the area where the fugitives actually were.

Baker introduced Doherty to former Lieutenant Colonel Everton J. Conger and former Lieutenant Luther Byron Baker of the detective force and was told that the two detectives would accompany his unit.[785]

Before noon, the Sixteenth New York Cavalry boarded the government gunboat *John S. Ide* at the Sixth Street Wharf. They steamed down Aquia Creek to Belle Plain Landing. It took seven hours for the gunboat to steam the sixty miles down Aquia Creek to its destination. Then, without pause, Doherty debarked his men and horses and march them south to the main road to Fredericksburg.[786]

Doherty and his men spent that night riding and knocking on doors that they passed. They asked everyone they met whether they had seen two men traveling together, one with a broken leg. Conger and Baker frequently rode ahead and pretended to be ex-Confederate soldiers looking for two friends. Their plan was to check all the physicians in the area and claim to be looking for two separate friends – one with a broken ankle. The doctors they visited, however, had not seen anyone fitting the description of Booth or Herold. By early Tuesday morning, April 25, the small cavalry unit arrived at "Bleak Hill – the home of Dr. Horace Dade Ashton." They questioned Ashton and stayed for a short time to rest. Dr. Ashton generously gave them breakfast and fed their horses before the men were mustered again to leave for the Port Conway ferry.

To cover more ground, Conger and Baker, along with five men, followed the Rappahannock River toward Port Conway. Lieutenant Doherty took the rest of his unit on a land route to Port Conway. Early that Tuesday afternoon, the two groups met near the ferry at Belle Grove, the home of Carolinus Turner. Turner gave the soldiers food. Doherty walked down to the ferry to check out the river and the size of the transport. There he met Dick Wilson.

Wilson, a black man, had helped William Rollins with shad fishing. When Doherty questioned Wilson as he did everyone he met, he learned that two men answering the description of Booth and Herold had been there the day before and had crossed the river to Port Royal.

Rollins was on the little wharf by the ferry when Doherty approached and described the men they were pursuing. From Doherty's description of Booth and Herold, Rollins knew immediately that they were the same men he had helped across the river the day before. His heart sank, for he realized that he had helped the men the army was hunting. Rollins feared that he would be arrested and tried as an accomplice for assisting the president's killers. He thought that the best way to avoid arrest was to tell all he knew. He told Doherty about the five men he had helped across, three of whom were Confederate soldiers and one of whom he knew to be William Jett as he had often taken him across.[787]

Rollins told Doherty that he had been asked by Booth to take the two to "Orange Court House" but had refused because it was too far away. Rollins related how Booth and Herold had then offered Rollins ten dollars to take them to Bowling Green. Rollins thought them "much anxious to get across the river." They claimed that they were brothers and that Booth was wounded at Petersburg. The three Confederates decided that they, not Rollins, would help Booth and Herold to their next destination. Rollins was arrested and taken as a guide.[788]

"Jett has a lady-love over at Bowling Green, and I reckon he went there," Mrs. Bettie Rollins told Doherty.[789] First, the cavalry unit had to get over the Rappahannock River, a slow and tedious business, since the ferry could transport only nine horses and men at a time. It was nearing sunset (April 25) when the soldiers and two detectives were on the southern side at Port Royal. They started at a gallop for the Star Hotel where Jett's girlfriend lived.

Doherty's exhausted troops had had no sleep except for occasional stops since getting off the *John S. Ide* the previous evening, and now they were in for more hard riding. Rollins led the men to Bowling Green. They passed the Garrett farm, not knowing that the assassins were concealed there.[790]

On their way to the Star Hotel, Doherty, Conger, and Baker stopped at "the Trap."[791] As it happened, Herold and Bainbridge as well as Jett and Ruggles had been there. The men had paid well for the ladies' favors; so when Doherty questioned the women, they claimed to know nothing. They were Southern sympathizers and did not want to betray Southern soldiers. They got no cooperation at first until they used the ruse of telling the women that the two men they were looking for had raped a young girl. Indignantly, Martha Carter and her daughters revealed that four men had visited the day before. Doherty showed the women pictures of Booth and Herold. The women recognized Herold; however, they could not identify Booth's photo or remember seeing a lame man. Four men had left on Monday and three men had been back just that afternoon but without Jett. Jett had stayed behind with Izora Gouldmen. Doherty, Conger, and Baker were disappointed at not finding a lame man; however, they were getting close, and finding Jett would lead them to Booth.[792]

Once outside, Doherty called his tired men to mount, and they were off at once for Bowling Green. It was not an easy ride. The horses and men were exhausted, hungry, and sleepy, yet they made good time and approached the little town between eleven and midnight.[793]

Just outside of Bowling Green, the cavalry dismounted. Half of the men rested with the horses; and Doherty, Conger, and Baker took the others to the Star Hotel. Once they had located the little building, the troops moved silently to surround it. When they were all in place, Doherty pounded on the door. After some delay, Mrs. Julia Gouldman opened the door and shouted, "What do you want? My husband isn't here!"

"We're not interested in your husband," Doherty returned. "You got any other men in the house?"

"Only my son, Jesse," Mrs. Gouldman lied. "He is recovering from a wound in the abdomen."

"Show us his room then, Ma'am. And I warn you, if anyone jumps out firing on us or any of my men, I swear we will burn the building down and we'll take you all as prisoners to Washington!"

Frightened, Mrs. Gouldman led the soldiers up one flight of stairs to her son's room. As they entered, Jett sprang half-dressed from his bed. He was quickly subdued. The wounded son lay still on another bed.

Jett admitted his identity and was read Stanton's proclamation about the consequences for aiding and abetting the fugitives. Doherty then shouted, "I have known your movements for the past two or three days, and if you do not tell me the truth I will hang you; but if you give me the information I want, I will protect you."[794]

"What do you want?" Jett asked

"We know you took Booth across the river."

"You are mistaken in your man."

"You lie!" A revolver was put against Jett's head. "We are going to have Booth. You can tell us where he is or prepare to die."

Feeling the cold metal against his temple, Jett decided to talk. "Booth is at the Garrett brothers' three miles this side of Port Conway. If you came that way you may have frightened him off, for you must have passed the place." Jett also told that Herold had come to Bowling Green with him and had returned that morning to the Garrett farm.[795]

It was somewhere between midnight and 1:00 a.m. on the twenty-sixth when Lieutenant Doherty and his troops left the Star Hotel. Booth had six hours to live.

Jett was forced to go with them, but the reins to his horse where held by the mounted soldiers who flanked him.

Doherty returned to the remainder of his unit at the outskirts of Bowling Green. The exhausted men were asleep, but Doherty roused them, and soon they were all riding back along the road they had just traveled. The night was dark, cold, and damp, and it was nearly two o'clock in the morning when the cavalry detachment, guided by Jett, arrived at the long crooked lane to the Garrett farmhouse.

Conger rode up beside Jett and Rollins. "These two stay here!" he shouted to the soldier guarding them. The guard nodded, his face haggard from exhaustion. Then Doherty led his men to the farmhouse where they immediately dismounted and raced to surround the house and its outbuildings. Baker thudded across the narrow porch to the front door and pounded on the front door of the Garrett house. He yelled, "Open up! Now!"

After what seemed too long, there was movement within. A window near the door opened slowly. Someone stood there just inside in the dark.

Baker lost not a moment but thrust his hand through the opening and grabbed the arm of Richard Garrett Sr.

"Open the door. Be quick about it!"[796]

Garrett opened the door, and immediately soldiers rushed in.

Baker demanded, "Where are the men who were here today?"

Garrett did not know where the two had gone. He had fallen ill and retired early that evening, leaving the problem of Booth and Herold to his sons. Meanwhile, the soldiers began to search the house. When they started to enter a bedroom, Garrett pleaded, "Don't go in, there are women undressed there."

"Damn the women," came Baker's reply. "What if they are undressed? We shall go in if they haven't a rag!"[797]

The soldiers burst into the room and searched but did not find Booth or Herald in the house.

Baker again turned to the ailing Garrett. "Where are the men who have been staying with you?"

Garrett spoke with a stutter that intensified when he was nervous. He tried again to make himself understood that he retired early and did not know where the men were.

Garrett began to tell the story of Booth and Herald's visit when Baker interrupted, "I don't want any long story. I just want to know where those men have gone!"

"Bring a rope, hang the damned old rebel, and we will find the men afterwards!" someone yelled.[798]

A rope was brought and knotted around Garrett's neck; and in his nightclothes, he was dragged into the yard. Awakened by the commotion, John Garrett came out of the corncrib. He ran across the yard and spoke to a nearby soldier, who immediately brought him to the farmhouse.

"Don't hurt Father!" the boy shouted, seeing his father with a rope around his neck. Colonel Conger asked the soldier who had brought John Garrett there, "Where did you get him from?"

"Who are you looking for?" John Garrett asked.

One of the soldiers replied, "Two men."

"Those two men are in the tobacco barn," John replied. "We were becoming suspicious of them, and Father told them they could not stay with us."

"Where are they now?" Baker demanded, forgetting the elder Garrett for the moment.

"In the barn, locked up for fear they would steal the horses."[799]

A soldier was ordered to the barn to check. He returned saying, "We got em, but the door is locked."

The soldiers abandoned the house and the elder Garrett and quickly surrounded the tobacco barn. John told them that his brother, William, still in the corncrib, had the key; and a soldier was sent to retrieve the key.

Once the key had been grabbed from William's hand, it was brought to Conger. He seized young John by the arm.

"Go into the tobacco barn, and get the two men to surrender," Conger commanded John Garrett.

"They are armed to the teeth and they'll shoot me down," John Garrett protested.

But Conger would not let the boy decline. The boy understood that he had no choice – perhaps the soldiers would shoot him if he refused.

Shaking, John Garrett approached the barn. The weathered wooden slats of the tobacco barn were set four inches apart to allow air to flow through during curing. However, no one could see into the dark interior.

Young Garrett opened the door with the key and disappeared inside.

There was the sound of muffled conversation, then Booth's theatrical voice thundered, "You have betrayed me, sir; leave the barn or I will shoot you!"

Baker shouted for the men inside to turn over their arms. If they did not, Baker shouted, "We shall burn the barn, and have a bonfire and shooting match!"

At the door, Garrett cried, "Let me out!"

Immovable, Baker shouted, "You can't come out unless you bring the arms!"

"He won't give them to me! Let me out quick!"

Baker relented and let the door open slightly, whereupon young Garrett rushed out, fearful that at any moment a bullet from Booth's gun would come smashing into his flesh.

Moments later, Baker again called to Booth and shouted that he would give him five minutes to surrender.

Booth replied, "Gentlemen, give me time for reflection." Then he added, "I am alone, there is no one in here with me."

To this obvious lie, Baker responded, "We know that two men are in there and two must come out!"

Booth continued, "Captain, I do not want to shed blood, I could kill you now where you stand if I wanted to." Baker suddenly realized that he was a dark outline against the bonfire the men had built.[800] Baker, Conger, and several soldiers near the barn were easy targets for the desperate men in the barn.

"Oh, Captain!" Booth's voice sounded again moments later. "There is a man in here who wishes to surrender."[801]

Herold was at the door. "Let me out!" he cried.

"You can come out if you bring your weapons with you!" was the reply.

Booth, from farther within, shouted, "I own all the arms, they are mine!"

Booth and Herold were both wanted alive; but one alive was better than none, so the concession was made. The door was opened slightly.

"Let me see your hands!" Baker shouted to Herold. Herold came to the door and was immediately grabbed, searched, and dragged away. He was bound up to a tree near the house.

At this point, there was a disagreement among the three commanders as to what to do next. Doherty wanted to wait until daylight in order to see Booth better and to more easily take him captive. Baker and Conger wanted to set fire to the barn immediately to force Booth out. Since Conger was in charge of the manhunt, his argument won out.

Baker warned Booth, "If you don't come out in ten minutes, we will set the barn on fire."

Booth, however, was still inhabiting his private world in which he saw himself as standing center stage in a great play about honor and bravery.

"Tell me who you are and what you want of me. It may be that I am being taken by my friends," Booth replied in his marvelous stage voice.

"It makes no difference who we are! We know you and we want you. We have fifty well-armed men stationed around this barn. You cannot escape," responded Baker, exaggerating the numbers of the cavalry unit.

After a dramatic pause, Booth, theatrical to the last, called out, "Captain, this is a hard case, I swear. I am lame. Give a lame man a chance. Draw up you men twenty yards from here, and I will fight your whole command!"

This was vintage Booth, acting out his last drama and showing his bravery and honor, but Baker and the others must have thought him an idiot. This was not a play, and Booth was a wanted assassin.

"We are not here to fight; we are here to take you!" Baker replied.

Booth continued his oratory, "Captain, I believe you to be a brave and honorable man. I have had half a dozen chances to shoot you. I have a bead drawn on you now, but I do not wish to kill you. Withdraw your men from the door and I'll come out."

The actor was insisting on living out his delusion.

"Your time is up. If you don't come out we shall fire the barn!" Baker shouted.

"Well, then, my brave boys, you may prepare a stretcher for me. One more stain on the glorious old banner,"[802] Booth replied heroically. Booth seemed to stand outside himself and watch himself act on the stage of life.

Conger stepped from behind the barn. "You ready, Baker?"

Baker nodded.

Conger disappeared again behind the barn. He quietly slipped through the night to the corner of the barn where hay was stored. Pulling a wisp through a crack, he set it on fire.[803] The hay blazed up quickly, and the fire began to race along, fed by the old dry furniture and other copious tinder. All stepped backward farther and farther as the flames began to grow. The inside of the barn lit up as if by floodlights, and Booth became visible through the openings between the slats. He leaned on a single crutch, holding a revolver and carbine in each hand. At last the crutch fell, and Booth stood still as the flames blazed to the roof. The heat was becoming intense. Baker cautiously inched forward and looked between the slats. He saw Booth standing hatless and erect "as beautiful as the statue of a Greek god and as calm in that awful hour."[804]

"Booth was standing under and within an arc of fire . . . . Not the brilliant lighting of the theater; the roaring of the flames was not like the swelling music of the orchestra," Baker later wrote melodramatically.[805]

A shot rang out, and Booth sank to the floor an immediate quadriplegic.[806]

As Booth lay unable to move, Baker and Conger pulled open the door. Accompanied by soldiers and the younger John Garrett, they rushed through the withering heat to Booth. They pulled him out into the yard, but the heat was still so great that they had to drag him some distance off. At last they laid him under an apple tree. John Garrett in the meantime was trying unsuccessfully to put out the fire.

Conger at first thought that Booth must have shot himself; however, Baker replied, "No, I had my eye upon him every moment."[807]

Booth was conscious but in terrible pain. "Tell Mother, tell Mother!" Booth said weakly but then fell into unconsciousness.

Soldiers crowded around to look at the assassin they had ridden so hard and long to catch. Booth, meanwhile, slipped into and out of consciousness. The heat from the blazing barn was increasing and reached Booth even under the tree.

With great difficulty, Booth whispered, "Captain, it is hard that this man's property should be destroyed. He does not know who I am." These words may have spared the Garretts from being put on trial as Dr. Mudd and Spangler were.

John Garrett, still trying to put out the fire, called to the soldiers to help him, and Baker ordered soldiers to help put out the fire. Conger, however, saw that it was impossible to save the barn and had the soldiers pull back.[808]

The heat from the flames became so intense that Booth was carried to the porch of the house where he was put on a straw mattress pulled out by Mrs. Garrett. A cloth was dampened "in brandy and water" and given "to him to suck as he was unable to swallow."[809] The moisture seemed to revive him. After a few moments, he opened his eyes and pleaded to those about him, "Oh, kill me, kill me."

Dr. Urquhart in Port Royal was sent for. When he arrived, he was immediately led to the Garretts' porch. He put down his leather bag and squatted beside the paralyzed man to examine the wound. Baker asked whether there were any chance of transporting Booth to Washington alive.

Urquhart said no. It would be impossible, and then he told those near Booth that he was going to die soon.

Booth dropped in and out of unconsciousness. He began to mumble. Baker could not understand him and thought he was asking if there was blood in his mouth. Baker looked and said there was none.

Booth at last said the phrase that so many dying soldiers had uttered, "Tell Mother I died for my country." Continuing to defend his actions, he said, "I did what I thought was best."

In agony, he asked to be turned on his face and then turned back over. The schoolteacher Lucinda Holloway, Mrs. Garrett's sister, wiped his face with a damp cloth.

Meanwhile, the burning barn collapsed with a crashing roar, and the sky was beginning to lighten with coming dawn.

Booth lay staring upward at the porch roof and at the hint of an increasingly blue sky. "Lift up my hands," Booth asked since he could not move. When Baker lifted Booth's hands in front of his face, Booth said, "Useless, useless, useless." These were his last words. At seven fifteen that morning of April 26, 1865, John Wilkes Booth died. He was two weeks short of his twenty-seventh birthday.[810]

*   *   *

Sergeant Boston Corbett, the man who shot Booth, was a religious fanatic. Corbett felt that he was put upon Earth to save men's souls and to oppose all evil. As one of Lieutenant Doherty's men, he found himself in the dark of night facing the epitome of evil for 1865 – John Wilkes Booth. Corbett claimed, "God Almighty had directed me to shoot."[811]

Corbett had been stationed at a large gap between the boards of the burning barn. From this vantage, Corbett could see Booth clearly by the light of burning hay. It was his bullet that pierced Booth in the side of the neck and went through on a slightly downward path, passing through three vertebrae and cutting the spinal cord.[812]

Conger demanded of Corbett why he had disobeyed orders and shot Booth; Corbett replied, "God Almighty directed me." Later Corbett was brought before Stanton on a charge of having disobeyed orders in shooting Booth. The secretary of war quickly disposed of the matter by saying, "The rebel is dead – the patriot lives – he has saved us continued excitement, delay and expense – the patriot is released."[813]

*　　*　　*

Just before Booth died, Conger departed for Washington to tell Stanton, Colonel Baker, and the world that Lincoln's killer was dead. He took with him items taken from Booth's pockets: the candle-spattered compass, a knife, a pipe, the appointment book with the first draft of the letter to Dr. Stewart along with the five dollar bill that was too much to give him, and Booth's belt and his weapons. Booth also had had with him photographs of five women: actresses Fanny Brown, Helen Western, Alice Grey, and Effie Germon. There was also a photograph of Lucy Hale.

While the Garretts prepared breakfast for the hungry men of the Sixteenth New York cavalry, Baker and a corporal quickly wrapped Booth's body in a saddle blanket and sewed the cloth firmly.[814]

Baker left with the body in the wagon and reached the Rappahannock River before the cavalry. The wagon with Booth's body traveled the thirty miles to the Potomac and the gunboat. Once some ex-Confederate soldiers coming the other way asked what was on the wagon, "A dead Yank?"[815] They reached the *John S. Ide* and, after getting Booth's body on board, headed north to Washington.

*　　*　　*

Conger reached Washington about five o'clock on April 26. He reported to Colonel Baker at once and briefed him on the capture of Herold and the death of Booth. Conger and Colonel Baker then left for Stanton's house to tell him the news. Most of the articles taken from Booth's person were given to Stanton. Stanton, upon seeing the belongings of Booth, was overcome with emotion and silently covered his eyes a moment with his hands.

Stanton, anxious that Herold should be interrogated and that Booth's body should not fall into Southern hands, ordered the *John S. Ide* to go directly to the Navy Yard. Secretary Stanton was obsessed with the belief that Booth's act was the signal for a reversal of Lee's surrender and the continuance of the rebellion, and he was afraid that John Wilkes Booth, dead or alive, might be a rallying point. Stanton directed that Herold and Booth's body should be transferred to the *USS Montauk*.

Sometime around ten-thirty that night (April 26), the *Montauk* met the *John S. Ide* as it came up the Potomac River. The gunboat came along side, and Booth's body was brought aboard. Forbidden to ask any questions, the crew was under orders to fire at any boat other than the tug that came near.[816]

At approximately one forty-five on the morning of April 27, silent soldiers brought Herold and Booth's body to the *USS Montauk* anchored off the Washington Navy Yard. Booth's corpse, still in the gray army blanket, was carried to a carpenter's bench on the forward deck of the *USS Montauk*, and a guard placed around it. Herold was immediately clapped into double irons attached by a chain to a thirty-two pound shot. The shot was carried by a guard whenever Herold had to move. Herold as well as all the others tried in the conspiracy (with the exception of Mary Surratt) were compelled to wear a canvas hood padded with an inch of cotton but with slits for breathing and eating.[817]

\*   \*   \*

Jett was taken prisoner, but Bainbridge and Ruggles fled to their homes in King George County. Ten days later, the two were arrested at night by Union cavalry. The two were taken to Washington and held in the Old Capitol Prison. They were not alone in their misery, however, for with them were Dr. Stewart, at whose house Booth had stopped; Charles Lucas, the Negro who had driven him to the ferry; and including Willie Jett, who had escaped from Captain Doherty but had been recaptured at his home in Westmoreland County.[818] Scores of other people, not involved, or only incidentally involved were also caught in the police dragnet and were imprisoned.

# PART 3

# CHAPTER 24

## *It Is the Body of J. Wilkes Booth*

On April 27, Commodore J. B. Montgomery, commandant of the Navy Yard, sent a message to Gideon Wells, secretary of the navy, "David E. Herold, prisoner, and the body of Wilkes Booth were delivered here at 1:45 this morning. The body of Booth is changing rapidly. What disposition shall be made of it? It is now on board the ironclad Montauk."[819]

At nine o'clock that same morning, Commodore Montgomery received the following order, "You will permit Surgeon General Barnes and his assistant, accompanied by Judge Advocate-General Holt, John A. Bingham, Major Eckert, William C. Moore, Colonel L. C. Baker, Lieutenant Baker, Lieutenant Colonel Conger, Charles Dawson, J. L. Smith, Mr. Gardner, photographer, and an assistant, to go on board the Montauk and see the body of John Wilkes Booth. Immediately after the surgeon general has made an autopsy you will have the body placed in a strong box and delivered to the charge of Colonel Baker, the box being securely sealed."[820]

Many people identified Booth's body. Charles M. Collins, a signal officer on the *Montauk*, stated, "I have known him personally about six weeks. I have known him by sight since 1862 . . . . I have not the least doubt that it is the body of J. Wilkes Booth."[821]

Charles Dawson, a clerk at the National Hotel, was brought on board the *Montauk*. He had known Booth since October 1863. "I distinctly recognize it as the body of J. Wilkes Booth – first from the general appearance, next from the India ink letters 'JWB' on his wrist, which I have very frequently noticed and then by a scar on the neck. I also recognize the vest as that of J. Wilkes Booth."[822]

Dr. John Frederick May, who had two years previously removed a fibroid tumor from the left side of John Booth's neck, also identified his body. Between April and May 1863, Booth went to Dr. John Frederick May and told him that he "was much annoyed by a large lump on the back of his neck, which had been gradually increasing in size." Booth asked Dr. May if the procedure would prevent him from acting. May later wrote, "I told him, if he would be careful not to make any violent efforts, it would not." Dr. May told Booth that if the wound was cared for, it would only leave a slight scar. The tumor was removed and the wound sewn very closely. For two weeks, Booth came regularly in order to have the wound dressed; however, one day, Booth returned to May's office with the wound torn open and "widely gaping. Charlotte Cushman, while performing with him in a play, had struck Booth in the neck, reopening the wound. The doctor now told Booth the wound would heal with a mark similar to a vaccination scar. Booth asked the doctor to say if questioned that the scar came from 'the removal of a bullet from his neck.'"[823] Booth was always the actor.

Now on the *Montauk*, Dr. May identified his former patient by the surgical scar on Booth's neck.[824]

An autopsy was conducted by Dr. J. Janvier Woodward of the Army Medical Museum. He had performed the autopsy on Lincoln just twelve days earlier. The official autopsy reads as follows:

> Case JWB: Was killed April 26, 1865, by a conoidal pistol ball, fired at the distance of a few yards, from a cavalry revolver. The missile perforated the base of the right lamina of the 4th lumbar vertebra, fracturing it longitudinally and separating it by a fissure from the spinous process, at the same time fracturing the 5th vertebra through its pedicle, and involving that transverse process. The projectile then traversed the spinal canal almost horizontally but with a slight inclination downward and backward, perforating the cord which was found much torn and discolored with blood. The ball then shattered the bases of the left 4th, and 5th laminae, driving bony fragments among the muscles, and made its exit at the left side of the neck, nearly opposite the point of entrance. It avoided the 2nd and 3rd cervical nerves. These facts were determined at autopsy which was made on April 28. Immediately after the reception of the injury, there was very general paralysis. The phrenic nerves performed their function, but the respiration was diaphragmatic, of course, labored and slow. Deglutition was impracticable, and one or two attempts at articulation were unintelligible. Death from asphyxia, took place about two hours after the reception of the injury.
>
> Signed, J. J. Woodward[825]

From Booth's neck, Dr. Woodward cut out and preserved Booth's third, fourth, and fifth cervical vertebrae and a portion of the spinal cord.[826]

Booth had not shot himself: the bullet wound was inconsistent with suicide – the shot was not fired close to Booth's head as demonstrated by the absence of powder burns on the skin.[827]

It was time for disposal of the body. That night, Booth's body was placed in a strongbox, securely sealed, and was given into the charge of Colonel Barker of the

War Department Detective Bureau. Stanton directed Baker to dispose of Booth's remains so that they would not "be found until Gabriel blew his trumpet."[828] With his nephew, Lieutenant Baker, Colonel Baker took the body from the *Montauk* at about three o'clock that afternoon and put it aboard a rowboat. They were careful to be seen also putting a heavy ball and chain into the boat. They did not conceal their movements from the men on the *USS Montauk*. The Bakers first rowed to Giesborough Point, where for years condemned government horses and mules had been taken to be shot. As they intended, rumors spread that uncle and nephew had dropped the body with the heavy ball and chain into the Potomac. *Frank Leslie's Illustrated Newspaper* (May 20, 1865) showed on its front page a drawing of a form completely wrapped in a blanket and tied to a board being lowered into the water in a secret nighttime burial.

However, the body was not dropped into the river. After a time, the Bakers rowed to the officer's landing on the arsenal grounds.[829] The body was placed in a small summerhouse, a rustic structure used by the officers and families as a waiting place for boats or as a shady spot for a picnic overlooking the river.

As it happened that Thursday afternoon (April 27, 1865), a military doctor, Dr. Porter, had taken his wife for boat ride down the Potomac. When they returned and were rowing toward the pier, soldiers ordered them away. The sentry yelled to him "that no persons were permitted to land at the pier and that he would fire upon [them] if [they] attempted to land." Porter, who was in uniform, ordered the sentry to call for the officer of the guard. When the officer arrived, he did a quick assessment and allowed the Porters to land their boat.

The Porters went home, but at midnight Dr. Porter was called to come back to the pier. He and the arsenal's military storekeeper, E. M. Stebbins, and four enlisted men were present as a team of horses pulled a cart. Dr. Porter pledged his word as an officer and a gentleman never to tell of what occurred on the night of April 27 until the need for secrecy passed. It was only in 1911 that he wrote of what happened that night. The enlisted men were members of the Ordnance Corps picked for their reliability and discretion. They also were all sworn to secrecy about what happened that night.

The group went to the summerhouse where Booth's body had been kept hidden and put it into a cart. The men marched along in complete silence, challenged by sentries as they were approaching their posts. The midnight march ended when they reached the Old Penitentiary. The building actually had not been used as a prison for many years. Booth's body was quietly carried to a ground floor storage room that was fifty by forty feet, large enough for the horses and the cart to go inside. The floor was unpaved, and a shallow hole had been previously dug.

Booth's body was put into the hole, which the men quickly refilled, "packed down and the surface smoothed off" so no trace of a hole could be seen. They then shoveled the remaining dirt into the cart and led the horses and cart away. The door to the storeroom was locked, and the key was taken to Secretary of War Stanton.[830]

In 1867, Booth's body was moved to one of the large store houses on the east side of the arsenal's parade grounds.[831] It was not until February 1869 that President Johnson released the bodies of Booth and those hanged for conspiracy to their families. Booth's family, with the rest of the country, had not known where John Wilkes Booth's remains had been for four years. At last, the Booths buried him in the family plot at Green Mount Cemetery in Baltimore.

# CHAPTER 25

## My Country, Right or Wrong

Booth knew that if his plan was successful, he would be a hunted man, and everyone around him – his family and friends – would ask why he had done such a thing.

In preparation, Booth put together a sealed packet in November 1864 with an explanation in the care of his sister, Asia.

After Booth's death in April 1865, Asia opened the packet her brother had given her. Inside was a letter to Samuel Chester, whom Booth had unsuccessfully sought to recruit. There were a letter and bonds for his mother and a transfer of an oil well to Junius Booth and one to his sister Rosalie.

Also in this packet was the famous "To Whom It May Concern" letter. It was an explanation by Booth of what he thought of the Southern cause and what he was planning to do to serve the Confederate cause.[832] Asia's husband gave the letter to United States Marshal William Milward, who turned it over to the *Philadelphia Enquirer*, which printed the letter on April 19.

On May 6, 1865, John Clarke gave a written statement to the judge adjutant's office, "John Wilkes Booth has repeatedly within, say, two years left at my house in care of his sister (my wife) large envelopes sealed and directed to himself, saying for 'safe keeping' as he was obliged to travel though the far west to meet his professional engagements – invariably stating that they contained 'stocks etc' – These envelopes have remained sometimes months, and he has called for them – About the latter part of November '64, while I was acting in New York, he left a sealed envelope at my house in Philadelphia in this way. During January he again visited my house and asked for it, took it and shortly after returned it, (or a similar one) and it was again placed as usual in my safe."[833]

In this bitter, rambling letter, Booth claimed to "have loved the Union beyond expression" but stated that "all hope for peace" was dead. He felt that the country had been established for whites.

Booth's letter claimed that the South was not and never had been fighting for the continuation of slavery. The Confederate cause, he said, was as noble and far greater than that of the founding fathers. And even if one assumed that they started the war for the wrong reasons, "cruelty and injustice have made the wrong become the right, and they stand now before the wonder and admiration of the world as a noble band of patriotic heroes. Hereafter, reading of their deeds, Thermopylae will be forgotten."

In the letter, Booth raved theatrically about the Union, Lincoln, abolitionists, and the South. "O, how I have longed to see her break from the mist of blood that circles round her folds, spoiling her beauty and tarnishing her honor."

The letter was dated only 1864.

My dear Sir:

You may use this as you think best. But as some may wish to know when, who and why as I know not how to direct, I give it (in the words of your master) – "To whom it may concern."

Right or wrong, God judge me, not man. For be my motives good or bad, of one thing I am sure, the lasting condemnation of the North. I love peace more than life. Have loved the Union beyond expression. For four years I have waited, hoped and prayed for the dark clouds to break and for a restoration of our former sunshine. To wait longer would be a crime. All hope for peace is dead. My prayers have proved as idle as my hopes. God's will be done. I go to see and share the bitter end.

I have ever held the South were right. The very nomination of Abraham Lincoln, four years ago, spoke very plainly of war, war, upon Southern rights and institutions. His election proved it. "Await an overt act." Yes, till you are bound and plundered. What folly. The South was wise. Who thinks of argument or pastime when the finger of his enemy presses the trigger? In a foreign war, I, too, could say "country right or wrong." But in a struggle such as ours (where the brother tries to pierce the brother's heart) for God's sake choose the right. When a country like this spurns justice from her side, she forfeits the allegiance of every honest freeman and should leave him, untrammeled by any fealty so ever, to act as his conscience may approve.

People of the North, to hate tyranny, to love liberty and justice, to strike at wrong and oppression, was the teaching of our fathers. The study of our early history will not let me forget, and may it never.

The country was formed for the white, not for the black man. And looking upon African slavery from the same standpoint held by the noble framers of our Constitution, I, for one, have ever considered it one of the greatest blessings (both for themselves and us) that God ever bestowed upon a favored nation. Witness heretofore our wealth and power: witness their elevation and enlightenment above their race elsewhere. I have lived among it most of my life, and I have seen less harsh treatment from master to man than I have beheld in the North from father to son. Yet, heaven knows, no one would be willing to do more for the Negro race than I, could I but see the way to still better their condition. But Lincoln's policy is only preparing a way for their total annihilation. The south are not, nor have they been fighting for the continuation of slavery. The first battle of Bull Run did away with that idea. Their causes for war have been as noble and greater far than those that urged our fathers on. Even should we allow they were wrong at the beginning of this contest, cruelty and injustice have made the wrong become the right, and they stand now (before the wonder and admiration of the world) as a noble band of patriotic heroes. Hereafter, reading of their deeds, Thermopylae will be forgotten.

When I aided in the capture and execution of John Brown (who was a murderer on our Western border and who was fairly tried and convicted before an impartial judge and jury, of treason, and who, by the way, has since been made a god) I was proud of my little share in the transaction, for I deemed it my duty that I was helping our common country to perform an act of justice. But what was a crime in poor John Brown is considered (by themselves) as the greatest and only virtue of the whole Republican party. Strange transmigration. Vice so becomes a virtue, simply because more indulged in.

I thought then as now that the Abolitionists were the only traitors in the land and that the entire party deserved the fate of poor John Brown, not because they wish to abolish slavery, but on account of the means they have ever used to effect that Abolition. If Brown were living I doubt whether he himself would set slavery against the Union. Most or many in the North do, and openly curse the Union, if the South are to return and retain a single right guaranteed to them by every tie which we once revered as sacred. The South can make no choice. It is either extermination or slavery for themselves (worse than death) to draw from. I know my choice.

I have also studied hard to know upon what grounds the right of a state to secede has been denied, when our very name United States, and the Declaration of Independence both provide for secession. But there is no time for words. I write in haste. I know how foolish I shall be deemed for taking such a step as this, where on the one side, I have many friends and many things to make me happy, where my profession alone has gained me an income of more than twenty thousand dollars a year, and where my great personal ambition in my profession has such a great field for labor. On the other hand, The South have never bestowed upon me one kind word; a place where I must become a private soldier or a beggar. To give up all the former for the latter, besides my mother and my sisters, whom I love so dearly (although they so widely differ from me in opinion), seems insane: but God is my judge. I love justice more than a country that disowns it, more than fame and wealth; more (Heaven pardon me if I am wrong), more than a happy home. I have never been upon a battle field; (sic) but, O my countrymen, could you all see the reality or effects of this horrid war as I have seen them (in every state save Virginia) I know you would think like me, and would pray the Almighty to create in the Northern mind a sense of right and justice (even if it should possess no seasoning of mercy) and that He would dry up the sea of blood between us which is daily growing wider. Alas, poor country. Is she to meet her threatened doom? Four years ago I would have given a thousand lives to see her remain (as I had always known her) powerful and unbroken. And even now I would hold my life at naught to see her what she was. Oh, my friends, if the fearful scenes of the last four years had never been enacted, or if what has been was a frightful dream from which we could now awake, with what flowing hearts could we bless our God and pray for His continued favor. How I have loved the old flag can never be known. A few years since and the entire world could boast of none so pure and spotless. But I have of late been seeing and hearing of the bloody deeds of which she has been made the emblem. O, how I have longed to see her break from the mist of blood that circles round her folds, spoiling her beauty and tarnishing her honor. But no, day by day, has she been dragged deeper and deeper into cruelty and oppression till now (in my eyes) her once bright red stripes look the bloody gashes on the face of heaven. I look now upon my early admiration of her glories as a dream. My love (as things stand to-day) is for the South alone. Nor do I deem it a dishonor in attempting to make for her a prisoner of this man to whom she owes so much misery. If success attends me, I go penniless to her side. They say she has found that "last ditch" which the North has so long derided and has been endeavoring to force her in, forgetting they are our brothers, and that it's impolitic to force on an enemy to madness. Should I reach her in safety and find it true, I will proudly beg permission to triumph or die in that same "ditch" by her side.

The letter was signed, "A Confederate, at present doing duty upon his own responsibility". The manner in which Booth signed the letter is unusual. The words "at present" were crossed out. Booth may have been acting independently in November but hoped to receive Confederate support in the future or had approached Confederate representatives in Montreal and been rebuffed. The letter was written after his visit to Canada.

\* \* \*

234 BRENDAN H. EGAN, JR.

Booth stated in this letter his intention to try to make "a prisoner of this man" who had caused the South so much misery. Added to the confessions of Arnold and Atzerodt and to the testimony of Chester, Booth's statements made a strong prima facie case for the existence of the abduction conspiracy. Both statements, the one in the letter and the one in the diary, were known to investigators and prosecutors, but neither was mentioned at the trial. Instead, Bingham had argued persuasively and effectively that the assassination of the president had been Booth's object from the beginning. Even though the dairy had been mentioned in the press, none of the defense attorneys mentioned or used the Booth letter or diary.

The *New York Times* of April 27, 1865, reported that Booth had at the time of his death a diary in which he had noted events of each day since the assassination and that the diary was in the possession of the War Department. The *Times* story was not completely correct. Booth did write in the diary on two occasions, but he did not write daily. The *New York World* on April 28, 1865, also reported on the diary under the byline of George Alfred Townsend. The "To Whom It May Concern" letter also had been widely reprinted in the newspapers.

\*     \*     \*

In the package that Booth had given to Asia was a letter to his mother. Booth wanted his mother, whom he dearly loved, to see that he had become a hero. He described himself in idealistic terms. He was, he said, a loving and dutiful son fated to "a noble duty for the sake of liberty and humanity due to" his country. He claimed to have suffered for four years, keeping his thoughts to himself, "Even in my own home constantly hearing every principle dear to my heart denounced as treasonable." Booth also complained that he had been "idle" in the Southern cause, a statement that implied he had not been as active a spy or smuggler as his sister Asia later wrote. Booth wrote theatrically that he began "to deem myself a coward and to despise my own existence . . . . I have borne it mostly for your dear sake, and for you alone have I also struggled to fight off this desire to be gone [from the North]." But a fate over which he had no control now "takes me from you dear mother, to do what I can for a poor oppressed downtrodden people . . . . I care not for the censure of the north. [Just] So I have your forgiveness, and [I] feel I may hope it, even though you differ with me in opinion."[834]

Booth had not joined the Confederate ranks at the beginning of the war, and he believed toward its end that he had missed the opportunity to achieve distinction. Flattered by the applause given him on the stage in the South, he became more violent in his verbal defense of the Southern cause than were most rebels. Booth had traveled the country, belligerently criticizing people who opposed slavery and secession. He felt, however, that while he had talked, other men had attained military recognition in the Confederacy. To become a hero, Booth felt that he must act quickly for the Confederacy or sink forever into insignificance.

Another aspect of Booth's personality, which helps to explain his actions, was that he was a romantic who liked the limelight and public adoration. On the last night of his life, Booth ate dinner at the Garrett farmhouse. One of the Garretts, not knowing that Booth was the man who had assassinated Lincoln, said that the assassin must have been well paid, to which Booth replied, "It is my opinion he wasn't paid a cent, but did it for notoriety's sake." If this recount is accurate, it well explains Booth's motives.

"When I leave the stage for good, I will be the most famous man in America," he had declared over the brandy glasses on the evening of the assassination. And at Garrett's farm, he had said that he believed the man who shot the president did it "for notoriety's sake."

Asia, in Philadelphia at the time of the assassination, thought that the assassination was caused by Lincoln's trip to Richmond. Asia wrote, "I believe that with the kidnaping scheme was laid to rest, although with curses, [John's] cherished hope of saving those he would have died to serve; but the fall of Richmond rang in with maddening, exasperating clang of joy, and that triumphant entry [by Lincoln] into the fallen city breathed air afresh upon the fire which consumed him."[835]

There is Booth
- the great Southern patriot and hero of Confederate history
- egoistical, "I will be the most famous man in America"
- reviving the CSA (Confederate States of America) singlehandedly by killing the hated Lincoln
- needing to do "something great and desparate" for his beloved country
- mad, unable to reason clearly

\*   \*   \*

Booth loved the South and identified with the Southern cause, having grown up in Baltimore, Maryland, a Southern city in a Southern-minded state. He hated Lincoln, whom he considered a tyrant, and had the idea that the federal government would collapse if Lincoln was dead. With the beginning of the Civil War though, Booth failed to join the Confederate forces. John was the only member of the Booth family who supported the cause of the South. Edwin Booth supported Lincoln and voted for Lincoln in the 1864 election.

Several of Lincoln's war measures infuriated Booth, such as the expansion of the army, the blockade of Southern ports after the surrender of Fort Sumter, the disbursement of two million dollars to the Union Army without the consent of Congress, and the suspension of the writ of habeas corpus so Lincoln could arrest and hold people indefinitely without charge or trial. Under this last measure, Lincoln ordered the arrest of thirty-one secessionist members of the Maryland State legislature the day before they planned to vote Maryland out of the Union. Lincoln took this drastic measure to prevent Washington from falling into Confederate hands. Booth, however, viewed Lincoln's act as pure tyranny and maintained that if the North won the war, Lincoln would become king.

This idea was exemplified by his admiration of Brutus, the assassin of Caesar, whom Booth considered a protector of liberty due to his murder of a tyrant. Booth compared himself to Brutus and to William Tell but stated that he was better than both. They had, he later wrote in his diary, personal motives for what they had done, whereas he himself had struck solely for the good of the Confederacy. Booth thought that eventually he would be considered a patriot.

Booth's namesake, John Wilkes, was an eighteenth century English radical whose repeated expulsions from Parliament in a fight for individual political liberty made him a hero of the common people. Wilkes's cousin, Elizabeth, married a London silversmith named John Booth, whose son, Richard, (John Wilkes Booth's grandfather) went to America to help the colonists fight for their independence.[836]

Far from being the ravings of one man, many Southerners shared Booth's indignation at what Lincoln had done and may have felt as Booth did that violent action against Lincoln and other Union leaders would save the Confederacy. The criticisms of Lincoln voiced by individuals and by newspapers fed Booth's own private hatred of Lincoln's "lawless tyranny." After General Lee surrendered his forces to General Grant on April 9 and after Lincoln's speech of April 11, Booth decided that the Confederacy's desperate condition necessitated desperate action.[837]

Booth had cursed his four-year idleness and said he had begun "to deem myself a coward and to despise my own existence." After March 17 when his conspiracy to kidnap Lincoln collapsed, Booth felt personal failure and humiliation. These feelings added to his anger at the terrible wrong he felt was being committed against the South. He focused his hatred on the man whom he deemed chiefly responsible. And Booth had to be further frustrated at having his deeply held political views ridiculed by his own family.

Suffering from depression ran in the family, and he appeared not to have escaped the family curse. When Washington citizens were wildly celebrating the end of the war, Booth fell into a dark mood and began to drink heavily "to drive away the blues." He could put away a quart of brandy within two hours and showed signs of becoming an alcoholic. When asked when he planned to go to Richmond, he replied despondently, "I never shall go to Richmond again." And then he repeated himself, "I never shall go to Richmond again."[838]

Those who knew Booth considered his deed the result of a vain nature and a lifelong desire for acclaim. They felt that he had enthusiasm without good judgment. He spoke indiscreetly on the Southern cause and had traveled the country belligerently criticizing people who opposed slavery and secession. He envied men who had attained military recognition. The idea of sinking forever into insignificance disturbed him.

On the evening of the assassination, Booth declared over his brandy, "When I leave the stage for good, I will be the most famous man in America." Booth needed fame and public adulation, and with his hatred of Lincoln, he saw only one answer, assassination.

Booth viewed himself as a savior of the Confederacy and believed that the Confederate cause was not lost. Johnson's army was still in the field; however, Booth did not know that Johnson was negotiating with Sherman for terms of surrender. Booth thought that some dramatic action might yet save his devoted Confederacy and that he was the man to take that action. He wrote in his diary, "For six months we had worked to capture, but our cause being almost lost, something decisive and great must be done." He saw himself as the man of the hour who could change the course of history and save the South.[839]

There was in Booth's character a flare for the dramatic, both in his personal life as well as on the stage. His passion and sympathy for the Southern cause, his guilt at having a lucrative acting career that made him rich while other Southerners fought and died, and his belief that he would be personally fulfilled by performing an act of greatness, led him to grab at assassination as the last available way to give his life meaning. He was like a drowning man grasping for something big enough to hold him afloat.

John Wilkes was his mother's favorite, and he had promised never to join the Confederate army.[840] In plotting to kidnap Lincoln, Booth was violating his promise to his mother; however, if successful, he felt he would be adored as a hero and remembered as the savior of the Confederate cause. He considered the murder to be an act of war against the Union and believed that Lincoln was a tyrant and dictator. He frequently called Lincoln King Lincoln.[841]

"Mr. Lincoln had acted oftentimes with the authority almost of a dictator, and had permitted his Secretaries, particularly the Secretary of War, a license of power greater even than he would himself have used. Individual rights had seemed for a time suspended." Men close to Lincoln and the people at large had trusted him; the people around him knew him and "detected not a movement of personal ambition in his exercise of power." They expected a restoration of their civil liberties at the war's end. "But men who were not near him could not so see him." One such man was John Wilkes Booth.[842]

Carl Sandburg pointed out that such views were shared by many educated individuals and newspapers and had been constantly written about throughout the war. Sandburg wrote that if Booth had been entirely ignorant of what the Confederacy thought of Lincoln and knew him only from the pages of the *New York World*, the *Detroit Free Press*, and the *Chicago Times*, Booth would have felt himself justified in going "forth with a brass pocket pistol."

Booth had wanted to kidnap Lincoln and use him as ransom to force the release of Confederate prisoners of war. His poorly organized attempt on March 17 failed, and he and his conspirators went their separate ways. Then quickly followed the fall of Richmond, the fight of Jefferson Davis, the surrender at Appomattox, and Lincoln's April 11 speech calling for what Booth call nigger citizenship. It was somewhere between the speech of April 11 and April 15 that Booth's mind turned to assassination.

On the evening of April 11, Lincoln delivered a speech from a White House balcony. Herold later thought that this was the fatal moment in which Booth decided on assassination when Booth uttered, "Now, by God! I'll put him through. That is the last speech he will ever make."[843]

Booth was now waiting for the opportunity for assassination, and he did not have long to wait. On the morning of the assassination, April 14, Booth learned that President Lincoln and General Grant would be at Ford's Theatre that night. If Lincoln and Grant could be killed, plus Seward, plus Johnson, maybe the South still had a chance to survive in the federal government disarray. This was the "something decisive & great" that motivated Booth on April 14. Perhaps he, John Wilkes Booth, could change history and save the Confederacy. After the assassination, Booth was shocked to read that the world, including his "beloved South," condemned him in the vilest of terms.

With the collapse of the Confederacy, Booth had no one to answer to and was now acting entirely on his own. Booth was now heavily drinking and saw himself as a tragic hero, giving up his wealth, his family, his fiancée, and his career. It was almost impossible for him not to draw the connection between himself and Brutus striking down the tyrant Caesar. Booth did not want to believe that it was too late, that the South was really defeated. In his first diary entry after assassinating Lincoln, Booth wrote, "But our cause being almost lost, something decisive & great must be done."

# CHAPTER 26

## *Organized to Convict*

The incredible precautions used in incarcerating the prisoners reflected the fear and paranoia of their captors. The *USS Saugus* was used to jail David Herold, Lewis Powell, George Atzerodt, Samuel Arnold, Edward Spangler, Michael O'Laughlen, and Dr. Samuel Mudd. Their hands were manacled by handcuffs set on each end of a ten-inch-long iron bar, and each man was attached by chains to a seventy-five-pound iron ball.

On April 28, the prisoners were transferred from the gunboat to the Old Penitentiary, a military prison at the U.S. Arsenal. Each prisoner was in his own cell, and the cells were separated by empty cells on each side so the prisoners could not communicate by "knocking or rapping." Each prisoner was guarded by four soldiers, all of whom were relieved every two hours: none of these soldiers ever guarded the same prisoner more than once. When all the regiments of a brigade had been used as guards, another brigade took its place. Stanton had ordered that not only were the prisoners not allowed be to talk to one another, they were not even allowed to talk to their guards.

And on April 30, Mary Surratt was also transferred to the Old Penitentiary, but her accommodations were not so severe. She had a furnished room, and her daughter, Anna, visited her daily.

Although the civil courts were functioning, Stanton wanted the conspirators to be tried quickly before a military commission. There the rules of evidence were less demanding and punishment was more likely to be swift. Stanton attempted to get the trial started even before Lincoln was buried. He asked Attorney General Speed for his opinion as to whether the conspirators "were lawfully triable before a military commission." Speed's opinion was that they were, and he agreed with Stanton and Holt that a trial by a military commission would be legal under what Judge Advocate General Holt termed "the common law of war."[844] It was Lincoln himself who in 1862 had given him this power. Under Lincoln's proclamation, civilians accused of "disloyal practices" came under military jurisdiction. Many people, including editors of Northern newspapers, considered the prosecution of civilians in military courts to be unconstitutional. Ironically, this proclamation was one that had thoroughly angered Booth and had fed the fires that led to his final violent act.

Lincoln had created Holt's position, and since 1862, Holt had often used military commissions to bring civilians under the jurisdiction of military courts.

Elated, Stanton ordered Holt to prepare the government's case. Stanton appointed Congressman John A. Bingham and Colonel H. L. Burnett as assistants. Burnett was the successful military prosecutor of the Copperhead leaders Clement Vallandigham and Lambdin Milligan.

Bingham, literate and well spoken, was elected to the House of Representatives from Ohio in 1854 as a Republican, and he served four terms before being defeated in 1862. After the loss of his House seat, he was appointed by Lincoln to the office of judge advocate. He held that position for two years and was reelected to the House in 1864. He was a demagogue, known for his forceful personality and lack of self-doubt.[845]

As judge advocate general of U.S. Army, Holt investigated and prosecuted the eight people who were charged. Holt was driven to see those responsible for assassinating the president punished, and he had little sympathy for the defendants.

Holt determined that no guilty party would escape even if it meant temporarily imprisoning many innocent ones. In the process, many people were falsely accused, and they angrily denounced the War Department for denying them due process and for intimidating witnesses. As time passed, and these men wrote in newspapers and magazines of their experiences, Democratic politicians and editors found the public increasingly responsive to their outrage. But at the time, the public demanded and approved of Holt's and Stanton's thoroughness and would have been far more critical of the department had it done too little to investigate and avenge Lincoln's murder. Only later did the public respond with outrage and condemn the War Department for having gone too far.

Holt, born in 1807, was a successful lawyer in Kentucky and Mississippi. He retired from the law when still in his forties, and he and his second wife, a daughter of U.S. Representative Charles A. Holohan of Kentucky, did a great deal of traveling. In Washington, Holt eventually became one of the social elite. As a Southern Democrat, he denounced legislation that impeded the recovery of fugitives slaves and supported the compromise of 1850. He was postmaster general (1859-1860) during the Buchanan administration. In 1859, he approved the nondelivery of abolitionist literature through the post office but was against the use of federal troops to prevent secession. He did, however, completely change his political stance when the Southern states seceded – he wanted to preserve the Union at whatever cost. In 1861 after a shakeup in Buchanan's cabinet, Holt became secretary of war. With Attorney General Edwin M. Stanton and Secretary of the Treasury John A. Dix, the Buchanan administration hobbled through its final months.[846]

Holt, a cultured Southern gentleman, had many friends. However, when he embraced the Union cause, many of his Southern friends became enemies, and his attitude toward them became vindictive. He felt strongly that Southern leadership should be severely punished. During 1861, he aided the Union cause by keeping his native state of Kentucky loyal to the Union.

Holt was in Charleston, South Carolina, on April 14, 1865, participating in the ceremonies at Fort Sumter. These ceremonies were conducted to celebrate the symbolic end to the Civil War. Later in a Charleston hotel, Holt delivered a speech advocating paroling Confederate soldiers, but not their leaders.

The idea of civilians being tried by the military was not universally accepted. Many in the press, most notably Horace Greeley, criticized the military proceedings as unconstitutional. Originally Holt proposed that the trial be conducted in secret. Although Stanton argued for an open trial, Holt convinced him that secrecy was the best and quickest way to get the conspirators convicted. When news that the trial was to be held behind locked doors was published, it brought such vociferous protest that Stanton rescinded the order.

Military tribunals had unlimited powers. They were the sole judge of the law and decided the admissibility of all the evidence submitted. These tribunals also handed out the penalty, and only the president could change their findings.[847]

Also under Stanton's orders, General Townsend selected the officers who would make up the military commission. Nine officers were appointed as judges with Major General David Hunter as the president of the tribunal.[848] Brevet Major General John F. Hartranft was to act as special provost marshal general during the trial, and his immediate superior was Major General Winfield S. Hancock, commander of the Middle Military Division, United States Volunteers.

Holt oversaw the Bureau of Military Justice as it collected evidence, and War Department investigators accumulated and evaluated evidence acquired by the many agency's detectives.

Stanton also actively collected evidence and examined witnesses. On April 26, Burnett sent a letter to General Augur, which stated in part, "The Secretary of War directs that you will deliver to Major Eckert the clothing worn by Payne at the time of his arrest, and any other garments connected with Payne that the Major may desire."[849] Stanton also spent a great deal of time trying to implicate Confederate leaders.

There was much evidence to organize and collate and statements to be taken. It had to be determined who had helped Booth, both in his conspiracy and in his escape. Four years of Confederate records in Richmond had to be sifted through. Not all the information they found was correct, for example, just ten days after the assassination on April 24, Stanton telegraphed General Dix in New York, "One of the assassins now in prison, who attempted to kill Mr. Seward, is believed to be one of the Saint Albans raiders"[850] Stanton was wrong in thinking that Powell was one of the St. Albans raiders.

\*　　\*　　\*

On May 2, President Johnson asked Stanton for the names of the Confederates against whom there was evidence of participation in the Lincoln assassination. Holt eagerly forwarded the names of Jefferson Davis, Clement C. Clay (once among Holt's closest friends), Jacob Thompson, Beverly Tucker, William C. Cleary, and George Sanders.[851]

At a cabinet meeting on May 2, Stanton presented the case against each of these Confederates. Johnson asked for the advice of his cabinet. Stanton, Secretary of Treasury Hugh McCulloch, and Acting Secretary of State William Hunter were in favor of Johnson's signing. Secretary of the Navy Welles wrote that he favored signing only if there was proof of guilt. Johnson signed.[852]

The proclamation read as follows:

> Whereas it appears from evidence in the Bureau of Military Justice that the atrocious murder of the late President, Abraham Lincoln, and the attempted assassination of the Hon. William H. Seward, Secretary of State, were incited, concerted, and procured by and between Jefferson Davis, late of Richmond, Va., and Jacob Thompson, Clement C. Clay, Beverly Tucker, George N. Sanders, William C. Cleary, and other rebels and traitors against the Government of the United States harbored in Canada:
>
> Now, therefore, to the end that justice may be done, I, Andrew Johnson, President of the United States, do offer and promise for the arrest of said persons, or either of them, within the limits of the United States, so that they can be brought to trial, the following rewards:
>
> One hundred thousand dollars for the arrest of Jefferson Davis.
> Twenty-five thousand dollars for the arrest of Clement C. Clay.
> Twenty-five thousand dollars for the arrest of Jacob Thompson, late of Mississippi.
> Twenty-five thousand dollars for the arrest of George N. Sanders.
> Twenty-five thousand dollars for the arrest of Beverly Tucker.
> Ten thousand dollars for the arrest of William C. Cleary, late clerk of Clement C. Clay.
> The Provost-Marshal-General of the United States is directed to cause a description of said persons, with notice of the above rewards, to be published.[853]

Stanton also had subpoenas issued to more than 340 witnesses, and he authorized the release of witnesses once they had given their testimony. Stanton removed the guards from Surratt's house on June 2. The dragnet pulled in hundreds of people. However, after all the interviews and investigations, Stanton and Holt decided that only eight would be formally charged in the assassination.[854]

\* \* \*

Each prisoner wore ankle bands attached by a chain to an iron weight. They wore these manacles continuously during their imprisonment and trial. The acting assistant adjutant general, a member of General Hartranft's staff, later wrote that "it must be confessed but little care was taken for their comfort. Indeed, it is beyond question that no prison of modern times was ever guarded with such rigid rules and severe discipline."[855] Because of her gender, Mrs. Surratt was never manacled and was treated with leniency.

The trial lasted until the end of June, and with the increasing summer heat, the manacled hooded prisoners suffered greatly. Their cells reached one hundred degrees during the day. Dr. Porter became alarmed; he felt that their treatment was inhuman and feared that they could lose their sanity or even die. He went to Stanton asking him to let the hoods be removed to ensure their health and well-being. Stanton, not wanting to lose the prisoners, agreed. Porter was also successful in gaining permission for the prisoners to have reading material although Stanton stipulated that anything they were given had be printed before 1835. Porter also convinced Stanton that if the men were to remain healthy enough to stand trial, they needed exercise; this they were at last permitted but under heavy guard. The men were allowed an hour of exercise in the morning and in the evening in the prison courtyard with Porter checking their health daily.

The military commission opened proceedings on May 9. When the charges were read against the prisoners, for Mary Surratt, they read that "on or before the 6th day of March, A.D. 1865, and on divers other days and times between that day and the 20th day of April, A.D. 1865, receive, entertain, harbor, and conceal, aid and assist the said John Wilkes Booth, David E. Herold, Lewis Payne [Powell], John H. Surratt, Michael O'Laughlen, George A. Atzerodt, Samuel Arnold, and their confederates, with the knowledge of the murderous and traitorous conspiracy aforesaid, and with intent to aid, abet, and assist them in the execution thereof, and in escaping from justice after the murder of the said Abraham Lincoln."[856] The charges of the other seven defendants read about the same.

A courtroom was prepared on the third floor of the Old Penitentiary (now Fort Leslie J. McNair). The room selected was long and narrow, fifty-five by twenty feet, with four iron-barred windows. Three wooden support beams were spaced evenly down the long axis of the room. The courtroom had limited seating, and the small number of people who attended had to have an authorized pass.

No one knew that Booth's body lay secretly buried just three stories below the courtroom.

General Hartranft maintained a logbook during the trial, and he described the daily routine of the prisoners,

> I took charge of eight prisoners in the cells of this prison about 2 o'clock on the 29th of April. I immediately swept out the cells and removed all nails

from the walls and searched the persons of the prisoners and took the articles mentioned and marked "A" from their persons which I enclose.

At 8 O'clock A. M., breakfast was given to the prisoners in my presence and under my personal supervision, which consisted of coffee, soft bread and salt meat. After they had finished breakfast, the bowl containing the coffee was removed. No other article was taken into the cell. The same system has been observed at each subsequent meal. At this same hour (8:00 A.M.) I also made a personal inspection of all the cells and prisoners, and found them as comfortable as could be expected under the circumstances. At 2:30 P.M., Dr. G. L. Porter reported by authority of the Secretary of War, for his daily inspection of prison and prisoners; he inspected the prisoners in my presence. I also made a personal examination of the cells and prisoners at this time.[857]

It was a forgone conclusion that all the defendants would be found guilty. The only question was what the sentences would be and who would be hanged. Many felt that Powell, Atzerodt, and Herold would be hanged. Who else would be executed was uncertain. The military tribunal had already determined the guilt of the conspirators at the start of the trial and that its main purpose was to "discover the degrees of guilt" and decide who should live and who should be hanged.[858]

The defendants were asked whether they wanted to hire counsel, and all replied that they did.

"To afford the accused opportunity to secure counsel, the Commission adjourned to meet on Wednesday, May 10 at 10 o'clock A. M."[859]

The eight defendants were able to procure attorneys who were not only courageous under the circumstances but qualified and capable. Herold acquired the services of Frederick Stone, an old family friend and prominent attorney in Port Tobacco. Arnold and O'Laughlen were both represented by Walter S. Cox, an established Washington attorney and a graduate of Harvard Law School. Spangler had none other than Thomas Ewing Jr., a Union general and former chief justice of the Kansas Supreme Court; Ewing's father had been a U.S. senator and a member of the cabinets of three presidents. Ewing also helped in the defense of Mudd and Arnold. Atzerodt was represented by William E. Doster, former provost marshal of Washington. Doster agreed to defend Powell until he could get his own attorney; however, when no one else would take the case, Doster continued his defense.

Doster later wrote that "this was a contest in which a few lawyers were on one side, and the whole United States on the other, a case in which, of course, the verdict was known beforeh and . . . . [The defendants] are presumed to be guilty and are called on to prove their innocence."[860]

Mary Surratt's attorney, Reverdy Johnson, was the Democratic senator from Maryland. Recognized as one of the nation's leading constitutional and trial lawyers, he had been attorney general under President Tyler and had served on the Maryland senate. When Reverdy Johnson withdrew as council after a disagreement with one of the judges, two young lawyers from his firm, Frederick Aiken and John W. Clampitt, continued the case. Johnson then acted only as a consultant to his two junior attorneys.

Aiken was an unseasoned attorney in his late twenties, and Mrs. Surratt's trial was his first major case.[861] John Wesley Clampitt was only twenty-six years old when he joined the defense, and it was also his first major case.[862]

The military commission issued a statement that "the prisoners will be allowed counsel, who shall file evidence of having taken the oath prescribed by act of Congress, or shall take said oath before being permitted to appear in the case."[863] On May 12, Brigadier General Thomas M. Harris questioned Reverdy Johnson's qualification to appear before the commission.

Harris objected "on the ground that he did not recognize the moral obligation of an oath designed as a test of loyalty, or to enforce the obligation of loyalty to the Government of the United States." Harris referred to a letter, dated Baltimore, October 7, 1864, in which Johnson questioned the binding effect of the loyalty oath "to be taken by the voters of the State as the condition and qualification of the right to vote upon the New Constitution."[864]

Reverdy Johnson was insulted that the tribunal would question his loyalty to the Union. He indignantly replied that he was a strong Union man and had been influential in keeping Maryland in the Union; that he was a senator in the Congress that created armies, generals, and military tribunals; and that he was accredited to practice law before the Supreme Court. "The objection being then withdrawn, Mr. Johnson accordingly appeared as counsel for Mrs. Mary E. Surratt."[865] But the damage had been done; Johnson thought that his argument with Harris had damaged his relationship with the judges, so he let his associates handle the case; and he only appeared twice during the trial. William Doster felt that "Johnson's absence during the rest of the trial had a bad effect on his client's cause, on account of the conclusion drawn by many, that he had given up her case."[866]

Using all the powers of the federal agencies, the government had a month to prepare the case against the eight conspirators. The defendants, on the other hand, did not "receive their charges until the day the trial opened and then they could only communicate sitting in chains, with a soldier on each side, a great crowd surrounding them, and whisper through the bars of the dock to their counsel." Stanton had ordered that the defendants could only speak to their attorneys within the presence of guards. Doster felt that "had counsel been closeted with the prisoners for weeks, with the charges in their hands and the war power of the Government at their disposal, the odds might have been more even."[867]

At the end of each trial day, the clerks transcribed the day's proceedings, and the previous day's proceeding went out to the Associated Press.

To the general public, Lewis Powell and Mary Surratt were the most interesting of the prisoners. Each day, Powell would sit in his chair, put his head against the wall, and occasionally look out the window. The *New York World*[868] reported that Powell sat "entirely unmoved either by anything said or done in the room, and never speaking to the counsel, not bold and defiant, but composed, indifferent and self-possessed." During the trial, Powell entered the courtroom in his stocking feet because his ankles were swollen from the tight iron bands; and he could not get his shoes on.

On Powell's behavior, Doster wrote, "During the first two weeks of the trial I could get nothing out of Payne either as to his previous history, or as to anything he might have to say in his own defense, or as to whether he wished to be defended at all. During all this time I knew very little more of him than the public generally, and not near as much as the prosecution, and was in great doubt whether to explain his conduct by lunacy, unparalleled stupidity or fear of prejudicing his cause by communications with his counsel."[869]

On May 12, the attorneys decided on a bold tactic – they would challenge the authority of the commission to hear the trial of civilians. The strategy was for the defendants to withdraw their pleas of not guilty and argue that the Constitution stated that civilians could not be tried by the military if civil courts were in session, and civil courts had never ceased to function in Washington.[870]

U.S. Attorney General James Speed replied that if the defendants had "committed the deed as public enemies, as I believe they did, and whether they did or not is a question to be decided by the tribunal before which they are tried, they not only can, but ought to be, tried by a military tribunal. If the persons charged have offended against the laws of war, it would be palpably wrong for the military to hand them over to the civil courts as it would be wrong in a civil court to convict a man of murder who had in time of war, killed another in battle." President Johnson quickly approved Speed's decision.[871]

The civilian attorneys for the defense had problems with the rules of evidence in a military tribunal. Doster wrote, "The court not knowing anything about the rules of evidence, ruled out practically everything the Judge Advocate objected to and admitted everything the counsels opposed . . . . The witnesses were many of them detectives in the government pay."[872]

The trial lasted for seven weeks, and the temperature in the courtroom kept going up as Washington's summer heat increased. Meanwhile, Secretary Stanton's fear that the rebellion would start again turned out to be unfounded. In late May, there was a Grand Review of the Armies filled with pomp and ceremony. Soon after this, the soldiers of the Union Army were mustered out; and the Civil War was over.

# CHAPTER 27

## *Sentenced to Hang*

The trial of the eight people charged with murdering Abraham Lincoln did not deal with any plots to kidnap Lincoln. Instead, Judge Holt chose to prove that the assassination, as carried out by Booth and others, was planned by the Confederacy in Canada and Richmond.[873]

There was much testimony about Confederate covert operations and their connection with the assassination plot. There was testimony about plots to destroy vessels and buildings and to burn steamboats; there was the City Point explosion, the burning of New York City, the attempt to introduce yellow fever to Union troops, the starvation of Union prisoners, and the St. Albans raid.

The theory that the Confederacy was behind the assassination was accepted by the judges during the trial, but some testimony supporting it was later revealed to be perjured. When the perjury became public, many people began to doubt the integrity of the military tribunal.

Four witnesses came forward to link Jefferson Davis and other Confederate leaders to the assassination. Henry Von Steinacker, Richard Montgomery, Sanford Conover, and Dr. James B. Merritt all claimed to have had contact with Confederate agents in Canada.

On May 12, the first day of testimony, Von Steinacker, an engineer officer in the Topographical Department on the staff of General Edward Johnson, was called as a witness for the prosecution. He testified that at a secret meeting, which he did not attend but learned of later from a fellow officer, the assassination of Lincoln was discussed. Von Steinacker's credibility was severely weakened when defense attorneys revealed that he had been a deserter from the Union Army. He had been tried and had been given the death penalty and then had escaped and joined the Confederate army. While in the Confederate army, he had been arrested for theft and for the abuse of Union prisoners but once again had escaped.

Montgomery testified that Jacob Thompson had told him that the South had so many friends in the North that Lincoln could be eliminated at any time. Montgomery alleged that in January, Thompson claimed Southern sympathizers had come to him with a plot to assassinate Lincoln, Stanton, Grant, and Johnson and that Thompson had approved the plan, subject to authorization from Richmond.[874]

James Merritt, a physician practicing in Ayr, Canada West, in April 1865, testified, "I was on confidential terms with the rebels in Canada because I represented myself as a good Southerner."[875] Merritt claimed that in October or November 1864, he met George Young, identified as "formerly of Morgan's Command," who told him that it was decided that "Old Abe should never be inaugurated."[876]

Merritt claimed that on April 5, he met a man named Harper who told him that "they were going to the States, and were going to kick up the damnedest row that had ever been heard of." Later Harper said that "if I did not hear of the death of Old Abe, and of the Vice-President, and of General Dix, in less than ten days, I might put him down as a damned fool . . . . When I found that they had left for Washington, probably for the purpose of assassinating the President, I went to Squire Davidson, a justice of the peace, to give information and have them stopped. He said that the thing was too ridiculously or supremely absurd to take any notice of."

The most incriminating and perjurious witness of the four was Sandford Conover. He was the *New York Tribune's* anonymous correspondent who had fled from his position in the Confederate War Department late in 1863 and whose articles about the inner workings of the Confederate government and of the life in the wartime South had fascinated readers during 1864. He had a flair for self-promotion and was well liked though arrogance. In October 1864, under the name of James Watson Wallace, he traveled to Canada and ingratiated himself with Montreal's Southern sympathizers.[877] Conover claimed to have been on intimate terms with all of the Southern leaders named in the president's May 2 proclamation.

Conover testified that Thompson had revealed a plan to assassinate Lincoln and that other officials had asked Conover to participate in the operation led by Booth. He testified that sometime between April 6 and 9 while he was in Thompson's office, Surratt had arrived from Richmond with letters from Davis and Confederate Secretary of State Benjamin. Thompson had read the letters and then stated, "This makes the thing all right."

Conover further stated that he continued to send stories about this assassination conspiracy, secretly to the *New York Tribune* from Montreal. He claimed that the paper had not published his warning "because they had been accused of publishing sensation stories."[878]

The *New York Tribune*, however, denied receiving these letters.[879] "It is either overwhelmingly conclusive of the complicity of the Confederate leaders in the assassination conspiracy, or it is an unmitigated lie from beginning to end," wrote the *New York Tribune* in response to Conover's accusations.[880]

Although Holt thought that Jefferson Davis and other Southern officials were guilty as charged, he and Stanton recognized that the evidence presented at the trial was only hearsay and was only as believable as the witnesses themselves.

Even while the trial was in progress, a flood of letters and affidavits denouncing Merritt, Montgomery, and Conover as liars and impostors was published in Canadian newspapers and reprinted in the United States. Justice of the Peace Davidson declared that Merritt's story about visiting him to seek an order arresting Harper and his associates was "a miserable fabrication containing not one particle of truth . . . . I know nothing about the man personally but from inquiry I find that his character stands very low in the neighborhood in which he lives."[881]

As for Richard Montgomery, it was later learned that he had a criminal record in New York.

Conover's testimony was at last dismissed as almost entirely perjured. His claim to having been on intimate terms with Thompson was refuted by publication of a letter from Conover, under the alias of James Watson Wallace, to Thompson on March 20, 1865, which began, "Although I have not had the pleasure of your acquaintance . . ."[882] After the trial, proof came to light that Conover had forged Confederate Secretary of War James Seddon's signature to letters written on department stationery and on other printed forms identifying Conover as a secret agent entitled to draw upon the funds entrusted to Thompson.

Despite all of the unfavorable publicity about himself, Conover wrote to Holt on July 26, almost a month after the verdicts were read, that he had continued to investigate the assassination conspiracy in order to implicate Davis, Clay, and others, and that he had located men of "unimpeachable character" who had been paid by the Confederate government to assassinate Lincoln, Johnson, and members of the cabinet. Holt did not reply, so on August 2, Conover wrote again, saying that if Holt wasn't interested he would take his new evidence and go to Mexico.

Holt wanted to believe that Conover was on the verge of finding startling new evidence and new witnesses that would cinch the case against Davis, Clay, and others. Therefore, Holt gave Conover the opportunity to present this new evidence.[883] He sent Conover a check for $150, which he supposed Conover would need "from the number of witnesses you seem to have on hand." Holt instructed Conover to do his work quickly and thoroughly and not to miss any important witnesses. Conover in the spring 1866 duly produced eight witnesses, each providing sworn depositions that the assassination was a Confederate conspiracy. To Holt, the case for the assassination as a Confederate conspiracy appeared stronger than ever.[884]

But in the end, Conover and all of his witnesses were completely discredited. In the fall of 1866, Conover (real name, Charles A. Dunham) was arrested and convicted of perjury and suborning perjury and was sentenced to prison for ten years. Later, Dunham confessed to his perjury saying he wanted to take revenge on Jefferson Davis, who had him imprisoned for six months in 1863.

Holt and the commission had been made to look inept and dishonest because Holt had brought in perjurers. The public came to doubt the integrity of the military tribunal, the evidence, and of Holt himself.

\* \* \*

After the testimony of these four witness, the trial was opened to the public on May 13.

The proceedings were reported in detail in the *Washington Chronicle* and the *Washington National Intelligencer* and summarized by other newspapers in the nation. The testimony showed that Arnold was not in Washington on the night of the assassination but had been far from the city for quite sometime. Charges against O'Laughlen were not strong, and the prosecution could not prove that he "laid in wait with intent to kill" General Grant. The two had been involved in Booth's abduction plot but could not be implicated in the assassination. The defendant Spangler was not given much attention and eventually was given a sentence of six years.

Everyone in the boardinghouse had been arrested. It was not until May 11 that Anna Surratt and Honora Fitzpatrick were released from Old Capitol Prison, although Anna returned daily to visit her mother.

It was not clear what was to happen to Mary Surratt and Dr. Samuel Mudd.

Like Lloyd, Weichmann saw and talked to John Ford while they were in prison. Some of their conversation were about Mary Surratt, with Weichmann giving her high praise saying, "She was an exemplary Christian woman, to him she had fully filled the place of mother, and in every relation of life she was eminently a consistent, pious lady." This was before Stanton and special prosecutor, Burnett, had spoken to Weichmann. Weichmann recounted to John Ford that when he was brought to Stanton's office, Stanton told Weichmann that if he didn't testify as the government wished he would be hanged.[885]

On May 13, Weichmann was called to testify for the prosecution. He spoke of his relationship with John Surratt and the Surratt family while living at the boardinghouse. Weichmann testified that Mrs. Slater and John Surratt smuggled messages and other dispatches back and forth between Richmond and Canada and that Booth frequently visited the boardinghouse and called even when John Surratt wasn't at home. Weichmann related that on April 11, Mary had sent him to find Booth to borrow his carriage so she could go to Surrattsville. Because Booth had sold his carriage, he gave Weichmann ten dollars to rent one.

Weichmann's testimony that Booth had frequently visited and talked to his alleged accomplices at the Surratt boardinghouse laid the basis for the charge that the plot had been hatched there.

Weichmann, although frightened because he had been threatened with prosecution if he did not cooperate, did go so far as to say that Mary was "exemplary and ladylike in every particular; and her conduct, in a religious and moral sense, [was] altogether exemplary."[886]

Reverdy Johnson, in one of his rare courtroom appearances at the trial, cross-examined Weichmann about the events of April 11 when he first took Mary Surratt to Surrattsville to see John Nothey about the money that he owed her. Near a place called Uniontown, just outside of Washington, Mary and Weichmann met John Lloyd and Mrs. Offutt on the road. Weichmann testified that he heard nothing about shooting irons at that meeting. He said that Mrs. Surratt had spoken to Mrs. Offutt about Gus Howell. Mrs. Surratt had said that she was going to see him and ask him to take the oath of allegiance so he could be released.[887]

Weichmann testified about the events on April 14. While he and Mrs. Surratt were in Surrattsville, he had written a note to John Nothey for Mrs. Surratt because she couldn't see well enough to write. In the note, she asked Nothey to pay her the money he owed her, or she would bring suit against him. The money was to be used to satisfy her indebtedness to George Calvert.[888]

On May 18, Weichmann was recalled by the prosecution. He testified to the events in the boardinghouse on March 17 and how Booth and the others acted after the attempted kidnapping of Lincoln.[889]

On Sunday, April 30, Stanton had him brought back to Old Capitol Prison. In a report on him, Colonel Wood wrote that Weichmann was an employee of the government in the Office of the Commissary General of Prisoners and that he was satisfied that Weichmann had "frequently purloined important papers which have been forwarded to Richmond by or through John Surratt."[890]

Ford became convinced from his conversations with Lloyd and Weichmann that Mrs. Surratt was innocent and that the two witnesses had been coerced. "Many yet living recall their fright," Ford later wrote, asserting that Weichmann had told him that "Secretary Stanton had, in a threatening manner, expressed the opinion that [Weichmann's] hands has had as much of the president's blood on them as Booth's."

Weichmann, testifying at the John Surratt inquiry in 1867, said he had been nervous at the previous trial. He contradicted some of his previous statements, thereby putting Mrs. Surratt in a more favorable light. At this second trial, Louis Carland, a former customer at Ford's Theatre, testified that Weichmann had told him in 1865 that if he had been "let alone and had been allowed to give his statement as he had wanted to, it would have been quite a different affair with Mrs. Surratt than it was," that his statements had been "written out for him," and that he had been "threatened with being charged as one of the conspirators" if he refused to swear to them. Weichmann, under examination, denied that he had made this confession but admitted that he had talked to Carland.[891]

John Clampitt, one of Mrs. Surratt's lawyers, felt that Weichmann, after testifying, had been stung with remorse because he had committed perjury in implicating Mrs. Surratt in Lincoln's murder. Certain "authorities of the War Department" had threatened to prosecute him as an accomplice in the conspiracy against Lincoln if he refused to offer testimony. Holt had rejected the first statement Weichmann had prepared with the remark that "it was not strong enough," whereupon, still under threat of prosecution, Weichmann had written a second and stronger statement, the substance of which he subsequently swore to on the witness stand.[892]

*   *   *

On May 13, John Lloyd testified against his former landlady. Lloyd told that at the behest of John Surratt, accompanied by George Atzerodt and David Herold, he had hidden two carbines with ammunition, a rope, and a monkey wrench in the Surratt Tavern. John Surratt had suggested that Lloyd dangled the carbines on a rope between the inner and outer walls of the dining room. John Surratt showed Lloyd how to hide them since he had lived in that tavern for many years.

Lloyd confirmed Weichmann's testimony about a meeting on the road with Mrs. Surratt in Uniontown on April 11. Lloyd claimed that Mary said to have the shooting irons ready and that someone would be calling for them in a few days. However, during cross-examination, Lloyd was "not altogether positive" whether she had mentioned the shooting irons.[893]

Lloyd said that when Mary visited Surrattsville on Friday, April 14, she again had told him to have "those shooting irons ready that night – there would be some parties call for them." Then Lloyd testified that she had handed him "something wrapped in a piece of paper" and that he only later found out that the package contained field glasses. (That was the package that Booth, back in Washington, had asked Mary Surratt to deliver to John Lloyd.) Lloyd claimed that Mrs. Surratt told him to have "two bottles of whiskey ready, and that these things were to be called for that night." Lloyd said that the items Mrs. Surratt referred to were picked up that night by Booth and Herold.[894]

Lloyd had gotten himself into a precarious position by lying to investigating officers on the evening of the assassination. He had maintained that Booth and Herald had not been at his tavern that evening, and he had misdirected John Clarvoe telling him that the best escape route was the Piscataway Road, when in fact, Lloyd knew that Booth and Herold had taken a road leading to the town known locally as T. B. Lloyd knew that if he did not testify the way the government wanted him to, he too could be charged as a conspirator; so he was motivated to implicate others while emphasizing his uninvolvement.

It is most probable that Lloyd did not even clearly remember what had happened the night of the assassination. Three witnesses had seen him on that afternoon and evening and confirmed that he was "very much in liquor."

On May 25, the day the defense began, Honora Fitzpatrick testified that she "bought a photograph of J. Wilkes Booth, and took it to Mrs. Surratt's house" and that "Miss Anna Surratt also bought one." Honora said that she didn't know that a photograph had been hidden behind a framed picture of Anna's.

Sometime between mid-March, Monday, April 3, 1865, Weichmann had given Anna Surratt the framed picture called *Morning, Noon and Night*. Anna Surratt testified, "I put a photograph of John Wilkes Booth behind it."[895] Anna was not fond of Weichmann, whom she called "that man Weichmann," because of his testimony against her mother.

Much of Mary Surratt's defense rested on the premise that she had not lied when she said she did not know Powell the night he was arrested at her home. She had not recognized him because she could not see him. Again and again, witnesses testified about Mary Surratt's poor vision. Honora testified, "Mrs. Surratt has complained that she could not read or sew at night on account of her sight. I have known of her passing her friend, Mrs. Kirby, on the same side of the street, and not see her at all . . . . Mrs. Surratt's eyesight is defective; I have often threaded a needle for her when she has been sewing during the day, because she could not see to do it herself and I have never known her to sew or read by gaslight." On redirect, Honora said of Powell that she "did not recognize him at the house, but I did at General Augur's office, when the skullcap was taken off his head."[896]

Eliza Holohan, another boarder, testified for Mary Surratt. She confirmed that Mrs. Surratt's eyesight was "defective." She told how she went to church during Lent and that "she was very constant in her religious duties."

About Powell, she related that Powell had been to the boardinghouse twice, once in February for a night and then for two or three days in mid-March.

Concerning George Atzerodt, Mrs. Holohan said that he was known in the boardinghouse as Port Tobacco, that she had seen the man at various times, and that he had dined once or twice at the boardinghouse. She said that Mrs. Surratt had objected to his boarding there because she found a bottle of liquor in his room.[897]

On May 27, Gus Howell, the Confederate courier, testified that Mary Surratt had poor eyesight. Howell recounted one incident about February 20 when "although the gas was lit in the hall, she failed at first to recognize me." He had stayed at the Surratt boardinghouse while he waited for Sarah Slater to return from Canada. Howell, trying to implicate Weichmann while protecting himself, said that he met Weichmann during his visits to the boardinghouse, and on one occasion, he had shown Weichmann "a cipher, and how to use it. Weichmann then made one himself." Howell testified that "the cipher I showed to Weichmann I learned out of a magician's book. I have been acquainted with it for six or seven years."[898]

Others involved in the drama testified to particular facts or events. George Calvert verified that he had sent Mary a letter on April 12 about the money she owed him. And Captain Bennett Gwynn testified that when he had stopped at Lloyd's tavern on his return trip from Marlboro on April 14, Mary had asked him to deliver a note to John Nothey that Weichmann had written for her. Gwynn testified that on April 14, he saw John Lloyd on the road coming from Marlboro, and Gwynn had noticed that he "had been drinking right smartly."[899]

The defense was hoping to show that Lloyd was so drunk that afternoon that Mary waited for him at the tavern, that he certainly could not remember what *anyone* had said, and certainly not that Mary had told him to get guns ready for pickup.

On June 13, Emma Offutt returned to the witness stand, this time for the defense. Mrs. Offutt began her testimony by saying that "on the evening of the 14th of April, Mr. Lloyd was very much in liquor, more so than I have ever seen him in my life."[900]

Then Frederick Aiken told the military commission "that at the time Mrs. Offutt gave her testimony before, she came here very unwell . . . . She had been suffering severely from sickness, and had taken considerable laudanum [a narcotic]. Her mind was considerably confused at the time, and she now wishes to correct her testimony in an important particular."[901]

Then Mrs. Offutt made a surprise announcement. She corrected her previous testimony, saying that she had been mistaken when she had earlier testified that Mrs. Surratt had not handed her the package. Now Mrs. Offutt testified that Mary had indeed given her the package and asked her to keep it at the tavern. Offutt was referring to the package that Booth had asked Mrs. Surratt to deliver. The implication was that Mary Surratt did not know the importance of the package and was willing to hand it over to anyone at the tavern. Mrs. Offutt put the package in the parlor.

When John Lloyd returned from his trip to Marlboro, she testified that Lloyd and Mrs. Surratt were "talking together at the buggy in the yard, I was in and out all the time. I did not see Lloyd go into the parlor, but I saw him on the piazza [porch], and I think from that that he must have gone into the parlor. He had a package in his hand, but I did not see Mrs. Surratt give it to him."

Mrs. Offutt told the court that Mrs. Surratt had said "that she would not have come down to Surrattsville that day, had it not been for the letter she received; and I saw business transacted while she was there." The defense was showing that Mrs. Surratt had only gone to the tavern on the fourteenth to conduct business, not to deliver Booth's message.

Mrs. Offutt also repeated what others had said – that Mrs. Surratt's eyesight was defective.[902]

On May 26, John Nothey on the witness stand confirmed that he met Mrs. Surratt on Tuesday, April 11, in Surrattsville, and that on April 14, Captain Gwynn had delivered a letter to him from Mary concerning the debt. Nothey said he "did not see her that day."[903]

Joseph T. Knott confirmed Lloyd's drunken condition when Lloyd returned to the tavern from Marlboro on April 14 testifying that "he was pretty tight that evening." Knott stated, "For some weeks past Mr. Lloyd had been drinking a good deal; nearly every day, and night, too, he was pretty tight. At times, he had the appearance of an insane man from drink."[904]

On May 30, Anna Surratt took the stand. After a few emotional moments at seeing her mother, she composed herself and began her testimony. Anna answered questions about George Atzerodt. She said that he called often at the boardinghouse, asking "for that man Weichmann."[905]

Anna reported that the last time Atzerodt had been at the boardinghouse, it had been Weichmann who had asked Mary to allow Atzerodt to stay the night. Anna reported that her mother had said, "Well Mr. Weichmann, I have no objection." Anna told about how later Atzerodt "was given to understand that he was not wanted at the house" because an empty liquor bottle had been found in his room.[906]

When questioned about Lewis Powell, Anna acknowledged that the first time he had come to the boardinghouse was at night and that he had left early the following morning. He came again some weeks later. At that time, everyone, except her mother, was in the parlor and had seen Powell when he arrived. Anna said that she recognized him as the man who had been there once before calling himself Wood. Anna had gone down to the dining room and told her mother that Powell was in the parlor; her mother commented that she supposed that he had come to see John.

Anna, in answering questions about Booth's visits to the house, said that she thought the last time that Booth was at the house was on Friday, April 14. She said that she had not seen him but that she "heard that he had been there." Anna further testified that her mother "went to Surrattsville on the Friday of the assassination" and her mother's "carriage was at the door [ready to depart] at the time Mr. Booth called."[907] Anna heard someone come up the steps when the carriage was at the door, and her mother was ready to leave. She said that her mother had spoken about going to Surrattsville the day before Booth came. When Booth arrived, he stayed only "a very few minutes," implying that Booth's visit had been coincidental.

Anna also testified about her mother's poor eyesight. She said that her mother had "often failed to recognize her friends" [because she couldn't see them] and that "she has not been able to read or sew by gaslight for some time past."[908]

On June 13, Rachel Semus testified as to Mary Surratt's character from the point of view of a slave,

> I have lived at Mrs. Surratt's house for six years; was hired to her by Mr. Wildman. She treated her servants very well all the time I was with her; I never had reason to complain. I remember Mrs. Surratt had Union soldiers at her house, sometimes a good many of them; and I know that she always tried to do the best for them that she could, because I always cooked for them. She always gave them the best she had, and very often she would give them all she had in the house, because so many of them came. I recollect her cutting up the last ham she had in the house, and she had not any more until she sent to the city. I never knew her taking any pay for it. I never heard her express herself in favor of the South; if she used such expressions, I did not hear them.

> Her eyesight has been failing for a long time, very often I have had to go upstairs and thread her needle for her because she could not see to do it; I have had to stop washing to go up and thread it for her in the daytime. I remember one day telling her that Father Lanihan was at the front gate, coming to the house, and she said, "No, it was not him, it was little Johnny [Surratt]."[909]

\*    \*    \*

On behalf of Mrs. Surratt, Reverdy Johnson said that she is "a woman well educated and, as far as we can judge, from all her past life, as we have it in evidence, devout Christian, even kind, affectionate and charitable, with no motive disclosed to us that could have caused a total change in her very nature, could have participated in the crimes in question, it is almost impossible to believe. Such a belief can only be forced upon a reasonable, unprejudiced mind, by direct and uncontradicted evidence, coming from pure and perfectly unsuspected sources. Have we these? Is the evidence uncontradicted? Are the two witnesses, Weichmann and Lloyd, pure and unsuspected? . . . If the facts which they themselves state as to their connection and intimacy with Booth and Payne are true, their knowledge of the purpose to commit the crimes, and their participation in them, is much more satisfactorily established than [that] of Mrs. Surratt."[910]

Aiken, in his final arguments for Mary Surratt, said that both Louis Weichmann and John Lloyd had had more intimate knowledge of a conspiracy than his client had. Moreover, Lloyd, in his drunken state on April 14, could hardly be considered a credible witness as to what anyone was doing or saying on that day. In fact, Lloyd testified that he was "quite positive she asked me about the shooting irons. I am quite positive about that, but not altogether positive."[911] Then Aiken reminded the court that the primary purpose of Mrs. Surratt's going to Surrattsville on the day of the assassination was to transact private business. Had she left the boardinghouse a little earlier, she would have missed Booth altogether and would never have delivered the package to Lloyd.

In regard to Mrs. Surratt's not recognizing Lewis Powell, Aiken reminded the court of her defective eyesight. The last time she had seen Powell, he had been impeccably dressed as a Baptist minister. When he appeared at the boardinghouse on the night of her arrest, he had been in the guise of a dirty, uncouthly dressed ditchdigger. Aiken spoke of Mrs. Surratt's fine reputation. He noted that the prosecution could not find one person to testify to the contrary. It was inconceivable that such a woman could conspire in the murder of President Lincoln.[912]

\*     \*     \*

The evidence against Mary Surratt was threefold. The first is the testimony of Louis Weichmann, who testified that on Tuesday, April 11, Mary Surratt wanted to borrow a carriage from Booth to go to Surrattsville and sent Weichmann to ask Booth for the carriage. Booth had, however, sold the carriage and instead gave Weichmann ten dollars to hire one. Weichmann testified that on April 14, Mary Surratt had a conversation with Booth in midafternoon just before she left for her second trip that week to Surrattsville. She had taken with her Booth's package containing the field glasses. Additionally, Confederate couriers Sarah Slater and Spencer "Gus" Howell had visited the Surratt boardinghouse as had Powell, Atzerodt, and Herold.

The second part is the testimony of John Lloyd. He testified that on March 18, John Surratt had Lloyd hide two carbines at the tavern. On Tuesday, April 11, Mrs. Surratt had met Lloyd by chance on the road and told him to get the "shooting irons" ready. And on April 14, she again met Lloyd this time at his tavern, and she had again told him to have the "shooting irons" ready, that the weapons would be called for that night. Mary Surratt had delivered a package to him to be given to those who called for them. That night, Booth and Herold had arrived at the tavern, and Herold said, "Lloyd, for God's sake, make haste and get those things," meaning the two carbines, ammunition, and the field glasses. The two fugitives left with one carbine and the damning field glasses.

The third body of evidence against Mary Surratt was the untimely arrival of Powell at her boardinghouse on the evening of the seventeenth, implying that Powell felt safe in looking to Mrs. Surratt for shelter.

*   *   *

In the case of Lewis Powell, Doster believed that the only hope for saving Powell's life was to have him declared legally insane. Doster called in the superintendent of the Government Hospital for the Insane, Dr. Charles H. Nichols, as well as Dr. James C. Hall to examine his client. Doster believed that Powell's actions were not normal and that Powell was not sane at the time he attacked Secretary of State Seward.

Both Dr. Hall and Nichols examined Powell, and they concluded that the war had affected his mind and that Powell was insane. Holt, however, called on several other doctors, including Surgeon General Joseph K. Barnes. Not surprisingly, Barnes and the other doctors found "no evidence of insanity in Paine."[913]

When the death warrant was read to Powell on July 6, 1865, he took the news in his usual emotionless manner. Powell was the only one of the condemned to eat a breakfast on the morning of the execution.

Major Thomas Eckert visited Powell frequently during imprisonment and up to the day before the execution. In 1867, Eckert was questioned about his May 2 visit by the Impeachment Committee of the Judiciary House Committee. When asked whether Powell had implicated others in the assassination, Eckert replied that Powell's answer "to that question . . . besides implicating John Surratt was, 'All I can say about that is that you have not got the one-half of them' . . . . I asked him if he left Gettysburg with a view to go to Baltimore to meet Booth. He said he did not. I questioned him very strongly on that and he laughingly replied that I must believe him; that his meeting with Booth in Baltimore was accidental."[914]

*   *   *

In the prosecution's closing argument, Bingham denied that there ever had been plans for a kidnapping because he could not believe that anyone would undertake a scheme that on its face was so obviously unworkable. Bingham told the tribunal that Booth had always intended to assassinate Lincoln. At the time of the arrests, only Arnold had mentioned a kidnapping plot, and only later did Atzerodt amended his confession to include participation in the kidnapping plot.

Doster and Cox had made references to kidnapping in their defense of Powell and O'Laughlen; but the lawyers for Herold, Mudd, Spangler, and Mrs. Surratt made no reference to a kidnapping. Bingham said that the alleged scheme to kidnap Lincoln from the theater and hold him for ransom "was but another silly device . . . to hide from the knowledge of his captor the fact that the purpose was to murder the President."[915]

Samuel Chester defended himself by saying he had only been approached to help kidnap Lincoln but had declined. Bingham dismissed these claims saying, "Failing to secure the services of Chester, because his soul recoiled with abhorrence from the foul work of assassination and murder, he found more willing instruments in others whom he gathered about him."[916] Chester was not prosecuted for failing to report the plot to authorities.

Bingham invoked the law on conspiracy: "The rule of law is, that the act or declaration of one conspirator, done in pursuance or furtherance of the common design, is the act or declaration of all the conspirators."[917] Even those defendants who had not directly participated were just as guilty; Bingham said, "Mary E. Surratt is as guilty as her son of having thus conspired, combined and confederated to do this murder, in aid of this rebellion, is clear. First her house was the headquarters of Booth, John H. Surratt, Atzerodt, Payne, and Herold. She is inquired for by Atzerodt, she is inquired for by Payne, and she is visited by Booth and holds private conversations with him. His picture, together with the chief conspirator, Jefferson Davis, is found in her house. She sends to Booth for a carriage to take her on April 11, to Surrattsville, for the purpose of perfecting the arrangement deemed necessary to the successful execution of the conspiracy, and especially to facilitate and protect the conspirators in their escape from justice."[918]

On June 7, John Holohan, testifying for the prosecution, said that the last time he had seen John Surratt was on the night of April 3. That night, John Surratt came to Holohan's room and asked him to "exchange some gold for greenbacks." Holohan had exchanged "$60 in paper for $40 in gold."[919] This was the gold that John had been given in Richmond to pay for his and Sarah Slater's trip to Canada. Holohan testified that George Atzerodt had gone to the Surratt boardinghouse several times to see John Surratt.[920]

After seven weeks, the trial ended on June 28.

\*    \*    \*

Deliberations were held in secret with Holt and Bingham sitting in and offering advice. The verdict and sentences of the military commission only required a two-third majority. The military officers on the commission generally agreed on the sentences of the defendants except for that of Mary Surratt.

When the commission was considering the fate of Mrs. Surratt, they at first proposed "to spare her life." The first ballot by the commission was not for hanging. However, Holt and Bingham suggested that, in the absence of the attorneys for the defendants, the testimony "be read over again and such interpretation placed upon it as they thought best." Holt then moved that Mary get the same judgment as others but that a recommendation for mercy signed by each member of the Commission to the President of the United States should be attached to the findings of the court martial. This was done.[921]

The verdicts for the defendants were decided on June 30. Mudd, Arnold, and O'Laughlen were given life imprisonment; Dr. Mudd had missed the death penalty by one vote. Spangler, whom the court believed took the place of Samuel Chester, was sentenced to six years of imprisonment. Powell, Herold, Atzerodt, and Mrs. Surratt received the death penalty.

John W. Clampitt told the *Chicago Times Herald,* "The question may be asked, why could not facts confirming the innocence of Mrs. Surratt be established before the military commission which tried her? It is my belief that the commission was *organized to convict* (italics his). It threw out wholesale the evidence for the defense and admitted that for the prosecution, which we could have shown beyond the peradventure of a doubt was perjury."[922]

# CHAPTER 28

## *The President Is Immovable*

When the commission reached its decision, Johnson and Stanton were severely ill.[923] Holt was able to see the ailing president on the afternoon of July 5 and brought him "a formal brief review of the case." No one else was present when Holt briefed Johnson on the tribunal's sentences. Johnson considered and approved the death sentences for Herold, Atzerodt, and Payne. What happened next, however, in the case of Mrs. Surratt is not clear. Years after the fact, Johnson and Holt disputed what occurred. According to Holt, President Johnson saw the recommendation for mercy, a contention Johnson later vehemently denied. Whether Johnson saw the clemency plea or not, he did approve the verdict for Surratt's execution.[924]

Judge Bingham later wrote,

> Before the President had acted on the case, I deemed it my duty to call the attention of Secretary Stanton to the petition for the commutation of the sentence of Mrs. Surratt, I did call his attention to it before the final action of the President . . . . After the execution I called upon Secretaries Stanton and Seward and asked if this petition had been presented to the President before the death sentence was approved by him, and was answered by each of those gentlemen that the petition was presented to the President and was duly considered by him and his advisers before the death sentence upon Mrs. Surratt was approved, and that the president and the Cabinet, upon such consideration were a unit in denying the prayer of the petition; Mr. Seward and Mr. Stanton saying that they were present.[925]

Attorney General James Speed said that he saw the record of the case in the president's office. Attached to it was the plea signed by "some members of the commission recommending that the sentence against Mrs. Surratt be commuted to imprisonment for life."

James Harlan, secretary of the interior, did not agree with Judge Bingham's assessment. Harlan did not remember hearing "in Cabinet meeting any part of the record of the trial or the recommendation of clemency." Harlan understood that the case had been examined by Speed and Stanton, the two cabinet members who were more concerned with the case.[926]

General R. D. Mussey, President Johnson's military secretary, said that the president had told him that the court had "recommended Mrs. Surratt to mercy on the grounds of her sex (and age, I believe). But that he said the grounds urged were insufficient, and that he had refused to interfere; that if she were guilty at all, her sex did not make her any the less guilty, . . . he told me that there had not been 'women enough hanged in this war'"[927]

*　　*　　*

There were no appeals made for Powell, Herold, and Atzerodt; however, there were many efforts to save Mary Surratt.

On the afternoon of July 5, Major Eckert, aide to Secretary of War Stanton, received orders to have a gallows built. The next morning, under the command of General John F. Hartranft, who had been a sheriff in Norristown, Pennsylvania, before the war, a scaffold was erected that would accommodate four people. General Hartranft gave the assignment of actually building the scaffold to Captain Christian Rath.[928]

*　　*　　*

The prisoners were told their fates on July 6, the day after President Johnson had signed the execution orders. Between 11:00 a.m. and noon, Major General Hancock told each prisoner individually of his sentence and that the sentences would be carried out the next day. Powell, the first to be told, took the news in his usual emotionless manner. He showed no surprise and took the announcement as if he fully expected it. Powell was the only one of the condemned to eat a breakfast on the morning of the execution.

Atzerodt was next. After being told of the sentence, he "showed great nervousness" and asked to see a minister. Herold, when informed of the death sentence, "trembled like a leaf." And finally, Mrs. Surratt was told. She "burst in a violent paroxysm of grief" and said, "I had no hand in the murder of the President!" Then she asked for Father Walter of St. Patrick's Catholic Church; Father Wiget, president of Gonzaga College; and John Brophy of the St. Aloysius School.[929] Fathers Walter and Wiget were with Surratt to her final moments.[930]

During the night of the sixth, Atzerodt, Powell, and Mary Surratt, all had relatives stay with them in their cells. Powell was asked if there were any relatives or friends he wanted to see; he replied no, that his family was too far away.

Powell's attorney William Doster had written a letter to Powell's father in Live Oak Station, Florida, on June 23,

The duty I have to perform is so repugnant to my feelings that only absolute necessity and the request of your son has driven me to it. The person who is now on trial here for assault upon Secretary Seward on the evening of the 14th of April says his name is Lewis Thornton Powell, and that the name of his father is George C. Powell of Live Oak Station, Florida; that he enlisted in the 2nd Florida Infantry and deserted from the Southern Army. He begs you to come on at once. Your safety is guaranteed.[931]

Powell did ask to see the Reverend Augustus P. Stryker, rector of St. Barnabas Church, an Episcopal church in Baltimore. Powell knew Rev. Stryker when he was in Baltimore. Rev. Stryker arrived about noon the day of the execution and so only saw Powell for about two hours.

\* \* \*

Father Walter heard Mary Surratt's last confession on July 6. Then he and Anna rushed to the White House to see President Johnson to plea for Mary's life. They met former Pennsylvania congressman Thomas Florence at the White House gate. Father Walter told Florence of his mission, and Florence remarked, "Father Walter, you and I are on the same errand of mercy. The President must not allow this woman to be hanged!" As the three entered the White House, they met General Mussey and former New York senator Preston King.

But President Johnson refused to see Anna Surratt or anyone else that day about clemency for Mrs. Surratt. When all Anna's efforts to see the president failed, Father Walter brought the tearful young woman back to the prison, arriving there about four-forty in the afternoon.[932]

John Brophy, who at the time was a professor of English at Gonzaga College and a onetime friend of John Surratt and Louis J. Weichmann, swore in an affidavit that after the trial and before Mrs. Surratt was executed, Weichmann told him that he was arrested as a conspirator and threatened with death by Stanton and Burnett unless he made statements revealing all he knew about the assassination and the Surratt household.[933] He was vulnerable, he told Brophy, because he (Weichmann) could be connected with the conspirators; he had become friends with Atzerodt, and the two of them had even been riding Booth's horses.

In an effort to save Mrs. Surratt, Brophy sent his original affidavit to President Johnson. The president did not respond to the affidavit. After she was executed, Brophy gave a copy of the affidavit, for publication, to the *Washington Constitutional Union*.[934]

Two of David Herold's sisters also were at the White House that afternoon to plea for their brother's life. They too were not allowed to see the president. The sisters did write a note to Mrs. Johnson asking "that she would not turn a deaf ear to their pleadings." But the note was not delivered with the reason given that Mrs. Johnson was "quite sick." The two sisters then asked if the note could be delivered to Mrs.

Patterson, the president's daughter. Again staff denied the request saying that Mrs. Patterson was "also quite indisposed."[935]

*     *     *

At about five o'clock on the afternoon of July 6, Clampitt and Aiken were sitting in their office, awaiting the findings of the commission, when they heard a paper boy on the street heralding the news of Mrs. Surratt's execution scheduled for the following day! "So sudden was the shock, so unexpected the result, amazed beyond expression at the celerity of the order of execution, we hardly knew how to proceed," wrote Clampitt.[936]

The two attorneys immediately went to the White House but were turned away by soldiers with fixed bayonets. The attorneys next went with Anna Surratt to see Holt to plea for a three-day stay of execution. But Holt told them, "I can do nothing. The President is immovable."[937]

It was nearly midnight when Clampitt and Aiken telegrammed Reverdy Johnson in Baltimore about the next day's execution. Johnson suggested that the two attorneys "apply for a writ of habeas corpus and take her body from the custody of the military authorities. We are now in a state of peace – not war."[938] The basis of the writ would be the one the attorneys had been using throughout the trial that the defendants should not be tried by a military court but by a civil court since there was a functioning civil court in the city of Washington.[939]

The two attorneys quickly wrote a writ of habeas corpus to stay Mary Surratt's execution. They requested that Mrs. Surratt be turned over to the city's Criminal Court at ten o'clock the following morning, July 7.

After reading and deliberating on it, Judge Wylie of the Supreme Court of the District of Columbia announced his decision, "I am about to perform an act which, before tomorrow's sun goes down, may consign me to the Old Capitol Prison."[940] With that, Judge Wylie signed the writ. The writ was given to a U.S. Marshal at four o'clock in the morning. At eight thirty that morning, the marshal served it to General Hancock. The writ directed General Hancock to produce Mary Surratt in court at ten o'clock that morning.

General Hancock sent word to President Johnson, who at ten o'clock suspended the writ. At about eleven thirty, General Hancock with Attorney General Speed appeared in court to report that President Johnson "had suspended the power of the writ in this case."

Attorney General Speed addressed the court briefly to explain the action of the federal government. Speed stated "that the suspension of the writ of habeas corpus was absolutely necessary in time of war for the preservation of the public liberties and the life of the Government in time of peace, and enforced with power and effect the right of the military authority to protect the life of the commander-in-chief of the army and navy by and through its own courts in such times."[941]

Judge Wylie felt that since the military had taken the case out of his hands, he "had no power to proceed further in it."[942]

It was in despair that Aiken and Clampitt returned to the prison to tell Mary Surratt.

\* \* \*

Father Walter, Mary Surratt's confessor, visited Powell the night before the execution. During the visit, Father Walter asked him, "Tell me, my friend, is Mrs. Surratt guilty?" Powell answered, "No, she is not. She might have known that something was going on, but she did not know what."[943]

Powell had summarized correctly. Mary Surratt knew that anti-Union activities were being planned in her house and had chosen not to know just what was going on in her own home. It was not that she was weak willed, she had doggedly ensured the education of her children, stood up to her drunkard husband, engaged in aggressive and successful church fund-raising, thrown out Atzerodt because he had brought liquor into the boardinghouse, and embraced Catholicism and then converted all her relatives.

Immediately, Father Walter wrote a letter to President Johnson recounting his visit with Powell and added that he believed Powell and was convinced that Mary was innocent. Father Walter was convinced that Powell was being truthful "as he was now beyond hope [and] that he would say what he knew about Mrs. Surratt."[944]

Powell felt responsible for Surratt's arrest and conviction. He naively spoke to Colonel Christian Rath, the executioner, and told him that "he wanted to know if he could not suffer punishment for her." Rath thought that he "really seemed to feel badly," that Powell felt he was largely to blame for her incarceration. The fact that he was captured in the cellar of her house led to her arrest. He said he would willingly suffer two deaths if they would save Mrs. Surratt from the noose. He denied that she was implicated in the plot to murder. His presence in her home and his "long acquaintance with her had made the trouble for her."

Later that night, Colonel Rath told Major Eckert of his conversation with Powell. Rath recounted that "early the next morning I was summoned before Secretary Seward. I repeated the story. The officials were considering the advisability of withdrawing the sentence of death pronounced upon her. Why it was not done I do not know."[945]

Powell continued to plea for clemency for Mrs. Surratt. He repeated to General Hartranft what he had told Father Walter the night before. From this conversation, Hartranft wrote a letter to President Johnson detailing that conversation. He wrote,

> The prisoner Payne has just told me that Mrs. Surratt is entirely innocent of the assassination of President Lincoln, and of any knowledge thereof. He also states that she had no knowledge whatever of the abduction plot, that nothing was ever said to her about it, and that her name was never

mentioned by the parties connected therewith. I believe that Payne has told the truth in this matter.[946]

Hartranft handed his and Father Walter's letter to John Brophy, saying, "I will furnish an Army conveyance and swift horses. Take it and drive like mad to the White House and give the President this note. I will delay the execution until the last moment or until I hear from you definitely and positively what the President's answer is."[947]

Powell's efforts to save Mary Surratt were well-known by all, and the press ran stories of it on the day of the execution.[948]

Powell also spoke to his counsel, William Doster, of Atzerodt's part in the conspiracy. He said, just hours before the execution, that Atzerodt "was innocent of any attempt to murder, and at the Herndon House, where Booth, Atzerodt, Herold and himself met on the evening of the 14th, he heard Atzerodt declare, when ordered by Booth to kill the Vice President, that he would not do it."[949] In all the statements given by the conspirators, there is a common agreement that none, except Booth, knew of the scheme to assassinate Lincoln until that fateful meeting on the evening of April 14 at the Herndon House.

\*       \*       \*

At home on the night of July 6, John Ford heard of the execution scheduled for the next day. He quickly wrote a letter to President Johnson and then took a train out of Baltimore at three o'clock in the morning to personally deliver the note to the president. In his letter, he implored President Johnson to delay the execution for a few days in order "to establish the truth, with a free hearing." Ford was making reference here to what he learned as a prisoner in Carroll Prison. He had heard of the threatening or outright torture of witnesses such as Lloyd, Weichmann, and Howell. "My memories of my contact with these witnesses, without whose testimony there was no shadow of a case against Mrs. Surratt, made the announcement of her conviction, and the intended swift and terrible execution of her sentence on the following day, a fearful horror." Ford told President Johnson in his letter that "justice could not be balked in any way by a brief delay."[950]

Ford arrived in Washington at six o'clock in the morning and stopped at the home of former postmaster general Montgomery Blair, who was still in bed. Ford left a message with a servant, requesting that Blair immediately take the letter to the president. Blair later told Ford that the letter did reach President Johnson, but to no avail; Johnson ignored his pleas.[951]

\*       \*       \*

On the evening of July 6, Assistant Secretary of War Thomas Eckert arrived at the home of Rev. Dr. A. D. Gillette (a clergyman from the First Baptist Church in

Washington) and told him that Powell had asked for him. Powell knew Dr. Gillette when he was in Baltimore earlier that year.

Gillette went to the prison and stayed with Powell during the night of July 6. They spoke about religious beliefs, and Powell told him that he was the son of a Baptist minister in Florida. Powell told Dr. Gillette that the "time for lies has passed" and that almost immediately after attacking the Seward household he had regretted his act.[952]

George Atzerodt's spiritual advisor, Rev. Dr. Butler, a Lutheran minister, had prayed with Atzerodt throughout the night.[953] Atzerodt was very emotional during his last night and into the day of execution. He shook and cried, saying he was afraid to die and that he was not prepared.[954] His mother arrived in Washington and visited him before he was executed.

Reverend Olds of Christ Episcopal Church administered the sacraments of the Episcopal church to Herold. Herold's sisters came to visit him that morning, and he bravely told them that he was ready to die. His sisters told him that his mother had not come because she was too ill.

*    *    *

At eight thirty in the morning of July 7, Anna Surratt and her friend, Mary Queen, went back to the White House to ask for a presidential pardon. Anna again met with General Mussey and "with tearful eyes and mournful sobs, entreated him to use his influence to enable her to see the President." Mussey then told Anna that "he had received peremptory orders not to allow any visitors to see the President." Anna was weeping bitterly. Senators King and Lane, in addition to the armed soldiers with fixed bayonets, had barred Anna's way to the president's office.[955]

As Anna stood there, not knowing what to do next, Mrs. Stephen A. Douglas arrived to plea for clemency for Mary Surratt. Despite Mussey's orders, Mrs. Douglas did get to see Johnson; however, she also failed to get clemency or a delay of the execution.

When Anna left the White House, she immediately became enmeshed in the gridlock of traffic heading for the scheduled execution. General Hancock, on his way to oversee the execution, saw Anna Surratt and got her through the traffic to the prison to visit her mother.

During this last visit, Anna, wanting to give her mother one last symbol of her feelings, placed a jewelry pin through the silk bow of her mother's black dress.[956]

From the *Washington Evening Star* of July 7, the headlines read,

EXTRA
THE EXECUTION
FOUR OF THE CONSPIRATORS HUNG!
PETITIONS FOR EXECUTIVE CLEMENCY

ATTEMPT TO STAY THE EXECUTION
INCIDENTS AT THE WHITE HOUSE
SCENES AT THE SURRATT HOUSE
SKETCHES OF THE CONDEMNED
THEIR PREPARATION FOR DEATH
PROSTRATION OF MRS. SURRATT
THE AGONY OF THE DAUGHTER
SCENES AT THE GALLOWS
INCIDENTS

At the time, the public supported the execution and its swiftness. The *Washington Chronicle* wrote,

> President may be assured that every loyal man in the country, of whatever party, will warmly and unflinchingly endorse his decision was wise, just, and befitting the head of a great people, desirous of establishing an impressive and salutary example of swift retributive justice in the case of the first resort to the bullet and dagger in this country . . . Doubtless there will be some to say, as they have said already, "But this is too short notice; these wretches ought to have longer time in which to prepare for their dreadful fate." Ay! but how much short was the time they allowed their hapless victim to prepare for his fate?[957]

Twenty-two-year-old William Coxhall was chosen for duty at the execution at the Old Arsenal Prison because he was part of the Invalid Corps and on duty at the United States Arsenal. He had had his finger shot off at a skirmish near Petersburg and had been transferred to Washington. As a member of the Invalid Corps, he was placed on duty at the United States Arsenal. Years later, Coxhall gave the following account of the execution,

> On July 6, the Invalid Corps reported for duty at the arsenal prison . . . . On that day when we reported for service, Colonel Christian Rath came in when we were assembled.
>
> •
>
> "I want four able-bodied men to volunteer for special duty," he said.
>
> None of us waited to hear what the duty was. We were ready for anything to break the monotony. Plenty of us stepped forward. Rath looked us over and walked down the line. He stopped before the man next to me and looked him over critically.
>
> "Where's your cartridge belt?" he asked.
>
> "I got doctor's permission to leave it off," the soldier said. "I've been sick."

"I don't want you," Rath told him. Then he looked at me.

"What ails you?"

I held up my hand to show the missing finger.

"Anything else?" he asked.

"Not a thing," I answered.

"All right," Rath said, "You're elected."

He looked us over some more and picked out the likely ones. We followed him into the yard of the arsenal and there we had the first hint of what we were to do. The gallows was standing, ready for the execution." After cleaning up the carpenter's debris, Rath assigned men their duties for the next day, July 7th. "D. F. Shoupe and I were chosen to knock out the posts beneath one of the drops. G. F. Taylor and F. B. Haslett handled the other one. Three others were chosen to bring in the prisoners, . . . And then that morning, a rehearsal was held in the prison yard . . . . For two hours we were drilled in dropping these exactly as though the prisoners were there. After rehearsal the soldiers dug four graves.

We reported early on the day of the execution. It was July 7, 1865, a terrifically hot day with the thermometer close to a hundred degrees. Before nine o'clock we were in the prison yard. We were told that the execution would take place around two o'clock. The first floor anterooms of the prison started to fill up with officers who watched proceedings from the open windows.

Newspaper reporters were on the job, and I picked up scraps of information from them. Three or four of Davy Herold's sisters had spent the night with him. There were six girls, I believe, and Davy was little more than a boy. Mrs. Surratt's daughter had attempted to reach President Johnson to plead for her mother but had been stopped on the way. She was trying to get an order preventing her execution. George Atzerodt had been visited by a woman with whom he lived. None but his lawyers and a minister had been with Lewis Payne. All this gossip helped to pass the time while we stood about and sweated under the boiling sun . . . . Gen. Winfield Scott Hancock had overall charge of the execution and he waited as long as he could hoping for Anna Surratt through the crowds and to the prison he reached General Hartranft and ordered him to proceed.

"God, not the woman, too?" Hartranft exclaimed.

"Yes, the woman too," Hancock answered.

At one-fifteen Generals Hancock and Hartranft emerged from the building where the prisoners had been held and the trial conducted. Mrs. Surratt was first, near fainting after a look at the gallows. She was flanked by two priests carrying crosses and reciting the service for the dead.

Herold was next, trembling and clearly frightened of what was to happen. Atzerodt shuffled along in carpet slippers, a long white nightcap on his head, under different circumstances, he would have looked ridiculous. Finally, Powell, who as he walked reached out and took someone's straw hat off the man's head and put it on his own. The temperature had reached a hundred degrees. The tops of the Old Penitentiary walls were jammed with soldiers, and ranks of them were drawn up in front of the scaffold. There were hundreds of civilians, many holding umbrellas to shield themselves from the blinding sun. The group climbed up the traditional thirteen steps leading to a gallows.

With the exception of Payne, all were on the verge of collapse. They had to pass beside the open graves to reach the gallows steps and they could gaze down into the shallow holes and even touch the crude pine boxes that were to receive them. But Payne was as stolid as if he were a spectator instead of a principal. Herold wore a black hat until he reached the gallows.

The condemned were led to the chairs and Rath seated them. Mrs. Surratt and Payne were on our drop, Herold and Atzerodt on the other. Umbrellas were raised above the woman and Hartranft, who read the warrants and the findings. Then the clergy took over, talking what seemed to me interminably. The strain was getting worse. I became nauseated, what with the heat and the waiting, and taking hold of the supporting post, I hung on and vomited. I felt a little better after that, but not too good.

Much has been made of what Mrs. Surratt said as she was being bound. I know what it was. They tied the bands pretty tight and she complained.

"It hurts," she said.

"Well," was the consoling reply, "it won't hurt long."[958]

Powell walked upright toward his death, and he was needing no assistance as he mounted the thirteen steps to the gallows platform. Powell kept asking if any word of a reprieve had come for Mrs. Surratt. While on the scaffold, just a few minutes before his death, he shouted to the crowd, "Mrs. Surratt is an innocent woman! She does not deserve to die with the rest of us!"[959]

Four armchairs were there, and in plain view on the ground below, four pine coffins. The condemned sat, and General Hartranft read out the warrants and findings, the execution order, in a low voice. Most people had never in the world expected Mrs. Surratt would be hanged. When he had knotted the four hangman's ropes the previous night, Christian Rath had believed that only three would be utilized; surely, thought Rath, President Johnson would extend the woman clemency. The clergymen continued offering prayers.

While Mary Surratt and Father Walter were on the scaffold, Mary turned to him and asked, "Holy father, can I not tell these people before I die that I am innocent of the crime for which I have been condemned to death?"

"No, my child", Father Walter replied, "the world and all that is in it has now receded forever; it would do no good, and it might disturb the serenity of your last moments."

Ropes were put around the necks of the condemned. From the second floor of the arsenal, William Doster and Anna Surratt had a view of the execution, she at one window and he at an adjoining window. As the rope was fixed around her mother, Doster writes that "she fell down in a swoon."[960]

At one twenty-six, the soldiers standing below the platform received their signal from General Hancock and pushed the supporting planks from below the platform. The five-foot fall quickly killed Atzerodt and Mrs. Surratt; however, Herold had drawn up his knees and slowly strangled to death. Powell took the longest to die, a full five minutes. The condemned remained there for fifteen minutes before they were cut down and pronounced dead by Assistant General Surgeon Porter.

The four conspirators were buried on the grounds of the prison, only a few feet from the scaffold.[961] On October 1, 1867, the bodies were moved and reburied in an arsenal warehouse next to the body of John Wilkes Booth. In 1869, just days before his term expired, President Johnson released the bodies to their respective families. It was at this time that he also freed the remaining prisoners at Dry Tortugas, Florida.

Before he died in March 1895, Father Walter spoke to John Clampitt and revealed why he had discouraged Mary Surratt from speaking on the gallows. Father Walter had been asked the day before the execution to administer to the spiritual needs of Mrs. Surratt. However, he was told by the messenger from the War Department that "he would not be allowed to see Mrs. Surratt on the day of her death unless he would pledge his faith and honor as a priest of God that after he had absolved her and she had received the sacrament he would prevent her from making any protestation of her innocence." In order to see Mrs. Surratt, Father Walter was coerced into encouraging her to go to her death without a last dying statement of her innocence.[962] Father Walter also declared that he believed Mary Surratt to be innocent in the assassination of Lincoln. The *New York World* and the *Boston Post* reported that "the confessor of Mrs. Surratt, the Rev. Mr. Walter, says – not revealing the confessional – that as God lives Mrs. Surratt was innocent of the murder of President Lincoln or of any intent or conspiracy to murder him."[963]

\*　　\*　　\*

The other four prisoners who went to jail – Mudd, Spangler, Arnold, and O'Laughlen – were not informed of the executions that afternoon of July 7. They did not get their usual exercise time that day. Close to midnight on July 7, the prisoners were marched from their cells to a steamer. From there, they began their journey to Dry Tortugas.

# CHAPTER 29

## John Surratt Trial

John Surratt was on the run from federal officials. He had left Canada for England and then traveled to Italy to work as a Zouave for the papal guards. Unfortunately for Surratt, Henri Sainte-Marie, who had been introduced to Surratt by Weichmann in 1863, was also working as a Papal Zouave when he recognized John Surratt. Sainte-Marie went to the American embassy in Rome and told the ambassador of Surratt's whereabouts, that he had "admitted his connection with the assassination of the President," and that he had also implicated Jefferson Davis, Judah P. Benjamin, and the rest of the Confederate Cabinet "as being privy to it.[964]

The ambassadors wrote dispatches to Washington that Sainte-Marie claimed that "the plot had been discussed at Richmond – that [Surratt] and Booth used to visit Richmond every week and that they had laid the scheme before Mr. Benjamin, that he had presented it to the cabinet, and it had undergone discussion there, and that money had been advanced to further the enterprise."[965] The U.S. government, upon hearing Sainte-Marie's claims, sent him $250 in gold. Later he got an additional $10,000 even though the reward for Surratt's capture had been revoked.[966]

Johnson's Cabinet sent an inquiry to Cardinal Antonelly at the Vatican, asking whether Surratt could be extradited to the United States. Because Surratt was a Catholic, he had been hidden initially by Catholic clergy in Canada and had then found his way to the Vatican. This church involvement later led to conspiracy theories involving the Catholic Church.

"I believe," Sainte-Marie wrote, "Surratt is protected by the clergy, and that the murder is the result of a deep-laid plot, not only against the life of President Lincoln, but against the republic, as we are aware that priesthood and royalty are and always have been opposed to liberty."[967] Sainte-Marie's Catholic devotion was obviously subordinate to his hunger for money.

Before Sainte-Marie's claims were proved false and was found guilty of perjury, Secretary of State Seward began to negotiate with the Vatican to arrest Surratt. It was a complicated matter because the United States had no extradition treaty with the Vatican.[968] While discussions were under way, the papal government took action on its own and arrested Surratt. However, in a spectacular escape, Surratt suddenly broke free from his guards, leaped off a high precipice, survived the fall, and fled to Naples. There he quickly boarded a ship about to sail for Egypt. A month later, on November 27, 1866, he was recaptured on board a ship docked at Alexandria, Egypt. From Egypt, he was eventually returned to the United States, more than twenty months after the assassination.

The hanging of Mary Surratt caused such controversy that Stanton and the U.S. government simply had avoided apprehending John Surratt even when they had the chance. As early as September 1865, Stanton and Seward were fully aware of Surratt's whereabouts in Liverpool and of Surratt's intention to go to Rome. Yet they had not arrested him. Henry Wilding, the vice-consul in the United States Consulate in Liverpool, had wired the State Department in Washington on September 30, one month after Benjamin also landed at Liverpool, that "the supposed Surratt has arrived in Liverpool and is now staying at the oratory of the Roman Catholic Church of the Holy Cross . . . . I can, of course, do nothing further in the matter without Mr. Adams's (U.S. Minister to England) instructions and a warrant. If it be Surratt, such a wretch ought not to escape."[969]

Wilding received a reply from William Hunter, the acting secretary of state, on October 13, 1865: "Your dispatches . . . have been received. In reply . . . I have to inform you that, upon a consultation with the Secretary of War and the Judge Advocate General, it is thought advisable that no action be taken in regard to the arrest of the supposed John Surratt at present."[970]

Wilding's informant, the ship's surgeon on the ship that carried Surratt to Liverpool, was so eager to pick up the $25,000 reward that he took his case to the U.S. consul in Montreal. That consul wired the State Department on October 25, "It is Surratt's intention to go to Rome . . . . If an officer could go to England, I have no doubt that Surratt's arrest might be effected, and thus the last of the conspirators against the lives of the President and Secretary of State be brought to justice."[971]

The ship's surgeon, fearful that he was losing his reward money, stated that "Surratt remarked repeatedly that he only wished to live two years longer, in which time he would serve President Johnson as Booth did Mr. Lincoln."[972] But it was too late for rewards; on November 24, 1865, Stanton revoked the rewards that had been offered for the capture of Thompson, Tucker, Sanders, Cleary, and Surratt. He later explained he had done it because he was convinced that the men were out of the country, and that if they were arrested, it would be by government representatives who had no right to claim rewards for performing their duty.

The delays in extraditing Surratt continued, and John Surratt did not arrive in the United States until late February 1867.

\* \* \*

Criminal case number 4731, *The United States v. John Harrison Surratt*, began on June 10, 1867. Surratt was then twenty-three years old, and the trial was a sensational national event that lasted sixty-two days. He was charged on a four-count indictment, three relating to the assassination and the fourth to an assault upon Lincoln. During the trial, which lasted from June 10 to August 10, Surratt's attorneys showed convincingly that he had been in Elmira, New York, at the time of the assassination. As part of Surratt's defense, Brigadier General Edwin Lee, a relative of Robert E. Lee, who had been appointed to succeed Jacob Thompson, testified on July 15 that he had sent John Surratt on a reconnaissance mission to Elmira on April 12. Surratt was to survey the prison and its surroundings to determine the feasibility of a prisoner outbreak. Surratt had arrived in Elmira on April 13, the day before Lincoln was assassinated. When Surratt learned of the assassination, he immediately fled Elmira for Montreal where he arrived on April 18.

Belle Seamen, Anna Surratt's cousin, sent a letter to her from Washington, Pennsylvania, dated April 20, 1865, when Anna was in the Old Capitol Prison. Being in prison, Anna may not have received this letter.

> My dear Anna,
>
> It was with feelings of deep regret that we heard the rumors of Cousin John being accused of the assassination of Mr. Lincoln. I was rejoiced to receive a letter from him written from Montreal. It was written on the 10th, mailed the 11th, and came here the 17th, which was just sufficient in my mind to clear him from all suspicion. The Provost Marshal, hearing I had it, came and demanded it. A copy of which is now in the hands of the authorities in Washington. Write at the earliest convenience, as we are all interested in your welfare. Love is yours and the assurance of the sincere love of,
>
> Your cousin,
> Belle Seaman[973]

Whatever his previous relations with Booth had been, Surratt could not have participated in Lincoln's murder. Indeed, Surratt was a less prominent figure at his own trial than the ghost of his mother, which was invoked over and over again to embarrass the government and impress the jury with how unfair the 1865 military trial had been. Mrs. Surratt was portrayed as the innocent victim of wartime hatreds and the desire for revenge.

More than two hundred witnesses were called during the trial; however, Surratt did not testify. It was a hung jury for Surratt; eight of the twelve were ready to vote for acquittal.[974] He was returned to prison to await another trial; however, in November 1868, his case was dismissed, and Surratt was set free.

\*     \*     \*

Two years later, on December 6, 1870, Surratt gave a public lecture at the Rockville, Maryland, courthouse. At this lecture, he confessed to having been a courier in the Confederate Secret Service Bureau since 1861 and admitted to having plotted with Booth. But he said emphatically it was only for the abduction of the president, an act he considered "rash, perhaps foolish, but honorable."

Surratt claimed that as a courier, the only money he had received from the Confederacy was $200 from Secretary of State Judah P. Benjamin on the Friday before the evacuation of Richmond. He was to deliver dispatches from Richmond to Canada. "That was the only money I ever received from the Confederate government in an any shape or form." As for the kidnap plot, Surratt told his audience, "Booth and I often consulted together as to whether it would not be well to acquaint the authorities in Richmond with our plan, as we were sadly in want of money, our expenses being very heavy. In fact, the question arose among us as to whether, after getting Mr. Lincoln, if we succeeded in our plan, the Confederate authorities would not surrender us to the United States again, because of doing this thing without their knowledge or consent. But we never acquainted them with the plan, and they never had anything in the wide world to do with it. In fact, we were jealous of our undertaking and wanted no outside help. I have not made this statement to defend the officers of the Confederate government. They are perfectly willing to defend themselves. What I have done myself I am not ashamed to let the world know."[975]

Surratt described the dispatches he delivered in Montreal to Confederate Brigadier General Lee as "only accounts of some money transactions-nothing more or less." His attorneys had tried to introduce these dispatches as evidence at his trial, but Judge Fisher had ruled them out, despite the fact that the government had tried to prove that they had relation to the conspiracy to kill Lincoln.[976]

\*     \*     \*

As CSA secretary of state, Benjamin was responsible for the Canadian diplomatic post, and it was Benjamin's messages to Canada, delivered by Surratt, that brought accusation against Davis. The accusation was that Davis knew of and approved Benjamin's actions. In truth, Davis was not happy about Benjamin's association with John Surratt and the Canadian delegation.

Although no court of law, reliable document, responsible investigation, or unperjured witness ever proved any connection between Davis and the assassination, in Davis's strict sense of honor, Benjamin was responsible for making the charges against him seem credible. The military, led by Stanton and Holt, saw John Surratt as the connection to Jefferson Davis. Davis was deeply shocked at the accusations. Benjamin, Davis's most trusted adviser and closest confidant, had caused unfounded charges to be brought against him by using a messenger whose mother owned the boardinghouse where the conspirators occasionally met.

That Benjamin had continued using as his most trusted courier a young man who plotted with Booth to abduct Lincoln was seen by Davis as a failure of Benjamin's judgment of profound proportion. Davis was sure that Surratt had, in his last meeting with Benjamin in late March 1865, told Benjamin of the abortive March 17 attempt to kidnap Lincoln. Davis felt that Mary Surratt had been threatened and hanged in order to force her son to surrender and that the federal government would stop at nothing to implicate him. For five years until Surratt's 1870 lecture, Davis felt that his personal honor and his role in history were in the hands of John Surratt, the young messenger of his former secretary of state.

*   *   *

During his last weeks as president in 1869, Johnson ordered that the bodies of Powell, Herold, Atzerodt, Mary Surratt, and Booth be removed from the warehouse on the arsenal grounds and turned over to their families. He also granted full and unconditional pardons to the prisoners at Dry Tortugas – Mudd, Arnold, and Spangler. O'Laughlen had died in a yellow fever epidemic at the prison in 1867.[977]

Johnson never revoked his proclamation of May 2, 1865, charging Davis, Clay, Thompson, and Confederate representatives in Canada with having "incited, concerted, and procured" Lincoln's assassination. But by 1869, no one took the charges seriously.

# AFTERMATH

Actors: Laura Keene, John Doytt, and Harry Hawk of the *American Cousin* cast were arrested on a Northern Central train near Harrisburg, Pennsylvania. John Lutz, Laura's lover, telegraphed the War Department in Washington for official permission to continue on their tour. Colonel Baker granted this request, saying that he knew of no reason for detaining them. Other actors of the company who remained in Washington were required to report to the police daily. None of the actors were able to get to their possessions and trunks in Ford's Theatre because the soldiers on guard had been ordered to let nothing in the building be removed. Several of the actors, including George Spear, asked the War Department for permission to obtain these possessions. Spear explained that it was impossible for him to continue his acting career without his wardrobe. The actors did receive authorization to retrieve their wardrobes, but Colonel Wells accompanied them to ensure they took only their own property. (Spear spent his last days in the Edwin Forrest home for retired actors near Philadelphia.)

Samuel Arnold: After his release, he lived with his father in Baltimore and worked as a butcher. Later he moved to Friendship, Maryland, and managed a farm. Arnold led a reclusive life. In 1902, he was interviewed by Edward Lollman of the *Baltimore American*, who published Arnold's memoirs in serial form from December 7 to 19. He died on September 21, 1906, and was buried in Green Mount Cemetery in Baltimore, Maryland.

Booth Family: Mrs. Mary Ann Booth and Rosalie lived secluded lives. Mary Ann Booth died in 1885. Joseph retreated into melancholy and buried himself in studies to become a doctor. He finally finished his studies and acquired a practice in New York City at the age of thirty-nine. Although he married twice, he had no child and died in 1902. Junius Jr. died in 1886. Although an actor, he was more successful as a theater manager in Boston. Junius's last job was as manager of a home for retired actors at Manchester-by-the-Sea. Edwin's acting career temporarily ended after his brother assassinated Lincoln. Later, however, he was slowly accepted again by audiences. His first acting engagement was on January 3, 1866, as Hamlet. By the mid-1880s he was restored to his place as one of America's leading tragedians. He helped in establishing the Players Club in 1888, which is still located in the same building near New York's Gramercy Park.

Booth's Burial: Mary Ann Booth desperately wanted to give her son, John, a proper burial. He had been, Edwin said, his mother's darling. Soon after John's capture and death, friends of the family asked the New York politician Thurlow Weed to query Secretary Stanton about the remains of John Wilkes Booth. The newspapers had reported that there were no remains, that the body was dumped into the Potomac River in April 1865. Stanton told Weed that Booth's body was in custody and that when public sentiment over Lincoln's death had cooled, the family could claim the body. Seven months after the assassination, Edwin wrote to Stanton:

> Mr. Thurlow Weed has delivered to me the message you were kind enough to send, and at the earnest solicitation of my Mother I write to ask if you think the time is yet arrived for her to have the remains of her unhappy son. If I am premature in this I hope you will understand the motive which actuates me, arising purely from a sense of duty to assuage, if possible, the anguish of an aged mother. If at your convenience you will acquaint me when and how I should proceed in this matter you will relieve her sorrow-stricken heart and bind me ever. (Gene Smith, *American Gothic: The Story of America's Legendary Theatrical Family – Junius, Edwin, and John Wilkes Booth*, 237-238. The source of this book is David Rankin Barbee, "Lincoln and Booth," [unpublished manuscript, Barbee Papers, Georgetown University, Washington, DC.])

Edwin received no reply to this letter. A year and a half later, he asked John Ford to help in gaining the release of his brother John's body to the family. Ford was still a Washingtonian of some influence although his former theater was now a government-owned building that housed, among other agencies, the surgeon general's office of the War Department. The building held the three cervical vertebrae of John Wilkes Booth which had been removed in the Montauk autopsy. These vertebrae had holes that revealed the fatal bullet wound he had suffered. "Do what you can," Edwin wrote Ford, "whatever you think can be done. I shall not forget it" (Arthur Kincaid, ed., *John Wilkes Booth, Actor*, [North Leigh, Oxfordshire, England, 1989], 38). But Ford was unable to accomplish much.

On September 11, 1867, Edwin wrote to the new secretary of war, General Grant:

> Having once received a promise from Mr. Stanton that the family of John Wilkes Booth could be permitted to receive the body when sufficient time elapsed, I yielded to the entreaties of my Mother and applied for it to the 'Secretary of War', I fear too soon, for the letter went unheeded – if, indeed, it ever reached him.

I now appeal to you, on behalf of my heart-broken Mother, that she may receive the remains of her son.

You, Sir, can understand what a consolation it would be to an aged parent to have the privilege of visiting the grave of her child, and I feel assured that you will, even in the midst of your most pressing duties, feel a touch of sympathy for her, one of the greatest sufferers living.

May I not hope that you will listen to our entreaties and send me some encouragement, some information how and where the remains may be obtained?

By doing so you will receive the gratitude of a most unhappy family, and will, I am sure, be justified by all right-thinking minds should the matter ever become known to others than ourselves.

I shall remain in Baltimore two weeks from the date of this letter, during which time I could send a trust-worthy person to bring hither and privately bury the remains in the family grounds, thus relieving my poor mother of much misery.

Apologizing for my intrusion, and anxiously awaiting a reply to this,

I am, sir, with great respect

Yr obt sert

Edwin Booth

(Reprinted in George S. Bryan, *The Great American Myth*, [New York: Carrick & Evans, 1940], 304)

There is no record of Grant's ever replying. Edwin tried again in February 1869 to write to President Johnson. At the time, John Wilkes's body was no longer buried under the Old Penitentiary. Because there were improvements and new buildings being constructed at the federal arsenal, and the section of the building under which Booth and the other four condemned defendants had been buried was to be razed, all the bodies were moved to a new location.

On a historical footnote, the body of Captain Henry Wirz, the commandant of the infamous Confederate Andersonville Prison, was also buried with Booth and the conspirators. Wirz's trial in which he was charged with inhumanity toward Union prisoners began on August 21, 1865. He was found guilty and was hanged at the Old Capitol Prison on November 10. He was the only person to be executed as a result of wartime activities.

On October 1, 1867, all the coffins were reburied under the dirt floor of a warehouse on the eastern side of the Washington Arsenal grounds.

In February 1869, with one month to go in his presidential term, Johnson in one of his last official acts pardoned the conspiracy trial defendants who were at Dry Tortugas. O'Laughlen, Spangler, Arnold, and Mudd had been sentenced to life imprisonment at hard labor and were at the island fortress of Dry Tortugas in the waters of the Gulf of Mexico, southwest of Key West. O'Laughlen had already died there during a yellow fever epidemic.

On February 10, 1869, Edwin Booth for the third time sent a letter to President Johnson, asking for his brother John's remains. Johnson at last acquiesced,

> Executive Mansion
> February 15th 1869
>
> The Honorable Secretary of War will cause to be delivered to Mr. John Weaver, Sexton of Christ Church, Baltimore, the remains of John Wilkes Booth, for the purposes mentioned in the communication.
>
> Andrew Johnson

Edwin retained the services of John H. Weaver, who conducted a cabinetmaking and undertaking business, to bury John in the Booth family plot at Green Mount Cemetery, Baltimore. On the afternoon of February 15, 1869, a furniture moving van, not a hearse that might attract unwanted attention, went to the grounds of the Washington Arsenal and picked up the body of John Wilkes Booth. Booth's initial casket had been a gun box with ink lettering of the single word "Booth" (William M. Pegram, "An Historical Identification: John Wilkes Booth," *Maryland Historical Magazine*, 8 [1913]: 327-31). Earlier in the day, coffins bearing the remains of David Herold and Mary Surratt had been taken away. Booth's body was recovered by Harvey and Marr, a local Washington undertaking firm, and taken to their establishment at 335 F Street around the corner from Ford's Theatre. Edwin Booth was not there to view his brother's remains, he was at the Booth's Theatre in New York. It was his brother Joseph Booth who fulfilled this family obligation.

On February 16, General Ramsay sent a memorandum to General Townsend, assistant adjutant general of the army,

> Sir:
>
> I have the honor to report that the body of John Wilkes Booth was, on Monday afternoon the 15th inst., delivered to the person designated in the order of the President of the United States of the same date. (Reprint in Bryan, *The Great American Myth*, 309)

The body was shipped in a pine box to Weaver's establishment on Fayette Street in Baltimore. Two days later, on February 17, Joseph, Rosalie, and Mary Ann Booth went to Weaver's to identify the body. Joseph was the one who confirmed that the body was that of his brother by his recognition of a "plugged tooth." The Booths had purchased a family plot in Green Mount Cemetery in Baltimore. The family planned to move the bodies of the elder Booth and Richard Booth from Baltimore Cemetery, as well as those of the Booth children buried at the Bel Air farm. On the afternoon of Saturday, June 26, 1869, John Wilkes Booth was buried at Green Mount Cemetery.

Rev. Fleming James, an Episcopal minister living in New York City, conducted the burial services. Rev. James was visiting the Reverend Dudley, rector of Christ's Church, in Baltimore. A messenger was sent to the rectory to ask Rev. Dudley if he would officiate at a burial service. Rev. Dudley was in the rectory that day, and Rev. James agreed to conduct the services. He had not asked the name of the deceased, and it was not until he reached the cemetery that he was told that he was to officiate at the burial of John Wilkes Booth.

When Rev. James returned to New York and his congregation learned that he had conducted services at Booth's funeral, he was fired from his position. Rev. James remained in Baltimore, and for many years, he was the rector of St. Mark's Episcopal Church on Lombard Street (William M. Pegram, "An Historical Identification. John Wilkes Booth – What Became of Him?" *Maryland Historical Magazine* 8 [1913]: 329; Francis Wilson, *John Wilkes Booth: Fact and Fiction of Lincoln's Assassination* [Boston: Houghton Mifflin, 1929], 293-295).

In the family plot were the graves of Junius Brutus Booth and his three children who had died in infancy. Eventually Mrs. Mary Ann Booth, Rosalie, Asia, and Joseph were buried there. At Edwin's direction, John Wilkes's grave remained unmarked until years later.

Asia Booth Clarke: Asia completed a memoir of her father, a project she had started with her brother John. She wrote a book about her brother John, which she kept secret, because her husband or her brother, Edwin, would have destroyed it. The last page was dated 1874. The book was kept in the family and finally published in 1938 as *The Unlocked Book*. In August 1865, Asia gave birth to twins. Asia and her husband, John Sleeper Clarke (who she married in 1859), left for England. It appears the marriage was not a happy one. John Clarke became a popular actor and theater manager. Asia died in England in 1888. In accordance with her wishes, her body was returned to Baltimore to be buried near her family, including John Wilkes Booth.

William C. Cleary: He was Jacob Thompson's secretary while in Canada; and after charges against him for complicity in the Lincoln assassination were dismissed, he returned to Covington, Kentucky, to practice law. He died in 1897.

Clement C. Clay: He is one of the Confederate representatives in Montreal; he was imprisoned with Jefferson Davis at Fort Monroe. Clay wrote to President Johnson on November 23, protesting that he was innocent of the charges against him. He claimed that he had "been absent from Canada for nearly six months" and therefore could not have attended the meetings described at the conspiracy trial. Clay asked for a speedy trial or a parole to Alabama. Public opinion was swinging the other way by this time, and it was more expedient to parole than try him; and so in April 1866, Clay received his parole. He returned to Huntsville, Alabama, where he died in 1882.

Boston (Thomas P.) Corbett: After leaving the army, Boston Corbett was in demand to make speeches as the killer of Lincoln's assassin. But requests for speeches ceased when Corbett delivered religious tirades and only a brief description of what had occurred at Garrett's farm. He wandered about the country working as a farmer and a hatter and taking other odd jobs. He wore his hair to his shoulders because, he explained, that was what Jesus had done.

In 1886, Corbett moved to Kansas where he regaled townspeople with his religious opinions, exhorting them not to play baseball on Sundays, as it was the Lord's day. His admonishment set him up for ridicule. It was a practice that set him up for ridicule.

In 1887, the Topeka Grand Army of the Republic secured for Corbett an appointment as a doorkeeper in the state legislature. When clerks and pages, holding a mock session, made fun of Corbett, saying, "The Reverend so and so will now invoke a blessing upon this legislature." Corbett, who was observing from the balcony, was greatly offended. He took out two revolvers and, in the name of God, opened fire. Fortunately no one was killed. Quickly the police arrived and apprehended Corbett. He was put on trial. (The prosecuting attorney was Charles Curtis, a future vice president of the United States.) The strange Corbett was found to be insane and was confined to a state institution in Topeka, Kansas. The following year, he escaped by jumping on to a horse, which had been carelessly left near the institute gate by the superintendent's son. The outspoken, opinionated Corbett was never found or seen again.

Mary Apollonia Dean: Mary, a resident at the Surratt boardinghouse, was born in middle to late 1854. She was at home with her parents at the time of the assassination. On December 19, 1872, she married Napoleon Bonaparte Grant in Fairfax County, Virginia. They had two children. Her husband died in a train wreck in February 1894, and she died three months later on May 14, 1894; she was thirty-nine. She was buried at St. Mary's Catholic Cemetery, Alexandria, Virginia.

Edward P. Doherty, Lieutenant, U.S. Cavalry: Doherty later served as general inspector of street paving in New York City. Doherty died on April 3, 1897.

Thomas T. Eckert: Major Eckert was to be appointed assistant secretary of war; and before he resigned his commission, he bore the rank and title of brevet brigadier general. He later became the president of the Western Union Telegraph Company.

Ford's Theatre: While the hunt for Lincoln's assassin was under way, the cast of *Our American Cousin* was ordered to perform the play again for a group of detectives reconstructing the events of the night of the assassination. Some of the actors were brought from the Old Capitol Prison and others, under orders to report to the police every day, were ordered to report to the theater. The actors went through their parts in the almost-empty theater and played until the moment when Harry Hawk had paused for the laugh he expected. "Turn you inside out, you sockdologizing old mantrap."

From that moment, the theater sat silent for over a hundred years. John T. Ford, finally freed, took it back and announced he would put on regular performances. On July 3, 1865, Ford placed announcements in the Washington newspapers, stating that his theater had not been sold and would reopen at the earliest possible moment but that the "private box occupied by our late lamented President will remain closed." However, before opening night, the government seized the theater. Stanton had decided that no more theatrical performances would be held in that theater. The War Department took it over for use as the surgeon general's office, finally paying Ford $100,000 for the theater (*Century Magazine*, February 1913). It was used as a warehouse until June 9, 1893, when the structure collapsed, killing twenty-eight people. It was rebuilt, with the presidential box restored to its original condition, as a theater and a museum with memorabilia of Lincoln's assassination. Ford died in 1894 in Baltimore.

Garrett family: Richard Garrett appealed to the U.S. Congress for damages done to his farm. This appeal was rejected. William and Jack Garrett were arrested and imprisoned at the Washington Navy Yard. After their released, they returned to the family farm.

Jennie Gourlay: Jennie was to have starred in a benefit performance of *The Octoroon* the following evening. She later married William Withers, who had conducted the band on the evening of the assassination.

Bennett F. Gwynn: Gwynn had attempted to help Mary Surratt to get a repayment of a loan from John Nothey and testified on her behalf at the conspiracy trial. He remained on his plantation until 1870 and then sold his land and moved to Baltimore. Gwynn died in August 1897 at the home of his daughter in Alexandria, Virginia.

Lucy Hale: She went with her father, mother, and sister to Spain. Lucy returned and eventually married a widower with several children, William E. Chandler (1835-1917). Through him, Lucy returned to the social position in Washington she had occupied earlier in her life. She annually contributed small sums to more than one hundred charities. She bore one son, who became a U.S. senator and secretary of the navy. One of her stepchildren, who later became a U.S. Navy admiral, long remembered her as "a thoroughly unpleasant woman, in no way a sensuous woman" (Stepson letter, October 9, 1944, Barbee Papers, Georgetown University). He remembered that at social events, she seemed always to be on the outskirts of the crowd. Even when she gave parties for her young son, she stayed in a hallway silently looking on. Eventually her widowed sister Elizabeth took over as the Chandler household's hostess. For many years, Lucy wore only black, as did her coachman, who drove black horses. She went about throwing newspaper clippings on the lawns of people she thought would be interested in reading particular stories (Richmond Morcom, "They All Loved Lucy," *American Heritage*, October 1970, 12-15; Terry Alford, *Alexandria Historical Society Annual*, 1990).

Thomas H. Harbin: One of those not arrested as a conspirator in the Lincoln kidnapping plot was Thomas H. Harbin. Harbin appeared at Ashland, Virginia, on April 28, 1865, and secured a formal parole as a member of Company B, First Maryland Cavalry. There were no records of Harbin for the next five years until he appeared as a clerk at the National Hotel in Washington, a job he held until he died on 18 November 1885. During the years at the National Hotel, Harbin often spoke of his wartime activities as a Confederate agent when he had called himself Wilson and reported directly to Jefferson Davis. Harbin said that after the assassination he had made his way to Cuba, then Great Britain, and then back to the United States when he thought it was safe to return.

Henry and Clara Rathbone: In 1867, Henry Rathbone married Clara Harris. Over the years, his behavior became more and more violent.

Holohan Family: The family moved to Baltimore in 1867, then to New Jersey, and then about 1874 returned to Washington. John Holohan died on July 3, 1877, of cancer. His son, Charles, was a stonecutter, and he died in Washington on November 11, 1909.

Joseph Holt: Holt remained in his position of judge advocate general until 1875. He died intestate on August 1, 1894 (*New York Times*, col. 2, August 20, 1894, 1).

Elizabeth Jenkins: Mary Surratt's mother converted to Catholicism. She died June 7, 1879, and was buried at St. Ignatius Catholic Church Cemetery, Oxon Hill, Maryland.

William Jett: About a year after the assassination, Jett took a job in Baltimore, traveling to and from Virginia. He married the daughter of a Baltimore physician. According to John L. Mayre, who identified himself as "a near relative of Mr. Jett, and our homes being only a mile apart at the time of" the assassination, Jett remained "fast friends" with his ex-sweetheart, Izora Gouldman, and her family despite the fact that he had married another. Jett was ostracized by friends and neighbors and forced to leave Virginia. According to Mayre, Jett was "respected by every one who knew him." Local people thought Jett helped in Booth's capture because Booth, while dying on the Garrett's front porch, asked, "Did Jett betray me?" Jett died of paresis in a hospital at Williamsburg, Virginia.

Thomas Jones: Jones remarried, and this marriage bore ten children. He was active in Maryland and Baltimore politics and owned a coal, wood, and feed yard in North Baltimore (George Alfred Townsend, "How Wilkes Booth Crossed the Potomac," *Century Magazine*, April 1884, 832).

Mary Todd Lincoln: Mary Lincoln left the White House in black mourning attire. She would wear black every day of her life but one, and that was her son Tad's birthday. With only one exception, she wrote on mourning stationery with the widest of black bands. Mary compulsively spoke about her husband's death and her own life story to anyone who would listen. She exhibited an irrational fear of poverty but also was subject to extravagant spending frenzies. She lived modestly in Europe and returned to the United States after a few years. She was devastated by her son Tad's death at age seventeen in 1871. She thought that electricity was the invention of the devil and used only candles. Her only surviving son, Robert, convinced that his mother was mentally unbalanced and had her committed to an institution in 1875. The first female lawyer in Illinois was able to plead for Mary's release and had her declared sane after nine months. Mary made another European trip and then went to Springfield to live with her sister. Mary always kept her carriage curtains closed when she took a drive. The end of her broken life came in the summer of 1882 on July 16.

Robert Lincoln: Robert Lincoln was twenty-one years old when his father died. Young Lincoln became the most successful presidential progeny in history, except for members of the Adams family. He became rich from his law practice and from his positions as president of the Pullman Company, secretary of war, and minister to Great Britain. It was his fate to be present at two succeeding presidential assassinations. He was by President Garfield within seconds of his being shot by a disappointed office seeker. It was in Robert Lincoln's carriage that Garfield was taken away from the railroad station where he had been shot. Years later, Robert was with President McKinley when an anarchist came from a reception line and shot the president.

Robert's absence from the first of all presidential assassinations, that of his father, never ceased to cause him agony. Had he been there, he reasoned, as the junior member of the theater party, he would have taken a seat behind the others and so, perhaps, would have been in a position to prevent Booth from entering the box. That he might have prevented all was "an obsession which he never outgrew" (*Saturday Evening Post*, February 11, 1939). Robert Lincoln died in 1926.

John Lloyd: Lloyd had been arrested on April 18, 1865, and was released from the Old Capitol Prison on June 30. He returned to Washington where he continued in his trade as a bricklayer. On December 18, 1892, his sixty-eighth birthday, Lloyd was supervising a construction project and climbed some scaffolding to inspect the work. The boards of the scaffold broke, and Lloyd fell to the ground. Some bricks on the scaffold fell on top of him. Almost two weeks later, he died from the injuries he sustained. His grave is only fifty yards from that of Mary Surratt at Mount Olivet Cemetery. His wife survived him for several years; there were no surviving children (*Washington Evening Star*, December 19, 1892; James O. Hall "John M. Lloyd, Star Witness", *Surratt Society News*, March 1977; Laurie Verge, "That Man Lloyd," *Surratt Courier*, April 1988).

John Mathews: The man Booth had entrusted to deliver a letter to the *National Intelligencer* had destroyed the letter in his hotel room but later told of its contents. Mathews remained in the theater world all his life, ending as an official of an actors' relief fund. His response to any mention of President Lincoln's death was to end the conversation and leave the room.

Dr. Samuel Mudd: After being sentenced to life imprisonment, Mudd and the other conspirators were sent to Dry Tortugas, Florida. This island prison was about seventy miles from Key West. Dr. Mudd made an unsuccessful attempt to escape on September 25, 1865. In the summer of 1867, yellow fever spread on the island; and after the prison's doctor died on September 7, Dr. Mudd took the position of prison physician and helped to stamp out the yellow fever epidemic. Dr. Mudd contracted the disease but recovered. It was this prison epidemic that killed O'Laughlen on September 23, 1867. A petition to President Johnson for Dr. Mudd's pardon was circulated at the prison and signed by all noncommissioned officers and soldiers on Dry Tortugas. This petition was ignored. However, Dr. Mudd was pardoned by President Johnson on February 8, 1869, and released on March 8, 1869; and he returned to his farm in Maryland. He resumed his medical practice and lived a quiet life on his farm, until on January 10, 1883. Dr. Mudd died of pneumonia. He was forty-nine years old. Sarah Frances, his wife, lived until December 29, 1911, and was buried next to him in St. Mary's Cemetery. In October 1959, President Eisenhower authorized a plaque at Dry Tortugas, honoring Dr. Mudd's efforts in combating the 1867 yellow fever epidemic.

Michael O'Laughlen: After receiving a life sentence at hard labor from the military tribunal, O'Laughlen was sent to Dry Tortugas in the Florida Keys with his fellow convicted defendants. He died during an outbreak of yellow fever at the prison on September 23, 1867.

John F. Parker: Lincoln's bodyguard was dismissed from the Washington Police Force sometime after August 13, 1868. He had been charged with gross neglect of duty on July 22, 1868, and this was his last offense and was dismissed. He then had successive jobs as carpenter, ship carpenter, and machinist. He died on June 28, 1890, of pneumonia, complicated by asthma and exhaustion. His wife died on January 1, 1904.

William Petersen: Petersen, who owned the boardinghouse where Lincoln died, was a German tailor. He later committed suicide by overdosing on laudanum. His body was discovered on the grounds of the Smithsonian Institution.

The Powell Family: Powell's attorney William E. Doster received a letter dated September 30, 1865, from Powell's father, George Powell. In the letter, George explained that he was quite ill and planned on traveling to Washington as soon as he was well. When his health was improved enough for travel, he set out and got as far as Jacksonville, Florida, when he heard of his son's execution and returned home. The Powell family had not fared well during the Civil War. One son was killed in action, one son was executed, and one son maimed in battle, although he went on to father sixteen children.

Lewis Powell: Powell's body was moved several times over the years, and only the whereabouts of his skull is now known. After being hung, Powell's remains were initially buried on the arsenal grounds. When the prisoners on Dry Tortugas were released and the bodies of those executed for the assassination were made available to their families, Powell's body was not claimed. According to James Cisogin in the *Washington Star* in 1869, Powell's remains were reinterred at Holmead Cemetery in Washington. A news article in the *National Republican* reported that all the bodies at that cemetery were being relocated so that the land could be used for land development. At this point, all trace of Powell's remains were lost until 1992 when the Smithsonian Institution discovered a skull with a tag that read "cranium of L. Paine hung at Washington, D.C. for the attempted assassination of Secretary of State William H. Seward in 1865." Further research into the Smithsonian revealed that the skull was turned over to the Army Medical Museum on January 13, 1885, close to the time of the closing of the Holmead Cemetery. The skull was then given to the Smithsonian on May 7, 1898 (*Surratt Courier*, March 1992).

Christian Rath: The hangman at the execution of the conspirators, worked for the Railway Mail Service between Grand Rapids and Detroit, Michigan, after the war. He lived in Jackson, Michigan, and died about 1905.

Henry Rathbone: Rathbone, who was in the box with Lincoln when he was assassinated, recovered from the knife wound and, in 1867, married his stepsister, Clara Harris. They were wealthy, respected members of Washington society. They had two sons and a daughter. One son, Henry Riggs Rathbone, served two terms as a congressman from Illinois in the 1920s.

The assassination preyed on Rathbone's mind, and he faulted himself for not preventing it. Depression, headaches, and stomach upsets afflicted him; and he resigned from the army. With his wife, he toured European spas, seeking relief for his health and mental condition. His health did not improve; and by 1881, Clara Harris Rathbone was telling relatives that in fits of temper, her husband threatened her life. She considered a separation or divorce but ruled it out for the sake of her children. Rathbone was posted in Hanover, Germany, after President Cleveland had given him an appointment in the U.S. Consul General's Office. Before daylight on Christmas morning of 1883, Clara awoke to find her husband fully dressed and wandering about her room. He said he wanted to see the children. She pointed out the earliness of the hour and, in his rage, pulled out a revolver and shot her. She died, and Rathbone tried to commit suicide, stabbing himself five times.

But Rathbone survived and was committed to a mental institution. Rathbone maintained that the walls of his asylum were hollow and contained spray apparatus blowing dust and gas on him and giving him headaches and chest pain. Rathbone died in 1911 at the age of seventy-four in the asylum, twenty-eight years after murdering his wife.

Real Estate: The H Street boardinghouse was lost to creditors on November 13, 1867, and the lower level of the boardinghouse is now a Chinese restaurant. The management does not allow visitors upstairs. The Surratt house and tavern in Surrattsville also fell to creditors on March 11, 1869. The old Surratt house and tavern fell into disrepair and quickly became dilapidated. In the 1970s and early 1980s, concerned local historians rescued the old tavern and restored it to its original condition. The property is now part of the Maryland-National Capital Park and Planning Commission.

Reward Money: There was a protracted battle over who deserved what percentage of the reward money for finding Lincoln's assassins. A congressional committee ultimately decided that the largest amount, $15,000, was to be given to Colonel E. J. Conger with diminishing sums down to $1,653.85 to each of the twenty-six enlisted personnel of the Sixteenth New York Cavalry for the capture of Booth and Herold.

By an act of Congress on July 28, 1866 (14 *Stat.* 341-2), the following sums of money went to fifty-three people named in the act to receive a share of the reward money.

Here are the following names and the share received for the capture of Booth and Herold:

| | |
|---|---|
| Colonel E. J. Conger | $15,000.00 |
| Lieutenant Doherty | 5,250.00 |
| General Lafayette C. Baker | 3,750.00 |
| Luther Baker | 3,000.00 |
| George Cottingham | 1,000.00 |
| Alexander Lovett | 1,000.00 |
| H. H. Wells | 1,000.00 |
| Twenty-six members of the Sixteenth New York Cavalry | 43,000.00 |

Here are the following names and the share received for the capture of Powell:

| | |
|---|---|
| Major H. W. Smith | $1,000.00 |
| Detectives: Richard C. Morgan, Eli Devore Thomas Sampson, W. M Wermerskirch ($500 each) | 2,000.00 |
| J. N. Kimball | 500.00 |
| P. M. Clark | 500.00 |
| Susie Jackson ("colored" as listed in 1866) | 250.00 |
| Mary Ann Griffin | 250.00 |

Here are the following names and the share received for the capture of Atzerodt:

| | |
|---|---|
| Major E. R. Artman | $1,250.00 |
| Sergeant Z. W. Gemmill | 3,598.54 |
| Six privates of 1st Delaware Cavalry, and civilian James W. Purdman ($2,878.78 each) | 20,151.46 |

George Foster Robinson: The nurse who defended Secretary of State Seward was promoted from private to commissioned officer. In 1871, a medal was endorsed by the Treasury Department, honoring Robinson's heroic efforts in saving the life of Seward.

William Rollins: He died in Virginia in 1901. At the time of his death, Rollins owned large tracts of farmland.

Sarah Slater: Nothing is known of Sarah Slater after April 4, 1865. However, her husband Rowan Slater wrote to his brother James, a clerk in a New York City retail store: "You wrote me that you heard that Nettie was dead. I hope she is in a better world. If you have any of the particulars about her, let me know. Of course placed in the situation that I am it is natural that I wish to know all, when did she die, where, and under what circumstances. Give me all the particulars so far as you know." No reply to this letter has been located (for a good history of Sarah Slater, see James O. Hall, "The Veiled Lady," *North & South Magazine*, August 2000).

Edman Spangler: After being pardoned by President Andrew Johnson and released in March 1869, he worked for John Ford in Baltimore until 1873. Spangler and Dr. Mudd had become close friends in prison; and after Spangler left Ford, Mudd gave Spangler five acres of land to farm. However, Spangler spent most of his time doing carpentry work for Mudd and others. Spangler's health slowly deteriorated and died on February 27, 1875. He was buried at the St. Peter's Church graveyard.

Henri Beaumont de Sainte-Marie: He died destitute in 1873 in Philadelphia. He was buried in Potter's Field.

Anna Surratt (Elizabeth Susanna Surratt): Two days after her mother's execution, Anna wrote the following letter:

> Washington, D.C.
> July 9, 1865
>
> Genl. Hartranft
>
> Genl Hancock told Mr. Holohan that you had some things that belonged to my poor Ma, which, with my consent you would deliver to him. Don't forget to send the pillow upon which her head rested and her prayer beads, if you can find them – these things are dear to me.
>
> Someone told me that you wrote to the President stating that the Prisoner Payne [Powell] had confessed to you the morning of the Execution that Ma was entirely innocent of the President's assassination and had no knowledge of it. Moreover, that he did not think that she had any knowledge of the assassination plot, and that you believed that Payne [Powell] had confessed the truth. I would like to know if you did it because I wish to remember and thank those who did Ma the least act of kindness. I was spurned and treated with the utmost contempt by everyone at the White House.
>
> Remember me to the officers who had charge of Ma and I shall always think kindly of you.
>
> Your Respectfully
> Anna Surratt

Anna Surratt married Dr. William P. Tonry on June 18, 1869, by Father Walter. Dr. Tonry, a chemist employed by the surgeon general's office, had an office in Ford's Theatre, which was being used as a government office. Dr. Tonry was fired four days after his marriage because he married the daughter of Mary Surratt. The young couple moved to Baltimore where the doctor established a business as an analytical and consulting chemist and chemical expert. Dr. Tonry received the first honorary doctorate ever given by Georgetown College. Eventually the couple had three sons and a daughter: William, Albert, Reginald, and Clara. Anna Surratt Tonry was sixty-one years old when she died on October 24, 1904, and she was buried next to her mother at Mount Olivet Cemetery.

Isaac Surratt: Isaac, Mary Surratt's oldest son, was arrested in September 1865 when he returned home after the war. He was eventually released and settled in Baltimore and was employed by the Old Bay Steamship Company until his death in 1907. Isaac never married. Isaac, as well as Anna Surratt and her husband, William Tonry, were buried next to Mary Surratt at Mount Olivet Cemetery, Washington, DC.

John Surratt: John Surratt was not tried a second time and was released. John Surratt taught school in Emittsburg and Rockville, Maryland. He had these teaching positions for a short period, and soon he and his brother Isaac secured positions with the Old Bay Line, a Baltimore steam packet company. By the time John retired in 1915, he was auditor and treasurer of the company. In 1872, John married Mary Victorine Hunter, a second cousin of Francis Scott Key; and the couple had seven children. In early 1916, John was stricken with pleurisy; and he appeared to have recovered. But then he was stricken with pleuropneumonia and died on April 21, 1916, at the age of seventy-two. He was buried in the New Cathedral Cemetery in Baltimore, Maryland (Obituary of John Surratt, *Baltimore Sun*, April 22, 1916).

Mary Surratt: On February 8, 1869, after four years of appeals by the Booth and Surratt families, President Johnson on February 8, 1869, released the bodies of the conspirators and Booth. Mary Surratt was buried in the Mount Olivet Cemetery, Washington, DC.

Surrattsville: The small Maryland town was renamed Clinton, Maryland.

Jacob Thompson: He is one of the Confederate representatives in Montreal; he fled to England but returned to live in Memphis, Tennessee, with his personal wealth still intact.

Beverly Tucker: After he published his open "Address to the People of the United States," Tucker stayed in Canada. In November 1865, the $25,000 reward for his arrest was withdrawn. He traveled through England, Mexico, and Canada and only returned to the United States in 1872. In 1889, Secretary of State Blaine appointed Tucker as Democratic member of a commission to Haiti. However, at the last minute, President Harrison withdrew Tucker's appointment. It is not known whether he lost this appointment because of his association with the assassination twenty-four years previously or because of the lack of harmony between President Harrison and his secretary of state Blaine. Tucker died in 1890.

Clement Laird Vallandigham: He was banished to the South but soon left for Canada. He ran in absentia in the 1863 Ohio gubernatorial election but lost. Vallandigham safely returned to the United States in 1864 and then ran unsuccessfully a number of times for public office.

Lew Wallace: After serving as a judge in the conspiracy trial, he presided as head of the military commission that tried and condemned Henry Wirz, the commandant of Andersonville Prison. He is the only Confederate to be executed by the federal government. Wallace is best known as the writer of *Ben-Hur*.

Father Walter: He was Mary Surratt's confessor and presided over Anna's wedding. He died on February 5, 1894, in Washington, DC.

Louis J. Weichmann: Weichmann never finished his theological studies; and on October 25, 1870, he married Annie Johnson of Philadelphia. The marriage ended when Weichmann moved out of the house, leaving his wife to take in boarders. There were no children from this marriage. In 1869, through the recommendation of Secretary of War Stanton and Judge Holt, he was appointed to a position in the Philadelphia Custom House. He lost this job in 1886, and he went to live with his parents in Anderson, Indiana. There he operated a business college. Weichmann wrote a book on the assassination, but it was not published until well after his death on June 5, 1902 (*A True History of the Assassination of Abraham Lincoln and of the Conspiracy of 1865* [New York: Alfred A. Knopf, 1975]).

Gideon Welles: He was Lincoln's secretary of the navy and remained in that post until 1869. He supported Johnson's reconstruction policy. His diary remains an invaluable historical source. He died in Hartford, Connecticut, on February 11, 1878.

Bennett S. Young: Young was the leader of the raid on St. Albans, and he was president of a number of railroads and of a bridge company in Indiana. He dedicated the Confederate Monument in Arlington Cemetery in 1914. He died in 1917.

# TIMELINE

| | |
|---|---|
| 30 June 1821 | Junius Brutus Booth and his common-law wife, Mary Ann Holmes, arrived in United States at Norfolk, Virginia. |
| 10 May 1838 | JWB was born in Bel Air, Maryland. |
| 18 Apr 1851 | Junius Booth was divorced from Adelaide Booth. |
| 10 May 1851 | Junius Booth married Mary Ann Holmes. |
| 30 November 1852 | JWB's father died on a river steamer near Louisville. |
| 23 Jan 1853 | JWB was baptized at St. Timothy's Episcopal Church. |
| 14 Aug 1855 | JWB's acting debut in *Richard III* in Baltimore. |
| 15 Aug 1857-19 Jun 1858 | JWB acted in stock at Arch Street Theatre in Philadelphia. |
| 27 Aug 1858 | Appeared with Edwin Booth as Richmond in *Richard III* in Baltimore. |
| 1858-1859 | JWB acted for a season at Old Marshall Theatre, Richmond. |
| 1859-1860 | JWB acted for a season at Old Marshall Theatre, Richmond. |
| 16 October 1859 | John Brown began raid on Harpers Ferry. |
| 18 October 1859 | Harpers Ferry raid ended with Colonel Robert E. Lee commanding and J. E. B. Stuart in the action. |
| 2 December 1859 | At John Brown's execution in Charles Town, Virginia. |
| 28 May 1860 | The 1859-1860 season ended at Old Marshall Theatre. |
| 31 May 1860 | Gave a benefit performance for himself and another at the Old Marshall Theatre in Richmond. |
| 1 October 1860 | JWB with Matthew Canning company in Columbus, Georgia. |
| 12 October 1860 | JWB accidentally received "flesh wound in the thigh." |
| 20 October 1860 | JWB recited the funeral oration of Marcus Antonius in Columbus, Georgia. |

| | |
|---|---|
| 26 October 1860 | JWB joined Matthew Canning company in Montgomery, Alabama. |
| 1 December 1860 | JWB's last performance in Montgomery, Alabama. |
| Early December 1860 | JWB was in Philadelphia with his family. |
| 16 December 1860 | Asia Booth Clarke wrote a letter saying, "John Booth is home. He is looking well, but his wound is not entirely healed yet: he still carries the ball in him." |
| 20 December 1860 | South Carolina seceded from the Union. |
| 7 January 1860 | Mississippi seceded from the Union. |
| 21 January 1861 | JWB began an engagement in Rochester, New York. |
| 2 February 1861 | JWB's engagement in Rochester closed. |
| 11 February 1861 | JWB at the Gayety Theatre, Albany, New York. |
| 11 February 1861 | Lincoln left Springfield, Illinois, for Washington. |
| 12 February 1861 | JWB fell on a dagger during his performance, inflicting a deep wound under his right arm. |
| 18 February 1861 | JWB returned to the stage after his knife wound. |
| 26 April 1861 | JWB's last performance in Albany, stabbed by Henrietta Irving. |
| 25 June 1861 | Gus Howell enlisted in the Confederate army. |
| 11 September 1861 | JWB opened the 1861-1862 season in Detroit. |
| 1 July 1862 | JWB closed 1861-1862 season in Louisville after appearing in ten cities, including Cincinnati, Indianapolis, St. Louis, Chicago, Baltimore, New York, and Boston. |
| 15 July 1862 | Joseph Booth left England for Australia. |
| 16 July 1862 | Gus Howell was discharged for disability. |
| 24 October 1862 | Gus Howell was arrested on the Potomac River for transporting rebels from Maryland to join the rebel army. |
| 22 December 1862 | JWB began a two-week engagement at Ben DeBar's St. Charles Theatre in St. Louis. He was reported to have said he wished the "whole damned government would go to hell." He was arrested, fined, and took the oath of allegiance. |
| 4 January 1863 | JWB ended his St. Louis performances. |
| 29 January 1863 | Gus Howell was arrested again. He was held for a month. |
| 11 April 1863 | JWB performed *Richard III* at Grover's Theatre in Washington, DC. Lincoln attended. |
| 3 July 1863 | JWB finished the 1862-1863 season in Cleveland. |
| 3 July 1863 | Battle of Gettysburg was won. |
| 4 July 1863 | Vicksburg fell to Grant. |

| | |
|---|---|
| ? July 1863 | New York City drafted riots; five hundred were killed; JWB was with his brother, Edwin, when riots broke out. |
| 28 September 1863 | JWB began the 1863-1864 season in Boston. |
| 2 November 1863 | JWB began a two-week engagement at Ford's Theatre. |
| 9 November 1863 | JWB acted in the play *The Marble Heart* with President and Mrs. Lincoln in the same boxes Booth would assassinate him seventeen months later. |
| 16 November 1863 | JWB ended his two-week engagement at Ford's Theatre. |
| ? November 1863 | JWB has engagement at John Ellsler's Academy of Music in Cleveland and began oil agreement with Ellsler Mears. |
| 22 December 1863 | JWB at the Union Theatre in Leavenworth, Kansas. |
| 2 January 1864 | JWB was stranded in St. Joseph, Missouri, in a snowstorm. |
| 5 January 1864 | JWB was still stranded in St. Joseph, Missouri. He did dramatic readings at Corby's Hall in order to raise money to get to the Ben DeBar's theater in St. Louis. |
| 1 February 1864 | JWB was in Nashville, Tennessee, for two weeks at the Wood's Theatre; it was reported that he met Governor Andrew Johnson and his secretary, William A. Browning. |
| 14 February 1864 | JWB's engagement in Nashville ended. |
| 15 February 1864 | JWB was in Cincinnati with a severe cold; he performed that night. |
| 26 February 1864 | JWB's last performance in Cincinnati, and he was still not feeling well. |
| February/March 1864 | Dahlgren's raid into Richmond. |
| 14 March 1864 | JWB was in New Orleans at the St. Charles Theatre with "severe hoarseness." |
| 3 April 1864 | JWB's last performance in New Orleans. |
| 25 April 1864 | JWB at the Boston Museum, Boston, Massachusetts, opening of *Richard III.* |
| 28 May 1864(?) | JWB finished in Boston with a matinee of *The Corsican Brothers*; this was his last extended engagement; his throat and voice continued to irritate him. |
| 10 June 1864 | JWB at the McHenry House in Meadville, Pennsylvania. |
| 29 June 1864 | JWB at the McHenry House in Meadville, Pennsylvania. |
| 30 June 1864 | JWB checked in to the Waddell House in Cleveland. |
| ? June 1864 | General Jubal Early led the army into Maryland. |

| | |
|---|---|
| ? July 1864 | Horace Greeley's abortive peace negotiations with Clay and Sanders. |
| 1 July 1864 | JWB was in Cleveland at the Waddell House. |
| 26 July 1864 | JWB at the Parker House, Boston. |
| 7 August 1864 | JWB was in Philadelphia. |
| ? Aug 1864 | JWB recruited Arnold and O'Laughlen. |
| Mid-August 1864 | JWB was in New York City for two weeks. He wrote that he was "laid up" with erysipelas of the arm. |
| ? September 1864 | Situation: Mobile Bay and Atlanta had fallen. Grant was laying siege to Richmond, then Petersburg; Sheridan active in Shenandoah Valley; Sherman marching to the sea. |
| 2 September 1864 | Atlanta fell to General Sherman. |
| 23 September 1864 | Edwin Gray Lee, cousin of Robert E. Lee, was promoted to brigadier general. |
| 27 September 1864 | Joseph H. Simonds, JWB's business agent, said JWB's oil business was entirely closed out by this date. |
| 1 October 1864 | Mary Surratt moved into her H Street boardinghouse in Washington, DC. |
| 6 October 1864 | Honora Fitzpatrick moved into the Surratt boarding house on H Street. |
| 16 October 1864 | JWB was in Newburgh, New York, on his way to Canada. |
| 18 October 1864 | JWB checked in to the St. Lawrence Hall in Montreal at 9:30 p. m. He occupied room 150. |
| 19 October 1864 | St. Albans raid, led by Lieutenant Young. |
| 23 October 1864 | General Robert E. Lee in Richmond. |
| 25 October 1864 | Lee wrote a letter to Davis. Lee recommended Davis not to prove Rev. Kensey Johns Stewart's "undertaking he proposes." |
| 27 October 1864 | JWB at the Ontario Bank in Montreal, purchasing bills of exchange that were later found on his body at Garrett's farm. |
| 28 October 1864 | JWB left Montreal. |
| 29 October 1864 | JWB signed a document in New York relating to the final disposition of his Pennsylvania oil properties. From NYC, Booth stopped in Baltimore and then on to Washington. |
| 1 November 1864 | Louis Weichmann moved into the Surratt boardinghouse. |
| 2 November 1864 | First hearing began for the St. Albans raiders. |
| 8 November 1864 | Election day, Lincoln defeated McClellan. |
| 9 November 1864 | JWB arrived at the National Hotel, Washington, DC. |
| 11 November 1864 | JWB left the National Hotel for "an early train" and traveled to lower Maryland to visit Dr. Queen near |

| | |
|---|---|
| | Bryantown with a letter of introduction from Martin (Canada); this was a Friday. |
| 12 November 1864 | JWB visited John C. Thompson, Charles County, Maryland. |
| 13 November 1864 | JWB was introduced to Dr. Mudd by Dr. Queen's son-in-law, John C. Thompson, at the St. Mary's Catholic Church. JWB went to the church with Dr. Queen and his family. He slept in Mudd's home that night. |
| 14 November 1864 | JWB returned to the National Hotel early evening. |
| 16 November 1864 | JWB deposited $1,500 in Jay Cooke & Company Bank in Washington, DC. JWB left the National Hotel for New York City to rehearse for *Julius Caesar* with his two brothers. JWB first arrived in Baltimore to met brother Junius and then continued to New York City. |
| 24 November 1864 | Maryland emancipated its slaves. |
| 25 November 1864 | JWB performed in Central Park with his brothers, Edwin and Junius, in *Julius Caesar*. |
| 27 November 1864 | JWB and his brothers, Edwin and Junius, were photographed together in their *Julius Caesar* costumes. |
| Late November 1864 | Powell escorted Captain Blazer to Libby Prison in Richmond unknown. JWB spent a few days in Philadelphia with his sister Asia; at that time, he gave her the "TO WHOM IT MAY CONCERN" letter. |
| 12 December 1864 | JWB arrived at the National Hotel. |
| 15 December 1864 | Colonel Edwin G. Lee, when en route to Montreal to take over the Confederate apparatus there, sent a communication from NASSAU to Secretary of War Seddon, requesting that Gabriel Edmondson of the "signal corps" be sent to him in Canada. |
| 17 December 1864 | JWB left the National Hotel "on a morning train" and spent the night at Dr. Queen's home. |
| 18 December 1864 | JWB met Mudd at St. Mary's Church and later met with Thomas Harbin and then later spent the night at the Mudd farm. |
| 19 December 1864 | JWB bought a one-eyed horse from George Gardiner. |
| 20 December 1864 | Thomas Gardiner delivered the horse to JWB at the Bryantown Tavern and rode back to Washington. Upon his return, Booth was accompanied by Ellen Starr. Booth did not check in to the National Hotel; instead he stayed with Starr at 62 Ohio Avenue, a bordello, operated by Mary Jane Treakle, Starr's sister. |

| | |
|---|---|
| 20 December 1864 | JWB cashed a check for $100 at Cooke's bank in the morning. |
| 21 December 1864 | Savannah fell to Sherman. |
| 22 December 1864 | JWB checked in at the National Hotel. |
| 23 December 1864 | Dr. Mudd arrived in Washington and checked in at the Pennsylvania House. He met with Booth at the National Hotel in the evening. They left the hotel together, meeting John Surratt on the street; Louis was present. |
| 24 December 1864 | JWB left the National Hotel for New York to be with his family for Christmas; on his way back to Washington, he met Samuel Arnold to buy a horse and buggy and to ship weapons to Washington. |
| 25 December 1864 | Powell saved the lives of two federal soldiers in Fauquier County, Virginia. |
| 30 December 1864 | JWB was known to be in Baltimore; he collected rent on the Harford Country Farm and signed receipt for this date. |
| 30 December 1864 | John Surratt took a job with the Adams Express Company. |
| 31 December 1864 | JWB arrived at the National Hotel. |
| ? December 1864 | General Edwin Gray Lee was sent to Canada to replace Jacob Thompson as Confederate representative to Canada. |
| 1 January 1865 | JWB entered the Surratt boardinghouse for the first time. This was also Anna Surratt's birthday. |
| 10 January 1865 | JWB left the National Hotel, his destination unknown. |
| 11 January 1865 | Second hearing began for five of the St. Albans raiders. |
| 12 January 1865 | JWB arrived at the National Hotel. |
| 13 January 1865 | John Surratt quit his job at the Adams Express Company. Lewis Powell (alias Paine) applied to provost marshal in Fairfax Country, Virginia, as a civilian refugee. He was sent to Alexandria and took the oath of allegiance. |
| 14 January 1864 | John Surratt met with Thomas Harbin in Port Tobacco. |
| ? January 1865 | John Surratt recruited George Atzerodt. |
| ? January 1865 | David Herold was recruited. |
| 20 January 1865 | JWB performed at Grover Theatre, Washington, in *Romeo and Juliet*; it was a benefit for Avonia Jones. |
| 21 January 1865 | John Surratt and Louis Weichmann arrived in Baltimore. |
| 22 January 1865 | John Surratt met Parr to introduce Powell in Baltimore. |
| 23 January 1865 | Powell sold a horse in Alexandria, Virginia, and went to Baltimore. |

| | |
|---|---|
| 24 January 1865 | General Edwin Lee arrived in Montreal and assumed control of CSA operations in Canada. |
| 28 January 1865 | JWB left the National Hotel for New York City in an attempt to recruit Samuel Chester; he returned in a few days. On his way to New York, he stopped in Philadelphia to pick up a sealed envelope and returned it to his sister on the return trip to Washington. |
| 31 January 1865 | Sarah Slater left Richmond for Montreal on her maiden trip as a courier. |
| 1 February 1865 | John Surratt checked in at the National Hotel. |
| 2 February 1865 | Sarah Slater met up with Gus Howell at Mattox Creek in Maryland. |
| 6 February 1865 | John Surratt was in Washington. |
| 7 February 1865 | The Holohan family moved in to the Surratt boardinghouse. |
| 9 February 1865 | JWB left Washington for Philadelphia and New York. |
| 10 February 1865 | JWB was in Philadelphia; he and Asia had their last meeting. |
| 13 February 1865 | JWB was in New York City; during his visit, JWB wrote a valentine to Lucy Hale. |
| 15 February 1865 | Sarah Slater arrived in Montreal; she registered at the St. Lawrence Hall. |
| 18 February 1865 | JWB left New York City according to Junius Booth Jr.'s diary entry. |
| 19 February 1865 | Gus Howell arrived at the Surratt house and stayed and waited for Sarah Slater's return. |
| 22 February 1865 | JWB arrived at the National Hotel. Sarah Slater arrived in Washington, escorted by John Surratt, and left immediately for Richmond with Howell. |
| 28 February 1865 | JWB left the National Hotel on a morning train. JWB met Powell in front of the Barnum Hotel for the first time in years. |
| Early March 1865 | Sarah Slater and Gus Howell left Richmond for Canada. |
| 1 March 1865 | JWB was assigned a room at the National Hotel. On March 2, 3, and 4, he was called at 8:00 AM by hotel staff. |
| 1 March 1865 | Powell was at the Surratt house. |
| 4 March 1865 | Lincoln's second inaugural. |
| Mid-March 1865 | Powell was living at the Herndon House, Washington. |
| 10 March 1865 | Sarah Slater arrived at the H Street boardinghouse of Mary Surratt on her way to Montreal. |

| 11 March 1865 | Sarah Slater left the Surratt boardinghouse for Montreal. |
|---|---|
| 12 March 1865 | Lewis Powell beat a black maid in Baltimore. |
| 13 March 1865 | JWB sent a telegram to O'Laughlen. |
| 14 March 1865 | John Surratt sent a telegram to David Preston Parr. |
| 14 March 1865 | Lewis Powell came out of jail after taking an oath of allegiance and went to Surratt boardinghouse. |
| 14 March 1865 | Arnold and O'Laughlen took a train to Washington from Baltimore. |
| 15 March 1865 | JWB reserved the presidential box at Ford's Theatre. John Surratt, Lewis Powell, Honora Fitzpatrick, and Mary Apollonia Dean attended the play *Jane Shore* that night. |
| 15 March 1865 | JWB held a general planning session with Arnold, O'Laughlin, Surratt, Atzerodt, Herold, and Powell for a meeting and for a midnight oyster dinner in a private room at Gautier's. |
| 17 March 1865 | JWB and conspirators attempted to kidnap Lincoln but failed when Lincoln was not there. |
| 17 March 1865 | Sarah Slater arrived in Montreal with dispatches from Richmond. |
| 18 March 1865 | JWB's last performance as an actor for the role Pescara in *The Apostate* at Ford's Theatre. |
| 20 March 1865 | Powell was in New York City at the Revere House Hotel. |
| 18 March 1865 | JWB's last performance at Ford's Theatre; it was a benefit performance for his friend John McCullough. |
| 18 March 1865 | John Surratt hid two carbines at the Surratt Tavern. |
| 19 March 1865 | Atzerodt moved into the Pennsylvania House in Washington. |
| 19 March 1865 | John Surratt saw Anna Ward and then Martha Murray about reserving a room for Powell on March 27. |
| 20 March 1865 | Arnold and O'Laughlin left Washington for Baltimore to find jobs. |
| 20 March 1865 | Powell was in New York City at the Revere House Hotel. |
| 21 March 1865 | JWB paid $50 on account and left the National Hotel on the 7:30 p.m. train headed for New York City with a stopover in Baltimore. |
| 22 March 1865 | JWB was in New York City for his brother Edwin's one hundredth performance of *Hamlet* at the Winter Garden. |

| | |
|---|---|
| 22 March 1865 | Sarah Slater left Montreal for Richmond with a letter from General Edwin Lee to Secretary Benjamin. She met Surratt in New York City, and he escorted her to Washington. |
| 23 March 1865 | Lincoln sailed to General Grant's headquarters at City Point on the *River Queen*. |
| 24 March 1865 | JWB arrived in Baltimore from New York City to see Arnold. JWB did not see him; Arnold was at his brother's farm. |
| 24 March 1865 | Arnold applied to J. W. Wharton at Old Point Comfort for a job. |
| 25 March 1865 | JWB was in Baltimore on his way to Washington and saw Arnold. Later he arrived at the National Hotel. |
| 25 March 1865 | Sarah Slater arrived in Washington and left the next morning with John Surratt for Richmond; for part of that day, Surratt was in Surrattville. They learned of Howell's arrest. |
| 25 March 1865 | Mary Lincoln's first tirade, this one with Mrs. Griffin. |
| 26 March 1865 | Mary Lincoln's second tirade, this one with Mrs. Ord. |
| 26 March 1865 | Slater left with John Surratt in Richmond from Surrattville. |
| 26 March 1865 | David Barry saw Mary Surratt and delivered a letter to her from John Surratt. |
| 27 March 1865 | Lewis Powell returned to Washington from a trip to New York City and checked in to the Herndon House under the alias of Kincheloe. |
| 27 March 1865 | Arnold sent Booth a letter from Baltimore. |
| 27 March 1865 | Sherman was at City Point and met with Lincoln and Grant. |
| 27/28 March 1865 | Lincoln on board the *River Queen* for conference with Grant, Sherman, and Porter. |
| 29 March 1865 | Surratt arrived in Richmond with Sarah Slater. |
| 30 March 1865 | Surratt was reimbursed ten twenty-dollar gold pieces for expenses to and from Montreal. Surratt was given a mission to return to Montreal with Slater with dispatches for depositing Confederate funds in English banks. |
| 1 April 1865 | Mrs. Lincoln returned to Washington alone. |
| 1 April 1865 | JWB left the National Hotel for a New York-Philadelphia train. |
| 1 April 1865 | Arnold accepted a position as clerk in a store in Old Point, Virginia. |

| | |
|---|---|
| 1 April 1865 | John Surratt and Sarah Slater left Richmond for Canada. |
| 1 April 1865 | Susan Mahoney, a black servant, was hired by Mary Surratt. |
| 2 April 1865 | The city of Richmond fell. President Jefferson Davis evacuated the city. |
| 3 April 1865 | General Edwin Lee began residency at the St. Lawrence Hall, Montreal. |
| 3 April 1865 | John Surratt returned to Washington. He heard about a detective at the boardinghouse asking about him. He slept in a hotel that night. |
| 4 April 1865 | JWB told members of his family that he was going to Boston. |
| 4 April 1865 | JWB was with a female in a Rhode Island hotel. |
| 4 April 1865 | Surratt and Sarah Slater left early for New York and then left New York that evening for Montreal by train. |
| 5 April 1865 | Secretary of State Seward had a carriage accident. |
| 5 April 1865 | Mary Lincoln with friends left Washington for City Point. |
| 5/6 April 1865 | JWB was in Boston. |
| 6 April 1865 | Mary Lincoln arrived at City Point about noon and visited Richmond without the president. |
| 6 April 1865 | John Surratt registered at the St. Lawrence Hall using the name John Harison and saw General Edwin Lee. |
| 7 April 1865 | President and Mrs. Lincoln and visitors visited Petersburg. |
| 7 April 1865 | JWB returned to New York City from Boston and had a conversation with Samuel Chester. |
| 8 April 1865 | Lincoln left City Point for Washington late that night. |
| 8 April 1865 | JWB arrived at the National Hotel. |
| 8 April 1865 | President and Mrs. Lincoln sailed from City Point. |
| 9 April 1865 | General Lee surrendered at Appromatox Courthouse. Lincoln arrived back in Washington about sunset. |
| 10 April 1865 | Sergeant Tomas Harney was captured by Union soldiers. |
| 10 April 1865 | Annie Ward shared a letter she received from John Surratt with Mary Surratt; JWB was at the house. |
| 11 April 1865 | Mary Surratt sent Weichmann to borrow JWB's carriage but did not have it and gave Weichmann $10 to rent a carriage. Mary then went to Surrattsville in the morning where she encountered Lloyd on the way. |

| | |
|---|---|
| 11 April 1865 | Lincoln gave his last speech from the balcony of the White House; JWB and Powell listened to it. JWB then stated that will be Lincoln's last speech. |
| 12 April 1865 | John Surratt left Montreal for Elmira, New York. |
| 13 April 1865 | John Surratt arrived in Elmira, New York. |
| 13 April 1865 | (Afternoon) JWB visited Grover's Theatre and asked about Lincoln's theater plans. |
| 13 April 1865 | General Grant arrived in Washington in the morning. |
| 13 April 1865 | Ten-year-old Mary Apollonia Dean left the Surratt boardinghouse for the Easter holidays. |
| 14 April 1865 | (2:00 a.m.) JWB wrote a letter to his mother. |
| | (8:00 a.m.) Atzerodt registered at the Kirkwood House; he seemed by the clerk between twelve and one there. |
| | (Early morning) JWB returned to National Hotel from staying the night with Ella Starr. He ate breakfast and had a shave at Charlie Wood's barbershop. |
| | (Mid-morning) JWB talked to Thomas R. Florence. He spoke of engagements in Canada and oil investments' loss. |
| | (11:00 a.m.) JWB was seen at the National Hotel. |
| | (11:00 a.m.) Lincoln's cabinet met with Grant; after the meeting, Grant told Lincoln that he is leaving that after to see his children in New Jersey. |
| | (11:30 a.m.) JWB learned that Lincoln and Grant will be at Ford's Theatre that night. |
| | JWB then went to Pumphrey stable to rent a horse. |
| | JWB then stopped at the Kirkwood House and wrote a note to Vice President Johnson. |
| | JWB then went to the Willard Hotel and saw Julia Grant. |
| | JWB then at the National Hotel, he ate lunch with Mrs. Hale. |
| | JWB then returned to the Kirkwood House to see if Johnson returned; he hadn't. |
| | (1:00 p.m.) Herold and Atzerodt were at Naylor's Stable. Herold rented a roan horse, and Atzerodt stabled a rented horse from another stable. |
| | (2:30 p.m.) JWB visited Mary Surratt. |
| | (3:00 p.m.) JWB was seen at the back entrance of Ford's Theatre. |

(3:10 p.m.) JWB was in the theater, with Maddox and Ferguson on the stage.

(3:30 p.m.) JWB was at the Star Tavern with Maddox and Ferguson.

JWB then left the Star Tavern and started for Pumphrey's stable.

JWB met Joseph Hazelton, talked with him for a moment, and gave him money for a stick of candy.

JWB stopped at Grover's Theatre and wrote a letter, presumably the one he gave to Matthews.

JWB left Grover's and went to Pumphrey's stable.

JWB left Pumphrey's and met Charles Warwick on the street (Reck and Asia Clarke).

JWB chatted briefly with James Maddox in front of Ford's Theatre.

(About 4:00 p.m.) Booth saw John Mathews and gave him a letter he wrote for the *National Intelligencer*.

JWB saw the Grants' carriage and galloped after it and saw General and Mrs. Grant.

JWB went to the Willard Hotel and confirmed that the Grants are leaving.

(Between 5:00-6:00 p.m.) JWB talked with John Devenay at the Kirkwood House. He left and went to Ford's Theatre and entered the theater to get a halter from Spangler.

Then JWB and Spangler put halter on the horse.

Then JWB, Peanuts John, Maddox, and Spangler drank at the restaurant next door to Ford's.

(Sometime after 5:00 p.m.) JWB was at the National Hotel; he saw Lucy Hale alone in the parlor.

(4:15 p.m.) Herold returned to Naylor's and picked up the roan horse.

(6:30 p.m.) JWB was at National Hotel for dinner with Lucy, Senator, and Mrs. Hale and Mrs. Temple and then went to his room.

(About 6:45 p.m.) Atzerodt returned to Naylor's, talked to Fletcher about another night's rental for his room, and left.

(7:00 p.m.) JWB left the National Hotel. Atzerodt returned to Naylor's stable and saddled his horse.

(7:30 p.m.) Atzerodt returned to Naylor's and requested Fletcher not to take off the saddle or bridle.

(7:30 p.m.) JWB had a drink with William Withers. (8:00 p.m.) JWB met with Herold, Powell, and Atzerodt at the Herndon House.

Then JWB went to the Star Saloon next to Ford's Theatre.

Then JWB came in and out of Ford's Theatre many times before the assassination; on one of these trips, JWB went to the stable and got his horse.

(10:00 p.m.) Atzerodt came for his horse.

(10:22 p.m.) JWB shot Lincoln.

(11:00 p.m.) Herold caught up with Booth near Soper's Hill, and the two rode to the Surratt Tavern.

15 April 1865     John Surratt learned of the assassination, thought of JWB and his connection to him, caught a train for Canandaigua, New York, and spent the night at the Webster House.

15 April 1865     JWB and Herold left Mudd's farm early evening. (At 9:00 p. m., JWB and DH got lost and met Oswald Swann.)

16 April 1865     (After midnight) JWB and DH arrived at Cox's farm guided by Swann.

16 April 1865     Jones visited JWB for the first time; he would help JWB for the next six days and five nights. During this time, JWB wrote his first diary entry.

17 April 1865     John Surratt left for Rouses Point and crossed into Canada. He registered at the St. Lawrence Hall as John Harrison.

17 April 1865     O'Laughlin was arrested in Baltimore.

17 April 1865     James A. McDevitt, John Holohan, and Weichmann left Washington for Canada in search of John Surratt.

18 April 1865     John Surratt registered again at the St. Lawrence Hall, Montreal.

19 April 1865     Funeral services were done for Lincoln in the East Room of the White House.

20 April 1865     George Atzerodt was arrested in Germantown, Maryland, at 4:00 a.m.

21 April 1865     Dr. Samuel Mudd was arrested at his farm.

21 April 1865     JWB crossed the Potomac River that night, got lost, and landed near John Hughes's farm. He made his second entry into his diary.

22 April 1865     JWB tried a second time to cross the Potomac River, this time crossed the river.

| | |
|---|---|
| 23 April 1865 | JWB landed near Quesenberry farm in the early morning hours. He was told by Harbin that Bryant will take them to Dr. Stuart's farm. JWB refused aid by Stuart and was taken to William Lucas's house. He threw the black couple out of the house and slept the night there. |
| 24 April 1865 | JWB was taken by Charles Lucas to Port Conway where he met Jett, Brainbridge, and Ruggles. |
| 24 April 1865 | Booth slept at the Garret farm in a bed. Herold slept at the home of Joseph Clarke, a friend of Bainbridge; during the day, Herold is at the Star Hotel. Lieutenant Doherty assembled cavalry in search of Booth. Lieutenant Doherty disembarked from the John S. Ide at Belle Plain Landing and began search of Booth at 10:00 p.m. |
| 25 April 1865 | JWB was asked to leave the Garrett farm, but he stayed for the night in the barn. Federal troops arrived, and JWB was killed. |
| 28 April 1865 | Gabriel Edmondson was paroled at Winchester, Virginia. He returned to Washington and had been listed in city directories after 1866. |
| 28 April 1865 | Powell, Atzerodt, Spangler, Herold, Arnold, Dr. Mudd, and O'Laughlen were transferred from the boat to the Old Penitentiary at the U.S. Arsenal. |
| 30 April 1865 | Mary Surratt was transferred from the Old Capitol Prison to the Old Penitentiary. |
| 16 September 1865 | John Surratt was on a ship from Quebec to England. |
| 27 November 1866 | John Surratt was captured in Alexandria, Egypt. |
| 19 February 1867 | John Surratt arrived in Washington, DC, to stand trial. |
| 10 June 1867 | John Surratt's trial began; sixty-two days later, a hung jury caused a mistrial. |
| 21 March 1869 | President Johnson pardoned the remaining conspirators. |
| 26 June 1869 | JWB finally was buried at the Green Mount Cemetery in Baltimore. |
| 6 December 1870 | John Surratt gave a public lecture in Rockville, Maryland. |

# ENDNOTES

1   The *Charleston Mercury* sums up the emotional feelings of the press in the secessionist states:

> If this were the beginning of our difficulties in the South, if our present position of embarrassment and danger were not the result of years of accumulated aggression and wrong, there might be some hope of a favorable change . . . But the distemper of the times has been gathering virulence through twenty years of progress and agitation. It has been fed by the strongest passions of our nature, and nurtured by the meanest. It has obliterated all the old party lines, which stood for a half century dividing the opinion of the country. The last to perish . . . was the Democratic party. That too has fallen. One by one all its cardinal principles have been surrendered in the North to an absorbing sectionalism. And now the South stands alone . . . before her a united North banded together against her rights and interests, threatening dangers. . . . The Northern people have forced upon us the conviction, reluctantly and slowly attained, that no submission on our part can win their forbearance, and no rights escape their violation, and that our safety rests in ourselves (Editorial, *Charleston Mercury*, June 7, 1860).

2   *Richmond Enquirer*, November 19, 1860.

3   Avery Craven, "Southern Attitudes toward Abraham Lincoln," November 6, 1860.

4   Craven, "Southern Attitudes toward Abraham Lincoln," November 12, 1860.

5   Edmund Ruffin, *Diary of Edmund Ruffin*, ed. William Kauffman Scarborough (Baton Rogue: Louisiana State University Press, 1972), entry for May 21, 1860.

6   The writ of habeas corpus (Latin for "you are to bring the body"), used since medieval times, required a person taken into custody to be brought before the court. The Magna Carta (1215) set forth concepts of due process of law and was later interpreted as including habeas corpus. Habeas corpus as we know it developed over time from principles of due process in English common law.

7   Harold M. Hyman, *A More Perfect Union: The Impact of the Civil War and Reconstruction on the Constitution* (Boston: Houghton Mifflin, 1973), 84-87; *Ex parte Merryman*, 17 Federal Case no. 0487, 1861. Taney quoted article 1, section 9 of the U.S. Constitution, which states, "The privilege of the writ of habeas corpus shall not be suspended, unless when, in cases of rebellion or invasion, the public safety may require it."

8   Robert S. Harper, *Lincoln and the Press* (New York: McGraw Hill, 1951), 151-52; Mahony was later nominated for Congress by the Democrats in his Iowa District, but he was defeated for the elected office (*Pen and Powder* [1888], 9-10). Mahony was arrested on August 14, 1862, at his residence in Dubuque, Iowa. He was released from the Old Capitol Prison in Washington on November 11, 1862, after signing "an oath, both of allegiance to the Government, and an obligation not to prosecute the Federal or state officers concerned in their arrest and imprisonment" (John A. Marshall, see the chapter on "Dennis A. Mahony," in *American Bastille* [Philadelphia: Evans, Stoddard, 1870], 403-416).

9   Noah Brooks, *Washington, D.C., in Lincoln's Time*, reprint (Athens, GA: University of Georgia, 1989), 106-111. Noah Brooks was a newspaper correspondent in his twenties, who personally knew Lincoln and spoke to him frequently.

10  Vallandigham, *Century Magazine*, May 1889.

11  *The Collected Works of Abraham Lincoln* (New Brunswick, NJ, 1953-1955), 9:260-269; also see *Century Magazine*, May 1889, 127-137 for a more detailed discussion of the legal arguments used in the Vallandigham case.

Gideon Welles wrote about Vallandigham in his diary. These notes reflect the feelings Wells had about arbitrary military arrests of civilians:

> The arrest of Vallandigham and the order to suppress the circulation of the Chicago Times in his military district issued by General Burnside, have created much [ill] feeling . . . . The proceedings were arbitrary and injudicious. It gives bad men the right of questions and advantage of which they avail themselves. Good men, who wish to support the Administration, find it difficult to defend these acts . . . . The President – and I think every member of the Cabinet – regrets what has been done, but as to the measures which should now be taken there are probably differences.
>
> The constitutional rights of the parties injured are undoubtedly infringed upon. It is claimed, however, that the Constitution, laws, and authorities are assailed with a view to their destruction by the Rebels, with whom Vallandigham and the Chicago Times are in sympathy and concert. The efforts of the Rebels are directed to the overthrow of the government, and Vallandigham and his associates unite with them in waging war against the constituted authorities. Should the government, and those who are called to legally administer it, be sustained, or should those who are striving to destroy both? There are many important and difficult problems to solve, growing out of the present condition of affairs . . . . A state of war exists; violent and forcible measures are resorted to in order to resist and destroy the

government, which have begotten violent and forcible measures to vindicate and restore its peaceful operation. Vallandigham and the Chicago Times claim all the benefits, guarantees, and protection of the government which they are assisting the Rebels to destroy. Without the courage and manliness to go over to the public enemy, to who they give, so far as they dare, aid and comfort, they remain here to promote discontent and disaffection.

While I have no sympathy for those who are, in their hearts, as unprincipled traitors as Jefferson Davis, I lament that our military officers should, without absolute necessity, disregard those great principles on which our government and institutions rest" (Gideon Welles, *Diary of Gideon Welles*, ed. Howard K. Beale, 3 vols. [1911; 1960, rev. ed.; 1991, repr.] 2:321-322, Wednesday, June 3, 1863, entry).

## FORMER PRESIDENT FRANKLIN PIERCE

In July 4, 1863 speech, Franklin Pierce, a former President of the United States, said that in states not actually experiencing the "ravages of war . . . the mailed hand of military usurpation strikes down the liberties of the people, and its foot tramples on a desecrated Constitution. Ay, in this land of free thought, free speech, and free writing – in this republic of free suffrage, with liberty of thought and expression as the very essence of republican institution-even here, in these free States, it is made criminal for that noble martyr of free speech, Mr. Vallandigham, to discuss public affairs in Ohio, even here, the temporary agents of the sovereign people, the transitory administrators of the government, tell us that in time of war the mere arbitrary will of the President takes the place of the Constitution, and President himself announces to us that it is treasonable to speak or to write otherwise than as he may prescribe (As quoted in Horace Greeley, *The American Conflict* [Hartford: O.D. Case, 1866], 2:497-498).

[12] Horatio Seymour

Horatio Seymour, republican governor of New York, wrote that those who differed "honestly, patriotically, sincerely, from [the Administration] with regard to the line of duty, are not men of treasonable purposes and enemies to our country." Governor Seymour went on to say, "If we agree that 'in times of war, Constitutions are suspended, and laws have lost their force, then we should accept a doctrine that the very right by which this Government administers its power has lost its virtue, and we would be brought down to the level of rebellion itself." The governor concluded his speech by asking the audience, "Shall we do as our fathers did under circumstances of like trial, when they combated against the powers of a crown? They did not say that liberty was suspended; that men might be deprived of the right of trial by jury; that they might be torn from their homes by midnight intruders." Horace Greely notes here tremendous and continued applause.

"If the public permits its constitutional liberties to be suspended," exclaim the lawyer and constitutionalist George Ticknor Curtis of Massachusetts, "it 'will be an end of this experiment of self-government." (Frank Freidel, ed., *Union Pamphlets of the Civil War* [Cambridge, MA: Belknap Press of Harvard University Press, 1967], 1:537).

*The War of the Rebellion: A Compilation of the Official Records of the Union and Confederate Armies*, 2nd ser. (Washington, DC: Government Printing Office, 1880-1901), 7:543-49.

13    Allan Nevins and Milton Halsey, eds. *The Diary of George Templeton Strong* (New York: Macmillan, 1952), 3:204.

14    Rufus Rockwell Wilson, *Lincoln among His Friends* (Caldwell, Idaho: Caxton Printers, 1942), 243.

15    Maria Lydia Daly, *Diary of a Union Lady*, ed. Harold Earl Hammond (1861-1865; New York: Funk & Wagnalls, 1962), 160.

16    Daly, *Diary of a Union Lady*, 240-241.

17    Freidel, *Union Pamphlets of Civil War*, 2:639.

18    "What Are We Fighting For?" *Old Guard*, April, 1864, 75-77; for similar rhetoric, see "The Infamous Message and Proclamation," January 1864, 15-17; and February 1864 issue. Burr was the editor from January 1863 to 1869.

19    *Old Guard*, May, 1864, 119.

20    Ibid., 224-225; also see Joseph George Jr., "'Abraham Africanus I': President Lincoln through the Eyes of a Copperhead Editor," *Civil War History*, September 14, 1968, 226-36.

21    Harper, *Lincoln and the Press*, 151-52.

22    John S. Rock, a black man, was admitted to the bar of the Supreme Court on February 1, 1865; his advocate and sponsor was Senator Charles Sumner of Massachusetts. William Wilkins Glenn, *Between North and South: A Maryland Journalist Views the Civil War*, ed. Bayly Ellen Marks and Mark Norton Schatz (Rutherford: Fairleigh Dickinson University Press, 1976) 145.

23    Army, Official Records, 1st ser., 14, p. 599.

24    Anna Ridgely, "A Girl in the Sixties: Excerpts from the Journal of Anna Ridgely," *Journal of the Illinois State Historical Society* 22 (October 22, 1929): 437-438.

25    Frank L. Klement, "A Small-Town Editor Criticizes Lincoln: A Study in Editorial Abuse", *Lincoln Herald* 54 (Summer 1952): 27-32.

26    Mark E. Neely, "The Lincoln Theme Since Randall's Call: The Promises and Perils of Professionalism," *Abraham Lincoln Association Papers*, 19-21.

27    Salmon P. Chase, *Inside Lincoln's Cabinet: The Civil War Diaries of Salmon P. Chase*, 24-27.

28    Benn Pitman, *The Assassination of President Lincoln and the Trial of the Conspirators*, ed. Philip Van Doren Stern (1865; New York: Funk and Wagnalls, 1954), 28.

29    David C. Mearns, *The Lincoln Papers* (New York: Doubleday& Company), 354-355; Mearns was director of the Reference Department of the Library of Congress and charged with the custody of the library's Lincoln collection.

30    John Hay, *Lincoln and the Civil War: In the Diaries and Letters of John Hay*, ed. Tyler Dennett, 2, entry for April 18, 1861.

Ficklin mentioned by Ms. Davenport has never been identified. However, a Benjamin F. Ficklin does appear in the *Investigation and Trial Papers Relating to the Assassination of President Lincoln.* In a letter from A. E. Fitzpatrick of Philadelphia, Ficklin is described as having "the ability to plan and the courage to carry out the villainous act just consummated." The writer of the letter claimed "that he goes by James Ficklin in Richmond" and was a successful blockade-runner. Arrested on April 16, 1865, Ficklin denied any connection with the assassination and was released on June 16, 1865 (*Investigation and Trial Papers Relating to the Assassination of President Lincoln,* microfilm M599, reel 7, file 51, frame 220-222, National Archives).

31  Frederic Bancroft, *The Life of William H. Seward,* 2 vols., (1900; 1967, repr.) 418; the letter was dated July 15, 1862.

32  Harold Holzer, *Dear Mr. Lincoln: Letters to the President* (Addison-Wesley Publishing, 1993).

33  Written by R. S. Bassett, October 17, 1860, from Mearns, *Lincoln Papers,* 293.

34  Seymour Ketchum to Abraham Lincoln, *Lincoln MSS,* November 2, 1864, from Library of Congress as quoted in David Donald, *Lincoln,* 549.

35  Written by Joseph Lee, Salem, Massachusetts, October 13, 1860; Holzer, *Dear Mr. Lincoln.*

36  Written by F. R. Shoemaker from Mearns, *Lincoln Papers,* 294.

37  Written by Joseph I. Irwin, November 12, 1860, from Mearns, *Lincoln Papers,* 307.

38  Wilson, *Lincoln among His Friends* (1942), What a Reporter Saw and Recorded, Henry Villard, 243.

39  Francis B. Carpenter, *Six Months at the White House with Abraham Lincoln* (New York: Hurd and Houghton, 1866), 62, 75.

40  Charles A. Dana, *Recollections of the Civil War* (New York: D. Appleton, 1898), 278.

41  Mearns, *Lincoln Papers,* 293.

42  Edward Neill, *Lincoln and His Mailbag: Two Documents,* 15, 41.

43  John Nicolay and John Hay, *Abraham Lincoln: A History,* 10 vols. (New York: Century, 1890), 10:286-287; the vice president had a reputation of more radical views than Lincoln.

44  Elizabeth Keckley, *Behind the Scenes: Or Thirty Years a Slave, and Four Years in the White House* (1868; repr., Buffalo, NY: Stansil & Lee, 1931), 118-121.

45  Leonard Swett, "The Conspiracies of the Rebellion," *North American Review,* February 1887, 187-188.

46  Holzer, *Dear Mr. Lincoln,* 359.

47  House of Representatives, *Assassination of Lincoln,* 39th Cong., 1st sess., Rep. 104, July 28, 1866, 21-22.

48  House of Representatives, *Assassination of Lincoln,* 22-23; John B. Jones, *A Rebel War Clerk's Diary,* ed. Earl Schenck Miers (New York: Old Hickory Bookshop, 1935), 264.

49  Stanton to Seddon, August 9, 1863, "Letters Received by the Confederate Secretary of War," file 518-S-1863, RG 109, National Archives; Seddon's response was sent August 17, 1863.

50   *Investigation and Trial Papers*, M599, roll 3, frame 23-26.

51   House of Representatives, *Alleged Hostile Organization against the Government within the District of Columbia*, 36th Cong., 2nd. sess., Rep. 79, February 14, 1861, 178 pages. "Resolved, That the select committee of five be instructed to inquire whether any secret organization hostile to the Government of the United States exists in the District of Columbia; and, if so, whether any official or employees of the Federal Government in the executive or judicial departments are members thereof."

52   Abraham Lincoln, *Collected Works of Abraham Lincoln*, ed. Ray P. Basler, 9 vols. (New Brunswick: Rutgers University Press, 1953), 4:190. There are three versions of Lincoln's speech – the version used appears in Lincoln's and Nicolay's handwriting, and the other two versions appeared in print.

53   Mearns, *Lincoln Papers*, 1:295-296; the letter was signed P. W. Curtenius, Adjt. Genl. M. M.

54   Ibid., 360.

55   Ibid., 359.

56   Ibid., 2: 358.

57   Ibid., 355-357; letter dated Washington, December 26, 1860.

58   Ibid., 398; E. B. Washburne was later appointed secretary of state in the Grant administration.

59   Later wrote under the pen name of Miles O'Reilly.

60   George S. Bryan, *The Great American Myth* (New York: Carrick & Evans, 1940), 61.

61   General Wadsworth, military commander of the District of Columbia, assigned the unit to Lincoln.

62   Charles Graham Halpine, *Baked Meats of the Funeral. A Collection of Essays, Poems, Speeches, Histories, and Banquets* (New York: Carleton, 1866), 108.

63   Smith Stimmel, "Experiences as a Member of President Lincoln's Bodyguard," *North Dakota Historical Quarterly*, January 1927, 9-10; this unit was also known as the Sixth Independent Troop, Ohio Calvary.

64   Benjamin Thomas and Harold Hyman, *Stanton: The Life and Times of Lincoln's Secretary of War*, 393-395; Bryan, *Great American Myth*, 66.

65   Stimmel, "Lincoln's Bodyguard," 13.

66   "Guarding Mr. Lincoln," *Surratt Courier Newsletter*, March, 1987; this is a reprint of an article originally published on April 28, 1888, in the *Ohio Soldier*, Chilicothie, Ohio.

67   Ward Lamon, *Recollections of Abraham Lincoln, 1847-1865*, ed. Dorothy Lamon Teillard, 258-276.

68   Holzer, *Dear Mr. Lincoln: Letters to the President*, 359.

69   Ibid., 336.

70   Gideon Welles, *Recollections of Events Immediately Preceding and Following the Assassination and Death of Lincoln* n.d.,ca. 1870, manuscript, Welles Papers, Huntington Library, San Marino, CA.

71   William O. Stoddard, *Inside the White House in War Times: Memoirs and Reports of Lincoln's Secretary* (New York: Charles L. Webster, 1890), 30-31.

72   Holzer, "Threats and Warnings," in *Dear Mr. Lincoln: Letters to the President*.

[73] Marie De Mare, "When Lincoln Posed," *New York Times Magazine* Section, May 9, 1937, 10.

[74] Carpenter, *Six Months at White House,* 62-63.

[75] Halpine, *Baked Meats of Funeral,* 108; Halpine has been described as a satirist and commentator on literary, military, and political affairs; an aide to General David Hunter and on General Halleck's staff; and a friend of Lincoln. Charles Halpine had been at the White House that day for presidential signatures on papers he had brought over from General Halleck's office. Halpine writes that the entire conversation "had probably not endured over ten or fifteen minutes; and it was the first, although not the only time, that I heard Mr. Lincoln discuss the possibility of an attempt to assassinate him."

[76] *Come Retribution: The Confederate Secret Service and the Assassination of Lincoln,* 234; who quoted an undated 1864 Beaver Dam Argus (Wisconsin) article.

[77] Pitman, *Assassination of President Lincoln,* 52.

[78] Henry T. Louthan, "A Proposed Abduction of Lincoln," *Confederate Veteran,* June 1908, 157-158; William Hanchett, "The Happiest Day of His Life," *Civil War Times,* November/December 1995; also see Davis to Taylor, August 31, 1889, C. Seymour Bullock MSS, Southern Historical Collection, University of North Carolina.

[79] Varina Howell Davis to Henry T. Loutham, May 10, 1898, Jefferson Davis MSS, University of Alabama.

[80] Joseph George Jr. "Black Flag Warfare: Lincoln and the Raids against Richmond and Jefferson Davis," *Pennsylvania Magazine of History and Biography* 115 (July 1991): 291-318.

[81] William W. Goldsborough, *The Maryland Line in the Confederate Army* (repr., Gaithersburg, MD: Butternut Press), 203.

[82] Sources for the proposed Johnson raid, William W. Goldsborough, *The Maryland Line in the Confederate Army,* was first published in 1869 by Kelly, Piet & Co. (Baltimore, 246-248) and revised in 1900 by Goldsborough; Butternut Press (Gaithersburg, Maryland) reprinted an edition in 1983 (203-208); Bradley Johnson in volume 2 of the twelve-volume *Confederate Military History,* published by Confederate Publishing Co. (Atlanta, 1899); George Booth, *Illustrated Souvenir of the Maryland Line Confederate Soldiers' Home* (1894); Bradley Johnson, "My Ride Around Baltimore in Eighteen Hundred and Sixty-Four," *Cavalry Journal* (September 1889): 250-260; *Surratt Society News,* March 1981. Also Irving Ditty, who was to command a company in the raid, testified before a congressional committee investigating the Hayes-Tilden election controversy and confirmed Johnson's story; he testified that "General Bradley Johnson gave me an intimation that there was to be a movement of very great interest. He would not tell me what it was precisely, but I have since learned from him and a book which he wrote that the intention was that a detail of picked men and horses, taken from my regiment, was to be sent to capture Mr. Lincoln between the White House and the Soldiers Home, and I believe that I was to have been sent with that detail. But the battle of Trevelyan's Depot interfered with the operation, and the order never was given (House of Representatives, *Miscellaneous Document 42,* 44th Cong., 2nd sess., February 1, 1877, 275).

It should be noted that Goldsborough first published this account in 1869; and Jefferson Davis, Robert I. Lee, Jubal A. Early, Wade Hampton, and Bradley T. Johnson, all were still living to read and dispute Goldsborough's account. None of the above individuals ever disputed Goldsborough.

[83] David Donald, letter from Lizzie W. S., dated July 1864, *Lincoln*, 548, original in *Lincoln MSS*, Library of Congress.

[84] Stimmel, "Lincoln's Bodyguard," 10. The soldiers' home was "on a slightly elevated plot of ground, well shaded by a beautiful grove. It was a pleasant country place, where the President could get a good night's rest."

[85] Interview with John W. Nichols, *Cincinnati Enquirer*, August 15, 1885, 12; "A Narrow Escape of Lincoln," *New York Tribune*, August 16, 1885; and John A. Logan, *The Great Conspiracy* (New York: A. R. Hart, 1886), 646n-47n, dated it August 1864.

Footnote: Lamon wrote, "One morning, however, in the month of August he came riding up to the White House steps, where I met him, . . . he said, "I have something to tell you!" The following is a retelling by Lincoln to Lamon of what happened the previous night. As a preface to narrative Lamon admits "At this distance of time I will not pretend to give the exact words of this interview, but will state it according to my best recollection."

Lamon quoted Lincoln as saying,

Last night, about 11 o'clock, I went out to the Soldiers' Home alone, riding Old Abe, as you call him [a horse he delighted in riding], (this is Lamon's insert) and when I arrived at the foot of the hill on the road leading to the entrance of the Home grounds, I was jogging along at a slow gait, immersed in deep thought, contemplating what was next to happen in the unsettled state of affairs, when suddenly I was aroused-I may say the arousement lifted me out of my saddle as well as out of my wits-by the report of a rifle, and seemingly the gunner was not fifty yards from where my contemplation ended and my accelerated transit began. My erratic namesake, with little warning, gave proof of decided dissatisfaction at the racket, and with one reckless bound he unceremoniously separated me from my eight-dollar plug-hat, with which I parted company without any assent, expressed or implied, upon my part. At a break-neck speed we soon arrived in a haven of safety. Meanwhile I was left in doubt whether death was more desirable from being thrown from a runaway federal horse, or as the tragic result of a rifle-ball fired by a disloyal bushwhacker in the middle of the night.

This was all told in a spirit of levity; he seemed unwilling, even in appearance, to attach that importance to the event which I was disposed to give to it . . . . I have about concluded that the shot was the result of accident . . . . No good can result at this time from giving it publicity.

However, Lamon wrote a few pages later, "It was impossible, however, to induce him to forego these lonely and dangerous journeys between the Executive Mansion and the Soldiers' Home. A stranger to fear, he often eluded our vigilance; and before his absence could be noted he would be well on his way to his summer residence, alone, and many times at night." However, after that August night, Lincoln never rode alone again. (The *Recollections of Abraham Lincoln* by Ward Hill Lamon was edited by his daughter Dorothy Teillard. Ms. Teillard placed the shooting incident in August 1862, and Nichols places the shooting in August 1864; the 1864 date is probably more accurate because Lincoln never rode alone after this incident [267-270]).

[86] Robert W. McBride, "Lincoln's Body Guard, the Union Light Guard of Ohio," *Indiana Historical Society Publication*, vol. 5 (1911): 20-21; in *Indiana Magazine of History*, December 1911, 143-144; Lamon, *Recollections of Abraham Lincoln*, 265.

[87] Leonard Swett, "Conspiracies of the Rebellion," 178-189; Swett was a house guest of Lamon at the time.

[88] William H. Crook, *Through Five Administrations: Reminiscences of Colonel William H. Crook*, comp. and ed. Margarita Spalding Gerry (New York: Harper & Brothers, 1910), 1-2.

[89] Crook, *Through Five Administrations*, 4; Crook went on to explain the necessarily behind the police bodyguards. He wrote:

> The reasons why the friends of Mr. Lincoln insisted on this precaution were almost as evident than as they became later. Marshal Ward Lamon and Secretary Stanton had been begging him, it is reported, since 1862 not to go abroad without protection of some kind. Mr. Lamon is on record as having said that he was especially fearful of the President's showing himself at the theatre. He considered that a public place of amusement offered an opportunity for assassination even more favorable than Mr. Lincoln's solitary walks or the occasional drive or horseback ride he took to the Soldiers' Home. Mr. Stanton is known to have been angered by a lack of caution which, on the part of a man so indispensable to the welfare of the nation as its President, he regarded as foolhardines . . . . He hated being on his guard, and the fact that it was necessary to distrust his fellow Americans saddened him . . . . But toward the end of 1864 so much pressure was brought to bear on him, particularly by Marshal Lamon and Secretary Stanton, that he finally yielded . . . . He told Lamon of a shot that had barely missed him one day when he was riding to the Soldiers' Home. (the incident at the Soldiers' Home was in August 1864 and William Crook did not arrived at the White House until January, 1865. Apparently Crook was told of this incident second hand, probably by Lamon or Lincoln perhaps on one of their nightly walks to the War Department.) Conspiracies to abduct or assassinate the President were constantly being rumored. At first he contended that if any one wanted to murder him no precaution would avail. Finally, although he was always

more or less of this opinion, the President gave way to the anxieties of those near to him (Crook, *Through Five Administrations,* 2-3).

[90] Nicolay and Hay, *Abraham Lincoln,* 10:286. Of Lincoln's attitude about assassination and security, they wrote:

> Although he freely discussed with the officials about him the possibilities of danger, he always considered them remote, as is the habit of men constitutionally brave, and positively refused to torment himself with precautions for his own safety. He would sum the matter up by saying that both friends and strangers must have daily access to him in all manner of ways and places; his life was therefore in reach of any one, sane or mad, who was ready to murder and be hanged for it; that he could not possibly guard against all danger unless he were to shut himself up in an iron box, in which condition he could scarcely perform the duties of a President; by the had of a murderer he could die only once; to go continually in fear would be to die over and over. He therefore went in and out before the people, always unarmed, generally unattended. He would receive hundreds of visitors in a day, his breast bare to pistol or knife. He would walk at midnight, with a single secretary or alone, from the Executive Mansion to the War Department and back. He would ride through the lonely roads of an uninhabited suburb from the White House to the Soldiers' Home in the dusk of evening, and return to his work in the morning before the town was astir. He was greatly annoyed when it was decided that there must be a guard stationed at the Executive Mansion, and that a squad of cavalry must accompany him on his daily ride; but he was always reasonable and yielded to the best judgment of others (Nicolay and Hay, *Abraham Lincoln,* 10:288).

[91] Pitman, *Assassination of President Lincoln,* 51; this incident was also mentioned by Nicolay and Hay in their ten-volume work *Abraham Lincoln: A History* (1890, 10:287).

[92] Otto Eisenschiml, "Did He, Too, Try to Kill Lincoln?," *Lincoln Herald,* June, 1946, 30-33.

[93] In 1907, Ripley published *Memoirs of the Capture and Occupation of Richmond, April 3, 1865* (New York: G. P. Putnam's Sons, 1907, 23, Library of Congress, Rare Book Room).

[94] Ripley, *Memoirs of Richmond,* 23.

[95] Ibid., 23-24.

[96] Ibid., 25; also see Donald C. Pfanz, *Abraham Lincoln at City Point* (Lynchburg, VA: H. E. Howard, 1989), 69.

It is speculated that there was a bombing plot involving Sergeant Thomas F. Harney. Thomas F. Harney, a Pennsylvanian teacher, enlisted May 1, 1962, at Corinth, Mississippi. He was wounded in October but recovered, and he returned to his unit only to be captured two months later. He was sent to the Gratiot Street Prison in St. Louis; and on June 2, 1863, he was exchanged.

General Rains apparently recruited him, and he was sent to Mississippi. Rains signed a requisition for a horse for Harney at Brandon, Mississippi, on July 12, 1863. (*Unfiled Papers and Slips Belonging in Confederate Compiled Service Records*, M347, reel 169, NA; this is a small sheet of paper which shows the requisition of the horse.) On Rains's staff, Harney worked in Charleston and Mobile in 1864. In June, he mined the James River at Richmond. In July, he was again sent to Charleston. (Biographical data from Tidwell and others, *Come Retribution*, no documentation given except for the requisition of a horse.)

At the end of March 1865, Harney worked in Richmond at the Torpedo Bureau. Just before Richmond was evacuated, Harney joined Mosby in Fauquier County. Upon his arrival at Mosby's headquarters, Harney was assigned to Company H, commanded by Captain George B. Baylor. Company H left Upperville, Fauquier County, on April 8, 1865, for Washington; and in two days, they were near Burke Station in Fairfax County, fifteen miles outside Washington. Here they were attacked by a detachment from the Eighth Illinois Cavalry under Colonel Charles Albright, and Harney and the three others were captured in the skirmish. On April 12, the four were brought to Old Capitol Prison in Washington. Colonel Albright's report of April 10, 1865, showed that Harney "brought ordnance to Colonel Mosby and joined his command." The *Washington Daily Morning Chronicle* for April 11, 1865, carried a little story about the Burke Station fight and quoted the prisoners as saying they had joined Mosby "from the army of Lee" a few days before.

The authors of *Come Retribution* argue that Harney was sent to assassinate Lincoln. *Mosby's Rangers* (New York: Simon and Schuster, 1990), 283. Addressing the issue of Mosby aiding Harney in an assassination attempt on Lincoln, Jeffrey D. Wert wrote, "The authors (Tidwell et al) argue that when the 8th Illinois Cavalry captured Thomas Harney of the Torpedo Bureau on April 10 at Burke Station the troopers foiled a plot to blow up the White House. Tidwell, et al writes that 'Harney had been sent to Mosby for passage through Union lines. It was a secret mission, but it could be reasonably argued that Mosby knew of the purpose.' If so," concluded Wert, "*it is out of character for the man and the officer.* Neither he nor any of his men, who wrote rather voluminously about their exploits, ever hinted of any link to the Booth plots. Until solid proof is forth coming, the case is unproven."

[97] Lamon, *Recollections of Abraham Lincoln*, 47.

[98] Nicolay and Hay, *Abraham Lincoln*, 289.

[99] Noah Brooks, *Washington, D.C. in Lincoln's Time*, 43-44.

[100] Breckinridge received Maryland's electoral votes.

[101] Allan Pinkerton (born in Glasgow, Scotland, August 25, 1819, and died on July 1, 1884) arrived in the United States in 1842 from Scotland and settled in Dundee, Illinois. He started as a barrel maker and became successful. One day in the forest while looking for trees to cut down for his business, he came upon a counterfeiting operation. He reported this group and helped capture the counterfeiting ring. Pinkerton was

subsequently asked by people in the town to do more detective work, and from this background, he was asked to become deputy sheriff, first in Kane and later in Cook County, Illinois. Soon he accepted an invitation to go to Chicago to join the Chicago police force as its first and only plainclothes detective. In 1850, Pinkerton went into detective work for himself as Pinkerton's North Western Police Agency. Railroads plagued by freight thefts in Illinois asked Pinkerton to set up a protective system. In 1855, Pinkerton started a new agency called Pinkerton's National Detective Agency with railroads as his major clients.

During the Civil War, Pinkerton was active in the Union cause, heading an organization engaged in spying on the Confederacy. When the war ended, Pinkerton resumed control of his agency and was instrumental in breaking strikes and in crushing the Molly Maguires. After his death, his agency continued to be active in the new American labor movement on the side of management, and Pinkerton's agents were widely criticized for their part in such labor disturbances as the Pullman strike (1894) and the Ludlow Massacre (Ludlow, Colorado, 1914). See also Horan, James D., *The Pinkertons: The Detective Dynasty That Made History* (1967); Morn, Frank, *The Eye That Never Sleeps: A History of the Pinkerton National Detective Agency* (1982); Pinkerton, Allan, *Criminal Reminiscences and Detective Sketches* (1879) and *Thirty Years a Detective* (1884); Rowan, Richard W., *The Pinkertons: A Detective Dynasty* (1931).

[102] Lamon, *Recollections of Abraham Lincoln*, 38.

[103] Ibid., 39.

[104] Mearns, *Lincoln Papers*, 442.

[105] Colonel Charles P. Stone's report, dated February 21, 1861, read as follows:

> A New York detective officer who has been on duty in Baltimore for three weeks past reports this morning [to Col. Stone] that there is serious danger of violence to and the assassination of Mr. Lincoln in his passage through that city should the time of that passage be known. He states that there are banded rowdies holding secret meetings, and that he has heard threats of mobbing and violence, and has himself heard men declare that if Mr. Lincoln was to be assassinated they would like to be the men-He states further that it is only within the past few days that he has considered there was any danger, but now he deems it imminent. He deems the danger one which the authorities & people in Baltimore cannot guard against. All risk might be easily avoided by a change in the traveling arrangements which would bring Mr. Lincoln & a portion of his party through Baltimore by a night train without previous notice (Mearns, *Lincoln Papers*, 442-443; Nicolay and Hay, *Abraham Lincoln*, 3:311-312).

[106] Lamon, *Recollections of Abraham Lincoln*, 42; Lamon quoted Lincoln, "I have thought over this matter considerably since I went over the ground with the detective last night. The appearance of Mr. Frederick Seward with warning from another source confirms my belief

in the detective's statement. Unless there are some other reasons besides fear of ridicule,
I am disposed to carry out Judd's plan."

[107]    Frederick Seward, *Reminiscences of a War-Time Statesman and Diplomat* (New York: G. P.
Putnam's Sons, 1916); Seward writes of the Baltimore Plot from pages 134-139.

[108]    Lamon, *Recollections of Abraham Lincoln*, 40.

[109]    (Benson J. Lossing, *History of the Civil War*,108-110) On December 7, 1864, Lincoln gave
a narrative account of the plot as he viewed it to Lossing, a historian of the day:

> I arrived in Philadelphia on the twenty-first. I agreed to stop over night
> and on the following morning hoist the flag over Independence Hall. In
> the evening there was a great crowd where I received my friends at the
> Continental Hotel. Mr. Judd, a warm personal friend from Chicago, sent for
> me to come to his room. I went and found there Mr. Pinkerton, a skillful
> police detective, also from Chicago, who had been employed for some days
> in Baltimore watching or searching for suspicious persons there. Pinkerton
> informed me that a plan had been laid for my assassination, the exact time
> when I was expected to go through Baltimore being publicly known. He
> was well informed as to the plan, but did not know that the conspirators
> would have pluck enough to execute it.
>
> He urged me go go right through with him to Washington. I didn't
> like that. I had made engagements to visit Harrisburg and go from there to
> Baltimore and I resolved to do so. I could not believe there was a plot to
> murder me. I made arrangements, however, with Mr. Judd for my return to
> Philadelphia the next night, if I should be convinced that there was danger
> in going through Baltimore. I told him that if I should meet at Harrisburg,
> as I had at other places, a delegation to go with me to the next place and
> then to Baltimore; I should feel safe and go on.
>
> When I was making my way back to my room through the crowd
> of people, I met Frederick Seward. We went together to my room, where
> he told me that he had been sent at the instance of his father and General
> Scott, to inform me that their detectives in Baltimore had discovered a plot
> there to assassinate me. They knew nothing of Pinkerton's movements. I
> now believed such a plot to be in existence.
>
> The next morning I raised the flag over Independence Hall and then
> went on to Harrisburg with Mr. Sumner, Major Hunter, Mr. Judd, Mr. Lamon
> and others. There I met the legislature and the people, dined and waited
> until the time appointed for me to leave. In the meantime, Mr. Judd had so
> secured the telegraph that no communication could pass to Baltimore and
> give the conspirators knowledge of a change in my plans.
>
> In New York some friend had given me a new beaver hat in a box and
> in it had placed a soft wool hat. I had never worn one of the latter in my
> life. I had this box in my room. Having informed a very few friends of the

secret of my new movements and the cause, I put on an old overcoat that I had with me and, putting the soft hat in my pocket, I walked out of the house at a back door, bareheaded, without exciting any special curiosity. Then I put on the soft hat and joined my friends without being recognized by strangers, for I was not the same man.

Sumner and Hunter wished to accompany me. I said no; you are known and your presence might betray me. I will only take Lamon whom nobody knew and Mr. Judd. (Lincoln's memory was incorrect here, only Lamon went with him) Sumner and Hunter felt hurt.

We went back to Philadelphia and found a message there from Pinkerton, who had returned to Baltimore. (This also is wrong, actually Pinkerton accompanied Lincoln all the way to Washington.) The conspirators had held their final meeting that evening and it was doubtful whether they had the nerve to attempt the execution of their purpose. I went on, however, as the arrangement had been made for a special train. We were a long time in the station at Baltimore. I heard people talking around but no one particularly observed me. At an early hour on Saturday morning, at about the time I was expected to leave Harrisburg, I arrived in Washington.

[110] Also see Allan Pinkerton, *History and Evidence of the Passage of Abraham Lincoln from Harrisburg, Pa., to Washington, D.C., on the Twenty-second and Twenty-third of Fecruary, 1861* (Chicago: Republican Press, 1868), 2-11, eighteen pages, the Pamphlet Collection of Library of Congress; this document has copies of letters from Felton, Judd, and others involved in the plan to secretly get Lincoln to Washington; Pinkerton's record book in Norma B. Cuthbert, ed., *Lincoln and the Baltimore Plot* (1949).

[111] Lamon, *Recollections of Abraham Lincoln*, 47, 261.

[112] Born on May 1, 1796, and died on November 30, 1852.

[113] On June 4, 1824, Junius Booth Sr. signed a one-thousand-year lease with Robert Hall for $733.20 for unimproved farmland in Hartford County, Maryland (HD 407, Hartford County Land Records, MD as quoted in Tidwell, *Come Retribution*). On April 25, 1833, in a deed of trust, Junius Sr. named Edwin Forrest as trustee for Mary Ann Booth, maiden name Mary Ann Holmes, and their children. (HD 16-97, Hartford County Land Records, MD as quoted in Tidwell, *Come Retribution*) Junius Sr. also kept a townhouse in Baltimore at 62 North Exeter Street where the Booth family usually spent the cold Maryland winters. Across the street were the O'Laughlens at 57 North Exeter.

[114] December 22, 1821-September 16, 1883.

[115] Rosalie passed away in 1889 at the age of sixty-six.

[116] November 13, 1833-June 7, 1893.

[117] F. A. Burr, "Junius Brutus Booth's Wife Adelaide," *New York Press*, August 9, 1891.

[118] Letter from Asia Booth to Jean Anderson, undated 1854, Peale Museum, Baltimore; quoted from Gene Smith, *American Gothic: The Story of America's Legendary Theatrical Family – Junius, Edwin, and John Wilkes Booth*, 59.

119 Asia Clarke, *The Unlocked Book* (New York: G. P. Putnam's Sons, 1938), 100; John Rhodehamel and Louise Taper, eds., *Right or Wrong, God Judge Me: The Writings of John Wilkes Booth* (Chicago: University of Illinois Press, 1997), 38.

120 Edwina Booth Grossman, *Edwin Booth: Recollections by His Daughter* (New York: Century, 1894), 227-228.

121 Clarke, *Unlocked Book*, 107.

122 Ibid., 106-107.

123 September 1858 through May 1859 and September 1859 through May 1860.

124 *Investigation and Trial Papers*, M599, roll 6, frames 491-492, statement of George Wren.

125 Gordon Samples, *Lust for Fame: The Stage Career of John Wilkes Booth* (Jefferson, NC: McFarland, 1982), 40, quoted a Letter to E. V. Valentine from George Crutchfield, Richmond, VA, July 5, 1909, original in the Valentine Museum, Richmond; Bryan, *Great American Myth*, also quoted this letter.

126 Bryan, *Great American Myth*, 87; also in Samples, *Lust for Fame*, 40, who quoted from *Richmond Enquirer*, November 28, 1859, 2.

127 In the star system of the day, managers brought in well-known performers for limited engagements, usually for one week. The star would receive top billing and a percentage of the revenues for his performances. Because of the summer heat, the Richmond theater season, like that in Philadelphia, ran from September to June, like the school year.

128 *Columbus Enquirer*, October 16, 1860.

129 Clarke to Jean Anderson, a friend of Asia, December 16, 1860, Peale Museum, Baltimore.

130 *Albany Atlas & Argus*, February 18, 1861.

131 H. P. Phelps, *Players of a Century: A Record of the Albany Stage* (Albany: McDonough, 1880), 325-326. It is an interesting historical footnote that on the evening of February 18, 1861, President-elect Abraham Lincoln was also in Albany on his inauguration trip to Washington; Booth was there playing Pescara in *The Apostate*. The last performance of Booth's life was at Ford's Theatre on March 18, 1865, playing Pescara in *The Apostate*.

132 George Alfred Townsend, *The Life, Crime, and Capture of John Wilkes Booth* (New York: Dick & Fitzgerald, 1865), 24.

133 H. P. Phelps, *Players of a Century*, 326-327.

134 "Edwin Booth and Lincoln," *Century Magazine*, April 1909, 919-920; a similar account is given by William Bispham in *Century Magazine*, November 1893. Later Robert told Adam Badeau, lifelong friend and at the time on General Grant's staff, of the near fatal accident; and Badeau told Grant, who wrote a letter to Edwin Booth offering to be of service to him if the occasion arose. Edwin replied that when Grant was in Richmond, he would like to perform for him.

135 March 17, 1862.

136 April 23, 1862.

137 Washington, April 27, 1863.

138 *Investigation and Trial Papers*, M599, reel 4, frame 0073-74.

139 *Washington Evening Star*, April 11, 1863; *Theatre Magazine*, December 1903, reproduces the playbill as does Rhodehamel and Taper, eds., *Right or Wrong, God Judge Me*, 87.

140 *Washington National Republican,* April 13, 1863.

141 Ibid., April 14, 1863.

142 Interview with Sir Charles Wyndham, *New York Herald,* June 27, 1909, 1-2; Wyndham first performed with Booth as Osric in *Hamlet* on April 14, 1863. Two years to the day later, Booth would shoot President Lincoln.

143 John Adam Ellsler, *The Stage Memories of John A. Ellsler,* ed. Effie Ellsler Weston (Cleveland: Rowfant Club, 1950), 123.

144 John T. Ford, "Behind the Curtains of a Conspiracy," *North American Review,* April 1889.

145 Clara Morris, *Life on the Stage* (New York: McClure Phillips, 1901), 101.

146 Morris, *Life on the Stage,* 98.

147 Ibid., 97.

148 Clara Morris, "Some Recollections of John Wilkes Booth," *McClure's Magazine,* February 1901, 299-304.

149 *Boston Herald,* January 10, 1890.

150 Anne Hartley Gilbert, *Stage Reminiscences* (New York: Charles Scribner's Sons, 1901), 57.

151 *Yesterday with Actors* (Boston: Cupples and Hurd, 1887), 142.

152 Townsend, *Life, Crime, and Capture* (New York: Dick & Fitzerald, 1865), 24.

153 Morris, *Life on the Stage,* 79.

154 Interview with Charles Wyndham.

155 "A Former Actress in 'Our American Cousin' Tells the Story of the Assassination of Lincoln," *Minneapolis Journal* (April 27, 1914).

156 *New York Sunday Telegraph,* May 23, 1909, taken from Francis Wilson.

157 Interview with Sir Charles Wyndham, 1-2.

158 Adam Badeau in *McClure's Magazine,* August 1893.

159 Katherine Helm, *The True Story of Mary, Wife of Lincoln* (New York: Harper & Brothers, 1920), 243.

160 On January 5, the *St. Joseph Morning Herald* (Missouri) printed the following notice, "J. Wilkes Booth . . . will appear at Corby's Hall tonight at half past seven, where our citizens will have an opportunity of hearing some of the finest dramatic reading ever . . . . Wherever he appears, Mr. Booth is greeted with unbounded favor . . . and we are confident our people will show their appreciation of splendid talent and acknowledged genius by turning out en masse tonight." January 6, the *Morning Herald* reviewed Booth's performance, giving him high praise; the paper also wrote of the extreme cold that night in Corby's Hall and on the noise the audience was making about in order to keep warm.

161 Booth wrote, "I have had a rough time John scince [sic] I saw you. It was hard enough to get to Leavenworth but coming back was a hundred times worse. Lost all but four nights of my St. Louis engagement. In St. Joe I was down to my last cent and had to give a reading to pay my way. It gave me $150 with which I hired a sleigh and came 160 miles over the plains. Four days and nights in the largest snow drifts I ever saw . . . . I will say this that I never knew what hardship was til them"(Wood Theatre, Louisville, January 23, 1864) (Ellsler, *Stage Memoirs,*126, reprints the letter; also see Mrs. McKee Rankin, "The

News of Lincoln's Death," *American Magazine*, January 1909, 259-262; John B. Horner, "John Wilkes Booth as Speculator," Surratt Courier, June 2000, 4).

[162] Rhodehamel and Taper, eds., *Right or Wrong, God Judge Me*, 101.

[163] *New Orleans Daily Picayune*, March 18, 1864, col. 1, p. 5.

[164] Ibid., March 20, 1864, col. 4, p. 1.

[165] It has been suggested by some historians that this illness was the beginning of the end of John Wilkes Booth's acting career and that the problem with Booth's voice was his lack of proper training and ability to control and project his voice. Kimmel wrote: "The day of reckoning had arrived. Wilkes' "hoarseness" was not due to a bronchial infection resulting from a severe cold but was the reprisal from the lack of early study and training in voice control. He knew his future as a star was doomed" (181). However, this voice problem did not keep Booth from fulfilling the longest professional engagement in his acting career. After twenty-two days of rest, Booth went on to perform for five successive weeks in Boston. There he gave thirty-four performances from April 25 to May 27 in eighteen different roles (Samples, *Lust for Fame*, 223).

[166] June 7, 1864; Rhodehamel and Taper, eds., *Right or Wrong, God Judge Me*.

[167] July 14, 1864; Ibid.

[168] Ibid., 110-117.

[169] Booth also played on November 25, 1864, Winter Garden, New York, as Mark Anthony in *Julius Caesar* to raise money for the purchase of a Shakespeare statue in Central Park. He appeared in this play with his two brothers, Edwin and Junius.

He played Romeo on January 29, 1865, Grover's Theatre, in Washington, DC, as a benefit for actress Avonia Jones.

March 18, 1865, was his last performance. It was at Ford's Theatre, Washington, DC, as Pescara in the tragedy, *The Apostate*. This also was a benefit performance, this time for his friend, John McCullough (*Washington National Intelligencer*, March 18, 1865).

[170] On East Nineteenth Street.

[171] Affidavit of Junius Brutus Booth, May 6, 1865, in *Investigation and Trial Papers*, M599, roll 2, frames 2061-68.

[172] Clarke, *Unlocked Book*, 124

[173] Ellsler, *Stage Memories*, 122-131.

[174] Pitman, *Assassination of President Lincoln*, 45.

[175] Ellsler, *Stage Memories*, 130. On April 25, 1865, a cashier at the McHenry House in Pennsylvania wrote a letter to Secretary of War Stanton describing an inscription scratched on a window pane at the hotel. The letter, in part, read,

Sir,

Recent dispatches, referring to a former and futile attempt upon the life of the late Abraham Lincoln by poison, have induced me to write you regarding a circumstance occurring at this hotel, where I have been cashier for a year and a half. Sometime ago the following words were observed to have been scratched upon a pane of glass in room No. 22 of this house, evidently done with a diamond: 'Abe Lincoln departed this life August 13, 1864, by the effects of poison.' I have this just as it appears upon the glass. In view of recent events, it was deemed best to take the pane of glass out and preserve it, and we have it safe. As to the date of the writing, we cannot determine. It was noticed some months ago by the housekeeper, but was not thought particularly of until after the assassination, being considered a freak of some individual who was probably partially intoxicated . . . . As to who was the writer, we can, of course, give no definite information. J. Wilkes Booth was here several times during last summer and fall, on his way to and from the oil regions. He was here upon the 10th and again upon the 29th of June, 1864, but does not appear to have been assigned that room, still he may have been in it in company with others who did occupy it.

The letter was signed "S. D. Page" (the text of his letter is in Ernest C. Miller, *John Wilkes Booth-Oilman* (New York: Exposition Press, 1947), 72-74; also see introduction to *Investigation and Trial Papers*, M599, roll 15, for a photograph of the inscription which was cut on the pane of glass). It has never been determined who wrote the inscription or when the inscription was scratched on to the pane.

[176] James O. Hall, "The Story of Mrs. Mary Surratt: A Lecture Delivered before the Docents of the Surratt House," *Surratt Society* (Clinton, MD, August 1977) and *Maryland Genealogical Bulletin* (Baltimore, MD, January 1931).

[177] Surratt Society archives has a copy of the receipt for Mary's enrollment; Mary was enrolled on November 26, 1835. In 1839, the school closed.

[178] On December 19, 1843, two-year-old Anna Surratt was baptized at St. Peter's Catholic Church. On September 20, 1847, John Jr. was baptized.

[179] Elizabeth Jenkins, Mary's mother, was later buried at this church in 1878, having outlived her daughter by thirteen years.

[180] Joseph George Jr., "'A True Childe of Sorrow,' Two Letters of Mary E. Surratt," *Maryland Historical Magazine*, vol. 80, no. 4 (Winter 1985): 403.

[181] Laurie Verge, "A Portrait of Mary E. Surratt," *Surratt Society News*, May 1981.

[182] Pitman, *Assassination of President Lincoln*, 131, Anna Surratt's testimony.

[183] On May 8, 1881, George Alfred Townsend wrote in the *New York Tribune* that he learned from a "gentleman prominent in that country" that "while there was considerable pity for Mrs. Surratt, her dignity had been much exaggerated, that while her husband was yet living an Italian priest who ministered in that part of the country got in such a flirtation with Mrs. Surratt that it raised a commotion, and he had to be sent to Boston to get him out of the scandal."

[184] George Alfred Townsend, "A Talk with Louis Weichmann," *Surratt Society News*, 1980.

[185] Alfred Isacsson, ed., "Some Letters of Anna Surratt," *Maryland Historical Magazine*, September 1959, 310-313.

186 Thomas Conrad, *Confederate Spy* (New York: J. S. Ogilvie Publishing, 1892), 128.

187 Louis J. Weichmann, *The True History of the Assassination of Abraham Lincoln and of the Conspiracy of 1865* (New York: Alfred A. Knopf, 1975), 19.

188 Weichmann, *True History of Assassination*, 24; years later, Sainte-Marie would turn John Surratt over to authorities in Rome.

189 One official Confederate document mentioned the Surratt Tavern as part of the Confederate Army Signal Corps. It is a quarterly report ending March 31, 1864, and written by Captain William N. Barker. It reads in part,

> We are only required to keep open lines by which Agents, Scouts, etc. can forward letters, papers, and light packages to the Depts. The lines are as follows:
>
> I. Mathias Point, King George Co. Va. Lieut. C. H. Cawood Commanding, via Allen's Fresh, Newport, Bryan Town, Surratt's Tavern, and to Washington (M437, roll 121, frame 0059, National Archives; this was discovered by Erick F. Davis of Baltimore in 1979; David W. Gaddy, "The Surratt Tavern-A Confederate 'Safe House'?" *Surratt Society News*, April 1979; also commenting on the Surratt Tavern was Conrad, *Confederate Spy*, 127-128).

190 Weichmann, *True History of Assassination*, 26.

191 During the time that John and Mary Surratt owned the H Street townhouse, it was lease to various individuals. For more information on the history of the boardinghouse, see Joan Choconas, "Mary Surratt's Boardinghouse," *Surratt Courier*, July 1988.

192 Weichmann, *True History of Assassination*, 27-28.

193 A tavern license was issued to John Lloyd on December 20, 1864.

194 Currently 604 H Street, NW, and a Chinese restaurant, which does not allow the general public in the second and third floors.

195 Pitman, *Assassination of President Lincoln*, 132, testimony of Honora Fitzpatrick.

196 Mary had a brother Zadoc and Olivia was his daughter. Harold Wang, "A Visit to the Surratt Boardinghouse, Washington, D.C.," *Surratt Society News*, August 1982, 5-6.

197 Source: Laurie Verge, "A Portrait of Mary E. Surratt," *Surratt Society News*, May 1981.

198 *Washington Star*, November 30.

199 Verge, "Portrait of Mary E. Surratt."

200 Ibid., 115.

201 Clarke, *Unlocked Book*, 116-117.

202 Samuel Bland Arnold, *Defence and Prison Experiences of a Lincoln Conspirator. Statements and Autobiographical Notes* (Hattiesbury, MS: Book Farm, 1943), 18. Arnold places the meeting "in the latter part of August or about the first of September"; however, because of Booth's lengthly illness with erysipelas, the meeting had to have been earlier.

203 *Investigation and Trial Papers*, M599, reel 4, frames 0198-99 and reel 6, frames 0286-89.

204 Arnold, *Defence and Prison Experiences*, 35.

205 Ibid., 36-38; "After a debate of some time, and his pointing out its feasibility, and being under the effects some little of wine, we consented to join him in the enterprise . . . . We seperated [sic] that afternoon and I returned to my brothers near Hookstown, Baltimore County, Md. Booth stating he would leave for New York the next day, to wind up his affairs, and make over his property to different members of his family, reserving enough to carry out his projected scheme, and would soon return" (Ibid., 19).

206 Ibid., 40; also see Arnold Confession in Appendix; in *The Unlocked Book*, Asia Clarke wrote of this illness.

207 Pitman, *Assassination of President Lincoln*, 45, testimony of Joseph H. Simonds Oil was found on the property in December 1864, and Ellsler received a bid for eighty thousand dollars. He wanted to sell and was trying to contact Booth when he received news of the assassination. At the news, all the bids were withdrawn. Ellsler finally sold the property for seven hundred dollars to the Allegheny Valley Railroad Company. Ellsler lost even this when his "bank was destroyed by fire and the money lost in the flames" (Ellsler, S*tage Memories*, 131).

208 Clay to Beverly Tucker, October 14, 1864, quoted by Oscar A. Kinchen, *Confederate Operations in Canada and the North: A Little-Known Phase of the American Civil War* (North Quincy, MA: Christopher, 1970), appendix 7, pp. 231-232.

209 Letters Received by the Secretary of War, Registered Series, 1801-70, M221, reel 221, National Archives; the date April 19 refers to the 1861 attack on Massachusetts troops en route to Washington by citizens of Baltimore.

210 *Official Records of the Union and Confederate Navies in the War of the Rebellion*, 30 vols. (Washington, DC: U.S. Government Printing Office, 1894-1914), 1 ser., vol. 2, pp. 714,728,735; 1 ser., vol. 15, pp. 374-77.

211 A letter written by Captain Robert D. Minor of the Confederate Navy to Admiral Franklin Buchanan states that Minor had been sent to Canada with twenty-two men to capture the federal gunboat "Michigan" on Lake Erie and to free the Confederate prisoners at Johnson's Island. The plot was not successful; however, Minor did write in his report the following:

> Finding Marshal Kane and some of our friends in Montreal, we set to work to prepare and perfect our arrangements, the first object of the plan being to communicate with the prisoners on Johnson's Island, informing them that an attempt would be made to release them. This was effected through a lady from Baltimore, a Mrs. P. C. Martin, then residing with her husband and family in Montreal, and whose husband did all in his power to aid us in every way (Union and Confederate Navies, 1 ser., vol. 2, pp. 824).

212 W. H. Gurley, consul at Quebec, kept the Department of State informed about the salvage of the "Marie Victoria" in a series of dispatches: *Investigation and Trial Papers*, M599, reel 7, file 52, frame 0225-0234.

Booth's trunk was salvaged from the Marie Victoria and sold at public auction in July 1865 by decree of the vice admiralty court. The trunk's contents brought about five hundred dollars. George Rankin, brother of the actor McKee Rankin, bought most of the articles. Eventually they came into the possession of Edwin Booth.

Mrs. Martin was listed in a later city directory as a widow.

[213] Kinchen, *Confederate Operations*, 47.

[214] Tidwell and others, *Come Retribution*.

[215] Kinchen, *Confederate Operations*, 47, 231-232; first letter was written to Secretary of State Benjamin on June 17, 1864, and the second on October 14, 1864.

[216] Ibid., 41.

[217] There was the testimony of William E. Wheeler on May 12, 1865: "I reside in Chickopee, Massachusetts. I was at Montreal, Canada, in October or November last, when I saw John Wilkes Booth, who was standing in front of the St. Lawrence Hall, Montreal. I spoke to Mr. Booth, and asked him if he was going to open the theater there. He said he was not. He left me, and entered into conversation with a person who was pointed out to me as George N. Sanders" (Pitman, *Assassination of President Lincoln*, 39).

John Deveny testified on May 12, 1865 that "in July of 1863, I was in Montreal, and left there the 3d or 4th of February of this year. I was well acquainted with John Wilkes Booth. The first time I saw him in Canada he was standing in the St. Lawrence Hotel, Montreal, talking with George N. Sanders. I believe that was in the month of October. They were talking confidentially, and drinking together. I saw them go into Dowley's and have a drink together . . . . I spoke to Booth, and asked him if he was going to play there, knowing that he was an actor. He said he was not. I then said, 'What are you going to do?' He said, 'I just came here on a pleasure trip.' The other Southerners, whose names I have mentioned, (Thompson, Clay and Tucker) I have seen talking with Sanders, but I can not say positively that I saw them talking with Booth" (Pitman, *Assassination of President Lincoln*, 38-39).

On May 29, 1865, Hosea B. Carter testified "some twenty or thirty Southerners boarded at the St. Lawrence Hall, and usually associated together, and very little with other people who came there, either English or American. I frequently observed George N. Sanders in intimate association with Booth, and others of that class, in Montreal" (Pitman, *Assassination of President Lincoln*, 38).

[218] "A Short Biography of George Sanders," *Biographical Encyclopedia of Kentucky* (Cincinnati: J. M. Armstrong, 1878), 538-41.

[219] Amos A. Ettinger, *The Mission to Spain of Pierre Soule, 1853-1855* (New Haven: Yale University Press, 1932), 316-335.

[220] *New York Herald*, September 6, 1864.

[221] In the *Diary of a Public Man*, Sanders was spoken of in an entry for February 28. The diarist wrote of a conversation he had with President-elect Lincoln at Willard's Hotel: "I told him, what I believe to be perfectly true, that the worst stories all originate with men like George Sanders of New York . . . they have been telling wonderful stories of conspiracy and assassination" (*North American Review*, August 1879, entry for February 28, 1861, 62).

222    Kinchen, *Confederate Operations*, 41, 42.

223    Alexandra Lee Levin, *This Awful Drama: General Edwin Gray Lee, C.S.A., and His Family*.

224    Pitman, *Assassination of President Lincoln*, 46, testimony of Robert Campbell; also see *Investigation and Trial Papers*, M599, roll 15, frame 0096, for a copy of the draft.

225    Under the Webster-Ashburton Treaty.

226    Chester testified:

In the early part of November last I met him in New York, and asked him why he [Booth] was not acting. He told me that he did not intend to act in this portion of the country again; that he had taken his wardrobe to Canada, and intended to run the blockade. I saw him again on the 24th or 25th of November, about the time we were to play 'Julius Caesar' in New York, which we did play on the 25th. I asked him where his wardrobe was; he said it was still in Canada, in charge of a friend. I think he named Martin in Montreal.

He told me he had a big speculation on hand, and asked me to go in with him. I met him on Broadway as he was talking with some friends. They were joking with him about his oil speculations. After he left them he told me he had a better speculation than that on hand, and one they wouldn't laugh at. Some time after that I met him again, and he asked me how I would like to go in with him. I told him I was without means, and therefore could not. He said that didn't matter; that he always liked me and would furnish the means. He then returned to Washington, from which place I received several letters from him. He told me he was speculating in farms in lower Maryland and Virginia; still telling me that he was sure to coin money, and that I must go in with him (Pitman, *Assassination of President Lincoln*, 44). Booth was actually doing. at this time, was scouting out a route through Southern Maryland and across the Potomac River to Virginia in a route he would take after he had kidnapped Lincoln.

About the latter part of December or early in January, (may be Jan 10-12, 1865) he came to New York, and called on me at my house, No. 45 Grove Street. He asked me to take a walk with him which I did. We went into a saloon known as the "House of Lords," on Houston Street, and remained there perhaps an hour, eating and drinking. We afterward went to another saloon under the Revere House, after which we started up Broadway. He had often mentioned his speculation, but would never mention what it was. If I would ask him, he would say he would tell me by-and-by. When we came to the corner of Bleecker Street, I turned and bade him good night. He asked me to walk further with him, and we walked up Fourth Street, because he said Fourth Street was not so full of people as Broadway and he wanted to tell me about that speculation. When we got into the unfrequented portion of the street, he stopped and told me that he was in a large conspiracy to capture the heads of the Government, including the President, and to take them to Richmond. I asked him if that was the speculation that he wished me to go into He said it was. I told him I could not do it; that it was an impossibility: and asked him to think of my family. He said he had two or three thousand dollars that he could leave them. He urged the matter, and talked with me, I suppose half an hour; but I still refused to give my assent. Then he said to me, "You will at least not betray me," and added, "You dare not." He said he could implicate me in the affair. The party he said were sworn together, and if I attempted to betray them. I would be hunted down through life. He urged me further, saying I had better go in. I told him "No, and bade him good night, and went home.

He told me that the affair was to take place at Ford's Theater in Washington, and the part he wished me to play, in carrying out this conspiracy, was to open the back door of the theater at a signal. He urged that the part I would have to play would be a very easy affair, and that it was sure to succeed, but needed some one connected or acquainted with the theater. He said every thing was in readiness, and that there were parties on the other side ready to co-operate with them. By these parties I understood him to mean the rebel authorities and others opposed to our Government. He said there were from fifty to one hundred persons engaged in the conspiracy" (Pitman, *Assassination of President Lincoln*, 44).

Chester recounts in his interrogation by detectives that Booth said "I carry a derringer loaded to shoot everyone who betrays us." The implied threat Chester felt was unfair and argued with saying: "It is very wrong, John, because I have always looked up to you as a friend and have never done you any wrong" (*Investigation and Trial Papers*, M599, roll 4, frames 140-142; also see "Chester's Interrogation on April 28, 1865," in *David Rankin Barbee Papers*, Georgetown University Special Collections).

Samuel Chester continued his testimony:

He [Booth] wrote to me again from Washington about this speculation; I think it must have been January. I did not keep my letters. Every Sunday I devoted to answering my correspondence and destroying my letters.

In January I got a letter from him, saying I must come. This was the letter in which he told me his plan was sure to succeed. I wrote back, saying that it was impossible, and I would not come. Then by return mail, I think I got another letter, with fifty dollars enclosed, saying, I must come, and must be there by Saturday night. I did not go, nor have I been out of New York since last summer. The next time he came to New York, which I think was in February, he called on me again, and asked me to take a walk with him, and I did so. He then told me that he had been trying to get another party, one John Matthews, to join him, and when he told Matthews what he wanted, the man was very much frightened, and would not join him; and he said he would not have cared if he had sacrificed him. I told him I did not think it was right to speak in that manner. He said no; but Matthews was a coward, and was not fit to live. He then urged me again to join, and told me I must do so. He said there was plenty of money in the affair; and that, if I joined, I never would want for money again as long as I lived. He said the President and some of the heads of the Government came to the theater very frequently during Mr. Forrest's engagements. I desired him not to again mention the affair to me, but to think of my poor family. He said he would ruin me in the profession if I did not go. I told him I could not help that, and begged him not to mention the affair to me.

When he found I would not go, he said he honored my mother and respected my wife, and he was sorry he had mentioned this affair to me; but told me to make my mind easy, and he would trouble me no more. I then returned him the money he had sent me. He told me he would not allow me to do so, but that he was so very short of funds, and that either he or some other party must go to Richmond to obtain means to carry out their designs (Pitman, *Assassination of President Lincoln*, 44-45).

227  John Thompson later described the meeting with Booth, "I was introduced to him by Dr. Queen, my father-in-law, about the latter part of October last, or perhaps in November. He was brought to Dr. Queen's house by his son Joseph. None of the family, I believe, had ever seen or heard of him before; I know that I had not. He brought a letter of introduction to Dr. Queen from some one in Montreal, of the name of Martin, I think, who stated that this man Booth wanted to see the county. Booth's object in visiting the county was to purchase lands; he told me so himself, and made various inquiries of me respecting the price of land there, and about the roads in Charles County . . . . On the next morning, Sunday, I accompanied him [Booth] and Dr. Queen to Church at Bryantown." That Sunday was November 13. Thompson continued, "I happened to see Dr. Samuel A. Mudd in front of the Church before entering, and spoke to him, and introduced Mr. Booth to him" (Pitman, *Assassination of President Lincoln*, 178).

228  Mudd, born December 20, 1833, was a slender man with a narrow face and a steady gaze. He also had thin sand-colored hair and a drooping mustache that merged with a goatee. When he was fifteen, Mudd had entered St. John's College and, after two years, had gone to Georgetown College and then studied medicine and surgery at the University of Maryland at Baltimore. Graduating in 1856, Mudd returned to the farm of his father, Henry Mudd, "a large land-owner" and slave owner living a few miles from Bryantown. Mudd started a medical practice and became a gentlemen farmer. At the age of twenty-four on November 26, 1857, Mudd married Sarah Frances Dyer, a young woman who

had just graduated from a convent school. Seven years later, he built a home for her on a portion of his father's land.

229 Booth's ledger sheet of deposits and withdrawals at the Jay Cooke & Company Bank, Washington, DC, is in the *Abraham Lincoln Papers*, Chicago Historical Society. Seven checks for cash were drawn against this account (Tidwell and others, *Come Retribution*, 343).

230 For a more detailed account of this Civil War incident, see Nat Brandt, *The Man Who Tried to Burn New York* (Syracuse: Syracuse University Press, 1986).

231 On this concern, L. Q. Washington, private secretary to CSA Secretary of War Benjamin during the war, wrote:

I was present at the time when Mr. (Jacob) Thompson received his instructions from Mr. Benjamin. They were oral and largely suggestive and informal. Much was left to his discretion and wisely; for he was an experienced and conservative man. But there was not a word or a thought that looked to any violations of the rules of war, as they exist, among civilized nations. As a matter of fact, Mr. Davis, Mr. Benjamin, General Lee and the other leaders of the Confederacy believed to the last that it was not merely right, but the wisest and best policy to maintain and respect every one of the humane restrictions in the conduct of war which are upheld by the publicists (L.Q. Washington to Lawley, Lawley MSS, Pierce Butler Collection, Tulane University, as quoted in Eli Evans, ed., *Judah P. Benjamin: The Jewish Confederate* [New York: Free Press, 1988]; also see Benjamin Butler, *Autobiography and Personal Reminiscence of Major-General Benjamin F. Butler* [Boston, 1892], 347-348).

232 Evans, *Judah P. Benjamin.*

233 Clarke, *The Unlocked Book*, 126.

234 Arnold, *Defence and Prison Experiences*, 20. "Fearful that the weight of his trunk might attract attention he (Booth) asked me to take part of them, which I did and sent them to him by express to Washington."

235 Gath, *Cincinnati Enquirer*, April 18, 1892.

236 Pitman, *Assassination of President Lincoln*, see testimony of Thomas L. Gardiner in page 71; for a more detailed treatment of the subject of Dr. Mudd's three meetings with Booth, see Edward Steers, *His Name Is Still Mudd: The Case Against Dr. Samuel A. Mudd,*" chap. 5. (This was the horse used by Powell on the night that Lincoln was assassination.)

237 The red-light district was known as Hooker Division since that area was frequented by men from General Hooker's Division. This is the derivation of the slang *hooker*, meaning prostitute. Mary Jane Treakle, Ella Turner Starr's sister, had a bordello at 62 Ohio Avenue.

238 *Investigation and Trial Papers*, M599, roll 6, frame 494.

239 As Jeremiah T. Mudd describes it, "It was a little in the night when we arrived in Washington; we put up our horses near the Navy Yard, and went to the Pennsylvania

House, registering our names for lodgings. We went to a restaurant on the avenue, . . . for supper, and staid [sic] there possibly an hour. We then went to Brown's Hotel, and afterward to the National Hotel, and there was a tremendous crowd there, and we got separated. I met a friend at the National, conversed with him a short time, then went down the avenue and visited some clothing stores, and returned to the Pennsylvania House. Dr. Mudd came in there shortly after me, and we went to bed" (Pitman, *Assassination of President Lincoln*, 190).

240   Pitman, *Assassination of President Lincoln*, see testimony of Mary Simms in page 170; Surratt was six foot three and had a prominent forehead, a large nose, sunken eyes, a goatee, and long light-colored hair. John Surratt was at St. Charles College at the beginning of the Civil War. In August 1862 after his father died, John left college. On September 1, 1862, he was appointed postmaster of the Surrattsville post office. It was soon after this that Surratt Jr. began to take an active part in sending information on Federal troops moving from Washington. He carried dispatches to Confederate boats on the Potomac. Because of its crossroads location, the Surratt Tavern soon became a relay station for Confederate couriers traveling up and the down the east coast. Surratt's dependability and success in slipping through Federal Union lines soon established him as a trusted and reliable Confederate courier to Canada. Surratt was called Little Johnny because although he was tall, he could slip in and out of any location in a variety of disguises. John reveled in the secrecy and the exhilaration of the life of a high-level secret courier. He knew all the streams, creeks, and backwaters and knew men with rowboats, rafts, or boats who could be paid to help. He would smuggle himself into Washington and then travel by train to Canada. He knew the Union capital and its countryside well.

241   Ibid., 114.

242   Ibid., 190.

In an affidavit written by Capt. George W. Dutton, commander of the guard detachment, on August 22, 1865, he wrote about his conversations with Dr. Mudd while en route to the Dry Tortugas. "He (Mudd) confessed that he knew Booth when he came to his house with Herold, on the morning after the assassination of the President; that he had known Booth for some time, but was afraid to tell of his having been at his house on the 15th of April, fearing that his own and the lives of his family would be endangered thereby. He also confessed that he was with Booth at the National Hotel on the evening referred to by Weichmann in his testimony; that he came to Washington on that occasion to meet Booth, by appointment, who wished to be introduced to John Surratt; that when he and Booth were going to Mrs. Surratt's house to see John Surratt, they met, on Seven Street, John Surratt, who was introduced to Booth, and they had a conversation of a private nature" (Ibid., 421).

Dr. Mudd, incarcerated at Dry Tortugas, an island off the southern tip of Florida, later heard that Captain Dutton written an affidavit about their conversation; he immediately wrote a responding affidavit. In his affidavit, dated August 28, 1865, Mudd vehemently denied Dutton's statement that he had confessed to knowing Booth, but he did admit to the meeting at the National Hotel where he introduced Booth to John Surratt.

[243] As quoted in Stanley Kimmel, *The Mad Booths of Maryland* (Indianapolis: Bobbs-Merrill, 1940), 196*

[244] Arnold, *Defence and Prison Experiences*, 20.

[245] Clara E. Laughlin, *The Death of Lincoln: The Story of Booth's Plot, Hid Deed, and the Penalty* (New York: Doubleday, 1909), 35, letter is reprinted; John Surratt's letter to Belle Seaman, 6 February 1865, Surratt Society archives, Clinton, MD.

[246] "I went with Miss Honora Fitzpatrick to a deguerrean gallery one day to get her picture; we saw some photographs of Mr. Booth there, and, being acquainted with him, we bought two and took them home. When my brother saw them, he told me to tear them up and throw them in the fire, and that, if I did not, he would take them from me. So I hid them. I owned photographs of Davis, Stephens, Beauregard, Stonewall Jackson, and perhaps a few other leaders of the rebellion. My father gave them to me before his death, and I prize them on his account, if on nobody else's. I also had in the house photographs of Union Generals – of General McClellan, General Grant, and General Joe Hooker" (Pitman, *Assassination of President Lincoln*, see testimony of Anna Surratt in page 131 and see testimony of Honora Fitzpatrick in page 132).

[247] *The Trial of John H. Surratt in the Criminal Court for the District of Columbia*, 2 vols. (Washington, DC: U.S. Government Printing Office, 1867), see testimony of Henry R. McDonough, Adams Express Company in 1:356-57; Weichmann, *True History of Assassination*, 70.

[248] In a confession published in the *Baltimore American* on January 19, 1869, there was a slightly different wording; Atzerodt said, "Harbin was in it first; he came for me with John Surratt during the winter."

[249] Richard M. Smoot, *The Unwritten History of the Assassination of Abraham Lincoln*, Clinton, MA: W. F. Coulter Press, 1908), 8-9; Rare Book Room, Library of Congress.

[250] The Powell family Bible shows April 22, and Lewis Powell's military records also show April 22.

[251] As a part of General A. P. Hill's Third Corps.

[252] Henry Bascom Smith, "Statement of Margaret Branson," in *Between the Lines*, (New York: Booz Brothers, 1911), 306, 309; the Branson family lived at 16 Eutaw Street, Baltimore, and it was a safe house in the Confederate courier system similar to the Surratt Tavern.

[253] On September 2, 1863.

[254] *Investigation and Trial Papers*, M599, roll 3, see letter of Samuel S. Bond to Colonel John A Foster, June 3, 1865, during the conspiracy trail.

[255] Betty Ownsbey, *Alias "Paine": Lewis Thornton Powell, the Mystery Man of the Lincoln Conspiracy* (Jefferson, NC: McFarland & Co.), 238; As Private Powell, he was listed on Company B rolls of the Rangers from October 1 to December 31, 1863, and in the fourth quarter 1864; the rolls show that Private L. T. Powell, Company B, is listed as being issued two shirts and two pairs of drawers.

It is not known why Powell went to Northern Virginia and why he joined Mosby's Rangers. There is plenty of speculation but no historical documentation that existed. The most likely scenario is that Powell's move to Mosby's Rangers was suggested by the Branson family, who were Southern sympathizers and part of the Confederate courier system.

[256] For an account of Captain Blazer's efforts at capturing Mosby, see Jeffrey D. Wert, "In One Deadly Encounter," *Civil War Times Illustrated*, November 1980, 12-19.

[257] Smith, *Between the Lines*, 258.

[258] *Philadelphia Weekly Times*, June 3, 1882, reprinted in its entirety in Betty J. Ownsbey, *Alias "Paine,"* appendix C.

[259] The *Alexandria Gazette* of January 23, 1865, reported that Powell, who now could call himself Lewis Paine, sold a horse.

[260] Smith, *Between the Lines*, 258.

[261] At 1211 Baltimore Street.

[262] Weichmann, *True History of Assassination*, 74.

[263] Ibid., 75.

[264] *Trial of John H. Surratt*, 1:206-7.

[265] Pitman, *Assassination of President Lincoln*, 97; Herold was born on June 16, 1842; he was the only surviving son among seven sisters. He studied at Georgetown College from October 1855 to April 1858 and at Rittenhouse Academy in 1859.

[266] Will of Adam George Herold, dated August 25, 1864, filed October 15, 1864. Register of Wills, Washington.

[267] *Investigation and Trial Papers*, M599, roll 4, frames 445-447.

[268] House of Representatives, Testimony of Thomas T. Eckert on 30 May 1867 before the Judiciary Committee, *Impeachment Investigation*, 39th Cong., 2nd sess., and 40th Cong., 1st sess., 674.

[269] *Washington National Intelligencer*, January 22, 1865.

[270] Rhodehamel and Taper, eds., *Right or Wrong, God Judge Me*, 134-135; Booth's letter to Orlando Tompkins is owned by Richard and Kellie Gutman, Boston.

[271] *Trial of John H. Surratt*, see testimony of John T. Holohan in page 669 and testimony of Eliza Holohan in page 688.

[272] *Investigation and Trial Papers*, M599, reel 16, frames 0170-0200, statement of Mrs. Mary E. Surratt, April 28, 1865.

[273] James O. Hall, "The Other Boardinghouse Residents – Mary Apollonia Dean and The Holohan Family," *Surratt Society News*, May 1984.

[274] *Trial of John H. Surratt*, see testimony of Eliza Holohan in page 689.

[275] James O. Hall, "The Saga of Sarah Slater," *Surratt Society News*, February 1982.

[276] Levin, *This Awful Drama*, 145.

[277] Ibid., 147.

[278] Pitman, *Assassination of President Lincoln*, see testimony of Louis Weichmann in page 119.

[279] R. D. Watson wrote to Mr. J. H. Surratt; in this letter, Watson asked Surratt to come to New York "on important business" and to respond immediately by telegraph.

March 19th, 1865

Mr. J. H. Surratt,

Dear Sir,

I would like to see you on important business if you can spare the time to come on to New York. Please telegraph me immediately on the reception of this. Whether you can come on or not – much obliged.

Yours truly,
R. D. Watson

P. S. Address care of Demill & Co.
178 1/2 Water St. New York, New York

Since Sarah Slater would have arrived in New York on her second trip from Canada on or about March 23, this letter may have been in connection with Mrs. Slater's arrival in that city, asking John Surratt to act as an escort for her to Washington (the letter to John H. Surratt is in *Investigation and Trial Papers*, M599, reel 3, frame 0114).

Roderick D. Watson was from Charles Country, Maryland. An educated man with poor health, he was arrested in Baltimore on March 18, 1864, on suspicion of being a blockade-runner. However, he was released when he took the oath of allegiance. Major General John A. Dix, who commanded New York military district, had Watson arrested again on May 8 and confined at the Fort Lafayette prison. He was released five months later on October 10, 1864 (for Watson's imprisonment and release date, see *Turner-Baker Papers*, M797, file 3413, National Archives; Turner was a major in the Federal army and a judge advocate in New York City; and *Selected Records of the War Department Relating to Confederate Prisoners of War*, M598, reel 85, frame 41, Fort Lafayette, National Archives). He was arrested twice as blockade-runner and with his association with Surratt; Watson was undoubtedly involved in the Confederate courier system.

280  Arnold, *Defence and Prison Experience*, 25, 49.

281  Surratt gave Barry a note to deliver to "Mr. Brooks" (real name Brooke Stabler) at Howard's Livery:

March 26th, 1865

Mr. Brooks:

As business will detain me for a few days in the country, I thought I would send your team back. Mr. Barry will deliver it and pay the hire of it.

> If Mr. Booth my friend should want my horses let him have them, but no one else. It you should want any money on them he will let you have it. I should like to have kept the team for several days but it is too expensive – especially as I have "woman on the brain" and may be away for a week or so.

Yours respectfully,
J. Harrison Surratt

The horses mentioned did not belong to Surratt, but to Booth.

282    *Trial of John H. Surratt*, see testimony of Oliva Jenkins in pages 750-51.

283    Ibid., See testimony of David Barry in page 752.

284    Ibid., See testimony of the hotel clerk J. B. Tinsley Jr. in 2:790-91.

285    Levin, *This Awful Drama*, 151-152.

286    *Investigation and Trial Papers*, M599, reel, frames     0353-57.

287    Weichmann, *True History of Assassination*, 84.

288    Ibid., 83-85.

289    William E. Doster, *Lincoln and Episodes of the Civil War* (New York: G. P. Putnam's Sons, 1915), 267.

290    *Daily Constitutional Union*, July 7, 1865, statement of Lewis Powell.

291    Richard H. Sewell, *John P. Hale and the Politics of Abolition* (Cambridge, MA: Harvard University Press, 1965).

292    Richmond Morcom, "They All Loved Lucy," *American Heritage*, October 1970, 13.

293    Morcom, "They All Loved Lucy," 14.

294    Later ambassador to Great Britain (1897-'98) and secretary of state (1898-1905).

295    Morcom, "They All Loved Lucy," 15.

296    *Philadelphia Press*, December 8, 1881.

297    Clarke, *Unlocked Book*, 198-199.

298    Kimmel, *Mad Booths of Maryland*, 346-347.

299    "A Sister's Thoughts: A Letter From Asia Booth Clarke," *Surratt Society News*, April 1985, reprints the letter from Asia to her friend Jean Anderson, original in the Peale Museum, Baltimore.

300    Smith, *Between the Lines*, 255-256.

The *Baltimore Sun* reported on March 15, 1865,

> Arrested as a Spy-Louis Paine was arrested on Monday last at No. 16 North Eutaw Street, charged with being a rebel spy. Major. Wiegel made a thorough examination of his case, and there not being sufficient evidence to substantiate the charge, he was released from the charge of being a spy, but held as disloyal. Upon taking the Oath of Allegiance, and engaging to go North of Philadelphia during the war, he was finally released (Local Matters, *Baltimore Sun*, March 15, 1865, 1).

Eighth Army Corps Papers, RG 93, Register 125, 411, National Archives, show the following information:

| | |
|---|---|
| March 12, 1865 | Lewis Payne, 16 N. Eutaw Street, Charge Spy, Imprisoned. |
| March 14, 1865 | Discharged and ordered North upon taking the Oath of Allegiance |

[301] A reprint of the parole can be found in Betty Ownsbey's *Alias "Paine"* in page 49.

[302] Smith, *Between the Lines*, 255-256.

[303] Ibid., 309; *Investigation and Trial Papers*, M599, roll 3, frame 1044.

[304] Ben Perley Poore, *Conspiracy Trial for the Murder of the President*, 3 vols (New York: Arno Press, 1972; repr., 1865), see testimony of Weichmann in page 76.

[305] Weichmann, *True History of Assassination*, 97.

[306] Poore, *Conspiracy Trial*, see testimony of Weichmann in pages 76-77.

[307] Weichmann, *True History of Assassination*, 97; Poore, *Conspiracy Trial*, 76.

[308] Weichmann, *True History of Assassination*, 97.

[309] Pitman, *Assassination of President Lincoln*, see testimony of Honora Fitzpatrick in page 121.

[310] Arnold, *Defence and Prison Experiences*, 38.

[311] Ibid., 22.

[312] Ibid., 22, 46, 48; John Surratt, "Rockville Lecture," *Washington Evening Star*, December 7, 1870; William Hanchett, "The War Department and Booth's Abduction Plot," *Lincoln Herald*, Winter, vol. 82, no. 4, (1980): 499-508. Also see the statements of Thomas Manning, watchman at Gautier's; and John T. Miles, one of the waiters, in *Investigation and Trial Papers*, M599, reel 5, frames 0285-94. Both of these witnesses remember Booth and six others about three or four weeks before the assassination.

[313] Arnold, *Defence and Prison Experiences*, 23; Arnold wrote:

> The next day as I was standing in front of Rullmans Hotel Penna. Avenue . . . in company with O'Laughlen, Booth riding by on horseback, stopped and called O'Laughlen. He conversed with him a short time and returned saying Booth wanted to see me. I went to the curb and met him. Booth apologized to me for the words he had used at the meeting, remarking he thought I must have been drunk in making the objections I did at the meeting in reference to his proposed plan of carrying out the abduction. I told him no – drukeness [sic] was on his and his party's part, that I was never more sober in my life, and what I said last night I meant and that this week should end my connection in the affair.

[314] *National Intelligencer*, March 18, 1865.

[315] *Washington Evening Star*, March 18, 1865.

[316] Arnold, *Defence and Prison Experiences*, 47.

317 Weichmann, *True History of Assassination*, 101.

318 Arnold, *Defence and Prison Experiences*, 47.

319 *Trial of John H. Surratt*, see testimony of William Norton in 1:510-14.

320 Arnold, *Defence and Prison Experiences*, 23-24; John Surratt, "Rockville Lecture."

321 Of this incident, Arnold wrote:, "Booth made enquiries [sic] at the encampment at which place the performance was to be held, and learned he, the President, was not there" (24); Tidwell and others in *Come Retribution* stated that Davenport told of Booth's appearance at the hospital some years later in an interview with a reporter for a Boston publication; no other documentation given.

322 Arnold recorded, Booth returned immediately seemingly very much excited cautioning care and descretion [sic] in our movements and in a hurried manner advising, seperation [sic] from one another and to return to different routes into the City, as he feared our movements were being overlooked" (Arnold, *Defence and Prison Experiences*, 48); Of the men who were there, only Arnold wrote about this incident. However, John Surratt gave a speech in 1870 in Rockville, Maryland, a city just a few miles outside of Washington. He spoke of the group's general intentions: "By the time the alarm could have been given and horses saddled, we would have been on our way through Southern Maryland towards the Potomac river" (Surratt, "Rockville Lecture").

323 Weichmann, *True History of Assassination*, 101-102; Pitman, *Assassination of President Lincoln*, see testimony of Weichmann in page 118.

324 Smith, *American Gothic*, quotes *Boston Globe*, June 17, 1878.

325 Owned by John Chandler Thompson.

326 Pitman, *Assassination of President Lincoln*, see testimony of John Lloyd in page 85.

327 On March 20, Powell was in New York City at the Revere House Hotel. There he wrote two letters, one to John Surratt and the other to Mary Branson in Baltimore (Weichmann, *True History of Assassination*, 101; *Investigation and Trial Papers*, M599, roll 3, statement of Mary Branson).
    Colonel H. H. Wells, in a letter to the chief of the New York Detective Police, wrote, "It appears by the statement of two woman in Baltimore named Branson, that one of them met Louis Payne alias, Louis Powell, alias Jim Moore at Gettysburg" and that Powell had used this alias while in New York (*Investigation and Trial Papers*, M599, roll 1, p. 36; H. H. Wells to John Young, May 11, 1865). Also in this letter, Wells stated that Branson confirmed that Powell did live with the Branson family beginning in the "middle of January." Mary Branson also confirmed that Powell left for New York City after March 14, 1865.

328 Arnold, *Defence and Prison Experiences*, 24, 48.

329 Michael W. Kauffman, "John Wilkes Booth and the Murder of Abraham Lincoln," *Blue and Gray Magazine*, April 1990, 24.

330 *Washington Evening Star*, March 18, 1864, 1.

331 *Trial of John H. Surratt*, see testimony of Weichmann in page 400; also in Weichmann, *True History of Assassination*, 119.

332 Arnold wrote about the letter, "I went out to my brothers at Hookstown Balto. C. and I returned March 25th to Baltimore I was informed at my father's that Booth had called

to see me and left a card requesting me to call upon him at Barnums Hotel. I found a letter there also from him for me, in which he stated he desired to give it another trial the week following and if unsuccessful [sic] to abandon it forever. The letter found in Booths trunk was in answer to this letter which I innocently wrote to prevent his undertaking it" (Arnold, *Defence and Prison Experiences*, 24).

333 Samuel Arnold, *Defence and Prison Experiences*, 24.

334

March 27, 1865

Dear John:

Was business so important that you could not remain in Balto. til I saw you? I came in as soon as I could, but found you had gone to Washington. I called also to see Mike, but learned from his mother he had gone out with you, and had not returned. I concluded, therefore, he had gone with you. How inconsiderate you have been! When I left you, you stated we would not meet in a month or so. Therefore, I made application for employment, an answer to which I shall receive during the week. I told my parents I had ceased with you. Can I, then, under existing circumstances, come as you request? You know full well that the Government suspicions something is going on there; therefore, the undertaking is becoming more complicated. Why not, for the present, desist, for various reasons, which, if you look into, you can readily see, without my making any mention thereof. You, nor any one can censure me for my present course. You have been its cause, for how can I now come after telling them I had left you? Suspicion rests upon me now from my whole family, and even parties in the county. I will be compelled to leave home any how, and how soon I care not. None, no not one, were more in favor of the enterprise than myself, and to-day would be there, had you not done as you have – by this I mean manner of proceeding. I am, as you well know, in need. I am, you may say, in rags, whereas to-day I ought to be well clothed. I do not feel right stalking about with means, and more from appearances a beggar. I feel my dependence; but even all this would and was forgotten, for I was one with you. Time more propitious will arrive yet. Do not act rashly or in haste. I would prefer your first query, *go and see how it will be taken at Richmond, and ere long I shall be better prepared to again be with you.* I dislike writing; would sooner verbally make known my views; yet your non-writing causes me thus to proceed.

Do not in anger peruse this. Weigh all I have said, and, as a rational man and a friend, you can not censure or upbraid my conduct. I sincerely trust this, nor aught else that shall or may occur, will ever be an obstacle to obliterate our former friendship and attachment. Write me to Balto., as I expect to be in about Wednesday or Thursday or, if you can possibly come on. I will Tuesday meet you in Balto., at [the] Barnum Hotel. Ever I subscribe myself,

Your friend,
Sam

Arnold's message to Booth indicated that Arnold at least asked Booth to take his plan to Richmond. This suggestion indicates that Arnold thought that Richmond was unaware of Booth's plans. (*Investigation and Trial Papers*, M599, roll 15, frames 101-103,)

Federal soldiers found this letter in a trunk in John Wilkes Booth's room at the National Hotel after the assassination. Arnold had become irritated with Booth's ridiculous method of kidnapping Lincoln in the theater. Arnold accepted a position as clerk in a store owned by a Mr. Wharton at Old Pond Comfort, Virginia.

335 Booth addressed the telegram to Louis Weichmann, Esq., at 541 H Street, Washington, the Surratt's boardinghouse address. Booth sent this message from the telegraph office at the St. Nicholas Hotel in New York City. The telegraph read, "Tell John [Surratt] to telegraph number and street at once" (*Investigation and Trial Papers*, M599, roll 15, frame 0096, a copy of the telegram is on microfilm). Eliza Holohan carried the telegram from the boardinghouse to Weichmann at work the office of the commissary general of prisoners. Weichmann in turn gave the telegram to John Surratt, who understood what the telegram meant. Booth wanted Weichmann to ask John Surratt what the Washington address of the Herndon House run by Martha Murray.

336 Reprinted in Bryan, *Great American Myth*, 141.

337 Pitman, *Assassination of President Lincoln*, see testimony of Anna Ward; Weichmann memories.

338 "The Last Days of Payne," *New York World*, April 3, 1892; also see Kauffman, "John Wilkes Booth," 24.

339 Lincoln, *Works of Abraham Lincoln*, 8:367-374.

340 Badeau dates for first outburst on March 26 and describes the ambulance as "a sort of half-open carriage with two seats" (Badeau was Edwin Booth's lifelong best friend) (Adam Badeau, *Grant in Peace: From Appomattox to Mount McGregor* (Hartford, 1887), 356-357, for Badeau's account of the incident with Mrs. Griffin.

341 Badeau wrote: "She was absolutely jealous of poor, ugly Abraham Lincoln" (Ibid., 357).

342 Ruth Painter Randal, *Mary Lincoln: Biography of a Marriage* (Boston: Little, Brown, 1953, 334-336; Justin G. Turner and Linda Levitt Turner, *Mary Todd Lincoln: Her Life and Letters* (New York: Alfred A. Knopf, 1972), 206-208, for addition accounts of this incident with Mrs. Griffin and Mrs. Ord.

343 Badeau, *Grant in Peace*, 356-358.

344 Ibid., 358-365; Horace Porter, *Campaigning with Grant* (New York: Century, 1897; repr., Bloomington: Indiana University Press, 1961), 420-430; Ishbel Ross, *The President's Wife, Mary Todd Lincoln* (New York: G. P. Putnam's Sons, 1973), 224-228.

Shortly before Mrs. Lincoln's arrival at City Point, Adam Badeau wrote that in a conversation with Mrs. Stanton, he asked a question about Mrs. Lincoln. Mrs. Stanton replied, "I do not visit Mrs. Lincoln." Badeau was uncertain what she meant. He assumed that the wife of the secretary of war must visit the wife of the President. "Understand me, sir," Mrs. Stanton repeated, "I do not go to the White House. I do not visit Mrs. Lincoln."

Badeau wrote: "Mrs. Lincoln repeatedly attacked her husband in the presence of officers because of Mrs. Griffin and Mrs. Ord, and I never suffered greater humiliation and pain on account of one not a near personal friend than when I saw the Head of the State, the man who carried all the cares of the nation at such a crisis – subjected to this inexpressible public mortification" (the preceding account was taken from Adam Badeau's *Grant in Peace*, 356-60; also see William T. Sherman's *Memoirs of Gen. William T. Sherman*, who also wrote of these tirades of Mrs. Lincoln [2:326-328]).

[345] *Scribner's Magazine,* January 1893, 34-35, for an account of the trip by Marquis de Chambrun; also Marquis Adolphe de Chambrun, *Impressions of Lincoln and the Civil War* (New York: Random House, 1952).

[346] William H. Crook, "Lincoln's Last Day," *Harper's Monthly*, September 1907, 519-530; Crook wrote that "the streets were alive with people, all very much exited. There were bonfires everywhere."

[347] *Trial of John H. Surratt,* see testimony of Honora Fitzpatrick in page 173; James O. Hall, "Saga of Sara Slater"; James O. Hall, "The Veiled Lady," *North and South*, August 2000.

[348] War Department files, *Investigation and Trial Papers*, M599, reel 6, frames 0233-0251, see statement of Mary Surratt, April 17, 1865.

[349] John Surratt's "Rockville Lecture," December 5, 1870; *Trial of John H. Surratt*, see testimony of Susan Ann Mahoney in page 714.

[350] War Department files, statements of Mary Surratt made on the seventeenth and twenty-eighth of April 1865.

[351] Surratt, "Rockville Lecture."

Surratt's statement in his Rockville lecture that servants had told him Booth was in Boston was confirmed by a letter from Alfred Smith of Newport, Rhode Island. In a letter dated April 16, 1865, he wrote Secretary of War Stanton,

> J.W. Booth was in this city on the 5th inst. arriving in the steamboat from New York on that morning, and going with a lady to the Aquidneck House registering his name "J. W. Booth and lady." After taking breakfast, they went out walking and were out till 2 P.M. when they returned to the hotel and requested dinner to be sent to the room for the lady, the excuse being indefinite–but before the dinner could be served, they left on the 3 p. m. train for Boston.

Booth's betrothal to Lucy Hale, daughter of a New Hampshire senator, did not prevent his having relations with other women.

On Sarah Slater's disappearance, see Aftermath.

352 *Investigation and Trial Papers,* M599, reel 6, frames 0233-0251, see statement of Mary Surratt, April 17, 1865.

353 Surratt, "Rockville Lecture"; Levin, *This Awful Drama,* 187; also see "Report of the Proceedings in Canada" by Special Agent C. W. Taylor, The David Rankin Barbee Collection, Georgetown University Library, Washington, DC. Lee wrote in his diary for April 6, "Letter by Charley from Mr. Benjamin" Surratt also used the alias 'Charley Armstong.'"

354 The *Boston Sunday Herald* on April 11, 1915 reported that "on April 17, just after the tragedy at the capital, the *Boston Advertiser* contained this statement: 'John Wilkes Booth was in this city no longer ago than last Monday and perhaps on previous days. He visited the shooting gallery of Floyd & Edwards in Chapman place, by the Parker House, and practiced with a pistol.' Booth was seen at various places around the city on 5 and 6 April 1865. The purpose of this trip to Boston is unknown. Booth may have been there to settle some real estate transaction and he had told members of his family in New York that he was going to see his brother Edwin who was on stage in Boston at the time playing Hamlet."

355 Pitman, *Assassination of President Lincoln,* see testimony of Samual Chester in page 45; *Investigation and Trial Papers,* M599, reel 4, frames 155-164, see statement of Edward Person.

356 Gideon Welles wrote in his diary of the emotions of the city that day, "It was raining on Palm Sunday, April 9. In the evening the night's stillness was broken by the cannonading of Federal forces near Washington D.C. The news of General Lee's surrender on April 9 had finally reached Washington. At daybreak, on April 10th, close to 500 cannons again fired in celebration. The nation seems delirious with joy. Guns are firing bells ringing, flags flying, men laughing, children cheering, all, all jubilant. This surrender of the great Rebel captain and the most formidable and reliable army of the Secessionists virtually terminates the Rebellion." Gideon Welles, *Diary of Gideon Welles,* 2:278, entry for April 10, Monday, Wells gives a very good contemporary account of the feelings of the people the week between Lee's surrender to after Lincoln's assassination.

357 Roeliff Brinkerhoff, "Tragedy of an Age: An Eyewitness Account of Lincoln's Assassination," *Journal of Illinois State Historical Society* (Summer 1973): 206.

358 *National Intelligencer,* April 11, 1865; Lincoln, *Works of Abraham Lincoln,* 8:393; also see William H. Demote, "The Assassination of Abraham Lincoln," *Journal of the Illinois State Historical Society* (October 20, 1927): 422-428; William H. Crook, "Lincoln's Last Day," *Harper's Monthly,* September 1907, 519-530; Stimmel, "Lincoln's Bodyguard," 29.

359 William Crook in his *Harper's Monthly* article said that "the whole city was brilliantly illuminated that night. The public buildings were decorated and, from the Capitol to the Treasury, the whole length of Pennsylvania Avenue bore witness, with flags and lights, to the joy everybody felt because the war was over" (September 1907, 524).

360 The Marques Adolph de Chambrun wrote under an April 12 heading: "Washington has been in a state of frenzy since the taking of Richmond: shouts, speeches, fireworks, nothing else is to be seen or heard. The 10th of April was proclaimed a legal holiday, a day of thanksgiving throughout the nation . . . . The South is subjugated, trampled down.

Its male population has been practically annihilated. Ruin, devastation and death, such are the results of audacious and absurd pretensions" (Chambrun, *Impressions of Lincoln*, 90-91).

John W. Clampitt, one of Mary Surratt's trial lawyers, wrote of the times: "The heart of the nation throbbed with joy. Exultant music filled the air. Flags and banners with peaceful mottoes festooned the cities of the restored Union, and illuminations, grand in conception and effective in result, turned night into day" (John W. Clampitt, "The Trial of Mrs. Surratt," *North American Review*, September 1880, 223).

[361] Pitman, *Assassination of President Lincoln*, see testimony of Annie Ward in page 135; Weichmann, *True History of Assassination*, 130-131.

[362] Weichmann, *True History of Assassination*, 133.

[363] In Nothey's words, "Some years ago I purchased seventy-five acres of land from John Surratt, Senior. Mrs. Surratt sent me word that she wanted me to come to Surrattsville to settle for this piece of land. I owed her a part of the money on it. I met her there on Tuesday (April 11th), in regard to it. On Friday, the 14th of April, Mr. Gwynn brought me a letter from Mrs. Surratt, but I did not see her that day." (Pitman, *Assassination of President Lincoln*, 126).

[364] Poore, *Conspiracy Trial*, see testimony of Louis Weichmann in page 80.

[365] Weichmann, *True History of Assassination*, 134; Pitman, *Assassination of President Lincoln*, see testimony of Gwynn and Nothey in page 126.

[366] *Trial of John H. Surratt*, see testimony of Bennett Gwynn in page 755.

[367] Maxwell Whiteman, ed., Biographical introduction to *While Lincoln Lay Dying: A Facsimile Reproduction of the First Testimony Taken in Connection with the Assassination of Abraham Lincoln as Recorded by Corporal James Tanner* (Philadelphia: Union League of Philadelphia, 1968); Emerson Reck, *A. Lincoln: His Last 24 Hours*, 144; Smith, *American Gothic*, 131.

[368] *Washington Star*, April 12, 1865, 1.

[369] William H. Crook, "Lincoln's Last Day," 524.

[370] Herold spoke of Booth's reaction to his attorney, Frederick Stone, who gave the information to George Alfred Townsend; Stone felt that this "was the occasion of the deliberate murder being resolved upon by Booth" (see Townsend's *Day of Catoctin* (New York: Appleton, 1886, 490, 490n); Powell reported the incident to Thomas T. Eckert, see *Impeachment of the President*, House report 7, 40th Cong., 1st sess., 1867, 674; also see Jesse W. Weik, *Century Magazine*, February, 1913, 560; William Hanchett, "Happiest Day," 84.

[371] *Investigation and Trial Papers*, M599, reel 6, frames 16-17, see statement of Edward Person.

[372] "For a period of about ten days before the assassination, he visited my place every day, sometimes in the afternoons, sometimes in the evenings. At this time he was out of an [acting] engagement and drinking quite freely, noticeably so, even for him, I thought . . . he sometimes drank at my bar as much as a quart of brandy in the space of less than two hours of an evening" (*New York Sunday Telegraph*, May 23, 1909, quoted in Francis Wilson).

[373] *Investigation and Trial Papers*, M599, reel 5, frame 0458-0488, see H. Clay Ford statement, April 20.

[374] Edwin A. Emerson, "How Wilkes Booth's Friend Described His Crime," *Literary Digest*, March 6, 1926, 58.

[375] Ms. Porterfield wrote: "I don't remember now just how I answered, of course I gave him the benefit of my recollection and judgment, but I do remember that the question, coming so abruptly and unsuggested by anything either of us had been saying, was most singular and unusual." She later wrote that the next night, she and her mother attended the performance of *Our American Cousin* and saw Booth leap from the presidential box to the stage. She, like many others, described the pandemonium that followed (Jesse W. Weik, "A New Story of Lincoln's Assassination," *Century Magazine*, February 1913, 559-562).

[376] Alexandra Lee Levin, "The Canada Contact: Edwin Gray Lee," *Civil War Times Illustrated*, June 18, 1979, 44.

[377] Levin, *This Awful Drama*, 153.

[378] Surratt, "Rockville Lecture."

[379] On Wednesday, April 19, Edwin Lee wrote in his diary, "Gave Messenger $40 expenses & $100 services, Charley." On this trip Surratt's cover name was Charley Armstrong (Levin, *This Awful Drama*, 154).

[380] *Trial of John H. Surratt*, vol. 1, p. 472; also see vol. 2, pp. 841-842, 845-846, 858, 895, 902-903.

[381] C. Dwight Hess testified: "On the day before the assassination he (Booth) came into the office during the afternoon, interrupting me and the prompter of the theater in reading a manuscript. He seated himself in a chair, and entered into a conversation on the general illumination of the city that night. He asked me if I intended to illuminate. I said yes, I should, to a certain extent; but that the next night would be my great night of the illumination, that being the celebration of the fall of [Fort] Sumter. He then asked, "Do you intend to" or "Are you going to invite the President?" My reply, I think, was, "Yes; that reminds me I must send that invitation." I had it in my mind for several days to invite the Presidential party that night, the 14th. I sent my invitation to Mrs. Lincoln. My notes were usually addressed to her, as the best means of accomplishing the object."

"Booth's manner, and his entering in the way he did, struck me as rather peculiar. He must have observed that we were busy, and it was not usual for him to come into the office and take a seat, unless he was invited. He did upon this occasion, and made such a point of it that we were both considerably surprised. He pushed the matter so far that I got up and put the manuscript script away, and entered into conversation with him." (Pitman, *Assassination of President Lincoln*, 99).

George Wren, an actor at Grover's Theatre and present with Hess when Booth was there, wrote, "It occurred to me that the reason he did not design to go again was that it would be disagreeable to him to witness the subjugation of the rebellion" (*Investigation and Trial Papers*, M599, roll 6, frame 0491-0496).

[382] Leonard Grover, "Lincoln's Interest in the Theatre," *Century Magazine*, April 1909, 949.

[383] As was revealed in Atzerodt's unpublished confession, "I overheard Booth when in conversation with Wood (a Powell alias) say that he visited a chambermaid at Seward's

house and that she was pretty. He said he had a great mind to give her his diamond pin" (Ownsbey, *Alias "Paine,"* 71).

[384] Pitman, *Assassination of President Lincoln*, see testimony of Honora Fitzpatrick in page 132.

[385] Turner and Turner, *Mary Todd Lincoln*, 218.

[386] Leonard Grover wrote: "To gain relief from the many importunates, he often sought the theater for rest and relaxation . . . . He was satisfied with being entertained and amused, and to have his mind taken from the sea of troubles which awaited him elsewhere" (Grover, "Lincoln's Interest in Theater," 944).

[387] Helm, *True Story of Mary*, 119-120.

[388] Grover, "Lincoln's Interest in Theater," 945.

[389] Carpenter, *Six Months at White House*, 52.

[390] Ibid., 160-161.

[391] *Lincoln Herald*, Summer 1957.

[392] November 10, 1863.

[393] *Lincoln Herald*, Summer 1957.

[394] Leonard Grover, the owner of Grover's Theatre, wrote that Lincoln was at the theater frequently "without guard or special attendance" (for a more detailed account of Lincoln's interest in the theater, see Leonard Grover, "Lincoln's Interest in Theater," 943-959 and Brooks, *Washington, D.C., in Lincoln's Time*, 71-72).

[395] Cornelius Cole, *Memoirs of Cornelius Cole*, (New York, 1908), 214.

[396] *New York Times*, April 17, 1865, "It is known that on frequent occasions he would start from the Executive mansion for his Summer country residence at the Soldier's Home without the cavalry escort, which often hurried and overtook him before he had proceeded far. It has always been understood that this escort was accepted by him only on the importunity of his friends as a matter of precaution." The *Times* went on to say that "the President before retiring to bed, would, when important military events were progressing visit the War Department, generally alone, passing over the dark intervening ground, even at late hours, on repeated occasions; and after the warning letters had been received, several close and intimate friends armed for any emergency were careful that he should not continue his visits without their company. For himself, the President seemed to have no fears" (Ibid., col. 3-4, 5, p. 1).

[397] Noah Brooks, "Washington in Lincoln's Time," *Century Magazine*, November 1894, 141.

[398] Cornelius, *Memoirs of Cornelius Cole*, 214.

[399] Lincoln's secretaries, Nicolay and Hay, wrote that "the sermons all day were full of gladness; . . . the country from morning till evening was filled with a solemn joy" (*Century Magazine*, vol. 39 (1890): 428).

[400] Mrs. M. E. Surratt:

> Dear Madam – During a late visit to the lower portion of the county, I ascertained of the willingness of Mr. Nothey to settle with you, and desire to call your attention to the fact, in urging the settlement of the claim of my late father's estate. However unpleasant, I must insist upon closing up

this matter, as it is imperative, in an early settlement of the estate, which is necessary.

You will, therefore, please inform me, at your earliest convenience, as to how and when you will be able to pay the balance remaining due on the land purchased by your late husband.

I am, dear madam, yours respectfully,
Geo. H. Calvert, Jr.

(Pitman, *Assassination of President Lincoln*, see testimony of George Calvert in page 126.)

[401] Weichmann, *True History of Assassination*, 164-165.

[402] James O. Hall suggested a scenario: "Would you do me a favor? Drop this package off with Lloyd and tell him that somebody will be by tonight to pick it up along with the weapons John left out there. And better keep this to yourself as there might be trouble if the wrong people hear of it" (James O. Hall, "John M. Lloyd, Star Witness," *Surratt Society News*, March 1977).

[403] Atzerodt, in his confession, made reference to this incident, saying, "Booth told me that Mrs. Surratt went to Surrattsville to get out the guns (two carbines) which had been taken to that place by Herold. This was Friday."

[404] *Trial of John H. Surratt*, see testimony of J. Z. Jenkins in 759.

[405] April 14, 1865

Mr. John Nothey,

Dear Sir:

I have this day received a letter from Mr. Calvert intimating that either you or your friends have represented to him that I am not willing to settle with you for the land.

You know that I am ready and have been waiting for these last two years; and now, if you do not come within the next ten days, I will settle with Mr. Calvert and bring suit against you immediately.

Mr. Calvert will give you a deed on receiving payment.

M. E. Surratt,
Administratrix of John H. Surratt
(Pitman, *Assassination of President Lincoln*, 126.)

[406] Ibid., see testimony of Emma Offutt in page 125.

[407] *Trial of John H. Surratt*, see testimony of John Lloyd.

408 Pitman, *Assassination of President Lincoln*, see testimony of James Lusby in page 129.

409 Ibid., see testimony of Richard Sweeney in page 129.

410 Ibid., see testimony of Bennett Gwynn in page 126.

411 Ibid., see testimony of Emma Offutt in page 125.

412 *Trial of John H. Surratt*, see testimony of Captain Bennett Gwynn in page 755.

413 *Investigation and Trial Papers*, M599, roll 6, frames 0170-0200. "Statement of Mrs. Mary E. Surratt, April 28, 1865, Carroll Prison"; *Trial of John H. Surratt*, see testimony of Captain Bennett Gwynn in page 756.

414 *Trial of John H. Surratt*, see testimony of Captain Bennett Gwynn in page 756.

415 Pitman, *Assassination of President Lincoln*, see testimony of James Lusby in page 129.

416 Weichmann, *True History of Assassination*, 172.

417 *Trial of John H. Surratt*, see testimony of Olivia Jenkins in page 746; Weichmann in his book stated that Mary Surratt answered the door and the caller was John Wilkes Booth although Weichmann admits that he did not see the caller (Ibid., 174).

418 Weichmann, *True History of Assassination*, 173.

419 *Trial of John H. Surratt*, see testimony of Eliza Holohan in page 689.

420 Seward, *Reminiscences of a War-Time*, 2254-255; *Galaxy*, April 1872.

421 Stanton had a reputation of being late, and Gideon Welles once wrote that Stanton "made it a point to be late."

422 Welles, *Diary of Gideon Welles*, April 14, 1865 entry, 282-283; Seward, *Reminiscences of War-Time*, 255-256; also see Moorefield Storey, "Dickens, Stanton, Sumner, and Storey," *Atlantic Monthly*, issue 145, pp. 463-465, Stanton told Senator Sumner of the dream; *Galaxy*, April 1872.

423 Seward, *Reminiscences of War-Time*, 257.

424 Turner and Turner, *Mary Todd Lincoln*, 219.

425 Ibid., 220.

426 Hanchett, "Happiest Day," 85.

427 Smith, *American Gothic*, 133.

428 Storey, "Dickens, Stanton, Sumner and Storey," 464.

429 *Lincoln: An Illustrated Biography* by Philip B. Kunhardt III and Peter W. Kunhardt contains photographs of the people who refused Lincoln's theater invitation.

430 The letter was addressed to "Mrs. M. A. Booth, No. 28 East Nineteenth Street, New York, N.Y." The *New York Herald* wrote that the letter was "all contained on one side of a half a sheet of note paper."

April 14, 2 A. M.

Dearest Mother:

I know you expect a letter from me, and am sure you will hardly forgive me. But indeed I have nothing to write about. Everything is dull, that is, has been till last night (the illumination).

Everything was bright and splendid. More so in my eyes if it had been a display in a nobler cause. But so goes the world. Might makes right. I only drop you these few lines to let you know I am well, and to say I have not heard from you. Excuse brevity; am in haste. Had one from Rose. With best love to you all, I am your affectionate son, ever,

John

*New York Herald*, April 30, 1865, col. 6, p. 1; the illumination here was also referred by William Crook in his book, *Through Five Administrations*, "On the evening of the 13th there was another illumination."

On March 28 Booth's mother wrote to her son, John, of her concern over his safety and well-being. She wrote:

I have never doubted your love and devotion to me; in fact, I always gave you praise for being the fondest of all my boys, but since you leave me to grief I must doubt it. I am no Roman mother. I love my dear ones before country or anything else. Heaven guard you, is my constant prayer.

Your loving mother.

(Collier's, December 17, 1924; Bryan, *Great American Myth*, 41; Rhodehamel and Taper, *Right or Wrong, God Judge Me*, 145.)

Of John Wilkes Booth's letter to his mother that he wrote in the early morning hours of April 14, Aldrich wrote: "It was an affectionate letter, such as any mother would like to receive from her son, containing nothing of particular moment, but ghastly to read now, with the thought of what the feelings of the man must have been who held the pen in writing it, knowing what overwhelming sorrow the next few hours would bring (Mrs. Thomas Bailey Aldrich, *Crowding Memories* [Boston: Houghton Mifflin, 1920], 73).

431 Mrs. Moss recalled that she shook hands with Booth at that time and, later in the day, shook hands with Lincoln (Helen Palmer Moss, "Lincoln and John Wilkes Booth as Seen on the Day of the Assassination," *Century Magazine*, April 1909, 591).

432 *Daily Constitutional Union*, April 15, 1865; Bryan, *Great American Myth*, 153.

433 *New York Tribune*, April 17, 1865.

434 The *Evening Star* read, "Lieutenant-general Grant, President and Mrs. Lincoln, and ladies, will occupy the state box at Ford's Theater to-night, to witness Miss Laura Keene's company in Tom Taylor's American Cousin."

In addition to this announcement, a paragraph in the City Items of the *Evening Star* read as follows:

Ford's Theatre.

Honor to our Soldiers!

A new and patriotic song and chorus has been written by Mr. H. B. Phillips, and will be sung this evening by the Entire Company to honor Lieutenant General Grant and President Lincoln and Lady, who will visit the Theatre in compliment to Miss Laura Keene, whose benefit and last appearance is announced in the bills of the day. The music of the above song is composed by Prof. W. Withers, Jr. (*Evening Star,* 3)

[435] William H. DeMotte, "The Assassination of Abraham Lincoln", *Journal of the Illinois State Historical Society* (October 20, 1927): 423.

[436] E. A. Emerson confirms this meeting in "How Wilkes Booth's Friend Described His Crime" (58-60); also see Amusements, *Washington Star,* April 14, 1865.

[437] It is an interesting footnote that when the Republican Convention in Chicago nominated Lincoln, a large number of delegates that night went to a local theater to see Laura Keene in *Our American Cousin.*

[438] Pitman, *Assassination of President Lincoln,* see testimony of Mary Ann Turner in page 75.

[439] In a confession by Atzerodt, on May 1, 1865, he wrote: "Booth never said until the last night (meaning Friday) that he intended to kill the President" ("The Lost Atzerodt Confession," *Surratt Courier,* October 1988; this confession was discovered by Joan L. Chaconas while looking through some old papers of William Doster, Atzerodt's lawyer in Goshen, Connecticut, in 1977).

[440] Pitman, *Assassination of President Lincoln,* see testimony of James W. Pumphrey in page 72.

[441] Originally, the rocking chair "had been in the reception room, but the ushers sitting in it had greased it with their hair," and Harry Clay Ford had it removed to the Ford's private rooms (Pitman, *Assassination of President Lincoln,* see testimony of Harry Ford in page 99).

It has been maintained for decades that sometime during that afternoon, Booth bored a small hole, using a gimlet (a small carpenter's tool), through the inner door leading to the president's box so he could see the president. He then loosened screws (on the keepers of locks) to both inner doors and propped a wooden rod behind the outer passage door, which, when properly arranged, prevented entrance from the outside. However, in 1962, Frank Ford, a son of Harry Clay Ford, wrote a letter that says in part "I say . . . unequivocally that John Wilkes Booth did not bore the hole in the door leading to the box President Lincoln occupied the night of his assassination . . . . The hole was bored by my father, Harry Ford, or rather on his orders, and was bored for the simple reason that it would allow the guard easy opportunity whenever he so desired to look into the box rather than open the inner door to check on the Presidential party" (Reck, *A. Linoln,* 75; letter from Frank Ford to George J. Olszewski, a Ford's Theatre historian, the letter is partially reprinted) Harry Ford maintained throughout his life that he thought it was "laughable" that Booth could do this on the day all knew the president would attend the theater in the evening and not be seen.

442  Pitman, *Assassination of President Lincoln*, see testimony of Joseph Burroughs, alias "Peanuts," in page 74.

443  Ibid., see testimony of Robert R. Jones, clerk at the Kirkwood House, in page 144.

444  April 25, 1865; *Investigation and Trial Papers*, M599, reel 3, frames 0596-0602, see Confession of Atzerodt.

445  Pitman, *Assassination of President Linoln*, 70.

446  John Y. Simon, ed., *The Personal Memoirs of Julia Dent Grant* (New York: G. P. Putnam's Sons, 1975), 154-155.

447  Interview with Mrs. Temple, *Chicago Daily Inter-Ocean*, June 18, 1878.

448  Porter, *Campaigning with Grant*, 498.

449  Ibid., 498-499; Julia Dent Grant, *The Personal Memoirs of Julia Dent Grant*, ed. John Y. Simon (New York: G. P. Putnam's Sons, 1975), 156; Porter, *Campaigning with Grant*, 499; this is also confirmed in John Matthews, letter to the editor, *National Intelligencer*, July 18, 1867, 2.

450  Welles, *Diary of Gideon Welles*, 255.

451  Sewell, *John P. Hale*, 222.

452  Ibid.

453  Crook, *Through Five Administrations*, 66-67; he repeated this conversation in "Lincoln's Last Day" (525).

454  Thomas Reed Turner, *Beware the People Weeping: Public Opinion and the Assassination of Abraham Lincoln* (Baton Rouge: Louisiana State University Press, 1982), 71, who quoted John A. Bingham "Recollection of Lincoln and Stanton," John A. Bingham Papers, Ohio Historical Society.

455  David Homer Bates, *Lincoln in the Telegraph Office: Recollections of the United States Military Telegraph Corps during the Civil War* (New York: Century, 1907_, 366-367; also see Badeau, *Grant in Peace*, 362; Bryan, *Great American Myth*,160-161.

456  *New York Sun*, April 27, 1913.

457  Crook wrote that "when we had reached the White House and he had climbed the steps he turned and stood there a moment before he went in. Then he said, "Good-bye, Crook."

It startled me. As far as I remember he had never said anything but 'Good-night Crook,' before. Of course, it is possible that I may be mistaken. In looking back, every word that he said has significance. But I remember distinctly the shock of surprise and the impression, at the time, that he had never said it before" (Crook, 67-68).

458  Pitman, *Assassination of President Lincoln*, see testimony of Mary Jane Anderson in page 75.

459  James Maddox, the propman at Ford's, said of Booth: "He had such a very winning way that it made every person like him. He was a good-natured and jovial kind of man. The people about the house, as far as I know, all liked him." In fact, Maddox was another one of those individuals who inadvertently helped Booth further his various schemes. Maddox testified that "I was employed at Ford's Theater as property man. In December last, I rented from Mrs. Davis, for John Wilkes Booth, the stable where Booth kept his horse up to the time of the murder of President Lincoln. Mr. Booth gave me the rent money monthly, and I paid it to Mrs. Davis" (Pitman, *Assassination of President Lincoln*, 75-76).

460  James Ferguson, *Saturday Evening Post*, February 12, 1927, 44, 46, 49.

461 Campbell MacCulloch, "This Man Saw Lincoln Shot," *Good Housekeeping*, February 1927, 115-116.

462 *New York Tribune*, April 17, 1865.

463 Pitman, *Assassination of President Lincoln*, see testimony of Pumphrey in page 72.

464 Poore, *Conspiracy Trial*, 1: 189-190, reprint of 1865 edition.

465 Impeachment Investigation, House Report 7, 40th Cong., 1st sess., 1867, 783. Matthews testified: "It was on the afternoon of Good Friday, April 14, 1865, at about 4 o'clock, that I met John Wilkes Booth (on horseback) on Pennsylvania avenue, at the triangular enclosure between Thirteenth and Fourteenth streets."

466 Ibid.; *National Intelligencer*, July 18, 1867.

467 Pitman, *Assassination of President Lincoln*, see testimony of John Devenay in pages 38-39.

468 Spangler wrote a statement, probably while he was imprisoned at Dry Tortugas, "In the evening, between five and six o'clock, Booth came into the theater and asked me for a halter [for his horse]. I was very busy at work at the time on the stage preparatory to the evening performance, and Rittespaugh went upstairs and brought one down. I went out to the stable with Booth and put the halter upon the horse. I commenced to take off the saddle when Booth said, 'Never mind, I do not want it off, but let it and the bridle remain'" (from Nettie Mudd, *The Life of Dr. Samuel A. Mudd*, [1906; repr., Linden, TN: Continental Book Company], 325).

469 Interview with Mrs. Temple, *Chicago Daily Inter-Ocean*, June 18, 1878; Statement of Henry Merrick, *New York Tribune*, April 17, 1865.

470 William A. Croffut, "Lincoln's Washington," *Atlantic Monthly*, January 1930, 55-65.

471 Reck, *A. Lincoln*, 79.

472 Letter to Francis Bicknell Carpenter, Chicago, November 15, 1865, in *Mary Todd Lincoln* (New York: Alfred A. Knopf, 1972), 284-285; William Crook also wrote of this carriage ride in in *Harper's Monthly*, 1907, 525.

473 "Mary, we have had a hard time of it since we came to Washington, but the war is over With God's blessing, and we may hope for four years of peace and happiness; we will then go back to Springfield and pass the rest of our lives in quiet. We have laid by some money, and during this term we will try and save up more, but I shall not have enough to support us. We will go back to Illinois, and I will open a law office at Springfield or Chicago and practice law and at least do enough to help give us a livelihood" (Katherine Helm, *True Story of Mary*, 255; Isaac Arnold, *The History of Abraham Lincoln and the Overthrow of Slavery* [Chicago: Clarke, 1866], 429-430).

474 William M. Stewart, "Reminiscences of William M. Stewart," ed. George Rothwell Brown, *Saturday Evening Post*, February 15, 1908; William M. Stewart, *Reminiscences of Senator William M. Stewart, of Nevada*, ed. George Rothwell Brown (Washington, DC, 1908), 190.

475 Starr, *Further Light on Lincoln's Last Day* (Harrisburg, PA: Private printing, 1930), 126; a facsimile of this note is printed.

476 Stewart, "Reminiscences of William M. Stewart," 190.

477 Isaac Arnold, *The Life of Abraham Lincoln* (Chicago: Jensen, McClurg, 1885), 431.

478 Thomas F. Pendel, *Thirty-six Years in the White House* (Washington, DC: Neale, 1902), 40.

[479]  Smith, "Lincoln's Bodyguard," 32.

[480]  Ford's Theatre was on the site of a Baptist church whose cornerstone was laid in 1833. It was converted into a theater by John T. Ford, a Baltimore theater producer. In early 1862, Ford remodeled the building for theatrical productions. On March 19, 1862, he reopened it as Ford's Atheneum for a spring season. In the 1800s, there was no summer theater season because the theater became too hot. In the fall of 1862, the regular season opened with John Sleeper Clarke starring in *Paul Pry and Toodles*.

However, a fire soon destroyed the building, and Ford constructed a completely new theater. There were seats for 2,400 people that sold for twenty-five cents to a dollar and boxes for up to ten dollars, including the double-size one for which President Lincoln paid. The theater was a success until December 31, 1862, when a fire caused by a defective gas meter left the theater in ruins.

On February 28, 1863, John Ford began construction on an even larger theater. After some construction problems – such as a lack of workmen, war supply problems, and bad weather – the theater was reopened on August 27, 1863. One newspaper's review said, "In magnitude, completeness, and elegance it has few superiors, even in our largest cities . . . . In fact, every improvement that genius could devise, and skill and wealth achieve, has Mr. Ford brought to his aid in the erection of this magnificent theatre" (*Washington Sunday Chronicle*, August 23, 1863).

[481]  Pitman, *Assassination of President Lincoln*, 229.

[482]  Ibid., 228; James B. Henderson testified that "I saw him (O'Laughlen) in this city on Thursday and Friday, the 13th and 14th of April. I do not know whether he visited J. Wilkes Booth on either of those day, but he told me on Friday that he was to see him that morning."

[483]  Ibid., 231.

[484]  "Samuel Arnold, was in my employ from the 2d of April to the 17th when he was arrested. He was employed by the week as a clerk. I was absent about three days during that time, but I have reason to believe he was there all the time, or I should have been told of his absence. Charles B. Hall testified that "I saw him every day" (Ibid., 241).

[485]  *Investigation and Trial Papeprs*, reel 3, frames 0596-0602, Atzerodt's statement of April 25, 1865; After his capture, Powell told Major Eckert that he was assigned the task of assassinating Secretary Seward. He told Rev. Gillette, just before his execution, that "until the morning of the fatal day, no crime more serious than the abduction had been contemplated." Moments before his death, Powell also told Rev. Gillette that "it was early in that day that he was instructed as to what was expected of him" ("Last Days of Payne").

[486]  *New York Evening Post*, July 8, 1884.

[487]  Pitman, *Assassination of President Lincoln*, see testimony of Joseph "Peanuts" Burroughs in page 74.

[488]  John E. Buckingham, *Reminiscences and Souveniers of the Assassination of Abraham Lincoln* (Washington, DC: Rufus H. Darby, 1894), 13; Buckingham wrote, "In looking back over the occurrences, I can see that Booth must have been under great stress of excitement,

although his actions did not seem to me at that time to be at all strange. He was naturally a nervous man his movements."

489 Pitman, *Assassination of President Lincoln*, 72.

490 Ibid., 81.

491 *Minneapolis Journal* (April 27, 1914).

492 "Guarding Mr. Lincoln," *Ohio Soldier*, April 28, 1888.

493 John F. Parker was born on May 19, 1830, in Frederick County, Virginia. He came to Washington in the early 1850s and worked as a carpenter. He married Mary America Maus on July 16, 1855, and by the 1860 census had three children and lived at 750 L Street. He enlisted for ninety days in the Union Army on April 11, 1861, and left when his enlistment was over. When the Metropolitan Police Force was organized on September 11, 1861, he became one of its first patrolmen. He lived at 750 L Street.

On October 14, 1862, Parker was charged with conduct unbecoming an officer and with the use of violent and coarse language. The owner of a grocery store had complained that officers were embarrassing him by loitering in front of his store. One of Parker's superiors, after arriving on the scene, was talking to a police recruit, whom he had found with Parker in front of the shop. Parker took personal offense at what the supervisor was saying.

The police board found that Parker had shown a disposition to be insubordinate. "The language he used, was exceedingly violent and disrespectful, and if permitted to be continued, must lead to insubordination," the report said. Parker maintained, however, that he had been jesting and had not intended to be disrespectful to his superior. This being his first offense, Parker was reprimanded and transferred to another precinct (Otto Eisenschiml, *Why Was Lincoln Murdered?* (Boston: Little, Brown, 1937), 12, who quotes from Records of the Metropolitan Police Department, Washington, DC. Also see Stanley Kimmel, "Fatal Remissness of Lincoln's Guard Unpunished," *Washington Star*, February 9, 1936; Reck, *A. Lincoln*, 162-163).

Again in March 1863, Parker went before the police board, charged with willful violation of the rules and regulations and with conduct unbecoming an officer. This time he was accused not only of having used "highly offensive language toward an officer named Pumphrey" and of having visited a house of prostitution kept by a Ms. Annie Wilson, but also of having been intoxicated and, after having gone to bed, having fired a pistol through the window. According to the official charges, Parker had, "after coming off of his beat at twelve o'clock, gone to the said house and to bed, with one of the inmates, Miss Ada Green." Parker maintained that he "was at a house of ill fame with no other excuse than that he was sent for by the Keeper." The employees of the house came to Parker's defense, and the Police Board found that no evidence could be produced to show that Parker had been "drunk or had fired a Pistol there as charged." The charges were dropped (Ibid.).

Only two weeks later, Parker was accused of being found asleep on a streetcar when he should have been walking his rounds, but the charges were dismissed on April 2, 1863. Parker claimed that he and another officer, named Williams, had heard the squawking of ducks and that they thereupon had entered the car to determine the cause of this commotion.

Only three months later, on July 1, 1863, Parker had to appear before the police board again. This time the complaint was that he had refused to restrain some "disorderly Negroes" and had used insulting language to the lady making the complaint. These charges were also dismissed on July 9.

In March 1865, John Parker was detailed to the White House as one of four security guards. He received this special duty despite a history of insubordination and a shoddy service record. There is nothing in his record that could be called a recommendation.

Policemen assigned to the White House were normally some of best and most respected members of the Metropolitan Police Department, for example, Thomas Pendel and William Crook, two policemen who remained in the White House for decades. With a history of insubordination and his shoddy record, it is not known why Parker was appointed to such a sensitive assignment. In addition, on April 3 and again on April 4, Mrs. Lincoln wrote letters for Parker exempting him from the draft (a facsimile of the letter Mrs. Lincoln wrote on behalf of Parker appears in Eisenschiml, *Why Was Lincoln Murdered?* 15). Mary Lincoln may have interceded on Parkers behalf to "protect her turf" (James O. Hall, "The Mystery of Lincoln's Guard," *Surratt Society News*, May 1982).

[494]  Campbell MacCulloch, "This Man Saw Lincoln," 112, 116.

[495]  Charles A. Leale, "Lincoln's Last Hours," *Harper's Weekly*, 7; Hazelton, *Good Housekeeping*, February 1927, 116.

[496]  Lamon, *Recollections of Abraham Lincoln*, 272, 275, 277.

Lincoln gave Lamon the following pass:

Allow the bearer, W. H. Lamon, and friend, with ordinary baggage, to pass from Washington to Richmond and return.

A. Lincoln.

April 11, 1865

On April 11, Lamon left for Richmond.

"Make me one promise?" he asked of Lincoln.

"What is that?" said the president. "Perhaps I can."

"I want you to promise not to go to the theatre during my absence."

"Well," said he after some conversation, "I will do the best I can." Then turning to John P. Usher, then the secretary of the interior, who was present at the interview, he said in substance, "Lamon is a monomaniac on the subject of my safety . . . . What does anyone want to assassinate me for?" (Leonard Swett, "Conspiracies of the Rebellion," 188-189; this conversation is repeated in Ward Lamon's book *Recollections of Abraham Lincoln* [274-275].)

[497] Crook, *Through Five Administrations*, 65.

[498] Reck, *A. Lincoln*, 93; *National Republican*, April 15, 1865 and June 8, 1865.

[499] William O. Stoddard, *Abraham Lincoln: The True Story of a Great Life* (New York: Fords, Howard & Hulbert, 1888), 459; John Nicolay, *A Short Life of Abraham Lincoln* (New York: Century, 1902), 537, writes basically the same version. If Forbes was given a card by Booth, Stoddard and Nicolay could only have gotten that information from Forbes himself.

[500] Roeliff Brinkerhoff, "Tragedy of an Age: An Eyewitness of Lincoln's Assassination," ed. Arthur M. Markowitz, *Journal of the Illinois State Historical Society* (Summer 1973): 208.

[501] E. R. Shaw, "The Assassination of Lincoln," *McClure's Magazine*, December 1908, 183–184; Captain Gatch was attached to Company G, Eighty-ninth Ohio Volunteer Infantry, and had just arrived in Washington that day. For a thorough examination of eyewitness accounts, see Timothy S. Good, ed., *We Saw Lincoln Shot: One Hundred Eyewitness Accounts* (Jackson, MS: University Press of Mississippi, 1995).

[502] Pitman, *Assassination of President Lincoln*, see testimony of James P. Ferguson in page 76.

[503] Ruth Painter Randall, *Mary Lincoln: Biography of a Marriage*; Reck, *A. Lincoln*, 102. Both of these sources quoted a letter from Dr. Anson G. Henry to his wife, Washington, April 19, 1865, a photostat is in the Illinois State Historical Library, Springfield.

[504] John Lattimer, *Kennedy and Lincoln: Medical and Ballistic Comparisons of Their Assassinations* (New York: Harcourt Brace Jovanovich, 1980), see the Lincoln autopsy.

[505] Pitman, *Assassination of President Lincoln*, see testimony of Henry R. Rathbone in page 78.

[506] Ibid., see testimony of James Ferguson in page 76; Ferguson testified that after Booth entered the presidential box, "I saw no more of him until he made a rush for the front of the box and jumped over. He put his left hand on the railing, and with his right he seemed to strike back with a knife. I could see the knife gleam, and the next moment he was over the box. As he went over, his hand was raised, the handle of the knife up, the blade down .... I saw the flash of the pistol right back in the box. As the person jumped over and lit on the stage, I saw it was Booth."

[507] James Ferguson, *Washington Star*, April 17, 1865, 1.

[508] Good, *We Saw Lincoln Shot*, 21;
Did Booth fracture his fibula while jumping from the presidential box? Some historians believed that in this jump Booth fractured the fibula of his left leg just above the ankle (Reck, *A. Lincoln*, 107). But on that night, no one reported that Booth limped or hobbled as he raced toward the back door. Others believed that Booth sustained his injury in a fall from his horse as he raced to the Surratt Tavern (Michael Kaufman has an excellent treatment of this subject in *Blue and Gray*, June 1990, 17; also see Good, *We Saw Lincoln Shot*, 19).

William Ferguson wrote in his book that "Edwin [Booth], when he was only fourteen, made his first appearance at Boston. His father permitted him to play the part of Tressel, in 'Richard the Third,' a rider who bears a message .... As he needed a spur, his father lent him one of his own, with the remark, 'Edwin, I hope you will wear it with credit.' Edwin, all dressed for the part, fastened the spur to the heel of his right boot .... When the father died, his theatrical wardrobe was divided between the boys. Before the assassination of the President at Ford's Theater, Booth had planned to make his escape from the theater on horseback, but the folds of the American flag, by which the box was draped, played a big part in American history when it tripped the assassin in his flight, by entangling itself in the prongs of his spur, it was the spur that Edwin had worn as Tressel, sixteen years before. It was strapped on his right boot" (William J. Ferguson, *I Saw Booth Shoot Lincoln* [Boston: Houghton Mifflin, 1930], 21).

[509]  Good, *We Saw Lincoln Shot.*

[510]  Ibid.

[511]  Dr. Samuel R. Ward, "Present When Lincoln Was Shot" Kessinger's Mid-West Review, April 1931, pp.22-23*

[512]  Hawk later wrote: "Booth dragged himself up on one knee and was slashing the long knife around him like one who was crazy . . . . It was then, I am sure, I heard him say: 'The South shall be free!' I recognized Booth as he regained his feet and came toward me, waving his knife. I did not know what he had done or what his purpose might be. I did simply what any other man would have done – I ran. My dressing room was up a short flight of stairs and I retreated to it" (Allen C. Clark, *Abraham Lincoln in the National Capital* [Washington: W. F. Roberts, 1925], 100).

[513]  Buckingham, *Reminiscences and Souvenirs*, 13.

[514]  Ford was interviewed in the *New York Evening Post*, July 8, 1884.

[515]  Emerson, *Theatre Magazine*, June 1913.

[516]  House Report 7, 40th Cong., 1st sess., see Mathews testimony in page 787.

[517]  Ferguson, *Saturday Evening Post*, February 12, 1927, 42; Ferguson's first spoken lines in his acting career had been directed toward Booth in Richard III.

[518]  "Lincoln's Washington," *Atlantic Monthly*, January 1930.

[519]  Pitman, *Assassination of President Lincoln*, see testimony of Withers in page 79.

[520]  Charles Taft, "Abraham Lincoln's Last Hours," *Century Magazine*, vol. 45 (February 1893): 634.

[521]  The distance from the stage up to the presidential box in the restoration of Ford's Theatre is ten feet ten inches. It is not known what the original height from the box to the stage was. In the conspiracy trial, there was testimony from Henry Clay Ford that he had been in the presidential box and that Spangler had handed him a hammer "from the stage." Considering the height of a man with an extended arm, the length of a hammer and the length of Ford's arm, perhaps the jump from box to stage was ten feet. Booth could negotiate a jump from this height and even slightly higher with little difficulty. John T. Ford remembered at the conspiracy trial that Booth was "a very bold and fearless man," and that Ford had "seen him make a similar leap without hesitation." Ford went on to say that "Booth had a reputation for being a great gymnast. He introduced, in some Shakespearian plays, some of the most extraordinary and outrageous leaps-at least they were deemed so by the critics, and were condemned by the press at the time." After one of Booth's leaps, the *Baltimore Sun* in an editorial the next day called him "The Gymnastic Actor" (Pitman, *Assassination of President Lincoln*, see testimony of John T. Ford in page 103).

522 Helm, *True Story of Mary*, 258.

523 *New York World*, February 17, 1924, sec. E, p. 8.

524 *New York Times*, February 14, 1926.

525 Jesse W. Weik, "A New Story of Lincoln's Assassination," *Century Magazine*, February 1913, 562; John Creahan, *The Life of Laura Keene* (Philadelphia: Rodgers Publishing, 1897), 27.

526 Charles Taft, "Abraham Lincoln's Last Hours," 635.

527 Leale, "Lincoln's Last Hours," 8.

528 Taft, "Abraham Lincoln's Last Hours," 635.

529 Leale's address was given before the commandery of the state of New York, Military Order of the Loyal Legion of the U.S., New York City, at its February meeting, 1909; Leale, "Lincoln's Last Hours," 8.

530 Chambrun, *Impressions of Lincoln*, 95-96.

531 Stewart, *Reminiscences of Senator William*, 193.

532 Taft, "Abraham Lincoln's Last Hours," 636.

533 Helen Nicolay, "Lincoln's Secretary," New York: Longmans, Green, 1949, 232-33; William H. DeMotte, "The Assassination of Abraham Lincoln," *Journal of the Illinois State Historical Society* (October 20, 1927): 422-428.

534 Official Orders, vol. 46, pt. 3, p. 736.

535 Pitman, *Assassination of President Lincoln*, see testimony of William T. Kent in page 82.

536 James G. Randall and Theodore C. Pease, eds., *Diary of Orville Hickman Browning*, 2 vols. (Springfield, IL: Jefferson's Printing and Stationery, 1933), 2:18-19.

537 Allan Nevins and Milton Thomas, eds., *Diary of George T. Strong*, 4 vols. (New York: MacMillan, 1952), 3:582.

538 "The Attack on Mr. Seward," *New York Times*, April 17, 1865, 4.

539 Patricia Carley Johnson, "I Have Supped Full on Horrors," *American Heritage*, October 1959, 61-101.

540 Seward, *Reminiscences of a War-Time*, 258-259.

541 Johnson, "Supped Full on Horrors," 61-101.

542 For a contemporary account of the evening, see *Washington Star*, April 15, 1865, 1.

543 Pitman, *Assassination of President Lincoln*, see testimony of Robert Nelson in page 158.

544 "Last Days of Payne."

545 Pitman, *Assassination of President Lincoln*, see testimony of Lt. John F. Toffey in pages 159-160.

546 Poore, *Conspiracy Trial*, 327.

547 Moorefield Storey, "Dickens, Stanton, Sumner, and Storey," 463-465.

548 Welles, *Diary of Gideon Welles*, 285.

549 Moorfield Storey, "Dickens, Stanton, Sumner, and Storey," 463-65; Welles, *Diary of Gideon Welles*, April 14, 1865 entry, 285-286.

550 Assistant Secretary of War Charles Dana wrote later that "they seemed to be almost as paralyzed as the unconscious sufferer with the little chamber. The surgeons said there was no hope. Mr. Stanton alone was in full activity" (Dana, *Recollections of the Civil War*, 274.) Two days later in a letter, James Tanner wrote that "Secretary Stanton was there trying

every way to be calm and yet was very much moved" (letter from Tanner to Henry F. Walch, April 17, 1865, *American Historical Review* 29 (1924): 516). And again years later, Corporal Tanner wrote that "though all that awful night Stanton was the one man of steel" (*New York Sun*, April 16, 1905, 7). Dr. Leale said of Stanton, "He was then the master, and in reality Acting President of the United States."

551  Pitman, *Assassination of President Lincoln,* see testimony of John Fletcher in page 145.

552  Leaving the Kirkwood on D Street and turning north at Tenth Street takes Atzerodt to Ford's Theater. If Atzerodt was at Naylor's near 10:00 PM, had a drink with Fletcher, left and went to the Kirkwood, left there and rode to Tenth Street, Atzerodt had to be near Ford's Theatre at the time of the assassination. Atzerodt was checking to see if Booth would really carry out his plans to murder Lincoln.

553  Pitman, *Assassination of President Linolcn,* see testimony of John Fletcher in pages 83-84.

554  Ibid.; Poore, *Conspiracy Trial,* see John Fletcher testimony in pages 326-330.
As Fletcher told General Augur, two men came to the stable on the late afternoon of April 3. The two men brought in two horses, one a brown horse, blind in one eye. The well-dressed man "said he was going to Philadelphia, and that he would leave the sale of his horse to Atzerodt; he left, and I have not seen him since" (if this man was Booth, then the date had to have been April 1, 1865, since Booth left for New York/Philadelphia later that day). Fletcher handed the second man a stable card, and he wrote his name on it. A few days later, the bay horse was sold. The one-eyed horse remained in the stable until Wednesday, April 12, when the charges were paid and the horse taken away.

555  Pitman, *Assassination of President Lincoln,* see testimony of John Lee in page 144.

556  Ibid., 70; William A. Browning testified that between four and five o'clock in the afternoon of the fourteenth of April last, "I left the Vice-President's room in the Capitol, and went to the Kirkwood House, where we both boarded. On going to the office of the hotel, as was my custom, I noticed a card in my box, which was adjoining that of Mr. Johnson's, and Jr. Jones, the clerk, handed it to me. It was a very common mistake in the office to put cards intended for me into the Vice-President's box, and his would find their way into mine; the boxes being together."

557  Ibid.; Browning testified: "I had known J. Wilkes Booth when he was playing in Nashville, Tenn.; I met him there several times; that was the only acquaintance I had with him . . . . I thought perhaps he    might have called upon me, having known me; but when his name was connected with the assassination, I looked upon it differently."

558  Sources for this section on Vice President Johnson is from Welles, *Diary of Gideon Welles,* 2:288-89; Storey, "Dickens, Stanton, Sumner, and Storey," 463-65; Buckingham, *Reminiscences and Souvenirs,* 61-63.

559  Taft, "Lincoln's Last Hours"; Clara Harris letter, April 29, 1865, *New York Historical Society.*

560  Pendel, Thomas F, *Thirty-six Years,* 44.

561  Leonard Grover, *Century Magazine,* April 1909.

562  In the biblical aspect, Haman, the chief minister of the Persian king Ahasuerus, planned the extermination of all the Jews in Persia, including the hanging of Mordecai, Equeen Ester's uncle. Haman himself was hanged after Esther, the Jewish wife of the king, intervened

(*Esther*, 3-7). (*American Historical Review* 29 (1924): 516; Whiteman, *While Lincoln Lay Dying*; also see Nancy Griffith, "Corporal James Tanner," *Surratt Society Newsletter*, August 1980, for more biography on the life of James Tanner.)

563    "At this hour the melancholy intelligence of the assassination of Mr. Lincoln, President of the U.S. at Fords Theater was brought to this office, and information obtained from the following persons goes to show that the assassin is a man named J. Wils [sic] Booth" (*Records of the Government of the District of Columbia*, National Archives; also see U.S. National Archives Web site (http://www.archives.gov/exhibit_hall/american_originals/lincoln.html) for a colored photocopy of entry.

564    Official Records, vol. 46, pt. 3, p. 756.

565    Porter, *Campaigning with Grant*, 499-500.

566    Official Records Armies 46, 1st ser., pt. 3, p. 756.

567    see Reck, *A. Lincoln*, 145-146 for a more detailed description of the newspaper stories of the assassination.

568    Army, Official Records vol. 46, 1st ser., pt. 3, p. 754.

569    *Saturday Evening Post*, February 11, 1939, for Nicholas Murray Butter remembrances of Robert Lincoln.

570    Pitman, *Assassination of President Lincoln*, 41, 235.

571    Ibid., 236.

572    Stanton to General Dix, Official Records vol.46, 1st ser., pt. 3, p. 871.

573    The only source of information that Booth's claim to have known how to use the cipher is Asia.

        At the conspiracy trial, Major T. T. Eckert testified: "I have examined the secret cipher found in Booth's trunk, and the other cipher just testified to by the Assistant Secretary of War, (found in Confederate Secretary of State Judah P. Benjamin's Richmond office) and find they are the same." At the trial, Major Eckert produced cipher dispatches bearing dates of October 13 and 19. "These dispatches which I hold in my hand are copies and translations of certain cipher dispatches which came from Canada; They passed through the War Department in this city, where copies were taken of them, and the originals forwarded to Richmond. These dispatches are written in the cipher to which this model and the paper found in Booth's trunk furnish the key" (Pitman, *Assassination of President Lincoln*, 41-42).

574    Turner, *Beware the People Weeping*, 46.

575    Edward Bates, *The Diary of Edward Bates*, ed. Howard K. Beale. *Annual Report of the American Historical Association*, 1930 (Washington: Government Printing Office, 1933).

576    David McDonald, *Hoosier Justice: The Journal of David McDonald*, ed. Donald O. Dewey, *Indiana Magazine of History* 62 (1966): 199.

577    General George S. Boutwell to General Benjamin Butler, April 20, 1865, *Letters to Benjamin Butler*, 5:598, Library of Congress; General Boutwell was later to be a radical Republican Representative and U. S. Senator from Massachusetts.

578    Mrs. Dixon's May 1, 1865, *Surratt Society News*, March 1982.

579    Leale, "Lincoln's Last Hours," 10.

580    Ibid., Leale address.
581    Taft, "Abraham Lincoln's Last Hours," 635.
582    Letter to the *New York Times*, April 17, 1865, 1.
583    There are many variations of what Stanton said the night. "Now he belongs to the ages" is most widely quoted. However, this is how James Tanner, Stanton's stenographer that night, recorded Stanton's words, and the version that seems the most accurate (Richard Bak, *The Day Lincoln Was Shot* (Dallas, TX: Taylor Publishing, 1998), 98; Taft, "Lincoln's Last Hours," 635; and Nicolay and Hay, *Century Magazine*, January 1890, 436. John Hay give the quote as being said before the Gurley prayer, and Taft gives the quotes after the prayer. Welles, *Diary of Gideon Welles*, April 15, 1865 entry, 288).
584    *New York Sun*, April 16, 1905, 7.
585    Taft, "Abraham Lincoln's Last Hours," 635.
586    Ibid.; also see Statement of Mr. Field, Assistant Secretary of the Treasury, reprinted in Clara E. Laughlin, *The Death of Lincoln* (Doubleday, New York, 1909), 303-308. For a personal eyewitness account of the assassination by Ms. Julia Adelaide Shepard, a young lady, who was at Ford's Theatre the night of the assassination, *Century Magazine*, April 1909, 917-918. This account is in the form of a lengthy letter to her father, written April 16, the day after the assassination, before memories were contaminated by future events. The letter tells of the audience's reaction, the crowds in the street, and the tension in the city.
587    Letter of Tanner to friend Hadley F. Walch, April 17, 1865, *American Historical Review* 29 (1924): 514-517.
588    Welles, *Diary of Gideon Welles*, April 15, 1865 entry, 2:288.
589    Ibid., 2:289-90.
590    *London Times*, April 27, 1865.
591    *The Assassination of Abraham Lincoln, Late President of the United States of America, and the Attempted Assassination of William H. Seward, Secretary of State, and Frederick W. Seward, Assistant Secretary, on the Evening of the 14th of April, 1865. Expressions of Condolence and Sympathy Inspired by These Events* (Washington: Government Printing Office, 1866), 717 pages, copy at the Surratt Society, Clinton, MD.
592    April 17, 1865.
593    Army, Official Records, vol. 46, 1st ser., pt. 3, p. 786).
594    Ibid., 787.
595    *National Intelligencer*, April 24, 1865, see under "The Occasion in Memphis."
596    Helen Nicolay, *Lincoln's Secretary* (New York: Longmans, Green, 1949), 232-233.
597    William C. Davis, *An Honorable Defeat: The Last Days of the Confederate Government* (New York: Harcourt, 2001), 387.
598    Stephen R. Mallory, "Last Days of the Confederacy," *McClure' Magazine*, December 1890, 244, Mallory was the Confederate secretary of the navy; Robert McElroy, *Jefferson Davis*, 2 vols (New York, 1937), 2:486; also see Jefferson Davis to C. J. Wright, May 11, 1876, *Jefferson Davis, Constitutionalist: His Letters, Papers, and Speeches*, ed. Dunbar Rowland (Jackson, MS: 1923), 7:513.

599  Davis's latest biographer, William C. Davis, was of the opinion that "Jefferson Davis would have recoiled from assassination just as he shrank from retaliatory executions of Federal soldiers" (William Davis, *Jefferson Davis: the Man and His Hour* (New York: Harper Collins, 1991), 620.

600  "Jefferson Davis and Abraham Lincoln," *Confederate Veteran,* June 1908, 245-247, Alexander Kelly McClure interviewed Jefferson Davis in 1880 in Beauvoir, Mississippi; McClure repeated this quote in his book *Our Presidents and How We Make Them* (New York: Harper & Robs, 1905), 201.

601  W. T. Walthall, "The True Story of the Capture of Jefferson Davis," *Southern Historical Society Papers* 5 (March 1878): 116-117.

602  Varina Davis, *Jefferson Davis: Ex-president of the Confederate States of America: A Memoir By His Wife* (Freeport, NY: Books for Libraries Press, 1890), 2:627.

603  *The World's Work*, February 1908, 9902.

604  Letter Davis to Crafts, Carl Sandburg, *The Lincoln Collector: The Story of Oliver Barrett's R. Great Private Collection* (1949), 292-293.

605  *Washington Evening Star*, April 21, 1865, 1; Richmond Whig, May 2, 1865, 2; Turner, *Beware the People Weeping*, 91.

606  Thomas M. Cook, *New York Herald*, April 29, 1865.

607  Charles Bracelin Flood, *Lee: The Last Years* (New York: Houghton Mifflin, 1981), 43-44, quoted J. William Jones, *Personal Reminiscences, Anecdotes, and Letters of General Robert E. Lee* (1874), Lee to Count Joannes, September 4, 1865, New York.

608  Levin, *This Awful Drama*, 153.

609  Smith, *American Gothic*.

610  April 17, 1865, 1.

611  Bryan, *Great American Myth*, 384.

612  Turner, *Beware the People Weeping*, 95-96.

613  Sherman, *Memoirs of Gen. William*, 349.

614  Putnam, *Memories of My Youth* (New York: Putnam's Sons, 1914), 431.

615  Interview of Sir Charles Wyndham, *New York Herald*, June 27, 1909, 1-2.

616  *Lincoln Herald*, Summer 1957.

617  Ellsler, *Stage Memoirs*, 130.

618  Morris, *Life on the Stage*, 104-105; "Morris, "Recollections of John Wilkes Booth," 299-304.

619  Gene Fowler, *Good Night, Sweet Prince: The Life and Time of John Barrymore* (New York: Viking Press, 1944), 29.

620  Bryan, *Great American Myth*, 244; Margaret Leech, *Reveille in Washington, 1860-1865* (Harper & Brothers, 1941), 398.

621  All grammar and spelling errors are Ella Starr; letter reproduced in George Bryan, *Great American Myth*, 244.

622  House Report 7, 40th Cong., 1st sess., 1867, see John T. Ford testimony in pages 532-535.

623  "The Lincoln Tragedy, Reminiscences of Harry Ford," *New York Evening Post,* July 8, 1884,; House Report 7, 40th Cong., 1st sess., 532.

624  *Washington Star*, April 15, 1865, 1.

625 Augur to Morris, telegrams, Letters Sent, Department of Washington, RG 393, National Archives.

626 Years later, journalists and historians put the various pieces of the puzzle together when people became less afraid to tell what they knew or what they did (see Gary R. Planck, *The Lincoln Assassination's Forgotten Investigator: A. C. Richards* [Harrogate, Tennessee, 1993]; Gary R. Planck, "Lincoln Assassination: The 'Forgotten' Investigation," *Lincoln Herald,* Winter 1980, 521-539.

627

Department of the Metropolitan Police
483 Tenth Street
Washington City, May 1st, 1865

To John F. Parker

Sir: Take notice that charges have been preferred against you to the Board of the Metropolitan Police, which charges are now on file in the office of the secretary of the board, at No. 483 Tenth Street, and a copy hereof annexed. You are hereby notified and required to answer the said charges in accordance with, and in the manner required by the rules and regulations for the government of the police force.

You will also take notice that your trial upon said charges will be in order, and will take place at a meeting of this board to be held at the office of the said board, no. 483 Tenth Street, in said city, on the third day of May, 1865, at 1 o'clock p.m. and will be continued from day to day until the trial is concluded.

T. A. Lazenby, Secretary

To the Board of the Metropolitan Police:

I hereby charge Patrolman John F. Parker of the 5th Precinct with Neglect of duty.

### SPECIFICATION

In this, that said Parker was detailed to attend and protect the President, Mr. Lincoln, that while the President was at Ford's Theater on the night of the 14th of April last said Parker allowed a man to enter the President's private box and shoot the President.

Respectfully,
A. C. Richards,
Supt.

(A facsimile of the report appears in Stanley Kimmel, "Fatal Remissness.")

[628] Although Stanton had been mercilessly severe during the war with poor country boys who had fallen asleep on sentry duty after long marches and had repeatedly criticized Lincoln for undermining the discipline of the army through his granting of clemency, Stanton was inexplicably silent on the issue of Parker.

Parker was not punished, reprimanded, or even immediately relieved of his White House duties. There is no evidence that Parker was in any way involved in the murder conspiracy. He had escaped prosecution, in contrast to Spangler, who had been tried and convicted for less, had slipped past the notice of the newspapers of the day and was ignored by the public. Parker was not even called as a witness in the conspiracy trial and apparently was ignored by Stanton – one of the unexplained mysteries of the assassination.

[629] Crook, *Through Five Administration*, 71-72.

[630] Ibid., 72; also see Crook, "Lincoln's Last Day," 527.

[631] William H. Crook, *Memories of the White House* (Boston: Little, Brown, 1911), 41.

[632] Pitman, *Assassination of President Lincoln*, see testimony of Burroughs in page 74.

[633] Ibid., see testimony of Sgt. Cobb in pages 84-85.

[634] Ibid., see testimony of Polk Gardiner in page 85.

[635] Ibid., see testimony of John Lloyd in page 86.

[636] *Washington Star*, January 24, 1909.

[637] *Chicago Daily Inter-Ocean*, June 18, 1878.

[638] Ibid.

[639] Ibid.

[640] William E. Doster, *Episodes of Civil War* (New York: G. P. Putnam's Sons, 1915), 36.

[641] Keckley, *Behind the Scenes*, 91-92; also see John E. Washington, *They Knew Lincoln* (New York: E. P. Dutton, 1942), 205-225.

[642] Brooks, Noah, *Washington, D.C., in Lincoln's Time*, 266.

[643] Army, Official Records, vol. 46, 1st ser., pt. 3, pp. 783-84.

[644] Reprint of handbill is in Ray Stannard Baker, "The Capture, Death, and Burial of J. Wilkes Booth," *McClure's Magazine*, May 1897, pp. 574-585.

[645] Reprint of proclamation is in Baker, "Capture, Death, and Burial," 574-585.

[646] *Trial of John H. Surratt*, testimony of Mrs. Lambert who lived on the south side of H Street between Fourth and Fifth streets.

[647] Weichmann, *True History of Assassination*, 411, Richards to Weichmann letter, April 29, 1898, letter reprinted in entirety; also see McDevitt's statement in *Indianapolis News*, April 14, 1894.

[648] *Trial of John H. Surratt*, see testimony of Honora Fitzpatrick in page 717.

[649] *Trial of John H. Surratt*, see testimony of John Clarvoe in page 696.

[650] *Washington Evening Star*, April 15, 1865; *Trial of John H. Surratt*, see testimony of John Holohan in page 672.

[651] *Trial of John H. Surratt*, see testimony of John Holohan in page 675; Weichmann, *True History of Assassination*, 218-219.

[652] *Trial of John H. Surratt*, see testimony of Eliza Holohan in page 689.

[653] *Investigation and Trial Papers*, M599, reel 6, frames 0233-0251, statement of Mary Surratt, April 17, 1865.

654   House of Representatives, Report 99, 39th Cong., 1st sess., reward for the Capture of Booth, to accompany H. R. no. 801, July 24, 1866.

655   Dialog source: Pitman, *Assassination of President Lincoln*, see testimony of Major H. W. Smith in page 121; and *Investigation and Trial Papers*, M599, roll 10, frame 122-124, statement of Major H. W. Smith.

656   Mary Surratt's statement April 17, 1865, at General Augur's headquarters.

657   Pitman, *Assassination of President Lincoln*, see testimony of Major H. W. Smith in page 122.

658   Ibid., see testimony of Honora Fitzpatrick in page 132; Fitzpatrick was brought in to see Powell at General Augur's office. She said, "I did not recognize him (Powell) at the house."

659   Ibid., 154; Lewis Payne was the spelling of his name during the trial.

660   Dialog source: Pitman, *Assassination of President Lincoln*, see testimony of Major H. W. Smith in page 121; and *Investigation and Trial Papers*, M599, roll 10, frame 122-124, statement of Major H. W. Smith.

661   William E. Doster, *Episodes of Civil War* (New York: G. P. Putnam's Sons, 1915), 267.

662   Mary Surratt's statement, April 17, 1865, introduction.

663   Mary Surratt's statement of April 17, 1865.

664   "Statements Made by the Alleged Lincoln Conspirators Under Examination, 1865," *Investigation and Trial Papers*, reel 6, 0170-0200.

665   Ibid.

666   John T. Ford, "Behind the Curtain of a Conspiracy," *North American Review*, 1889, 484-493.

667   Leech, *Reveille in Washington*, 399.

668   *New York Tribune*, April 22, 1865.

669   *Chicago Daily Inter-Ocean*, June 18, 1878; John T. Ford repeats this story in the *Washington Evening Star*, December 7, 1881.

670   *Washington Evening Star*, December 7, 1881

671   Washington, *They Knew Lincoln*, bib., 254.

672   For an excellent treatment of orders given and received in the early hours after Lincoln was shot, see Turner, *Beware the People Weeping*.

673   Ibid., 105, cited Almarin Cooley Richards, Benjamin Butler Papers, Library of Congress.

674   A Committee on War Claims stated that James L. McPhail, while provost marshal of the state of Maryland, and other members of his detective force "were instrumental in causing the arrest of Arnold and McLaughlin, by giving information and advice." (House Report 325, 43rd Cong., 1st sess., 1874, 1, and House Report 742, 1874, 1-3).

675   A copy of the confession, the original having been lost or destroyed, can be found in the M619, reel 458, frames 030-0312, National Archives; a more readable confession was given to the *Baltimore American* by McPhail and published on January 18, 1869; also see Arnold, *Defence and Prison Experiences*, 52.

676   Pitman, *Assassination of President Lincoln*, see testimony of William Wallace in page 221.

677   Percy E. Martin, "Surprising Speed in the Identification of Two Baltimore Conspirators," *Surratt Society News*, October 1978; see also Army, Official Records, vol. 46, 1st ser., pt. 3, pp. 806, 821.

678    Arthur R. Loux, "The Mystery of the Telegraph Interruption," *Lincoln Herald* 81, no. 4 (Winter 1979): 284-87; also see David Homer Bates, *Lincoln in Telegraph Office*, 116-118.

679    Loux, "Mystery of Telegraph Interruption," 235-36.

680    John C. Brennan, "John Wilkes Booth's Enigmatic Brother Joseph," *Maryland Historical Magazine*, Spring 1983, 22-35; grammar errors copied as written; also in Rhodehamel and Taper, *Right or Wrong, God Judge Me*, 79; original letter in the Mapden-Booth Theatre Library, The Players, New York City.

681    John C. Brennan, "John Wilkes Booth's Enigmatic Brother Joseph," *Maryland Historical Magazine*, Spring 1983, 22-35.

682    Ibid.

As part of an interview with Joseph before Major General Dix, on May 12, in New York City, Joseph was asked:

> Q.   Have you ever been insane, Mr. Booth?
> A.   Yes, sir.
> Q.   For how long a time?
> A.   For several months. I was insane in Panama.
> Q.   On your return?
> A.   Yes, sir. That news made me insane.
> Q.   You was [sic] troubled before you went away from time to time?
> A.   Yes, sir.
> Q.   Have you any idea how long you was [sic] troubled on your way here?
> A.   Two or three days aboard ship, when I heard the news. Two or three days out before I began to get my thinking faculties.
> Q.   You have had several attacks of it in your lifetime?
> A.   Yes, sirs
> Q.   Do you remember how old you was[sic] when you had the first attack?
> A.   No, sir. About 10 or 12 I think.
> Q.   Have you ever been confined for that?
> A.   No, sir. It was melancholy insanity.

683    Mrs. Thomas Bailey Aldrich, *Crowding Memories*, 72.

684    Ibid.; Francis Wilson, *John Wilkes Booth: Fact and Ffiction of Lincoln's Assassination* (Boston: Houghton Mifflin, 1929), 280.

685    *Surratt Society News*, September 1985.

After the death of Orlando Tompkins, the ring descended to his son, Eugene Tompkins; and upon his death, the ring came into the possession of a man identified only as Mr. Kilby. To the ring, he added the inscription "April 6, 1865" ("Actions of Booth for Fifty Years a Mystery," *Boston Sunday Herald*, April 11, 1915).

686    April 24, 1865.

687    Wilson, *John Wilkes Booth*, 281.

688    Ibid., 282.

[689] *Century Magazine*, November 1893.

[690] Otis Skinner, *The Last Tragedian* (New York: Dodd, Mead, 1939), 142; Aldrich, *Crowding Memories*, 74-76. One such letter read: "You are advised to leave this city and this country forthwith. Your life will be the penalty if you tarry 48 hours longer. Revolvers are already loaded with which to shoot you down. You are a traitor to this government (or have been until your brother's bloody deed). Herein you have due warning. Lose no time in arranging for your departure. We hate the name of Booth. Leave quick or remember. [signed] Outraged Humanity."

[691] Smith, *American Gothic*.

[692] John S. Clarke affidavit of May 6, 1865, National Archives.

[693] Clarke, *Unlocked Book*, 130.

[694] Wilson, *John Wilkes Booth*, 283-284, who quoted Emil Benlier from an article "printed in the papers at the time"; see also in Osborn H. Oldroyd, *The Assassination of Abraham Lincoln* (Washington: O. H. Oldroyd, 1901), 96-97.

[695] The present University of Maryland in Baltimore.

[696] Gath, *Cincinnati Enquirer*, April 18, 1892.

[697] Mudd, *Life of Dr. Samuel*, 31.

[698] *Investigation and Trial Papers*, M599, reel 6, frames 0205-0211, statement of Richard Stuart, and reel, frame 0095, statement of William L. Bryant.

[699] *Investigation and Trial Papers*, M599, reel 6, frames 0205-0211, statement of Richard Stuart.

[700] Samuel Cox Jr. annotations in Thomas Jones's *J. Wilkes Booth;* see also Steers, *Still Mudd*, 50, 149, fn. 6.

[701] Mudd, *Life of Dr. Samuel*, 32.

[702] Michael Kaufman, *Blue and Gray Magazine*, June 1990.

[703] Pitman, *Assassination of President Lincoln*, see testimony of Bean in page 203 and testimony of Frank Bloyce in page 177.

[704] Ibid., see testimony of Farrell in page 219; Hardy in testifying the same day as his friend Farrell will put the time as just before sunset, and sunset that day was 6:45 PM. If Farrell is correct, the time fits the time frame given by Mudd; however, if Hardy is correct and Mudd only arrived at 6:30 PM, then there is a two and a half hours gap, and where was Mudd? An idea recently put forward by Dr. Edward Steers is that Mudd went to see William Burtles. Burtles was a known Confederate sympathizer who was involved in the Confederate courier route operating in Prince George and Charles County, Maryland. Burtles lived three miles south of Bryantown, a round trip of six miles on horseback would take about one and a half hours and with time needed to talk to Burtles that would have filled the missing two hours. And as we will see later, when Booth and Herold got lost and come across a black farmer, Oswell Swann, it is first to Burtles farm they ask Swann to take them. Perhaps Mudd was alerting Burtles that Booth and Herold would be coming by later that night.

[705] Pitman, *Assassination of President Lincoln*, see testimony of John Hardy in page 218.

[706] Ibid., see testimony of Farrell in page 219.

707 Statement of Samuel Cox Jr. to Osborn Oldroyd in *Assassination of Abraham Lincoln* (Washington, DC: Privately published, 1901), 269.

708 Mudd, *Life of Dr. Samuel*, 33.

709 Pitman, *Assassination of President Lincoln*, see testimony of Benjamin Gardiner in page 212.

710 Ibid., see testimony of Dr. George D. Mudd in page 206.

711 Ibid., see testimony of George Mudd in page 208.

712 Mudd, *Life of Dr. Samuel*, 30-35.

713 Pitman, *Assassination of President Lincoln*, see testimony of George Mudd in page 208. George Mudd explains in his testimony:

> There were four detectives, who asked me to go up in a room with them. (Tuesday afternoon) They there questioned me very particularly relative to this affair. I stated to them what I have already stated here; and upon my inability to answer all their questions, they ordered their carriage and asked me to direct them the way to Dr. Samuel Mudd's house. I accordingly went with them to Dr. Samuel Mudd's house. I was outside of the door, and saw him coming, and told him, as he entered the house, that the detectives had come there for the purpose of ascertaining the particulars relative to the matter which he had spoken to me about, and that I had made the statement to the military authorities which he had made to me on Sunday, and that they were up there for the purpose of making special inquiry in reference to it.

714 Pitman, *Assassination of President Linolcn*, see testimony of Lieutenant Alexander Lovett in page 87.

715 Ibid.

716 Mudd made two statement prior to his arrest; both were made on April 21, 1865. The first will be referred to as the voluntary statement and this was handwritten by Mudd. The second statement was made later in the day and drafted by Colonel H. H. Wells and signed by Mudd; this statement will be referred to as the Wells statement. Copies can be found in the *Investigation and Trial Papers Relating to the Assassination of President Lincoln* (M599, reel 5, frames 0212-0239); also reprinted in "From War Department Files, Statements Made by the Alleged Lincoln Conspirators Under Examination, 1865," Surratt Society, Clinton, Maryland, 1980; Steers, *Still Mudd*, appendix A and B). In both the voluntary statement and the Wells statement, Mudd denied knowing that the stranger who stayed at his house for approximately twenty-five hours was Booth even though Booth and Mudd had met three times before.

In an AFFIDAVIT CONCERNING CERTAIN STATEMENTS MADE BY DR. SAM'L A. MUDD of Captain George W. Dutton, he wrote that "during a conversation with Dr. Mudd, on the 22d of July, he confessed that he knew Booth when he came to his house with Herold, on the morning after the assassination of the President; that he had known Booth for some time, but was afraid to tell of his having been at his house on the 15th of April, fearing that his own and the lives of his family would be endangered thereby. He also confessed that he was with Booth at the National Hotel on the evening referred to by Weichmann in his testimony; that he came to Washington on that occasion to meet Booth by appointment, who wished to be introduced to John Surratt; that when he and Booth were going to Mrs. Surratt's house to see John Surratt, they met, on Seventh street, John Surratt, who was introduced to Booth, and they had a conversation of a private nature."

On August 28, Mudd wrote a statement, in response to the allegations made by Captain Dutton, in which he said that the statement "that I confessed to having known Booth while in my house; was afraid to give information of the fact, fearing to endanger my life, or made use of any language in that connection, I positively and emphatically declare to be notoriously false." In this statement, however, Mudd does admit to the December 23, 1864, Washington meeting.

Thomas Jones wrote a book, published in 1893, detailing the events surrounding his participation in hiding Booth and Herold until getting them across the Potomac. A copy of Jones's book was owned by Samuel Cox Jr. Of particular interest in this privately held volume is a series of annotations made in margins and blank pages of the book by Samuel Cox Jr. Jones's book with Cox's annotations resides in the *Maryland Historical Society*. In 1877, according to Samuel Cox Jr., after Dr. Mudd's release from prison, he and Dr. Mudd were candidates for the Maryland state legislature. The two men canvassed Charles County together during this period and, according to Cox, privately discussed the events of 1865 concerning John Wilkes Booth and David Herold. Cox wrote that Mudd confided to him that he recognized Booth when he came to his farm with a broken leg. Mudd maintained that Booth said nothing to him about shooting Lincoln. Booth and Herald told him that they had just crossed the Potomac and that Booth's horse had fallen and broken his leg. Mudd told Cox that "he believed the statement, and knew nothing different while he was ministering to Booth's suffering." Mudd said he learned of the assassination when he went to Bryantown that afternoon to mail some contraband letters received from the South. A Union cavalry picket stopped him just outside the town and told him the news about Lincoln and Booth. Mudd's first impulse was to "deliver him up" to the military in Bryantown. Upon reflection, he decided to go back and "upbraid" Booth for treachery and the danger he had placed him and his family. When Mudd threatened to turn Booth in, Booth pled passionately, and Dr. Mudd compromised by asking him to leave immediately. (In 1901, Osborn H. Oldroyd interviewed Samuel Cox Jr. and was told the same account by Cox that appears in his annotations in Jones's book. Oldroyd published the account in his book, *Assassination of Abraham Lincoln*, privately published in Washington, DC, in 1901 [265-269]; Samuel Cox Jr., *J. Wilkes Booth* [Chicago: Laird & Lee, 1893].)

Cox also told Oldroyd that "from statements made to me, I believe Mudd was aware of the intention to abduct President Lincoln, but am confident he knew nothing of the plan of assassination" (statement of Samuel Cox Jr., 269).

77 All these points have been originally researched by historian Michael Kaufman. *Saturday Evening Post*, February 12, 1927, 42; also see *We Saw Booth Kill Lincoln* for an analysis

of the many eyewitness accounts of the assassination; M599, reel 4, frames 442-485 for Herold's first interrogation, in particular frame 457; testimony of "Peanuts" Boroughs and Sergeant Cobb.

[718] Pitman, *Assassination of President Lincoln*, see testimony of Washington Briscoe in page 145.

[719] Statement of George A. Atzerodt on April 25, 1865, *Investigation and Trial Papers*, M599, reel 3, frames 0596-0602, National Archives; Atzerodt said, "[I] then walked up 4 1/2 St. and there met a Stranger who asked me where he could find a Hotel to stop at and I told him to come to the Pa. House and he did so. He was a Stranger to me, and I never seen him before and have not since."

[720] Pitman, *Assassination of President Lincoln*, see testimony of John Greenawalt in page 146.

[721] Ibid., see testimony of John Greenawalt in page 147.

James Walker, a servant at the Pennsylvania House, confirms the time of Atzerodt arrival at "about 2:00 in the morning." Walker testified that "he (Atzerodt) left between 5 and 6 in the morning. As I was going out for a hack to take a lady to the 6:15 train, I overtook him about thirty steps from the door; he was walking along slowly. Another man came to the house about the same time that night, and occupied the same room. He went away a little earlier, to take the 6:15 train . . . . He had no baggage that I saw . . . . They (Atzerodt and Thomas) had no conversation in my presence" (Pitman, *Assassination of President Lincoln*, see testimony of James Walker in page 147).

[722] Ibid., see testimony of John Caldwell in page 148.

[723] Statement of William R. Gaither, *Investigation and Trial Papers*, M599, reel 3, frames 0548-53 ; Gaithersburg was named after the Gaither family and is located immediately north of Rockville, which is immediately north of Washington, DC.

[724] Pitman, *Assassination of President Lincoln*, see testimony of Hezekiah Metz in page 149; Metz testified, "On the Sunday following the death of Mr. Lincoln, the prisoner, George A. Atzerodt, was at my house, and eat his dinner there . . . . He was just from Washington. We were inquiring about the news, and a conversation came up about General Grant's being shot-for we had understood that he had been shot on the cars-when Atzerodt said, as I understood, "If the man that was to follow him had followed him, it was likely to be so. Atzerodt passed in the neighborhood by the name of Andrew Attwood; that was the name by which I knew him" (Ibid., see testimony of Hezekiah Metz in page 149).

Somerset Leaman supported Metz's testimony when he testified that "while we were at the dinner table, my brother asked him the question again, whether General Grant was killed or not, and he said, 'No, I do not suppose he was;' and he added 'If it is so, some one must have got on the same car that he did.'" (Ibid., see testimony of Somerset Leaman in page 152).

[725] Ibid., see testimony of Hartman Richter in page 153.

[726] Ibid., see testimony of Sergeant L. W. Gemmill in page 149.

Sergeant Gemmill described the arrest:

I first went to Mr. Purdun's house to get him as guide to Mr. Richter's. When I knocked at the door, Richter asked me twice who it was before he would let me in. I told him to come and see. When he came to the door, I asked him if there was a man named Attwood there; he said no, there was no one there; that he had been there, but had gone to Frederick, or to that neighborhood. I then told him that I was going to search the house, when he said that his cousin was up stairs in bed. His wife then spoke up, and said that as for that there were three men there. He got a light, and taking two men with me, went up stairs, where I found Atzerodt lying on the front of the bed. I asked him his name, and he gave me a name that I did not understand, and which I thought was a fictitious one. I told him to get up and dress himself; and I took him to Mr. Leaman, a loyal man, who knew him. Mr. Leaman told me it was the man, meaning Attwood.

[727]   Entries in *Investigation and Trial Papers,* M619, reels 455 and 456, National Archives; these entries relate to reward claims.

[728]   *Investigation and Trial Papers,* M599, reel 6, frames 0227-0029.

[729]   Ibid., frame 0227; the route that Booth and Herold took that night came from Herold's interrogation on the *USS Montauk,* April 27, 1865, Ibid., reel 4, frames 0442-85; report by Colonel H. H. Wells giving a summary of his interview with Samuel Cox, Ibid., reel 4, frame 0207, NA; statement of Mary Swann, Ibid., reel 6, frames 0160-0162.

[730]   Thomas A. Jones, *J. Wilkes Booth* (Chicago: Laird & Lee, 1893), 78.

[731]   George Alfred Townsend interview with Thomas Jones, in "How Wilkes Booth Crossed the Potomac," *Century Magazine,* April 1884, 822-832.

[732]   Jones, *J. Wilkes Booth,* 68.

[733]   Townsend, *Century Magazine,* April 1884; see also in Jones, *J. Wilkes Booth,* 70-72.

[734]   Jones, *J. Wikes Booth,* 71, 73.

[735]   Ibid., 74-78.

[736]   Ibid., 80.

[737]   Townsend, 829; Jones, *J. Wilkes Booth,* 79.

[738]   Jones, *J. Wilkes Booth,* 80; Jones had written: "I mentioned to Booth that I had seen a horse grazing nearby, and he said it belonged to him. I told him and Herold that they would have to get rid of their horses or they would certainly betray them; besides, it would be impossible to feed them."

[739]   Mrs. Margaret C. Powers of Stafford, Virginia, wrote to Stanley Kimmel the following narrative:

The man who disposed of the horses was Mr. Franklin Robey (Cox's overseer). He told my father many years after the war, when he was a near neighbor, just how he did it, and the facts as I recall them are as follows:

There was a spot in the marsh where a limb of a large tree extended out over the water, deep enough to cover the horses after they were shot. He rode one horse and led the other out as far as he could in the water, climbed on the limb, and shot them. They sank out of sight, and I'm sure few ever knew what became of them. Mr. Robey, in my father's opinion, was a man of integrity, and thoroughly reliable, and there was never a doubt in our minds as to his story. Only a short time before my father's death, in 1932, at the age of eighty-five, we were discussing the book by Jones, and he remarked that he regretted so much that Jones had not known at the time he wrote the book what became of the horses" (Kimmel, 360).

This story is confirmed by Samuel Cox Jr., who said, "I am the only person living who knows where the horses ridden by Booth and Herold were taken and shot by Franklin A. Roby, who lived upon one of Colonel Cox's farms" (Oldroyd, *Assassination of Abraham Lincoln*, 269).

Jones did write, "During my week's attendance on the two men I never once saw Herold's horse, and saw Booth's only on the one occasion already referred to. I had no hand in the disposition of them; and do not remember, if I ever knew, the exact day that Herold removed them . . . . In the dense growth that covers the swamp there is a large area of quicksand covered with water. It is my opinion that the horses were led into this quick-sand and shot there, and that their own weight sunk them" (Jones, *J. Wilkes Booth*, 81-82).

It does appear that Robey, who knew the swamp, shot the horses with or without Herold's help. It is a fact "that not even a bone of them has ever been discovered" (Jones, *J. Wilkes Booth*, 82). Jones states that Franklin Robey did know of Booth and Herold's whereabouts and that Robey did see Booth (Jones, *J. Wilkes Booth*, 73).

[740] Townsend, *Century Magazine*, April 1884, 828.

[741] Jones, *J. Wilkes Booth*, 93.

[742] Jones, *J. Wilkes Booth*, 93; also see Buckingham, *Reminiscences and Souvenirs*, 63-65.

[743] Jones, *J. Wilkes Booth*, 101-105; also see *Reminiscences and Souvenirs*, 64; and Townsend, *Century Magazine*, April 1884, 822-833.

[744] Jones, *J. Wilkes Booth*, 94.

[745] William Hanchett, "Booth's Diary," *Journal of the Illinois State Historical Society* (February 1979): 39-56.

Some of what Booth wrote is factually incorrect. For example, on his first night of riding, Booth did not ride sixty miles, but closer to thirty. Also his broken bone, although very painful, was not "tearing the flesh" since Dr. Mudd later stated that "there was nothing resembling a compound fracture."

[746] Matthews' letter to the *National Intelligencer*, July 18, 1867, 2; Committee on the Judiciary, House Report 7, 40th Cong., 1st sess., 783; noted that Booth referred to Powell by his alias Paine.

John Mathews had fled Ford's Theatre with other actors with shouts of "burn!" "hang!" and "lynch!" from the crowd gathered about the theater. Later that night, Matthews went to his room in the Petersen House. It was then that Matthews remembered the letter that Booth had given him earlier. In the safety of his room, Mathews opened the letter. It "was written on a sheet of commercial note paper, coving three pages." Matthews claimed that "the first two pages were written in the spirit and style of the Philadelphia letter, he had left with his sister Asia back in November 1864. It was only at the concluding paragraph that anything was said bearing upon what had transpired."

Mathews asked himself, alone in his room, what to do now. "I thought to myself, 'What should I do with this letter?' It could only convict him. If this paper be found on me I will be compromised, no doubt lynched on the spot. 'If I take it to the newspaper office it will be known and I will be associated with the letter, and suspicions will grow out of it that can never be explained away, and I will be ruined.'"

Alarmed, Mathews threw the letter into his fireplace and burned it. He was the only one who ever saw what Booth had written; and two years later, he said that the last paragraph went about as follows:

> For a long time I have devoted my energies, my time and money to the accomplishment of a certain end. I have been disappointed. The moment has now arrived when I must change my plans. Many will blame me for what I am about to do; but posterity, I am sure, will justify me. Men who love their country better than gold or life.
> J. W. Booth, Paine, Herold, Atzerodt.

About June 1, a few days after John T. Ford was released from Carroll prison, he met John Mathews on the streets of Washington. Ford testified at the impeachment hearings for President Johnson recounting this conversation. "After some further conversation, Mathews said to me,

> I will tell you something about that letter. On the afternoon of the day of the assassination, at about four o'clock, I was going up Pennsylvania avenue; John Wilkes Booth came riding down on horseback, and we met between Seventh and Eighth streets, He was very much excited. He drew a packet from his pocket and handed it to me, saying, 'I wish you, no matter what occurs, to deliver this at the office of the Intelligencer to-morrow morning.'"
> Mathews went on to say, "He was very excited in his manner, and was apparently somewhat under the influence of liquor. He seemed to impress upon me, very seriously, the importance of keeping it a profound secret, and to be sure to deliver the letter faithfully . . . . I took it reluctantly, and put it in my side pocket, and kept it until late that night."

He said the assassination so frightened and bewildered him that when he went home, he remembered that Booth had given him this letter or package. He put his hand in, his pocket, and drew it out. In view of the great excitement prevailing, he resolved to break it open and read its contents. He did break it open and read it. It contained a justification of Booth's intended act. Mathews thought it was written on the day he received it. It went on something in the style of Booth's diary, claiming that he was called upon to do this murder and that he would do it, and for no other purpose than to serve his country, or something of that kind, quoting all the famous assassinations of history to justify the deed. Mathews said that after reading it, he made up his mind to destroy it; fearing that, if found upon his person, it might cost him imprisonment or probably his life. He therefore put it in the fire (Judiciary Committee, House of Representatives, Impeachment Investigation, 40th Cong., 1st sess., 1867, 533).

[747] Jones, *J. Wilkes Booth*, 96.

[748] George Alfred Townsend interview with Thomas Jones, in "How Wilkes Booth Crossed the Potomac," *Century Magazine*, April 1884, 830; also Jones, *J. Wilkes Booth*, 99.

[749] Townsend, *Century Magazine*, April 1884; Jones, *J. Wilkes Booth*, 100-101.

[750] Townsend, *Century Magazine*, April 1884, 829.

[751] Jones, *J. Wilkes Booth*, 101-105.

[752] Ibid., 106.

[753] Townsend, 830.

[754] Ibid., 109; Jones had purchased this boat for eighteen dollars one year earlier.

[755] Townsend, 830; also Jones, *J. Wilkes Booth*, 109-110.

[756] A few days after Booth had been killed, suspicion turned upon both Jones and Cox. Swann, the black man who had taken the fugitives to Cox, had talked to the authorities; soldiers came and arrested Jones and took him to Bryantown. He was kept for eight days in the second story of the tavern where Booth had stopped in his December meeting with Mudd and Harbin and in sight of the country Catholic church where Booth first met Dr. Mudd and others six months before. Cox was also held there but was sent to Washington in two or three days. Eight days later, Jones was sent to the old Carroll prison in Washington where he was incarcerated for six weeks. Cox was held for seven weeks (Townsend, *Century Magazine*, April 1884, 832).

[757] *Investigation and Trial Papers*, M599, reel 6, frames 0014-0015.

[758] Ibid.

[759] Mary Swann, a black servant, lived on the Cox farm, stated: "On Easter morning some men came to the house. Did not see faces. One had stick in his hand and was leaning on it. Did not see any horses. Do not know whether entered house or not. Do not see them eat or drink" (Statement of Mary Swann, *Investigation and Trial Papers*, M599, reel 6, frames 0160-0162).

Another black servant identified only as A. Swann and described as being in charge of Colonel Baker and living at the Cox house also gave a statement. She said that there were two men at the house on Easter morning, but that "admittance was refused" and that she "could not see their faces" and did "not know who they were." She also stated that "Nobody got them anything to eat or drink that I know of" (*Investigation and Trial Papers*, M599, reel 6, frames 0163-0164). It is now believed that she lied to protect the life of her employer.

[760] Jones, *J. Wilkes Booth*, 111.

[761] Hanchett, "Booth's Diary," 39-56.

Much has been made by historians of the sentence: "I have a greater desire and almost a mind to return to Washington and in a measure clear my name." Some historians have postulated that Booth might name accomplices in high places, but there is no documentation for such a conclusion. Booth's statement in light of his painful broken leg, his being out in the cold and in the rain for several days, his overwrought mental condition, and his flair for the melodramatic, can be taken as nothing more than a momentary flight of fancy.

762 Quesenberry's ancestry is quite interesting. She was born Elizabeth Rousby Green in 1826. Her genealogy included a Revolutionary War general and a governor of Maryland. One of her sisters had married into the family of George Washington and another was the wife of Don Angelo de Iturbide, a brother of the Emperor Maximilian. She was a widow with three children to raise; her husband Nicholas died in 1863 (Kaufman, *Blue and Gray Magazine*, June 1990).

763 Townsend, *Century Magazine*, April 1884, 831.

764 Statement of Elizabeth R. Quesenberry, *Investigation and Trial Papers*, M599, reel 5, frames 0556-59; Federal officers later located the satchel and found Mrs. Quesenberry's initials inside it. She was later arrested and taken to Washington on the steamer *John S. Ide*. She was released for lack of evidence; it is not known if Mrs. Quesenberry knew who they were.

765 William L. Bryant affidavit, *Investigation and Trial*, reel, frame 0095.

766 Stuart Visit, *Investigation and Trial Papers*, M599, reel 6, frames 0205-0211.

767 Quotes taken from Statement of William Lucas, *Investigation and Trial Papers*, M599, reel 5, frames 0144-47, NA.

768 Booth had written two notes. The one indicating a payment of $2.50 was delivered to Dr. Stuart (the one he decided not to send, indicated a payment of $5.00). The original copy of the note mentioning payment of $5 was found on Booth after his death (Judiciary Committee, House of Representatives, Impeachment Investigation, 40th Cong., 1st sess., 1867, 677).

769 Military Ranks
The correct military ranks of the three Confederates are not definitely known. They have been listed as privates and as Major Ruggles, Captain Jett, and Lieutenant Bainbridge ("Pursuit and Death of John Wilkes Booth," *Century Magazine*, January 1890, 443). At the time of their arrest, Ruggles and Bainbridge were listed as privates. William S. Jett later testified that he "was formerly a member of the Ninth Virginia Cavalry," and "more recently, I was stationed in Caroline County, Virginia, as commissary agent of the Confederate States Government." At the conspiracy trial, he did not give his rank but did state that at the time the three met Booth and Herold that "we were all dressed in Confederate uniform." Also during his testimony, he referred to Ruggles as Lieutenant on three occasions; and concerning Bainbridge, he only referred to him as a "young man."

In a letter Nannie Burton Marye wrote to Mrs. Marguerite DePont Lee in Washington:

First I would like to say that neither of the young men you mention, Bainbridge, Ruggles or Jett held any commission in the Confederate army, but were simply enlisted men. My cousin, William S. Jett was only eighteen years old at the time of the surrender, and had been in the army a very short time. (letter quoted in Otto Eisenschiml, "Why Was Lincoln Murdered")

770     Ruggles wrote:

> I observed there a wagon, drawn by two very wretched-looking horses. In the wagon were two men. On seeing us approach, one of them came towards us, and, finding that we were Confederate soldiers, said that his name was Boyd, and that his brother had been wounded severely in the leg while escaping from prison, where they had been for some time. He furthermore said that their negro driver, Lucas, refused to take them any farther, and that they were anxious to get on their way, and asked our aid. I at once said we would help them; and while discussing the speedy coming of the scow, [ferry] the other got out of the wagon, and walking with evident pain, with the aid of a rude crutch, came towards us. He apparently mistrusted his companion, for as he came forward he said, "I suppose you have been told who I am?" Thinking he meant that Herold had told us they were Confederate soldiers, escaped from prison, I answered in the affirmative. Instantly he dropped his weight back upon his crutch and drawing a revolver said sternly, with the utmost coolness, "Yes, I am John Wilkes Booth, the slayer of Abraham Lincoln, and I am worth just $175,000 to the man who captures me." (That was the sum recent newspapers had been quoting.)
>
> In response to his defiant words I said that we had been told that Lincoln's slayer had been captured; [either one of thousands of rumors circulating about or perhaps he had heard of the capture of Powell and Atzerodt] but that, though we did not sanction the act as an assassin, we were not men to take "blood money"; and that having promised his friend, who proved to be Herold, to take them across the river to a place of safety; we would do so . . . . Booth replaced his weapon at my words, and, thanking us said he was utterly unable to walk. I dismounted and we lifted him upon my horse . . . . I noticed that his wounded leg was greatly swollen, inflamed, and dark, as from bruised blood, while it seemed to have been wretchedly dressed, the splints being simply pasteboard rudely tied about it. That he suffered intense pain all the time there was no doubt . . . . When the scow arrived Peyton Washington (a black man in the employ of Rollins) ferried us across the river (*Century Magazine,* January 1890, 243-44).

771     The foot was much swollen and seemed to trouble him greatly. The crutch he carried was rough and ungainly . . . . His beard, of a coal-black hue, was of about two weeks' growth and gave his face an unclean appearance. Over his shoulders drooped a long gray shawl, which he said had served him well in covering the telling initials "J. W. B." done in Indian

ink on his right hand. These letters he showed to us to establish his identity (*Century Magazine*, January 1890, 244).

772   "Pursuit and Death," *Century Magazine*, January 1890.

773   *Century Magazine*, January 1890.

774   Quotes from Betsy Fleet, ed., "A Chapter of Unwritten History" *Virginia Magazine of History and Biography*, October 1963, 387-407; *Century Magazine*, January 1890.

775   *Century Magazine*, January 1890.

776   Ibid., and October 1963; also see Fleet, "Chapter of Unwritten History," 387-407, for the dialogue.

777   M169, reel 457, frames 0499-0511, National Archives, interrogation of John M. Garrett on May 20, 1865.

778   *Century Magazine*, January 1890, 445.

779   Fleet, "Chapter of Unwritten History," 387-407.

780   M169, reel 457, frames 0499-0511, National Archgives, statement of John Garrett on May 20, 1865.

781   "My father and brother had talked over the matter and arrived at the conclusion that something must be wrong with these men judging from their suspicious actions," later wrote Richard Garrett. The Garretts thought that perhaps "they were guerrillas who had done something to cause them to fear arrest" (Fleet, "Chapter of Unwritten History," 387-407).

782   The tobacco barn was filled with valuable furniture entrusted to Garrett's care by rebel neighbors who supposed it safely hidden under a covering of fodder and hay (Ibid.; also described by Garrett's sister-in-law Lucinda Holloway in a letter entitled, "The Capture and Death of John Wilkes Booth" [Confederate Museum, Richmond, Virginia]).

783   M169, reel 457, frames 0499-0511, National Archives, statement of John M. Garrett.

784   *Century Magazine, January 1890*, 446.

785   Ibid., 447; Luther Baker was Colonel Baker's nephew.

786   Ibid.

787   Ibid., 445; Doherty's remembrances.

788   *Investigation and Trial Papers*, M619, roll 457, frames 551-561, National Archives, statement of William Rollins, dated May 20, 1865.

789   Ray Stannard Baker, "Capture, Death, and Burial," 574-585.

790   *Century Magazine*, January 1890.

791   The building no longer existed; its site is located in a restricted area of Fort A. P. Hill.

792   Report of Lieutenant Edward P. Doherty to Lieutenant Colonel J. H. Taylor, Washington, 29 April 1865, M-619, reel 456, frames 0273-84.

793   Everton Conger and Luther Baker joint letter to Secretary of War Stanton on December 24, 1865.

794   *Century Magazine*, January 1890, 448; the accounts of events at the hotel in Bowling Green vary according to who is telling the story – Doherty, Baker, or Conger – because of the rivalry and possible reward among these officers. Their statements regarding the part each one played in the roundup are a confused mass of contradictory testimony. An article by

Luther B. Baker is reprinted in the *Journal of the Illinois State Historical Society* (December 1946): 425-446.

795 *Investigation and Trial Papers*, M619, roll 456, frames 275-284, National Archives, report of Lieutenant Doherty.

796 Baker, "Capture, Death, and Burial," 580.

797 Townsend, *Life, Crime and Capture*, 31-37.

798 Fleet, "Chapter of Unwritten History," 387-407.

799 Ibid.; also Statement of John M. Garrett, *Investigation and Trial Papers*, M169, reel 457, frames 0499-0511, and M619, roll 456, frames 275-284, report of Lieutenant Doherty.

800 Fleet, "Chapter of Unwritten History," 397; *Investigation and Trial Papers*, M169, reel 457, frames 04990511, statement of John M. Garrett.

801 *Century Magazine*, January 1890; *Investigation and Trial Papers*, M619, roll 456, frames 275-284.

802 Baker, "Capture, Death, and Burial," May 1897; *Century Magazine*, January 1890; L. B. Baker, "An Eyewitness Account of the Death and Burial of J. Wilkes Booth," *Journal of the Illinois State Historical Society* (December 1946) 425-446.

803 Fleet, "Chapter of Unwritten History," 387-407.

804 Ibid.

805 Baker, *Journal of the Illinois State Historical Society* (December 1946).

806 A wound of the spinal cord in his neck produced complete paralysis of the arms, legs, and lower portion of the trunk, but respiration and the action of the heart continued. This is because the nerves that cause paralysis came from the cranium and not from the spinal cord. An uninjured brain left Booth's mind active in a helpless body.

807 Baker, *Journal of the Illinois State Historical Society* (December 1946).

808 The United States Government refused to pay Garrett for the loss of his tobacco barn, but Edwin Booth years later sent him money to rebuild it.

809 Fleet, "Chapter of Unwritten History," 387-407.

810 Doherty, Baker, and Conger each described the scene in a way that stressed his own central role. Doherty claimed to have overruled Baker about the acceptance of Herold's surrender to have grabbed Herold by the wrists and pulled him from the barn. Doherty also claimed to have been the first to reach Booth after Corbett's shot was fired. In Doherty's 1890 reminiscence, he even claimed to have caught Booth before he touched the ground (Doherty, "Pursuit and Death," 448-49.)

Some writers of fact and faction contend that Booth escaped through a rear door in the barn and left another man in his place. But of all the many people who were at Garrett's farm when Booth was killed, not one reported at the time that the tobacco barn had a rear door. The Garretts ridiculed the escape story. Booth had stayed in their home for two days, and they all asserted that he was the same man who was taken from the barn to their porch and who died there.

Baker, Conger, and Doherty all wanted the reward money for apprehending Booth. The three wrote of what happened on the hunt for Booth, and their report differed wildly: Each report showed that its writer was the one who did all the work and deserved the money.

Baker and Conger maintained, in a report signed jointly and dated December 24, 1865, that Lieutenant Doherty was "the mere commander of the soldiers" and that Baker and Conger "often gave orders directly to them." They stated that Baker alone had communicated with Booth about surrendering, pulled Herold from the barn, and was the first to reach Booth inside after the fatal shot had been fired. Baker and Conger further maintained that "Lt. Doherty took no part in the communications with Booth and Herold, and was absent from the door when Booth was shot." Baker stated that Conger had left him in charge of Booth when Conger: attempted to put out the fire in the barn, went to find the soldier who had fired his arms against orders, and gathered the articles from Booth's pockets and departed with them for Washington about twenty minutes before Booth's death (the affidavit is reprinted in L. C. Baker, *History of the United States Secret Service* (Philadelphia: L. C. Baker, 1867), 532-38; also see *Trial of John H. Surratt*, 318-19; House Report 7, 40th Cong., 1 sess., 1867, 485-487; and Baker, *Journal of the Illinois State Historical Society* [December 1946]: 441).

Conger was later asked by a congressman if he had ever left Booth after the attempt to put out the fire. "No, sir; I did not," Conger replied. "I may not have staid directly by his side all the time until he died; but I did not leave the porch, so far as I remember." Congress believed Conger and awarded him fifteen thousand dollars, which was the leader's share of the reward money. Conger not only left Booth's side, but left the area to return to Washington (House Report 7, 40th Cong., 1 sess., 1867, 327).

Doherty present his version of events in "Pursuit and Death."

[811] Baker, "Capture, Death, and Burial," 574-585.

[812] *Century Magazine,* January 1890, 449; Doherty's remembrances: Doherty defended Corbett, saying that Corbett saw Booth leveling his carbine to shot and that Corbett had fired to disable Booth's arm. Booth, however, had made a sudden move, and the bullet struck Booth in the neck.

Richard Garret refuted this story, saying that Booth had made no movement to fire upon anybody (Fleet, "Chapter of Unwritten History," 387-407).

[813] Kimmel, *Mad Booths of Maryland*, 365.

The "patriot" had had a long career of abnormal and masochistic behavior. His name had originally been Thomas, born in England in 1832. As a child, his family had settled in Troy, New York. There, Corbett grew up to become a hatmaker. He married; however, his wife and only child died in childbirth. Corbett began to drink.

Corbett moved to Boston to make hats, and while living there, he became interested in religion. He went into it in a big way, and the good news was that he gave up liquor. The bad news was that he lost all perspective and became a shouting street evangelist. Calling himself Boston, after the city of his "rebirth." Corbett became a common sight standing on soapboxes and proclaiming his view of religion. His fellow hatters found they could make him fall to his knees and pray if they uttered an obscenity, which we can imagine they took great delight in doing.

It was in 1858 that Corbett, absorbed in his visions of pure spirituality, was brought low by his acquired loathing of sex. Two prostitutes, seeing the self-styled evangelist, set about to entice him. Their sidling, touching, and suggestive language, however, was not lost on Corbett. He recognized at once what they were about, yet their blatant sexuality overcame his mental defenses. He was aroused.

Angry, he had stomped to his lodgings. He was furious that his growing male organ had betrayed him and had not obeyed his spiritual direction.

*If thine eye offend thee, pluck it out!* he must have thought. He went to his hatmaking tools and selected a pair of heavy scissors. With these, he genitally mutilated himself, cutting away the offending part so that impure thoughts could never come into his mind again.

Needless to say, the operation was rather painful. Corbett knew only that he must get closer to God. Holding packing against his wound, he made his way to the house where the prayer meetings he attended were held. The fellow believers assembled there saw at once that he was badly hurt and insisted on taking him to Massachusetts General Hospital.

It was a month before Corbett recovered. But as he had planned, now he could devote himself fully to his calling – finding evil and destroying it. He enlisted in the army in New York and served with distinction. He single-handedly fought against more than two dozens of Colonel John S. Mosby's raiders and earned Mosby's personal respect. Later, Corbett was captured and sent to the infamous Confederate prison camp at Andersonville. Luckily for him, however, he was exchanged and returned to duty. His fellow soldiers called him the Glory to God Man.

It is possible that Corbett's odd behavior was induced by mercury poisoning. In industrialized areas during the nineteenth century, many deadly occupational diseases were known. These included the mercury poisoning familiar to hatters, who used mercuric nitrate in the preparation of felt. (The nervous Mad Hatter in Alice's Adventures in Wonderland is a portrayal of a person suffering from the nerve damage caused by mercury exposure.)

Details of Corbett's life is described in Lloyd Lewis, "The Glory-to-God Man," in *The Assassination of Lincoln* (Lincoln, Nebraska: University of Nebraska Press, 1994), 246-258; Albert Reid (a Kansas neighbor), *Scribner's Magazine,* July 1929.

[814] Baker, *Journal of the Illinois State Historical Society* (December 1946): 446.

The wagon was owned by Ned Freeman, the black man who through the aid of John Garrett, Booth had hired for ten dollars to take Herold and himself to Fredericksburg. Baker got the ten dollars from John Garrett and made his own arrangements with Freeman.

[815] Baker, "Capture, Death, and Burial," 574-585.

[816] Impeachment of the President, House Report 7, 40th Congr., 2nd sess., 409.

[817]
> April 22, 1865
> Commander J. B. Montgomery
> Commandant, Navy Yard

Washington, DC

The Secretary of War requests that the prisoners on board the iron clads belonging to his department shall have for better security against conversation, a canvas bag put over the head of each and tied around the neck with a hole for proper breathing and eating, but not for seeing, and that Payne be secured to prevent self destruction.

G. V. Fox
(Assistan Secretary of the Navy Department)

Arnold described the hood as follows: "This covering for the head was made of canvass [sic], which covered the entire head & face dropping down in front to the lower portion of the chest, with cords attached, which were tied around the neck and body in such manner, that to remove it, was a moral impossibility" (Arnold, *Defence and Prison Experiences*, 57). The hoods had small circular openings for the nose and mouth.

Secretary Stanton ordered that all the male prisoners have a thick padded hood over his head with only holes for eyes and a slit for the mouth. The order applied to about forty prisoners in the penitentiary, not just the seven conspirators immediately connected with the assassination. One such prisoner was Burton N. Harrison, private secretary to Jefferson Davis and father of New York congressman Francis Burton Harrison (George L. Porter, "How Booth's Body Was Hidden," *Magazine of History*, April 1911, reprint in the Surratt Society Library).

[818] Ruggles wrote: "After the trial, by a strange mistake I was sent to Johnson's Island, where as a Confederate prisoner I had passed half a year; but after a few days spent there I was returned to Washington, and after taking the oath of allegiance I was released" (*Century Magazine*, January 1890, 446).

[819] Porter, "Booth's Body Was Hidden."

[820] Ibid.

[821] *Investigation and Trial Papers*, M599, reel 4, frames 0351-0352.

[822] *Investigation and Trial Papers*, M599, reel 4, frames 0354-0355; there were others who saw the body of Booth and gave statements that the body was that of John Wilkes Booth, see Ibid., frames 0356-0359 and 0366-0369.

[823] "The Mark of the Scalpel," *Records of the Columbia Historical Society*, vol. 8, 1910, p. 51-68.

[824] *Investigation and Trial Papers*, M599, reel 4, frames 0360-0365.

[825] Lattimer, *Kennedy and Lincoln*, 69-70.

[826] These were placed in the museum of the Medical Department of the Army, which was initially located in the former Ford's Theatre after the government had taken the building. In a sense, part of Booth's returned to the place of the assassination. The medical museum is now housed at the Armed Forces Institute of Pathology on the Walter Reed Army Hospital campus in Washington, DC, and the three vertebras are on display there.

[827] For a complete accounting of the medical aspects of Booth's death and the ballistic testing, see Lattimer, *Lincoln and Kennedy*, 67-88.

[828] Luther B. Baker, *Journal of the Illinois State Historical Society* (December 1946): 445.

[829] Baker, "Capture, Death, and Burial," 574-585.

[830] George L. Porter, "How Booth's Body Was Hidden," *Magazine of History*, April 1911; Baker, *Journal of the Illinois State Historical Society* (December 1946).

[831] Now currently Fort McNair in Washington, DC; Porter, "Booth's Body Was Hidden," April 1911.

[832] Clarke, *Unlocked Book*, 127.

[833] *Investigation and Trial Papers*, M599, reel 7, folder 82, frames 0407-0412.

[834] Hanchett, 46-47; see Lincoln Log, May and June 1977, 1-4, for the complete text of the letter.

[835] Clarke, *Unlocked Book*, 139.

[836] Genealogical data from Gene Smith, Chapter 1, *in American Gothic*.

[837] *Civil War Times*, November/December 1995, 80.

[838] *While Lincoln Lay Dying*, Wilson, *John Wilkes Booth*, 81-84.

[839] Booth's diary can be found in its entirety in *Trial of John H. Surratt*, 1:310-311.

[840] Edwin Booth once asked his brother John why he did not join the Confederate army. To which he replied. "I promised mother I would keep out of the quarrel, if possible, and I am sorry that I said so." Edwin Booth wrote of this conversation in a letter dated July 28, 1881; the letter in its entirety is reprinted in Edwina Booth Grossman, *Edwin Booth: Recollections by His Daughter* (New York: Century, 1894), 227-228.

[841] Grossman, *Edwin Booth*, 227.

[842] Woodrow Wilson, *History of the American People*, (New York: Harper & Brothers, 1901), 4:261.

[843] Impeachment of the President, House Report 7, 40th Cong., 1 sess., 1867, see testimony of Thomas T. Echert on his conversations with Powell in page 673; George Alfred Townsend, *Katy of Catoctin* (New York: Appleton, 1886), 490; Herold told this story to his attorney Frederick Stone, who repeated it to George Alfred Townsend.

[844] Beale, *Diary of Gideon Welles*, 303-305; Henry Lawrence Burnett, "Some Incidents in the Trial of President Lincoln's Assassins," in James G. Wilson and Titus M. Coan, eds., *Personal Recollections of the War of the Rebellion* (New York, 1891), 189-190, located at the Library of Congress, microform no. 43153.

[845] William E. Doster characterized the conduct of Judge Advocate General Holt and Special Judge Advocate Burnett as both "courteous and moderate." However, he wrote of Bingham that his "mind seemed to be frenzied and his conduct violent" (Doster, *Episodes of the Civil War*, 281).

[846] Henry S. Foote, *Casket of Reminiscences* (Washington: Chronicle Publishing, 1874), 98-101; Nicolay and Hay, *Abraham Lincoln*, 2:362-63; 3:130-31.

[847] R. A. Watts, acting assistant adjutant general under Judge Advocate Holt, "The Trial and Execution of the Lincoln Conspirators," *Michigan History Magazine*, vol. 6, no. 1 (1922): 99.

[848] Major General David Hunter: President of the Military Commission, his maternal grandfather was a signer of the Declaration of Independence; he knew Lincoln personally and had accompanied him on his inaugural train and his funeral train to Springfield. He lived in Washington until his death on February 2, 1886.

Major General Lewis Wallace: Served in the Mexican War as a first lieutenant. Promoted to brigadier general in September 1861 and major general in March 1862. He was the president of the military commission that tried and hanged Henry Wirz, commandant at Adersonville. General Wallace is best remembered as the author of the novel *Ben Hur*.

Brevet Major General August V. Kautz: He was born in Germany. He commanded a division in the Twenty-fifth Corps.

Brigadier General Albion P. Howe: He had participated in the Mexican War and had served on frontier duty. Promoted to brigadier general in June 1862, he was a member of the guard of honor that escorted Lincoln's body to Springfield. General Howe retired from the army in 1882 and died in 1897.

Brevet Major General Robert S. Foster: He was promoted to brigadier general of volunteers in June 1863 and later promoted to brevet major general. He resigned in September 1865. He died in 1903 in Indianapolis after serving as city treasurer, city marshall, and president of the city board of trade.

Brigadier General Thomas M. Harris: He was a medical doctor before the war and was promoted brigadier general on March 29, 1865. He left the army in 1866 as brevet major general. He later wrote a book on the Lincoln assassination and died in 1906.

Lieutenant Colonel David R. Clendenin: Clendenin had been assigned to the Eighth Illinois Cavalry.

Colonel B. Comstock: He was on General Grant's staff. Colonel Comstock was dismissed from the military commission because he believed that the trial should be in a civil court. He also did not like the idea of the prisoners being chained twenty-four hours a day.

Brevet Colonel Horace Porter: He was on General Grant's staff and was present when Mrs. Lincoln had one of her jealous tirades at City Point. It is not known why, but he was dismissed from the military commission.

The replacements for Colonel Comstock and Colonel Porter were Brevet Brigadier General James A. Ekin and Brevet Colonel Charles H. Tompkins (Pitman, *Assassination of President Lincoln*, 18).

849 *Investigation and Trial Papers*, M599, reel 1.

850 Army Official Records, vol. 47, 1st ser., pt. 3, p. 301.

851 Thomas and Hyman, *Stanton*, 424; also see Hans L. Trefousse, *Andrew Johnson: A Biography* (New York: W. W. Norton, 1989); W. W. Cleary, "The Attempt to Fasten the Assassination of President Lincoln on President Davis and Other Innocent Parties," *Southern Historical Society Papers* 9 (July and August 1881): 313-325, which contain a reprint of the May 2 proclamation.

852 Welles, *Diary of Gideon Welles*, 2:299-300.

853 James D. Richardson, comp., *A Compilation of Messages and Papers of the Presidents*, 11 vols. (Washington: Bureau of National Literature and Art, 1907), 6:307-8.

854 Pitman, *Assassination of President Lincoln*, 17.

Special Orders, No. 211


On May 6, the adjutant general's office of the War Department issued Special Order no. 211 in compliance with President Johnson's executive order of May 1. Item 4 read as follows:

4. A Military Commission is hereby appointed to meet at Washington, District of Columbia, on Monday, the 8th day of May, 1865, at 9 o'clock A.M. or as soon thereafter as practicable, for the trial of David E. Herold, George A. Atzerodt, Lewis Payne [sic], Michael O'Laughlen, Edward Spangler, Samuel Arnold, Mary E. Surratt, Samuel A. Mudd and such other persons as may be brought before it, implicated in the murder of the late President Abraham Lincoln and the attempted assassination of the Honorable William H. Seward, Secretary of State, and in an alleged conspiracy to assassinate other officers of the Federal Government in Washington City, and their aiders and abettors.

Brigadier-General Joseph Holt, Judge Advocate General, U.S. Army, is appointed the Judge Advocate and Recorder of the Commission, to be aided by such Assistant for Special Judge Advocates as he may designate.

The Commission will sit without regard to hours. By order of the President of the United States.

(Signed)

W. A. Nichols
Assistant Adjutant-General

[855] R. A. Watts, "The Trial and Execution of the Lincoln Conspirators," *Michigan History Magazine* 6, no. 1 (1922): 81-110.

[856] Pitman, *Assassination of President Lincoln*, 20.

[857] Quoted in Betty Ownsbey, *Alias "Paine,"* 109-110.

[858] Doster, *Episodes of the Civil War*, 1915, 264, 259.

[859] Pitman, *Assassination of President Lincoln*, 18.

[860] Doster, *Episodes of the Civil War*, 257, 259.

[861] Frederick Argyle Aiken was born in 1837 in Boston, Massachusetts. He graduated with high honors from Middlebury College, Vermont, and then from Harvard Law School. He became editor and part proprietor of the *Burlington Sentinel* from 1858 to 1859; he was the Washington correspondent for that paper. During this time, he married Sarah Weston of Vermont. He was a Democrat and once worked for the National Democratic Committee. On April 5, 1861, Frederick Aiken had written a letter to Jefferson Davis that he wished to "offer his pen to the cause rather than his blood" to the Confederate cause. No reply from Davis has been documented" (Trindal, 149; Aiken's letter was found by James O. Hall and Mike Musick in the National Archives, Washington, DC), His desire to join the Confederacy was short-lived; in the early years of the war, Aiken was on the staff of Winfield S. Hancock's staff with the rank of captain. In Aiken's obituary, it was written that Aiken was "in several engagements, during one of which had two horses shot under him, and received injuries, the ultimate effect of which, no doubt, hastened his death." After the trial, Aiken was admitted to the Supreme Court of the United States and practiced there and in the district courts until 1868 when he returned to journalism. In 1877, he became city editor of the *Washington Post* (*Washington Post*, December 24, 1878, 2).

862 *Washington Post*, December 24, 1878, 2; Clampitt was born in Washington in 1839 and served in the Union Army.

863 Pitman, *Assassination of President Lincoln*, 22

864 Ibid.

865 Ibid.

866 Doster, *Episodes of the Civil War*, 264.

867 Ibid., 260.

868 May 31, 1865.

869 Doster, *Episodes of the Civil War*, 264.

870 Pitman, *Assassination of President Lincoln*, 22-23.

871 Johnson issued the following presidential order:

> Whereas the Attorney-General of the United States hath given his opinion: That the persons implicated in the murder of the late President Abraham Lincoln, and the attempted assassination of the Honorable William H. Seward, Secretary of State, and in an alleged conspiracy to assassinate other officers of the Federal government at Washington city, and their aides and abettors are subject to the jurisdiction of and lawfully triable before a military commission.

872 Doster, *Episodes of Civil War*, 260.

873 Pitman, *Assassination of President Lincoln*, 29.

874 Ibid., 24-25.

875 Ibid., 36.

876 Ibid., 35.

877 Hanchett, 72.

878 Pitman, *Assassination of President Lincoln*, 28-29.

879 *New York Tribune*, June 6, 1865, col. 2, p.4.

880 June 6, 1865, col. 1 and 4

881 *Investigation and Trial Papers*, M599, roll 7, frames 0120-31.

882 W. W. Cleary, "Attempt to Fasten Assassination," 313-25; Sandford Conover, *Testimony of Sandford Conover, Dr. J. B. Merritt, and Richard Montgomery, before Military Court at Washington Respecting the Assassination of President Lincoln and the Proofs Disproving Their Statements and Showing Their Perjuries* (Toronto: Lovell & Gibson, 1865), 1-65; also see Stuart Robinson, *Infamous Perjuries of the "Bureau of Military Justice," Exposed* (Toronto, 1865), Rare Book Division, Library of Congress.

883 Army, Official Records, 2nd ser., pt. 8, pp. 931-33.

884 Ibid., 934-45, correspondence between Holt and Conover.

885 John T. Ford, "Behind Curtain of Conspiracy," 484-493; Charles Benjamin, *Recollections of Secretary Stanton*, 766; Thomas and Hyman, *Stanton*, 426, 138-139.

886 Pitman, *Assassination of President Lincoln*, 115.

887 Ibid., see testimony of Weichmann in pages 113-120.

888   Poore, *Conspiracy Trial*, seen testimony of Weichmann in pages 69-110.

889   Pitman, *Assassination of President Lincoln*, see testimony of Weichmann in page 118.

890   Trindal, 138, quotes report of Colonel William P. Wood, superintendent of Old Capitol Prison, on Louis J. Weichmann, Bureau of Military Justice Records, National Archives.

891   *Trial of John H. Surratt*, see testimony of Lloyd in page 290; Carland, 815, and Weichmann, 444; Ford, "Behind Curtain of Conspiracy."

892   "An Interview with Colonel John W. Clampitt," *Chicago Times Herald*, March 23, 1865, 1.

893   Poore, *Conspiracy Trial*, 117.

894   All quotes from Pitman, *Assassination of President Lincoln*, 85-86.

895   Ibid., see testimony of Anna Surratt in page 131.

896   Ibid., 132.

897   Ibid. 132-133.

898   Ibid., see testimony of Howell in page 133.

899   Ibid., 126.

900   Ibid., 125.

901   Ibid.

902   Ibid., see testimony of Offutt in page 125.

903   Ibid., see testimony of John Nothey in page 126

904   Ibid., see testimony of Joseph T. Knott in pages 126-127.

905   This will substantiate John Holohan's testimony at John Surratt's trial two years later (*Trial of John H. Surratt*, see testimony of John Holohan in pages 669-70).

906   Pitman, *Assassination of President Lincoln*, 130-131.

907   Ibid., see testimony of Anna Surratt in page 131.

908   Ibid.

909   Ibid., see testimony of Rachel Semus in pages 137-38.

910   Ibid., see argument of Reverdy Johnson in defense of Mary Surratt in page 263.

911   Ibid., 293.

912   Ibid., see argument of Frederick Aiken in pages 289-299.

913   Ibid., see testimony of Dr. Nichols in page 161, Dr. Hall in page 164, Surgeon-General Barnes in page 167, Dr. Morris in page 167, and Assistant-Surgeon Porter in page 168.

914   House of Representatives, The Impeachment Committee Investigation (Washington, DC: Government Printing Office, 1867), see testimony of Major Thomas T. Eckert in pages 673-75.

915   Pitman, *Assassination of President Lincoln*, 390.

916   Ibid., 382.

917   Ibid., 390.

918   Ibid., 392.

919   Ibid., see testimony of John Holohan in page 139.

920   Two years later, John Holohan testified at John Surratt's trial that Atzerodt had gone to the house to visit Weichmann (*Trial of John H. Surratt*, 669; John Holohan testified for the defendant, John Surratt).

921   "Colonel John W. Clampitt," 1.

922   Ibid.
923   *Washington Evening Star*, July 7, 1865, col. 4, p. 2.
924   The petition for clemency reads as follows:

> To the President:
>
> The undersigned, members of the Military Commission appointed to try the persons charged with the murder of Abraham Lincoln, etc., respectfully represent that the commission have been constrained to find Mary E. Surratt guilty, upon the testimony, of the assassination of Abraham Lincoln, late President of the United States, and to pronounce upon her, as required by law, the sentence of death; but in consideration of her age and sex, the undersigned pray your Excellency, if it is consistent with your sense of duty, to commute her sentence to imprisonment for life in the penitentiary.

After examining the papers that Judge Holt brought from the commission, President Johnson issued the following order:

> Executive Mansion
> July 5, 1865
>
> The foregoing sentences in the cases of David E. Herold, G. A. Atzerodt, Lewis Paine [sic], Mary E. Surratt are hereby approved, and it is ordered that the sentences in the cases of David E. Herold, G. A. Atzerodt, Lewis Payne and Mary E. Surratt be carried into execution by the proper military authority, under the direction of the Secretary of War, on the seventh day of July 1865, between the hours of 10 o'clock A. M. and 2 o'clock P. M. of that day.
>
> It is further ordered that the prisoners Samuel Arnold, Samuel A. Mudd, Edward Spangler and Michael O'Laughlen be confined at hard labor at the penitentiary of Albany, New York, during the period designated in their representative sentences.
>
> Andrew Johnson
> President

(Pitman, *Assassination of President Lincoln*, 249; *Washington Star*, July 6, 1865, col. 1, p. 2)

However, Stanton was instrumental in having the four convicted conspirators originally ordered to be sent to the Federal Penitentiary in Albany were sent instead to the Dry Tortugas Military Prison in Florida on July 16, 1865. Stanton and the president discussed this change and decided to transfer the prisoners to "a part of the country" where it would be difficult to serve a writ of habeas corpus (Welles, *Diary of Gideon Welles*, July 17, 1865 entry, 334).

925 *Century Magazine*, January 1890.

926 Ibid.

927 Joseph Holt Papers, R. D. Mussey to Holt, August 19, 1873, Georgetown University Library.

928 An interview with Christian Rath, "Hangman of President Lincoln's Assassins Tells His Story," *New York Press*, September 4, 1898.

929 *Washington Evening Star*, July 7, 1865. 2.

930 John W. Clampitt, "Trial of Mrs. Surratt," 238; *Washington Star*, July 6, 1865.

931 Letter is reprinted in Ownsbey, *Alias "Paine,"* 134; the original is in the General Ethan Allan Hitchcock Papers, Library of Congress.

932 *Washington Evening Star*, July 7, 1865, co. 5, p.2; The Reverend J. A. Walter, "The Surratt Case," *Church News*, Washington, DC, August 16, 1891.

933 *Washington Constitutional Union*, July 11, 1865; *Washington Post*, January 7, 1908, 3.

934 John Brophy's affidavit, *Washington Constitutional Union*, July 11, 1865.

935 *Washington Evening Star*, July 7, 1865, col. 5, p. 2; Johnson's illness for two days prior to the execution was also reported in the *Washington Morning Chronicle*, July 8, 1865, col. 1, p. 1.

936 Clampitt, "Trial of Mrs. Surratt," 234-235.

937 Ibid., 235.

938 Ibid., 236.

939 Ibid.

940 Ibid.

941 *Washington Evening Star*, July 7, 1865, col. 5, p. 2.
The Executive Order suspending the writ of habeas corpus reads as follows:

Executive Office, July 7, 1865, 10 A. M.

To Major-General W. S. Hancock, commanding, etc.

I, Andrew Johnson, President of the United States, do hereby declare that the writ of habeas corpus has been theretofore suspended in such cases as this, and I do hereby especially suspend this writ, and direct that you proceed to execute the order heretofore given upon the judgment of the Military Commission, and you will give this order in return to this writ.

Andrew Johnson, President

(Reprinted in Clampitt, "Trial of Mrs. Surratt," 237.)

942 *Washington Evening Star*, July 7, 1865, col. 5, p. 2.

After Surratt's execution, R. A. Watts, acting assistant adjutant general, was in Judge Holt's office "when the execution was mentioned. I said that all the officers at the prison were much surprised that, because of her sex, the sentence of Mrs. Surratt had not been commuted."

"The substance of Holt's reply was, that the President believed that she had been as guilty as any of the others, but added that he might not have insisted on her execution, but for the imprudent action of her attorneys in obtaining the writ of habeas corpus. According to Holt, the application angered the President, who would not tolerate any attempt to force him into any action and who promptly ordered the execution to be carried out." Holt's claim, however, seems unlikely; President Johnson had refused to see anyone about commuting Mary Surratt's sentence the day before the writ was issued. (R. A. Watts, "Execution of Lincoln Conspirators," 105).

[943] Quoted in Betty J. Ownsbey, *Alias "Paine,"* 137; from an undated clipping from the *New York Herald* entitled "The Hanging of Mrs. Surratt."

[944] Rev. Walter's letter to President Johnson, RG 153, Judge Advocate Office, box 3, unnumbered item, National Archives.

[945] "Hangman of President Lincoln's Assassins Tells His Story," *New York Press*, September 4, 1898.

[946] *Washington Constitutional Union,* July 11, 1865; Clampitt, "Trial of Mrs. Surratt," 240; a copy of the letter is reprinted.

[947] *Sun*, Baltimore, MD, Sunday, July 7, 1901; *Washington Constitutional Union*, July 11, 1865.

[948] *Washington Constitutional Union,* report in the July 7, 1865 edition, "Payne made a confession last night, and exonerated her, Mrs. S., of all complicity in the conspiracy" (2).

[949] "The Conspirators: Payne's Farewell to His Counsel," *Washington Evening Star,* July 10, 1865.

[950] Ford, "Behind Curtain of Conspiracy."

[951] Ibid.

[952] Dr. Gillette, in a sermon the next Sunday, told his congregation that Powell had been "frank and candid, a member of the Baptist church and possessing a well cultivated mind" and that Powell said he was ready to face his death. Rev. Gillette also told his congregation that, "until the morning of the fatal day Payne claimed that no more serious crime than that of the kidnapping of the President had been planned as far as he was involved." Powell had repented of his deed and hoped for a heavenly, if not earthly, pardon. He had inquired of the health of Frederick Seward and said that he owed him an apology for the injuries he had caused. Finally, mentally exhausted and emotionally drained, Powell slept for about three hours (the statements made by Powell to Gillette were published by the minister's granddaughter, Mrs. Amy Gillette Bassett, in her 1961 book, *Red Cross Reveries* (Harrisburg, PA: Stackpole Company), 88-103; also see *New York World*, July 11, 1865; the *Boston Post*, July 8, 1865; *Washington Daily Morning Chronicle*, July 10, 1865, on Rev. Gillette address to his congregation on his sixteen hours with Powell.

[953] *Evening Star*, Washington, DC, July 7, 1865.

[954] *Boston Post*, July 8, 1865.

[955] *Sun Sunday*, Baltimore, MD, July 7, 1901.

956     Doster, *Episodes of Civil War*, 276.

957     *Washington Chronicle*, July 7, 1865, col. 2, p. 2.

958     Harlow Hoyt, *Town Hall Tonight* (New York: Bramhall House, 1955), 148-152. In this book, Hoyt recounts a conversation he had with William Coxhall, the soldier who pulled the support from under Mary Surratt and Lewis Powell in the execution. Hoyt was a young boy when Coxhall "told of the incidents of that execution when he hanged Mrs. Mary Surratt and Lewis Payne on that hot July day in 1865" (may need to get permission from publisher to use the extensive quotes).

      The *Boston Post* of July 8, 1865, described Mary Surratt: "She was so physically prostrated that she had to be lifted on to the steps leading to the scaffold. In addition to this, her limbs were so heavily manacled that her steps were impeded. She was accompanied by two officers and two Catholic clergymen. Once on the platform and seated in the chair, she seemed at this moment to be in a fainting condition, leaning on her left arm, and looking sorrowfully upward; a soldier held an umbrella to protect her from the hot sun. She was attired in a plain black dress and black bonnet. As she sat there before the noose was adjusted, one of the Catholic priests administered the service of that church, and held a cross to her lips."

959     Amy Gillette Bassett, *Red Cross Reveries*, 90; Mrs. Bassett was the granddaughter of Dr. Gillette.

960     Doster, *Episodes of Civil War*, 276.

961     In November 1865, Henry Wirz, the commandant of Andersonville, was hanged after his conviction of war crimes at that prisoner of war camp. He was buried next the four condemned Lincoln conspirators.

962     Interview of Clampitt with Father Walter, *Chicago Times Herald*, March 23, 1895.

963     *New York World*, July 11, 1865; *Boston Post*, July 8, 1865.

964     Leo F. Stock, ed., *United States Ministers to the Papal States: Instruction and Dispatches 1848-1868*, 2 vols. (Washington, D.C.: Catholic University Press, 1933), 1:359-360, 367, 377-78, 381-82, 388, 401.

965     The reactions of Johnson's cabinet to this sensational disclosure were described in the diaries of Orville H. Browning, a former senator from Illinois and the secretary of the interior under Johnson. James G. Randall and Theodore C. Pease, eds., *Diary of Orville Hickman Browning*, 2 vols. (Springfield, IL: Jefferson's Printing and Stationery Company by the Trustees of the Illinois State Historical Library, 1933), 2:100; Browning also recorded Seward's response to the letter: "Mr. Seward expressed his belief that Booth and Surratt had conferred with Benjamin upon the subject, and that Benjamin had encouraged and subsidized them; but he did not believe that the matter had ever been under discussion before the Richmond Cabinet or received the countenance of other members of the Cabinet than Benjamin."

966     House of Representatives, Executive Document no. 9, 39th Cong., 2nd sess., 1866, 9-10; Letters from the Secretary of War Ad Interim Relative to a Claim of Sainte Marie for Compensation Furnished in the Surratt Case, 40th Cong., 2nd sess., 1867, 24.

967     Quoted in G. S. Bryan, *Great American Myth*, 387.

968     Eli Evans, *Judah Benjamin*, 335.

[969] House of Representatives, Executive Document No. 9, 39th Cong., 2nd sess., Consular Message no. 538, pp. 3-7.

[970] Ibid., Consular Message no. 476.

[971] Ibid., Consular Message no. 236.

[972] Ibid.

[973] *Investigation and Trial Papers*, M599, reel 3, frames 0749-0751.

[974] *Trial of John H. Surratt*; Edward Pierpont was one of the prosecutors and later became attorney general of the United States, and Richard T. Merrick was a special prosecutor at the trial of Guiteau for the assassination of President Garfield.

[975] Lecture on the Lincoln Conspiracy, *Lincoln Herald* 51 (December 1949).

[976] Ibid.

[977] *Washington Star*, February 8, 13, 15, 1869.

CPSIA information can be obtained
at www.ICGtesting.com
Printed in the USA
LVOW12s2310060716

495393LV00001B/69/P